NOT BEHIND THE BIKE SHEDS

The magic and the mayhem of
a lifetime in teaching
(and related escapades)

Barrie Day

Created through the Create Space Publishing Platform

Create Space
4900 La Cross Road
North Charleton SC 29406
USA

© B.N.Day

First Printed 2016

ISBN 978-1503242692

Dedications

To
Sue, Katie and James,
my cherished travelling companions.

And to
Charlie, Harry, Mason and Max.
This was my journey, boys.
What will yours be like?

And to Allen Freer,
my inspiring English teacher,
who lit the fuse.

ACKNOWLEDGEMENTS

Apologies to my wife, Sue and my children,
Katie and James.
I hope I haven't caused you too much embarrassment by
broadcasting your lives to the world.

.

Thanks to Joby Davey for
his assistance with the cover design.

And thanks to Sue for her much
valued help with editing and Caroline Carey and Julie
Jackson for help with proof reading.

CONTENTS

LIST OF ILLUSTRATIONS

Front Collage clockwise from top: Ponce girls' soccer, Ponce Spirit Week, *Grease* production, Challenger launch, Sue's father on Jamaican beach, Golden Gate Bridge, San Francisco, Jamaican 3rd yr. class, Newman flood, Rocky Horror trip – Katie and Dawn.

PART ONE

NOT BEHIND THE BIKE SHEDS

PART TWO

NOT IN FRONT OF THE INSPECTORS

PART ONE

NOT BEHIND THE BIKE SHEDS

1972-84

CHAPTER THE FIRST 1972-73 Staffordshire

A CASE OF EROTIC CONDOMS

June 1972 Tamworth College of Further Education.

Here I was, a trainee 'lecturer', four weeks into the placement, chalk like dandruff on my collar and fingers stained with ink from the leaking Gestetner copier. Things were not going so badly apart from my Thursday afternoon class of day-release mechanical engineering apprentices. These unlikely lads were sent by their employers one day a week to the college to gain some basic qualifications in their occupational field. But they were forced to sample what was called social or liberal studies. This was where I came in. To breathe some aesthetic light into the dark satanic world to which these poor wage-slaves had been condemned as they grubbed daily over their gear-boxes and grease guns.

There was no clear curriculum to work from so I designed a mouth-watering menu of delights to nourish the souls of these ne'er-do-wells. I tried introducing them to elements of social history, fine art, music, political ideas. They would grunt and scowl or go to sleep. The only part of the lesson where they seemed to show some interest was when I handed out the worksheets. They would press these to their noses, close their eyes and, with that look of bliss of the Bisto kids, try to get high on the chemicals from the copier. Then they would burp and fart and fashion paper aeroplanes from my work sheets and fire them around the room.

This was the final placement of my PGCE (Post Grad Certificate of Education) year and I was to teach social studies and sociology to a variety of full-time and day release students. Disillusioned with my initial intention of becoming a high-powered marketing executive I had now chosen education as my career route. Keen to salvage some self respect after bottling out of industry, I had it in mind to become not a mere 'teacher', with its image of ink-stained fingers and chalk dusted clothing, but a 'lecturer'. This was more me. Rarefied scent of academia; sun-kissed lawns with eager students sitting at my feet drinking the nectar of my words. There were 'lecturers' in Colleges of Further Education so I asked my tutor if I could be fixed up with a final placement in such a college.

And here I was. Tamworth Tech. in Staffordshire. It was a rather dreary, red-brick building with paint flaking from the metal window frames. The corridors were gloomy and painted hospital green but luckily I found that most of my lessons were to be taught in a temporary classroom behind the main building. The windows looked out on to a playing field and beyond was the undulating landscape of south Staffordshire. While the flaky, red brickwork sapped something of my energy, the touches of green landscape were invigorating. This was not bad, not bad at all.

One Thursday afternoon I decided to try a multi-media approach. I would take in the college tape recorder and slide projector and start the lesson with some dramatic newspaper photos and tapes of recent pop songs, the lyrics of which might illuminate my chosen area for discussion. So, for our discussion of personal finances, I would use the Beatles' *Money*; for a discussion of teenage angst I chose Cat Stevens' *Father and Son* and the Beatles' *She's Leaving Home*. This approach was a winner, I just knew it.

With a spring in my step and aiming to impress them with tape recorder, projector, tapes and colourful worksheets, I opened the door of the portacabin which served as my Thursday afternoon classroom. They were all there, my platoon of recalcitrant greasers with Gary Summers, the cocky, curly-headed loud mouth grinning near the front. Many of them were only a few years younger than I was – stocky young men with developing beer guts, long hair and leather jackets. Some were so big that their thighs seemed to spill down the sides of their chairs.

I smiled, as usual, and adopted an exaggerated cheeriness to disarm their hostility. I was two steps through the door and heading for my desk at the front of the class when Summers hissed, 'Now!'

A salvo of chalk like a hail storm erupted from the hands of every member of the class and peppered me. I had time to blink, take it all in, hold the following dialogue with myself: 'Don't panic. Don't show weakness, that's what they want. Stay cool, stay calm. Smile.' I took the final two steps and reached my desk, placed the tape recorder on the floor. I turned to the class, 'A nice way to show your appreciation lads. Thank you, now let's get on with the lesson.' Some laughed, some jeered, some scowled. I just quaked in my shoes.

I bluffed and fumbled my way through the rest of the lesson and vaguely recall some discussion stimulated by the songs I'd chosen. I think someone slept through most of it and when the bell went they elbowed their way past the desks and chairs and jostled each other out of the door and left the room which looked like a bombsite. 'See you next week, sir,' chirped Summers.

By July, the class of thirty had dribbled away to about fifteen. Following the chalk pelting incident, I was increasingly restless on Wednesday evenings, trying to dream up something different to get me through the one hour lesson the following afternoon. My sleep that night would be fractured and haunted by vivid waking dreams. The apprentices would be nine feet tall and three feet wide leering down at me with broken toothed grins and brandishing monkey wrenches and wheel braces. Frequent dreams involved me sitting at my desk at the front of the class bluffing away but unable to move as I was naked from the waist downwards! (Psychoanalysts, step right in.)

But inspiration finally arrived just after midnight. My wife, Sue, thrust my *AA Book of the Car* in front of me. 'Give them a quiz. You've tried everything else.'

What a brilliant idea! I would test their knowledge of engines, gear boxes, rules of the road and so on. It couldn't fail. I cleverly devised around sixty questions which would certainly fill the hour-long lesson. I would divide and rule, splitting them into teams which would help to take the heat off me. Redirect the aggression so that they channelled their belligerence towards each other – great psychology BD.

It was a hot summer's day, that memorable Thursday afternoon as I approached the portacabin once again. 'Can we go outside, sir. Go on, it's too hot in here. Can we, sir. Go on!' Summers was there, squawking like a demented magpie.

We trouped outside on to a patch of grass, a slight hollow, between four other portacabin classrooms. We sat on the grass and students in the other classrooms gazed down on us. My roughneck mechanics liked the idea of being put into teams and there was some friendly wrestling on the grass and some competitive banter. But at least it wasn't directed at me. The psychology was working. Clever old me.

I had seated myself in the centre and they had spread themselves in the two teams on either side although some had moved behind me so they were somewhat outside my line of vision. No matter, they were quiet and the quiz started well. Summers was not his usual loud-mouthed self, neither was his side-kick Dillon. For once I seemed to have got his measure. There was good-humoured competition between the two sides and I felt that, after the debacle of the chalk throwing incident, I had at last re-established something of my authority. They found the questions quite demanding and the scores were fairly even. This was good education I thought, they're learning from each other, there's tolerance, sensible questioning, effective listening, all the ingredients of what a good lesson should contain.

With ten minutes to go, I realised that there was some commotion from the classrooms which bordered our little grassy amphitheatre. Faces at the windows, a teacher leaning out of a classroom door, smiling. I sensed an admiring look from him and thought, yes, at last I'm winning some professional respect.

It was the sniggering from behind me that made me turn, that and a curious farting noise. I turned to see two huge misshapen balloons, one pink, one blue, floating up into the air. Another zig-zagged off into the bushes. And then all the boys were rolling on the grass laughing.

They weren't balloons. They were erotic condoms floating in all their obscene beauty on the warm summer air. And it was Summers' toothy grin which then assailed me. 'Hey sir, I've got a case full here. Something for the weekend, was it?'

*

OF HAIR CUTS AND COW PATS

Despite the chalk salvo and the airborne condoms, I managed to complete my PGCE training year in the summer of 1972. Then I secured my first teaching job that summer and started at the newly formed King Edward VI Comprehensive School, Lichfield, on September 6th 1972. Little did I realise the historical significance of 1972 in the educational chronology.

It was the first year of ROSLA – Raising Of The School Leaving Age. This was a major state initiative designed to improve the educational backbone of the nation. Keep youngsters in school for an extra year, so they leave at 16 not 15 and you thereby enhance the nation's pool of skills, intelligence and aptitude.

Laudable indeed. However, the reality was quite different. Those students with skills, intelligence and aptitude would have stayed on anyway. It was the less-able, the no-hopers, the rebels who were now being forced to postpone their escape from the daily punishment of state education and stay chained for another year. What to do with them though? How to prevent anarchy and outright rebellion? This was where I came in; a bearded liberal with a sociology degree – the perfect agent to ameliorate the situation.

All round the country Headteachers were losing sleep and living the waking nightmare of how to contain, for another year, the antisocial underbelly of their schools. To solve the problem, the government was cascading ROSLA money like confetti. At some schools ROSLA units were being hastily built and equipped with teenage-friendly coffee machines and comfy seating to thwart the rebellion. Not so at KES Lichfield. Here they employed me, invested in some glossy new social studies work packs, and stiffened their sinews.

The Headmaster, the irascible Mr 'Piggy' Hardcastle, as the less respectful used to call him, drew up his battle strategy for the war on two fronts. For many years he had basked in the honour of being Headmaster of the noble KES Grammar School, Lichfield, founded in 1495. On its honour roll were no less than Dr. Samuel Johnson, compiler of the first English dictionary and David Garrick, the actor. But now the illustrious Mr Hardcastle found himself Headmaster of the new hybrid 'Comprehensive school' – an amalgamation of the traditional King Edward's Grammar School at the bottom of the hill near St. John's Street with the impostor at the top of the hill - Kings Hill Secondary Modern. Not only did Headmaster Hardcastle have to swallow the pill of this new policy of 'comprehensivitis' but in the same year he and his senior managers had to come up with some way of preventing rebellion in the ranks of the fifteen year olds forced to stay in school another year.

Things were not looking rosy. A rearguard action was required. I imagined him ordering a new armoury of canes from the official cane makers, Leatherem & Bumwack, and practising on the flower heads in his country garden during the summer holidays. Any slippage of standards must immediately be quashed.

And so the Headmaster, with gown flying, went into action. Rarely did he venture up the hill to the Kings Hill campus where I was based. I'm convinced he and many of the old grammar school teachers viewed the school up the hill as an unfortunate wart on the rump of a school of status and noble tradition. But when the Headmaster did make a foray up the hill, he did it with his inimitable gusto. He came to make his mark, to prevent 'slippage' and maintain the old codes. We're talking about 1972 – the time of David Bowie who was breaking all conventions with his androgynous Ziggy Stardust persona - but at King Edward's the Head was mounting a spirited rearguard action.

One afternoon late in the Autumn term, I am invigilating a school exam. All is quiet, only the scratch of pens on paper, the squeak of a chair, the sigh of a bewildered candidate. The door bursts open and there stands 'Piggy' blowing like an angered bull. He goes round the room at full pelt doing a hair check, gown billowing like the wings of a vampire bat. 'No more than half an inch over the collar!' he roars peering over the cowed heads of the pupils. His eyes light up when he finds his first prize. 'You boy, into town, at the double, to Mr Priddle. He's waiting for you. Get it seen to!'

The poor miscreant has to leave his exam paper and his half finished sentence to get his hair cut. A couple more victims are summarily ejected and then 'Piggy' turns on his heel and heads for the door. With a final flourish he turns, leers at us, narrows his eyes and hisses, 'And remember, not behind the bike sheds!' With that he's away down the corridor leaving the dust dervishes whirling in the doorway. We all look at each other, raise eyebrows, collectively sigh and get back to the exam.

Such was the subtle handling of the shifting cultural landscape of the early Seventies at King Edward's, Lichfield.

But all was not well in other respects. By Christmas the novelty of the job and the place was wearing off. I was teaching geography to low level exam classes, not a subject I'd been trained to teach and social studies to low ability ROSLA students. Admittedly Bill, the Head of the social studies department, had invested in some trendy new discussion packs full of dramatic newspaper stories or photos of things like the religious rituals of the Dyaks of Borneo or a homeless vagrant sleeping in the doorway of a shop with a bottle of brown ale by his cheek. These new curriculum materials were 'state of the art' and intended to stimulate earnest discussion of social issues at home and abroad. We would sit in circles passing round these various stimulants and the students sometimes showed mild interest for a few minutes. But the girls were much more concerned to pass round magazine pictures of David Cassidy or little Michael Jackson, the two current pinups for pubescent girls in 1972.

For a couple of lessons a week I had the 'privilege' of teaching down the hill on the old grammar school site. And what a contrast. When I first entered the staff room the difference in atmosphere was palpable. Male dominated, dusty, gloomy – it reminded me of the grammar school in Birmingham I had attended as an eleven year old for a couple of years and which I hated. Hated it for its dark oppressiveness, the black cloaked schoolmasters who were dangerously eccentric and who threw chalk and wielded canes as though we were the enemy. And here at King Edward's there was the aloofness of the older masters, none of the friendly banter which was a feature of the King's Hill staffroom. Here it felt stuffy and unfriendly. And the pupils were different too. Here were the A stream kids – clean uniforms, middle class, precocious, products of a system that is self-fulfilling: tell a child he's bright, that he's A stream material, set high expectations and he'll perform accordingly. Label a child D stream, expect little of him, and you'll get the disaffection which such humiliation is bound to breed.

So here I was in the old grammar school teaching geography to classes of smart, precocious 13 year olds. It should have been rewarding after the testing times and disaffection I so often encountered up the hill. But somehow it wasn't. Was it me or the pupils? Probably something of both. I certainly wasn't inspired by teaching the import and export figures of Rotterdam or Kuala Lumpur or drawing diagrams of how volcanoes worked. I had taken A level geography but had never intended to pursue it further. And here I was, in my first year of teaching, being manacled to a subject which didn't inspire me.

Basically I had taken the wrong course at university. My old English teacher, the remarkable and inspirational Allen Freer, had warned me. 'Think of your soul, Day,' he chimed one afternoon when I passed him in the corridor. It was the summer of my fifth year and we were deciding on options. I was flirting with doing economics and dressing myself up as a marketing executive in a big corporation just like my uncle who was a big cheese at Dunlop. I had visited his plush office, seen the size of his mahogany desk, seen the deference his personal secretary accorded him, driven in his big six cylinder car – and yes that's where I saw myself heading. It was economics for me and to hell with soul-searching.

But it was not to be, not yet anyway. There were not enough takers for economics so I was back with dear old Freer and A level Literature. The first year of A level we studied Shakespeare's *Antony and Cleopatra*, T.S Eliot's *The Waste Land*, George Eliot's *Middlemarch* and, most significantly, D.H. Lawrence's *Sons and Lovers*. And that year strange things happened. Chords were struck in me, things read and things said in class which resonated gently but deeply. What Lawrence and Eliot were writing about triggered something in me which I didn't really understand but which left me unsettled and restless. There was something 'out there' which was tugging at me but I didn't know how to respond. I just felt a kinship with what I was reading and the ideas that Freer was peddling in our seminars.

However, by the end of my two years in sixth form there was still no contest. The big six-cylinder car, the mahogany desk and the prospect of a fat salary were beckoning far stronger than any soul nourishment. I was accepted on to a five year industrial training course with an international company which would groom me for the executive status to which I aspired. A year training before university, three years at university studying Industrial Economics, then a final year back in industry to refine my grooming – that was the key to my future. I was following in uncle's footsteps.

By the second year of my university course in Nottingham I was stumbling hopelessly. I didn't understand the economic theories, found the accountancy lessons an utter bore, couldn't do the statistics and only found solace in the sociology, my subsidiary subject. My year in industry prior to university had been a novelty at first, but the work I was given, whether it was in a personnel department or in marketing, sales or accounting, became increasingly unrewarding.

My final placement in the summer vacation of 1970 was at a company in Leicestershire which made tubing for car exhaust pipes. Curiously, the factory was located at Desford, out of town in open countryside, quite incongruous really but for me it sealed my decision. While supposedly working on some report for the personnel department I would spend hours gazing out of the windows watching the tractors in the fields, watching the golden dust clouds rising as a combine harvester made its way across a field of wheat. And I remembered Lawrence's writing – his characters' empathy with the heavy scent of flowers at dusk, or with a sunset or birdsong at dawn. I remembered the themes of *The Waste Land,* the craving for water in a barren landscape and my teacher's words, 'Think of your soul!'

But what to do? I wrote to the company saying I would be no use to them and, after a rather searching final interview with my training officer, climbed out of the industrial ditch into which I had jumped. Back at Nottingham, having scraped through my end of year exams, I negotiated to change my degree subject from economics to sociology. Thus I embarked on my final year at university and a new direction. Sorry uncle, it was not to be.

And thus it comes to pass, that on a Wednesday afternoon in March 1973 I am sitting in a classroom with a motley crew of 14 year old ninth stream no-hopers trying to engage with the fertility rituals of the Dyaks of Borneo.

Jamie Tomkins: So why do the boys go off in the forest, sir?

Me: It's one of their customs.

Angela Utterworth: When my dad comes back from his trips he always brings loads of ciggies through customs.

Derek Bailey: Your dad was flogging them on the market. I saw him.

Angela: No, he wasn't.

Derek: Yes, he was.

Charmaine Williams: Can we go on a trip, sir?

Me: Well, I'm not quite sure....

Derek: Go on, sir. Nobody ever takes us anywhere.

And I suppose that's how our camping trip to Wales came about. A chord of compassion was struck somewhere in me and the thought of the fresh air of the Welsh hills was certainly tempting.

The school had some old scout tents and an ageing minibus and with the blessing of the Deputy Head, well it was a kind of blessing: 'You want to take who? Where? You must be mad!' I set to work organising my first extra curricular event. Ten of them signed up, ten of my third year, ninth stream social studies class. Most of them lived on the council estate on the north side of the town. None of them had camped before, none of them had been far from the shops before.

We left just after lunch on a Friday afternoon in May, heading for the A5 which snaked its way to north Wales. I had co-opted a crew of like-minded King's Hill colleagues to help execute this grand plan. There was Will, the art teacher, the bane of 'Piggy' Hardcastle's life because he sported long, black locks and wore colourful shirts. Most of the fourth year girls were in love with Will. Then there was Bob the woodwork teacher, who played guitar and amused the King's Hill staffroom with his dry northern wit. Peroxide Jenny who taught French was along to oversee the girls as well as my wife, Sue, who would drive our car and bring the food, our frame tent and the cooking gear.

The kids, five girls and five boys, were excited and chatty as they boarded the bus, although the little trio of Alison, Kelly and Charmaine, looked like three timid mice about to face a mauling by the local tom-cat.
Alison: Can we sit near the front, sir?
Kelly: She gets sick, sir.
Charmaine – no words just a baleful look and a tight clutching of a copy of *Jackie*.

The bumptious Derek Bailey was organising the crew on the back seats and dispensing the contents of a huge bag of 'Pick 'n' Mix'. I checked again that we'd got the sick bucket to hand while Bob and Will stowed bags and camping gear at the rear of the bus. Mouthy Laura Turnbull and her friend, Diane Tickell, were wrestling the lads for the prime spot in the middle of the back seat.

And so the trip began – the weather looked promising, Radio One was playing *Crocodile Rock* by Elton John and as we joined the line of Friday afternoon traffic on the A5, I felt a fine sense of achievement at pulling all this together. On the back seats the bubble of noise and activity was subsiding. Derek Bailey was still cramming fluorescent pink sweets into his mouth and Tommy Stephens' mouth but most of the party had glazed over, hypnotized by the frieze of fields and trees and traffic which passed by the mini bus windows.

The campsite was not far from Llangollen. It was a simple site, close to a farm with a basic toilet block and a couple of taps and rubbish bins. Bob, Will and I had found it during the Easter break when we went off for a recce. We reckoned that the canal basin in the town and some of the historical sites around would at least provide a distraction if the weather turned bad.

With about half an hour to go and with the mountains closing in, the road began to wind more severely. The sky was now greying with bunched clouds and the mountain moorland looked somewhat wild and bleak. I was 'riding shotgun' with Bob driving as Tommy Stephens made his way to the front. He was looking somewhat sickly.

'Please sir, can we stop, I think I want to be......'

Projectile vomit, somewhat sweet smelling and pink, landed on my shoulder and splattered the dashboard.

'I think 'sick' was the word you were looking for,' murmured Bob as he swung the bus into a lay-by. Tommy heaved and hawked into the grass at the roadside for a few moments while we mopped and disinfected the mess. I changed my shirt and had stern words with Derek Bailey about not giving out anymore sweets.

'It's okay sir, I ain't got none left,' he chirruped.

'I wonder why,' muttered Bob.

We finally turned through the gate to the campsite at around six o'clock. The kids spilled out on to the grass and then stood in a huddle somewhat bemused.

'Is this it then? Are we here?'

'There's nowt here.'

'Where's the shops?'

'Urrgh, sir, what's that?'

'That's a cow pat.'

'A what?'

'Just don't step in it.'

'I need toilet, sir.'

'Over there, that almost white building.'

'You what!'

'Just go and have a look. It's quite clean.'

'You kiddin', sir?'

'No, we're deadly serious,' said Bob.

And so it started.

While they tiptoed their Doc Marten boots between the cow-pats in the direction of the toilets we set to work erecting the tents. I had noticed the sky getting greyer and the clouds louring the mountain tops but it was still dry and we were ever hopeful that we'd get the camp set up before it rained. The two scout tents were of thick green canvas with wooden tent poles. They were big enough to sleep eight. We pitched the girls' tent a short distance from the boys' but closer to the frame tent where Sue and Jenny were to sleep, just in case the girls needed some reassurance during the night. The grass was somewhat sloping but if the kids slept with their heads uphill there shouldn't be a problem. Bob, Will and I would sleep in Bob's super lightweight Everest Expedition tent with its brilliant yellow fly sheet. In Bob's tent, even in the grimmest of weather you could convince yourself the sun was out.

It took about an hour to get the camp set up and it was now getting dark. We were just banging in the last of the tent pegs when the first rain started to fall. Big drops splattered on the canvas. Not an encouraging sound. We dragged the kids' bags from the minibus into the tents and as the heavens opened scurried under the canopy of the frame tent.

'Just in time,' crowed Will.

'Anyone seen the kids?' asked Jenny.

'Didn't they go to find the toilets?'

'That was an hour ago.'

We peered through the curtain of rain-drenched gloom and listened for voices. Bob went off to check the tents and the toilet block. In torchlight, Sue and Jenny began organising the kitchen area and sorting the food while Will investigated the mysteries of how to light a Tilley lamp. A match was struck, Will started pumping the lamp and the mantle of the Tilley lamp erupted into white light. The kettle hissed on the camping stove and suddenly all felt well with the world.

'Dying for a brew,' grinned Will rubbing his hands together. 'Any flapjack?'

'I'll flapjack you in a minute if you don't get those kids out of the rain. We don't want them soaked in the first hour,' said Jenny.

There was the patter of running feet and Bob appeared dripping in the doorway of the tent. 'No sign,' he said.

'Where on earth have they gone?' said Jenny frowning.

I felt a slight clenching of the buttocks and heard the voice of a newsreader in my head, 'Teacher sacked as school party disappears in the Welsh mountains.'

I pulled on my anorak and ventured out of the warmth into the wet darkness. There were no other tents in the field and only a light from the toilet block. The humps of the mountains hemmed in the field and above the skyline there was a darkening evening sky. I ventured to the top of the field peered around and then shouted. 'Derek! Laura! Charmaine!' I listened intently. Only the sound of a tumbling stream nearby and the bleating of a distant sheep. I shouted again. 'Tommy! Diane!' Nothing. Just the rush of the stream and the splatter of the rain on the hood of my anorak.

Then I spotted something. Faint pin pricks of red in the darkness at the bottom of the field. I went towards them. One of them glowed brighter for a second and then dimmed.

They were shivering together under a tree clutching cigarettes. I could see their pale faces now. They were like a huddle of sheep, corralled by a circling wolf.

'What on earth are you doing out here?'

A flurry of timid voices:

'Derek said there was a monster.'

'We saw it, sir, it was a going to trample us.'

'Probably just a cow or a sheep,' I said.

'But it was scary, sir.'

'And there were things in the bushes and vampires, sir.'

'And Charmaine doesn't like it here, sir. She wants to go home.'

'We're not going home. We've only just arrived. Now put the fags out and come in out of the rain. Follow me.'

I led the gaggle of bedraggled specimens up the field to the tents.

'And remember, there are no vampires in Wales.'

'How d'you know, sir?' asked Derek Bailey.

'I just know, that's all. Teachers know everything.'

The rain eased for a time. The kids' dampened spirits revived as they munched on hot dogs and warmed their hands round mugs of tea. Will foraged for some dry twigs and we turned the barbecue grill into a semblance of a camp fire. Bob strummed his guitar and taught the kids some rather risqué drinking songs and by ten o'clock we sent them to sort out sleeping bags and make their last expedition through the darkness to the toilet block. Jenny went into the girls' tent to settle them down and I went to check on the boys' tent.

Not what you'd call organised. Derek Bailey sat on his mound of 'stuff' shuffling a deck of cards, surrounded by sweet wrappers and empty drinks cans.

'Quick game of poker, sir?'

'Not now, Derek. Just get yourself ready for bed.'

'But sir, it's early yet.'

13

'Bed.'

'Oh, sir.'

'Bed!'

Jamie Tomkins, a scrawny , pale faced lad whose dad had died recently was unrolling his sleeping bag. 'Hey sir, those were good hot dogs.'

'Glad you liked them. How're you doing? Getting sorted?'

'Not bad, sir.' There was a slight pause and then he said, 'Sir?'

'What is it, Jamie?'

'My dad was in the scouts. Me mam showed me these badges he had.'

'What kind of badges?'

'He had to learn stuff. How to make tent pegs out of wood and how to build a camp fire.'

There was a loud fart from Derek Bailey's direction. 'Sorry, sir. My mam says I don't digest my food properly.'

'Sounds like she's right,' I said.

'But what I don't understand,' went on Jamie, rather earnestly, 'is what cows are for.'

'What d'you mean, what are they for?'

Jamie sat back against his backpack and frowned. 'Well, you see them in fields, but what are they for? You can't ride them like a horse.'

'Well, they give us milk and meat.'

Jamie considered this reply for a moment and then said, 'But down our way, we get our milk from the co-op man and meat comes from Mr Perkins, the butcher. He sometimes gives us bones for Tilly our Jack Russell.'

'Don't try to explain, sir, Jamie's just thick,' chirped Tommy who was trying to shuffle Derek's deck of cards. 'He don't understand nothing. I'll put him right.'

'We'll talk about it tomorrow, Jamie, okay?' I said.

'Okay, sir. Thanks, sir.'

The remaining two, Stevie Watson and Iain Dickinson arrived from their expedition to the toilet block. Stevie, tall and skinny, was a quiet, inoffensive lad who was mad about fishing. Iain, was the opposite - short and dark and prone to losing his temper and getting into fights. His father ran a car crushing business and Iain claimed he drove old stock cars in races, cars which he and his dad had welded together from old parts.

'Okay, lads?'

They nodded and grunted and went to their corner of the tent away from the garrulous Derek and Tommy.

14

'Ten minutes, and then it'll be lights out. Right?' I said standing at the door of the tent.

There was a general muttering and another loud fart from Derek.

'Don't gas them in there, Derek, will you,' I said.

'It's them sausages, sir. They don't agree with me.'

I wasn't sure whether I had dreamt it or actually heard something. I shone the torch on the face of my watch. 3.30a.m. Rain was continuously splattering on the tent and I could hear the wind in the trees. Then I heard it again. 'Sir? Sir?' just outside the tent. Will and Bob were still asleep. I unzipped the door of the tent to see Laura Turnbull shivering in a dripping anorak.

'Sir, there's a stream running through the middle of our tent.'

'A what?'

'We can't sleep, sir. Everything's soaked.'

'I'll be with you in a sec.'

I groaned inwardly. This was turning out to be a disaster. 'Bloody Welsh weather,' I cursed.

Outside the rain wasn't as heavy as I'd thought. A lot of the splattering on the tent was from the trees nearby. The ground was squelchy under my bare feet and the water oozed between my toes. I looked inside the girls' tent and shone the torch on two huddles of despondent figures all looking at me helplessly. They had moved either side of a rivulet of water which was coursing its way through the middle of the tent.

'Who pitched this tent on top of a stream?'

'I think you did, sir,' said Laura.

'No, no it was Mr Hardwick and Mr Hall. I'll have words with them in the morning. Sorry girls. We'll have to move you.'

Luckily the boys' tent was still quiet. I roused Sue and Jenny and we moved the girls into the frame tent. Poor miserable wretches clutching their sleeping bags, they looked like refugees from a war zone. Sue lit the gas and got a kettle boiling and made them some hot chocolate while Jenny checked the state of their clothes and sleeping bags. 'Not too bad,' she told me. 'I think the sleeping bags are still usable, but they need a change of clothes.'

While she supervised the girls I went across to the boys' tent. I poked my head inside. It was steamy and stinky but at least they were still quiet. 'Thank god for small mercies,' I said looking skywards. The clouds were broken and the sheen of the moon threw the branches of the trees into strange unearthly shapes. I remembered the Deputy Head's words, 'You must be mad.'

15

I was starting to agree.

I zipped up the door of the frame tent at around 4.15. The girls were settled, finally. Not much chatter between them, just the odd murmur and then from the little round face of Charmaine came the words, 'Are we having an adventure, sir?'

'Something like that, Charmaine. Not very exciting is it.'

'It bloody isn't,' muttered Laura.

I must have slept, for when I opened my eyes it was light. I listened. No rain. No wind. Just Will snoring and Bob breathing heavily. And was that a blistering sun beating down on us or just the teasing sheen of Bob's bright yellow tent kidding me?

It was 7.15 and I could hear some movement from the boys' tent. I poked my head outside and blinked in the bright sunlight. There is a merciful god after all, I thought. Maybe I'm just being tested for some higher calling.

Will let out an extended yawn, spread his long arms wide and exclaimed, 'Wow, what a great night's sleep. That whisky nightcap idea was a winner.'

Bob groaned and farted, which prompted the distant voice of Derek Bailey to shout, 'Nice one, sir.'

A new day had begun.

The weather was kinder to us that day. After breakfast we piled the dirty dishes together and I gave the job of washing up to Derek, Tommy, Laura and Diane.

'But this is work, sir. Me mam didn't pay for me to come and do work,' moaned Laura.

'No, Laura, this is campcraft. It's part of learning about camping.'

'Camp crap more like,' muttered Derek.

'What was that, Derek?'

'Please, sir, I need a crap, sir. I can't wait.'

I nodded reluctantly and waved him away.

'Hey, sir that's not fair, look at him, he's laughing,' whined Diane.

I turned but he was too quick for me. I just saw a fat backside jogging towards the toilet block.

We drove in the direction of Llangollen but stopped near a small waterfall at the roadside. 'Right, everybody out,' I said. 'We're going to climb a mountain.'

There were collective groans and complaints which I ignored.

'You said we were going to some shops, sir,' twined Laura.

'Later, Laura. That's the treat part of the day. But first you've got to earn it,' I smiled.

Bob leaned towards me and murmured, 'Forget the character-building bollocks. Let's just get to a pub.'

'And Mr Hall has kindly offered to lead the way,' I called out.

We trekked up a valley following the course of a small stream. Bob was leading and Charmaine and Kelly were following, trying to weld themselves to Will's long arms. I stood at the rear and watched with some satisfaction as my little expedition sallied forth. Their spirits were lifting led by the irrepressible Derek with his never-ending supply of sweets and good humour.

I caught up with Jamie Tomkins. 'Did you sort out with Tommy about the cows?'

He turned, 'What, sir?'

'You asked about the cows last night. Tommy said he'd explain to you what cows were for.'

'Oh yes, sir. I've got it now. But I'm not sure about it, all this killing. It's not right really, just so I can have me Sunday dinner.'

'What about the milk?'

'Me mam was feeding our babby with her milk. It's a bit like that, init it, sir?'

'I suppose it is.'

'It's interesting init, sir.'

'Yes, Jamie, it is.'

We made it to the top of a small knoll which gave us a view over hills to the south. Will made them sit down and then pointed to a grey turreted building in the distance. 'See that building over there. That's Chirk Castle.' He lowered his voice and levelled his eyes at them. 'It belongs to the Myddleton family who've lived in the castle for over four hundred years.'

'Get away,' said Derek, 'no-one can live to be four hundred years old.'

'Not the same people, silly, the descendants of the family,' said Will. Then his voice took on a quiet, quivering tone. 'But beware. You mustn't mock the Myddletons – for the bloody hand could track you down and kill you.'

Ten pairs of eyes swivelled in Will's direction.

'What's the bloody hand then?' asked Laura, tilting her head, not quite sure whether to be drawn into this.

Will turned to her. 'The bloody hand is part of the coat of arms of the Myddleton family and there are strange legends as to its origin.'

No interruptions now. He had them hooked.

'One legend tells of an argument between two brothers over who should inherit the castle. It was agreed the brothers would run a race and whichever one touched the castle gates first was the winner. But just as the leader was about to touch the gates, a friend of the other brother drew his sword and cut off the hand of the first brother.'

'Why didn't he use his other hand?' asked Derek.

'Cos he was rolling around in agony, stupid,' replied Laura. 'What was another legend, sir?'

Will stooped and resumed with his voice aquiver and his eyes slowly ranging round the faces of the group. 'Another legend tells of one of the brave Myddletons who was fighting in a battle dressed in a white cloak. His sword arm was badly bleeding and he placed his hand on his cloak leaving the imprint of the bloody hand. The cloak was raised in the air like a flag to rally the troops. They won the battle and the bloody hand then became the family symbol.'

Ten open mouths, wide eyes, held breath. Then Jamie broke the spell. 'Can we see it, sir, the bloody hand?'

'That's where we're heading when we've finished the walk,' I said.

'To shake the bloody hand,' said Derek, shoulders hunched, arms akimbo doing his monster impression.

Charmaine leaned towards Will. 'How d'you know all this, sir?'

'Well, Charmaine, when I was at college I was studying art and design and I saw a picture of the iron gates of Chirk castle. They're really beautiful. And I did a bit of research about them. Do you know, the Davies Brothers who designed and made the gates in the early 1700s were only paid two shillings a day.'

'Remember when we had shillings, sir, before the new money come in,' chimed Derek, 'you could buy twenty four gob-stoppers for two shillings, sir.'

'Not sure they had gob-stoppers in those days, Derek,' said Will, 'but you never know. History is full surprises.'

There was lots of chatter and excitement in the minibus as we drove the few miles to Chirk Castle. Derek was still doing his monster impressions, Laura and Diane were flouncing their scarves and putting on 'posh lady' accents, and Iain Dickinson seemingly lost in a battle somewhere was punching the air and giving Steven an animated account of car crushing and how it was like the machines they used to bash down the walls of castles.

They spilled out of the bus and then suddenly stopped and went quiet when they caught their first sight of the castle.

18

'Cor, sir, look at that!' said Jamie, eyes wide. 'Never seen nothing like that before.'

There it was, at the end of a tree-lined drive on the top of a low hill, its great rounded towers squatting heavy and impregnable beyond the trees.

'It's a bit scary, sir,' murmured Charmaine, clasping on to Will's arm. 'Are there ghosts?'

'Who knows?' he replied. 'Lots of people have lived and died there and on the ground where we're walking lots of battles have been fought and lots of blood spilt.'

'D'you think there's metal and stuff, you know, swords and daggers under the ground, sir?' asked Iain. 'My dad's just got this metal detector and you can find stuff, coins and treasure. I'll have to get him to come here.'

We climbed the path through the trees and approached the main gate. The towers of the gate house dwarfed us and between them was the arch of the main gate. Above the arch was the coat of arms; a knight's helmet, two growling dogs on either side baring their teeth and above the helmet a single hand.

'There it is, sir, the hand, see it there at the top,' said Jamie in a kind of hoarse whisper. 'The bloody hand.'

'Bloody hell, it really is,' muttered Derek, open-mouthed and, for once, lost for words.

Charmaine, Alison and Kelly moved closer to each other and stared upwards. 'I don't like it,' murmured Charmaine. 'To think of that boy running that race and having his hand chopped off. It's horrible.'

'It's only a legend,' said Laura, 'might not be true.'

We spent an hour touring the castle and during that time I saw another side to the kids. Laura didn't always stick with Diane; at times she hung back, gazing up at tapestries, running her hand over the contours of statues and carvings. In the weapons room Tommy just stood for several minutes with his nose pressed against the glass of a cabinet full of old weapons. Even when Derek shouted from the next room, 'C'mon Tommy, get a load of this,' Tommy just ignored him and continued to study the contents of the glass case. At last he turned to me and said, 'Clever, weren't they, the olden days people. I never knew that before.'

We wandered out of the castle and the kids played tag round the massive domed yew trees as we went down the path to see the famous gates that Will had talked about.

'There it is again,' said Jamie excitedly, pointing to the top of the gates. 'The bloody hand.' It was not so easy to spot among the complex filigree of iron work which the Davies brothers had fashioned for two shillings a day.

Most of the group stood back gazing up at the gates but it was Laura who went right up to them and ran her hand over the intricate patterns and shapes. Will went and stood beside her and explained about some of the features. She continued to gaze and run her hand slowly over the curves and spirals of metal. And then she murmured, more to herself than to Will, 'It's just beautiful.'

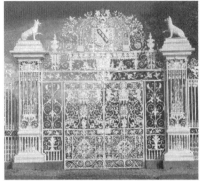

As soon as they saw the shops the magic was gone. They were urban kids again, brash and mouthy, searching for sweets and souvenirs. Laura had her arm linked in Diane's as they marched in step across the bridge over the River Dee gleefully chanting some rhyme they had learned; Derek was in seventh heaven when he found a Woolworths selling Pick'n'Mix and the other girls lost themselves in the world of soft toys and souvenirs. Steven found a fisherman to talk to, Jamie was exploring the barges moored along the tow path while Iain got told off when he tried to close a lock gate.

That evening we played rounders in a field near the campsite and later sat round a campfire and tried to toast marshmallows on sticks. I looked at their faces, reddened by the firelight. Derek and Tommy were playing with some toy Derek had bought in a joke shop, Iain was whittling a stick with his souvenir penknife, Jamie was sorting through a collection of stones he'd picked up and Charmaine was fiddling with the dress of a Welsh doll she'd bought. Laura and Diane had their arms round each other and were gazing into the fire trying to remember the words of pop songs.

My first extra-curricular trip. Maybe it wasn't so bad after all. Maybe they had been touched in some way. Maybe, just maybe, something had penetrated through that hard defensive shell so many of them seemed to wear. 'But they've got to survive on the streets,' said Jenny sometime later when I expressed this. 'You're just a romantic. These kids are realists, pragmatists. They've got to be tough to survive. They can't wander round with their heads in the clouds all day. Life's not sweetness and light you know.'

But I wished it could be for them, if only for fleeting moments.

CHAPTER THE SECOND 1973-76   Jamaica

JUMPING SHIP

All that we have, while we live, is life;
And if you don't live during your life, you are a piece of dung.
And work is life, and life is lived in work
Unless you're a wage slave.
While a wage-slave works, he leaves life aside
And stands there a piece of dung.

D.H.Lawrence goading me again in one of his *Pansies* poems. I closed the book and wondered why I felt so dissatisfied. I didn't quite feel like a piece of dung but not far off. Here I was a young man of twenty-four married to a lovely wife, in a secure job and having not long moved into a pleasant house in a sleepy Staffordshire village. To anyone else it probably looked like a pretty good start to a life. But something was missing.

The teaching was often boring, I felt uninspired and, furthermore, I used to sit in the staff room and listen in to the chat which came from the corner where the English teachers gathered. And it confirmed what I now knew. My old English teacher, Allen Freer, had been right. I should have studied English Literature.

Also I felt starved that I'd never been anywhere. When my university friends took off for the long summer vacation on the hippy trail to Katmandu or San Francisco, what was I doing? Compiling figures on how many paper clips had been used by the sales department in a firm making exhaust pipes in darkest Dudley.

I shared my thoughts with Sue.

She shrugged, 'Okay, let's change things then. Let's take off somewhere.'

'You mean it?'

'Well, you're not so great to live with at the moment.'

'What about the house?'

'We'll rent it out.'

'Are you sure?'

'Yes, I'm sure you're not great to live with at the moment.'

We started scanning the Times Educational Supplement 'Overseas' section. I found a job in Papua New Guinea but then I heard on the news that a volcano had erupted quite close to the island where the school was located so we crossed that one off the list.

Then one Friday evening I put the paper in front of Sue. I'd drawn a red circle round one of the adverts: 'The Priory School, Kingston, Jamaica, seeks to recruit teachers for the new academic year…'

'Jamaica? Where's that exactly?' she said.

'I'm not sure. Caribbean somewhere.'

'Thought you were a geography teacher.'

'No, I'm not a geography teacher, I just happen to be lumbered with teaching geography.'

She nodded, 'I think it's next to Cuba,' she said. 'Sounds exotic. Why not?'

And she was right: three months later we were standing on the deck of a cargo ship sailing through the Windward Passage towards the north coast of Jamaica staring at the blue misty hump which was the island of Cuba.

But what a three months it had been. We had been interviewed in London by Henry Fowler, the retiring Headmaster who had founded The Priory School in 1944. It was an international school with students drawn from around twenty four countries. Henry Fowler was very different from 'Piggy' Hardcastle. He was charm personified, and seemed genuinely pleased to offer both of us jobs. It was a two year contract with a tax incentive to stay for a third year. The school would pay our air fare and we could have accommodation in the staff apartments near the school.

While we were heading for Jamaica, Will was escaping to a new job in Sweden. It was he who mentioned that it was possible to get a passenger ticket on cargo boats.

'I'm getting a slow boat to Bergen,' he said. 'Why don't you get a slow boat to Kingston.'

We looked into it. Sure enough there were cargo boats plying the Atlantic between the West Indies and Britain carrying tropical produce in one direction and machinery and industrial goods on the return journey westwards. Some of them had cabins for passengers. 'What d'you reckon?' I said to Sue as we scanned a brochure we'd received from The Jamaica Banana Producers Company.

As usual she was carefully reading the small print. Finally she looked up and nodded, 'A banana boat to Jamaica? Does it get any more bizarre than that. But so what. Let's try for it.'

We secured tickets on a ship called the *North Star* and on the afternoon of September 1st 1973 found ourselves heaving our suitcases up the gangplank of the ship. The *North Star* was moored at Sheerness Dock, on the Thames estuary. It was a slim, white, Scandinavian cargo boat chartered by the banana company and it had twelve cabins for passengers at the rear of the ship. There was a small sun deck with a plunge pool and deck chairs. Just off this deck was the passengers' lounge with wood panelled walls, a small bar and the dining-room. At  the moment the plunge pool was empty and roped off and from the rope hung a wooden sign showing the following chalked words:

SHIP: NORTH STAR
DEPART: 2.00PM 1st SEPT.
DESTN: JAMAICA

Unreal. This was all unreal.

The ship finally moved away from the dockside at 2.30p.m. The sky was overcast and by late afternoon we were off Broadstairs and could see the winking light of the North Goodwin light ship. By then I was the only one on deck. Sue was sorting things in the cabin and we hadn't yet met the other passengers. The wooden notice board banged incessantly against the hand rail on the afterdeck, the wind gusted, tuning the steel rigging and by evening the lights of Hastings and Sittingbourne were winking faintly off the starboard side of the ship. The English Channel was a dark, undulating blanket flecked by the ropes of surf furling from the wake. This was it. No turning back now.

We were on a bearing of 200 degrees, our speed was 18.6 knots and the distance to Kingston was 4300 miles. I knew all this, not because I'd suddenly become a great geographer but because the purser posted little slips of white paper on the passengers' notice board giving us information about our location. I was using these to trace our route on an old Phillips School Atlas.

However, despite the reassuring lines which I was drawing on the map, it was a disconcerting experience being at sea for eleven days. On September 3rd, our third day out, we said goodbye to the black lump of Flores, the most westerly of the Azores islands and the last land you see as you head west. For the next six days we were out of sight of any land. We saw no ships and very few birds. I was religiously drawing my pencil lines on the map each day as a kind of reassurance that we knew where we were but when you then went up on deck there was just an empty sea and a 360 degree horizon. We could have been anywhere although the straight stream of the ship's wake and the position of the setting sun suggested we were in fact travelling steadily westwards.

To be surrounded by endless sea, with no solid reference points except the moving ship is like being lost in some equation devised by Einstein. Add to that the society of a quirky collection of passengers and you feel you've arrived in some Agatha Christie neverland.

First there was the writer, Lawrence Dame. He would be in his late sixties; shortish, stocky, shaved head, small silver goatee and a gold earring in his left ear. (This was at a time when the only men who wore earrings were gypsies or pirates) Each day he wore a different headpiece. On some days it was a green army beret, on others a red Egyptian fez with a black tassel; sometimes it was a straw hat with a coloured band round it. He would always be up on deck before anyone else, generally doing his yoga exercises. During the day he would pace the deck with his little notebook and pen, making jottings. I'd never met a writer before and was instantly in awe. To see a writer in the very act of the creative process was a rare privilege indeed, especially to me who had always had aspirations to write.

Sue reckoned he was a phoney but I put her straight. 'A phoney? But he's got twenty articles to write before we reach Jamaica, and he's written novels, and had a world exclusive for the New York Times.'

She shook her head. 'You're just gullible.'

But what clinched it for me was when I was leaning on the deck rail on the day we were passing through the Windward Passage. I was peering towards a misty humped shape on the horizon. Lawrence came over to me and leaned on the rail. 'Cuba,' he nodded, sagely. 'You know Barrie, I was with Hemingway the week before he shot himself. Fine man but a sad end.'

'And he was with Hemingway the week before he shot himself,' I reported back to Sue sometime later.

'A phoney, I tell you. You'd believe anything,' she said dismissively.

Then there was Mary Arthurs, the ageing plantation owner's wife, who strode twenty circuits of the deck every morning and waved you away with a 'Can't stop, still fifteen left to do.' Her accent was home counties, and she had the pale leathery complexion of an English aristocrat who's been in the tropics too long.

There was a quiet, neat, Indian doctor, Doctor Patel, who avoided company but smiled politely when you met him before bowing slightly and turning away.

Next, was Bridget, a young teacher from Bolton who was taking up a job on the north coast. She was gutsy and full of optimism about this adventure which her parents had tried to warn her against. She spoke in a wonderful slanting northern accent: 'I tauld them, people are people, muther – just because they're black dun't mean they dun't need educatin' and dun't think and feel like we do. But they think I'm going to end up in a cooking pot in some jungle clearing. I tell you. Parents!'

Then came Mr and Mrs Bennett – Jamaican, in their sixties, returning 'home' after being in England for twenty five years. He was a squat, square shouldered man with a serious look on his face while huge Mrs Bennett was straight out of the West Indian story books of 'big mammas'. She moved as if doing a rolling rumba, feet shuffling, shoulders, hips and arms all seeming to move independently. She smiled and huffed and swatted the air with a handkerchief. 'We's heading home after arl dis time a hengland. Me cyarn wait!' she exclaimed on the first day as I tried to edge past her with my suitcase. Sadly she spent most of the voyage in her cabin under a mountain of blankets groaning with sea-sickness. However, each evening when all the passengers assembled for dinner at the captain's table, Mr Bennett would be there dressed smartly in a suit and each evening, whatever we were eating, he would excuse himself with, 'If nobody don't mind,' and then proceed to empty the dish of fiery chilli pickles on his meal and breathe fire breath over whoever was sitting next to him.

Finally, there was the Irish mother and her three bright-eyed, freckle-faced children – Brian, Barry and Geraldine. She was the wife of a production manager who was supervising the building of the new Guinness plant in Kingston. She'd been back to Ireland for the summer and was returning for the children to start the new term at school.

This was the cast which peopled that strange summer of 1973 – our voyage into the unknown – it was like being in a who-done-it novel where you waited for the next chapter to unfold, always pinching yourself that this was in fact real. At night we stood on deck and marvelled at the dome of the heavens, the starry brilliance, the ink black sea and the dished highway of moonlight stretching away from the ship to the moonlit horizon.

During the day we fashioned some sort of routine. Breakfast at 8.30. Sun-bathing 9-10. Keep-fit 10-10.30. Swimming, reading and deck games with the Irish children until 11.30 when the bar opened. Drinks in the bar and then lunch. Siesta 2-3.00. Tea at 3.15. Shower and dress for evening. Bar open at 6.00 (double measures and duty free prices.) Dinner at 7.00.

Mr Bennett turned out to be something of a religious fanatic. He was desperate to save all our souls before it was too late. One morning after breakfast he joined me on deck. I was trying to spot flying fish with my binoculars. 'God will provide for him who gibs,' he proclaimed. He leaned over the deck rail looking down at the surf foaming away from the side of the ship, took a shilling piece from his pocket and rotated the coin between thumb and first finger. The sun glinted for a second on its surface. He motioned to me with the coin, 'I gib te get.' Then he chants, 'In de name ob de fader, son and Holy Ghost.' With that he tosses the coin over the handrail. It spins down and disappears into the surf. 'Dat's for de fishes,' he says. 'God will provide for him who gibs.' He touches my shoulder. 'Wash clean your spirit, clean like de sea.' He nods to me and to himself and walks away.

By the fifth day the sea had calmed to a carpet of barely shifting silk. The drama of the first few days when we rolled through a lively sea of surf crests and troughs was seemingly over. We had not seen another ship for three days. No birds, no flying fish. Nada. We heard no news of the world. It might have disappeared for all we knew. We were in limbo – suspended between worlds. The past was somewhere behind us, beyond the wake. The future somewhere ahead of the bow of the ship.

However, not so the night of day 5. At 4.30a.m the fire alarm shattered the ship. Never imagining there was a real emergency, we cursed out of bed and grumbled along to the lounge where we were supposed to assemble in such a situation. The crew rushed here and there. The young Irish mother from the next cabin worried her children along the corridor to the lounge. The Jamaican in his blue pyjamas stood in the corridor scratching his head while his wife stood lumped at her cabin door squealing, 'Whas arl dis noise. Is we sinkin'!' The writer who was always up in the early hours reading or writing, shuffled around like a seer nodding benignly that he is never surprised by anything and could we have some tea. Tea! Then in strode the planter's wife, buttoned-up, kilted, holding her life-jacket in her hand and informed us that she'd been up on deck standing by the starboard lifeboat for the past five minutes, had given up waiting and come down to see what in heaven's name was happening. Finally a shy, apologetic steward appeared and nervously told us it was a false alarm. After ten minutes discussion and minor grumbles that at least they could have provided a pot of tea we went off to our separate cabins leaving the writer shuffling back to his book muttering something about 'Tea, tea.'

In the morning I check the passenger noticeboard as usual. The Ship's Position note reads:

6.9.73 :Wind SW.
Temp: 83
Position: N33.42 W43.56
Dist. From Sheerness 2323.
Direction 243.
Dist. to Kingston 2041.
Speed 19.87

Alongside this note is an embossed card with blue edging which reads: *This evening, September 6th 1973, Captain Svensen invites the passengers to join him and his officers for a celebratory dinner. Drinks in the bar at 6.30pm. Formal dress required.*

.

'Only 2000 miles to go and tonight it's posh nosh,' I announce to Sue who is sitting up reading in bed.

'Posh nosh?' She looks up from her reading.

'With the captain. Special dinner. We have to dress up.'

'Not another of friend Lawrence's little stories?'

'No it's on the noticeboard. And anyway I haven't seen Lawrence yet.'

I see him later at lunch. He leans across his lobster salad and, moving the condiments aside, tells me in confidence that he's fallen in love with the Irish 'colleen'. 'I'm crazy about her, Barrie, and I think I'm in with a chance.' He nods, 'There's the party tonight. I'm going to write her a sonnet this afternoon.'

I can't tell whether he's serious or not. I just smile and feel rather foolish at his confiding in me.

Later that afternoon, up on deck I watch him from behind my sun-glasses. He is sitting writing in a notebook. I look on jealously at the creative artist in a spontaneous act of literary creation, the first real writer I have ever met.

A short while later he comes slowly towards me with a piece of paper in his hand. Once again in confidence he says slowly, 'Don't tell the children but I've written this for their mother. Let me know what you think.' He nods and I feel somewhat embarrassed by the confidence and honour he is bestowing on me in handing over his original draft:

Do not cast my love away
Let it last if only for a day
Let's be carefree
You and me...
Just like the sea.....

It goes on for two pages in that vein. I return it to him humming a nod and give a non-committal smile. Maybe he's having an off day I tell myself.

Sue walks over from the plunge pool and settles down on the sun-lounger beside me, 'Another literary gem was it?'

'What?' I murmur.

'You and Lawrence exchanging ideas?'

'Oh that. He was just asking my opinion on the opening to a short story he's writing.'

'Any good?'

'Pretty impressive, I tell you. Wish I could write like that.'

For the Captain's party that evening we all assemble in the bar at around 6.30pm. It is the first time we have had to dress with a hint of formality and at first we all feel somewhat inhibited decked in our collective finery. Mr Bennett is in his usual dark suit but tonight Mrs Bennett appears in a frothy pink sequined dress and wearing a black tinselled bow in her hair. It is the first time she has appeared at dinner in six days. 'Oh my lawd,' she beams. 'Yous arl lookin' so pretty. I miss you arl but I's feelin' much better, tank you.'

Lawrence appears wearing a kilt and a Scottish tweed jacket. He tells me he has Scottish ancestry and was in the Scots Guards fighting in the jungles of Belize. Tonight his head is newly shaved and polished and his goatee trimmed. He nods and smiles and makes his way across the lounge to sit near to the Irish mother.

The children scurry round and scatter peanuts on the floor in their excitement. Brian, the oldest at 11, is given the privilege of lighting cigarettes for people. Geraldine, his nine year old sister, looks on enviously as her brother flicks Mr Bennett's cigarette lighter and holds it to the tip of his cigarette. Mr Bennett smiles and tousles Brian's head. 'Promise me bwoy, you never take up smoking,' he says. 'It the devil's habit, but me a weak vessel.' His wife shakes her head and tuts.

The Captain arrives with two of his officers. They are dressed smartly in white dress uniforms. He greets us and announces that we will see land tomorrow and that we are all invited to the bridge at around 11a.m. to witness the event. We take our seats and the table bubbles with excitement at the news. Courses of hot and cold dishes are served by waiters in white uniforms, the wine flows, the candlelight casts jewels in every glass, the laughter simmers and Mr Bennett pronounces in a somewhat slurred voice that, 'God is wid de ship and de crew and ever one of us, helpin' us to Kingston town.'

When the meal has finished, the Captain takes up his accordion, the children dance and the first officer tries to caress the Irish mother's leg. Bridget, the teacher from Bolton, swoons with her arm round the Captain's shoulder, his collar loosened as he plays on with great gusto. Lawrence, his face flushed and eyes glazed keeps chanting, 'Open fire! Aren't we having fun.' The quiet doctor is slumped in a comfy seat and the planter's wife has disappeared. Mr and Mrs Bennett start arguing. He is drinking too much she says and she pouts as he shouts across the room, 'Shut yo mout woman, shut it nah.' She glares back dangerously, rises and then turning, waves her handkerchief and beams, 'Sleep well my darlins. The queen is off to her chamber.'

Sue and I join in the dancing, and eventually we all finish in a makeshift 'Auld Lang Syne' circle with the children still awake and dancing in the middle.

In the early hours I awake to the thrumming of the engine and a throbbing head. But then I remember we shall see land today and I drift back into a fitful sleep.

At around 10.30 we assemble at the foot of the gangway which leads up to the bridge. Normally passengers are not allowed into this forward area but today is different. I'm not sure what I'll see. I picture a cartoon tropical island, a small mound of land with a single palm tree. Who knows? But I'm excited that's for sure. I hadn't reckoned on being so disconcerted by not seeing land for several days. A feeling of total dislocation, no fixed points of reference, everything moving, the sea and sky and empty horizon. And ourselves similarly adrift from all that was known, all that was familiar. It's both scary and exciting.

We mill around on the bridge, peering out through the wide glass window at the sea and the sky ahead. The horizon shows nothing of interest, just a line, misted by the heat haze. Yesterday we saw sea-weed floating on the sea. It hinted at beaches, rocks, tidelines and there were sea birds following the wake and hovering just above the deck.

'See something there!' shouts one of the Irish children.

Everyone turns and looks to where he's pointing.

'Just a cloud, Brian,' replies his mother.

'No, I see something.'

We look again. The horizon is less a line, more a smudge now. It's a low, long dark smudge across a section of the horizon. And yes, yes, sure enough it's land.

Clapping and cheering, we hug and congratulate ourselves that we have come through, that we have all survived something. Mrs Bennett does a dance with little Geraldine, even Lawrence breaks his composure and takes the hand of the Irish mother for a brief waltz, while Bridget hugs the captain. He tells us that it is one of the Turks and Caicos Islands, the most southerly of the Bahamas.

By early afternoon we are passing through the Windward Passage between Haiti and Cuba. This is when Lawrence tells me of his sojourn with Hemingway. We are leaning on the starboard deck rail. Cuba is a vague shape in the blue mist translucency.

'You must come and visit my place, Barrie, visit my little kingdom of Horse Guards and see my shack on my mountain top that I built nearly thirty years ago,' he says. 'It's deep in 'Back a Bush' country near Mandeville. I was the first white man to settle in that district in 1946. I want to take you to see the real Jamaica. We need to do an expedition into the Cockpit Country. Nobody lives there. It's just bush, hog hunters, wild hogs and the glory of the forest.'

Later I casually drop this out to Sue. 'And he wants to take me to a place called the Cockpit Country, and to see his shack on his mountain.'

'Shack on a mountain? Expedition? Is he going to wear his kilt and play the bagpipes as well?'

'You wait. We'll see. I happen to believe him.'

Sue gives me one of her looks, shakes her head and returns to her reading.

The next day it is the dark hump of Jamaica we see in the distance. We are due to dock in Montego Bay for immigration and then sail round the eastern end of the island during the night to arrive in Kingston early the next morning. By now spirits are high. As the ship awaits the arrival of the pilot to guide us into Montego Bay port, we gather on deck for an impromptu party. Mrs Bennett has picked up the local RJR radio station on her little transistor radio and she is leading a conga round the deck to a tune called *Ramgoat Liver*. The children are wild with excitement, the plantation owner's wife claps her hands and Bridget brings up the rear while I snap photos of this historic moment.

Leaning on the deck rail I watch as the Jamaican landscape distils itself out of the haze. I am entranced. It is so green, so lush. I had imagined a dry parched landscape like Spain which is the only hot country I've ever visited. This is quite different.

Immigration is a stern event. A reality check. We've arrived and there's serious business afoot. The immigration officers are in no mood for frivolity. They come on board, check our passports with barely a word, give us some dark looks and then leave. And suddenly we realise the interlude of the voyage is almost over and our new lives are about to hit us.

Early the next morning I rise to see mist-shrouded mountains off the starboard side. I check my map of Jamaica. These are the Blue Mountains which rise to 7402 feet at Blue Mountain Peak. Kingston is tucked below the mountains behind a sinewy spit of land nine miles long called the Palisadoes Peninsula. It was at the tip of this peninsula that Port Royal, the infamous haunt of the pirate Henry Morgan, was located before most of it disappeared beneath the waves after the earthquake of 1692.

The ship moves slowly round the tip of what is left of Port Royal into the huge bay of Kingston harbour. Ahead of us the sprawl of Kingston emerges from the early morning mist – factories, warehouses and a few high rise buildings in the downtown area. Beyond this spreads the city, and then further, where the hills begin, there are houses dotting the slopes; in the far distance rises the massif of the Blue Mountains.

By nine o'clock the ship is near the dockside. A seething mass of black humanity, like worker bees, surge around it: dockers, hustlers, men with trucks and fork lifts, women with mops and buckets, some carrying bundles and sacks on their heads all waiting for the ship to dock.

The ropes are secured. The gangplank lowered and suddenly the corridors are filled with noise and people. We start collecting up our belongings when a small, rotund, pink-faced man with glasses and wearing a crumpled cream linen suit appears in the cabin doorway. 'Is it Barrie and Sue Day? I'm Trevor Williams, your new Headmaster.' He extends a limp, sweaty hand which we both shake and then he eyes the cabin. 'So this is what the school pays for, is it?'

We're not sure what we're supposed to say to this, so we just smile with some bewilderment. We had expected the tall, gracious, Henry Fowler who had interviewed us in London, not this rather edgy Englishman who seems somewhat out of his element in the cut and thrust of the dockside.

We start to manoeuvre suitcases down to the dockside only to be accosted by faces and voices and waving arms:

'Tek yuh bag, nah man?'
'Me a carry it feh yu, lady.'
'Come nah man, me ave a truck.'

As I go to locate our cabin trunks and cope with this somewhat aggressive hustler with a truck, I look back to where I have left Sue. She stands with her suitcase, marooned on the dockside, a lone white figure amidst a surging frenzy of black bodies, noise and utter confusion. Our new Headmaster has disappeared into the throng and I have a strong desire to be back on board the ship adrift on a silent, empty ocean. Too late. Our cabin trunks have been hauled on to a truck. The hustlers are in charge and we squeeze ourselves into the back seat of a taxi. 'Follow de truck man,' yells a guy in shades and a woolly hat. The taxi driver nods and we edge through the throng. Sue looks at me. I shrug. No going back now. The future elbows us forward.

*

WHEN BOB MARLEY WAS OUR NEIGHBOUR
AND A BEETLE WAS KING OF THE ROAD

'Maths? I can't teach maths!' The nerves in my stomach twitched violently. I was scrutinising my timetable which the Head's secretary had handed to me. Maths, English and Social Studies. Well, the last two were okay but where did maths come from? I had only just scraped through at GCE O level when I was sixteen.

'What's the matter?' asked Sue who was studying her own timetable.

'I'm down to teach maths. I don't know the first thing about teaching maths.'

A young woman next to me, another newly arrived teacher named Pascale, added, 'Well I'm down to teach English, and I'm French.'

On hearing that, Sue turned smiling and said to her, 'Well I'm down to teach French and I should be teaching English. How about if we swap?'

'Great idea,' replied Pascale.

'But what about this maths?' I moaned as Sue and Pascale went to find the senior teacher who'd devised the timetable.

'Don't worry,' said Sue, 'I'll give you some evening classes.'

It was two days before the start of the new term and this was a training day. We had had a week to settle into our apartment and get our bearings. A week to discover that the heat and humidity during the day were unbearable. A week to find that mosquitoes revel in the arrival of tender new European flesh.

Several other couples had arrived from England. Jenny and Jim Gervasio were our next–door neighbours. They had travelled on a Fyffes cargo boat and had not enjoyed the luxury we had experienced. Jenny had been sea-sick for most of the voyage. Jim was an economics and social studies teacher. He was a quick-witted, sharp intellectual, infused with the passionate Italian blood which had flowed in his grandfather's veins. Jim and I were to teach the social studies lessons throughout the secondary part of the school. Jenny was a science teacher, calm, serene and gentle in manner.

Another early notable was John Batten, the senior teacher. He was a jovial and welcoming bear of a man with an impressive beard who taught maths and devised the timetable.

The Deputy Head and long term friend of the founder, Henry Fowler, was Patrick Bourke. With the physique of a six foot six stick insect, he was a gentle, benign, philosopher who was enthusiastically developing his counselling department and willing to spend hours talking about Gestalt therapy, Beat poetry and the psychological theories of R.D.Laing.

It was a school like no other. The staff were of various nationalities, some on short term contracts like us, others like the very English Norah Hernould who was celebrating her eighteenth year at the school. She would be in her fifties; a delicate, bird-like woman who spoke with a gentle home counties accent and taught English and RE. She and her Belgian husband, a violinist, ran a guest house called Green Gables in uptown Kingston. The students loved her. She quelled eruptions of bad behaviour in her lessons with a caressing, 'Now, my dears, this is not what we expect at Priory School. You know your mother and father wouldn't approve. Now let's find a more civilised way of proceeding, shall we?' Generally this worked. If the verbal caress failed, however, she was not averse to a more waspish response but generally her gentle tone melted the hormonal heat of most boys' disruptive behaviour.

The student body boasted twenty four nationalities. Although predominantly Jamaican, the next biggest contingent was American and Canadian, the sons and daughters of managers of US and Canadian companies. Then there were pockets of British, south American, and central American students as well as a few from south-east Asia. It was indeed a classic melting pot of cultures and races.

The Priory School stood on Hope Road in the uptown area of Kingston. A wide driveway curved round to the front of an impressive old plantation house. Steps mounted to a pillared porch which opened into a wide entrance hall. Wooden balustrades ran round the upper and lower balconies of the old building which acted as the administrative hub of the school. The floors were polished mahogany and overhead, ceiling fans paddled the humid warmth into sluggish movement. In the mornings, at break time and after school, the balconies were where we congregated to mark books, moan about students or simply enjoy some semblance of a breeze which might waft its way through the fronds of  the palmettoes which bordered the old house.

Priory was number 32, Hope Road. Two hundred yards up the road was number 56, Hope Road, the old plantation house bought in 1972 by Chris Blackwell for his Island Records enterprise. This modest property was set to become the cauldron of a musical revolution stirred by the snagged rhythms and blood pulsing bass beat of the new musical style called 'reggae'. It was the early days of this revolution. Bob Marley, the genie who stirred this cauldron, was as yet little known beyond the slums of Trenchtown, in western Kingston. But when he and his entourage moved into number 56, Hope Road in 1973, they lit the flame beneath the cauldron and started stirring. And it was in this same house that Bob Marley would be shot and wounded in December 1976.

Oblivious to the murmurings of revolution on our doorstep, Sue and I had innocently moved into an apartment in a block just across the playing fields from the school. Apart from Bob Marley, our other close neighbour was Michael Manley, the newly elected charismatic leader of the left leaning People's National Party or PNP. From the back patio of our apartment we could throw water melon pips over the fence on to the grass which bordered the PM's back lawn. How cool was that.

I looked again at my timetable. Maths aside, the rest looked exciting. I was teaching English for the first time and to a GCE O Level group. This was a baptism of fire. Among the bundle of papers in my mail box was a memo from Marie Gregory, the Head of English. Attached was the syllabus for the O level Literature exam: Thomas Hardy and Shakespeare; *Far From the Madding Crowd* and *Henry V*. I had some preparation to do.

In addition the Headmaster had asked if I would take on the role of House Head. I agreed as I'd never done this kind of pastoral role before and also it meant a modest increase to my salary. At Priory there were three houses – named after the prestigious British and North American universities of Oxford, Princeton, and McGill. The house system was used mainly for generating some healthy competition within the school and functioned principally in the organisation of sports events. Sports Day and the annual Swimming Gala were two of the key events in the school calendar when the house system came into its own. However, each morning there would normally be a house assembly for announcements and for sorting out teams for school competitions.

I quickly discovered that Oxford house had the reputation of being the poor relation of the three houses. Generally the sports trophies were an annual tug-of-war between Princeton and McGill with Princeton usually triumphing. Oxford house hadn't featured in the trophy stakes for years. So, how to generate some Oxford pep - this was the next challenge.

Talking of challenges, within the first couple of weeks we were desperate to get a car. This proved anything but straight forward. We'd seen an advert in the local supermarket for a rather sporty looking Austin Allegro and went round to see it. It was red with black trim round the mudguards and had a kind of rally driver cool about it. The owner talked convincingly about the advantages of the car's unique hydrolastic suspension which, he said, was superb for riding the huge potholes which were a prominent feature of Jamaican roads. Sue and I nodded to each other and felt that now the car issue was sorted. However, we needed a bank loan to buy the car and this involved a personal interview with the bank manager.

'You want to buy a what?' he said frowning. 'A haustin hallegro?'

'Yes,' I nodded, 'it has this special kind of suspension which I think might be good for Jamaican roads.'

He leaned back in his swivel chair and shook his head, 'Who tell you that? The man sellin' you the car, I bet.'

'Yes he was quite convincing,' I said, looking across at Sue and seeking some moral support.

'Hydrolastic shit, excuse my French,' he said. 'Those cars are garbage. I'm not lendin' you money to buy a car like that.'

'Oh,' I said, rather crestfallen and surprised that a bank manager would take such a personal interest in the type of car I was buying.

'How long you staying in Jamaica?' he said.

'Two years, maybe three.'

He nodded, 'I guess you be explorin' the island, tekin the back roads, that type of thing?'

'I hope so,' I replied.

'Only one car I'll lend you money on then - a VW Beetle. That's the car for you. Strong suspension, reliable. Go find yourself a VW and then come back and see me again. Maybe then I lend you the money.'

And that was the end of the interview.

We took up the search again and eventually found a bright orange Beetle for sale - four years old and owned by a Chinese Jamaican. It drove like a tank, seemed to have over-sized wheels but they certainly rode the potholes and the bank manager was happy to give us the loan.

The next challenge was to get it tested and licensed. This involved a drive downtown to the testing centre. It was about three miles out on the Spanish Town Road west of Kingtson. I was a little nervous about going into this part of Kingston. This stemmed from some advice we'd being given at a cocktail party a few days earlier. All the newly arrived teachers had been invited to a welcoming party at the home of

Marie Gregory, the senior mistress at the school. She lived in a spacious house on Stony Hill, one of the uptown districts which looked down on the sprawl of Kingston. The party was mainly attended by white ex–patriates.

We drove there with Jim and Jenny in their newly acquired VW Beetle. Same bank manager it seemed.

Early in the evening I was cornered by an Englishman who'd lived in Jamaica for a year. He worked for a British insurance company.

'Never drive downtown, if you can avoid it. And always drive with the windows up, especially at traffic lights. That's where they'll leap out on you.'

'Leap out on you?' I said.

He leaned close to my ear, 'And always check your rear mirror for car jackers.'

'Car jackers?'

'They wear dark glasses.'

'Most people do,' I said.

'Hustlers. Everyone's a hustler. After whatever you've got. Don't trust anybody.'

I spoke to Sue later in the evening. She had been speaking to the man's wife who had warned her about the problem with servants.

'But we don't have servants,' Sue had said.

The wife nodded, 'Very wise. We had to sack ours as well. Dishonest were they? Stealing from you I expect.'

Across the room Jim was engaged in a heated discussion with an American man about Third World debt and the policies of the new prime minister, Michael Manley. From the American I heard the phrases 'Communist takeover' and 'Castro's latest protégé' and saw Jim getting quite animated.

'Wow,' said Jim later as we all left. 'I don't believe what I'm hearing here. They're all paranoid.'

Hence my nervousness a few days later as we headed downtown to the vehicle testing station. At first we had the windows tightly closed and then, when we were in danger of asphyxiation, I lowered the window a fraction. The air outside was hot and humid. My eyes were everywhere, especially at traffic lights and my pulse was racing. I gripped the steering wheel, my foot hovering over the accelerator.

It was like joining some kind of circus. Cows wandered the central reservation on Hope Road, goats nosed the garbage in the gutters, there were slow-moving donkey carts and motor cyclists 'fish-tailing' their bikes in and out of the moving line of traffic. This 'fish-tailing' style

of driving a motor-cycle was a classic example of Jamaican 'cool'. It involved squaring the shoulders, holding the arms rigid and steering the bike with the hips, tilting the bike this way and that to change direction but keeping the upper body rigid, the head held in a pose of casual arrogance. It didn't matter that your bike was a sputtering 50cc heap of flaking junk, the pose was 'king-of-the-road' cool. Add to the bikers the truck drivers swigging beer and banging their arms against the doors of the trucks in time to the reggae beat from the huge speakers in shop doorways and you get an idea of the Hope Road street circus.

We passed the clock tower at Half Way Tree and then the Carib cinema at Crossroads and now the buildings looked more tired, the pavements packed with people. Small wagons and trucks were parked at the roadside selling drinks and coconuts.

Sue was poring over the newly purchased map of Kingston. 'I think we need to take a right round here.'

'Are you sure?'

'No, I'm not sure but we need to get to Spanish Town Road.'

'Okay, here we go,' I murmured taking a deep breath.

Narrow streets snaked darkly away from the main street and I glimpsed decaying signs of human habitation, heaps of rusting corrugated iron, roughly hammered together to form a house. Children ran barefoot along the muddied roadside skimming hoops, dogs and goats scavenged among the spilled garbage and inside the rust hulks of abandoned car bodies.

The streets narrowed and I nosed the car slowly forward between the oncoming throng of brown bodies which brushed the side of the car as they passed. Women were sitting cross-legged on the pavement on bits of old sacking selling small heaps of yams, paw-paws and green bananas. Young men, seemingly menacing, swaggered to the music which beat its pulse from every street corner.

We came to a junction which opened on to a main road. There were warehouses and dockside cranes. Now we were on Spanish Town

Road. A few miles on we found the Kingston Vehicle Testing Centre. Inside the gates of the testing station was a big open concrete area. A few cars were lined up and I took my place at the end of the line.

As I headed for the office an engine roared into life. It was the big American car at the front of the queue. With grit flying, the car hurtled across the concrete, was jammed into a rear-wheel skid, shaved the edge of the earth bank which bordered the square and came slithering to a halt in a cloud of dust. The engine revved again and the car reversed at speed for thirty yards. Tyres squealed to a halt. The engine roared again and the car skidded forward, swerved to the right then to the left and ended up back in front of the office with the dust swirling.

A young Jamaican in a woolly hat slid out of the driver's seat, slammed the door and swaggered imperiously back towards the main office of the testing centre.

A figure burst out of the office, a short squat American waving a hat in his hand. 'Hey you some kind crazy cowboy? That's a new car!'

The youth cast a disdainful glance at him. 'Cool,' he nodded impassively, 'man, the car's cool.' He strolled on into the office. The car had been tested.

Inside the office people slouched against the walls. There was no queue as such. In the centre of the room was a desk piled high with papers behind which sat a fat Jamaican eating a mango, thumbing through a newspaper. I went across to him.

'Excuse me.'

'Wait over there,' he mumbled without looking up.

I took my place against the wall and felt the eyes watching me. I was hemmed in. The only white person there now that the American had left.

'Hey, white bwoy, gimme a cigarette nah,' said the stubbled black face next to me.

'Er, I'm sorry....I don't..'

The face frowned, 'Smoke the weed man?'

'What?'

'Hey you foolin' me?'

'Don't know what...'

'Ganja.'

'Pardon?'

'You not know ganja yet?'

He threw back his head laughing silently. 'Jesus Christ.' The eyes glinted. He touched me lightly on the arm. 'Where you come from?'

'I just got here…'

'You a English man?'

'Yes, that's right.'

He stood leaning on the wall, nodding slowly and smiling, rolling an unlit match between his teeth. He too wore a woolly hat on his head and had a tee shirt which read 'Legalise It' across the chest. I squirmed under his gaze, couldn't understand his accent, couldn't read this situation at all. Then he nodded and in a gentle voice murmured, 'Relax man. Peace and love.'

Another voice; the man behind the desk, 'Hey that your VW?'

I went forward. 'Yes…'

'Log book?'

'Here it…'

'Form?'

I fumbled in my pocket and handed him the test form. Through the open louvres of the office I watched my car spinning round the test area, heard the tyres squealing, brakes jammed, gears grinding and eventually, after a couple of swerves, saw the car chugging to a halt in front of the office. The driver loped back inside, threw a casual nod to the man behind the desk who stamped my log book, wrote something on the white form and held it out without looking up.

'Next,' he growled.

The classroom where I taught most of my lessons that first year was typical of most of the classrooms on the Priory campus. There was open brickwork on two sides for ventilation, paddle fans hung from the ceiling and the roof was a kind of corrugated aluminium. In some rooms they had the American style single desks with a wooden writing area attached to the seat frame. Tough if you were left-handed as the desk tops were shaped to favour right-handed writers. At the front of the classroom was the teacher's desk and behind that the blackboard. Chalk was dispensed from the school secretary's office – one box of white per term and one stick of each colour 'To be used sparingly,' said Mrs Phillips. When I asked for a board rubber, she frowned and one of the office staff giggled.

'They're called 'erasers' over here, Mr Day,' she said rather sternly.

'Oh, right,' I nodded, not quite understanding the significance of this correction.

That is until Jim put me right. 'Rubbers in America are condoms, so asking for a 'board rubber' sounds like asking a condom which is hanging around waiting for some action.'

I nodded, trying to do the semantic gymnastics and get the joke. 'Oh, yeah, I see what you mean,' I smiled limply.

'C'mon, I'll show you the audio visual side of things,' and I followed him along the corridor to one of the stock rooms. 'Not quite cutting edge technology but better than nothing,' he said. There was a reel to reel tape recorder and a 16mm projector on a trolley. Jim showed me a slide projector which took single slides but if you changed an attachment to the lens could show film strips of still photographs. I'd used one of these on my teaching practices and on one occasion tried playing some music to accompany the slide show. It didn't really impress the class as my choice of music was obviously not to their taste. There was a booking system for this equipment and you had to fill in your name and the date and the required equipment so that one of Mrs Phillips' assistants could organise things and avoid clashes.

And that was it. Technology in 1973 was pretty basic and 'chalk and talk' was very much the diet for most students in most lessons.

In the English department stock cupboard there was a reasonable stock of class reading books but the best resource was the American anthologies which I'd never encountered before. Standard issue in all American high schools, these anthologies were a gold mine of quality literature. They contained short stories, complete short novels such as George Eliot's *Silas Marner*, a variety of poetry, essays and non-fiction texts all in one book. I was almost salivating as I thumbed the pages. I felt that finally I was getting closer to what I should be teaching. I thought of Allen Freer, my teacher. He might be quite proud to see me now.

Then there was social studies. Jim, who was Head of social studies, presented me with some new books. It was a series published by Longman entitled *The People Who Came*.

'These will shake up some assumptions,' he said as he handed a set of the books to me.

'What d'you mean?'

'Well, they shift your centre of gravity from what I would call the Mercator mentality which places Europe at the centre of the world, to seeing the Americas as central.'

'I see,' I said, not really understanding.

He went on enthusiastically, 'It's the history of the Caribbean from the point of view of those on the receiving end of European exploration. Columbus is not the great conquering hero we in Europe are brought up to believe. From the point of view of the Arawaks, Aztecs and Incas, he's a murdering thug.'

'Right,' I nodded. 'I see what you mean.'

'Have fun,' he said and went off to find his class.

As for the maths, or math as the American students called it, it was always a trial and often a test of wits between me and the brighter students. I bluffed through my first lesson by a mixture of administrative time-wasting, getting the students to fill in forms, giving out books, outlining procedures and then giving them a test, 'Just to see what you can do,' I said.

'How was it?' asked Sue later that day.

'Well I didn't exactly have to teach them anything,' I said, 'but when I mark this test I'll get some idea of what I'm up against.'

I had thumbed through the maths text book which I was to use. Maths was all so alien and so vague in my memory. Apart from checking my bank balance and doing a little mental arithmetic during shopping expeditions I managed to live my life without encountering long division, decimals and trigonometry.

The night before each maths lesson I would thumb through the text book, check the exercises that I would be setting and then ask Sue for help with areas I was stuck on. It was fairly basic stuff, and I found my memory for algebra and geometry wasn't quite so rusty after all.

One afternoon, I was doing what I thought was a simple subtraction calculation on the board – 'See how we borrow from the tens, pay back to the units,' I was saying, when a voice from the back piped up, 'Please sir, I've never seen subtraction done like that before.'

It was Noel Hampling, a studious Canadian kid whose father was a senior manager at the Alcan plant. I felt like the proverbial duck - calm on the surface, but feet paddling like mad under the water. 'Ah well Noel, this is the British way of subtraction. You see the British invented a lot of mathematical practices…'

'But I thought math came from the Arabs.'

'Refined and further developed by the British and then of course probably modified by the colonists and that's where the problems arise.'

'I'll ask my dad about this, but it looks weird to me.'

Later that evening I mentioned this minor altercation to Sue. She frowned. 'You were doing what?'

'Borrowing and paying back.'

She shook her head pityingly, 'That method hasn't been used since the nineteen fifties. No wonder he didn't know what you were doing.'

'Well, what is it now then?'

'Decomposition.'

'What's that?'

'It's how you teach subtraction.'

'Well, nobody told me.'

She put her hand to her mouth and laughed. I threw an exercise book at her and after a brief skirmish gave in and subjected myself to the humiliation of another lesson in how to teach maths.

*

COCKPIT COUNTRY A GO-GO

It was in late September that I went to my mail box at school and found a creased air-mail envelope. My name and the address of the school were written in a spidery, almost illegible script. It was from Lawrence Dame - an invitation to trek across the Cockpit Country, stay overnight at a place called Windsor Caves and trek back the following day. He would act as guide for the expedition.

I'd told Jim all about my encounters with Lawrence on the boat and when I mentioned the proposed expedition in the Cockpit Country he was bubbling with enthusiasm. 'Definitely count us in on this one. Jenny will be up for it and my friend Chris who we met on the boat. He's teaching downtown but he'll be with us like a shot.'

I showed the letter to Sue. She raised her eyebrows when she saw the words 'Horse Guards Plantation' across the top of the letter. She gave me a wry smile, 'So now we'll see who was right. Do you honestly think 'Horse Guards Plantation' will be a shack on the top of a mountain?'

I shrugged. I had to admit it didn't seem likely. In his letter Lawrence listed what we would need on the trip: canteens for water, torches, insect repellent, Bandaids, rain gear. We had no backpacks but after some enquiries round school, managed to procure some old rucksacks from the local Girl Guide Association. No frames to them and they had old leather straps but at least they were better than nothing.

We set off early on a Saturday morning in mid-October. It was the week-end of our half term break. Jim and Jenny's orange VW followed ours out along the Spanish Town Road west of Kingston, one of the few dual-carriageway roads on the island. Three miles out of Kingston we passed the famous Tom Cringle's Cotton Tree, a huge twisted grey tree trunk used as a gallows during the time of slavery. The road wound between acres of newly planted sugar cane, the countryside green and spreading - to the right towards the mountains and to the left towards Old Harbour and the sea.

43

By-passing Spanish Town, we continued on towards May Pen. The road was not so good now but certainly adequate by Jamaica standards. Our trusty VW rode the pot-holes well and we nodded our thanks to the bank manager.

May Pen was a sizeable market town with a prominent clock tower in the centre. Women sat grouped among their vegetables and other produce in the shade of the market stalls. Dogs and goats chewed in the gutter while on the roof tops squatted a huddle of blue-black John Crow vultures.

Towards Mandeville the countryside began to change. There were forested hills and shallow valleys and the road was more enclosed and banked as we came into banana country. Trees canopied sections of the road which narrowed, winding and climbing with lush foliage on either side. Smallholdings of banana and yam hugged the hillsides and occupied clearings in the valley bottoms. Along the roadside were wooden stalls with wood smoke rising. Women were carrying wood bundles and tending barbecues made from oil drums and the rich smell of roasting yam drifted with us. Further on there were orange stalls sagging with bags of green oranges.

'The Mocho Mountains,' commented Sue studying the map. She pointed to the green forested slopes to the right of us. 'We take a right soon, I think.'

Just before we got to Mandeville we saw a minor road, sign-posted 'Mile Gully'. The hills and mountains were rising on both sides of the road now. The road was full of pot-holes. Finally we stopped and asked a man herding some goats the way to John's Hall and Horse Guards Plantation.

'Wha yuh seh?' he says leaning in at the window. His face is deeply lined and frosted with grey stubble.

'Horse Guards,' I say slowly. 'Lawrence Dame. A Canadian man with a shaved head and an earring.' I do a kind of pantomime of head shaving.

The lines deepen on the old man's face and he rubs his chin. Then suddenly his eyes widen. 'Yuh mean Captain Laurie? Me know him. Him a live a John's Hall. It a likkle way up up.' He gestures with his stick. 'Yuh tek a lef a Mile Gully sign den look fe dem gate at roadside. Me unerstan yuh now. Yuh a hengland?'

I nod, 'Yes, we just arrived last month. Working in Kingston.'

He shakes his head and stabs his stick into the dirt, 'Bad people dem inna Kingston. Country people differen.' He moves back from the car and waves. 'Stay well,' he says.

We turned at the Mile Gully sign, drove on a few miles along a red dirt road bordered by plantations of bananas. Eventually we spotted a wooden sign with faded blue letters: 'Horse Guards.' We turned up a steep track. There were several wooden cabins, animal pens and the rusting hulk of a pick-up truck. Beyond, a concrete path led up the hill to a squat red-roofed building perched on the top of a small hill.

Some small children emerged from one of the cabins followed by a tall woman in a flowery dress. She smiled when she saw us, pearly bright teeth in a wide open face. She raised her arms in a gesture of welcome, 'Is it Mr Barrie?'

I got out of the car and shook her hand.

'Kathleen,' she said, 'I look after the Captain. I his housekeeper.'

'Pleased to meet you, Kathleen,' I replied.

She greeted the others and then ushered us up the concrete path to the red roofed house on the top of the hill.

'He been sufferin' wid a likkle chill this past week and me tell him dis Cockpit Country walk is so much foolishness. But...' and she throws up her hands, 'him a stubborn ol' goat.' She shakes her head and giggles a little.

'Have you known him long?'

She stopped on the path. 'Me was a likkle girl of twelve years when im fust come here. Me ad never seen a white person before dat. Him come waving him stick in de air and sayin', 'I come in peace.' We never seen a person like dis before. Den im buy im some land and im build dis house. Dat was twenty years ago around de time ob de coronation of Queen Elizabeth. Me remember we hav a big party.'

When we got nearer the house Kathleen called out, 'Lawrence, Mr Barrie and him frens come nah.'

It was a small, single storey concrete building with a red tin roof. I nudged Sue and nodded. 'Told you, didn't I . Shack on a mountain top.' Lawrence emerged from the doorway wearing a kilt and a khaki shirt. He raised his arms in a gesture of welcome. 'Jamboree time,' he said. 'Come Kathleen, we need a feast. We need to kill the fatted calf for our English friends.' He turned and called over his shoulder, 'Come Maria, meet my English friends.'

From the doorway appeared a young woman, slim, pretty, combing her afro and smiling shyly. She wore a stylish maroon Kariba suit.

'Maria's coming with us too. She's a stunning dancer from May Pen. They call it go-go dancing, isn't that right, Maria?' The young woman looked down at her hands and smiled. 'I want to show her the beauty of the Cockpit Country.'

I glanced across at Kathleen but she was already heading back down the path.

There was no fatted calf that evening, just mountains of the staple Jamaican dish they call 'rice and peas' – a combination of rice and purple beans which lend the rice a subtle shade of pink. It was washed down with pink lemonade made from sweet syrup and squeezed lemons. We had brought some Red Stripe beers and Lawrence produced a bottle of whisky.

After we had eaten, he outlined the plan for the following day. Starting early we would drive to a small town called Troy on the south east corner of the Cockpit Country and leave the cars with his friend, Mr Stewart, who owned the store in the town. We would then trek north to a place called Windsor and either sleep in the caves there or on the balcony of the old abandoned Windsor Great House. The Troy to Windsor trail was reputedly built by soldiers of the British Army in the 1700s. This was the time of the Maroon Wars waged against runaway slaves. The trail we were to take was only one of  three ways through this strange almost impenetrable area. On the Sunday we would then trek south back to Troy. It sounded straightforward enough and as it was our half term break we had an extra few days holiday after the weekend to recover. We might need it. Apparently the average life expectancy of a soldier after arriving in Jamaica in the 1700s was a mere three years.

Lawrence's 'shack' was indeed a modest affair. There was one bedroom with an ex-army iron bedstead in the middle. A piece of washing line was hung round the room and from this hung various items of clothing. On a table there were some toy soldiers and some books and there were a couple of chairs. That was it. A small kitchen and washroom extended from the back of the house. The toilet was an earth closet some way from the house, up a narrow path between bushes. At the top of the path was a wooden hut and the 'throne' was sited on top of a column of rocks packed together with earth. Beneath the throne was a gaping hole which opened into the pit of the closet. Not a place for relaxed musing.

With no room for us or anyone else inside the house, we were to sleep in sleeping bags out on the concrete porch at the front of the house.

Jim, Jenny and Chris would sleep in a small wooden hut somewhere down the hillside.

As Sue and I wriggled into our sleeping bags and tried to find some comfort on the hard concrete porch, I smiled smugly and nudged her. 'Shack on a mountain top. Told you, didn't I.'

She turned her head a little. 'Just wait till our illustrious captain gets us lost in the jungle tomorrow. Then we'll see who's smiling. Goodnight.'

It was, in fact, a still, starlit night and mosquito free. There were muted night sounds coming from the surrounding hills and valleys but there was nothing muted about the giggles and gruntings and rhythmic squeak of bed springs which emanated from inside Lawrence's shack where he and the nubile Maria were happily cavorting on his ex-army bed.

After a somewhat fractured sleep and nursing numb buttocks from our concrete mattress, I was awoken just before dawn by the figure of Lawrence emerging fully dressed from his house. 'Early start, Barrie,' he said. 'We need to rouse the rest of the squad.' And with that he raised a pistol into the air and fired a single ear-splitting shot. It echoed around the hills and set birds and livestock scuttling and squawking. 'That should get em roused,' muttered Lawrence.

And so the day began.

We drove the few miles to Troy, parked the cars behind Mr Stewart's store and assembled our gear ready to start the trek. A gaggle of local children stood watching this curious collection of intruders. And when we set off out of the village towards the forest trail, the gaggle had grown to a crowd of twenty or more who danced and giggled in our wake.

Lawrence stopped and turned to face the crowd. He held up his gun. 'We come for the peace of the forest,' he shouted. 'Go home, all of you.' This time he didn't shoot, but held a dramatic pose of frowning threat. The children nudged each other and gradually melted away. Lawrence put away his gun, hoisted his leather rucksack on to his back, adjusted his army beret and, gesturing with his walking pole, said, 'Onward. Let's conquer the Cockpit Country.'

We must have looked a motley crew to the family who were emerging from the forest carrying bundles of firewood. Chris was leading, brandishing his newly acquired machete. He told us that Leonard, the Rastafarian caretaker at his downtown school had spent a morning sharpening the machete to razor sharpness and he proceeded to impress us by slicing cleanly through a number of fallen tree branches. Following Chris were Jim and Jenny and Sue and then came Maria, carrying on her head Lawrence's raingear, an Afghan shepherd's cloak, whilst peeling a grapefruit she had picked from a tree along the trail. I followed Maria and Lawrence brought up the rear.

Later in the day when he was lagging far behind and I suggested he moved ahead of me, he said, 'Never walk behind me, Barrie. Jungle training you know. I might shoot you. A soldier never forgets.'

That day we trekked for nine hours expecting to arrive at Windsor Great House where we would spend the night. I had bought maps of the area from the Kingston Geographical Survey office, but really they were useless. A semblance of a trail was marked on the map running south to north through this uninhabited landscape of conical limestone hills and thick forest. There were no rivers as the limestone was porous and surface water disappeared into underground gullies and tunnels and there were no landmarks to speak of. Generally the trail hugged the side of the hills and so we never gained any height or a viewpoint from which to see a horizon and we were never right at the bottom of the valleys which seemed to disappear into a tangled mattress of foliage and jagged limestone. Sometimes the trail broke out of the canopy of the forest but often it was a shaded jungle path with trailing lianas hanging high above our heads and bromeliads clinging to the trunks of the trees. I had brought a compass so I was checking that we were travelling roughly north but beyond that we were reliant on Lawrence as our guide. We had brought only a little food and water expecting to return the following day.

By dusk with the light fading we were flailing along an overgrown jungle path. Chris' machete was now necessary to hack our way through fallen limbs and liana vines. We were stumbling around, slipping and sliding on the wet undergrowth. Finally Jim stopped. 'This is madness,' he said. 'It's going to be dark in half an hour and we don't seem to be anywhere.'

Throughout the day we often had to wait for fifteen or twenty minutes for Lawrence to catch up with us. The group was frequently spread out over probably half a mile of the path with the bald head of Lawrence a tiny dot just visible way down the trail behind us.

This time when he finally arrived Jim voiced our feelings. 'Lawrence, this is getting crazy. We're falling over each other, someone's going to break an ankle. There's no sign of this Windsor Great House. We need to think about stopping here for the night.'

He shook his head. 'If I was alone I would be pressing on. It's just around here, around the next hill.'

But it wasn't round the next hill. With darkness falling we had emerged from the forest into a more open bushy area. This would have to be our campsite we decided. Using the machetes we cleared a circle of undergrowth and spread our sleeping bags on to the wet ground. We had brought no tents as we were supposed to be on the verandah of the legendary Windsor Great House. But whether the place existed or whether it was a figment of Lawrence's fertile imagination, no-one dared to guess. We prepared a supper of soggy pitta bread, tinned sausages and fruit. Chris cut some thin branches which we stuck in the ground, mounting candles on top of them to give us some light. There was a kind of sinister magic about this little campsite glowing like a halo against the wall of black forest foliage and the starry blue-black sky.

I must have slept a little but it was a sleep fragmented with dreams of nightmare figures coming out of the darkness brandishing machetes. But it didn't rain and, thankfully, there were few mosquitoes.

The next day we trekked for hours. By now we were very low on drinking water, there being no surface water in the Cockpit Country and spirits were very subdued. It was overcast and misty and by late morning the thunder was rolling around the hills.

Then it rained. It rained like I'd never seen before. Spears of rain, bullets of rain, rain which made a mockery of our so-called 'waterproofs'. But amidst it all the sparky Maria kept smiling as she balanced not only Lawrence's drenched Afghan shepherd's cloak on her head but also shouldered his now drenched and leaden leather Alpine rucksack. At least we were able to collect rainwater in our billy cans for drinking. When the rain eased, however, the mosquitoes came dancing out of the steam which rose from the forest floor. They bit us through our shirts, spiralled around our heads and stabbed the backs of our necks. Our insect repellent was certainly not repelling these little savages.

By late afternoon the landscape had started to change. The hills were getting lower, the valleys wider and there were signs of cultivation. We were emerging somewhere, thank goodness.

It turned out to be the village of Sherwood Content, on the north east edge of the Cockpit Country and several miles north-east of Windsor Great House. I checked the map and it was clear we had taken a wrong turning several miles back. We had turned east instead of west but at least we had arrived somewhere before night fell.

A throng of locals gradually assembled to stare and point as our bedraggled, motley band stumbled into the village. Among the bevy of children there probably was a girl called Jennifer. Little did we know in 1973 that this isolated village of Sherwood Content would become world famous thirty five years later. For it was here that in 1987 Jennifer Bolt gave birth to a little boy. She called him Usain and in the 2008 Beijing Olympics he became the fastest man on the planet. Yes, maybe she was amongst that gaggle of staring children who giggled and nudged us on that rain-soaked evening Maybe it was a relative of hers who drove us in his minibus at break-neck speed in the darkness along dirt roads back to Troy where we'd started. Who knows?

In an article he wrote about the trip, published in the Jamaica Daily Gleaner of November 11ᵗʰ 1973, Lawrence ends by quoting Maria's words: 'Whaffor you tek me into Cockpit? Why not stay home an' stick pins in ourselves?' 'My dear Maria,' he responds, ' I wanted to show you how beautiful the Cockpit County is.'

When I showed the article to Sue, she gave me a wry smile but withheld any further comment.

*

STEPPING ON EGG-SHELLS

'Sir, why we must study Shakespeare?'

The question came from Huey Morrison, a Jamaican student who sat at the back of the senior class. It was one of my early lessons with them and I had just issued copies of the set text, *Henry V.* I didn't know Huey, but with his impressive afro and a pair of piercing dark eyes he was clearly a character to be reckoned with.

'I have to agree, Huey, it wasn't the best play the exam board might have chosen. It was in fact written to stir the hearts of Englishmen in the sixteenth century, not people living four thousand miles from England in the nineteen seventies.'

'So why we have to read it?'

'Because I want you to get a good grade on the exam paper.'

He interrupted, 'I don't mean this play but why Shakespeare at all?'

'Well first, it's part of our heritage.'

'Your heritage not my heritage. My heritage is Africa, not Europe.'

Ah. There was the rub. I had to choose my words carefully.

'But both Europe and Africa are part of your heritage. Heritage doesn't only mean the positive things you inherit; they may be negative too.' I decided not to skirt the issue he was obviously driving at.

'If you're referring to slavery then both Europe and Africa are linked. They're both part of your heritage. The language we're speaking might be Spanish if history had worked out differently. England is part of your heritage whether you like it or not.'

The other students were watching this early sparring with great interest. I was back on my heels thinking fast.

'There are certain things, Huey, that people have to face whether they're living in Jamaica in 1973, China in 1800 or England in 1600. Let's consider this question for a moment; what are the regular things that all human beings and human societies cope with?'

I watched their faces. Scanned this fascinating mix of races and cultures that made up the class – American, Jamaican, Venezuelan, Canadian, British, Costa Rican. I waited for a hand to rise. Huey just stared, waiting to make his next move.

A hand rose hesitantly. It was the American girl, Amy, who sat near the front. 'D'you mean like friendship or conflict, that type of thing?'

I nodded.

Someone else suggested 'love and death.' Another mentioned 'war and the struggle for power.' These were sharp, intelligent students. I held up my hands, 'Huey asked why we should study Shakespeare. I would say that of all the dramatists that have ever lived, it's Shakespeare who is the genius who was able to explore these universal themes so effectively.'

'But sir, the language don't make much sense,' said Huey.

'It will, Huey. Give it time. This play, *Henry V,* may be about a particular event in English history but it's also about a young man having to prove himself, having to fight for a principle, having to convince an army of exhausted soldiers that they can win a battle against overwhelming odds. Like any politician new to power, just like, say, the Jamaican Prime Minister, he has to prove himself worthy of the job. He has to face opposition. He has to choose the right words to encourage his supporters. So we have to think beyond the play itself to appreciate what Shakespeare's playing around with.'

I paused, waiting for Huey's next shot. But he just stared back at me. I continued, 'How about if we give the play a chance? And maybe we'll find Shakespeare is worth studying after all.' I raised my hands in a kind of shrug as I looked back at Huey. His eyes were still locked on me but he gave the faintest of nods and didn't bother to reply.

There were other skirmishes as the weeks passed. Another exam text which was difficult for many of them to swallow was Thomas Hardy's *Far From The Madding Crowd.* A novel, which starts with a central character who is a sheep farmer, isn't necessarily going to grab young Jamaicans and Americans who don't get to see many sheep and shepherds in a lifetime. Fortunately the feisty character of Bathsheba Everdene appealed to the Seventies mood of female assertiveness and many of the students were quickly drawn into the tangled threads of the novel.

Later in the term I heard about a film library in Kingston from which I managed to borrow a 16mm copy of the 1967 feature film starring Julie Christie and Terence Stamp. I felt strangely nostalgic watching John Schlesinger's sweeping panoramic camera shots of the Dorset landscape while outside the temperature was in the eighties and humidity cloaked us in a blanket of sapping heat. But the students were enthralled and even Huey began to tolerate the novel with a little more patience. He had started referring to 'the bitch Bathsheba' until Michele, a sharply intelligent Hispanic girl from Miami, challenged him during one lesson and suggested that Sergeant Troy was the 'man-bitch' of the book.

'You cyarn have a 'man-bitch'. Dem no such thing,' protested Huey.

'Why not. He's a double-dealer like her,' said Michele.

'But you don' call a man a 'bitch'.'

'That's the trouble isn't it. The language of insults is heavily biased to favour men. What's a woman who sleeps around called?'

'A slag or a whore, of course,' replied Huey.

'And a man?'

Huey smiled and rocked back on his chair. He nodded, 'Him a stud.'

'Exactly,' said Michele.

'Wha yuh mean?' frowned Huey.

'I mean the language favours the male. So we need some new words to describe men. So I'm starting with 'man-bitch' to describe Sergeant Troy.'

I watched Huey's face and Michele's unwavering look at him.

'Jus' so much foolishness,' said Huey shaking his head. 'Troy is a regular dealer. Him know what him want and how to get it.'

'So he tramples on people,' said Michele. 'He's just a man-bitch.'

*

In my social studies lessons I also felt an unsettling but interesting sense of dislocation. It was dislocation from what had been my view of the world, what Jim had referred to as the Mercator mentality. Gerardus Mercator was the Flemish map maker who, in 1569, positioned Europe at the centre of his world map projection. It gives Britain and Europe a prominence which certainly prejudices one's view of other countries as being of secondary importance. In addition I was now teaching from this set of Longman Social Studies books Jim had ordered called *The People Who Came*, books which presented European history very differently from what I had been exposed to when I was a student. In these books, Columbus and Pizarro are not the heroic Spanish conquistadores who 'discover' and 'open up' the New World to the heathen hordes. Rather they are the invaders who brutally subdue and corrupt the ancient civilisations of the Incas and Aztecs. It is their greed for gold not their innate bravery which drives their actions.

Then come the English, Drake and Raleigh, the heroic gentlemen of the glittering Elizabethan court who had inspired my sense of adventure as a young boy. They arrive to plant the English flag in various random tracts of foreign land and claim it for Her Majesty, paying little heed to the indigenous native peoples who already live there. And in the next century, come the slavers and the pernicious Triangular Trade between Europe, Africa and the Americas.

As we worked through the various chapters in the books and read about the slaughter of the native peoples by the white European invaders and of the grim realities of slavery, the issue of race became central. Some of the American students in the class came from the Deep South. Their fathers worked for the American aluminium company Alcoa, based in Alabama, and Alcoa was now mining the bauxite deposits in Jamaica. So for them, to be to be sitting in a class of mixed races was something entirely new. Many of the schools in the south had been segregated and integration was only recent. It was only in 1963 that Martin Luther King had been leading his 'freedom marches' in America.

Now in Jamaica there was a similar mood of restlessness. It was not restlessness from the type of segregation which had existed in America but restlessness to conjure a new, more authentic identity free of the vestiges of colonialism and the domination of western capitalism or 'Babylon' as it was coined in Bob Marley's lyrics. It was a hunger for an identity rooted in Africa, often inspired by the religion of Rastafarianism and the yearning to go 'back to Africa'.

As we drove the streets of downtown Kingston or shopped in the uptown malls, the snagging beat of reggae from street corner sound systems vibrated the heat and seemed to bounce off the pavements and rumble in your belly. There was no getting away from breathing this new air of change. And it was in 1973 that two hundred yards up Hope Road from where I was teaching, Chris Blackwell at his Island Records base was working with the young Bob Marley on the seminal *Natty Dread* album which would be released in 1974 and which would catapult Bob Marley into the music stratosphere worldwide.

It was interesting that during the first term as I started to understand more about Jamaica, its history and its politics, I became increasingly intrigued with Huey Morrison who seemed to personify this restlessness that was in the air. In class he spoke in an accent heavy with dialect and street slang but at other times, when he was, say, speaking to a senior teacher, he would use Standard English with a more gentle Jamaican lilt. He seemed caught between worlds. There was the world of old Jamaica, the Jamaica of his parents, who would have seen Independence in 1962 and would have grown up looking to Britain as the mother country and model of civilised standards. But for him there was this new emerging world, a world of music which preached of revolution and promised a new dignity for the oppressed. Also there was the new Prime Minister, the young charismatic Michael Manley, who had sniffed the scent of restlessness and the hunger for change and was wooing the revolutionary left and making overtures to Fidel Castro in Cuba. He didn't wear the uniform of suits and ties favoured by Western politicians and the opposition JLP party but, like many African leaders, favoured Kariba bush suits and, like them, carried his polished cane, his 'rod of correction'. No wonder Huey questioned our studying of Shakespeare and Thomas Hardy. These were the shackles he was eager to cast off.

*

HURRICANE GILDA MEETS MR BOND

Nobody told us about the October rainy season; about the tropical depressions which spiral up from the mid-Atlantic. Nobody warned us about hurricanes. Of course we should have done our homework instead of being seduced by images of gently waving palm trees, turquoise seas and white sand beaches.

When we arrived in Jamaica it was humid and hot but, as September moved on, heavyweight rain clouds built up over the Blue Mountains in the afternoons. Mornings would be quite pleasant but by mid-afternoon the skies darkened and without warning the clouds would explode their cargo of bullet-sized raindrops. This bombardment would last for around fifteen minutes and I always hoped it would occur during one of my afternoon maths lessons. For when it rained teaching was impossible. The clatter of rain bullets on the tin roof of the classroom was deafening. Sometimes if the rain was slanting it sprayed in through the open walls flooding the floor and causing a scrabbling to save books from getting soaked. The gravel paths between the classrooms were turned into small streams and the roads beyond the school gates became rivers of orange water. The roadside gulleys were swirling torrents, great for sailing boats, and local children would run out in the warm rain to fire their homemade craft into the maelstrom and dance and squeal as their little craft went speeding down the gutters.

But late in October, not long after we had survived our Cockpit Country expedition, there came, not just heavy rain but Hurricane Gilda. The hurricane didn't exactly hit Jamaica; at the last minute it changed direction and cut a swathe through Cuba. But Jamaica caught the swirl of winds and rain which were flung from Gilda's skirts. Six inches of rain fell in six hours. Mountain roads were washed away, houses tumbled down the landslips which gashed the sides of the mountains and out of the valleys oozed mud flows which carried the wreckage of homes and lives.

School was closed for several days and so some of us volunteered to try to help out. Many of the homeless were being housed in the sports stadium in downtown Kingston. We collected supplies of clothes and provisions from local charities and made our way to the stadium. There was debris everywhere: wrecked shops, overturned cars, houses without roofs. The wide, deep concrete flood gulleys, normally dry, were seething brown rivers carrying debris from the mountains. The skies remained heavily blanketed with grey cloud for several days and if it wasn't raining there was a mizzle of soaking wetness in the air. Inside the stadium was a scene of dejection with families squatting on sacks and blankets with their few salvaged possessions beside them. We helped in the kitchens for a while and then returned to the school to check on the state of things there.

There was some minor damage to the science block and the roof of the old great house had leaked in several places but generally the school had not been too badly affected.

In the shops there were always shortages of various supplies but, with the hurricane, people had cleared the shelves of rice and flour and there were long queues at the gas stations where we were rationed to twenty dollars of gas per car.

The gloomy damp weather persisted for several days and this coincided with the arrival of the new James Bond film, *Live and Let Die*, at the Carib cinema in downtown Kingston. Sue and I had seen the film in England when it was released in July and had enjoyed the usual swashbuckling Bond escapism. The film had even been awarded Oscar nominations and subsequently won the 1975 Evening Standard Best Film Award. So it seemed the perfect antidote to a damp Friday evening.

About eight of us from school drove downtown beyond Half-Way Tree to Crossroads, a part of Kingston which was new territory for us at night. By now some of the paranoia about the dangers of downtown Kingston, which had been planted at that early expatriate cocktail party, had receded and we had more measured feelings about being on the Kingston streets. Nevertheless, there were regular shootings reported in the Daily Gleaner and the Daily News so as we queued for our tickets, eight white faces among a noisy throng of Jamaicans, we were hardly relaxed. We went inside, found our seats and sank into the anonymity of the darkness.

The film is set in the Caribbean and Roger Moore plays Bond. He is faced by the villain, Mr Big, a black drug baron, who keeps a personal psychic guide, the beautiful Solitaire, played by the white actress, Jane Seymour. Mr Big is aided by his entourage of black henchmen including Tee Hee who has a pincer for a hand and the wild-eyed voodoo witch doctor character of Baron Samedi. After the usual chases, shootings and smart moves, Bond saves Solitaire from the evil clutches of Mr Big and the villains are defeated. When I had watched the film in England and read the reviews I had not questioned the scenario on which the plot is based. But watching in a Jamaican cinema with a predominantly black audience it didn't take long for me to be awoken to the blatant racial overtones of the film. White knight rescues white princess from the evil clutches of a band of sub-human black villains.

Within half an hour of the film starting there were the first hoots of derision from the audience. At first these were isolated but as the film progressed and the racial clichés and stereotypes became more obvious the audience started to erupt with anger. People stood up and waved their fists at the screen. Beer cans and bottles were thrown and, as Bond stole Solitaire from under the nose of Mr Big, the villains were cheered and the hero booed and we sank further into our seats.

There was real indignation in that audience and in the newspapers the following day where there were sweeping condemnations of the film for what was seen as its blatant racism.

As I read the reviews I shook my head at myself. It was certainly sobering to have a mirror held up to your own naivety.

MORE CLASSROOM BLUNDERS

Whereas teaching maths was an ongoing trial, by contrast, teaching English was an unfolding joy. I had been poorly trained in the teaching of English on my PGCE course and so it was a case of learning on the job. But from the outset I delighted in exploring texts with students and trying to help them to appreciate the writer's craft. One of the early short stories I tackled with my class of fifteen year olds was Jack London's *To Build A Fire*. London's detailed descriptions of trekking through a sub-zero Canadian landscape with only sled dogs as companions was perhaps a little beyond the general experience of most of the class – snow had never fallen in Jamaica to my knowledge – but even so the text held the class' interest and I felt I was making ground.

Many of the American students found the English teaching style quite a shock. They were not used to open discussion. In American classrooms a student would sit at a single seat with a wooden writing board attached. These 'desks' were arranged in separate rows and the main interaction was one-to-one between teacher and student. For students to be sitting and working alongside each other and encouraged to discuss with each other and with the teacher was something they found unfamiliar. But they quickly warmed to it and often became the more vocal members of a class.

I'd always sensed that teaching English was where I really wanted to be. The first term in Jamaica confirmed that. No question. It also confirmed the other side of the coin. Encouraging students to write, generated hours and hours of marking. Typically, weekday evenings would find Sue and me wading through piles of exercise books. Often it was tedious if it was work testing recall of knowledge of a literature text or a topic in social studies. It was then that a couple of glasses of Appleton rum and Coke helped to make the task more bearable.

But sometimes, where the task invited more creative expression of ideas, opinions or feelings, you might come across a piece of writing which smouldered and scintillated and where the student's voice purred across the page. Then marking could become a joy. It could even create a close bond with some students who were interested in writing and keen to get feedback on their efforts. Over several months this subtle nudging of a student could work wonders for their confidence, their writing style and their delight in putting pen to paper. I doubted that any other subject allowed such an intimate insight into the minds of students. It is not too much to say that for many students writing was a kind of conduit from the soul. And they could be mortified by a trite, dismissive teacher's comment on a piece of writing they had struggled with. I know I alienated a number of students in those early days when I was getting a handle on how to respond to a piece of work or when their book was the last in the pile I had been wading through.

I remember early on in the term, the American girl Amy looking very anxious as she waited behind after our lesson. She held her book open at the last piece of work I had marked. She was almost tearful.

'Mr Day, I think I'm failing in English. I never got bad grades at home. Can you tell me what I need to do?'

I looked at the work and the mediocre mark I'd given. My comment was pretty dismissive. Amy had misunderstood what she had to do and I had written 'LISTEN NEXT TIME!' in capital letters at the bottom of the page. Probably more a reflection of my own tiredness than the quality of the work. I apologised for causing her so much worry and tried to wriggle out of my feeling of guilt by explaining again what she had done wrong. She nodded and thanked me. She still looked crestfallen as she went out of the classroom. It was a salutary lesson for me about the impact, for better or worse, that my teaching could have on a student.

It happened again later in the term when we had our first Parents' Evening. Sometimes the students would sit with their parents and listen to the teacher's comments. Others preferred to stay with their friends out in the hall while their parents sat with the teacher. On this occasion a well-dressed American lady, Mrs Purcell, sat down opposite me. Her husband worked for Alcoa in Alabama and he was on a three year contract in Jamaica. This lady was formidable and she didn't hold back. Her opening words were, 'Charlene wants to know why you don't like her.'

I was thrown. I tried to recall what Charlene was like in class. It was my first year social studies class and Charlene was not one of the students who had come to my attention. She was quiet, diligent. I rarely had cause to speak to her. And yet she thought I didn't like her. Where had she got that from?

'I'm sorry, Mrs Purcell, but I can't imagine where Charlene's got that idea from.'

'Well, she's very upset, Mr Day and I thought you ought to know.'

I thanked her for her frankness and tried to reassure her that Charlene was working hard, achieving well and that I couldn't remember any occasion when I had spoken sharply to her. 'I'll speak to her next time we have class and try to reassure her. Maybe she's a little over-sensitive and has misconstrued some throwaway comment I made. I'm sorry to hear she's upset.'

Mrs Purcell nodded and thanked me. I explained something about the work we were doing in social studies and how well Charlene was achieving. Finally, she left but I doubted that she was entirely placated.

As with the incident with Amy it was part of a steep learning curve for me as a new teacher. In delivering a lesson to a class of thirty individuals, I would have in mind the points I was attempting to put across to them. I would try to present and shape the subject matter in a way appropriate to the age and maturity of the students. I would spice it with illustrative anecdotes and humour. I might throw in some improvised drama to illustrate a historical event or a scene from a literary extract we were reading. What I now realised was that I had no control over the thirty versions of my lesson that the students were compiling. My encounter with Mrs Purcell was sobering. The power of the teacher was a scary responsibility and I had to be mindful of that at all times.

And really, I only had to recall my own experiences at school to confirm this realisation; how particular teachers, the things they said or didn't say could uplift or depress you, switch you on or switch you off. I thought fondly of Mr Freer, my all time inspiration for great teaching. How did he do it? Did he know the effect he was having on me? It was complex and difficult to fathom. And though I aspired to teach like him, so far, I wasn't getting very close.

*

BRIEF ENCOUNTER – DOWN MEXICO WAY

Weekdays could be a trial when the humidity was high and the marking relentless. So our weekends were precious. This was when we tried to explore more of the island. Often we would take off with a group of friends and rent a house on the coast or in the hills or we might drive up into the Blue Mountains where the air was cooler. On Sundays, if we were in Kingston, we would often buy the Sunday Gleaner and then drive out to the Hellshires peninsula south-west of the city. This was an area of hilly scrubland, as yet undeveloped, with sandy tracks leading through the bush to white sand beaches and an aquamarine sea. It was classic Caribbean. Back from the shoreline were some shelters roughly constructed from driftwood where local women cooked bammies and fish. Bammies were made from cassava dough and deep fried. They were cooked over charcoal in large circular pans filled with bubbling oil and into which went whole fish, freshly caught. If anything was a conduit to my soul it was carrying a plate of this food and an ice cold Red Stripe beer back to the beach with a view of the surf breaking on the distant reef.

As the end of term approached, the weather became more settled and much more pleasant. Lower humidity, wall-to-wall blue skies, and lower temperatures   meant there wasn't the build up of thunderous clouds in the afternoons. The hurricane season was over and we welcomed the two week Christmas break. We decided to travel to Mexico.

For the first week of the holiday we flew to Merida, the main city on the eastern Yucatan peninsula of Mexico. What a cultural contrast that was. We were mesmerised by the Indian clothing, the food, the markets, the stunning Mayan pyramids of Chichen Itza and Uxmal but we hadn't anticipated Montezuma's Revenge! They call it 'Inca Two-Step' in south America but it's just the same – when the bowels and the stomach decide that this holiday indulgence is just too much to handle.

It was Sue who was struck down and who lay languishing in the hotel room for a day. Somehow I escaped and in the evening decided to take myself off for a stroll round the town square in Merida. It was, after all, the day before New Year's Eve, the day of my birthday and it led to a memorable encounter.

The evening was warm, the fountains in the main square sparkled with rainbow light, there was a gentle pulse of marimba music from the bars around the square and I sat down on a bench to savour the scene. There were a few others out strolling, the odd dog nosing the dustbins. For a moment, I noticed a couple across the square, silhouetted by the arc lights around the fountains. He was big, loping and square shouldered and she was petite, delicate looking, walking lightly like a dancer alongside him, gesturing all the time with her hands. They passed by a short distance away and then a boy on a bike rode up and stopped in front of me. He was smiling, curious about the gringo sitting in the square.

'Merican? Vacation time?'

I smiled and shook my head, 'English.'

He nodded and looked at me for moment. 'Never meet a English man.'

'You learn your English in school?'

He nodded. 'Not good student.'

'You speak good English,' I said.

He shook his head and turned away. Then he pointed at the couple I'd seen earlier. They were walking across the square again. He grunted and gestured with his thumb and used a word I didn't understand. The he laughed and got on his bike. 'Good lucky,' he said and rode off.

I wandered along the side of the square where smoke was rising from the food stalls. Some of the women were making tortillas, shaping small balls of corn dough and slapping them flat on a round metal plate sprinkled with flour and then baking them in small blackened ovens. There were pots of beans in a black chocolate sauce and chickens being gutted and barbecued. But the smell and sight of food was not what I needed. Montezuma might be about to take his revenge on me too.

I went and sat near the fountains and a moment later the couple I'd seen earlier, re-appeared, again silhouetted by the fountain lights. She was still very animated, gesturing and dancing along beside the hulk whose shoulders were hunched with hands thrust into his pockets. They stopped for a moment and then came towards me.

'She' turned out to be a 'he'. Tight black trousers, pointed black shoes with Cuban heels, purple shirt, black waistcoat and waves of dark hair.

'Good evening,' he said, 'd'you mind if we speak with you?' A gentle intonation, impeccable English laced with a Mexican lilt.

'No, of course not,' I replied, rather disconcerted by my mistake over his gender.

He sat down on the bench, his body half turned towards me. Hulk looked on, shoulders still hunched, head thrust forward in a sort of vacant gaze.

'Can I ask what is your name?'

'Barrie,' I said.

He leaned forward and touched me lightly on my knee, 'Barrie is a very beautiful name,' he purred. 'And you are English, not American?'

'Yes, that's right.'

He tilted his head slightly, 'I could tell you are not American. You are very gentle, Barrie. Not like Americans.' He extended a hand of slender manicured fingers. 'My name is Edwardo, and this is my friend Peter.'

I shook the limp hand and nodded at Peter the hulk.

'Is this your first time in Mexico, Barrie?'

'Yes, that's right. It's a fascinating country.'

I was treading water here. Couldn't read the social cues. Had never been chatted up by another guy before and Mr cool Edwardo was so clearly at ease and on his own territory. But I wasn't sure about the hulk; whether he was along for security or just filling the space.

Edwardo put his index finger to his lips for a second. 'Barrie,' he purred again and then dropped his finger to rest on my knee for a moment, as if for emphasis, 'you must let us buy you a drink and show you our wonderful Merida.'

I was doing quite well to appear so calm when my pulse was racing and my feet paddling madly under the surface. But then I remembered my trump card.

'That is kind, Edwardo, but I'm afraid my poor wife is very sick and I must get back to the hotel to find out how she is. I only came out for a moment.'

He tutted and smiled and looked sideways at me. 'What a pity, Barrie, when I was sure I had found a new friend.' He shrugged. 'C'est la vie. You see, I speak French as well.'

Then, to my relief he stood up, extended his hand again and after I'd shaken it, waved. 'Au revoir, Barrie, my English friend. Come Peter.'

And off they went. I had to admit he had a certain kind of charm.

When I got back to the hotel, Sue had recovered somewhat and I was able to tell her of my ordeal and narrow escape. She didn't seem to take me very seriously.

'You should have gone for a drink instead of disappointing the guy. It is your birthday after all.'

'But you don't understand. I might have been sold as white slave traffic.'

She shook her head, 'Don't flatter yourself. You know, sometimes, you're such a drama queen.'

*

CHEER-LEADING AND HEAVY MANNERS

The world of the school was, to an extent, an enclosed world away from the cut and thrust of the streets. But things were happening beyond the walls of the school which would gradually seep into our world. By the spring of 1974 Prime Minister Manley had continued his move to the political left under his banner of democratic socialism. He increased the bauxite levy which foreign companies like Alcoa and Alcan had to pay, nationalised certain key industries and showed an increasingly friendly tone towards communist Cuba. There were rumours of young Jamaicans going to Cuba to be trained in the brigadista movement aimed at setting up communist cells in Jamaica. Political tensions between the two main parties, Manley's PNP and Edward Seaga's JLP, increased resulting in more shootings and more gun crime.

There was talk in the Priory staff-room and in the newspapers about America getting the jitters and that maybe the CIA might be supplying guns to the JLP. Certainly Manley was intent upon trying to restore Jamaica's pride in itself. He had introduced an adult literacy programme and offered the unemployed jobs in public works projects.

A mile from the school, at Half Way Tree where we often went to shop, the new sound from the street-corner sound systems was the gut-thumping beat of Bob Marley's new *Natty Dread* album. The songs spoke of the rawness of life in the Kingston ghetto, of police aggression, of the threat of revolution - 'a hungry mob is a hangry mob'. They sang of the corrupting power of capitalism or 'Babylon' and the healing power of Jah – the Rastafari name for God. As the temperature rose through March and April so did the shootings. And on April 1st a new genie was unveiled on a street below Crossroads. It was Michael Manley's answer to gun crime - The Gun Court. Styled like a wartime POW camp it was a prison for the indefinite detention of gunmen. It squatted on a stretch of a downtown street for everyone to see. Painted blood red, there were high wooden watch towers at each corner, coils of

razor wire on the tops of the high fences and atop the high wire gates in huge letters was the sign 'GUN COURT'. It aimed to intimidate and it did for a while. Furthermore, there was a new government dictat that all scenes involving the use of guns had to be cut from any film shown in cinemas. This was Manley's strategy of 'heavy manners'.

In the uptown area, there was tension but it was not like that in Trenchtown and Tivoli Gardens where the political gangs fought out their turf wars. Life at school went on pretty much as normal. The Priory soccer team had reached the final of the Kingston secondary school championships and were playing St. Joseph's at the city soccer stadium downtown.

Amy and some of the other American girls had formed a cheer-leading squad to pep up the team. Cheer-leading was unheard of in Jamaica and the sports coach, Peter Chavannes, was sceptical about this group of girls, the majority being white, prancing around with pom-poms on the touch line. But the girls  were insistent and the boys on the team seemed to enjoy it so he raised no objection. Each afternoon Amy and her squad of five other girls practised their routines, doing cartwheels, handstands and jumps and refining their chants. In the event of the opponents taking the lead they would chant, 'That's all right, that's ok, we're gonna beat you anyway!'

The day before the match I was out on the sports field working with some of the Oxford House athletes. As House Head it was my job to get the teams ready for Sports Day which would be held in a few weeks time. On that afternoon it was the relay team which needed practice and Amy's younger sister Zoe was one of my key runners in the 200m relay. Amy's cheerleaders were practising in a corner of the field. They were very excited about performing at the stadium for the final the next day.

'Do you have cheerleading in England, Mr Day?' asked Zoe.

'No we don't. I've never really seen it before.'

'What d'you think the Jamaicans will make of it at the game tomorrow?'

'I'm not sure.'

At the end of the afternoon, Amy walked over breathless and sweating. It was hot and humid in the afternoons now and not the time to be doing a frenetic work-out. As usual she was smiling and full of enthusiasm. 'I think we're just about ready,' she said. 'What d'you reckon?'

I nodded, 'Looks good to me. Let's hope the boys do justice to all your hard work.'

By the time we arrived at the stadium downtown the following afternoon the stands were packed with St Joseph's students. There were few white faces in a predominantly black audience. When Amy's little squad appeared on the touch line in their short blue skirts and yellow tops there were a few whistles. But when they ventured out on to the field and started waving their yellow pom-poms and doing their chants there were hoots and jeers. The girls carried on with their routine but they were unsettled and were looking at each other nervously. Then the two teams appeared and the jeers gave way to wild cheering and chanting from the crowd.

The game was a disappointment for the Priory team. They were two goals down at half-time and I could hear Amy talking to the other girls about their duty to pep up the team. 'That's what we're here for. That's what we would do back home.'

But they weren't 'back home'. And when they stepped over the touchline on to the field and started their next routine a hail of missiles exploded from the crowd. It was mainly oranges but it was enough as they splattered on to the ground around Amy's squad. A couple of the girls were hit directly and they covered their heads and one fell to the ground. The crowd was wild with excitement and the jeering increased.

Eventually the referees appeared and the two teams emerged for the second half. Amy's cheerleaders were bundled into the stand where they huddled together nursing their bruises and their stung pride.

When Priory scored a goal the tension increased. Now oranges were being hurled between the two sets of supporters. Police vans appeared outside the ground. We got word that there could be trouble outside the ground after the match and if Priory had levelled the score I think the consequences could have been worse. Priory was seen by some as an uptown rich kids' school and for it to beat a downtown school, especially in the current political climate, was a recipe for mayhem.

Sure enough as soon as the final whistle went and we hurried to reach our cars, missiles started falling around us. But now it wasn't just rotten fruit it was stones and small chunks of rock. The Priory team were quickly hustled into a minibus before any fights broke out. By now the crowd had swelled with the addition of people off the street who were whistling and jeering at us. The sides and roof of the bus were struck repeatedly as we skidded out of the car park.

Like our experience at the Carib cinema watching the Bond film, this was a side of Jamaica which was new to us. Tension and resentment were seething just beneath the surface. Whether it was racially driven – the sight of white girls on the field and a couple of light skinned boys on the team – who knows? Jamaican crowds were lively at the best of times. But it was not pleasant and with Michael Manley talking of introducing curfews, road-blocks and soldiers on to the streets to curb the gun crime and political violence, the prospects were far from rosy.

*

ESCAPE TO THE HILLS

Towards the end of the spring term Sue and I decided to review our situation. The heat and humidity were draining and we felt the need to escape from a life dominated by school. Initially it had been great to have an apartment just across the road from the school campus. Our neighbours were other young expatriate teachers who were on short contracts like us and so there was a ready made social life on our doorstep. By April the novelty had evaporated. We wanted to breathe some different air and meet different people from those we saw every day at work.

One week-end we drove to the west end of the island and stayed in a charming old plantation house called Saxham. It was located not far from Negril at Green Island. We had heard about this place from some friends who worked at the university hospital and it turned out to be the perfect antidote to the oppressive atmosphere in Kingston. It was run by a delightful old lady called Miss Katy. She was like a fragile bird, with slender fingers, thin arms and skin like parchment and she directed operations from a rocking chair in a room which overlooked her plantation of coconut palms. Her eyes danced and her face was kindly as she spoke gently but firmly to Evelyn, her housekeeper, to bring us tea or serve our meals.

There was only one other guest staying at Saxham that week-end and this was the warm-hearted and garrulous Shirley. She worked at the teacher training college in Kingston teaching drama. She was a fair-skinned Jamaican married to the Head of Maths at the university. We talked about our frustration with the heat and tensions of Kingston and our intention to find somewhere to rent out of the city.

'You may or may not be interested but we have a very simple cottage on our property which is available. I have to say it's very basic so it may not be quite what you want,' replied Shirley. 'Added to which its location is not very convenient.'

'Where is it exactly?' asked Sue.

'Irish Town.'

'Where's Irish Town?'

'Only about one hundred and fifty bends out of Kingston up a mountain road in the Blue Mountains.'

She was right. The road to Irish Town started at the top of Old Hope Road near the Papine market and then over a distance of around twelve miles and one hundred and fifty bends the road rose from sea level to around four thousand feet. But as you climbed the switchback road, the air got fresher, the urban sprawl gave way to small settlements, roadside rum bars and smallholdings growing banana, ackee, mango and yam. There were clumps of giant bamboo and eucalyptus trees sifting the breeze at the roadside which fell away into blue misty space. And in the distance, Kingston became a mirage merging into a haze of sea and sky.

Ultimately, the road crosses the ridge of the Blue Mountains at a height around 5000feet and then drops down the north side of the mountain range winding down to Buff Bay on the north coast just west of Port Antonio. A few miles above Irish Town stands the army camp of Newcastle. The camp was built in 1842 on the site of the Newcastle coffee plantation. The idea was that at 5000ft British troops would not succumb to yellow fever in the numbers that perished when based down in Kingston. This proved to be true and until 1959 Newcastle was used by British and Canadian regiments serving in Jamaica.

It was a different world here in the mountains. The air was fresher, there was no humidity, the vegetation changed and became almost that of a cool temperate latitude. There were clusters of pine trees and eucalyptus; rhododendrons, roses and wild strawberries grew in the gardens. The country people disliked the Kingston city slickers and preferred their slower, safer, more traditional pace of life. There were no grills or bars on the windows and doors up here.

The first time we drove the road we were following Shirley's directions. We were excited that maybe this was the place of escape we were looking for, away from the tensions and heat of Kingston. But the road was tortuous and the idea of driving this everyday to and from school was not, at first, something we wanted to contemplate.

At Irish Town the road levelled out and there was a cluster of houses and small-holdings atop a small plateau before the road started its climb up to Newcastle. We were looking for a track which branched off somewhere on the right but were not having much success. I stopped to ask a local man who was sitting on the step of one of the rum bars. He nodded and pointed the way to where the 'Doctor' lived. I thanked him and commented on how different it was up here from Kingston. He was quick with his reply, 'Dem Kingston folk, like animal. Dem live in cages like in a zoo. Dem wutless! Kingston full of criminal and gunman. Up here it more civilised living.' He waved his stick in the air and shook his head. I waved back and returned to the car.

'That was said with feeling,' murmured Sue.

A sandy track wound down from the main road. It was shaded by mango and eucalyptus trees and was pitted and potholed. But then we saw the sign to 'Mandala'. This was it.

Shirley and Martin's house commanded a superb view to the south over the lower mountain ridges to the hazy Liguanea Plain and Kingston. It was built on the Bermuda Mount ridge which ran east from the centre of Irish Town for a mile before falling steeply away to valleys in the north and south. The view north was dominated by Catherine's Peak, a conical mountain which rose to over 5000feet. Mandala House was a single storey timber framed bungalow with a balcony running all around the one side. Shirley was a keen gardener and the flower beds were bright with nodding hibiscus and exotic bird-of-paradise flowers.

There was a hedgerow of pink azaleas in full bloom and other lush greenery and flowers.

We followed Shirley down the slope behind her house to a flight of steps which curved round to reveal a small patio and white wooden cabin with a pitched roof clad in wooden shingles. This was Mandala Cottage.

'I said it was simple,' smiled Shirley, 'and certainly not big enough to swing a cat around.'

It was timber framed, clad in a single layer of planking. We stepped into a wood-floored living room in the corner of which was a door leading to a tiny toilet and shower. The living room led through to a miniscule kitchen and on into a bedroom. This room had a tin roof, floor to ceiling louvres at the front and a permanently fixed double bed three feet off the ground.

Below the cottage there was an area of level ground which looked as though it had once been cultivated. Tall eucalyptus and pine trees dominated the slopes of the hillsides around the cottage and there were thickets of massive green bamboo curving thirty feet into the air. Along one side of the small patio was a hedge of peach and white azaleas. On the other side were pink and red hibiscus bushes. Lower down the hillside were mango and grapefruit trees, trees with yellow and pink flowers and bushes hanging with bright red lobster claw blossoms. The nearest neighbours were quite a distance away down the hillside, their wooden rooftops and slow coiling woodsmoke just visible among the greenery. Out across the valley was the misty shape of Catherine's Peak. As we stood gazing in a kind of wonder at this Shangri-la place a humming bird swooped to one of the hibiscus blooms, hovered, wings a mechanical blur, dipped its long orange beak into the flower head and then sped off through the trees.

'It's a sign,' I said to Sue.

'What of?'

'Not sure but it's a sign.'

We hadn't said very much so far.

'So what d'you reckon?' I said.

'I'll have to get used to those bends.'

'What about the place? Small kitchen, tiny loo; a ladder to get into bed, a tin roof?'

She gave a slight shrug then smiled, 'It has a good feeling. And anything's better than Kingston.'

*

PEP AND DREAD

As Head of Oxford House I watched the approach of May 23rd with some trepidation - Sports Day. Each Tuesday we held house assemblies. Oxford house assembled under the old poinciana tree in front of the main building. This was Oxford's territory. McGill and Princeton houses met at other designated places on the campus. I would stand on a bench and give out notices about various events and school issues flanked by my two house captains, Cyril Bailey and Margaret Gregory. But in early May it was Sports Day which dominated the agenda. I had checked over the recent history of Sports Day winners and there was a clear pattern. McGill and Princeton fought it out while Oxford always trailed in third place. This year we had to make history and some pep was needed.

Inspired by Amy's cheerleaders and also remembering our reading of *Henry V* I sat down to compose an Oxford rallying chant – something to inspire the troops in the face of overwhelming odds. After a couple of hours of agonising over various ideas for rhyme, rhythm and scansion I finally came up with my secret weapon to put one over on Princeton and McGill. I unveiled my masterpiece at the next House assembly.

'So this year it's going to be different,' I said, my eyes passing slowly over the heads ranged in front of me. 'This year is Oxford's year. No more the dominance of Princeton.' I measured my words slowly, emphasising them with Shakespearean theatricality. 'No more the dominance of McGill.' Pause for effect. 'This year is the dominance of

Oxford!' I could sense a stirring of the blood in my audience. Fidgeting and chatter had ceased. They were hanging on my every word. 'I have composed a cheer that will lift us when we're down. Which will send a message to the other houses that this is Oxford's year. This is how it goes:

> Give us an O let's go
> And an X that's next
> And an F are you deaf!
> And an O we're going to show
> That we R what we R
> The house that's Dread
> OXFORD!!!

'Now repeat after me: Give us an O......'

They picked it up quickly and were really taken with the whole pep rally mood. Then I held up my hands: 'But that's not all.' I nodded at Cyril and Margaret who had collared six volunteers. The six came forward each bearing a big cardboard sign which I had laboured over the previous weekend. Each piece of cardboard bore a letter painted in Oxford blue. This time when we did the chant each letter was held up in turn and this time the chant was almost loud enough to blast the pods from the poinciana tree. I was delighted.

At break time Jim, who was in Princeton house, came across with his cup of coffee and said, 'What on earth was all that caterwauling about from the Oxford assembly?'

'So you heard,' I replied.

'We could hardly miss it.'

I nodded smugly, 'Just a bit of pep. Raise the spirits. Impressive was it?'

He smiled and shook his head, 'We're a little more subtle in Princeton. You see we have talent and history on our side. Bluff and bluster don't go very far in the grand scheme of things. But don't give up trying. Princeton always enjoys a little healthy competition.'

Increasingly visible around the campus this term was Pat Bourke, the kindly Deputy Head and resident philosopher-king. Apart from being the Director of Guidance and Counselling, he was the staff photographer for the yearbook. Always smiling, always engaging, this spindly, somewhat wacky six foot six character would wander round the school at various times of the day, shouldering his long lens camera until he spotted a choice moment to capture for posterity.

One break time I was heading for the tuck shop when he fell in step with me. 'Barrie,' he said, 'memories mark our lives. It's where we define who we are – where we've come from and where we're going. The camera is the great interloper in time.' With that he stopped, raised the camera, pointed it at two students sitting on a bench eating their patties and captured the moment. He looked across at me and waved. 'Wittgenstein, I think,' he called, ' or was it Walt Disney?'

Pat had an office and sitting area adjacent to the upper balcony of the main admin building. His door was always open and whatever time of day you called in on him, if he was free, he would offer you a seat, a cool drink and he would recommend some book he was reading. He was fascinated by new ideas in counselling and psychology and was keen to try out group therapy sessions with students. He recommended that I read the work of the Scottish psychologist R.D.Laing.

'*The Divided Self,* Barrie, that's the classic,' he said picking a paperback from his desk and thumbing through it. He went on, 'I'm wrestling with it at the moment but it's dynamite. You know Laing reckons that the insane are saner than the sane. Can you believe it!' He leaned forward resting his elbows on his long bony thighs. 'They call it 'anti-psychiatry' and I can't believe what I'm reading.' Then he held up a hand, 'But, Barrie, we musn't forget what's really important. Just look over there.' He had turned his head and was pointing out over the balcony. 'See over there. The poui trees are in bloom.'

A short distance across the campus there was a blaze of pink and yellow blossom.

'When you and I and R.D.Laing have turned to dust the poui trees will still conjure wonder with their blossom.' With that he clapped his hands, stood up and exclaimed, 'I'll have to turn you out, Barrie, I just remembered an appointment I'm about to miss.'

In that summer of 1974 the school honoured Norah Hernould, one of the other staff I had particularly warmed to. Norah had been at the school for eighteen years. She had been one of the early teachers at Priory who, with the school's founder, Henry Fowler and Pat Bourke, had helped to develop the philosophy and unique atmosphere of the school. As a young woman she had graduated from the Royal College of Music in London before moving to Jamaica with her Belgian husband. Norah had the voice of a home counties member of the Women's Institute but a somewhat fragile, careworn face and body. She was a plucky post-colonial survivor who had lived through the turbulence of

Jamaican independence in the nineteen sixties and was now one of the 'old guard' at the school. She had a passion for literature, drama and music and her students seemed to love her. But they could be disarmed when her usual gentle kindly manner switched to a steely reprimand if occasion demanded it.

Outside school Norah's life was dominated by trying to keep 'Green Gables' running efficiently. We had visited her little hotel and restaurant on Half Way Tree Road several times enjoying the Green Gables' fish and chips which were legendary. She seemed to run the place single-handedly, her husband was rarely in evidence. Green Gables had clearly seen better days but Norah, this sinewy strip of a woman, was the sort who would fight on regardless.

One afternoon when classes were over, we all assembled under the old poinciana tree and Norah was presented with gifts to mark the eighteen year milestone in her career at Priory. As a newcomer you couldn't help but realise that this school was something special and different. It was a place of great energy and a place which generated huge loyalty. Staff, like Sue and me, came on short term contracts from all over the world and this seemed to energise the place and give it a dynamic which conventional schools with a stable staff maybe don't enjoy. But it needed people like Norah to maintain the continuity and perpetuate the ethos.

'My dears,' she said after Pat Bourke had given the main address, 'I feel a bit of a fraud. I'm not retiring you know. Can't afford to and really wouldn't want to. But I have to tell you, it's a funny thing how this school still inspires me. My god, it frustrates me at times and wears me out but it still inspires me.' She looked round at the assembled faces. 'You new teachers won't quite understand what I mean but I predict that eighteen years down the line in your teaching careers or whatever career you choose to follow, you'll remember Priory as being a pretty special kind of place.'

The formalities were followed by drinks and cake and it was then that Norah came across and sat by Sue for a moment. She placed a hand gently on Sue's arm. 'Listen my dear, I've been wanting to enquire as to whether you might be willing to tread the boards. You see there's this play I've been wanting to put on for years now. It's a little Victorian melodrama called *Gaslight* and I thought that with all this new talent coming into the school I might finally find the right people to get the job done. And Susan, you seem perfect for the part of the maid, so I took the liberty of bringing you a copy of the play to look over. What d'you think?'

Sue was completely thrown. 'Well, er, I don't know Norah. I've never really acted.'

'But my dear, we are all actors and you seem to have the verve and spirit that the part needs. The maid is quite a feisty young woman. Now it's unlikely we'll be able to put this on before the summer but I thought maybe towards Christmas. It gives you plenty of time to make a decision.'

'Well, I'll have to read it and think it over.'

'Of course you will, my dear.' She patted Sue's arm and got up. 'Well hasn't this been wonderful. People are so kind. I don't deserve all this.'

And with a wave she was gone. I looked at Sue. She shrugged, 'Me on the stage as a maid?'

'First time for everything,' I said. 'It's not by any chance a French maid?'

Sue frowned and tapped the book on the top of my head, 'Dream on.'

In those last weeks of term as the temperatures rose, the humidity thickened and the clouds started to build up over the mountains, so the move to Mandala Cottage proved to have been the right move. We got used to the switchback ride and the one hundred and fifty bends and in fact as you ascended higher into the mountains the pressures and tensions of school and Kingston fell away.

At four thousand feet the air was cooler, sometimes stirred by a gentle breeze blowing from the north down over Catherine's Peak. Humming birds visited us frequently, sipping from the feeder of pink syrup we had placed on the edge of the patio. There were both the tiny bee humming birds and the more glamorous 'Doctor Birds' with their iridescent green and black plumage and their long tail feathers.There were no mosquitoes, no need for a noisy air-conditioning unit; we sank into sleep to the chatter and murmur of cicadas.

*

Despite my best efforts and the lusty chanting of the Oxford students, history repeated itself on Sports Day and Oxford crawled in third after Princeton with McGill winning overall. I say 'crawled' but that's unfair as there were isolated moments of true blue glory. Cyril Bailey, the house captain won the senior long jump and Amy's younger sister Zoe won the 400m but so often the colour sequence was the red of McGill then yellow then blue.

On the evening of Sports Day a party was thrown by Michael Matalon the house captain of McGill. All the Priory staff were invited along with the McGill students.

When someone mentioned that the party was in Beverley Hills I thought it was a joke. But it was no joke. The eastern end of Kingston harbour is backed by a ridge of hills called Long Mountain. At the lower, north western end of this ridge is Beverley Hills. It is where some of the wealthiest people in Jamaica choose to build their mansions. The Matalons were one of the long-established Jamaican families who lived here.

Until that evening we'd never had cause to drive to that area. But now I saw what the higher echelons of Jamaican society looked like. The mansions were built out from the hillside, often on concrete stilts providing balconies which commanded stunning views over Kingston, the harbour and the Palisadoes Peninsula beyond. The houses blazed with light and were furnished with great taste and elegance. And while we all danced to the The Four Seasons' *Oh What a Night*, sipped Appleton rum punch and gorged on barbecued ribs, I looked across the city to the shanties of western Kingston barely a couple of miles away. I remembered the drive through the tin shacks of Trenchtown on my way to get the car tested. And I looked around at the house where I was partying. Now I understood a little of what Bob Marley was protesting about and why the talk of revolution was not just in the lyrics of reggae music. The inequalities were stark; they were obscene. 'Babylon' gazed down on the sufferers with seeming disdain. But, according to one lyric, Babylon was on a 'thin wire'.

It was true, Michael Manley had started to wield his 'rod of correction' to bring about greater equality but it would be a slow process, too slow to satisfy the impatience of the gunmen. *A hungry mob is a hangry mob* Bob Marley sang on the new *Natty Dread* album in the song *Them Belly full (but we hungry)* .

How long before the mobs took to the streets and headed up the hill, I wondered.

*

NEW TERM

To leave the island for the summer holiday was to breathe a very different sort of air. We flew to Lima in Peru and started a five week trek. A thirty six hour bus ride on a cranky old bus packed with local Indians took us to the Amazon basin. We swam with pirhanas in the Ucayali river, gasped with altitude and wonder at the Inca ruins in Cuzco and Macchu Picchu, walked on the floating islands of Lake Titicaca and took a hair-raising bus-ride through the Andes into Bolivia.

It was an exciting trip but when our plane touched down on the tarmac in Kingston I was ready to jettison the rucksack and get back up the mountain to the tranquility of Mandala Cottage.

A few days before the start of term we drove down to the school. Scanning the class lists showing my new tutor group and my teaching groups I found some old names from last year but also a lot of new ones. I would be taking my senior GCE English group through to their second year of the course and similarly with some of the social studies groups. There were new literature texts to explore and that in itself was exciting.

The start of term, in fact, brought some disruption to the campus as there was a big building project to erect a new teaching block incorporating a hall and gymnasium and some more modern classrooms. Jim was taking over as Head of Princeton house and Chris Skrimshire as Head of McGill. I had high hopes that this year maybe Oxford could pull off a coup.

Most importantly, a new cohort of teachers had arrived. It seemed that Norah's life-long ambition to stage the melodrama, *Gaslight,* and play the part of the deranged wife might well happen with the arrival of a new drama teacher called Andy Rashleigh. Andy, a personable, quick-witted young man from London was keen to establish a drama department, something which had never really existed at Priory. He was already talking about a production of Miller's *The Crucible* sometime during the year. In addition there was the gentle giant, Colin Lago, a close friend of Andy, who was employed to teach Outdoor Pursuits and who later started to assist Pat Bourke in developing the counselling department.

Another new arrival was a tall American called Richard Gainer. Built like a quarter-back, he was to teach maths. He and his girlfriend, Connie, had moved into the apartment we had vacated when we moved to Mandala. Richard appeared quite a shy sort of person, rarely joining in the social chit-chat in the staff–room. I tried a couple of times to draw him into conversation but it was always hard work. However, away from school he was different. Within the first few weeks of their arrival he and his girlfriend could be seen riding around on powerful trail-bikes, the type of bikes rarely seen in Jamaica. Each weekend they would take off exploring the back-roads of the island.

'Not a wise thing to do,' commented someone in the staff-room one breaktime. 'A lot of the local boys would give anything to get their hands on bikes like those.' There was much tutting and shaking of heads among the older staff. According to Jim and Jenny who lived next door, each Sunday evening Richard and Connie would roar into the car-park, bikes caked in mud and red dirt, off-load their back-packs and with a cursory wave to their neighbours close the door of their apartment and that was that.

The other surprise that autumn was the news that teachers' salaries were to be doubled in the UK. In its wisdom, the Houghton Report of 1974 recommended an unprecedented salary increase of around 45%! The word was that Priory salaries would have to follow suit. There were celebrations all round.

For my year 3 English class I had chosen to start with the brilliant short story *Flowers for Algernon* by Daniel Keyes. It was in the standard issue American anthology but I'd never read a story like it. It focuses on a radical experiment by two doctors to use medicines to raise the intelligence of a mentally sub-normal man called Charlie Gordon. Charlie narrates the story through the diary which the doctors require him to keep during his treatment. As you read you watch the gradual improvements in Charlie's written language and realise the experiment is working. Charlie ultimately achieves super intelligence and is giving learned papers to international conventions of psychologists. But then he notices that Algernon, the mouse on whom the experiment was tried several months earlier, is going into a decline. The race is now on for Charlie to use his new found intelligence to stop his own decline.

My class were spellbound by it. I got them to keep their own 'reader's diary' of their reactions to the story. I'd never tried this technique before and it was a revelation to me as a new English teacher to see the power of personal writing. Many of the students commented movingly on their personal reactions to the story but gradually the 'reader's diary' became a vehicle for their musings and reflections on a variety of subjects which concerned them. I didn't grade these diaries but gave my own response to their ideas and opinions. With some students this set up a kind of dialogue which progressed over the weeks – me responding to their comments and sometimes the more confident ones responding to my comments. Now, instead of viewing my students as a 'class', I had separate threads to each of them through the diaries. This

76

totally changed my relationship with the group and once again I realised that teaching English was the place where I wanted to be. It was a subject like no other.

My problem however, was that I didn't have a degree in English and so getting a job back in England teaching English would be a major problem unless I gained the necessary qualifications. But how to do that? The question hung at the back of my mind throughout that year.

With my senior English group we were preparing for the mock exams at Christmas. They would take the GCE O level exam the following June. We had completed *Henry V* and Huey Morrison was not scowling at me quite so much. I'd won some approval from him when I put him centre stage during a poetry lesson. I'd discovered the wonderful dialect poetry of Louise Bennett in her collection *Jamaican Labrish* and decided it might be a way to close the distance with young Huey. I called him back at the end of a lesson and showed him the book.

Like many young Jamaicans, Huey tended to adopt a pose of exaggerated arrogance and disdain at times, head thrown back and slightly tilted so that, in every sense of the phrase, he was 'looking down his nose' at me. It wasn't 'cool' to be spending extra time with the teacher and he listened suspiciously, while flicking his afro with his long toothed comb.

'I couldn't begin to do justice to these poems, Huey. Listen.' And I attempted to recite the first verse of the poem *Six Nil*, a poem which refers to the 1947 soccer match between Jamaica and Trinidad when Jamaica lost six nil.

Huey's face cracked and his pose of disdain melted as he doubled up and snapped his fingers and clapped his hands.

'Was it that bad?' I said.

He laughed and shook his head. 'Let me see this t'ing.' He looked over the poem and I could see him mouthing it silently to himself.

'Would you do it for the class next lesson?'

He looked at me for a moment.

'This is your heritage after all,' I added.

He remembered our earlier exchange. Pointed a finger and nodded, 'Cool. Yeah I'll do it.'

Giving him a platform changed everything. The class were held by his performance, he relished the applause and Jamaican dialect became woven into our English lessons. I made some progress that day.

Some weeks later at lunchtime Huey stopped me as I was crossing the campus. His manner had changed. He was less 'edgy'.

'Hey Mr Day, sir. I been checkin' out Louise Bennett. Some cool poems she written.' He held up a copy of *Jamaican Labrish*.

'That's great, Huey. Did you find another one to perform?'

I was surprised when he nodded, 'But not Louise Bennett. This one my grandmother tell me about.'

'And you're going to perform it for the class?'

He nodded.

'Can I see it?'

He gave me a copy of *Song of the Banana Man* by the Jamaican poet Evan Jones. I could see why it appealed to him. It was about the pride of a working man faced with the prejudice of the foreign tourist. It was about Jamaican dignity and self belief. It was Huey's kind of poem.

The following week he performed it for the class. Not only did he have a powerful, expressive voice but there was a talent for drama there as he lived and breathed the emotion of the poem and the passion of the banana man.

The class loved it and, after the applause, students who had always been wary of him, especially the girls, were chatting to him and he was glowing. That day he left the class walking even taller than usual, but with more light in his eyes now rather than the usual brooding darkness.

But for every occasion in teaching when things go well, there are other times when the ground wobbles under your feet and the class are looking at you watching and waiting for your response. I was teaching my third year social studies class and we were at a chapter in the book about colonial expansion in Africa and the Americas. I was explaining about the tensions in South Africa between the British and the Dutch and I felt it was appropriate to mention the issue of apartheid.

During the early 1970s apartheid was a hot topic in British newspapers and on university campuses. Tensions in the black townships were growing which eventually led to the riots in Soweto in 1976. There was controversy about English cricket rebels going to South Africa to play when South Africa had been banned from international cricket competition. But when I wrote the word 'apartheid' on the blackboard there were few students who knew anything about it.

I explained about the system of separating white and non-white races and then realised that the class were looking around at each other quizzically. In a school like Priory where there were so many nationalities and so much racial variety and in a country like Jamaica, whose motto was 'Out of Many, One People', the issue of who was 'white' and who was 'non-white' was confusing. But I also realised the very phrase 'non-white' was negatively loaded. So, Laura from Costa Rica, whose skin was a golden, bronze colour was asking, 'What would I be?' Carin who was Chinese Jamaican and who had pale brown skin was asking the same question. Jackie who was dark brown Jamaican was stroking her fingers along her arm and frowning. And I realised I had raised the issue of race in a way which had somehow destroyed an innocence about racial stereotyping. I had introduced a self consciousness which might well be troubling to some. I felt I had crossed a line which maybe didn't need to be crossed.

Later in the lesson when the class was quietly working on written work and I was walking up the aisles between the desks, one of the students stopped me. It was Francine, a black English girl who had recently come with her parents to live in Jamaica. She had grown up in Brixton and spoke with a London accent. I had to stoop down next to her desk to hear what she was saying. She clearly didn't want the rest of the class to hear.

'You know sir, what they call me over here? A mongrel.'

I didn't know what to say.

She continued, more to herself than to me. 'All this 'Back to Africa' stuff, it doesn't mean a thing to me. I don't feel I belong anywhere. In England I'm not accepted as real English. And in Jamaica, well, they laugh at the way I speak and anyway I don't really like it here. I miss my friends and going up town on the bus. And it's too hot. Know what I mean, sir?'

'I think so, Francine.'

'So, I'm a misfit, a mongrel. Great isn't it,' she mumbled.

*

WHITE LEGHORNS AND BLUE MOUNTAIN COFFEE

Autumn at Mandala meant clouds over Catherine's Peak, mist filling the valleys in the early morning so that as we drove down the mountain road to school, it was like cruising through a floating world. Evenings were cool and to sit outside sometimes meant a blanket was needed. So I constructed a crude barbecue pit which we could use for cooking but also for a small outdoor fire. Then the evenings could be magical.

Sometimes we could hear drumming coming from lower down the valley below Bermuda Mount. Shirley explained that it was the local pocomania group, a religious cult who worked themselves into a frenzy with whirling and dancing and writhing about on the ground.

'Not for the faint-hearted,' she pointed out.

One Saturday morning I launched into my chicken project. I decided I wanted to construct an ethnic chicken coop. Just behind the cottage there were towering stands of bamboo with stems the thickness of your arm. I set to work with my new machete (made in Birmingham, England, of all places) to cut bamboo for the frame of the coop. Bamboo proved amazing material to work with. It split easily along the grain, could be sawed and slotted to make joints, split in half to make water troughs and gutters.

After a couple of hours I had my frame constructed and started to cover it with chicken wire. It was to be sited about thirty yards away from the cottage across a flat piece of ground which I intended to dig over for an allotment. Shirley had told me of a local man who lived near Strawberry Hill and who sold young 'point-of-lay' chickens.

The following week we came home with six white Leghorns and introduced them to their new bamboo home. This was our first venture into the 'good life' and we now waited impatiently for the first laying. I had also started digging over what was to become the vegetable plot and while doing so made a discovery. Among the tangle of foliage and undergrowth which fell away down the slope beneath the eucalyptus and mango trees, there were some bushes covered in small green and red berries. We had no idea what they were.

'Coffee,' said Shirley. 'That's genuine Blue Mountain coffee. Not that those few bushes will yield much but it's the real McCoy. The Japanese go crazy for it and in fact they've completely cornered the market in Jamaica.'

It was true. I found out later that eighty per cent of the coffee grown in the Blue Mountains went to Japan. That's why you rarely saw it on sale and when you did it was ridiculously expensive. Among coffee aficionados it was spoken about in hushed tones. And yet here it was growing in our back-garden. The fact that the berries were turning red meant they were ripe for picking. So I set to the task.

When you see roasted coffee beans on sale in a shop you have no notion of how they get to that state of perfection. I was now about to find out.

The ripe berries are the texture of olives. They have a soft outer skin which has to be removed. Beneath this is a moist transparent underskin which coats the light brown bean. How to proceed?

To soften the outer skins I immersed the beans in a bowl of water. I tried treading them to remove the skins but that didn't work; they just squidged around under my feet and between my toes. Then I had an idea. I fetched the food blender from the kitchen, put in a few soaked beans and switched on the power on the lowest setting. The beans whirred around in a blur for a few moments. When I stopped the machine – eureka! There were the beans and there were the skins all nicely separated. I processed the whole batch that I'd picked which weighed in at about two pounds.

Now I had the beans but how to remove the soft husk? On coffee plantations they lay out the beans on wide, flat concrete barbecues and leave the sun to dry them out, raking them and turning them every so often. So I covered part of the patio with a table cloth and spread out my booty of golden beans. I couldn't believe I was handling the genuine article – real Blue Mountain coffee. Wait till I told the folks back home about this.

It took several days for the soft moist coating of the beans to dry out and form a papery husk. Then came the next challenge; how to remove the husk from the bean. It peeled away cleanly but to do each bean by hand was out of the question; it would take hours. I turned to the blender again and on the slowest speed and with only a handful of beans, so that they weren't crushed, it seemed to work. Inside the blender were a clutch of naked little beans nestling in a nest of chaff. To separate the beans from the chaff I got the fresh air fan from the cottage, set it going, then dropped the beans from a height and watched the chaff blow away. This was high tech winnowing and suddenly the phrase 'separating the wheat from the chaff' made complete sense.

Now I had my beans ready for roasting. This was it. The final frontier.

I'd heard that coffee was roasted dry so I used a cast iron pot and set it up on the stove. The unroasted beans have no real smell, it's only in the roasting that the aroma is born. I turned up the gas and put the beans in the pot, watched and waited, moving them around slowly with a wooden spatula. A feint aroma. A little smoke.

And then a sudden shriek from the garden. Sue was down at the chicken coop and something was wrong. I dashed outside, down the path, across the vegetable plot. We'd heard movement in the woods on several nights and feared that local dogs might be after the chickens. So far we had lost none but this might be the first time.

I saw Sue stooping down inside the pen. The chickens appeared to be there. And then she turned round. She was holding up a white egg. 'Ta da! Our first egg!' she exclaimed.

I'd seen eggs before but an egg from our own chickens - it was like giving birth. And I suppose in some ways it was. I took it into the palm of my hand. It was still warm, the shell pure white and smooth.

'Any more?' I asked.

'Just the one, but it's a start,' replied Sue. 'We could have it for breakfast with some of your coffee.'

Coffee! I glanced back at the cottage. There was a coil of black smoke coming out of the kitchen window. I dashed back to the kitchen, wafted away the smoke and shoved the pan away from the gas flame.

No seductive aroma. No warmly burnished beans. No subtle Blue Mountain bouquet. Just a pile of charred black beads in the bottom of the pot.

Sue arrived a few moments later. 'High roast, was it? I thought Blue Mountain coffee was meant to be mild?'

Then she looked in the pot. 'Oops. Sorry. Did something go wrong?'

*

OF FRIENDS AND FOWLES

The arrival of Andy and Colin certainly breathed some new life into Priory. In November, Colin organised a hike to Blue Mountain Peak attended by twenty students and a number of staff. We all hiked up to a camping hut for the night and then got up at 4.30a.m. and headed for the summit to watch the sunrise. Blue Mountain Peak, at 7402ft, is surprisingly thick with trees and bushes even at that height and to watch the sun rising over a hazy Caribbean Sea and scan the broad ridged spine of the island was truly memorable.

Andy organised his first production – a Christmas show of music and drama sketches but he was also keen to put on stage Norah's Victorian melodrama. The first rehearsals were to be after the Christmas break and so Sue started reading the script in earnest and trying to learn her lines.

To mark the end of a busy term we organised a barbecue up at Mandala and it was there that Colin gave me a well thumbed copy of a book called *The Magus* by a writer I'd never heard of - John Fowles.

'I think you might enjoy it,' he said.

For the Christmas break Sue and I explored Mexico and Guatemala and on that holiday Colin's book proved a welcome distraction from dodgy airplane rides and lengthy bus journeys. But to describe it as a 'distraction' is to understate the book's impact on me. I was mesmerised by the writing, by its enchantment, by the teasing convolutions of the plot, by the ideas woven into the dense fabric of the text.

When we returned from Mexico I immediately headed for the local bookstore to enquire about other work by Fowles. It turned out that his first novel *The Collector* was published in 1963; then came a book of his philosophical musings called *The Aristos*. *The Magus* was published in1965 and then *The French Lieutenant's Woman* in 1969.

I managed to get second-hand copies of the first two books and ordered the last. This was something new. Not since my teenage reading of D.H Lawrence had I been so inspired by a writer. And the fact that Fowles was still only forty-eight and apparently making major waves among the literary establishment was excitement indeed.

During our trek through central America, Sue and I had also decided that we would return to England for the summer holiday so that I could try to find a post-graduate course that might furnish me with a qualification in English. Hopefully I could get a place on a course for the autumn of 1976 when we would finally leave Jamaica. And then maybe, just maybe, I could get a job in an English school teaching English.

Another development in the spring of 1975 was meeting some new neighbours, the Megevands. They had bought a bungalow called 'Mirabelle' which lay a short distance below the cottage a little further along the Bermuda Mount road. The house looked out over the valley towards Guava Ridge. Their eldest daughter, Katarina, was in my senior English class and their younger daughter, Regine, was in the junior school at Priory. They had bought 'Mirabelle' as a week-end retreat and, after they had closed up their restaurant, they would drive up on a Saturday night to the welcome cool and calm of the mountains.

They were a fascinating family. Katie was a light-skinned Jamaican born in the parish of St Mary in north-eastern Jamaica. Her grandmother was black and her sisters were darker than she was. She could pass for white and it was this that had set up some rivalry between her and her sisters. The old Jamaican adage: 'If you're white, you're all right, if you're brown stick around, if you're black stand back' had worked to Katie's advantage. She was a confident, feisty teenager who left Jamaica for London when she was sixteen to work in advertising. There she met Philippe, an ambitious young Swiss who was working in one of the big London hotels learning his trade as a hotelier. In the Sixties, newly married, they moved to west Africa where Philippe ran his first hotel as a manager. A short while later they were back in Jamaica managing the Silver Sands Beach Club on the north coast and it was there that Katarina was born.

The next move was to Haiti to run another hotel. But in Haiti the Megevands became targets of the corrupt regime of Papa Doc Duvalier. He and his murderous henchman, the Tonton Macoutes, maintained a reign of terror throughout the island during the nineteen sixties. He devised various methods by which to judge the loyalty of his citizens. At certain times people were ordered to stand on their balconies banging saucepans. If you were seen not be supportive, it was likely that you would be black listed, possibly arrested and then never heard of again. It was estimated that Papa Doc's regime of terror was responsible for 30,000 deaths and many more forced into exile.

Philippe had always been a very forthright and principled young man with a sharp business mind. His hotel in Port au Prince was popular and developing well when he heard through the Haitian 'grapevine' that he and his family were possible targets of the Tonton Macoutes. It was time to move. On the pretext of going on holiday to Jamaica they left their home and their business and headed for the airport. Little Katarina was even questioned as to why she was taking so many dolls and teddies on holiday. All except one were taken from her just before the family boarded the plane. And that was that. One life over. Another had to start in Kingston.

So they started from scratch with a small eating place. Philippe worked in the kitchen, Katie fronted the restaurant and they began to rebuild their lives. By the time we met them in 1975 they owned one of the most acclaimed eating places in Kingston – The Continental Restaurant. Philippe was also in demand for orchestrating state banquets at King's House, the residence of the Governor General.

During our remaining time in Jamaica and in the later 1970s, the Megevands became an important barometer for measuring the social and political temperature of this increasingly volatile country. But in our early meetings it was simply their lively company which we so enjoyed.

Around noon on a Sunday we would wander down the lane below Mandala to the Megevand's bungalow. Typically Katie would be down amongst her swathes of anthuriums, hibiscus and azaleas cutting and pruning while the girls played table tennis on the patio. As soon as we arrived, Philippe would appear. Always dapper, he would be dressed in his tailored shorts and a well-pressed sports shirt, his long cigarette holder clamped between his teeth.

'Salut, mon brave, so you think you can whoop the maestro today do you?' He would eject the girls from the patio, thrust a cold Red

Stripe beer and a table tennis bat into my hands, park his cigarette holder in an ash tray and take up his position at the end of the table.

Sue would drift away to chat to Katie and help collect flowers from the garden and Philippe and I would thrash away for an hour trying to out play each other.

The afternoon would be whiled away at the dinner table. Philippe would have conjured from the kitchen a piece of fillet steak, a tossed salad and a couple of bottles of fine red wine while Katie entertained us with anecdotes about the quirks and foibles of Jamaican politicians and country folk. She wrote a weekly column for the Sunday Gleaner entitled *What's a Day Without Laughter* and her observations were sharp and often hilarious.

And thus the Megevands became closely woven into our lives at Mandala. They broadened our grasp of things Jamaican and, more importantly, prepared us for the storm clouds which were gathering.

*

OF AGENTS, ROADIES AND LUVVIES

For the moment we were more than oblivious to the wider social rumblings in the country. We were preoccupied with school and with living the adventure which was Jamaica. Sue's 26th birthday was celebrated down on Hellshires Beach with a barbecue and improvised game of cricket. Jim and I had snorkelled out to the reef with our spear guns and caught a clutch of lobsters and some small fish. Sue, Jenny and Pascale sliced up fresh pineapple, mangoes and bananas, the barbecue sizzled with chicken, seafood and peppers and there were chilled Red Stripe beers in the cooler.

Colin borrowed a machete to fashion a cricket bat and wickets out of some driftwood and Andy entertained us with his anecdotes of the theatre and green room scandals. After the meal we played a frenzied game of beach cricket, swam in a crystal clear aquamarine sea, puffed on Jamaican cigars and dunked slivers of pineapple in glasses of Appleton rum. It was a way of life which could have been taken from the TV adverts for Bounty bars – the beautiful young things enjoying a life of sun-bleached hedonism.

But now the nights were increasingly punctuated by the distant throb of police helicopters and pierced by the beams of searchlights. From high up on our mountainside at Mandala we could hear the rhythmic droning and sometimes spot the thin laser beams of light as these sinister insect machines swung low over the downtown streets. The

Manley government had introduced curfews in an effort to thwart the increasingly brazen activities of the gunmen. Manley's championing of Fidel Castro, his visit to Cuba and his increasing of the bauxite levy on the American and Canadian aluminium companies had upset the hierarchy of power in the west. America was not happy. The Jamaican middle classes were getting the jitters and the US Secretary of State, Henry Kissinger, arrived that year to check Jamaica's pulse.

At school this coincided with our own local crisis. The newly-arrived American maths teacher and his girl-friend were absent one Monday morning. They had not arrived back at the staff apartments on their trail-bikes the previous night. There was general consternation and murmurings in the staff room. By the end of the week when they still hadn't appeared, people feared the worst. A special assembly was held at which prayers were offered for the safe return of the two young people. Any day we expected news of two bodies being found in some remote ditch in the bush. But no word came from the police. A week passed and then another. Still no news.

Several weeks later the school received a brief telephone call from America. It was Robert Gainer's father. His son was safe back in America with his girlfriend. Would the school send his belongings from the apartment?

The Head replied that the school would not and gave the Gainers four weeks to clear the apartment otherwise the contents would be auctioned for charity.

And that's how I came to acquire part of Robert Gainer's record collection which included Joni Mitchell's *Blue*, Carole King's *Tapestry* and James Taylor's *Mud Slide Slim*. There wasn't a lot on sale at the auction but it was an event tinged with mystery. Why had they disappeared in such curious circumstances? Where did they go on their week-end jaunts along the back roads of Jamaica? And why didn't they come back to collect their stuff?

It finally emerged that when your cover is blown, a CIA agent doesn't hang around to pick up his belongings!

Life went on. The school timetable was re-jigged to cover Gainer's classes. Rehearsals for *Gaslight* were proceeding apace and Andy reported that a 'tour' was being organised. After a three night run at the school, Norah's play would be taken round the island to a venue in Mandeville and to the prestigious private theatre of Paul Methuen in Montego Bay. It was now time for Sue to get the jitters in her role as Nancy, the maid.

'But I've never even performed on stage before and we're going on tour?'

'You'll be fine,' I said. 'You're good. You know your lines. I've been watching rehearsals.'

'You promised you wouldn't.'

'I know.'

'I said you couldn't watch until I'd got some confidence in doing the part.'

'Yes I know but I couldn't resist having a peep. You're good. You bob a cute little curtsy. How's your costume?'

She gave me a sideways look. 'It's a Victorian, floor length black dress.'

'Not a French maid style then?'

'Not a French maid style. Straight-laced Victorian.'

The production at school was a resounding success. Norah lived the part. Her normal thin, diminutive frame took on a powerful gravitas and charisma that was quite startling as she faced off against the rotund bullying frame of Vin McKie who played her sinister husband, Mr Manningham. There was the kind of tension between them that was reminiscent of the nerve-snagging tension between Elizabeth Taylor and Richard Burton in the 1966 film production of *Who's Afraid Of Virginia Woolf.* Norah shed tears of joy on the second curtain call. This was the fulfilment of something she'd wanted to achieve for so long.

It was reviewed in the *Daily Gleaner* on June 18th. I was sitting on the patio at Mandala having just driven up from school when I came across Christopher Philip's review. It was glowing in its praise: *'Norah Hernould's Manningham was touching, sometimes gently amusing, hysterically frightening and always convincing....*It went on ' *Susan Day, as pretty a Nancy as you could want has an obvious bent for comedy...* '

Sue was inside the cottage taking a shower. She hadn't seen the review. When she emerged I said, 'Did you know you have a bent for comedy?'

'I've got a what?'

'Christopher Philip, renowned theatre critic of the *Gleaner,* says you have a 'bent for comedy'.'

She raised her eyebrows, 'Really? Is it good to have that?'

'Of course.'

'What are you reading?'

'A very glowing review about your prowess as an actress.'

'Let me see that,' she said grabbing the paper.

'Impressive, huh.' I said, nodding sagely. 'You did well.'

She smiled. 'Not bad. Pretty good for a novice. But will it be as good on tour?'

'First stop Mandeville, next week-end. We'll soon see.'

But Mandeville was another story. It was a good job Mr Christopher Philip was not reviewing that production.

We left school on the Friday afternoon after packing the set, the lights, costumes and all the other paraphernalia in a red Ford Transit van. We were crammed to the gunnels. Colin, Andy and I rode in the van, the others came by car.

'So where are we performing?' asked Andy.

Colin and I shrugged. 'Somewhere in Mandeville,' replied Colin. He fished out a piece of paper from his pocket. 'St Gabriel's school, Maggotty Road, Mandeville. It's something Vin has arranged. He knows people there. Says they're really hot on theatre.'

'Maggotty Road?' exclaimed Andy. 'Doesn't sound very promising. But, the provinces are beckoning. Let us rise to the calling. Drive on.'

It was a tortuous drive. Friday afternoon on the Spanish Town Road is a definite challenge. Drivers are high on either the coming weekend or the weed or both – overstuffed trucks and country buses blasting their claxons, motor cyclists fish-tailing in and out of the traffic, taxi-drivers following their own version of the highway code as well as regular motorists in everything from clapped out Morris Oxfords to sleek BMWs with darkened windows – it was a free-for-all and Colin gamely steered our own overstuffed red van along the weaving stream trying to keep in view the other cars in our convoy.

It was getting dark as we finally wound our way along the streets of Mandeville searching for our venue. After a couple of enquiries we pulled up on a piece of waste ground opposite a low building. We weren't exactly in the middle of the town more on the outskirts. It almost felt rural.

'Are you sure we're in the right place, Vin?' asked Andy.

Vin emerged from the car he had been travelling in with Sue and Norah. He nodded, 'This is St Gabriel's.'

'Not exactly the West End is it,' said Andy.

'Don't worry. They really love theatre in Mandeville. You wait.'

We waited while Vin located the school caretaker who seemed somewhat bemused by our arrival. It seemed he wasn't expecting us.

As we started to unload the scenery flats from the van I was aware of a rustling in the bushes and movement in the darkness. The street lights caught the whites of several pairs of eyes staring at us. A little group of children had assembled to watch our progress. We carried the lighting gantries into the school hall. At one end was a small low stage. There were chairs stacked around the walls.

'No reception committee, then?' asked Andy.

'It is all rather quiet,' murmured Norah. 'Vin, my dear, you did send those posters and the publicity material.'

'Of course,' replied Vin.

'But did they arrive and did anyone do anything with them?' muttered Colin as we heaved the scenery flats into place and started screwing them together.

Sue and Norah started putting out the chairs as a few adult faces peered through the doorway. 'Wha' happenin'?' said an older man with a grey stubbled face. 'Is it a church meeting?'

Andy who was at the top of a ladder fixing one of the spot-lights called out, 'We're putting on a play, a Victorian melodrama. You'll love it. Go tell all your friends and family. Go tell the whole of Mandeville.'

The old man nodded, 'Carnival come to town,' he chuckled.

One or two more folks hovered at the doorway. The gaggle of children had grown somewhat and there were one or two local youths in woolly tams slouched against the door jamb watching us with a degree of suspicion.

The curtain was due to rise at 7.30 although there was no actual curtain in this makeshift theatre space. The stage itself was not very deep or wide and so entrances and exits would be a major challenge if not impossible. But the crucial thing was the lighting. The whole play rests on the way the evil husband tinkers with the gaslights dimming them and brightening them as part of his scheme to drive his poor wife mad. Whether the primitive lighting circuitry in this school hall would cope with subtle shifts in voltage was debatable. Colin was the lighting man and he was not very hopeful.

'I'm not putting money on this,' he murmured as he plugged in the dimmer board.

The lighting flickered as he moved the dimmer switches gingerly, awaiting some kind of explosion. But God was smiling and the stage lights brightened. There was clapping from a small group of children who had taken up the seats on the front row. By 7.15 a few more people had peered in at the hall entrance and tentatively stepped inside.

They were just curious locals. This was certainly not the Mandeville theatre-going set who clearly knew nothing of our production.

'Are we charging for this?' asked Andy.

'I'll ask Norah,' I suggested.

I found her in a small box-room behind the stage dressed in her long black dress and applying her make-up.

'Doesn't seem as though we were expected. There aren't many people out there.'

Norah sighed quietly, 'I shall have stern words with Vin later. But in the meantime, my dear, let's just treat this as another dress rehearsal. I'm sure these local people might enjoy a Victorian melodrama. We have a duty to put on the show now we're here.'

'And what about charging?'

She thought for a moment. 'How about if we mention at the start that there will be a charitable collection at the end of the production. I fear that if we try to extract money from these local people, they'll all disappear and then where would we be?'

I reported back to the others. Andy was not chuffed. 'I know we're bloody amateurs but we're not a charity.'

But like the true actor he was Andy took centre stage at 7.30 and, so that the audience knew what was coming, delivered a kind of Shakesperean prologue to the row of little children at the front, the huddle of older people in the middle and the group of slouching youths at the back.

'Good evening, theatre–goers. We are the Priory Players from Kingston and we've driven three hours this afternoon to bring you our play called *Gaslight*. It's what is called a Victorian melodrama....'

I was watching the faces – the staring eyes and open mouths of the little children at the front, the puzzled expressions of the adults, the frowns of the 'rude boys' at the back.

'.....it's not a comedy but a very gripping story of a man who tries to drive his wife mad. It's set in Victorian times, that's about a hundred years ago so you'll find the costumes different from today.' He opened his arms wide. 'So enjoy the show, and remember children,' he said looking sternly at the open mouths on the front row, 'no giggling, no laughing, this is M-E-L-O-drama!' He finished with a flourish, turned on his heel and then remembered and turned back. 'Oh yes, and we're performing in aid of charity. There will be a collection box at the door for your contributions. Give generously.' And with that he made his exit through the door at the rear of the set. The children looked at each other, huddled closer and fidgeted nervously.

The performance started quite well but the audience were far from attentive. They didn't really know what was going on. They mumbled and murmured, got up and went out, came back in, brought their friends, while the children on the front row alternately gasped and giggled at this old white lady in a long black dress, yelling and screaming at her husband in his tail-coat. And when Andy as the red-bearded, rotund Inspector Rough appeared towards the end and harrumphed around the stage, the old grey-stubbled veteran in the audience announced to nobody in particular, 'Him Sherlock Holmes, me know it a'ready!'

It was as Andy was handcuffing the villainous Mr Manningham and Norah was about to deliver her climactic final speech that the fuse board exploded with a flash. There were squeals from the children as we were plunged into darkness. Then I heard a frantic clapping from Colin, which prompted the audience to join in. They thought this was the way it ended.

And so it did that night.

We dismantled the set and the lights by hurricane lamp. The old caretaker hovered around us with his bunch of keys. 'Me find the play a likkle confusin',' he said.

'Not quite Samuel Beckett was it,' said Andy, 'but this evening's production had, I feel a somewhat Ibsen-esque surrealism about it.'

Norah stepped forward. 'But did you enjoy it?' she said touching the old man gently on his arm.

The old man nodded, 'Oh yes mistress, but it need some songs to liven it up a likkle. Singin' is what nourishes the soul.'

Norah nodded. 'That's a good idea. Thank you for your suggestion.'

'No problem,' replied the old man.

'And don't forget the charity box,' called Andy, from the back of the van.

'You'll be lucky' said Colin picking up the empty box. 'I think we put this one down to experience.'

The third and final leg of the grand *Gaslight* tour took place a week later in Montego Bay. What a contrast this was from the farce in Mandeville. We were hosted by the flamboyant Paul Methuen, a prime mover among the culture vultures of the north-west coast around Mobay. He lived in an old plantation house on what had been the once prestigious Fairfield estate. He and a worthy band of theatre lovers had set up the Montego Bay Little Theatre which had opened its doors only a month before we arrived.

91

The theatre itself was housed in a split-level timber building which was once the tennis pavilion overlooking the famous grass courts of the Fairfield Country Club. It had been inspired by the Little Theatre in Kingston which Henry Fowler, the founder of Priory School, and his wife Greta had opened in 1961. Goaded in part by the stinging comment of Bernard Shaw when he visited Jamaica in the early twenties: 'What! No dramatists in Jamaica? Then no civilisation here,' the Fowlers had worked tirelessly to establish a theatre in Kingston. Its purpose was to promote art in all its forms from live theatre and dance to art exhibitions and education. We had attended a number of thrilling performances of the Jamaica National Dance Company at the Little Theatre in Kingston. At that time the National Dance Company was led by the charismatic Rex Nettleford who was a brilliant choreographer of contemporary dance.

In Montego Bay it was Paul Methuen who led the charge to establish the theatre. So our arrival just over a month after the opening of the new theatre was a cause for great excitement among the luvvies of Mobay and their friends in Miami.

'Welcome, welcome my dears. How marvellous to entertain a group of travelling players.' He waved his arms, wafted a handkerchief at the humid air. 'I feel like Prince Hamlet welcoming the actors to Elsinore. Oh how wonderfully Elizabethan that sounds.'

He was dressed in a pink silk shirt, white trousers and white shoes. Tanned and smiling with a head of dark wavy hair, he led us into his home. It was a place of white walls, polished wooden floors, white paintwork; sunlit and airy. The walls were adorned with art work and there were bookshelves and collections of framed photographs. We had been told that he was good friend of Prince Philip who on royal visits to the island would escape from his royal duties to visit his friend Paul. On a bookshelf I later spotted a photo of the two of them standing together relaxing in the garden at Fairfield.

So here we were in the rarefied echelons of a very different Jamaican society. Paul Methuen had a reputation for being a brilliant theatre practitioner and had been responsible for many of the Shakespeare productions which had played on the Kingston circuit in the 60s and early 70s. He had owned a property at 72, Hope Road, in Kingston where he had set up a garden theatre in the 1960s. So to finally open the doors of the new theatre at Montego Bay was a major milestone in his career.

The performance would take place the following evening so we could at least relax after the drive from Kingston and set up the following day. Paul was an indulgent host. A sumptuous buffet was prepared for us, drinks flowed and he spent time talking with great animation to Norah and Andy about the state of modern theatre.

'My dears, we are so starved over here. And we struggle so. I read the reviews of things showing in London's West End and on Broadway and at times I feel so bereft in what sometimes feels like a cultural desert. But then I walk in my garden, feed my humming birds and tend my flowers and remember that it is here that I'm needed. And with our new theatre opening, I could not be more inspired.'

Norah, who at school so often looked frail and careworn, glowed in these surroundings. She sat like a delicate bird, settling her feathers, and mused on a way of life which had passed her by. Music and theatre had been in her blood since she was young but Jamaica had taken its toll.

'Oh, I know my dear,' said Paul, 'I just don't know what is going to happen to this country. But whatever does happen we have to put our faith in the arts which have such transcendent power to heal and to pave the way to better things.'

Norah smiled and nodded. It was clear to the rest of us that the daily grind of trying to run an ailing guest house and manage the stresses of school teaching were wearing her down. But here, in this world away, there was a kind of respite and tonic in which she delighted. On stage the following evening she gave the performance of a lifetime.

Many in the audience had flown in from Miami especially for the event. They arrived like a flock of exotic birds, the women swathed in silks and chiffon, some with flamboyant large brimmed hats and the men in Kariba suits and colourful cravats. Paul was in his element meeting and greeting his flock of devotees. The foyer of the small theatre was decked out with flowers and the pastel shades of the house lights created a deliciously comforting ambience. And, when the house lights dimmed and the stage was illuminated by the spots and floodlights and the curtain drew back to reveal the interior of a Victorian town house, the audience was transfixed.

I managed to escape from backstage during the second half and stood at the rear of the theatre to watch the climax of the play. Following the Mandeville fiasco we had re-painted the scenery flats and the stage set looked impressive. Norah's performance was electrifying and although I had seen the end of the play many times I too was held by the taut power of her voice and her stage presence.

When the curtain finally fell the audience applauded rapturously and on the third curtain call were on their feet with Paul shouting, 'Bravo! Bravo!'

He went up on stage and thanked the Priory Players for their 'scintillating performance' and hoped we would return again with our next production.

'There's going to be a 'next production'?' ventured Colin, as we started dismantling the set.

'This is just the beginning,' responded Andy.

'Too nerve-wracking for me,' said Sue.

Norah just beamed, 'My dears, this has been one of the special moments of my life. Nothing could ever match it. I have lived with the idea of this play for so many years and now finally we have brought it to life. And I thank you all for helping to make it happen.'

We returned to Paul's house for drinks and a welcome night's sleep. The following morning we packed away our things, thanked Paul for his hospitality and took the north coast road back to Kingston.

It was a good way to end our second year at Priory. We had booked our flights back to England for the summer but had heard little news of what was happening across the Atlantic. Then two letters arrived, one from my father and one from Will who had left Sweden and gone to Japan. He was now working in a college near the city of Nagoya and all was well in the land of the midnight sun.

My father's letter was less joyful. Britain was 'going to the dogs'. Inflation was running at 24% and petrol had gone up by 70% in the year! The Conservative party had chosen, of all things, a woman leader – someone called Margaret Thatcher and the IRA was threatening to explode more bombs in London. Just a warning, he said, that England in the summer of 1975 wasn't the rosiest of places to be going back to.

*

ENGLAND – THAT ENGLAND

Strange to be back in the old country. The air was certainly sharper and invigorating after the high temperatures and humidity in Jamaica. And having been away for two years you noticed things. Our white faces were no longer significant; we weren't a minority anymore and that felt more comfortable. There were no queues at the petrol

94

stations and the petrol price at 72p a gallon was much cheaper than in Jamaica. The supermarket shelves were full and house prices had rocketed while we'd been away. Our little semi in Staffordshire which we'd been renting out was now worth double what we paid for it.

But, after the initial novelty of our return and meeting up with family and friends, it began to feel mildly oppressive. There was a tired mood about England. In Jamaica we felt we were living 'on the edge' somehow with its unpredicatability which, at times, was unnerving but always exciting. Here, in England, everything seemed safe and predictable. The news was dominated by strikes, union disputes and the American debacle in Vietnam. The only other real drama of the summer came when the test match at Headingley had to be abandoned after supporters of the armed robber George Davis vandalised the pitch. Apart from that, little on the English landscape had changed.

One week of the holiday was spent in Dorset in a caravan belonging to my aunt and it was during that week that we happened to visit Lyme Regis. We indulged in things English – real ale and meat pasties for lunch and cream teas in the afternoon. It was when we were browsing in the local branch of W.H.Smith that Sue came across to me with a book.

'Didn't you order this back in Jamaica?' She was holding a copy of John Fowles' *The French Lieutenant's Woman.*

I looked at the cover. 'It never arrived and then I forgot about it.'

'I'll get a copy but I get first read.'

I checked the shelves and found another Fowles' book – *The Ebony Tower,* published the previous year.

Sue devoured the book in four days and when she handed it over to me said, 'I think you'll love it . And it's set in Lyme Regis. How about that.'

On the plane back to Jamaica I finished reading *The Ebony Tower,* Fowles' first book of short stories. A couple of the stories drew me in but not like *The French Lieutenant's Woman* which had me utterly intrigued but confused. Described as 'a post-modern Victorian novel' it was a book like no other I had ever read. At one point, at the start of chapter thirteen, Fowles holds up the plot and starts talking to the reader about the process of constructing the novel. This was a new kind of writing to me and it was the first time I had heard the term 'post-modern' to describe a style of writing. The term was unfamiliar and I was reminded once again that my knowledge of literary terminology was pretty limited.

One of the purposes of returning to England that summer was to try to find a university course which would equip me with an English degree and allow me to apply for jobs teaching English when we finally returned. After thumbing through countless course directories and making various phone calls, I finally located a post-graduate course at Lancaster University which might accept me. It was a one-year MA degree based on English and American literature but linked with social and art history. It sounded just what I was after. But I would have to prove my literary credentials before they would accept me. They needed an extended essay on a literary topic of my choice by the end of November and my future in teaching was resting on it.

An idea started to emerge that maybe Fowles' work could be the focus of my essay. I was sure it had literary merit but I wondered if universities might be 'sniffy' about contemporary writers being a valid subject for study. My new bible had become Fowles' book of philosophical musings - *The Aristos* and since Colin gave me *The Magus* back in September I had now read all that Fowles had written. Being so new, there would obviously be no body of critical commentary on Fowles' work so I would be venturing into uncharted territory. This might or might not be in my favour.

*

We arrived back in Jamaica in early September, a week before the start of the new term. It was a joy to open up the cottage door of Mandala. There was the smell of polish and the floor boards shone. Verna, the young girl who cleaned for Shirley, had obviously been down to freshen up the place. Across the yard, the chickens looked healthy enough. But my attempt to grow some vegetables on the hillside below the cottage  was a disaster. The cauliflowers had bolted, the cabbages had provided a feast for the slugs but there were a few tomatoes which looked edible. Below the cottage I noticed mangoes on the trees and grapefruit sagging on some other branches. All was not lost. Across the valley the mist was curling down over Catherine's Peak and the sky was stunningly blue. England was a world away – part of another life.

At school there were a few new faces but the start of term was a routine we were now used to. My timetable looked good – English and Social Studies and some new literary texts to choose. I went down to the English stock room to look at what was available. There was a new set of Edward Braithwaite's *To Sir With Love*. I'd seen the film some years ago. It starred Sidney Poitier in the part of a young teacher in a rough school in London and I remembered a very young Lulu singing the theme song at the end. The film dealt head on with the issues of racism and the struggle of a young teacher with a class of very difficult students. It might be an interesting one to do with my 3rd year class. I also had to select a Shakespeare play for my O level English group. I checked the syllabus to see the choice of set texts. It had to be *Romeo & Juliet*. I'd studied it at school so I knew something about it. It was a long time ago but I still remembered something of the passion and the tragedy of the play. But then reading it and teaching it were very different processes. I had some preparation work to do.

*

OF INCA SLINGS AND UPTOWN GUNMEN

'Sir, why didn't the Inca ride in a carriage like a normal king would. Why was he carried on this weird throne thing. Looks kinda wobbly to me.'

The question came from Harold, younger brother of Amy who had organised the cheerleaders. It was a social studies lesson with my first year class. Harold was eleven, bright, precocious. We were three weeks into our study of the Spanish conquistadores and today we were looking into Pizarro's campaign against the Incas.

'They didn't know about the wheel,' I replied.

'What do you mean 'didn't know about the wheel'?'

'The tribes in America had never come up with the idea of a wheel for transport.'

'Are you kidding me?' chirped Harold, his brow furrowed under his mop of fair hair. 'So what did the horses pull?'

'They didn't have horses.'

'You are kidding me. What about those masses of horses you see in cowboy films on the prairies ?'

'Hollywood got it wrong. There were no horses, or cows for that matter, until the Europeans brought them over.'

He sat there at the back of the class, lost for words, for a moment at least. 'Well I'll be darned,' he muttered shaking his head. 'What about gunpowder? I know the Chinese had gunpowder way back.'

'Not in the Americas. That's why the Spaniards had such an advantage. Horses, gunpowder, steel blades and metal armour. The Incas had none of those.'

I told them about Pizarro's first dramatic meeting with the Inca, Atahuallpa, on the high Peruvian plain outside the city of Cajamarca; how it was the Inca's first encounter with a horse and mounted rider. How Hernando de Soto, one of Pizarro's best riders, put on a display of his horsemanship to intimidate the Inca.

'Let me read you an account of that event,' I said picking up my copy of   William Prescott's classic *The Conquest of Peru*. I perched on the edge of my desk, waited for them to settle and started reading. '*Observing that Atahuallpa looked with some interest on the fiery steed that stood before him, champing the bit and pawing the ground with the natural impatience of a war-horse, the Spaniard gave him the rein, and striking his iron heel into his side, dashed furiously over the plain; then, wheeling him round and round, displayed all the beautiful movements of his charger and his own excellent horsemanship. Suddenly checking him in full career, he brought the animal almost on his haunches, so near the person of the Inca, that some of the foam that flecked his horse's sides was thrown on the royal garments......*'

I paused. Looked up. Thirty pairs of eyes staring at me.

Harold could not contain himself, 'So what happened? What did the Inca do?'

I shook my head slowly, 'He didn't flinch. Even with the breath of the horse touching his face, he didn't blink.'

'Wow. Some guy,' nodded Harold.

'But some of his men cowered and showed their fear and that night it is said that Atahuallpa had them executed for shaming the Inca people in front of strangers.'   I got up from my desk and went across to my cupboard. 'The Incas didn't have horses and gunpowder and steel, but they did have a lot of these.' With a flourish I held up the replica Inca sling I had bought in Peru two summers ago. 'With one of these slings an Inca warrior could unseat a Spanish soldier from his horse at one hundred yards. C'mon, I'll show you. Everyone outside.'

I had practised a little with the sling but wasn't confident that I could pull this off. We all trouped on to the playing field and I sat them down.

'Could an Inca warrior hit that goal post over there,' chirruped Harold. 'Go on, try and hit it.'

The preparation for this lesson had involved collecting a selection of small round stones from the school driveway, so I was well prepared. I selected one and pressed it into the pouch of the sling. Slowly, I started swinging the sling around my head. Finally, having gathered speed I let go of one end of the sling. The stone whizzed through the air missing the goal post but hitting a bench on the far side of the football pitch.

'Go, sir,' shouted one of the girls.

'Try again, sir,' shouted Harold's friend Kevin.

I reloaded the sling, whirled it around my head and let fly. This time the stone somehow fell on the floor behind me.

The class fell about pointing and laughing.

'That's me off the team,' I said. 'What happened there?'

'Would they rip out your heart for something like that?' quipped Harold.

'The Incas didn't rip out hearts, Harold, that was the Aztecs.' I loaded one more stone, whirled again and this time the stone whistled through the air, just missing the goal post. 'Okay, demonstration over. Back to the classroom,' I said.

'Pretty neat, sir,' commented Harold as we made our way back. 'I reckon I'm going to try and make one of those slings. Try it on the golf course near our house. See if I can hit a golfer at a hundred yards.'

*

On the last Sunday in September, Sue and I made our way down the track from Mandala to pay our usual midday visit to the Megevands. There was a pleasant breeze blowing up the valley gently shifting the broad banana leaves and bringing down some of the blossom from the trees. Katarina and Regine were in the garden playing badminton. Philippe, cigarette holder clasped firmly between his teeth, was swearing down the telephone. 'Swines!' he was shouting. 'What the hell is going on in this god-forsaken country!' He slammed down the telephone receiver, put his hand to his head for moment and then came across to us shaking his head.

There had been a shooting at the restaurant the previous evening. Six gunmen had stormed into the place looking for the office to grab the takings.

Philippe went on, 'One of them put a gun in Katie's back and screamed at her to show them where the safe was. People were screaming and falling to the floor. Then they couldn't find the office and that's when one of the customers pulled a gun and shot one of them.

99

Only wounded him and then they left. They shot holes in the ceiling and there was blood all over the floor.'

Katie emerged from the house carrying some cold Red Stripes. 'Hey, Philippe my love, calm yourself nah man. We survived it. We still here to smell the flowers and feel the breeze. Don't upset our visitors.'

She had bruising on her arm where the gunman had held her and a mark on her face where he had pushed her against the wall. She sat down and looked across at us. 'Life can be a bit of a bitch at times.'

We didn't know what to say. It was like looking over the edge into a dark place where we had never ventured. Like discovering that one of your colleagues was a CIA agent, or hearing in the staffroom that trained guerillas were infiltrating the country from Cuba. You felt like a child, naive and rather foolish. That you had been wearing rose-tinted glasses when in fact the world was a very different shade.

Philippe continued, 'They're trying to force me to let my staff join a labour union. Left-wing scum. But I've talked to my staff. They don't want a union. They say they don't need a union. I pay them higher than the usual rate. They know me. I picked Bully, my chef, out of the gutter six years ago. He was begging me for a ten cent outside a supermarket and living in the wreck of an abandoned car. I said, Pick youself up boy and come and work for me. I'll pay you more than a ten cent.'

And that's what Philippe had done. Under his patient tutelage, Bully, his head chef, had graduated from being a scrawny kid washing dishes to what he was now – a young man with pride and dignity who was a respected chef in one of the most prestigious restaurants in Kingston.

'Something is badly rotten in the state of Jamaica, Barrie,' said Katie. She gave a half smile, 'Are you impressed that I can quote Shakespeare to you the morning after almost being shot up?' She went on, 'Let me tell the story. When Manley was elected in '72, with his sparkling personality and seeming dedication to the land of his birth, we were there cheering him along. He had intelligence, charm, wit and strode like the Joshua he claimed to be. And when the PNP won by a terrific landslide we cheered and toasted the victory, we guzzled champagne, we sang and we danced. It was like Christmas and Carnival and a Sweepstake Grand Prize all wrapped into one. A heavy weight had lifted from the shoulders of all Jamaica. We hugged strangers in the streets and all was peace and love and euphoria.'

She drew on her cigarette, blew out the smoke quickly and shook her head, 'The feeling didn't last long. Success went to Manley's head and in no time he was riding rough-shod over people, institutions and traditions. He wasn't happy to work with what he had. Improve this and better that. No, he wanted to shake up the whole bag, change the whole shibang. Above all he wanted to make history overnight and be able to say 'I, Michael Manley did it.'

She looked across at Philippe and took a sip of her beer; drew slowly on her cigarette. 'We both felt he had some damned good ideas. He was sincere in many ways but he wanted everything at once yet he didn't have the money or the skills. His advisors were young and idealistic, wet behind the ears, fresh out of university and they all wanted it to happen now. Manley encouraged the unions; the businessman became a 'dirty capitalist' and overnight was blamed for the ills of the country. Get the Chinese, get the Syrian, get the white people. This is black man time now. That's how it is coming across. And the guns started coming in. Seaga arms his JLP people, Manley arms his PNP guys and,' she shrugged, 'you see what happen. We have the Gun Court, we have indefinite detention, curfews and now people start to leave the country. Lots of our friends are  leaving or have left, taking their skills with them, smuggling out their money. Philippe has felt strongly about staying and fighting for what we have worked so hard for. He has always had faith in the Jamaican people whom he has come to love. In fact in my little Gleaner column – *What's a Day Without Laughter,* I said he represented S.O.U.L. – Sticking Out, Unwilling to Leave. As against what I called A.F.R.O.s – Adamant Foreigner Return Overseas. But after last night, it'll never be the same for us.'

Her eyes were moist, and Katarina came across and put her arm around her mother's shoulders. Regine leaned against Philippe's arm and made circles with her toe in the dust.

Again we were lost to know what to say. Philippe took his daughter's hand and looking across at Katie said, 'Thank you for the resume my darling but let us celebrate that we are still here to drink some fine French wine and eat some fine filet. Come Barrie, a swift game of table tennis and then, a la table mes amis!'

By late 1975 the world we had conjured for ourselves in Jamaica was haemorrhaging. I suppose it was a mixture of things. Our return to England in the coming summer was beckoning. My essay on John Fowles had been completed and in early December I received a letter which confirmed my place at Lancaster University for the academic year starting in September of 1976. But the bubble of our naivety had been punctured by a series of events which brought home to us that Jamaican society was heading towards possible implosion. The Megevands' shooting, the curfews, the downtown gang warfare, the rumours of CIA subversion and Cuban infiltration became the backdrop to our daily lives. School life continued, but now, more and more things intruded.

In early December I helped organise a school trip to the Brimmer Hall Plantation near Port Maria on the north coast. It was for first year students and would show them a working plantation as well as the history behind the estate. To get to Brimmer Hall you take the road north out of Kingston to Castleton following the river valley of Wag Water. In places the road is narrow, running between steep hillsides and it was here that the bus was held up by a group of young men. They stood in the middle of the road with their arms held up. There were no guns in view but it was likely that they were armed. Two of them came on board. They wore leather jackets and woolly tams. They were collecting money they said for 'good causes'. They weren't overtly threatening but the students were nervous, as I was. We handed over money and the bus was waved on. It was quite literally 'highway robbery'.

Then soon after the Christmas break came the news that Norah had been beaten up at Green Gables. Gunmen had broken in, she had resisted and had been badly knocked around. She'd been taken to a local hospital and there was a plea for friends to give blood. In Jamaica there was no effective blood bank that patients could freely call on. You had to have a stock of blood credited against your name in order to qualify for a blood transfusion.

A number of us went straight from school to the hospital. Lying on the hospital bed watching the blood oozing from a tube in my arm into a plastic bag was a moment of forced reflection. We would always be outsiders in a society like this. There were expatriates who stayed for years and years and lived a curious life of privilege and detachment. But the real Jamaica was somewhere else. It was in the harsh cut and thrust of business and commerce, in the graft of the local farmers who eked out a modest living from the red earth. It was in the lives of the poor folk who lived in the tin shacks of Trenchtown on the edge of survival day in day out. We were privileged visitors and our time was almost over. Now reality was biting. I had to further my career. We wanted to start a family. It was time to close this chapter and open another.

After three days we were allowed in to visit Norah. There were vases of flowers around her bed. She was propped up but her slight frame seemed to have shrunk even further. Her head was bandaged and her face was blotched with purple bruises. Her thin arms showed more bruising and lacerations which had been poorly bandaged. She lifted one hand to us as we approached the bed and sat down.

'My dears, how kind,' she whispered. 'People have been so thoughtful.' She tried to smile. I held her hand. Sue found a vase for the flowers we had brought.

'They didn't manage to finish me off. I think they thought I was a mad woman when I started fighting back.'

It was a struggle for her to speak and her voice trailed away. She sipped some water and closed her eyes for moment. Then she went on, 'How is Andy? The poor dear came for a quiet drink and ended up in a gunfight.'

Andy told me the story later; how he had gone for a quiet drink with Norah to talk over an idea for another production. They heard what they thought was a gun-shot in the bar. Norah leapt up and rushed to the bar and and threw herself at one of two masked men. They struggled, she was hit and knocked down, then other drinkers joined in the fray and the two intruders ran off empty-handed.

When Norah was released from hospital we brought her up to Mandala for a few days of convalescence. She spent much of the time in the rocking chair gently rocking and dozing in the shade of the poinciana tree. In the evenings she would reminisce about her time in Jamaica, about her early hopes, the challenges of teaching, of running Green Gables and raising two boys.

'….Life is always about adjustment and compromise..' she nodded gently, 'but it must be inspired by a wider vision - a vision of how life could be and should be, inspite of what you're faced with day in day out. Without that vision I would have been destroyed by this beautiful and frustrating island. You know, Barrie, for years Henry Fowler and I would meet each Friday afternoon to review the week. We kept alive a vision of how the school could be, a vision beyond the daily routine. But we also celebrated the joy of particular moments in the week. We would laugh somewhat irreverently about the foibles of some colleagues and the antics of the students but it was always a joy. And it is that teasing puzzle - to combine the wider vision with the joy of the moment which is the key.'

She looked at us, this bruised survivor. Her eyes were starting to find some glint of life again and she smiled her gentle smile, 'Am I rambling again? Forgive me. But I have to say, I think I'm feeling a little better.' She eased herself forward and I plumped up the cushions in her back. Then she pointed towards the blue-black silhouette of Catherine's Peak, stark against the starlit sky. 'Now here's a thing. Did you know that when Oscar Hammerstein was writing the lyrics for *The Sound of Music* he wasn't in the Alps. No, he was in a little rented house just up there beyond Catherine's Peak.' She nodded, 'It's true. So next time you hear the words *The hills are alive with the sound of music* remember the Blue Mountains of Jamaica and this wonderful place. As if you'd ever forget it.'

*

CLASSROOM EXCURSIONS

'But just one minute longer and she would have known!' said Stacey.

'She wouldn't have to kill herself,' added Candace.

'Why didn't Friar Lawrence just tell her about the plan. Why didn't he!'

We had just read the death scene in *Romeo and Juliet*. There was murmuring, frowning and consternation among some of the students at the end of the scene where the young lovers kill themselves.

Michele, always the sharp one, just smiled and shook her head, 'But that's the point. That's why Shakespeare is a god. He doesn't give you what you want. He keeps the audience wanting more. Man, that's just brilliant.'

Desmond was nodding, 'This thing is a tragedy, right?'

I nodded back.

'An' tragedy is when you expect one thing but it doesn't turn out like you want?'

'It depends,' I replied, 'on the nature of the disappointment. Would it be tragic, for example, if an eighty-five year old woman was expecting to go shopping and she fell down dead? That's one kind of disappointment. Is it tragic though?'

It was one of those priceless moments in the classroom. The class were held, balanced on the threads of the moment – the emotion of the play, the tension of the debate and the stirring of their thinking. I let the question hang in the air, slowly scanned the faces - waited.

It was Desmond who came back. 'Is it like, when something happen but it not suppose to happen. Like in the play they are too young to die.'

I nodded, but said nothing. Waited a little longer. Watched the faces.

Desmond went on, 'Like it's not fair. That there's no justice in what happen?'

'Exactly,' I said, 'that feeling of injustice, that somehow the gods have not been kind; that they've been playing tricks with us.'

'And we're victims of forces beyond our control,' added Michele.

The clock was ticking towards the end of the lesson. It was a pity to break the spell but spellbound they had been and that was enough in itself.

I held up my hand and nodded, 'Great work today class. We'll finish the play next time. In the meantime, for homework, see if you can come up with examples of what you think would be classed as tragic events. But you have to explain why you would rate them as tragic. We'll listen to your ideas next lesson.'

The following lesson was with my third year group. We were several chapters into *To Sir With Love* and it was going well. It was new to me, this gritty account of Edward Braithwaite's experience of teaching in the East End of London in the 1950s. Admittedly I wasn't black and wasn't like Braithwaite in being confronted by the endemic racism of 1950s England, yet I could identify closely with many of the scenarios in the book. I remembered my roughneck apprentices on teaching practice in Tamworth and my bottom sets of social studies students in Lichfield. Braithwaite's presentation of the dynamics of a lone teacher with a new class are brilliantly instructive. I realised that the way the teacher establishes a relationship with the class is much the same the world over. All classes test and try out a new teacher in various ways. All classes try to push the limits. There is always the honeymoon period when the power struggle is bubbling just under the surface. The class is watching your every move, reading the cues – the way you sit, stand, move around the classroom. They listen to the tone of voice, listen and watch for signs of nervousness which they can exploit, gauge just how far they can go.

This was the class of Charlene from Alabama, whose mother on that first Parents' Night asked why I didn't like her daughter. It was the class of the feisty Danish-Canadian girl, Elizabeth, who always sat near the front; of the Venezuelan girl Marina, and Jose from Costa Rica. It was a rich melting pot of races and backgrounds and they knew nothing of England of the 1950s.

Some of the Jamaican students were clearly shocked and confused. They may well have imbibed from their parents the rosy notion of Britain as the mother country, civilised streets paved with opportunities, extending its welcoming hand to its Commonwealth children. And yet here is the young Braithwaite faced by crude racism and children whose horizons stretch only as far as the end of their street.

The American students were also confused by this portrayal of England. It seemed that their image of England and the English was that gleaned from a diet of period drama where people are well-dressed, polite and all take tea in the afternoon. Braithwaite's portrayal turned their assumptions upside down.

But it was perhaps the insight that the book gave about teaching which was most valuable. It is first person narrative and Braithwaite shows it from the inside. He exposes the teacher's vulnerability and the power of students to destroy a teacher's confidence. I could almost see my own students looking at me more quizzically as we delved further beneath the surface.

'So, Mr Day, have you ever had students like this?' asked Elizabeth.

'Like what?'

'Like the boy in the story who is always causing trouble? Have you ever lost control of a class?'

How much to reveal? Was Elizabeth deliberately bating me or was it genuine curiosity? A bit of both I reckoned. But I went ahead and told them of when I was pelted with chalk. They laughed and then Jose said, 'What would you do if we pelted you with chalk?'

I smiled and shook my head, 'But you wouldn't would you? I think I know you all well enough.'

Elizabeth nodded, head tilted a little. 'Tricky being a teacher, isn't it? I never thought about it before.'

*

ENDGAMES

By the spring of 1976 we were living in a Kafkaesque world of shifting mirrors. There were claims and counter claims. In the staff room there were rumours about further CIA and Cuban infiltration; of government employees planning moonlight flits to Miami; of business people syphoning millions of dollars out of the country to banks in North America.

And in the midst of all this we carried on teaching our classes, preparing for Sports Day and other school events while seemingly the world beyond the school was a bubbling cauldron on the verge of boiling over.

Oxford came in third again on Sports Day despite some energetic chanting and flag waving and some heroic efforts by the Oxford relay teams. As a gesture of gratitude for their efforts and to mark the end of my term as Head of Oxford House I arranged a week-end away for the Oxford students. Pat Bourke had a house on the north coast near Port Antonio and with his two children being stalwarts of Oxford he was only too willing to lend us the house for the week-end.

On a Friday afternoon in May our little convoy of mini buses and cars set off on the road to Annotto Bay and the north coast. There were about twenty students and six staff. Over the mountains, along the valley of Wag Water, we emerged on the coast at Annotto Bay and turned east towards Buff Bay and Port Antonio.

As we drove and once again drank in the views and the landscape, I felt the utter sadness and tragedy of this country. So much of the island was achingly beautiful. The word 'Jamaica' comes from the language of the original inhabitants of the island – the Arawak Indians; their word was 'Xaymaca' meaning 'land of wood and water.' On the drive to Port Antonio we passed rivers of clear water cascading down the northern slopes of the Blue Mountains. The mountains themselves were clothed in lush greenery, thick forest, coconut and banana plantations, exotic poinciana trees with their vivid red flowers. Along the roadside were swathes of poinsettias, the plant we buy in England as a 'Christmas rose' – a single plant in a pot which drops its red leaves by New Year.

Yet here there were hedgerows of them alongside banks of nodding yellow and pink hibiscus, pink and white oleander. To the left the sea – the Caribbean in all its shades from pearly silver where the waves broke on the shoreline, through bands of aquamarine, turquoise and out to the deep, deep blue of the open sea. All too beautiful and yet back in Kingston the country was tearing itself apart.

But this weekend was respite and a welcome escape. And we were coming back to one of my favourite parts of the island. On several occasions we had stayed at the resort called Goblin Hill a few miles east of Port Antonio. The resort comprised a collection of modern guest houses built on a hill overlooking San San Bay. Pat Bourke's house was a short distance round the bay built on a high bluff which gave it a stunning view of the whole of the bay. The bay itself was horseshoe-shaped with a small island – Nina Khan's Island - a short distance from the white sand beach which was lined with coconut palms. At low tide you could wade out to the island, which was named after the wife of the Aga Khan who had given it to his wife as a wedding gift. She had ideas of keeping leopards on the island until she discovered they could swim.

We were there for the weekend and I had allowed some Princeton interlopers to join our happy Oxford crew. This was profound generosity on my part considering it was Jim and his wife Jenny – Jim, the Head of the victorious Princeton house. But we were generous in defeat as Jim was gracious in victory.

'You know, Barrie, I reckon if you stayed on for another five years then you might be able to groom this feckless bunch into a winning team,' he said sipping his Red Stripe and leaning back in his chair.

There were hoots of derision from some of the students and a few watermelon pips flung in his direction.

'Hey, Mr Gervasio, yuh tekin' a risk showing off that yellow Princeton shirt in the Oxford camp,' said Patrick, the Oxford house captain.

'We might have to dunk you in Blue Hole tomorrow, you know,' added Amy.

'Patrick, I admire a house captain who faces defeat with such bravado. Maybe you'll be a politician one day,' said Jim.

It was a rare joy spending time away from the classroom with a group of students like these - a far cry from that first school trip to Wales with my ne'er-do-wells. The first evening after a barbecue we played silly games; Steven, always the natural comedian did his Charlie Chaplin impression and told some jokes. Then Josh tuned his guitar and played and they sang and the evening drifted on. They took no real organising – they were fun, energetic, considerate to each other. I watched and mused on the unique educational maelstrom which was Priory School. This rare mix of backgrounds, cultures, races – Jamaicans, North Americans, Europeans, South Americans, Canadians, British, Asians – we had most parts of the globe represented on this terrace high above a starlit Caribbean. It was an educational melting pot which would be a touchstone for me for the rest of my career.

The following day we trouped down to the beach and took the path to Blue Hole, a famous Jamaican tourist spot which was located at the east end of the bay. It was a circular inlet backed by steep cliffs. Reputedly a collapsed underwater limestone cavern, it was so deep that the water was an abyss of deep blueness – hence the name. We swam, some water-skied, others stayed on the beach and snorkelled or sun-bathed. They bought burgers and jerk pork from a local food stall and then played volleyball and beach cricket. And so the week-end passed, a week-end of laughter and good humour.

Finally on the Sunday morning we headed back over the mountains to Kingston. It was a good way to mark the approaching end of our Jamaican chapter.

*

Strange how when you know you're moving on, the present slips away so quickly. Thoughts turn to the next chapter. Jim was going to Bristol to study law. Colin, emulating his mentor, Pat Bourke, was going to Keele to train to be a counsellor. Andy wanted to break into professional acting and script-writing and I had to qualify to be a bona fide teacher of English.

But first Sue and I would fly to the USA. It would be our first time and we were planning to drive up the east coast and then fly out from New York back to England.

When I mentioned this in one of my English classes word spread along the grapevine and we had invitations from several families to stay with them. First there would be a few days with Lisa's family in Alabama. Her father worked for Alcoa and his contract was coming to an end. Then there was an invitation from Amy to stay with her family in

Pennsylvania. Her father's contract with his company was also coming to an end and the family were returning home for Amy to start college and her sister Zoe and brother Harold to take up places at their local high schools. For us, the summer of '76 was starting to feel like stepping on shifting sands, exciting and scary, nothing firm to hold on to – things ending but no clearly defined future.

*

PARTING IS SUCH SWEET SORROW

Julie Chang actually cried out, 'No, no!' when Leonard Whiting gulped the poison at the feet of his sleeping lover and Olivia Hussey then plunged the dagger into her own chest. Julie, usually so mouthy and opinionated, put her arm round Francine who sat next to her and stared opened-mouthed at the screen.

I had managed to get a copy of Zeffirelli's *Romeo and Juliet* from the Kingston film library. And finally as the credits rolled, Nino Rota's haunting theme music moved on the sultry heat of the afternoon. No-one spoke. Some rested their heads on the desks. Others stared out of the open windows. Normally it was the boys who were restless and fidgety when something emotional was broached. But not this time. Even they were quiet.

It was Michele who broke the spell. 'This country is a tragedy,' she murmured, more to herself than the class.

'What d'you mean?' I asked.

She shook her head, 'It shouldn't be like this. All this shooting and gangs and ting. Like in the play – just stupidity and foolishness. Men and their pride.'

'Always, you say it men fault,' chimed in Derek.

'Well, look at Tybalt, full of himself. 'Prince of Cats', Mercutio call him. It like the gunmen in Kingston. Always spoiling for a fight.'

She was right of course. Montague, Capulet, PNP, JLP. Turf wars and feuding. The same old story.

It was indeed tragic what was happening to the country. Here was Michael Manley, full of good intentions and the whole thing, after three years, the whole dream falling apart around him. The latest revelation was an apparent plot to overthrow the government. Pink leaflets had been published by the Agency for Public Information and distributed nationwide. They were headed:

PLOT TO OVERTHROW GOVERNMENT
Jamaicans, Know Your Enemies And Be On Guard

The leaflet gave information about a plan aimed at overthrowing the PNP government and linked to the JLP Senator and Deputy leader Pearnel Charles and the JLP candidate Peter Whittingham. It cited that in the St Ann Area there was a cell of : *22 trained men with supplies of 200 rifles, 100 sub-machine guns, 2 barrels of gun powder and 50,000 anti-government pamphlets.* In Wittingham's brief case there were anti-government leaflets which stated the following: *Michael Manley and his Government are dedicated Communists and we intend to destroy them at all costs'.* The Pamphlet mentioned *WEREWOLF – a 'militant underground movement'* and stated: *Werewolf is now willing to take up arms against this communist regime and purge them from our shores.*

As a result, a State of Emergency had been declared. There were tanks at intersections in downtown Kingston, soldiers with sub-machine guns at road-blocks, curfews from nine in the evening, helicopters droning low over the streets probing with searchlights, daily reports of subversion, infiltration, corruption, murder.

'How long will you stay?' I asked Philippe.

It was the Sunday of our last week-end. They had come up to Mandala to help us with our final packing and to say goodbye. Philippe was stretched out on the settee which we had dragged out on to the patio while we were sorting out our things. Katie was trying on one of Sue's sun hats which was being left behind. The girls were inside the cottage looking through our collection of books.

He took a sip from the cold Red Stripe I had given him and shrugged, 'We have so much to lose here. Two homes, a business, friends. What d'you do, run away and leave it all to the jackals?'

'We'll stay a little longer, until after the election and see what happen then,' said Katie. 'But it's not looking good.'

It was a sad parting. Not knowing where and when we might see them again. It had been a short but intense friendship. They had helped us make some connection with the real Jamaica, whatever that was. We had laughed with them, mused, discussed and argued and dined on some fine filet and French Merlot from Philippe's kitchen.

'And yes, the old Bard was right,' said Katie, giving us a last hug. 'Parting is indeed such sweet sorrow.'

And the leave-taking at school was similarly charged. The final lesson with my third year class was quite emotional. We had finished reading *To Sir With Love* some weeks earlier and curiously, as the narrator, Braithwaite, consolidates his relationship with his class of

111

dysfunctional adolescents, so my relationship with my own class seemed to have assumed a special kind of understanding. Through following Braithwaite's skilful narrative they had come to understand a lot more about the complexities of teaching – the stresses, the anxieties but also the pleasure in a teacher seeing students make progress and realise something of their potential.

As I walked into the classroom for the final lesson so the soundtrack from the film of *To Sir With Love* started up. And there were my class, Elizabeth, Charlene, Sumya, Curtis, Robert and the others standing round my desk in the middle of which was a big, round chocolate cake inscribed with the words:

Good luck. Thanks Mr Day

Alongside was a ring binder in which each of them had written a comment alongside their photograph. On the inside cover of the folder was written:

Dear Teacher and fellow students, We hereby take this occasion to make this presentation of a little token of our appricication (sic) on behalf of our excellent education. We regret this termination for it has been a good association. Hoping we will follow your instruction and our brains will be in just as good condition for our many examinations. TO YOU SIR, WITH LOVE.... .

Their personal comments ranged from the sentimental, to the jokey. Robert, from Canada, one of the sharpest minds in the class wrote in a spidery script :

TANKS A LOT FER LERNING ME SUCH GOOD INGLISH.
BECOZ OF YOUS I AM WOT I AM NOW

I looked at their faces and it was one of those moments which stay with you and which you live off long after the event; a moment which reassures you during the times in teaching when things aren't going so well – times of frustration, exhaustion and disillusionment.

You recall what it can be like when there is that close and unique bond between a teacher and a class, something so difficult for anyone outside of teaching to understand.

The final school assembly was equally moving. The staff stood on the stage and we looked over the sea of faces of the student body as the Headmaster announced which teachers were leaving. It numbered fifteen and included some of the key figures who had energised the school during the past three years – Jim, Chris and me- the three House Heads; Andy, Head of Drama, Colin, Head of Outdoor Pursuits, Jenny, Head of Science, Sue, Head of Girls' PE – the list went on and the shock to the students was palpable. Some shed tears and you felt a sense of betrayal at leaving them and at seeing the look of tugging helplessness in their eyes.

For me it was the first time I had experienced the breaking of this bond. In my first job at Lichfield I had not built up a very close relationship with classes and individual students but here at Priory it had been so different. I started to appreciate the unique privilege of being a teacher.

*

That summer we set foot on north American soil for the first time. We flew initially to Mobile, Alabama and stayed with Lisa's family. We were enveloped in southern hospitality and the sing-song lilt of the Alabama drawl with its stretched vowels and words which seemed to be chewed upon before being sung to the listener.

'Now, what y'all drinkin'?'

This from Lisa's father, a squat, jovial man who pours himself a whisky and soda before we set off for a drive to the Gulf coast. Obviously this is the southern way so we all leave the house holding our drinks and get in the car. Lisa's father places his whisky in the drinks holder on the dash board.

'Y'all set now? Let's get us some shrimp.'

What comes as a complete surprise is how much the English accent is revered by Americans. We first encounter this when we meet Ralph, one of Lisa's father's friends. We go to his huge beach house, a sun-bleached wooden structure set in the sand dunes near Mobile. Ralph is six foot six, a giant of a man with old world courtesy. He shows us his house with its broad deck, stunning views, rustic furniture and Indian blankets on the leather sofas. And this is only his second home. This guy clearly has money with his Lincoln Continental in the drive, his shiny pickup and his shrimp boat down on the dock. But he's not a talker. He leans forward and listens intently as we chat, nodding, not saying much. Finally he clears his throat and says rather nervously, 'I feel I'm been educated just listening to you guys.'

We're not sure what to say. The comment is so unexpected. Here we are, in awe of this lavish southern life style and yet he's in awe of us? It doesn't make sense.

Before we leave the south, Lisa's mother prepares a Sunday lunch, southern style. The table sags with the weight of food, most of it coated in a golden deep fry coating. There's fried chicken, corn bread, barbecue ribs, grits, fried shrimp, lobster tails, pork fritters, coleslaw and what they call 'collard greens'.

'Now thar's a theng you might like to take back to England,' says Lisa's mother. She shows us an old recipe which catches the Alabama twang:

Resipee for Cukin Kon-Feel Pees

Gether yo pees 'bout sun-down. The florin day, 'bout leven o'clock, gowge out yo pees with yo tum nale, like gowgin out a man's eye-ball at a kote house. Rense yo pees, parbile them, then fry 'em with som several slices uv streekt middlin' incouragin uv the gravy to seep out and intermarry with yo pees. When modritly brown, but not scorcht, empty into a dish. Mash'em gently with a spune, mix with raw tomaters sprinkled with a little brown shugar and the immortal dish ar quite ready. Eat a hepe. Eat mo and mo. It is good for yo general helth uv mind and body. It fattens you up, makes you sassy, goes throo and throo yo very soul. But whey don't you eat" Eat on. By Jings. Eat. Stop? Never, whil thar is a pee in the dish.

'Come, Lisa, read this to Mr and Mrs Day.'

'Nah momma.' Lisa squirms with embarrassment.

'I'll do it,' volunteers Charlene who's come over to join us for the meal. She reads the recipe in an exaggerated southern drawl. We applaud and then sit down to eat. First we hold hands round the table and Lisa's father says grace.

They are warm, welcoming people and by the time we leave we understand something of what people mean when they talk of the hospitality of the South.

'Now y'all come and see us agin soon,' says Lisa's mother and I feel she means it.

We then took the train north to West Chester, Pennsylvania where Amy's family lived. In Jamaica, we had only ever met her parents

114

at school Parents' Evenings. So it was, with some apprehension, that we arrived at Paoli station to meet Judy, her mother.

We needn't have worried; she and her husband, Hal, were a delight, full of good humour and endless generosity. They took us to New York for a day and we wandered in Central Park, down Broadway and then took the elevator to the top of one of the Twin Towers. At the top it was silent, so far from the city streets that there was no traffic noise and we gazed across the city past the Empire State Building and watched helicopters flying far below between the office blocks and across the Hudson River.

One afternoon Zoe brought two of her school friends in to meet us. They sat on the swing seat on the verandah giggling.

'Go on then,' Zoe said to us, 'speak.'

The two friends stared at us, wide-eyed.

'What d'you mean?' I asked.

'They've come to hear the English accent.'

More giggling then one says, 'We love the accent. We just couldn't wait to hear it.'

'I've been telling them all about our British teachers in Jamaica. They couldn't wait to meet you.'

Margie, the smaller of the two girls bubbled with excitement, 'Zoe says you don't call it the bathroom you call it something else.'

'Yes we have bathrooms in England, it's where you take a bath,' I said.

'But what about the other… you know.'

'You mean the toilet, or the loo.'

They rocked back on the swing seat hooting with laughter.

'Or it's sometimes called the WC,' added Sue.

'What's that mean?' asked Harold.

'Stands for water closet.'

More hoots of laughter from the girls.

'Okay, then,' said Harold adopting a more serious expression, 'So where d'you put the luggage in a car?'

'In the boot of course.'

'You are kidding, Mr Day,' he said smirking. 'A boot goes on your foot.'

'Okay,' I said, ' so where do *you* put luggage in a car?'

'In the trunk, of course,' replied Harold.

'No, that's what elephants have for a nose,' I said.

And so the banter and hilarity went on. We compared the food we ate, the names for everyday objects. They thought that calling a flashlight a 'torch' was priceless. For them it conjured images of cave men with flaming sticks.

By the time we left for England we felt a real friendship had been initiated and we talked of future visits across the 'pond'.

On the flight home Sue nudged me out of my dozing. 'Quite a three years wasn't it. You should write a book about it.'

I smiled. 'Maybe. One day. We'll see.'

CHAPTER THE THIRD 1976-77 Lancaster

OF FORSTER AND PHEASANTS

The old red racing bike which I had bought from a junk shop in Lancaster was just about coping with its new routine. I had to attend tutorials at the university twice a week and my route along the Lune valley and then through the town was a distance of about seven miles. Our rented accommodation was a converted stable at Halton Park, west of the city, on the estate of Geoffrey Bowring, the Lord Lieutenant of Lancashire. It was a world away from Mandala Cottage. The gamekeeper's house was just across the yard from our front door while behind the stable at the end of a long drive stood the impressive sandstone mansion of our landlord.

This was the year when I had to get an English degree so that I could pursue my career as a genuine teacher of English. So, my ageing red racing bike had quite a responsibility to stay the course, taking me back and forth on the fourteen mile round trip twice a week.

We had little money. The gratuity which was supposed to be paid to us at the end of the three year contract in Jamaica was frozen in a Jamaican bank under the terms of the country's current State of Emergency. I was following events there via the overseas edition of the *Daily Gleaner* which came every month and via letters from the Megevands. Things were not looking good.

Sue became the essential breadwinner. She travelled to Heysham High School each day as a supply teacher teaching Art. She didn't relish it and she was getting hassle from the management of the school for wearing trousers. Despite the strides made by women's lib in the Sixties, trousers for women teachers at Heysham High School in 1976 were verboten. But with no money and a wardrobe of only summer clothes, trousers were the warmest things to wear on those chilly autumn mornings. The other female staff at the school urged Sue to resist the pressure to conform. For years they had been pressing for a change to the dated dress code and here was their chance. Tensions mounted. Sue resisted. More pressure. More resistance. Finally senior management capitulated and trousers for women teachers were tolerated and for a short time Sue was a champion among the female staff at Heysham.

Meanwhile, I was pedalling back and forth on a Tuesday for my tutorial on English Literature with the eminent Margery Middleton, acclaimed guru on the works of George Bernard Shaw. On a Thursday it was American Literature with a young tutor called John Labbe. Apart from the tutorials there was simply a huge reading list to get through on 19th and 20th century literature, literary theory and social history.

While Sue grafted at the Heysham chalk face, I wrestled with the diverse joys and challenges of such topics as Modernism, Black American writing, Beat poetry, Post-Structuralist literary criticism. There were a few lectures on art movements of the 20th century – Futurism, Vorticism, Cubism and on aspects of social history to broaden the context but essentially it was literature which absorbed all my waking hours. There would be an examination at the end of the course the following summer and a dissertation to submit on a subject of my choosing.

During the day I had the run of the Halton Park Estate – its woods, lanes, river banks and rolling pastures. In the morning I might be wrestling with the works of William Faulkner, Henry Miller or William Carlos Williams. After several hours I would take a walk up the track, along the river and back through the woods, snatch a quick coffee and then start the next reading session which might be Forster, Strindberg or Pirandello. I'd never experienced such intensity of study, chewing through such a gristle of ideas and writing styles. It was not easy but it was exhilarating.

That year the memory of our Jamaican experience was kept alive by letters from former students; from the feisty Michele who was now in Miami at a junior college and from Amy's family in Pennsylvania.

Early in the first term I cycled to the university with high expectations of taking part in lively tutorials but I soon learned that it was one thing to be an acclaimed expert on the works of Shaw, but another to know how to orchestrate a productive tutorial. Alas, the eminent Margery Middleton was hopeless as a tutor. There were eight of us in the group and we would often sit around in silence with dear Margery fidgeting nervously, rarely making eye contact and struggling to get any sort of discussion going. One day she arrived complaining of a migraine and told us to conduct the tutorial ourselves while she lay on the floor behind us, a handkerchief over her face, groaning quietly. Her tutorials were truly painful and disappointing - not what I had hoped for at all. By contrast the tutorials on American literature with John Labbe were lively, engaging and good humoured and I quickly learnt there was a real art to good tutoring.

One chilly November morning I arrived early for a tutorial. I went to the cafeteria for a coffee. The latest copy of the *Jamaican Daily Gleaner* had arrived that morning and I was eager to catch up with events. The headline was shocking: *A bomb exploded on an Air Cubana aircraft en route from Cuba to Jamaica. The mid-air explosion killed all seventy-eight passengers. Anti-Castro groups in Miami claimed responsibility.* Letters from the Megevands talked of a situation close to civil war. They were torn between staying and leaving. The situation was grim.

That first term I was reading a range of books by black writers - Eldridge Cleaver's *Soul on Ice,* Franz Fanon's *The Wretched of the Earth,* the novels of James Baldwin, Aime Cesaire's narrative poem *Return to My Native Land* - books which expressed the frustration, the humiliation and the anger of the black race in post-colonial and racially segregated societies. Michael Manley's ideological battle in Jamaica was rooted in an attempt to change the plight of the black 'sufferers' but his political experiment had gone sour in the cauldron of violence which had erupted there. By 1976 Bob Marley's lyrics and the snagging pulse of reggae were stirring the dust in communities in British cities. In fact, just before I left Jamaica, Huey Morrison caught me one break time and held up a copy of a book of poetry he'd received from a cousin in England.

'Hey Mr Day, sir, trouble comin' to the streets of London. Me tell you, this book is somethin' else.'

The book was called *Dread Beat and Blood* and was by a young Jamaican poet called Linton Kwesi Johnson. He had come to Britain in 1963 and grown up in London..

'Listen to this,' said Huey.

We stood under the old poinciana tree and Huey read me a poem called *Reggae Sounds.* It was written in dialect and had a heavy pulsing rhythm. Huey's head was bobbing and his feet stepping as he read: *Shock-black bubble-doun-beat bouncing...rock-wise tumble-doun sound music.....*

When he had finished he looked at me smiling and shaking his head, 'This poetry is hot, man. I have to thank you, Mr Day, for turning me on to this literature. I never thought studyin' literature would get under my skin, but, man, this...' He waved the book in the air, 'this is the start of somethin' in England. Thomas Hardy soon be turnin' in his grave.'

I smiled, we shook hands and off he went, head down, fingers flicking through the pages of the book. I was not to know then that Huey's words would prove prophetic in a few years time.

Towards the middle of the term the winter weather started to bite. Our converted stable became a draughty ice box of a place. My daily walks along the Lune valley, through the woods and over the fields were often done with hands thrust into pockets, shoulders hunched against the wind which shivered the surface of the river. The horizons of

Caton Moor and Black Fell were nudged by blankets of grey mist, while the crows struggled up the valley in ragged flight against the force of the wind.

That term I was wrestling with Saul Bellow's *Dangling Man,* Kafka's *The Castle* and Sartre's *Nausea;* wrestling with the paradoxes of existentialism, the 'inner' and 'outer' lives we inhabit, trying to make sense of a reality of shifting mirrors. I felt very much akin to Bellow's 'dangling man' idea: I had few attachments to the real world (whatever that was) was adrift with books and ideas, with walks along the river and through the woods. Sue would return each day from work as if from another planet with tales of problem students and petty squabbles in the staff-room and I half-listened to her voice which battled against the cacophony of voices from the books I was reading.

However, Christmas brought some welcome focus to my sense of detachment. On a frosty, starlit evening we enjoyed a new Year's Eve reunion with friends from Jamaica. Jim and Jenny arrived from Bristol where Jim was re-training as a lawyer. Colin arrived from Keele where he was studying to qualify as a counsellor. Andy had driven up from London. He had recently won a small part in a BBC police drama as a detective and was also trying some scriptwriting for radio. Chris and Pascale were living locally with Chris also at the university. We were all treading new paths and it was fascinating to swap thoughts on how things were unfolding. We drank well, ate well, laughed a lot and ended the evening with *Auld Lang Syne*, mulled wine, a log fire and a somewhat sombre toast to the future of Jamaica.

By January I was absorbed by Doris Lessing's *The Four-Gated City.* She described so well the fine edge of awareness that I, myself, had felt on arriving back in England, seeing a culture from the outside, freshly, seeing it in all its relativity, with me on the outside, the observer, free in my isolation. And then the gradual, imperceptible clouding of that freshness of vision, the dulling of that fine edged sensibility, like the first rain on a new window pane, my view blurring, my self being sucked into the fog of a new social reality. Uncanny, how sharply Lessing's theme reflected my own state of mind.

On the eleventh of February 1977 at midday my thoughts were brought much more closely into focus with a phone call. It was Sue.

'I've just come from the doctor's. It's positive. I'm pregnant!'

My knees wobble, stomach leap-frogs, 'Are you sure?'

'Of course I'm sure. There are signs you know. But I wasn't going to say anything until I was certain.'

'When?'

'End of September .'

'Wow. Think I need to get a job.'

'I think you do. See you later.'

A father. Me a father! No time for dangling now. This is serious. And wonderful. And I am awash with wonder and terror.

Reality was really starting to bite. I started scanning the Times Educational Supplement for jobs. It was a little early for September jobs to be advertised but still I had to get moving. This term Sue had moved schools and was now teaching fifteen girls in a class at Casterton School near Kirkby Lonsdale - a far and welcome cry from the cut and thrust of Heysham High. But her burgeoning presence reminded me daily that I must do well on this course and secure a job for the September term.

Sometime later, two jobs appeared in Cumbria, one at Appleby Grammar School and one at a comprehensive school in Carlisle. I applied for both.

Something else which focused my mind that spring was the news that John Fowles had re-written his novel *The Magus* and his publisher, Jonathan Cape, was launching the revised version in May. This posed a major problem for me. I had agreed with my tutor that my dissertation would be on the works of Fowles. The deadline was October and here was Fowles re-issuing one of his key novels after a re-write. So my task would be to re-read the original version published in 1966 alongside the revised version and note the changes. Only then could I proceed with my examination of Fowles' work as a whole. Thanks Mr Fowles. Just what I needed!

That spring, another book jarred my sensibilities and opened new trains of thought. I was in the university bookshop browsing the shelves and bookstands when I lighted on the Abacus and Picador publications. A book called *Total Man* by a psychologist named Stan Gooch caught my eye and from the blurb seemed to connect with things I was reading on the course but in a very original way. He was looking at the way human society, institutions, literature, mythology, linguistics, art are rooted in a kind of dualism; that the structure of the human brain dictates that man is predisposed to construct a dualistic view of the world. Gooch was analysing duality in literature, legend, religion, social institutions and linking it with Jungian psychology, and linguistic theory. This was exhilarating stuff which synthesised aspects of what I'd studied for my sociology degree with what I was now studying for a literature degree. Brilliant. But not likely to help me get a job for September.

Meanwhile the estate farmyard was alive with activity. Derek, the gamekeeper, had been hatching pheasant eggs over the past few months and for several weeks the chicks had been snuffling around in small pens placed on the lawn behind the stable block. I had watched the whole process with great interest. At the egg stage soon after Christmas, Derek had been closely attentive to the eggs which were kept warm under incubator lights in a shed behind the stable. From our bathroom window I could see Derek's weathered face haloed in the darkness of the hatching shed as he pored over the trays of eggs monitoring their progress. When the eggs hatched his stubby hands were gentle with the fluffy balls of life which skittered around in the straw as he topped up their water or scattered their feed.

By late March, the young pheasants were big enough to be taken to the pens in the woods just up the valley. On my daily walks along the river and up through the woods I made a point of checking their progress. Their growth was rapid and they were soon stepping lightly through the ferns and leaves searching for grubs and insects and always wary of my intrusion into their woodland haven.

In mid-April replies came from the two schools. I was offered interviews at both, just one week apart. Things were looking up.

During the Appleby interview Sue sat in the car and stared out across a bleak moorland landscape contemplating a possible future there. Appleby lies on the west side of the Pennines east of Penrith. The school was on a hill above the town with open views across treeless moors. For me there was a certain wild romance about the location. Echoes from *Wuthering Heights,* the poetry of Ted Hughes and the novels of D.H.Lawrence spun in my head as I sat waiting to be called for the final interview. I really liked the atmosphere of the English department here and Andrew Austin, the Head of English, was good-humoured, gentle in manner but clearly passionate about literature and the power of education to change the lives of young people. I could

work with him. This could be a great starting point for my new career as an English teacher.

'So what happened on your first degree course, Mr Day? It seems you drifted somewhat. Industry was it? Then what? Why the change of direction?'

The question was from one of the governors and I felt he'd touched the nub of my so far chequered career. I was a waverer. Unreliable. Couldn't hack it in the real world of industry. So chose teaching. The old adage 'Those who can, do. Those who can't, teach.'

I stumbled through a reply and found all the confidence that I thought I had was somehow dribbling away. Andrew Austin tried to rescue me with some questions about the literature I enjoyed and finally, the Headmaster looked at me over his glasses and said, 'You said you liked D.H Lawrence. The author of Lady C ?'

While I was explaining my enjoyment of Lawrence's work, a look passed between the Head and another of the governors. He folded his hands together and concluded with, 'If you've no questions then that will be all, Mr Day. Thank you. Please wait outside.'

A short while later I crossed the car-park and saw Sue's face trying to read mine. I shrugged, 'One down, Carlisle here we come.'

She sighed, 'I'm so relieved. I couldn't imagine living up here. It's so desolate.'

'Yeah, you're probably right,' I nodded. The initial sense of romance about the place had quickly fled in the face of my failed interview and the sagging grey rain clouds which were elbowing their way across the Lakeland fells.

The following week we drove further up the M6 to Carlisle. The city was new to me. The school, St. Aidan's Comprehensive, was located near the centre of the city. It was an attractive old red sandstone building with newer blocks behind. Very different from Appleby which had been quiet and isolated, this place buzzed with energy, noise and young staff. The Head was a short, rotund man, with rimless glasses, and a balding head. Put him in a frock coat and he might have come straight from a Dickens novel. Across the table at the interview, however, I was only aware of the piercing gimlet eyes and the enigmatic smile which played around his mouth. He gave little away.

After the initial tour of the school I joined some of the staff for lunch, little realising that this was all part of the interview process. Roger, the Head of English, impressed me greatly. He was an unusual blend of the softly spoken intellectual and the rugged countryman. As our conversation revealed more detail, I felt he could have stepped out of a Thomas Hardy novel – Gabriel Oak from *Far From the Madding Crowd* came to mind. He farmed a small holding south of the city, was a Cumbrian wrestler, spoke with a Northumberland lilt and laughed easily. This was my man. If I had to choose a mentor, this unusual Renaissance man would be my choice. But there were three other candidates and a final interview to get through.

However, what marked the interview here as being so different from the Appleby interview was that my apparent 'chequered' history seemed to be viewed more positively. The Headmaster was interested that I'd changed tracks, that I'd taught abroad and that I was deliberately steering a new path towards teaching English.

'What is it about English that you find so important,' he asked.

I talked about my experiences in Jamaica, about the 'conduit to the soul' that writing offers. I mentioned Huey Morrison discovering poetry and the impact of studying *Romeo and Juliet.* I seemed to talk too much, but there was some nodding from both the governors and the Head and some gentle but searching questioning from the Head of English.

When it was over I was back out in a waiting room with the three other candidates immersed in this curious procedure which is peculiar to interviews for teaching jobs. After you've spent the day with the other candidates, getting to know each other, comrades in an excruciating trial of wits, you then sit around after the interview and wait for one to be asked back in. It feels like a betrayal of the curious camaraderie which has built up during the day.

I expected that they were all English graduates steeped in three years of studying English literature. They would know Chaucer and Beowulf; they would have studied Elizabethan poetry and Restoration Comedy, they would know the works of Swift, Wordsworth and Tennyson. I had studied none of these and yet here I was presuming I was qualified to become second in an English Department and teach GCE and A level English literature. Who was I kidding?

As I waited, so my initial optimism waned. I thought of Sue and the child she was carrying and the need for us to find a home. The dangling man had hit the ground with a bump. This would have been such a great place to work. No matter, I would have to start looking for other jobs.

Then the door opened. This was it. Roger came in. He looked round the room. His eyes fell on me. He nodded, 'Mr Day, would you follow me please.'

The three of us celebrated that night – Sue, me and the nameless little soul that she was carrying. Maybe it was the wine or perhaps the rhythm of Bob Marley's *Lively Up Yourself* playing on the record player which caused it but Sue suddenly took my hand and placed it over the curve of her stomach. At first nothing. Then, for the first time, under my finger tips a flutter, a feather touch of movement. Incredible, wondrous. I put my head against the place. 'Yes, baby, I got a job. All we have to do now is find somewhere to live – and pass those exams.'

Exams started in June with a list of questions from which I had to select six. I then had a week to complete these before attending the supervised three and a half hour exam two weeks later.

One morning, during the week I was struggling to complete my exam essays, the early morning air was riven with the scream of a chainsaw. Just what I needed! I looked out of the window which faced the drive to see a truck, two men in overalls and one levelling a chain saw against the broad trunk of a tree on the edge of the drive. I rushed outside to find Derek, watching a few yards away.

'What's happening,' I shouted against the scream of the chainsaw. 'Why are they felling the tree?'

'Diseased and it might fall on the stable or on my house. It's a lime. Been there ever since I can remember.'

We looked on, watching the spine of the tree being surgically severed. It was skilful work cutting so that the tree fell safely. It had a girth of almost three feet at its base. The canopy of pale green leaves was thirty or forty feet from the ground.

They made a horizontal cut and then one at an angle to meet the first cut. The wedge was removed with heavy mallets and crow bars. Then came a pause as if nature was taking a breath. The leaves of the tree shivered and then the tall trunk began to tilt. There was a crack like a pistol shot and the canopy started its rapid descent crashing in a heap of leaves and smashed branches on to the grass beside the drive.

Derek nodded. 'That was well done,' he said.

For the rest of the morning the chain-saws whined as the huge trunk of the tree was cut into sections. I was saddened by what I had seen and by the way the majestic tree was being unceremoniously sectioned for firewood. When there was a lull in the cutting I ventured across the drive. I asked if they could slice me off a section of the trunk. They shrugged and nodded.

Later that afternoon I carried away a circular section of the trunk, about three inches thick and three feet in diameter. The cuts of the chainsaw obscured the ring markings of the trunk but I felt that with some sanding and planing I could make something of my rustic souvenir – a table, maybe, to mark our year in Lancaster and the place where my first child felt the pulse of life.

On the day after I handed in my final essay I cycled into Lancaster to collect the book – the newly published copy of Fowles' revised version of *The Magus*. I'd never heard of an established author withdrawing a book from circulation, re-writing it and then a publisher re-issuing it. It seemed an odd thing to do and from my point of view a real inconvenience, given the catalogue of things already facing me in the coming months – complete exams, find somewhere to live, sell house in Staffordshire, vacate cottage in Lancaster, prepare for new job, write dissertation.

Yet, as I took the book from its brown paper bag, I was buzzing with excitement. It had a purple dustcover and the title in large gold letters. Below the title two black images – one of a Pan figure with a goat's head and long curving horns and the other the mask of a young girl. I waited until I'd found a table in a nearby coffee-shop before opening the book. My fingers were tingling. Ever since first reading Fowles and then waiting for each new publication I had been mesmerised by his work – the ideas, the style, his powers of description, the enchantment.

I started with the Foreword in which Fowles gives a resume of his writing career, the genesis of *The Magus*, its poor reception by some critics but its enduring popularity with readers. He mentions the influences of Jung and Alan Fournier's book *Le Grand Meaulnes* and of his own experience as a young teacher on the Greek island of Spetsai. It was unexpectedly honest, frank, and very revealing.

When I got back to the flat I found the original copy and placed the two versions side by side. It was a case of reading a couple of sentences of the original and then the same sentences in the new version. Tedious but intriguing; like literary detective work.

The first change comes on the fourth page where he changes *'I was interviewed'* to *'was cursorily scrutinized'*. Further on I started finding other changes of individual words or phrases. Sometimes it was clearly because the earlier version sounded dated, but there were other examples where the change was more subtle. It was a shift of tone, of mood, hardly there but enough to feel you were close to the purring of the writer's mind. Later in the book there were added paragraphs and even added scenes. And the final two pages were reworked, seeking, I supposed, to make the ending clearer.

It took me a week to complete the readings but it was a process which taught me more about the power of language, its shifting tones, the nuances of meaning contained within a word or phrase, than any number of books on literary style could have taught me. It also took me inside the mind of Fowles which was useful in preparing me for the dissertation I had to submit by the end of October.

*

A few days before our final departure from Halton Park, we were awoken by noise and activity in the farmyard. For several days Derek, the gamekeeper, had been taking the tractor up the track to the woods where the release pens for the pheasants were located. And for the past few weeks, on my daily walks, I had noticed pheasants wandering freely in the woods. This day was the culmination of all his hard work, his nurturing of the birds, the care and concern he had lavished over the past few months. His big day had arrived.

There was the roar of powerful engines in the yard and up the drive to the big house. Land Rovers and other four-wheel-drive monsters came through the gates and disgorged men dressed in green Barbour coats and flat tweed caps, who nursed polished shotguns under their arms. They strutted and joshed and commanded one side of the farmyard while their dogs, spaniels and retrievers, chased with wagging tails round the feet of their masters. These men talked in those accents which start in the back of the throat and seem to force the speaker to stiffen the neck and emit a kind of choked laughter. Across the yard was an untidy huddle of a different breed. Here was a group of shorter men in green waterproof capes and coats leaning on long sticks and poles, heads down, talking in low murmurs. These were the beaters whose job it was to flush the pheasants into the air for the guns to blast from the sky. It was like theatre, toffs and their underlings about to engage in a drama on the banks of the Lune River with Derek, the redoubtable director of this drama, scurrying around checking last minute details.

The farmyard emptied and for a short while there was quiet, just the breeze and the birdsong. Then came the first squawking of pheasants echoing from the direction of the woods and, soon after, the valley resounded to the boom of shot-guns.

The shoot lasted a couple of hours before the guns fell silent. Soon there were voices in the farmyard again, the barking of dogs and the two groups took up their positions on opposite sides of the class divide. Guns were zipped into gun cases and the dogs settled down panting on the gravel. Finally a ruddy-faced Derek nodding and half-smiling made his triumphal entry driving a tractor which carried a trailer brimming with the booty of dead birds. Fine, golden brown feathers, scarlet flashes on the heads, bloodied beaks, clenched, muddied claws.

Such a curious paradox, the job of a gamekeeper; from the weeks of sensitive nurturing to this celebration of the slaughter. Some would say it was just another type of farming but it was the nature of the slaughter which jarred, the joy in the kill. Derek was congratulated, money was passed round, the pheasants strung into braces, and then the actors departed.

It was indeed a curious piece of theatre which marked the end of our chapter of living at Halton Park Estate.

CHAPTER THE FOURTH 1977-83 Cumbria

NEW HOUSE, NEW JOB, NEW BABY

'But I don't want to live in a 'quiet cul-de-sac' and I certainly don't want to be 'within walking distance of the city centre'.' Sue gave a sigh and placed another set of house details on to the 'reject' pile. So far the details of forty two houses were on the reject pile and only two on the 'possibles' pile.

We had been spoilt. Our first house had been in a quaint Stafforshire village. Then came Mandala Cottage and then Halton Park. We wanted a house with some character and some history and a plot of land. Somewhere of the ilk evoked in Andrew Marvell's poem *The Garden:*

> *Ripe apples drop about my head;*
> *The luscious clusters of the vine*
> *Upon my mouth do crush their wine:*
> *The nectarine and curious peach*
> *Into my hands themselves do reach....*

-maybe vines, peaches and nectarines was expecting a little too much but an apple tree and a potato patch would be just fine.

But time was pressing. It was early June. My new job started in a few months time. The baby was due in September. Could we really afford to be so choosy?

We drove to one of the two 'possibles' near Longtown, north of Carlisle. But it wasn't right. It had a sad decaying air to it and the landscape around seemed somewhat bleak and featureless. So we set off along the Solway Plain west of the city to view the other property. Flat, flat, hardly a hill in sight apart from the tantalising skyline of the Lake District hills to the south, an area where the properties were totally out of our price bracket.

Finally we drove down the main street of a small village close to the Solway coast. The house stood at the end of a lane. It had been a row of three sandstone cottages but two had been knocked into one and this was for sale. The front door was a yucky bright orange and the sandstone porch and window surrounds were lime green. Built around 1800, it had once been a farmhouse. At the rear there was a cobbled yard and old out-buildings - a stable, a coal shed and a huge empty barn attached to the rear of the house. Inside, the house was grubby and scuffed and there were patches of damp on the flowered wall-paper. Beyond the house were fields and a wide sky. The sun was warm on the old sandstone walls, the swallows were spiralling in and out of the open door of the barn and in the garden there were some old apple trees. 'Ripe apples drop about my head....'

After viewing the house, we wandered up the lane.

'There's a lot of work,' Sue said.

I nodded.

'And we've very little money.'

I nodded again.

'Slates off the roof, corner of the barn crumbling, damp in some of the rooms, no central-heating.'

'Not the kind of house to bring a new baby into,' I said, feeling my spirits sinking. 'So you want to forget it then?'

Sue frowned, 'I'm not sure. But there's something about it that I like. Could be a great place to bring up a family. What d'you reckon?'

I looked back at the lane end, at the house front with its warm sandstone, at the leaning chimney stack and the sky and fields beyond. I nodded, 'It could be a good home for us. Quite a challenge though.'

A challenge of a different sort was starting at St Aidan's. To borrow a phrase from Laurie Lee's *Cider With Rosie* , the place 'roared like a rodeo'.

'C'mon you shiftless, witless lumps, come and swallow your medicine! Let's see if we can weedle some wisdom into those torpid brains of yours. Ah, Mr Morris, and how are your guinea pigs today? If you don't finish that book this lesson I'll tell your mother to lock you in a cage with those furry fiends until the job is done. Do we understand each other?'

This was my first meeting with Mike, part English department, part geography. During my first week I was using my free time to visit members of the department. I had been forewarned about Mike. 'Caustic melodrama but with good intentions' was how Jean, another member of the department, had described him.

Mike had a passion for children's literature. He and the Head of Special Needs had developed a new method for raising the profile of reading. Each Tuesday for a double lesson of eighty minutes groups of fifty lower school students trouped towards his room. Mike would stand, filling the doorway with his large frame and harangue the students with mock-friendly jibes as they approached. Once inside, each student sat at a separate desk equipped with headphones, cassette player, book, story tape. They would follow the story listening to the tape and then settle to answering the questions which accompanied the tape.

'Right, you reprobates, let's immerse ourselves in the delights of literary magic. Headphones on. Any problems put your hand up.' He turned to me and winked, 'They love me really.'

Mike was typical of what I came to know as the St Aidan's style – unconventional, unpredictable but inspiring. Generally, the place was pretty manic, buzzing with energy, activity, enthusiasm.

The staff-room, for a start, was anything but a respite from the frenzy of the classroom. It was almost as frenetic. There were two ends divided by a half partition wall. One end was occupied mainly by the science and maths teachers. This was normally a fug of smoke from the cigarette and pipe-smokers. At the other end the English department sat round the coffee table in the centre of the room; the few religious ed. and history staff would occupy the benches by the windows. It was territorial in one sense but pretty fluid in another. There was a lot of healthy banter between members of different departments and little time to relax. Staff would balance their coffee and biscuit in one hand while engaging in exuberant chat about this or that new idea or new project. No-one seemed to walk or amble, all seemed to rush and scamper from class to class while at lesson changes the narrow corridors would be packed with an elbowing throng of 1200 students moving in various directions.

This was the maelstrom into which I was pitched in the September of 1977. My title was Second in the English Department and as such I had to deputise for the Head of Department when he was absent. At last I felt had arrived. I had been switching tracks to get to this position ever since abandoning my abortive flirtation with industry and the world of economics. And when I heard from Lancaster that my Masters degree in English was assured, I finally felt I could start to build a career as a teacher of English.

*

'Try this with your second years,' said Jean. She handed me a book called *The Twelfth Day of July* by Joan Lingard. We were down in the 'dungeon' level of the school sorting through the book stock in the English stock room. I was in need of class readers for my lower school classes.

'It's set in northern Ireland. Deals with Protestant/Catholic tensions but in a very readable way. It raises a lot of important issues which our kids won't be aware of.'

'Thanks. Any ideas for first years?'

She moved between the piles of books stacked on tables and on the floor of the stockroom.

'This never fails,' she said and handed me Roald Dahl's *Danny Champion of the World*. 'It's a wonderful book,' she added.

Jean was always warm, friendly, helpful. I came to know her as the beating heart of the department. She had worked in Africa and was the dynamo of the local Oxfam shop. She adorned her classroom with William Morris fabrics and Aubrey Beardsley prints; she provided cakes for departmental meetings, costumed the school drama productions and was the person to turn to in time of need. She was sharply intelligent and mothered the rough-cut rogues in the bottom sets with her quick wit and her soothing words. She would work tirelessly to help  them find some semblance of self-belief and pride before they were launched into the harsh world of the streets.

'What about third year?' I asked.

'Ah, tricky one. When you have girls with newly heaving bosoms pining for pop singers, sitting alongside little boys who are still playing marbles and collecting football stickers it's not easy to find class readers which work.'

She edged along the stacks of books and then passed me a copy of Jack London's *Call of the Wild*. I'd come across this book in Jamaica. Gender neutral, it had action, adventure and pathos and focussed on a German Shepherd dog called Buck who is kidnapped and forced to work as a sled dog during the Klondike gold rush in Canada.

'I know this one,' I said. 'It could work well. Thanks.'

We made our way back along the dark corridor of the 'dungeons'. This floor, part way below ground level, housed a number of classrooms and the Bursar's office. But at the end of the corridor there was an even darker passageway leading to a door into the underground lair of Harry, the caretaker. Like most caretakers I'd met, he was generally grumpy. Not surprising when you consider what they have to put up with. Cleaning and polishing each day only to have your good works scuffed and spoiled by the legions of little oiks who invade the

131

premises each morning. Harry was a big, hunched man with the proverbial wart on the end of his nose. At around 3.35pm, just after the bell for the end of school had rung, a cloud of cigarette smoke would billow from the opening door of his room and Harry would appear like some ancient wizard herding the team of female cleaners before him. He was like a character from Raymond Briggs' *Fungus the Bogeyman*.

'Nah then gals, good work you know. I'll be round checkin' up later.' They would be stubbing out their ciggies, collecting mops and brooms to do battle with the litter and grime of the corridors and classrooms. Harry would stand for a moment, hands on his haunches nodding and then he would shuffle back into his little grotto.

'Try to keep on the right side of Harry,' said Jean. 'It's not easy, but it pays to keep him on our side.'

Another key member of the English department was Tricia: tall, elegant, bird-like with a braid of long hair coiled high on her head. She spoke with a soft home counties accent and for several years had written and broadcast for the BBC Radio *Woman's Hour* programme. Like Jean, she could disarm the most obnoxious teenage waster with some well-chosen verbal poniards. She could transform belligerence into compliance with her humour and kindness and drew a devoted following from her students.

John, the oldest member of the department was part-time. He farmed a small-holding on the Caldbeck fells where he kept sheep and crafted fine wooden furniture. He was quiet, somewhat reserved but quickly melted into chuckling humour at the gentle teasing of Tricia and Jean.

Finally there was Roger, the multi-faceted Head of Department, the true 'Renaissance man' – teacher, farmer, Cumbrian wrestler, eloquent in Chaucerian old English and with a passion for Shakesperian drama, Japanese haiku and Belted Galloway cattle: for me he was the perfect mentor.

Many of the St Aidan's staff were relatively young and it quickly became clear that the Headmaster's philosophy was to recruit staff with energy and talent, then give them space to try things out – the old adage 'enough rope with which to hang yourself' was often quoted but typically that didn't happen. Instead there was verve and imagination bubbling away in most departments.

It was a time of great experimentation. The Newsom Report of 1963 had opened up a major debate about education, especially for average and below average pupils. It had recommended the raising of the school leaving age, broadening extra-curricular provision, providing residential experience for all pupils, extending the use of audio-visual aids, moving away from the streaming of pupils and above all giving average and below average pupils access to the best teachers. It had stimulated the move to comprehensive education and so by the nineteen seventies many of the Newsom recommendations were being instituted in the more forward-thinking schools. St. Aidans, led by its visionary Headmaster, had fully embraced this climate of change and welcomed the casting off of the shackles which had hemmed in teachers and their pupils for so long.

During the first week in the school I sat in various meetings, mesmerised by the catalogue of activities planned for the year. The geography department was planning field trips at home and abroad, some combining with biology to set up environmental studies projects. The English department was planning theatre trips to Newcastle and in the summer term there was a week long trip to Stratford-Upon-Avon for the A level literature students. Cross-curricular projects were planned combining art, history and English. The Head of art was seeking more funds to equip a disused local primary school with television cameras to establish a T.V. studio. An Old Tyme Musical Hall was mooted for the Christmas term and a drama night for Hallowe'en. Funds were being raised to purchase a mini-bus for the school. There were working parties going down to the Lake District to continue refurbishing the school's outdoor centre. The list went on and on. Each night I left school exhausted but exhilarated, my head buzzing with the energy of the place.

*

That first week I returned home to a house being gutted and dismembered. The kitchen was being replastered and as part of the mortgage agreement we had to have the whole place sprayed top to bottom with Rentokil woodworm treatment. Sue, now heavily pregnant and with just a few weeks to go before the birth, perched herself on a stool near the door of the kitchen and cooked our evening meal on a two-burner camping stove. There were no modern kitchen units or surfaces to work on just a glass fronted cabinet with a drop down enamelled metal worktop. We were certainly back to basics.

That first week-end I mixed my first ever bucket of mortar. I read the instructions from my newly purchased DIY book not believing that this gunge I was mixing would actually set hard. My task was to rebuild the bottom corner of the barn which was crumbling owing to the cows in the field behind the house rubbing their backsides against the brickwork. This rebuild was another requirement of the mortgage company before they would release the whole of the mortgage. While I laboured at my brickwork Sue lay in the sunshine and the baby began to kick and punch obviously liking the warmth and brightness.

'Not long now, baby,' I said addressing Sue's belly-button and feeling the kicking through her skin. 'Just three weeks. Be patient, little one.'

But 'little one' was not patient and the following Saturday demanded a hearing!

At 6a.m. Sue's waters broke. No contractions yet but there was no time to waste. We drove into Carlisle with the petrol gauge flickering on zero. This was not planned. I had thought we had another week to get prepared. I quickly pulled into the nearest petrol station and started filling up. I couldn't believe the world was continuing as normal. I wanted to scream, 'BUT MY WIFE'S HAVING A BABY. DON'T YOU REALISE WORLD. THE UNIVERSE IS TILTING!'

We arrived at the hospital at 8 a.m. We were checked in and taken to a delivery room. And there we waited. Nothing happening. For four hours nothing happened.

Finally, at noon, a nurse came in, put Sue on a drip and within half an hour the contractions started. No panic. Sue does not panic. She breathed her way slowly through each contraction refusing the offer of gas and air to ease the pain. She was determined to be in control.

Meanwhile, my brain scrambled to remember the part I was supposed be playing in all this. We had attended ante-natal classes of the local National Childbirth Trust – a very feisty organisation which was working hard to shake up archaic birth procedures in the nation's hospitals. Where, once, fathers were banished to a waiting room during the birth, NCT devotees resisted the steely glare of old fashioned matrons and insisted on the father being present throughout. Not only that, I had a crucial role to play at the moment of what was called 'transition', when the mother has a strong urge to push but the baby is not quite in position. This is where I came in. We had gone through this routine at a class a few weeks ago. We had to choose a song and at the key moment of transition I had to force Sue to make eye contact and then sing our song and so distract her from her urge to push.

So here I was, contractions coming fast now, Sue's eyes rolling back while she struggled to breathe through the pain and me yelling, 'Look at me, look at me!' and banging the side of the bed singing, 'Show me the way to go home…I'm tired and I want to go to bed……..'

The attending nurse raised her eyebrows but I didn't care what she thought. From barely having a walk on part in this whole drama I was now centre stage and unstoppable. Sue's glazed eyes came into focus and she mouthed, 'Show me the way…..'

'That's it,' I said, 'show me the way....'.

And now Sue was back in control, eyes bright, pushing, pushing into our world this little head of dark hair followed by a glistening body. It was September the 17th. Katie had arrived and I was a father.

*

GROWING PAINS

There was a squeal from the back of the class. 'Mr Day, Mr Day tell him to stop it!'

I was registering the class at the beginning of the day. I looked up to see little Kevin Foster holding his bag close to his chest and grimacing while Wendy and Deborah clung to each other in the corner of the room.

'He's got a rat in his bag,' squealed Wendy pointing at Kevin.

'No I aven't. Don't like rats.'

'You're a liar, Kevin Foster.'

'No I'm not.'

'Look in his bag, sir.'

I made my way to the back of the class. The other children watched and waited.

'I don't keep rats. Don't like em,' repeated Kevin still clutching his bag.

'What's in the bag Kevin?' I said calmly.

Kevin's big brown eyes looked up at me, 'Sir, it's just for English. Mrs Pocock told us we had to do a talk on our interests.'

'And?'

'So I brought in Freddy.'

'Who, or rather what is Freddy?'

Deborah started bleating from the corner again, 'I told you, sir, he's brought in his rat. It's in his bag. He's always talking about his animals.'

'S'not a rat!' shouted Kevin.

'Hush, Kevin,' I said stooping down beside a now distressed little boy. 'Show me Freddy, will you?'

'He's probably over-excited now, sir.' Kevin opened the top of his battered blue rucksack. There was a musty smell of animal pee and then a little pink nose covered in silvery white fur appeared. 'He's a ferret, sir.'

135

'I can see that,' I said as a squirming little silvery body with bright pink eyes was pulled out of the bag and then cradled against Kevin's chest.

The other children plucked up courage to move closer and have a look.

'Did Mrs Pocock know you were bringing Freddy in?' I asked.

'No, sir. Will she mind?'

'I'm sure she'll be delighted,' I said, knowing Tricia's aversion to cats. 'And where's Freddy going to be for the rest of the day?'

'I could take him home at dinner time, sir.'

'I think you'd better, Kevin, just so he doesn't get unsettled. And not everyone likes animals like this you know.'

'Well they oughta. My nan says stroking her cat everyday has kept her alive, and she's eighty eight.'

'You're probably right, Kevin.' I stood up. 'Well, I'd better finish marking my register before the bell goes for first lesson. Put Freddy back in your bag and settle him down again. When's English with Mrs Pocock?'

'First lesson, sir.'

'Right, Kevin. After the lesson you keep Freddy safely in your bag. No taking him out to show people, right?'

'Right, sir.'

'And I hope your talk goes well. I'll be checking with Mrs Pocock at breaktime.'

'Yes, sir,' nodded Kevin. 'Thank you, sir.'

Like me, most of the St Aidan's teachers were form tutors as well as being subject teachers. This involved registering the class each morning, reading out notices, liaising with parents and taking a tutorial lesson each week. Tutorials were intended to tackle topics of social and personal interest pertinent to the age of the students. This would be done through discussions, worksheets or sometimes a film or slide show. Many teachers grumbled about these lessons. They were comfortable delivering lessons on their own subject but when it came to managing open discussions on Third World poverty, Crime and Delinquency or Teenage Pregnancy, it was a different matter.

That September I had been given a first year form as my tutor group. I would be attached to this group for their first three years before they moved up to what was called Middle School. My tutor room and the room in which I did most of my teaching was room 14. It was in the old part of the school and was accessed via a balcony which overlooked the old hall. The balcony, with its iron balustrade, was supported by cast iron columns topped with ornate filigree iron work. The hall was a charming relic from the early days of the school when it had been the County High School for Girls. With its highly polished parquet floor and vaulted ceiling it had something of the feel of a baronial hall.

I caught up with Tricia at break in the staff room, or rather, she caught up with me.

'You might have warned me,' she said. 'Gives a whole new meaning to the verb to 'ferret' in your bag for something.'

'Yes, I'm sorry but I didn't know until just before the lesson, then it was too late. How did it go?'

She nodded slowly, 'Entertaining at first. Kevin's very knowledgeable. But then he handed Freddy to someone else who dropped him and then it was chaos. Kids standing on chairs and desks, girls screaming while friend Freddy does a circumnavigation of my classroom. Oh and then the Headmaster pops his head round the door, frowns and says, 'Everything okay, Mrs Pocock? Looks like fun.' 'Just a ferret on the loose Headmaster,' I shouted back. 'Very good. Carry on then,' he replied and left me to get on with it.'

'Well done,' I said. 'And Freddy's back in the bag?'

She smiled and nodded, 'Freddy's back in the bag.'

*

My timetable included top set GCE O level classes and lower CSE exam sets. CSE or Certificate of Secondary Education was the exam course aimed at those students who couldn't cope with the demands of the O level syllabus. However, a grade 1 at CSE level was rated as equivalent to a GCE level pass. In addition to preparing work for these classes, I also had to face my first A level Literature groups.

I had looked over the A level syllabus before term started and chosen the texts I would be teaching. I was sharing the lower sixth literature group with Roger. Each of us would teach a Shakespeare play, then there was a prose work, a selection of poetry and what was termed a 'long poem'. This was my chance to fill in some of the gaps in my knowledge of pre-20th century literature. For the Shakespeare I chose *Antony & Cleopatra*, for the novel – Thomas Hardy's *Tess of the D'Urbevilles,* the poetry of Ted Hughes some of which I'd studied on the Lancaster course and finally Gerard Manley Hopkins' long poem *The Wreck of the Deutschland*. Quite a formidable set of texts to prepare in addition to those I would be teaching for the GCE and CSE groups.

Roger talked me through the O level syllabus. He had joined up with a number of other Cumbria schools to pilot a new English syllabus administered by the Joint Matriculation Board or JMB. It was called 'Alternative D' and was as far away from traditional O levels as you could get. It was examined entirely by coursework. Twelve assignments had to be completed during the two years of the course, one of which had to be done under exam conditions and the rest had to show evidence of a student's ability to write in different styles and respond to different texts. There was a free choice of literature texts but they must include a study of a Shakespeare play, a novel, a selection of poetry and two works of drama by a recognised playwright.

'And do they get a language and literature qualification at the end of the course?' I asked.

'Yes,' said Roger, ' it's called 'Dual-Certification. It's brilliant. It just liberates you to be really imaginative in the way you tackle texts, writing, and reading. We've only been doing it for a couple of years but it's transforming our teaching.'

'But how does the Exam Board make sure all the schools are working to the same standards?' I asked.

'We have to attend these standardising meetings every term. We're sent sample material by the Board – actual essays which have been submitted for the exam and we have to mark them blind, first individually, then together as a department. Finally we go to the regional meeting to compare our assessments. Only then do we get told what grades the assignments were given by the Exam Board.'

'And it works?'

He nodded, 'It's fascinating how in a group discussion of a piece of writing you will eventually arrive at a consensus. Now that's something you ought to do. Apply to become an exam moderator. That would really help with your career development.'

Me, an examiner? I'd assumed examiners were some rarefied breed of experts who floated somewhere in the ether detached from the cut and thrust of a grimy classroom. But when Roger handed me a circular from the JMB asking for teachers to apply to become moderators it set me thinking.

I floated the idea with Sue that evening. 'I think I might apply to become an examiner for the O level English exam.'

She glanced up from the chair where she was feeding Katie. 'What does that involve? And more importantly, do they pay you?'

'I'm not sure exactly how it works but you have to attend a couple of meetings in Manchester at the JMB offices. They send you sample scripts to mark and then in the summer you get batches of scripts from different schools which have to be marked.'

'Sounds like a lot of work to me. And you've only just started your job.'

'Yes, I know. But Roger thinks it would help my career development.'

'Well, I'm not sure. But how about if you help your career development as a father and go and change Katie's nappy? I'm feeling pretty whacked.'

'Fine,' I said, picking up the new member of the family. 'I'll talk it over with Katie. See what she thinks.'

But I knew really that this wasn't the year to embark on yet another venture. As usual, Sue's instinct was right. We had quite enough to be going on with. Various major building projects were planned for the house so somehow we had to start saving our money.

I decided to buy a motor bike. This would save on petrol and would leave the car for Sue to use. I'd had motor bikes when I was younger and enjoyed the exhilaration of fresh air and the open road. By hunting through the classified section of the Cumberland News each Friday I located a few suitable bikes and after several viewings finally bought a red Suzuki 175cc from a man in Upperby.

It was twelve miles into Carlisle each day, mostly on country roads and the autumn weather was still warm. I would set off around 7.30a.m. and get to school in time to get myself organised. My arrival often coincided with the arrival of the Headmaster who was driving in from his house in a village west of Carlisle.

The sight of him always made me chuckle. One of his many eccentricities was his love for his Reliant Robin – a small three-wheeler car. It only had space for two seats and had a rear end which made it look like a small van. These little three-wheelers were notoriously unstable and, being made out of fibre-glass, were vulnerable to being squashed flat under the wheels of trucks and buses. But this didn't seem to phase the Headmaster. He drove with a benign expression of private amusement on his face, his domed bald head peering over the top of the steering wheel, a newly picked rose always prominent in his button-hole. He was a man of few words and, if his arrival at the car-park happened as I was parking my bike, he might nod but rarely stopped to talk. Once he ventured across the gravel to me and proffered, 'But was Wordsworth really in an incestuous relationship with Dorothy? That's the question.' Then, without waiting for a reply, he turned, went a few paces, stopped to smell the scent of one of the roses in the garden by the school entrance and then proceeded into his office.

It was one afternoon when I was riding home that the inspiration came to me. In anticipation of Hallowe'en I'd set my second year class to compile their own anthology of poetry on the theme of 'the supernatural'. I had put together some boxes of poetry texts and some colourful non-fiction books on 'spooks' and 'witchcraft' from the school library and from the 'dungeon' stock room. There were coloured pencils and plain paper available and for our Friday afternoon double lesson we all enjoyed a relaxing but productive time. It was a mix of reading, writing, discussion and good presentation. They had to copy out each poem they had chosen, illustrate it, make comments on why they had chosen the poem and also compose poetry of their own. I sat at my desk thumbing through various anthologies looking for good poems to read to them while the class buzzed with enthusiasm and genuine industry.

'Look at this, sir, it's daft.'

I looked up to see the pinched face of Terry Jarvis.

'Hello, Terry. What have you found?'

'This thing about what they did to witches, it's crackers.'

He was holding a book of illustrations about witches. 'They used this thing called a dunking stool. Look here's a bit of poetry.'

'Can you read it to me?'

Terry frowned, took the book from me and placed his finger under the first line of the quotation: *"I'll speed me to the pond, where the high stool....On the long plank hangs o'er the muddy pool. That stool, the dread of every scolding queen."*

'What's it mean, a 'scolding queen', sir?'

I scanned the page and the illustrations, 'Ah, it's talking about how they used to punish women who were nosy gossips or who used bad language, by dunking them in the river.'

Terry grinned, 'Hey, sir, they could do wi' one of them down our street.'

'Is that right?' I smiled back.

Terry's face frowned again. 'But it's this thing what they did to witches that's daft. They dunk them an if they sink and drown it means they're not a witch but if they float they are and then they burn them. So they're dead either way. How crackers is that?'

'Doesn't seem very fair does it?' I said. 'I think that in those days they were more worried about the woman's soul than her body. If she was proved innocent by sinking then her soul would go to heaven; if she floated she was guilty and going to hell anyway.'

Terry shook his head, 'Sounds batty to me.'

'How's your project coming along?'

'Pretty good sir, I think I'll write a poem about the dunking stool.' He thought for a moment, then started mouthing, 'If they thought you were a fool. They'd stick you in the dunking stool.' He grinned, 'How's that for a start sir?'

I nodded, 'Pretty cool, Terry, pretty cool.'

'Hey sir, stool, fool, cool – I could use that. Thanks, sir,'and off he went back to his desk.   That afternoon I had found quite a rhythmic poem about witches: '*Witches glide in evening flight, Leering through the louring light....* and I started to formulate an idea of putting music to it for the Hallowe'en drama evening which I had agreed to help with. Riding home that afternoon, I started to compose a tune which fitted the words of the poem. I sensed that a tune in a minor key would sound suitably sinister. I was not great on the guitar but I could strum a few chords and I pictured myself under a single spot light in a darkened hall singing this brooding, moody composition to set the tone at the start of the Hallowe'en drama night.

'Sounds a great idea,' commented Graham, the Head of Drama when I caught up with him at break the following day. 'I'm getting my students to produce some posters to stick around school and I'll post a notice in 'Weekly Notes' for the form tutors to read out. Somehow Graham managed to speak with his bent pot pipe still clamped firmly between his teeth. It was generally not alight but always firmly lodged beneath his moustache. He went on, 'But I'm rather worried about the take up for this drama evening. We don't want it to be a damp squib. I was wondering whether we should offer maybe a Hallowe'en disco after the drama to boost the attendance.'

'Whatever you think,' I said. 'I'm the new boy here. I'll just help wherever I can.'

Each time I rode to and from school the mood music I was composing for the drama evening sounded ever more impressive as I sang it inside the acoustic dome of my motor bike helmet. I was looking forward to my first involvement in producing a drama event. I'd watched Andy in Jamaica fire his drama students with such enthusiasm and I wanted to try to emulate his success. Although it was Graham who would be producing the drama pieces, I was pleased to be involved in the event, even in a minor role.

*

Another new challenge that first term was teaching A level English Literature. I had not taught sixth formers before and when I saw them around the school they seemed very mature and worldly-wise. Maybe it was the fact that they didn't have to wear school uniform that made them look more grown-up but I assumed that A level lessons would be quite challenging faced by these young adults who had just scored success in their O levels.

In fact the reality was quite different. My class consisted of seven girls and three boys. Within the group there was an ability spread from Kiera at one end with eight grade As and one B at O level through to Michael who had predominantly C grades and one B. Despite their achievements at O level the previous summer they did not exude the confidence and flare in lessons that I had anticipated. Just the opposite. It seemed that those with lower grades were intimidated by the brighter students with the A grades and so were reluctant to speak, but then the A graders, especially the girls, felt it wasn't 'cool' to come across as too intelligent so they also said very little. Trying to get a discussion going about the books we were studying was like trying to get the proverbial 'blood out of a stone'. I thought back to my excruciating seminars at Lancaster where nobody spoke and the tutor struggled and I realised that teaching ten intelligent seventeen year olds required a very different set of teaching skills from teaching thirty thirteen year olds.

Nobody teaches you how to teach A level. It is assumed that if you understand literature you can teach about it. But I quickly realised that teaching sixth formers is less about telling them things than asking the right kind of questions. It was Jean in one of our department meetings who had first used the terms 'open' and 'closed' questioning. I'd never heard the terms before.

'Closed questions are those which can only be answered with a 'yes' or 'no' answer,' she explained. 'They generally start with words like 'Do you? Have you…? Will you…?' They're useless at opening up discussion. They don't draw anything out. Whereas 'open' questions which start with 'What d'you think about….?' ..or 'How do you feel about….?'..or 'What are your thoughts on…?' - they force the respondent to say something.'

I reckon I instinctively used more open than closed questions in my teaching but now, with my new A level group, I had to work doubly hard to open things up and break down their inhibitions. Another thing I quickly realised was that the seating layout in the small teaching room had a marked effect on the group dynamics. The rooms were typically laid out with tables in rows facing the front and most of the teachers left them like that. But this meant that the more reluctant students could hide behind the others or take seats at the back and try to avoid eye contact. So after the first lesson I rearranged the seating into a horseshoe shape so that there was more of a group feeling and everybody was, in a sense, exposed. This certainly helped, although I imagine initially the students felt less comfortable.

I had two double lessons a week with the group and decided I would focus on the novel *Tess of the D'Urbervilles* for the Monday lesson and as a contrast use the Thursday lesson for the Ted Hughes poetry.

I loved Thomas Hardy's writing and as a seventeen year old spent several months reading through many of the novels. This was after my interest had first been aroused by studying him for O level with dear old Mr Freer. Our set book was *Under The Greenwood Tree* and I remember Freer going into ecstasies at what he called the 'sensual climax' of the book. It occurs when the lovesick hero Dick Dewy is visiting the enticing school teacher Fancy Day. The scene takes place in her kitchen where he helps with the washing up and their hands touch under the water. I can hear Freer's voice even now, 'Ecstasy of ecstasies' he swooned. 'This is a great example of the subtlety of Hardy's sensuality.'

At that moment one of my smart-alek friends, Terry Cook, put up his hand and said, while keeping a straight face, 'Sir, could we call it a kind of Fairy Liquid fulfilment?'

There was a muted titter as we watched Freer's reaction. He could explode in laughter or anger in equal measure with this kind of goading and you were never quite sure which way he would go. This time, his eyes glinted, 'Bravo, Cook. Class, please note Mr Cook's fine example of alliteration, but sadly applied to a rather crass and cheapskate attempt to mock the artistry of one of our great literary masters.'

For me, there was something about Hardy which struck a deep chord. After reading several of the novels, I had driven to Dorset and camped near the various locations Hardy uses in the novels – Maiden Castle, Lulworth Cove, Durdle Door. They were all imbued with the mix of romance, sensuality and melancholy which infuses Hardy's writing. I had chosen *Far From The Madding Crowd* to teach in Jamaica and showed John Schlesinger's wonderful 1967 film version to the students at Priory. Now it was the tragedy of *Tess of the D'Urbevilles* and I was excited at the prospect of teaching the novel.

The first problem was how to ensure the students actually read the book. It was too easy for a student to buy from W.H.Smiths a set of *Coles Notes* which summarised themes, plots and chapters, and then never actually read the book. The Penguin edition was four hundred pages long - a lot of reading for a student new to sixth form and enjoying a burgeoning social life and the more relaxed regime.

After several lessons I was beginning to get a 'fix' on how they were coping. Clearly most of them were doing the reading. However, a couple of the boys were less engaged and their poor marks reflected this. I saw each of them separately after the lesson.

'Have you actually read the chapters I set?' This was to Mark - tall, popular, sharp but utterly distracted by his new found love life with his 'rock chick' Samantha who was heavily into her art and music. They were forever draped over each other in the sixth form common room.

He frowned, squirmed a little and said, 'It's a bit of a girly book.'

'A 'girly' book? What d'you mean?'

He shifted in his chair again, 'Well at the start the girls are all dancing around and then the main character's a girl, isn't she?'

'You'd prefer a male protagonist, would you?'

Mark shrugged.

'Can I ask how you see English Literature – what it's about?'

He sniffed, looked out of the window, shifted in his chair again. 'Stories, plays, poems, is that what you mean?'

'No I mean, what does the subject deal with? What's it about? You've chosen to study it for two years so you should know what you're getting yourself into.'

'Well I did all right at O level and I liked the poetry we did and *Lord of the Flies* was great.'

Now I was making some progress. 'Okay,' I nodded. 'If you enjoyed *Lord of the Flies* then stick with *Tess;* it has so much more. The best literature holds a mirror up to us and shows us what being human is all about. And *Tess* shows us every aspect of the human condition – young love, betrayal, hardship, tragedy, even murder. Give it a chance, Mark, but you must do the reading otherwise there's no point continuing.'

He nodded, 'Okay, sir.'

He was desperate to end this interview but I hoped I had got through to him. Time would tell though, as would his written work.

My other worry was Michael. His O level grades were much lower than Mark's. He was shy, something of a loner and had had to really graft to get into sixth form.

'It's so long, sir. I've never read a book this long before. I don't know how I'm going to manage to get through it. And the language is difficult. I get to the bottom of a page and wonder what I've been reading about.'

I sympathised with him. I remembered so clearly that same feeling when I was confronted with George Eliot's *Middlemarch* for A level. It was the thickness of a door-stop and, like Michael, I found the nineteenth century style impenetrable at first. I told him of my own experience as a sixth former.

'It's like you have to hear the sound of the language in your head, Michael. It's a bit like hearing a new piece of music which is strange at first but then grows on you. At first the writing will seem very dense and, yes, you'll have to read paragraphs over more than once to get the gist of what's going on. But believe me, after you've read a few chapters, you'll begin to hear the rhythm of the language and it won't sound so strange. And, I tell you, the story is very powerful.'

'I'll give it a go, sir. I really want to get my A levels. So much depends on it.'

My heart went out to him. He was not a shirker but then A levels were not designed to be easy.

*

In 1977 students who broke the rules might still get beaten on their backsides. Corporal punishment was still available as a last resort for 'modifying behaviour' although it was rarely administered to girls. It was probably what accounted, in those days, for the lack of direct 'in your face' challenge to a teacher's authority at St Aidan's. Yes, there would be minor skirmishes with some students but the underlying fear of being caned or slippered tended to keep things in check. And this ultimate threat was what gave two of the key teachers at St Aidan's their status as the 'hard men' in the school. There was Ted, the senior teacher and Roger the Head of fifth year who had cultivated the thrusting chin, the rasping tone and the stern look which intimidated the hardest of the fifth year lads. Ted and Roger were the ultimate deterrent and it meant the Head never had to deal directly with disciplinary issues and would certainly have been strongly averse to administering corporal punishment himself. He was too much the detached philosopher-king although, when pushed, he could use words like well-honed lances to cut to the quick of a dispute with a student.

Having said which, the general atmosphere at the school was not one of a teacher-pupil power struggle. The air we breathed at the school was full of good humour and humanity. The children laughed easily, they were courteous and pleasant in an earthy, genuine kind of way. The catchment of the school was predominantly working-class, down-to-earth and sometimes rather down-at-heel. These were not generally children from monied backgrounds but from honest, hard-working families.

'Please sir, Jeremy Barstow stinks.'

This was not shouted out but half-whispered to me during a lesson by a quiet, well-mannered girl called Lucy. I looked round to locate the said Jeremy Barstow. He was sitting alone in the corner, half whistling to himself whilst gleefully colouring the cover of his Hallowe'en poetry project with broad sweeps of his coloured crayon.

'Please, sir,' continued Lucy, 'he's started chewing garlic and his clothes stink of it. No-one wants to go near him.'

'Okay, Lucy, thanks for letting me know,' I whispered back to her.

I wandered up and down the aisles supposedly looking at the students' progress on their projects but making my way towards the corner and the garlic aura that surrounded Jeremy Barstow. It hit you at a distance of around two metres but became like a thick fug as you ventured inside his 'ring of confidence'.

'Look at what I done, sir,' he said holding up the cover of his project and smiling with a half chewed garlic clove mashed between his yellow teeth. The smell was overpowering. It came from his hair, his clothes and his skin. I turned my head away and coughed.

'I've done me six poems, sir, and I'm making up one about vampires.'

'Right,' I said, looking at the cover of his Hallowe'en poetry project. It had gravestones and a cloaked figure with grinning, blood-soaked fangs. Even the project reeked of garlic.

'Could I speak to you for a minute, Jeremy? Just come outside for a moment.'

He followed me outside the classroom on to the balcony which overlooked the old hall. At least there was some semblance of fresher air here.

'Jeremy, you're chewing. Chewing's not allowed in class. You know that, don't you.'

He looked up at me. Tousle haired, school tie yanked half round the collar of his shirt, his school sweater wrinkled and frayed at the cuffs. 'Oh sorry, sir. But I was drawing vampires and I suddenly had this thought. You can't see a vampire in a mirror. But here I was drawing this vampire and he's looking at me and I'm looking at him and it's like I'm looking in a mirror and so I thought I better chew some garlic, just to be on the safe side, you know?'

I shook my head, 'Sorry, Jeremy, I don't quite understand.'

146

'Well, sir, you know it's Hallowe'en soon and that's when the souls of the dead walk the night; well that could include the vampires couldn't it. So we've all got to be careful, be prepared like.'

'How, d'you mean 'prepared'?'

'Well we don't want vampires sucking our blood, do we? And we won't if we chew the garlic.'

'Who told you that?'

'Me dad. He's big on vampires. Took me on the train to Whitby. That's where Count Dracula came ashore. Have you ever been to Whitby, sir? It's really spooky. At night they shine this light on the wall of the ruined church on the cliff and there's shadows of the gravestones and it's where it all happened, you know, Dracula and all that.'

'But that was just a story; it was all made up by a writer named….'

'Bram Stoker,' interrupted Jeremy. 'I know all about it, sir. Me dad's been reading me the story.'

'I see,' I said nodding slowly trying to get back to the point of this little interview which was not difficult considering the noisome aroma which emanated from Jeremy and the area around him. 'But, first Jeremy you've got to stop the chewing in class. And secondly, vampires aren't real, they're only made up by writers like Bram Stoker.'

'What about the devil, sir? He's not made up and he doesn't like garlic either.'

'That may be true, Jeremy, but the point is, once you chew the garlic it loses its power. You're meant to keep the garlic dry in a little bag round your neck. You know how garlic smells pretty strong.'

'Don't notice it really, sir.'

'That's because you're the one chewing it. You should only chew it when you think vampires may be around and that's not going to be in school. Otherwise the power is gone and you're defenceless.'

His little smiling face clouded to a frown. He had stopped chewing. Then there was a slight trembling of the lower lip. 'But, sir, I aven't got any more with us. I've chewed me last clove. What am I gonna do getting home when it's dark?'

'Well, Jeremy, if you feel you must be prepared, put a garlic clove in a little bag and keep it ready in your pocket. But remember you mustn't chew it. You've just got be prepared, like you said.'

He nodded. The sparkle had gone from his eyes. He stared blankly at my midriff. Then he murmured, 'I better tell me dad, sir. I don't think he knows either. And Hallowe'en's not far off is it?'

'Just ten days, Jeremy.'

'Right, sir. Thanks for the advice, sir. No more chewing then.'

'No more chewing, Jeremy.'

I glanced through the window of the classroom door before going back inside. There was some chatter but most were busy with their projects. Jeremy returned mutely to his corner. I caught Lucy's inquiring look. I nodded and gave her the thumbs up. She smiled.

A week later, she caught up with me in the corridor. 'Sir, just thought I should tell you, Jeremy's okay now. No more garlic. Except when we're doing cookery. If anyone needs some for their cooking he's always got this little bag in his pocket. Don't you think that's weird, sir?'

'Not with Hallowe'en just round the corner, Lucy. We all have to be prepared. Just ask Jeremy about it.'

*

During the autumn, renovations on the house had continued. We now had a partly refurbished kitchen built from some new 'flat pack' units which I had installed with the assistance of my brother while Sue was in hospital. The heating in the house was still pretty limited: open fires in the two living rooms and a kind of yucky cream enamel range in the fireplace of the kitchen which helped to heat the hot water.

As the temperature dropped in October so the house began to wheeze with draughts round the old sash windows and under the doors. Upstairs there was no heating but we had acquired a couple of paraffin heaters from a second-hand shop in an attempt to counter the growing chill in the house but they weren't the best way of combatting the falling temperature.

We had devised something of a grand plan of changes to the house. There was of course the empty barn attached to the back of the house which invited some kind of renovation. I had visions of knocking through to the barn from the upstairs to create another bedroom and a study but more immediately there was the challenge of just surviving the winter and keeping little Katie healthy. The walls were thick sandstone but in some rooms the plaster was damp and crumbling. The bathroom was basic with old, chipped enamel units and cold lino on the floor. There were two small damp rooms on the side of the house. These, perhaps, could be knocked into one, to make a living-room overlooking the garden.

Then there was the 'garden' itself. It wasn't really a garden as such, just a sizeable rectangle of soil on which some neighbour had been allowed to plant potatoes for the past few years. At one end was a small patch of grass with a washing line and which we could mow to create a lawn and play area for Katie. The rest was soil scattered with clumps of weeds. The garden was bordered by a hawthorn hedge and at the roadside corner was an old ash tree. To the rear of the house was a large field given over to grass for grazing cattle. A small strip of land behind our outbuildings bordered the field and gave us a south-facing view towards the Caldbeck Fells and the hazy outline of Skiddaw and the mountains of the Lake District. It was a place of big skies, clouds elbowing their way from the Atlantic eastwards towards the Pennines. A good place to return to after the frenzied pace of life at St. Aidan's.

*

'So how's the Hallowe'en drama night coming along? Isn't it the day after tomorrow?' Sue asked one evening.

'Yeah, it's okay, I think. Graham's been rehearsing the sketches and I've been helping with the staging and lighting.'

As yet I hadn't told her I was opening the show with my newly composed *Wild Witches* song. I'd been singing it on my motor bike each day and rehearsing it at school with my guitar in my form room after school. It was a simple but haunting little piece, structured around the keys of A minor and E minor which I felt gave a suitably sinister mood.

'Yes, and Graham's asked me to open the show with a song I've been working on.'

Sue looked up from her sewing. 'You've composed a song? You didn't tell me. What's it like?'

'Oh it's nothing really, just a bit of mood music to set the tone of the evening.'

'Mood music?'

'Yes, it's based on a poem about witches which I came across. I just put a few chords to it and we're using it at the start.'

Sue nodded, and looked rather quizzical. 'Can you sing it to me?'

I laughed, 'Not really. My guitar's at school. That's where I've been practising. I couldn't really do it justice just singing acapella.'

'Acapella?'

'Unaccompanied.'

'I see. Well, it all sounds very impressive.'

'And there's a disco afterwards. We thought that might bring in a few more punters.'

We were right. When the doors were opened on the *St Aidan's Hallowe'en Drama and Disco Night*, hordes of lower school students streamed into the hall dressed up in their masks and cloaks and sporting vampire teeth and waving luminous wands.

'Quite a turnout,' said Graham. 'Didn't expect this many. Let's hope they'll tolerate an hour of drama before the disco starts.'

It was then I felt the first flutter of nerves. Not surprising really as I'd never before performed in public on my own. But I had anticipated a little nervousness and so had cunningly stuck a small piece of paper with the words to *Wild Witches* on the top edge of the guitar where no-one could see, just in case.

The clock ticked towards seven-thirty. I stood behind the red velvet curtains which were drawn across the stage. I had checked that my chair was there just in front of the curtains and that it was on the chalk mark on which the single spotlight would be focussed. A few moments earlier I had peered round the edge of the curtains to check what kind of audience we had. The hall was packed, packed with excited lower school students. I spotted some of the lower school toughies and some of the more mouthy girls. They weren't here for the drama. It was the disco they'd come for. And I thought about my idea of setting the tone and ambience with my opening song. I hadn't imagined a hall heaving with excited youngsters. I'd had in mind a more esoteric gathering of drama devotees.

Graham gave me a nod, the house lights dimmed and I stepped round the edge of the curtains and took my place on the chair. The spotlight erupted with a white light which blinded me for a second. I could see nothing of the audience, just sensed something rather monstrous palpitating in the darkness. There were a few giggles, and then the monster settled itself. My fingers were hot and moist and I glanced at the paper with the words stuck to the top of the guitar. I took a breath and then heard a strange sound in the darkness. It was something far away, a thin reedy voice singing some words about 'gliding darkness......bats in flight', and there was the tinny sound of a guitar but it was out of tune with the voice which quivered in the blinding light. And I felt the monster in the darkness start to move and palpitate again.

Then I realised it was my voice singing the wrong verse and it was my guitar playing the wrong chords. I stopped. Took a breath. Still I could see nothing but white light and the dark hump of the audience beyond.

I laughed nervously, 'I'm terribly sorry but I seem to have my capo in the wrong place. Just a moment.' I fumbled with the capo which was not in the wrong place, trying to appear calm and in control. I glanced again at the words of the song, checked my fingers were in the position for the opening chord, took a breath and started again. It was slightly better but it was nothing like the wonderful resonance that I'd achieved inside my motor-bike helmet out on the open road riding to and from work. It was more a thin, warbling sound like you'd hear from someone drowning at sea a long way off.

There were some muted jeers from the audience and I'm sure I heard some kid's voice grunting, 'Geddimoff.'

I stammered to a finish, picked up the chair and retreated behind the curtain vowing to myself that I would never perform in public ever again. But then I remembered I was due to start the second half in the same way by singing a second song. It was there in the running order: INTERVAL then *Mr Day's Song*. What to do!

I bumped into Graham a short while later. 'How did it go?' he said. 'I didn't hear the start, I was doing make-up.'

'Slight problem with the guitar strings,' I murmured. 'The heat I think.That spotlight, er..affecting the tuning.'

'But at least we're up and running. Can you believe the number of kids out there. It's mayhem.'

The clock ticked on. The audience seemed mildly contained by the drama pieces. There was no deliberate disruption. It was more a case of kids in the audience not being used to sitting quietly in a theatre and not knowing that you don't rustle sweet wrappers or chat to your friends when it's boring.

Meanwhile my mind was thrown, jettisoned to some other planet. I was going through the motions of helping with props and moving scenery but the whole thing was becoming an out of body experience. I just knew I couldn't face that chair, that spotlight and that audience again.

During the interval I crept around out of sight of Graham and found a spot at the back of the stage behind some old scenery screens. And there I hid. I kept checking the time, heard the three-minute bell, heard the audience return from the canteen where the refreshments were being served, heard the audience settling itself into the rows of seats, heard the one-minute bell and then heard Graham's voice, 'Anyone seen Mr Day?'- heard the message passed around as I sweated in shame in my hiding place. And then came Graham's blessed words, 'Well we'd better start without him.'

I let out a hesitant sigh of relief and then my mind scrabbled around for an excuse. I allowed five minutes to elapse before emerging from my hiding place.

'What happened?' said Graham when he saw me a short while later. He was obviously far from pleased.

'Sorry, but I thought the one minute bell was the three minute bell and I was in the loo. Think I must have picked up something. You know, gippy tummy.'

Graham shook his head, 'Well, anyway, we're back on track. It seems to be going okay.'

'That's good. Sorry, Graham.'

'These things happen.'

But they're never going to happen again, I said to myself, never, ever.

'So how did it go?' asked Sue when I got home. 'How was the mood music?'

I frowned and stroked my chin, 'Not quite how I'd planned it,' I said.

'What d'you mean?'

'There was this huge audience and, well, I don't think some of the kids had been to the theatre before so they were a little restless. Not as attentive as I'd hoped.'

'Well, never mind, maybe next time it'll be better, and remember it's only the first time you've performed on stage on your own.'

'Suppose so,' I murmured.

And it'll definitely be the last, I thought to myself.

*

AND THE BEAT GOES ON

Book Your Xmas Turkey. See Bill – Metalwork Dept. - the notice was pinned to the staff notice board.

'What's this about turkeys in the Metalwork Department?' I asked Jean as we gulped down a quick mug of coffee at morning break.

'No they're not *in* the Metalwork Department – it's just Bill, he rears them at home.'

'At home? You're kidding.'

'No, he's got a smallholding somewhere in the Eden Valley.'

'Another one with a smallholding. How do these people do it? So what are his turkeys like?'

'Wonderful. You've never tasted better. I've already booked mine.'

At lunchtime I headed into what was foreign territory for me – the Woodwork and Metalwork Department. It was in a separate block away from the main school building, not somewhere I had ever visited. As soon as I went inside and smelt the oil, saw the heavy grey machinery, the overalls hanging up, it took me back to my brief sojourn in industry. I remembered the dark interiors of factories in the west

Midlands, oil-stained operatives crouched over noisy machinery making exhaust pipes and bicycle parts. It seemed a lifetime away.

At the far end of the workshop someone in a brown overall was sharpening a chisel on a grindstone. I went across to him. 'I've come about turkeys.'

He couldn't hear me and continued drawing sparks from the edge of the chisel. I moved round in front of him into his line of vision. He was an older man with small hairs sprouting from his ears, a shiny bald patch edged by tufts of grey hair. Finally he looked up and switched off the machine. I waited for the noise level to subside.

'Turkeys. I wanted to ask about turkeys. Bill, is it?'

He frowned and gestured with his thumb, 'In the office. Bill's in there.'

Bill was a slim young fellow with short curly hair and a boyish smile.

'I saw your notice. Wondered if I could book a turkey,' I said.

'Of course. I'll put you on the list. Barrie, isn't it?'

I nodded. 'So how many turkeys do you keep?'

'Oh, it varies but we're doing about thirty this year. There's plenty of demand and it's nice to have a wodge of pocket money on Christmas Eve.'

Ideas started buzzing in my head. I couldn't wait to tell Sue. She was in the middle of feeding Katie when I arrived home.

'And he buys them as chicks in September from this farmer in the Eden Valley near a village called Great Corby. He rears them during the autumn, but you can't feed them on scraps you have to get the right feed which can be expensive. But it's offset by what you make when you sell them at Christmas. And at an average price of a pound for a pound, when you're selling a twenty-five pound turkey, and Bill's raising thirty this year well that's ......a lot of money.'

'Seven hundred and fifty pounds,' said Sue.

'What d'you think?'

'About buying a turkey?'

'No, about us raising turkeys next year.'

'Where?'

'Well, we could clear one of the outbuildings and keep them in there. We could start with a few. See how it goes.'

'But you don't know anything about raising turkeys.'

'Well, it can't be rocket science.'

'What about the killing, the plucking, the dressing?'

'It can't be too difficult. I'll ask Bill when the time comes. It's only an idea and as Bill says it's nice to have a wodge of pocket money on Christmas Eve and we can certainly do with it.'

Sue turned baby Katie to face her, 'What d'you reckon, Katie, should daddy keep some turkeys?'

'No, it's not just me, it's a family project. Next Christmas Katie will be old enough to take notice. She could even help.'

'Aged one?'

'Well maybe the following year.'

I took Katie from Sue and jiggled her in the air. 'You'll help daddy pluck turkeys won't you, my little love.' Her brown eyes were just starting to focus on things and I was convinced that some real rapport was developing between us. She gurgled and chuckled as I jiggled her above my head. There was a hiccough and then a splurge of milky puke landed on my cheek.

'I think you got your answer,' said Sue laughing.

That first winter was a real test for us. The house was freezing and draughty. We only really lived in the kitchen and adjoining dining room huddled round the open fires, our backs cold from the draughts. The paraffin heaters were marginally effective but the heat they emitted was a damp heat which reeked of paraffin. The two rooms on the west side of the house facing the garden were too cold and damp to use. They faced the full blast of the west wind, the rain and at times the snow. In fact by January there was a strange white mist covering the carpet and the curtains in these rooms. It was as though we had our own mini weather system operating there, the rooms blanketed in a misty layer of damp.

My epiphany came one bitter evening in January when I was changing Katie's nappy in an ice cold bathroom. I looked down at this little squirming bundle of new life and said, 'Right, my little love. This cannot go on. We're not spending another winter in this sort of cold. We need central heating. We can't afford to have it done so there's only one answer - daddy's going to do it.' This time Katie didn't puke at me but gurgled back. She was in full agreement.

After school the next day I went straight to W.H.Smiths and bought myself another DIY book: *How To Install a Central Heating system*. From then this was my new bedtime reading. The game was afoot. Cry God for Harry....etc!

*

'Right, put your pens down, relax and listen. I'm going to read you a story.'

At first when I said this to a class there would be a tricky few moments. The boys tended to chunter things like, 'We're not infants, sir.' Or 'We are out of the playgroup, you know.' They tended to associate listening to stories with something childish which you grew out of. But I felt strongly that listening to a good story was central to the appreciation of what writing could do, so I persisted.

I would continue with, 'There are certain rules, though, once I've started: no interruptions, no talking. You can put your heads down on the desk. You can go to sleep but no snoring, absolutely no snoring.'

Then I would start. After the first few times of doing this I didn't need to worry. They knew what to expect and they enjoyed it and for the duration of the story we would be transported. And as a reader I was starting to develop my own skills. I varied the pace of the reading depending on what was happening. I varied my tone of voice to convey mood and create atmosphere. I had always had a good ear for accents and could mimic Cockney, Yorkshire or west country accents with no problem and my Jamaican accent would have impressed Bob Marley. But what was essential was finding the right material.

I scoured anthologies and collections for good short stories until I had a set of books on my personal bookshelf behind my teacher's desk which contained sure-fire stories for different age groups. I wasn't just reading to the younger classes but to all ages. Many of Roald Dahl's stories worked with the younger students but his *Tales of the Unexpected* were often quirky and bizarre enough to appeal to the wayward minds of older students. Similarly, Ray Bradbury's short stories had the brevity that I needed for the last fifteen minutes of a lesson but also had the suspense and skilful twists of plot and setting which grabbed the students' attention. I used stories by Maupassant, Poe, Hardy as well as stories by contemporary writers – anything which could transport my students into the parallel worlds that the imagination can conjure and leave them glazed and spellbound. Few ever really fell asleep but many entered that magical trance state where their immediate worries were forgotten and the world became a different place.

Then I would finish the final sentence and wait without speaking or moving. I would watch them gradually emerge from that other world back into the moment. They would blink, look at each other and look round the class with a sense of slight bewilderment and sometimes slight embarrassment that for a while they had forgotten themselves. And then the bell would ring and reality would slap them back into focus again. As they left the room there might be: 'Thanks sir. That was okay that was.'

Or 'Good story, sir.' or simply a sigh, a benign smile and a 'Bye, sir.'
That was all I needed to know it had worked.

*

'You're a pusi.....pusillan....'

'Pusillanimous, moron,' corrected David who was sitting beside
Robert.

'Yeah, that's it,' grinned Robert, 'you're a pusillanimous, you
are.'

He was shouting across at dark-eyed Deborah whom he clearly
fancied.

'You can't be a 'pusillanimous'. That doesn't make sense, does
it, sir?' answered Deborah.

'No Deborah, you're right,' I replied. 'It's an adjective not a
noun. It's like you can't say you're a 'good-looking'. It's an adjective –
it has to be good-looking something.'

'Like me,' added David. 'I'm a good-looking something.'

'In your dreams,' muttered Deborah.

It was my fourth year CSE group. They were a third set – a
group of chatty, lively, uninhibited youngsters, very different from
teaching a top set. Typically a top set contained brighter but more self
conscious students, less willing to readily voice their ideas. With a third
set it was different. You really had to have your wits about you. The time
of day would affect their mood, as would problems with friends,
conflicts on their street – it all got brought into the classroom and
affected how well they would settle to their work.

'But I think Jimmy Porter's really mean to Alison. She seems
quite nice really,' commented Rachel.

'Don't you think she's a bit wet. And that's why Jimmy's got it
in for her?' added Stephen.

We had just finished reading the first Act of John Osborne's
Look Back In Anger. It was one of the books the department used for the
CSE Mode Three Literature course. Mode Three was an alternative to a
conventional exam. It was where the school designed its own course, had
it approved by the examination board and then had the students' folders
of work checked and validated by a visiting moderator at the end of the
course. The folders had to show evidence of the study of plays, poetry
and fiction.

It was the first time I'd taught *Look Back In Anger* and when I
first read it I felt it was rather difficult for fifteen year olds. But it was
early days and students can surprise you. This was a Thursday morning

lesson and we were doing some preliminary work on the main characters. I'd given out the dictionaries and set the students to write a list of adjectives and to find quotations which they might use to illustrate something about the characters.

'Anyway, Robert,' I said, 'when Jimmy calls Alison 'pusillanimous' what does he mean?'

'It's not in my dictionary, sir.'

'Are you sure? Look again.' I went down the aisle and stood by his desk while his finger with its bitten finger-nail inched its way down the page of 'p' words. 'It's *pu* not *pa*,' I said. 'I think you're on the wrong page.'

'Found it!' shouted Deborah.

'Wait on,' said Robert,' I'm nearly there.'

But Deborah was not waiting: 'Pusillanimous....lacking courage, faint-hearted, shrinking from risks,' she read. 'Sounds a bit like you, Robert.'

'It says 'cowardly or 'timid' in my dictionary,' he replied. 'I'm not cowardly or timid. You ask David. I'm always beating him up.' He aimed a fist at David's arm and a friendly tussle began.

'Okay, you two, enough's enough. Let's focus on the play, shall we? What else have we got to say about these characters?'

The horseplay subsided and the class settled again.

'Why is Jimmy so mean to Alison?' asked Heather. 'He's just nasty and she seems so quiet and gentle.'

I didn't answer but waited to see if anyone else would volunteer an idea.

'She's posh isn't she, sir?' added Rebecca a quiet girl with mousy hair who sat on the front row. 'But I'm not sure about him. He uses quite big words and he's reading a posh newspaper but he doesn't seem very posh himself.'

'Cliff seems nice but Jimmy's a bit nasty to him as well. Jimmy seems to have a big chip on his shoulder,' added Heather.

I raised my voice to quell the murmur of chatter, 'Heather's just suggested that Jimmy Porter has a 'chip on his shoulder'. D'you think she's right?'

'Doesn't seem a very happy kind of bloke,' said Ben from the back of the class. 'I'd just bop him.'

'Yes okay, Ben, and on that erudite note I think we'll finish for today. Homework is to finish making your character notes on Act 1 and don't forget to find some quotations to support your comments.'

'Found another 'pu' word for Jimmy, sir,' said Robert as he passed my desk on his way out. 'How about 'pugnacious' – it means he likes a fight. A bit like me really?'

'Brilliant, Robert. But don't go throwing that 'pusillanimous' around too much, will you. You might get bopped by someone who's a bit pugnacious.'

'Nice one, sir. See ya.'

*

JIVE TALKING

Bill's turkey certainly won the approval of the in-laws on Christmas Day. The meat was rich and succulent and the flavour was unlike any previous Christmas dinner I'd tasted. During the after dinner dozing with Katie asleep on my lap I mused on the prospects for the coming year. One thing was certain, turkey rearing was high on the agenda of autumn projects. There was the central heating to install and I wanted to build on a bedroom for Katie and knock through into the barn and create a study from an existing hay loft. At school I was still teased by the idea of getting involved in drama production although my days of performing were firmly consigned to the coffin of failed endeavours.

When I returned to school for the new term the students were buzzing. Something was in the air and they were all affected. It was disco fever. The film *Saturday Night Fever* was showing in cinemas throughout the country during the spring of 1978 and its effect was amazing. Between lessons some of the fifth year lads would draw applause from the girls and jeers from the boys by trying out the 'Tony Romero strut' which John Travolta had portrayed so brilliantly in the film. School dances were changed as well. During the autumn term there was little finesse in the way the boys danced. When the pounding screech of a punk track was played, the floor would clear and in the space the boys would take over barging and jumping in their manic 'pogoing'.

Away in Jamaica we had missed out on the rise of the punk phenomenon. So when I returned and saw youngsters with spiked, dyed hair wearing ripped clothing and with eyebrows and cheeks pierced with safety pins it was something of a shock. In school there were small groups of nascent punks, generally dressed in black, girls with eyes heavy with eye shadow and spiked hair a different luminous shade each week. They were repeatedly sent to the senior mistress to remove the make-up and be admonished for their hair but this only served to fire up their rebellious spirit.

Now it was different. At the Valentine Disco in February when the Bee Gees' tracks from *Saturday Night Fever* came on, the dancers formed lines and did intricate moves in varying formations. This was now the essence of 'disco cool'.

The pogoing punks were in retreat but they would go down fighting. They were generally pretty anti-social but with news that the Sex Pistols had broken up and Johnny Rotten was at war with Sid Vicious they had more reason to vent their outrage at anything that moved. When a group of the boys attempted to pogo into the disco dancers a minor scuffle broke out. Three of the teachers bundled the punks out of the door, a window was smashed and loud cheers erupted from the dancers as the beat of *Stayin' Alive* filled the hall. Tony Romero look-alikes preened themselves in the centre of the dance floor and the strutting began. Disco had taken over.

*

Other changes were in the air that spring. One morning I was browsing the staff notice board, particularly the section given to information about new training courses. One that caught my eye concerned a new A level called 'Communication Studies'. It had been recently launched by the Associated Examining Board and there was an introductory course being presented by the Chief Examiner at Higham Hall, the residential training centre in the Lake District. It sounded interesting and when I mentioned it to Roger he was very encouraging. I put in a request to the Head and a few days later found in my pigeon hole a scribbled note back from him approving my request.

'Hey, what are you looking so pleased about?' It was Jean, cradling a cup of coffee.

'Just this.' I showed her the Head's scribbled note. 'It's for a day's course at a place called Higham Hall.'

'Lucky you,' said Jean. 'Higham's great. The food's wonderful. What's the course?'

I showed her the details.

'Sounds interesting.'

'Roger reckoned it might combine well with English Lit. at A level. Could be an attractive combination for students looking for something different.'

'Keep me posted,' said Jean. 'I wouldn't mind getting involved in something like that.'

On a spring morning in March I set off driving south towards the Lake District. It proved to be a milestone in the direction my teaching career would take.

The Chief Examiner who ran the course was an inspiration. A man in his sixties with a shock of white hair and a friendly smile, he talked passionately about the need for courses which bridged the divide between traditional academia and the real world.

Communication Studies, he said, had been designed to embrace elements of the arts as well as psychology and sociology. It explored theories of interpersonal communication and mass communication. It offered students the chance to gain a critical understanding of the way films, newspapers, television and radio programmes were constructed and their impact on audiences.

But above all, the way it was examined was revolutionary. Students would sit conventional essay based exams but in addition they would have to demonstrate their own communication skills by producing a project aimed at a clearly defined audience. It might be a publicity campaign involving the design of posters, leaflets, brochures. It might be a radio programme, or a short television programme. And finally they would have to show their personal communication skills by doing a live presentation to an examiner and an audience of their peers.

Following the initial presentation, we broke for coffee and I mingled with the thirty or so other teachers from around the county. There was an enthusiastic buzz in the air. This was a course like no other. It was liberating for the teacher to venture into areas which the traditional curriculum failed to embrace but it was liberating for students to show their initiative. We were all hooked.

In the final session, the plenary at the end of the afternoon, the Chief Examiner issued a warning.

'You may be fired up now but believe me you'll encounter some resistance to a course such as this. You're going to have to sell it to your Head, the governors, to parents and students and there's a lot of prejudice out there. The universities view new subjects like this with great suspicion. Any subject which deals with the real world of such things as television, newspapers and film is a prime target for the traditionalists to condemn as a 'Mickey Mouse subject'. A subject which has an element of practical project work at A level is likely to be viewed as 'soft'. But believe me there's nothing easy about this subject. It tests students in ways which no other subject comes near. It equips students to be critically aware of such things as media manipulation and the power of propaganda but it also tests them as people – whether or not they can stand up in front of an audience and communicate effectively. Few jobs involve writing essays, but every job and every waking hour involves interpersonal communication. This subject should not be an 'add-on', rather it should be at the heart of the school curriculum. And there's your challenge.'

I drove away from Higham feeling inspired and invigorated. My task now was to try to get the subject of Communication Studies into the A level options for the coming September.

*

Back at school, faced with the pragmatic and the prosaic rather than the rarefied idealism of Higham, I considered the implications of running such a course as Communication Studies. If the students were to make TV and radio programmes we would need cameras and recording equipment. If we were to study television and film we would need access to video players. In 1978 there were about four in the whole school. It was the early days of video and there was an ongoing battle between the manufacturers to establish a standard format. Would it be Sony's Betamax or JVC's VHS? While the battle went on, schools were caught in the middle. So, 'JD' Wilson, the school's beleagured but ever resourceful technician, trundled both a Betamax and a VHS video player around on a trolley with a television on top. There was one trolley on the ground floor and another on the upper floor and to secure the use of this highly prized equipment you had to book well in advance to avoid clashes with other departments. JD kept a library of VHS and Betamax tapes with the recordings of programmes made for schools as well as a few commercially produced tapes which the departments had bought. It wasn't a great resource bank but compared to many schools it was distinctly ahead of the game.

Before I'd even broached the subject with the Headmaster, I sensed that maybe the climate at St. Aidan's was encouraging for my new course. Roy, the Head of Art, had already set up a small TV studio called Aidanvision in a disused primary school near the city centre. The school had bought up some ageing studio cameras from Border Television and students were already making studio based programmes.

But then there was the issue of students' project work. To produce brochures and leaflets was quite a challenge. At my first school in Lichfield and at Priory in Jamaica the only way to reproduce copies of printed material was by using a spirit duplicator or by running off copies on a Gestetner machine. This involved producing an original on a specially carbonised 'skin' which was then attached to a printing roller which took it through a container of alcohol based spirit. It was a smelly and rather messy process which generally resulted in ink-stained fingers and smudged copies. The students didn't object as they could get a vague 'high' by sniffing the chemicals soaked into the paper.

However, things dramatically improved later that spring when it was announced that the school was acquiring something called a 'Xerox photocopying machine'. These machines were revolutionary. They somehow photographed your original, stored the information and could then run off dozens of copies. No chemicals. No mess. Just clean black and white copies. They couldn't do colour but this was progress indeed.

When the gleaming, grey beast was unveiled with great ceremony, there was a hushed reverence in the reprographics room. This sleek machine was like a visitation from outer space. This was the future. And this would certainly make our lives easier.

For weeks, I'd geared myself up for the meeting with the Head. I had prepared my case, anticipated counter arguments and the prejudices the Chief Examiner had warned of. But I needn't have worried. He was ahead of me.

'Sounds like a great course,' he said. He sat behind his desk, hands forming a steeple, blue gimlet eyes levelled at me. 'Just what we need. It's about time the curriculum started to address the needs of the late 20th century. Talk to Roy about using the studio at Aidanvision. And get Jean on board. She'd be good for you to work with.'

'So, we're going ahead for September then?' I ventured.

He stood up and clapped his hands, 'Of course. No point dithering. I'll let the governors know. You do the groundwork.'

'What about materials and resources?'

'I'll add something to the English Dept. budget. Tell Roger.'

And that was it. I left his room in a haze of disbelief and a vague terror about what I had got myself into.

As well as thinking my way into teaching this new A level and keeping on top of the rest of my timetable I had to get prepared for my spring term residential week at Little Langdale. All first year form tutors were required to accompany their classes to the school's residential centre in the Lake District. Few schools had such places but, as with a lot of initiatives, the Head had pushed the school into embracing another key recommendation of the Newsom Report – that pupils should have some experience of education in a residential context. So in 1975 the school had acquired the lease on a disused primary school in the Little Langdale valley. It was very much a shell with no facilities for sleeping or catering for large groups. But with the enthusiasm of the St Aidan's staff and parents who held fund-raising events and organised working parties, the place was beginning to be transformed. Or at least this was what I was told.

'Just one big dorm and a couple of toilets and washbasins,' said Jean.

'For thirty pupils?'

'And it can be cold, so take some long johns.'

'But I don't wear long johns.'

'I'm serious,' she added, sipping her coffee one break time, a week before I was due to go. 'They get snow in May in those valleys and it's only the end of March. But listen, you'll enjoy it. And anyway, John McNicholas will be in charge. He's an old hand and he was a quartermaster in the army so he'll make sure things run smoothly.'

Memories of my camping trip to Wales with my third year misfits in Lichfield came back. I thought I ought to forewarn my class about what to expect.

In our next tutorial period I outlined the arrangements. We would leave on the Monday morning in three minibuses, returning the following Friday afternoon.

I saw Kevin Foster's hand shoot up in the air.

'And no Kevin, you can't bring your ferret. Get your little sister to look after Freddy.'

'But he's no trouble, sir. And he'll keep me warm at night in me sleeping-bag. My brother says it can be so cold there it could freeze the balls off a brass monkey.'

'That's rude, sir,' squealed Amanda Thompson. 'Tell him, sir.'

I smiled. 'Calm down, Amanda, I know it sounds rude but in fact it's not rude at all.'

'He said 'balls' sir and that's rude.'

'Depends what balls we're talking about.'

'Now you've said it, sir. That's disgusting.'

'Hold on, Amanda.' I held my hands up and lowered them slowly. The rest of the class were all watching and waiting. 'Take a few deep breaths and listen.'

Her eyes were staring at me, her lips pressed firmly, her little cheeks puffed up and red.

'Now then, the word 'balls' is not in itself rude. We have tennis balls, snooker balls and cannon balls. And in fact that's what Kevin was referring to.'

Kevin's face was a picture of confusion. 'Was I?'

'Yes, Kevin. A brass monkey is part of a cannon on a ship. It was a kind of brass plate on which cannon balls were stored. When it was very, very cold the brass would contract and the cannon balls might topple off the plate on to the deck. So we get the phrase 'Cold enough to freeze the balls off a brass monkey.'

There were a number of giggles coming from members of the class. Kevin still looked very confused.

'Please, sir. I don't think my brother knows that it means that.'

'I'm sure he doesn't but now you can tell him, can't you.'

He nodded.

'And remember, no Freddy otherwise you'll be sent straight back home. Understood?'

He nodded again, looking somewhat crestfallen.

I turned to Amanda. 'And are we happy, Amanda, that Kevin was not being rude?'

She was still pouting. 'I'm not sure, sir. I don't think Kevin knew all that stuff about ships and things. I think he was just being rude.'

'No I wasn't,' said an indignant Kevin. 'I saw about it on Blue Peter, so there. And I read about ships and stuff.'

'Good, that's settled then,' I sighed looking at my watch. 'So, I reckon we're in for an interesting week at Little Langdale. Make sure you give your letters from Mr McNicholas to your parents then they'll know what you have to bring. Anyone who's confused about anything wait behind after the lesson.'

The bell rang and everyone filed out except Peter Withins, a rather earnest little boy. He looked up. 'Please, sir, Robert said something about monkeys having tentacles. Well that's not true is it, sir? And how could they freeze off? It's impossible seeing as they don't have them in the first place.'

'You're absolutely right. Peter. Robert's obviously a little confused. I shouldn't worry too much about it though.'

'Yes, sir, thanks, sir.' He shouldered his overstuffed backpack and shuffled off down the corridor.

*

THE LITTLE LANGDALE EXPERIENCE

Thirty twelve year olds, away from the security of home in a draughty old school house which was reputedly haunted – it was always going to be memorable.

Our three minibuses wound their way out of Ambleside to Skelwith Bridge and then left the main road to snake along a narrow lane into the Little Langdale valley. There were three staff on the trip: me,

John McNicholas, the Head of First Year, and Julie, one of the parent volunteers. The morning was bright and the clouds whipped round the craggy shoulders of the Old Man of Coniston as our little convoy descended the final hill into a hamlet of stone cottages. There was a pub, a telephone box, a post office and a steep approach to a line of buildings, the last of which was the old school house.

'My brother said the school is haunted,' said Tracey Dobbins. 'He said a little girl died in the attic.'

'Okay, Tracey, we don't need to hear any tall stories just now thank you,' said John. 'Collect your rucksack and go and wait inside.' John was a reassuring presence on the trip and I was glad he was in overall charge. At school, he taught science but in addition, as Head of First Year, he had an important pastoral responsibility. He'd worked tirelessly to get the old school into a usable condition and was chairman of the Little Langdale committee which ran the centre. When the school took over the place in 1975 there was simply this big open room with a cast iron stove squatting against one wall, a small kitchen area, two toilets and little else. In the past three years a team of volunteers led by John had installed an upper floor to create a dormitory which at present was divided simply by a curtain down the middle – boys on one side, girls on the other, staff in the middle to preserve decorum.

In the downstairs space there was a collection of old armchairs and a couple of sofas, a stack of metal framed chairs and some trestle tables. There were two washrooms but no showers. A quick dunk in a mountain lake or river was the nearest anyone would get to taking a bath.

After unloading rucksacks, sleeping bags, crates of bread, milk, breakfast cereal and boxes of other provisions, the children ate their packed lunches and then assembled for their first expedition. Most of them were town kids who had never spent time in the country. They were kitted out with the school's walking boots and waterproofs but some didn't cope well with muddy tracks and cow pats.

I followed behind a little clutch of girls and listened in to their chatter.

'Oooh, I ate this clart round mi feet.'

'D'your boots pinch yer toes? Mine do.'

'My fingers are freezin'.'

'I wish I'd got a blue anorak like yours but they only had this green one left.'

'Anyone got any chuddy?'

'What's chuddy?' I asked.

'Chewing gum, sir. Want some?'

165

'Thanks,' I said and took a piece of 'chuddy' from the sticky fingers of little Dawn Armstrong.

'Are you married, sir?' said Deborah who had linked arms with Dawn.

'Yes.'

'Kiddies?'

I nodded, 'Just one. Katie, born last September.'

'Ahh, how lovely,' said Deborah.

We followed the path down to an old pack-horse bridge called Slaters' Bridge. The boys ran along the river bank and threw stones and found sticks to slash at the hedgerows.

'What a lovely place, I love this little bridge, don't you, sir,' said Bridget, a tall, willowy girl who tended to drift on the fringes of the groups of the more mouthy girls. 'I always think these will fall down but they must have been here for years and years.'

'They did a lot of quarrying in this valley,' said John, 'and these bridges would be used by the miners to get to and from work.'

'What were they quarrying for, sir?'

'Various metals - lead, iron ore and building stone.'

'Must have been a hard life for the wives, sir, with no electric.'

'It was, Bridget. We don't know we're born.'

'Sir, that's what me dad says. He says, 'You don't know you're born gal'. He often says it.'

I loved the banter, the easy mingling of the children in a way which school so often inhibited. Some of the girls were joining the boys to throw pebbles into the lake. They were free of the constraints of the classroom where twelve year old boys didn't socialise much with twelve year old girls. Give them a year or two and things would be very different, no doubt. But at twelve, girls were seen as strange squawky, giggling creatures and to the girls, boys were generally stinky little oiks who collected stickers and endlessly kicked footballs.

We explored further up the valley, passing waterfalls, a dead sheep, a rusting tractor and watched a farmer rounding up sheep with a young border collie. The children had been told to bring sketch pads and a notebook and we stopped by a spinney of silver birch trees so that they could do some drawing. There were still a few snowdrops out and a few clusters of daffodils.

For half an hour there was just a murmur of conversation and the scratch of pencils on paper. The children were very intent on their work but when a few of the boys started to fidget and get restless it was time to round things off.

'Okay,' I said, 'we'll finish off the sketches this evening but I want you to just sit for a moment and listen.' I moved them in closer so that they could hear me.

In my rucksack I had brought a copy of Dorothy Wordsworth's Journals and Wordsworth's famous 'Daffodils' poem. I explained the background, that William and Dorothy had been walking along the shores of Ullswater near Gowbarrow Park on their way to Grasmere. And then I read them Dorothy's account of first seeing the daffodils in the woods: *'I never saw daffodils so beautiful; they grew among the mossy stones and about them, some rested their heads upon these stones as on a pillow for weariness and the rest tossed and reeled and danced and seemed as if they verily laughed with the wind that blew upon them over the lake...'*

Then I read them Wordsworth's poem. *'I wandered lonely as a cloud.....Ten thousand saw I at a glance/Tossing their heads in sprightly dance......*

I didn't need to make the point, they picked up the inference immediately.

'So William nicked his ideas from his sister then,' blurted Gareth.

'Well not exactly, but he certainly used her journal for reference.'

'Yeah and nicked her best lines,' added Gareth.

'I like her version better,' said Bridget. 'It's much more descriptive.'

'But no-one ever talks about Dorothy. You only hear about William Wordsworth. Why is that?' asked Marjorie.

'Good point,' I nodded. 'At that time men wielded the power. A lot of women writers could only get published if they used a man's name. Anyone heard of the writer George Eliot?'

A couple of hands went up.

'Well George Eliot was a woman and her real name was Mary Ann Evans.'

Another hand went up. 'We were doing about it in history. How women weren't allowed to vote and how they used to smash windows in London.'

'Suffragettes,' shouted Kevin. 'I remember now. They forced food down their throats in prison.'

'That's gross, Kevin Foster,' said Wendy.

'So what, it's true.'

167

I raised a hand, 'Okay, troops, it's getting chilly so we need to make a move. When we get back Mr McNicholas will let you know who's on kitchen duty tonight.'

'Have we gotta do work? I thought this was a holiday,' piped Gareth.

'Sorry, Gareth, but we need your expertise in the kitchen. Mrs Dickinson was telling me about the scrumptious pizza you made in her cookery class.'

Gareth's expression changed. 'She did? Well it was pretty good, I must say.'

'So you see, we need you.'

He nodded slowly. 'S'ppose so then.'

Back at the centre the children checked which teams they were in. Some were laying the long trestle table, others were helping John in the kitchen, while another group filled the log basket beside the old iron stove.

Later, when their stomachs were full of John's hot-pot and the washing-up team were finishing off their jobs we stoked up the log-burner and settled them down to fill in their notebooks on the day's events. Some wrote little but others filled several pages.

'Hey check this out,' called Gareth. He'd found the cupboard full of board games. He and Kevin set out a draught board and were happily occupied for the next hour while some of the girls set up a game of 'Downfall'.

'Sir, what d'you think of my drawing?' Bridget handed me her sketch pad. There was a finely shaded sketch of a clump of daffodils against a boulder part covered with lichen.

'Bridget, you're a true artist. This is pretty impressive. Well done.'

She smiled, 'Thank you, sir,' and wandered back to her seat.

This easy, relaxed coming and going was a joy. I noticed some of the friendship groups had changed. Two of the boys were playing cards with two of the girls; Kevin and Gareth's vociferous game of draughts had drawn an audience of a couple of girls and even earnest little Peter Withins had found a chess partner in Jeremy Payne. This was a different kind of education. Difficult to quantify. You couldn't test or measure its value. You had to be there.

At 9.30 John called time on the games and we gathered them into the corner near the fire. He outlined the programme for the next day, congratulated them on their behaviour and handed over to me. I'd decided I would read them a story each night and that first night I chose

Roald Dahl's *The Hitchhiker*. I put on my best Cockney accent for the mysterious hitchhiker whom the narrator picks up in his car. I wove the tension into the air as the plot develops and, for a moment, as I was reading, glanced up. They were caught in the spell, some looking straight at me, hanging on my words, others staring into the fire. When the story finished there was a collective sigh and a sluggish shifting around and a few yawns.

'Good story, sir. Can you read another?' asked Gareth.

'Bedtime, Gareth,' I said shaking my head. 'Can't spoil you, can we. Right, girls upstairs first. Ten minutes and into sleeping bags and then the boys will be up.' I clapped my hands. 'Let's go!'

Sleeping arrangements were novel to say the least. As there were no separate dormitories the girls would wash and get into their sleeping bags on one side of a dividing curtain. Julie stood on the girls' side of the curtain and settled them down while I marshalled the boys into the room to get ready for bed on the boys' side of the curtain. Then one of us was supposed to mount guard to prevent any 'hankypanky' as John called it.

'Tell us another story, sir, go on. My mam used to tell me stories at bedtime when I was little,' came the strident voice of Lindsay Thomson from the far side of the dorm.

'Shut up, Lindsay, I bet you brought your teddy bear with you,' shouted Robert. The boys sniggered.

'So what if I did, Robert Gilbert. Better cuddling my teddy bear than having you anywhere near me.'

'Okay you two, settle down,' I said.

A loud fart erupted from the boys' side followed by whooping and giggling.

'That's typical,' called Lindsay. 'I bet it was farty pants Foster.'

'Wasn't so,' called back Kevin, 'it was Daniel.'

'Okay,' I said, raising my voice a little, 'just settle down. We have a busy day tomorrow and you'll all need a good night's sleep. Anyone who causes any more disturbance will spend the night sleeping in the wood shed. And I mean it.'

I waited. The threat seemed to work and I sat on my bed for another quarter of an hour while they settled into sleep.

*

We had three days of bright spring weather. We climbed the fells, followed the course of mountain streams down the valleys from the flanks of the Old Man of Coniston, explored the caves and the quarry near the village, paddled in the ice cold waters of Blea Tarn at the head of the valley. We played silly games in the evenings and sang songs round the old iron stove. Each morning Mrs Williams at the Post Office next door welcomed the children into her shop for the daily haggle over how much pocket money to spend and which sweets they would choose.

On the morning of the last day we took our final walk down to Slaters' Bridge. John spent some time doing some pond dipping with them, collecting little water critters in jam jars and getting them to do sketches in their notebooks. And before long it was time to make tracks back to school.

Gareth, normally one of the bright sparks of the class was distinctly subdued.

'Sir, I don't want to go home. Do we ave to?'

'Fraid so, Gareth. Why?'

He sat down on the river back beside me and dibbled his bare feet in the water.

'Didn't think it would be like this, sir.'

'What d'you mean?'

'Never been away from home before. Makes you kind of look at things different.'

'Like what?'

He shrugged. 'Things.'

I waited. And then said, 'What kind of things?'

But he didn't answer. Just flicked his stick in the water a couple of times.

'Doesn't matter, sir.' He looked up and threw his stick like a spear across the water. 'Think I may bring me dad back here one day. He likes fishing.'

I glanced around at this gaggle of different personalities who made up my class. They had bonded well and I felt quite protective towards them. The thought that I would be their form tutor for the next two years and watch their growing filled me with pleasure. To be able to nudge and support them through the difficult years of adolescence would be a challenge but it would be fascinating.

There was a mix of tears and singing in the minibuses on the drive back to Carlisle. As we emerged from the mountain valleys and came back into the world of towns and traffic and shops it was as if we had been under a spell in a parallel world for a while, a world lost in time where life was simpler. Now we were back.

As we turned the final corner we could see parents waiting at the school gates. I wondered what stories they would tell about the week and how they would reflect on what they had experienced. Impossible to know. But I knew from my own experience of school trips as a student, that such trips could be life-changing and their effects profound.

*

OF CHALK AND CHEESE

Easter marked the great switching on of the new heating system at home. For weeks I had been channelling copper piping under floor-boards, through sandstone walls, linking up radiators and finally connecting up to the boiler in the kitchen. We had lived in total disruption since January, stepping across floor joists, avoiding loose planks, clearing piles of old plaster and sandstone debris. Finally, on April 20th 1978 at 11a.m. my hand was poised to switch on. I mentally retraced the course of the pipework and plumbing with its myriad of bends, joints, stop-taps from the holding tanks in the loft through connections to wash basins, radiators, kitchen boiler.

Sue's parents were staying with us and each had been positioned at a strategic point in the system where leaks were likely to occur. Harry was on the landing where there was a spaghetti of copper pipes heading in all directions; Bunty was in the cupboard under the stairs where the main manifold which fed the radiators was located; Sue and Katie were in the kitchen watching for leaks from the joints on the boiler and I was ready to do a rapid circuit of all rooms to check for sudden gushes.

'Ready?'

Muffled voices came back from the various parts of the house. I turned the tap. Heard the tinkling of water through the pipes. Waited for the first shout. Scooted from room to room. No jets of water; no drips. Unbelievable!

And then when we lit the boiler in the kitchen and felt the first murmur of warmth in the radiators it was indeed a time for celebration.

That evening we gazed at the glow of the flames from the kitchen stove and, for the first time since moving in, felt that the house was settling more comfortably around us.

But there was no time for indulging in sweet reflection. Next up was the conversion of an empty loft space into a bedroom for Katie and also to create a study from the hayloft in the barn which adjoined the rear of the house. That would be planned for the summer holiday. Meanwhile there was the summer term to get through.

*

171

My new A level course in Communication Studies was scheduled to start in September and Jean would be teaching it with me. There was a lot of reading to do on the subject and the more we delved, the more it sped off in so many directions. There was the psychology of interpersonal communication, linguistics, semiotics, theories of mass media effects – it was all fascinating stuff but something of a mountain to climb.

I put together a flyer for the current fifth year students who were choosing subject options for the coming year and gave a talk after school one evening. There was a lot of interest and quite soon we had a cohort of around sixteen interested students. How to resource the subject was going to be the real challenge. Being such a new area, there were few text books on the subject; it was going to be more a case of gleaning material from wherever we could and re-working it into a form that the average sixth former could digest. One rich vein of materials was the new education unit set up by the British Film Institute. They were starting to produce booklets on various aspects of film analysis as well as study guides for specific films.

'So what is semiotics? Sounds a bit rude to me,' said Jean. We had arranged to meet once a week after school to try to get our heads round the subject and decide who would teach the different aspects of the course.

'Not easy,' I replied, scratching my head. 'It's to do with how we read signs.'

I had encountered semiotics during my year at Lancaster and wrestled with the impenetrable texts of the French theorist Roland Barthes and the linguistic theories of Ferdinand de Saussure.

'It's to do with the way meanings are generated, say, in adverts. So for example, the use of words, colours, objects, body language – they all act as signs which generate meanings to us. Does that make any sense?'

'Mmm,' nodded Jean, 'maybe you need to talk me through some examples. And we need to look at some past exam papers and work through them.' She looked at me with raised eyebrows and pointed to her own face. 'See this sign? It means I'm somewhat confused. I can see this isn't going to be easy. But hey, it's gonna be fun.'

Good old Jean. Of all the teachers I would have chosen to work with on something like this, she was the one; always good-humoured, possessed of a razor sharp intellect and boundless energy and enthusiasm.

*

It was in the nature of teaching that almost every day you were veering from the sublime to the ridiculous. At one end of the spectrum you might be exploring subtle intellectual nuances of a literary text while at the other end there were the likes of Danny Fleming and his mate Ricky Armstrong who squatted like unexploded bombs at the back of my fourth year lower set group. With them it was not intellect which you needed but wit and staying power. If you didn't keep one step ahead of them they would eat you up and spit you out. They were a double act, Ricky the weasel playing court to bully-boy Fleming.

Each Thursday afternoon I was catapulted from one end of the spectrum to the other: a double lesson of A level literature followed by the last lesson of the day with year four set five.

At the start of this particular Thursday afternoon, I had been attempting to lead the sixth form group through an understanding of Shakespeare's uses of verse structure. This can be quite a dry and clinical area of study if you're not careful but we were exploring an early section of *Antony and Cleopatra* where Enobarbus describes Antony's first sight of the woman who would steal his heart and soul. What delighted me was Mark's enthusiasm for the play. Mark, who had been so luke warm when he started the course, dismissing *Tess of the D'Urbervilles* as a 'girly' story. However, from seeing him with the sultry Samantha walking down the street or in the sixth form common room, it was clear he knew all about being besotted and he obviously found empathy with Antony's intoxication with Cleopatra.

'That line about Cleopatra…,' said Mark almost feverish with excitement as he thumbed through his copy of the play, '…where he says something about food.., that Cleopatra… let me find it.. that she makes men hungry for her.'

'*Other women cloy..*' started Kiera, who had already found the quotation.

'No wait,' said Mark, 'let me find it. Yeah here it is, it's brilliant.' He sat back in his chair and caught his breath for a moment then started reading: '*Other women cloy the appetites they feed, but she makes hungry where most she satisfies.*' Mark nodded to himself and then looked up. 'Wow, that's brilliant. Some woman, eh.'

We explored the variety of metrical patterns and rich alliterative touches in Enobarbus' famous speech about Cleopatra's barge: *The barge she sat in like a burnished throne burned on the water.....* We noted the way Shakespeare's use of iambic metre changed to a dactylic metre with its stress on the first rather than the second syllable in the line

- Purple the sails and so perfumed that the winds were lovesick with them...

'It just oozes with sensuality,' said Stacey. 'I love it.'

'I find it really sexy,' said Mark.

'Well you would, it's all you think about,' murmured Kiera.

'Yeah, but you can see the tragedy of the guy. Me and Sam watched the old film on video last week – the one with Liz Taylor and Richard Burton. I know it's not the Shakespeare play but at least you get a feel for the story. It was brill.'

I left the rarefied air of the sixth form block and switched into survival mode for the final lesson of the day.

'Can't we watch tele, sir. I'm knackered?' This was Danny Fleming, kicking aside a chair as he made his way to the back of the class.

'Go on, sir,' added Ricky Armstrong, 'Mrs Leggett, just gave us grief in chemistry just cos we broke a couple of test tubes. Danny's gotta go see Jeffreys after school. Cane most likely.'

'Shut yer face you, don't remind me. And anyway it was your fault,' grumbled Fleming.

'Okay, boys, I get the picture. But no, we're not watching tele, we're reading.'

'I hate reading,' mumbled Fleming.

'That's cos you're thick,' murmured Alison Blacklock, who always sat right at the front of the class and generally started the lesson by checking her makeup in a little pink mirror which she kept in her white plastic handbag. 'Shall I give out the books?' she said. 'You're looking a bit peaky, sir.'

'Am I, Alison?'

'We are a bit of a pain aren't we, sir?'

She went round the twelve students who made up my bottom set group giving out copies of Steinbeck's *Of Mice and Men*.

'Is teaching a really shitty job, sir?' she said returning to her seat.

'No, Alison. It gets tiring at times but, no it's not sh.. you know what.'

She laughed, 'Aren't you allowed to say 'shitty', sir?'

'Not in front of the children, Alison. Now what page did we get to?'

'This is the story about the mongo guy, isn't it, sir?' chimed Ricky rocking back and forth on his seat in the corner.

'Lennie and George,' I said, 'what can you remember about them?'

'Lennie's the retard,' shouted Fleming.

'Bit like you,' murmured Mary. Mary Foster was a plain, solitary girl with short black hair who generally sat on her own near the window. She didn't seem to connect with the others in the class and was a target for all kinds of ridicule. The problem was, she didn't shy away from mouthing back to the others.

'What did you say, pizza face?' growled Fleming.

'I said,' started Mary, turning to face him.

I cut in quickly, 'Okay you two, can you finish off this little tiff after the lesson, the rest of us would like to get on with the story,' and raising my hands to the rest of the class added, ' wouldn't we ladies and gentlemen?' I'd quickly learnt that ladling politeness and courtesy on rough necks like this lot generally disarmed them. They weren't quite sure what was happening but seemed to like the apparent respect I was showing them.

'Ooh, you havin' a tiff with Mary?' sang Ricky.

'Shut yer face, you,' said Fleming. 'What page is it?'

We were well into the book and they found the story fascinating – the strangely touching relationship between the wily George and the bear-like Lennie who had the mind of a six year old. The scenes of violence, aggression, the pathos of Lennie and the protectiveness of George were ingredients which really grabbed their attention. I did my best American accents, reserving a laboured hillbilly type drawl for Lennie and once the group settled to listening it was the best way to spend the last lesson of an afternoon.

As I read, I was all the time glancing up to check the response of the group. It didn't take much for someone like Armstrong to destroy the lesson with some stupid prank so while I read I kept my eye on the corner where Fleming and Armstrong were sitting.

I could see Armstrong grinning and scribbling something on a bit of paper while glancing across to where Mary Foster was sitting. Fleming beside him was seemingly absorbed in the book but Armstrong was clearly up to something. So while continuing with my reading I got up slowly and strolled down the aisle towards the corner where he was sitting. I stood behind him, still reading, without having disturbed the flow of the story. And by chance I had arrived at the point in the story where Curly, the fiery son of the boss is picking on Lennie in the bunk house. So I let rip close to Armstrong's ear with: *'What the hell you laughin' at? Come on, ya big bastard. Get up on your feet. No big son-of-a-bitch is gonna laugh at me, I'll show ya who's yella!'*

Armstrong, who clearly hadn't been following the story turned towards me with a shocked expression half-thinking I was talking to him.

I kept up the pace of the reading with the description of Curley slashing his fist across Lennie's face and then Lennie grabbing his fist and crushing his hand. Armstrong was back searching his book probably to find whether the word 'bastard' was really there. I strolled back towards my desk, still reading, still holding the tension of the story. I glanced at the clock on the wall. Ten more minutes. We were almost home and dry.

And that's how it was most lessons with a group like this. You never knew what might erupt. They lived with problems at home, problems on their streets, grief with the other kids at school who treated them as low life. Set five, after all, doesn't get much lower in the eyes of other kids and other teachers. So it was always tricky and always a relief when the end of the lesson arrived.

While Alison collected the books and the others started packing up their bags, Ricky Armstrong was chuntering something to Fleming. He turned and lifted his head in my direction.

'Did you call me a bastard, sir? I could ave you for that.'

'Weren't you following the story, Ricky? And anyway why on earth would I want to insult you. You're one of my best students.'

Fleming fisted his mate on the arm. 'See, stupid, I told you, he was just reading the story. You're a nut-case, you are.'

*

OF SANDSTONE AND SUNSHINE

I listened to the banter in the staff-room. There was talk of setting off for France as soon as the term finished, five weeks camping in the Dordogne, hiking in the Alps or jetting off to some villa in Majorca. It all sounded mouth-watering but sadly it wasn't for us. Our car did well if it got us a few miles down the motorway without something falling off. It certainly wouldn't have got us to France and in any case we had no money to spend on such holidays. Any spare money we had was allocated to more bags of cement or building blocks. No, our summer would be spent at home on the next project of building Katie a bedroom.

She was just starting to walk, pulling herself up with the handle of her little wooden trundle cart and stepping unsteadily along behind it. In the garden, while Sue hoed away the weeds, Katie crawled among the rows of beans and peas inspecting worms and beetles. Summer was indeed bursting out all over. The England cricket team was riding high with a new young player called Ian Botham scoring a hundred runs and taking eight wickets in the test match. At school all the talk among the kids was of the new film *Grease* starring John Travolta and Olivia

Newton-John. It was a classic American high school romp set in the late nineteen–fifties, with great music and great dance routines. The summer disco at school rang to the sound of *Grease Lightning* and *You're The One That I Want* along with the ever popular Bee Gees tracks from *Saturday Night Fever.*

The year had gone well. I felt I had finally arrived at becoming a genuine English teacher. From my wayward flirtation with the world of economics and industry I had successfully changed tracks. Allen Freer might well be proud of me. If only he knew.

On the last day of term I drove to school towing the new trailer which I had recently bought for seventy pounds from the Carlisle Saturday morning auction. It weighed a ton being made of welded angle irons from old bedsteads. It had no suspension but a fixed axle and big wheels from an old Austin Maxi. Empty, it jumped around behind the car like a demented kangaroo but when it was weighed down with cement bags or half a ton of sand and gravel it purred along quite happily. I had towed it in to collect the scaffolding which I was hiring for a couple of weeks in order to build Katie's new bedroom.

So while many of the staff were setting off to catch their ferries to France, I was towing the trailer at a very slow speed back home laden with a heavy consignment of scaffolding. I hadn't realised that the overhanging steel sections would cause the trailer to sway violently from side to side at any speed over fifteen miles per hour. The trailer tyres were squashed almost flat under the weight and I doubted that we would make it beyond the outskirts of Carlisle before some disaster struck. But luck was with me and, after a painstakingly slow journey, I finally pulled up outside the house. The summer holiday had begun.

I looked along the sloping roof on the west side of the house. The plan was to break into what was an empty loft space, remove the roof and build on to the existing ground floor wall. It was a scary business. I had barely laid a brick before let alone built a fully fledged stone and block structure and I was half tempted to turn the car round, return the scaffolding and spend the summer doing something less daunting. But then I'd made this commitment to the little toddler whom I tucked up in bed each night. She deserved a room of her own to grow up in. There was no turning back.

To seal the deal and dispel any doubts I went and got a ladder, climbed up to the sloping roof and ripped off half a dozen tiles. Now, with a gaping hole in the roof, there was definitely no turning back.

In fact I was not on my own in this ambitious summer project. Peter, a good friend from the Midlands who had experience of building, had offered to stay with us for a couple of weeks and oversee the whole thing.

That summer I learned to use a chisel and a mash hammer, to cut sandstone to an appropriate shape and size. I began to read the sandstone graining and be able to anticipate how it would cleave. I learned to use a cement mixer and to mix the right proportions of sand and cement so that by some miracle of science, what had been a viscous gloop magically hardened overnight. I never believed it would happen and each morning I would go and poke my fingers into the mortar joints we had laid the previous day and find the miracle had happened again. And so, gradually, the walls grew.

The weather was perfect through late July and August and from the top of the scaffolding there were clear views of the Scottish hills to the north and the rounded peak of Criffel just across the Solway. To the south were the Lake District fells and the prominent outline of Skiddaw while overhead there was always the big sky of pillowed cloud drifting east from the Atlantic. Below in the garden Katie toddled among the rows of cabbages and raspberry canes with her bucket and spade collecting garden treasures.

On August 16th I had a break from the building work. It was A level results day and although I didn't have any upper sixth students I knew most of them quite well and hoped they had achieved the grades they needed for college and university places. Results day was a new experience for me. There was ecstasy and agony in almost equal measure. Some students erupted with whoops of joy when they opened their brown envelope and discovered their grades. Others, their faces blank, went off quietly and stood away from the jubilation. So much hung on these results. They dictated the direction your life would take. I thought of my own lower sixth students. This would be their day next year and I felt the true weight of my own responsibility towards them.

In addition, here was I, having the gall to launch a brand new A level course in September – me, a mere pip-squeak in terms of teaching experience. But what the hell. The course would be great and I would try to ensure that in two years time it would be a day of smiles rather than tears.

In the last week of the holiday the roofing contractor arrived to seal the roof with roofing felt. He was a short, squat man in a grubby flat cap and tar smeared overalls and he was accompanied by a younger version in a baseball cap. They were like a couple of gremlins from the underworld with their drum of hot bitumen bubbling and steaming on the gas burner on the back of their truck. I sat on the grass with Katie to watch their progress. The outside work was virtually complete and with the roof done the room would be weather-proof before I returned to school.

'So what d'you reckon Katie, did we do a good job?'

She was picking dandelions, shaking them and watching the seeds drift away in the air. Her little brow was furrowed with concentration.

After the roofers had gone I took her up into her new room. The walls needed plastering and there was lots still to do but I perched her on the window sill and we looked out across the garden and the fields beyond. In the corner of the garden I had planted a few pine saplings. They were only a few feet tall at the moment but they would grow as Katie grew and maybe provide a touch of woodland magic for her.

I tapped the walls with the side of my fist as we left the room. They felt solid. Not bad for a novice builder. Not bad at all.

*

MORE RURAL MANOEUVRES

'Sir, I saw that postural echo thing outside the staff-room. It was Mr Jeffreys and Mr Slater,' said James one of my new sixth formers.

'And I found I was doing it in the sixth-common room,' added Gillian. 'I didn't realise. I was talking to Jane and she was leaning against the notice-board with one foot crossed over the other. And there was I doing the exact same thing. Susan shouts out, 'You're doing postural echo,' and everybody looks at her and thinks she's gone loopy. And she just announces, 'It's okay, you wouldn't understand. It's communication theory'.'

We were into our third week of lessons on the new Communication Studies course and in the middle of a unit on non-verbal communication. We had been looking at some sections from Desmond Morris' new book *Manwatching*. They loved it because unlike most subjects they could observe it themselves. Whether it was noting the

179

dynamics of non-verbal exchanges or analysing the way language register changed according to context they instantly recognised the concepts. Jean, who was teaching the mass communication part of the course also talked of the students' enthusiasm.

'They're complaining that I've spoilt their enjoyment of watching films as they're now looking out for camera angles and pace of editing.'

'But they love it really,' I added.

She nodded, 'They're just so enthusiastic. This morning I discovered that James Forrester is a whizz on the films of Hitchcock. He gave the class a mini lecture on the camera shots used in the *Psycho* shower scene. Do you know that we never actually see the dagger piercing the victim's flesh? We think we do but it's the mind of the audience that makes the connection between a series of rapid close-up shots. According to James, this is Hitchcock's use of 'montage'.'

'Wow,' I said, 'I think I need to do a lot more swotting up for this course. I don't know much about film techniques.'

'Don't panic,' replied Jean, 'just get the students to run your lesson. It's a doddle.'

As the term progressed I panicked less. The course was running well, Jean was doing a brilliant job and we met once a week after school to swap progress reports. One afternoon I had sent my students into the city centre to sit and make notes on non-verbal communication. They had to observe people's use of hand gestures, body posture, facial expressions, the distance between people when they spoke.

They reported back next lesson.

'And we did this test in the common room,' said Rachel. 'We had reckoned from what we'd seen in town that the usual distance English people seem happy when they're in conversation is around a metre. So we tried talking to people but gradually closing down the distance.'

'It was hilarious,' added Vicky, 'you could see people taking a step back to re-establish the distance.'

'It was like a dance going on around the common room,' said Richard. 'As we stepped forward, they stepped back.'

I nodded. 'They say that's what happens when diplomats from different countries meet. In Italy the comfortable distance when Italians speak to each other is much closer than the English. So it's like you saw in the common room; Italian diplomats pursue the English round the room with the English all the time stepping back and the Italians trying to get closer.'

I loved their enthusiasm and the more I read of the subject the more it fascinated me. There was a huge body of theory about how the communication process worked in different contexts. From the subtle dynamics of interpersonal communication there was a whole range of theories about the effect of mass media messages on people. Did watching violence on the screen make people violent? How did adverts exploit people's fears and fantasies? Did the James Bond films reinforce gender stereotyping?

I told the class of my experience of watching *Live and Let Die* in a Jamaican cinema; of the anger of the audience at the racial undertones of the film; the way the government started to cut out gun scenes from films because they assumed that watching violence encouraged people to be violent. The class enjoyed the anecdotes and I milked the fact that my close neighbour for a while had been Bob Marley.

'So you met the guy?' asked Richard, wide-eyed. Richard lived for his music. He played guitar in a local band and had the Rastafarian colours decorating his folder.

'I never met him,' I said, ' but the house where he was shot in 1976 was a couple of hundred yards up the Hope Road from the school where I taught.'

'That's awesome!' exclaimed Richard. 'You know I saw his concert at the Rainbow in London. It was so cool. They played from the new *Exodus* album. And did you hear about the peace concert back in April, the way he brought together on stage the leaders of the two parties.'

I had read about this in a copy of the Jamaican overseas paper, and Katie Megevand had mentioned it in one of her letters. Apparently, at the so-called 'One Love' peace concert, designed to defuse the state of near civil war in the country, Bob Marley had brought up on stage Michael Manley, the prime minister and Edward Seaga the leader of the opposition. He had joined their hands and then launched into the song *One Love*.

'Some guy,' nodded Richard, 'but man, that reggae beat is a swine to play. Our drummer goes nuts when he has to do it.'

I had recently received a disturbing letter from Katie and Philippe in Jamaica. They had stayed on trying to make things work but the shootings were moving uptown and the catalogue of murders and civil disorder grew weekly. Philippe's restaurant had been targeted by left-wing gangs and he had ended up handing over the whole business to his staff to be run as a workers' co-operative. Just as a few years earlier they had had to leave everything in Haiti - business, home, personal belongings, now they faced much the same scenario. Under the State of Emergency no money could be taken out of the country. The middle classes had fled in droves to Miami and there was no market for selling a business or any other property. So Katie, Philippe and the girls were planning to leave again and try to start a new life in Martinique. Our own lives paled into insignificance compared to what they were having to cope with.

I had also heard recently from Will who had left Sweden and was now in Japan, teaching technical English at a private university in Nagoya. Many of his adult students were from the big Toyota car plant in the city. He was having a ball and was dating a Japanese girl named Kayo. Our lives at the school in Lichfield seemed light years away.

*

That autumn we introduced five young turkeys to our little homestead. Bill had given me the address of the farm on the River Eden, just east of Carlisle from where he always bought his turkeys. I drove out of the city, crossed the river Eden at Warwick Bridge and then, following the river for a few miles, climbed the hill to the village of Great Corby. A couple of miles on I saw the sign to *Brocklewath* and drove down a long narrow lane for two miles, crossed a cattle grid and then stopped the car. I was on the lip of the valley side looking down at a broad bend in the majestic River Eden. Below, to the right, were some wooden barns and, to the left, a farm house with a thin plume of smoke drifting into the air. It was a stunning location.

A steep single track road snaked down the valley side and I parked near one of the barns. The farmer, Mr Roper, a squat ruddy-faced fellow was happy to set me off on my new turkey venture.

'You don't mind the competition then?' I said.

He shook his head. 'You have a go lad. I don't think your five will do much against my five thousand.'

And so I drove home with my new family of livestock.

Little Katie was intrigued, her rosy face all a-giggle. Sue was just mildly sceptical about the whole venture.

'So you're going to kill these little creatures yourself when the time comes?'

'Listen, if it's true what Bill says these won't be little creatures in December, they'll be mini-monsters that I'll be wrestling with. And yes, I'm going to dispatch them. Not sure how but I decided that if I'm going to dabble in a bit of farming I've got to do the lot, killing, plucking, dressing.'

Sue nodded slowly, with that slight raising of the eyebrows that hinted that she still had to be convinced.

I had created a turkey pen across the yard in one of the outhouses: there was clean straw, a feeding dispenser which I had picked up at one of the Saturday morning auctions at Dalton's Mart down Botchergate. My five white birds seemed quite contented with their new home. At first they stepped warily around the pen but when I left them their little beaks were pecking happily at the feed in the feeding trough.

My new career in farming had begun.

*

NEW KID ON THE BOARD

My application to become a moderator for the O level English examination had been accepted and in October I had to attend my first meeting in Manchester. It was held at the offices of the Joint Matriculation Board or JMB near the university on Oxford Road. I had always harboured the notion that people who sat on 'Examination Boards' were some fusty, rarefied breed of higher learning. I was soon to find out.

When I took my seat in a room of forty other moderators I saw a collection of fairly ordinary looking teachers of different ages, dressed casually apart from the JMB officer, Donald Leeming, who co-chaired the meeting. He was dressed in a dark suit and sat alongside the Chief Moderator, Philip Harris, who was Head of English at a large comprehensive school in London. We sat at tables arranged in a huge circle facing the top table where the Chief Moderator sat.

So this was what an 'Exam Board' looked like. And here was I, feeling like some interloper about to be found out, taking my place beside the rest of them. We were given bundles of papers which contained statistics from the previous summer examination, sample papers from candidates which had to be sifted and selected and which would then form this year's Trial Marking material. It was the Trial Marking material which went to every school and which set the bench mark of standards by which teachers would judge their own candidates' work.

The first part of the morning was given over to a review of the previous summers' exam results, some complicated statistical analysis which I struggled to understand and some discussion as to whether it was necessary for candidates to submit a folio of twelve assignments rather than say, ten. It was interesting listening to the debates. Despite their casual appearance , there were some really sharp people round this circle of tables. I was impressed. Donald Leeming himself, as well as being meticulous as an administrator, clearly had a passion about this course which was so different from conventional final examination courses. This was his baby. He had nurtured this English course from its infancy with the help of Philip Harris, a course which was revolutionary in being examined entirely by coursework. Since its inception a few years previously, it had exploded in popularity across the country. Many schools still followed conventional final exam-based English O level courses but more and more were seeing the benefits of coursework.

I knew from working with my own O level group the joy of being able to choose my own literature texts to suit the group; to be able to devise interesting reading and writing assignments free of the constraints of a conventional syllabus.

Only the previous week I had set an assignment which had ignited the imagination of my students.

'I want you to write a letter to your future child, to be opened on their sixteenth birthday. I want you to describe what it's like being a sixteen year old in 1978.'

They stared back at me. No-one spoke.

I continued. 'What I'd really like is for you to do two copies, one for your exam folder and one that you put in an envelope and place in a safe place and keep for your child's sixteenth birthday.'

It was Tina who spoke first. 'Sir, I just got shivers down my back. That's really weird, thinking of me having a child of sixteen. Can't get my head round that.'

From the back, Martin Jones raised his hand. 'So, let me get this right. I'm writing about what it's like being sixteen, but it's for my own sixteen year old child?'

'Right,' I nodded.

He frowned. 'What if I don't want children, sir?'

'Don't be pedantic, Martin. It's hypothetical.'

'What's pedantic, sir?' retorted Martin.

'It means to be rather picky, concerned with small details; from the Latin, 'pedes' meaning a foot. So it means when you're thinking in a rather slow, plodding fashion rather than as the usual, sharp, alert, quick-thinker that I know you to be.'

He nodded, half smiling. 'Okay, sir, I get the point.'

'And 'hypothetical'?' asked Richard, who sat next to Martin.

'It means when you make an assumption which may be imaginary.'

Richard nodded. 'Two new words. You're working well today, sir.'

'Thank you Richard. Now listen for a minute, everyone. First, to get you thinking, take a blank sheet of paper and do one of the spider diagrams I've been getting you to do. Write in the middle of the sheet 'Me at sixteen'. Then just fill the sheet with thoughts about what your life is like, what the world is like and most important, what your hopes and dreams are at age sixteen. When your child reads this you're probably going to be in your forties. What will your life have been like?'

The class was buzzing. Their thoughts were racing. I went round listening in on snippets of the chatter:

'You'll have six kids....'

'I'll be bald like me dad, I'm sure I found a grey hair this morning.'

'I'm going to be driving a swanky car and have a blonde beside me.'

'D'you think some of us might be dead already....?'

I allowed the bubble of chatter to continue for about ten minutes, then settled them down to collect their thoughts on paper.

Two weeks later when I collected in their completed assignments I was eager to read them. Marking this type of work was a joy. The assignment had really stirred their thoughts and feelings. Some were quite moving in their descriptions of home life, their feelings for friends and members of the family. Others were fascinating in the ways they revealed aspects of the student's personality which were entirely new to me.

And this was the delight of this course. It was the reason why the teachers sitting in the meeting were so passionate about the course. It ignited the writing and the interest of their students in so many ways and produced superb results even for weaker students.

On the train back to Carlisle I felt tired but elated. It had been a long meeting but I felt I had been part of something significant, something which touched education across the whole country. I'd met teachers from Cornwall, Wales, Northumberland, Norfolk. They were equally passionate about their work and if Leeming, the JMB man, was right, more and more schools were intending to change to this new syllabus. Education was in ferment and teachers were driving the changes. It was a great time to be a teacher.

*

LET'S JUMP THE BROOMSTICK...LA LA

The newspapers of 1978 had stolen a line from the opening of Shakespeare's *Richard III* and branded the season *The Winter of Discontent*. The unions were in uproar over the government's attempts at pay restraint; dustbin men were on strike and rubbish was piling up in the streets of London; dead bodies were crowding the morgues as the gravediggers had stopped digging and angry workers were marching on the streets in a number of cities. Prospects for the coming year might have looked bleak.

But not for us. In our little Cumbrian homestead our glasses were more than half full. The five turkeys had grown into huge white strutting specimens. They had piled on the pounds and eaten their way through dozens of bags of feed. There was nothing attractive about them, though. They had cold eyes and sharp beaks and were unremittingly cruel to each other. A ruthless pecking order was in place which relegated the smallest and weakest to the far end of the feeding line. Seeing the bald patches and bloodied skin on the heads and necks of the weaker birds and the strutting arrogance of the largest, I now realised where the term 'hen-pecked' came from. So when it came to the time for their slaughter there would be little sentiment to distract me from doing the deed. However, I knew that it would not be easy and that Christmas dinner for me might well be a slice of pizza if I couldn't face tucking into one of the turkeys I had just killed.

I revisited the metalwork department to consult Bill about how you kill a turkey.

'Various methods,' he said. 'You can't wring their necks like you would a chicken, they're just too big and strong. But there's the paraffin can method.'

'Paraffin can method?'

'You know those large blue paraffin cans with the narrow tops. Well some people put the turkey in the upturned can, pull its neck through the hole and slit the throat. Either that or they shoot it with an air gun. Bit bloody though.'

'Isn't it difficult to stuff it into the can?'

'Not really. The thing about chickens and turkeys is that if you hold them up by their legs they go into a kind of trance. They stay completely still so it's possible to lower them into the can. But I just found it too complicated.'

'So what d'you do?'

'The broom-handle method.'

'What's that?'

'I'll show you.'

Bill went and got a broom and laid it across the floor and stood just behind it.

'First you pick up the bird by its legs. It'll flap a bit but then just hang there motionless with its head curved upwards. You hold the legs in each hand, lower the curved neck to the ground, place the broomstick across the neck, step lightly on one end of it, then, always moving slowly and quietly, place your other foot on the other end of the broom stick. When you're balanced you then press down firmly with both feet and pull on those legs. The bird will flap for a few moments and then it's all over.'

I nodded, trying to picture the sequence of events.

'Then you hang it up and start plucking. Don't let it go cold as they're much harder to pluck when cold.'

'What about the cleaning out,' I asked.

'The dressing? You don't do that until about two days before Christmas unless you're going to freeze the bird. It can hang for a week in a cold shed quite happily as long as it hasn't been dressed.'

'Right,' I said. 'Thanks. I'll let you know how it goes.'

'Good luck.'

I left the workshop with my head buzzing trying to remember all that Bill had told me.

Term finished on a Tuesday. Christmas Day was on the Saturday, so I had to carry out the slaughter the weekend before then. The pressure was mounting, fuelled by the fact that a few weeks ago three friends had all asked Sue if they could each buy a turkey for their Christmas dinner. At the going rate of £1 for a pound weight, we stood to earn the princely sum of around £80. The offer was too tempting and Sue had readily agreed.

'You did what?' I said, when I arrived home from school and she told me.

'Well you were saying you wanted to be a farmer.'

'But not the first year. It might all go belly-up.'

'Well it better not. They're expecting great things from you.'

'Gee thanks.'

The responsibility for three families' Christmas dinners was very daunting. What if I botched the slaughter, or failed to pluck and dress the birds properly? What if the meat was tough?

With my head awash with doubts and a rather muddled memory of Bill's explanation of the 'broom-handle method' I crossed the yard carrying a broom on the final Saturday before Christmas.

'Can I help?' called Sue.

'No. What a man's gotta do, a man's gotta do,' I called back.

I went inside the outhouse and looked into the turkey pen. Their beady eyes were expecting food. 'Not this morning, I'm afraid, my dears,' I murmured. I was eyeing them, deciding which one to go for first. Not the biggest. Not the smallest with its tufty, pecked head. I chose one of middle size.

It was true what Bill had said. Once you held the bird upside down by its feet, it was completely still, the wings were outstretched, the head curving upwards, eyes staring. I took the bird into the adjacent shed and, holding the legs together with one hand, lowered the curved neck to the ground. With some difficulty, I then reached for the broom and placed the handle across the curve of the neck. I placed my right foot lightly down on one end, took the legs firmly in each hand and lowered my left foot lightly on to the other end of the broom handle. Think of Christmas dinner, I told myself and pressed down firmly with both feet while pulling on the bird's legs. There was a violent flapping of the wings, much stronger than I had expected and I almost lost my balance but managed to hang on until the flapping stopped. It was only a matter of seconds but the drama and tension of it all was quite a shock. I had snuffed out a life.

I admit I didn't feel comfortable about it but I had embarked on this project and had to see it through. I hung the bird up by its legs and had my first go at plucking. Bill had said to start at the legs and work down. The fine down of the lower legs came out easily. It was was soft and cleanly white. The more flesh I exposed the better I felt. It was starting to look like 'meat' rather than a lifeless bird.

To pluck the whole bird took half an hour and by the end I was ankle deep in a pile of soft white down. I moved on to the other birds and had something of a battle holding on to the biggest one, but the real test was killing the smallest. I had resisted calling him 'baldy' but despite this, the little fellow still stood out from the rest as something of a character.

'Sorry, baldy, but I've got to finish the job.' And although it was physically easier to dispatch this one, I didn't feel comfortable until it was completely plucked and I could start to imagine it as someone's dinner.

My reservations about the killings faded completely when the turkey was carved on Christmas Day. The meat was moist, the juices flowed into the gravy and when I tasted the meat I was convinced. A farmer's life for me, tra la.

'Well done, turkey man,' said Sue as she took her first taste. 'Didn't daddy do well.'

Katie in her high chair signalled her approval by banging on her new Flopsy Bunnies dish with her plastic spoon and making a noise which was a mixture of singing and shouting.

'And another thing,' said Sue. 'Thought I'd save the news until today. There could be another mouth at the table next year.'

'Why, who's coming?' I had visions of the in-laws joining us for Christmas dinner next year. But then with the turkeys weighing in at over twenty five pounds there was no shortage of meat. And with my plans to double the number of turkeys next year we could feed an army.

'I'm pregnant, silly. Happy Christmas.'

*

OF MICE AND MALLET MAN

Whenever the wind blew extra hard we would lie in bed and wait for the next clatter. I would grind my teeth as another slate slid off the barn roof and smashed in pieces in the yard. Another fifty pence down the drain for that was the price of replacement Welsh slates. Most of the slate laths were rotten, some of the beams were worm-eaten and many of the slate nails were rusted. With plans to convert one end of the barn into a study in which I would write my best seller there was no question; the Easter holiday job was re-roofing the barn.

In the middle of the spring term the school's supply of heating oil ran out as a result of the tanker drivers going on strike so we gained a couple of extra days holiday. School was as manic as ever but at least I was feeling more established. My new A level course was coming along nicely and we'd been trying out making some short video sequences. The problem was there was no easy way to edit video apart from 'crash editing' which involved linking two video machines together and transferring from one to the other the bits of video you wanted. The result was a very jerky sequence but it was fun and it was a new area for all of us.

My English classes were not giving me too much grief although Danny Fleming in five set five was becoming harder to handle especially in the Thursday afternoon lesson. He was generally morose and hell bent on disruption. Basically he was ready to leave school and was itching to join his dad's second-hand car business. He'd outgrown school and every day was a trial for him and for the rest of us. And of course sidekick Ricky could always be relied upon to wind him up.

I tried a new tack. We were revising *Of Mice and Men.* They had really been held by the drama and pathos of the final scene where George opts to shoot his friend Lennie.

'Okay, so what should happen to George?' I asked.

'Whadya mean?' asked Ricky.

'Well he's just murdered Lennie. He's got to be punished hasn't he?'

'But he had no choice,' said Alison. 'He did it out of kindness.'

'That Curley guy would've made him suffer,' added Danny. 'Didn't he tell the other men to 'shoot him in the guts'.'

I was impressed that Danny had remembered the quotation.

'So what? He's still murdered Lennie. He's got to be punished,' I said shrugging.

'But you can't call it murder,' said Danny. He was getting quite heated about it. The rest of the class were quietly listening and watching. They didn't normally see Danny Fleming taking things seriously.

'He did it deliberately,' I persisted.

'Isn't it what they call 'mercy killing'?' put in Alison.

I held up my hands. 'I tell you what. How about if we put George on trial? We'll set up a court room and the jury can decide.'

'Who's going to be the jury?' asked Mary Foster who usually spent most lessons gazing vacantly out of the window.

'You are.'

'Just me?'

'No, Mary, I mean about eight of you will need to be jury, then what else do we need? Anybody know how a courtroom works?'

I knew that Danny's older brother had been in court recently and wondered how much he knew.

'There's a prosecutor and then the guy who speaks for the person who's on trial,' said Jamie Finn. Jamie normally doodled his way through the lesson drawing cartoons but today even he was showing some interest.

'The defence lawyer,' I said.

'That's him,' nodded Jamie.

' I wanna be the judge,' called out Danny. 'Can I have one of those hammer things they bang?'

Ah, crunch time. Danny could make or break this little project. It would depend what mood he was in. Should I gamble or not?

'On one condition, Danny,' I said.

'What's that?' he frowned.

190

'You have to wear a judge's gown and more importantly you have to be in control at all times.' I watched his face. He was still with me.

He nodded and then nudged Ricky, 'Hey, if you shan us up I'll welt you with me hammer.'

*

'Danny Fleming in charge? You must be mad,' said Marjorie Leggett, the Chemistry teacher. She had overheard me at the coffee machine telling Jean about my proposed mock trial lesson. 'That boy needs locking up like his brother. He's dangerous. Regularly smashes my test tubes. He's evil!' With that she walked off to the other end of the staffroom.

Jean and I sat down. 'It's a bit of gamble, but hey, nothing ventured....' I said.

'I tell you, give lads like that a bit of responsibility, stop treating them like they're dangerous and they can be putty in your hand.'

'Yeah but you have the motherly touch. I've seen you at work. You just charm them.'

'Well sounds like you're doing okay. Give it a whirl. I'll lend you a black gown from the costume cupboard,' said Jean.

'And maybe I could get a small mallet and a block of wood from the woodwork department. I'll go and see Bill.'

'Why not video the whole thing? That would be a real coup, catching Danny Fleming on camera acting as a judge in a court of law.'

'You reckon? Isn't that pushing it a bit far? What if Danny flips?'

'He won't,' said Jean. 'I tell you, treat him like an adult and he'll surprise you.'

Before the day of the mock trial we spent a lesson doing some preparation work. Those who were taking on the roles of witnesses who would be called to testify had to write down some ideas for what they might say. They had to remind themselves of the story and of the characters' attitudes to Lennie and George. I took aside Alison and Jimmy who were the two lawyers along with Danny and explained the procedure for calling witnesses, asking questions and challenging unfair questions.

Most of the time Danny was only half listening. 'What about me ammer sir and me costume? I need to check it out. I don't want to look like some daft bugger.'

191

I showed him the black gown that Jean had found from the costume cupboard and he tried it on. He nodded. 'Ay, that'll be cushti. An me ammer?'

'Tomorrow,' I said. 'You'll get that tomorrow.'

When they arrived for the lesson the next day the room was set out like a court-room with two rows of seats for the jury, a row at the back for the witnesses, two tables on either side of the blackboard for the prosecution and the defence lawyers and in the middle the judge's table. But it was when they saw the video camera set up on the tripod I nearly had a revolt.

'I'm not doing it in front of the camera, you can forget that,' said Ricky who was taking on the role of Curley.

'Me neither,' said Tony who was playing Slim.

'Me mam says it's not allowed, taking film of us. She read it in the papers,' chimed Mary Foster, always mouth first, mind following sluggishly behind.

Then Danny appeared in the doorway and immediately Ricky was in his face. 'Look, Danny, he's got the camera. We're not doing it, are we? No-one's gonna do it if that camera's on and that's final init, Danny?'

Danny pushed past him and went over to his table. He unfolded the black gown and put it on and then took from a plastic bag the mallet and block of wood Bill had provided. He took his seat, adjusted his gown and banged the mallet down on the table. 'This court is in session. Now get yerselves bloody sorted!'

I'd never seen a transformation like it. Their behaviour was amazing. The two lawyers asked some probing questions and the witnesses made an attempt to keep in character. Some read their replies from bits of paper they had prepared and only half-listened to the questions. A couple of times this prompted Danny to bang his mallet and harangue them with, 'Listen to the question will yer. That's not what you wuz asked.'

The whole thing lasted for half an hour and ended with Danny passing judgement. I'd given him a piece of paper with some lines he might want to use.

'Right, we've heard everything now and it's time for me to say what's to happen to George. From what we've heard tha's two sides. George has killed a man, but he's not a murderer. He did it cuz he loved his mate Lennie. And that's that. So my sentence is that...' he paused for a moment; '... George should have to go and work with mental patients in a hospital for no money for a year cuz he seems to understand those type of people.'

With that, Danny banged his mallet and shouted, 'Court dismissed!'

I switched off the camera and gave them a round of applause.

We then viewed the playback on the television monitor and I watched their faces. They were enthralled. Ricky was fidgeting as usual but Danny was smiling and nodding when he saw himself on the screen. He nudged Ricky, 'Look at that eh! That's me there. I'm like a real actor a bit like that John Revolta.'

'Travolta, dummy,' said Alison.

'D'you fancy me now, then?' said Danny turning to Alison.

'Not quite,' replied Alison, 'but I have to say, you acted quite cool today. Quite grown up. You should do it more often then I might fancy you.'

There was a chorus of shrieks and wolf whistles and Danny Fleming, for the first time, was lost for words. His face was crimson. He turned on Ricky, 'What are you laffin' at, moron?'

When the bell rang for the end of the lesson, Danny pushed Ricky out of the door ahead of him. 'See you, sir', he called. 'Smart lesson that.'

Alison turned to me as she left the room, 'He's all right really, in't he, sir.'

I nodded. 'See you next time, Alison. Well done.'

It seemed I had made a little progress with the class and with Danny. But it was short-lived. The next lesson he threw his exercise book out of the window when I drew his attention to some errors in his written work. 'Sick of this friggin' place,' he growled and folded his arms. Then he pushed Ricky off his chair and stormed out of the room. Alison shook her head. 'Not your fault, sir. His boyo was sent down for ten years yesterday. He's been like it in every lesson.'

I went across to the window. Danny's dog-eared exercise book lay in the grass and was being soaked by the rain. I was inclined to leave it there. At times it felt pretty futile that you could have any impact on someone like Danny. I turned back to the class and went over to where Alison was working quietly by herself in her usual place on the front row.

'Alison, would you mind going and getting Danny's book out of the rain?'

She nodded and put down her pen. 'Probably not much in it worth saving but it is his own work after all.' She closed the door behind her.

And that was the point you had to hold on to. However minimal the signs of progress, it wasn't completely futile. Thank you, Alison.

*

SUMMER IS A-COMIN' IN…

Re-roofing a forty foot barn was quite a challenge and although Sue was still willing, she was not really able to help in her usual way. Now five months pregnant the sight of her at the top of the step-ladder passing up rolls of roofing felt was not really in the interests of mother and future baby. So I banned her from helping.

I had stripped off the old laths and replaced some of the rotten purlins. Now it was time to roll out the roofing felt and secure it with the new laths. The problem with roofing felt is that it tears very easily. It's basically a thin, brittle layer of bitumen reinforced with some thin woven chord. If you nail it and then it moves, the nail hole widens into a gaping hole. And with roofing felt, holes mean a potentially leaking roof.

It was the first week of the Easter holiday and on the morning when I was rolling out the felt there was little wind. Before I could nail the first lath to hold the felt in place, however, the forty foot length casually slid down the roof and I had to start again. I had to 'monkey step' my way the length of the roof above the gaping space of the barn itself to reposition the felt and hope it would still be there by the time I reached the other end forty feet away. The third time it glided down the roof I was ready to give up. I needed another pair of hands.

Quite by chance our friends from Whitehaven called in for a coffee that morning on their way to Carlisle. They were dressed up for 'big city' shopping.

'How are you at Superman impressions?' I said to Alan.

He looked at me with a look of total incomprehension.

'You must have seen the new Superman film, with Christopher Reeve and seen him flying,' I added.

Alan shook his head, 'Don't know what you're on about.'

'Well, in the film, Superman does this amazing flying sequence. And I just wondered whether you could replicate it on my roof?'

Alan looked at Sue and tapped his finger against the side of his head. 'What's he on?' he said to her.

'I think he wants some help roofing the barn,' she said.

I'd helped Alan with a couple of DIY jobs on his own house, so he owed me a favour. He followed me up the ladder in his smart blue coat and on to the scaffolding.

'What I need you to do is lie out along the ridge of the roof, one foot and hand on one side, one foot and hand on the other to hold the roofing felt in place while I fix a couple of battens. And if you'd seen the Superman film you'd know what I was talking about.'

Alan nodded. 'Is it safe?'

'Of course it's not safe. But then Superman has special powers of survival.'

'Just get on with it, will you.'

I should have had my camera handy. Alan spread-eagled along the ridge of the barn roof was a sight to behold. 'Bloody get on with it before I take off!' he said between gritted teeth.

Within half an hour I'd got enough laths in place to stop the felt from sliding and ripping. 'So now you need to go and see the Superman film and you'll know what I was talking about,' I said.

'Superman my arse,' replied Alan. 'Listen, Clark Kent, I've got an old septic tank at my house that needs replacing and you're just the man for the job. I'll book you in. But bring your wellies. It needs emptying first. But don't worry, I'll be generous. I've got a shovel and bucket you can borrow.'

By the end of the Easter holiday we could finally rest easy in our bed. I could lay my hand on Sue's rounded stomach and feel the kicking of a new life and not worry about the clatter of falling slates. The barn roof was secure and I could turn my attention to creating a study from the old hay loft at the end of the barn which adjoined the house. Yes, a study in which to write those novels and travel books, to emulate D.H.Lawrence and all those other artists who seemed to inhabit that rarefied world of winters in the south of France and summers in the Alps.

But there was a winding road to travel yet and I was about to be consumed by a frenetic summer term.

*

'This is brilliant,' murmured Jean.

'Whose is that?' I asked.

'It's Tina's diary piece on *Romeo and Juliet*. What a writer she is.'

'What d'you reckon?'

195

'It has to be an A grade. It's off the scale. And her poem about the death in winter moved me to tears. You must be delighted.'

I was. I had watched Tina Stephens' development over the two years I'd been teaching her. I watched her in class, that distant gazing out of the window and then the intense concentration on a piece of work. She was much like Michele, whom I'd taught in Jamaica; that same maturity of thought and style at the tender age of sixteen. And this was the culmination: her GCE folder of twelve pieces of work which would be sent to the exam board for the final moderation.

We were sitting round a large table – Roger, John, Tricia, Jean and me with all our students' folders ranked along the table top from the highest at one end to the lowest at the other. We had two days off timetable to do the final standardising of the GCE and CSE folders. Each of us had graded our own students and now it was a case of checking each others marking before the sample folders were sent off to the Board for the June meeting. And I would be at that meeting in my new role as an exam moderator. A week at the JMB offices in Manchester. It was both scary and exciting.

Two years. It had gone so quickly. I thought of my A level literature class to whom I would soon say goodbye and I remembered Mark Denning's dismissal of *Tess of the D'Urbervilles* as a 'girly book'. How he had matured in his two years in the sixth form. He had ditched the sultry Samantha and taken up with a girl from a neighbouring school. But what a change in his attitude. He had devoured the work on Ted Hughes with a passion. 'It's like he sticks a blade under your skin and starts probing for the bone,' he said in one lesson. I shivered at the simile while the rest of the class took a sharp intake of breath. And now he was applying to read for a Business and Combined Arts degree at Birmingham University. He'd got a place; now he just needed the grades. I told him of my early ventures into the bowels of the industrial Midlands.

'Can't picture you on the factory floor, sir,' he said.

'It was good in a negative kind of way,' I replied. 'It's why I enjoy teaching so much. I have no illusions about the world of offices and smart suits.'

He smiled. 'I have to thank you sir. I've enjoyed your lessons. Really made me think. I was a bit of a pillock at the start.'

I shrugged. 'But look at you now. You're going to do well.'

I remembered myself at that age – full of pretensions, youthful arrogance and utter naivety. It takes a long while to work things out.

My last few lessons with my GCE and CSE groups were quite touching. We had shared a lot. Exploring literature together had brought up a range of issues and provoked heated debate. The CSE group had been moved by the pathos of Billy Casper's plight in *Kes*. They had been stirred by the courage of Beatie Bryant in Arnold Wesker's *Roots* and had written well on Wilfred Owen's poetry.

'If only he hadn't gone back to the front when he came out of hospital. Why did he do that, sir?' asked Jenny Simons when we read about the circumstances of Owen's death.

'I don't know, Jenny. Maybe a sense of honour and loyalty to the men in his command. He didn't want to abandon them.'

'So sad though when it was so close to the end of the war. Is that what irony means, sir?'

I nodded. 'It was sadly ironical that he died so close to the war ending. You're right – that's irony. Well done.'

Little moments when understanding flares in the mind of a student. That's what you treasured as a teacher. It was also interesting reading the folders of your colleagues' classes - a way of sharing ideas and seeing what was possible with groups of different abilities.

But the big issue remained. Would they get the grades they needed and deserved? The results came out in August and I knew it would be as nerve-racking for me as it would for the students, especially the A level students; their university places were dependent on their grades.

In mid May I held my final lesson with the A level group before they went on study leave. We recapped on key features of the set books: the themes of *Antony and Cleopatra,* the key moments in *Tess,* the imagery and structure of Hopkins' long poem *The Wreck of the Deutschland.*

Towards the end of the lesson Stacey said, 'I'm going on a little trip to Dorset in the summer holiday, sir. Thought I'd look up Hardy's birthplace.'

'Don't miss the Hardy museum in Dorchester,' I added. 'I think there's a reconstruction of Hardy's study there with his desk and chair and pens and such like.'

'That book really got to me,' continued Stacey. 'Tess was such a victim and Angel was such a tool.'

'I don't think you should say that in an answer – Angel was a bit of a tool,' said Mark. 'But you're right, he was a bit of a tool.'

'I was reading some of Hardy's poetry over Easter,' continued Stacey. 'So much was written out of guilt after his wife died. Thought I might read *Far From the Madding Crowd* in the holidays.'

I told them of my experience of teaching it in Jamaica, of the tussle between Michele and Huey and Michele's description of Sergeant Troy as a 'man-bitch.'

'Must have been fun, teaching out there,' said Mark.

'It was. Very memorable. Indelible in fact,' I said, my mind drifting back to Caribbean skies and the Blue Mountains.

We had recently had a letter from Katie and Philippe. They were now in Martinique trying to set up a little guest house. Regine was in school but Katarina had been unable to go to college as they were so short of money; most of it was still locked up in Jamaican banks. The tone of Katie's letter lacked her usual verve and wit. She was bitter and angry and worn down by the injustices they had had to cope with.

I said goodbye to my sixth formers and promised to see them on results day. Strange how close you got to your students over a two year period. You knew something of their innermost thoughts and feelings and at times got close to the essence of what seemed to make them tick. Then suddenly they were gone and the distance loomed up between you all again and there was a real sense of loss.

*

My week in Manchester as a GCE moderator was memorable. It was intensive work but at the same time inspiring beyond belief. My eight brown packages of exam folders from my eight schools had arrived three weeks prior to the meeting. Every evening and most of each weekend were spent poring over the piles of folders, reading the assignments, checking on the schools' standards and making sure the assignments met the examination criteria. There were schools from the London area, from Devon, from Yorkshire, north Wales and the Midlands.

The teachers on the examination panel were equally varied. It was a melting pot of personalities; from the London teachers who were typically cavalier and extravert, to the acerbic wit of the teachers from the north of England. Most of us were lodged in a small hotel in Rusholme, off the Wilmslow Road and each evening we would take to the streets of Manchester to find somewhere to eat, drink and put the world to rights. There was animated debate about the recent election of Margaret Thatcher as prime minister and the direction in which the country was heading. It was all lively and invigorating, like breathing a different kind of air from that in rural Cumbria.

'So it was good then?' asked Sue when she picked me up from Carlisle station.

I looked at the two of them – my little family – Sue blooming in the final stages of her pregnancy, her face glowing and bronzed from the summer sunshine; Katie, all smiles and rosy cheeks and arms outstretched for a cuddle. I nodded, 'Yes, it was great. I learnt a lot.'

'So you'll do it again next year?'

'Definitely. It'll pay for a few more bags of cement.'

'It had better pay for more than that. There's going to be another hungry mouth at the table remember.' She winced and put her hands over her swollen abdomen. 'This one's desperate to get out. Never stops kicking.'

I felt the tiny movements beneath the surface of her dress - mysterious and wondrous. 'How long now?'

'Doctor reckons the end of August.'

'Just gives us enough time to get that wall knocked down in the lounge.'

'I thought you might say that. Are you sure you know what you're doing?'

'Silly question. Of course not.'

*

OF GIRDERS AND GOOFBALLS

One thing I did know was that I needed to buy three girders to support the ceiling where the dividing wall was to be removed. If it wasn't done properly we might one day find some poor visitor perched on the loo and falling through the floor of the bathroom to join us in the lounge below.

New girders or 'RSJs' as they were known in the trade were expensive so I was on the hunt for second hand ones. The only place to go was Dalton's Mart in Botchergate. It was a classic Carlisle institution where, at the Friday afternoon auction, building materials of all kinds would be sold and where on a Saturday morning there was an indoor auction selling household goods. I had been keeping an eye on Dalton's auction yard each week. You could inspect the things during the week and just before the end of term I spotted exactly what I needed – RSJs of pretty much the right dimensions for spanning the lounge.

Roger agreed to cover my classes for the Friday afternoon and around noon I set off for the auction which started at one o'clock. I had never attended an auction before but I knew that you had to play a canny game of keeping your cards close to your chest. I watched the others in the yard, mostly old farming types in flat caps who were hunting around the machinery, stacks of bricks, wooden planks and steel sheeting. Not wanting to give away that I was a real hick in the world of auctions, I wore my old waxed jacket and wandered around trying to look knowledgeable, inspecting a pile of planks here and a mound of old field drains there. I kept an eagle eye on my girders watching to see if anyone took a particular interest in them. So far so good.

At one o'clock a small man with a clipboard and something which looked like a rubber cosh came out of the office and took up a position at the far end of the yard. This was Mr Dalton, the auctioneer. The gaggle of around twenty punters gathered in a group around him. I stood at the back to watch the proceedings. My girders were half way down the yard so it would be a while before we got to them by which time I should have picked up a few tips on how the whole thing operated.

'Right gentlemen; Lot number one – twelve rolls of chicken wire and six fence posts. Anyone like to start the bidding.'

There was a bit of shuffling and coughing but nobody spoke.

'C'mon gents, we've a lot to get through this afternoon. Now, anyone like to offer a couple of quid for this lot.'

There was a grunt and a slight nod from one flat cap.

'Right we have two pounds.'

Another grunt.

'Three, any advance on three?'

A nod and a hand slightly raised.

'Four, I'm bid four pounds. Do I see five? C'mon gentlemen, dig deep now. Four pounds. Any advance?' He glanced quickly round the group. 'No? Then selling for four pounds; going once, going twice, going three times for four pounds.' And with that he thumped his clip board with the black rubber cosh.

We proceeded down the yard towards my girders. I reckoned I'd got it sussed now. Don't bid too early. Keep cool. Don't let on you're too keen. Even so I could feel the nerves beginning to tingle as we moved ever closer.

Finally, the auctioneer climbed on top of a pile of corrugated iron sheeting and stood looking down at my three girders. This was it.

'Right gentlemen, Lot twenty three, always in big demand. Anyone like to start us off?'

I waited, watched and saw an old flat cap to my right nod and hold up his hand.

'Right we have five pounds.'

A grey haired fellow in the middle of the group nodded.

'And seven pounds.'

I waited, cards close to my chest. Powder dry. Keeping cool.

'Eight pounds.'

A nod from grey hair.

'Ten pounds.'

I needed to enter the fray. I caught the auctioneer's eye, nodded and mouthed 'Twelve'.

'Twelve pounds.'

Heads turned and looked in my direction.

Flat cap continued bidding.

'Fourteen pounds.'

I held up one finger.

'Fifteen pounds.'

I saw grey hair shake his head.

Flat cap nodded.

'Sixteen pounds.'

Right, I thought, let's increase the pace a little. I mouthed 'Twenty'.

The auctioneer's eyebrows lifted a little. 'Twenty pounds I'm bid.'

I saw flat cap shake his head.

'Are we done gentlemen. Do I hear any advance on twenty pounds?'

I waited. There was no response. I was home and dry. I'd done it.

'Lot twenty three, sixteen sheets of corrugated iron going for twenty pounds...'

'Wait a minute,' I stammered. 'Corrugated iron? I thought we were bidding for these RSJs.'

The auctioneer sighed and shook his head. 'That's Lot twenty four, lad.'

There was a collective muttering and shuffling from the punters. Then flat cap was nominated again as he had the next highest bid. The clip board was 'coshed' and the auctioneer turned to the three RSJs.

But of course, I'd blown it. They knew and so did flat cap who pushed the bidding up and up to my final bid of thirty five pounds. At that point he shook his head and baled out. I was sure he nudged his friend and smiled, the old bugger.

At least I had secured them. Now I was faced with having to transport them home. I had two hours before the yard closed then everything bought had to be removed or you lost it. The girders were a foot too long and Bill had said he would cut them if I could get them to the metalwork department. I'd negotiated with the school office for the use of the 'Green Goddess', the old school bus, for an hour. It had a door at the back and an aisle between the seats where I could lay the girders. Roger joined me when I drove back to the auction yard in the bus; he'd agreed to help lift the girders in.

'How did it go?' he asked.

'Pretty good. Think I got a good deal.'

'Have you been to that type of auction before?'

'No it was my first time.'

'Takes a while to get to know how those old guys operate. They're a wily bunch.'

'Oh it was fine,' I lied. 'I just kept my cards close to my chest and kept them guessing.'

'Quick learner, eh,' smiled Roger.

'Something like that.'

*

ROCK-A-BYE SWEET BABY JAMES

James Taylor's lilting lullaby became the soundtrack to that summer. I brewed pea-pod wine, put the final coats of paint on the study and then prepared to knock down the wall in the lounge. Things were going swimmingly until the morning of August 17th.

6.30a.m. Sue: I'm gushing. My waters broke.

Me: What!

Sue: It's okay. I'm not going to be rushed this time.

Me: What d'you want me to do?

Sue: Run me a bath.

The contractions were coming spasmodically, lasting around thirty seconds. I felt the little mite inside kicking in its strange in-between state – 'of' and 'not of' this world. Its feeble little kicks made me want to weep at its helplessness. Boy or girl? We had no idea.

'And phone the hospital will you, and check on Katie.'

I marvelled at Sue's calmness, at the great mystery of the female body in its fullness. And I felt somehow puny and inconsequential.

7.30a.m. Breakfast. Katie is mopping egg yolk with her 'soldiers' oblivious to the enormity of what's happening. I remember the little wooden trike that we must take to the hospital – a present from the new baby.

9a.m. Contractions coming every ten minutes. Sue, her eyes closed, breathing through them. Me, holding my breath until she opens her eyes again and relaxes. She nods: 'I'm okay. Let's go.'

9.20a.m. I pull in for petrol. Can't believe this happened last time as well. Should have filled up yesterday. The cashier tells me to hold on while she tots up the pump figures. She smiles and mutters about the weather and the boss who keeps an eye on her and how it's awful for people on holiday and look at the rain and how the figures won't balance. And all the time I'm burning to shout at her: 'BUT I'M GOING TO HAVE A CHILD AND WE'RE ON OUR WAY NOW AND THERE'S MY WIFE AND ISN'T IT WONDERFUL AND AREN'T FEMALES AMAZING WHAT THEIR BODIES CAN DO AND WILL IT BE A BOY OR A GIRL AND ISN'T IT EXCITING AND TERRIFYING!'

But I just wait and watch her broad back bent over her cash book and say nothing as my fingers beat rapidly on the counter.

9.30a.m. We arrive at our friend Helen's house to drop Katie. I feel a terrible sense of betrayal as Katie's bright eyes look questioningly at us as Sue tells her that we have to go to see the doctor.

'Katie come doctor,' she says, her eyes filling.

'No, just mummy and daddy.'

'Katie, please!' tears welling up.

Helen takes her and distracts her with her own children's toys as we sidle out.

9.45a.m. We arrive at the hospital. Sue is positively blooming, hair sleek and shining, face slightly flushed, eyes bright. She's so much in control with this one. As for me I'm as lost and useless as ever.

9.50a.m. A staff nurse takes her into the inner sanctum of the Labour Ward. The doors close and I am given a seat in the corridor. I settle down with my bag containing camera, sandwiches, flask, magazine, an anthology of poetry, a novel and at the bottom the leaflet *Instructions for Expectant Fathers.* I am prepared for a long wait.

There is the distant rumble of a trolley and around the corner a pink-coated coffee lady arrives. She smiles and pours me a cup of weak warm coffee. 'First time?' she asks.

'Second,' I reply.

She nods, 'You'll be fine.'

I fidget, sip the coffee, check the decor of the corridor, the pale green walls, the shiny red lino flecked with white streaks, the noticeboard with its faded picture of a smiling mother and baby. Mothers in dressing gowns waddle haltingly along to the television room.

There is the muted sound of a baby's cry, the slamming of doors, footsteps along passageways, a telephone ringing and the smell of disinfectant. A toilet flushes, a tap is run. A door opens and a doctor in a white coat goes up the corridor.

I finger the leaflet which I have read many times before. I remember my role of distraction at the transition phase, to stop Sue pushing. Eye contact. And we're using the same song we used with Katie – *Show Me the Way to Go Home*, despite the withering looks from the midwife last time; it worked then and it'll work again.

10.50a.m. A door opens and a nurse beckons me into the Delivery Room. I expect to see Sue in bed but she's sitting on a chair, hands on her hips. Her eyes closed with each contraction. They're coming every two minutes now. She grips my hand, lips pursed, eyes bright. I feel the kicking again. Not long now, little one.

11.20a.m. The midwife places pink and blue labels and wrist tags on a table beside the bed. The great question – boy or girl? I don't care as long as Sue is okay and the baby's healthy.

11.30a.m. A breezy trainee doctor comes in all smiles and all knowledge. 'Good morning. Everything looking good is it?' The midwife raises her eyebrows just a fraction and replies, 'Fine doctor. Not long now.'

11.45a.m. Stronger contractions. Sue panting her way through them, eyes closed, eyebrows twitching with the pain of it, her hand gripping mine. Then she relaxes, smiles at me, nods, 'It's okay. It's going to be okay.'

12.00. Sue moves on to the bed, sitting up, gets comfortable. Waits for the next one. I check my bag and my camera. With Katie's birth the camera jammed and we ended up with some strange blurred photographs. This time I have to get it right. No second chances.

12.45p.m. A nurse wheels in a trolley. Sue panting and grunting 'Out, out!' and it's every minute now and I'm sure it's now that I have to keep her focused. But she shakes her head, 'I'm okay,' she murmurs breathing hard. 'I'm okay, this one's not hanging around.' Her face contorts with the next contraction.

1.07p.m And finally…a small patch of the dark head visible… another contraction and within seconds the head of dark hair and the little glistening body slithering out and the nurse holding the baby up by its little legs, the twisted umbilical chord, a tiny penis, the purple scrotum like a ripe plum. We have a son! Sweet baby James. I point the camera. The shutter clicks. I turn the winder. Camera jammed again.

'We don't need pictures,' gasps Sue. 'Just look at him. Isn't he wonderful.'

*

Half an hour later I left the hospital and went to collect Katie. When we got back to the ward I sat her on the bed next to Sue. 'This is James, our new baby, your new little brother.'

Katie looked at the little bundle with the mop of black hair. She stretched out a finger and touched his head then looked at us and then looked back at the baby.

'And he's brought you a present. It's under the bed.'

She climbed off the bed and found the wooden trundle bike. Little brother was instantly forgotten as she propelled herself up and down the ward.

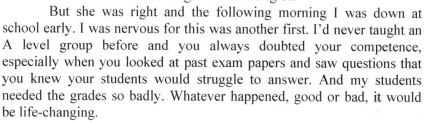

'What a day,' I said.

Sue nodded, 'And we have a son.'

I picked up the sleeping bundle. His eyes were closed and I watched for the tiny flutter of his breathing, marvelling at the miracle of it all.

'Isn't it results day tomorrow?' said Sue.

'How on earth did you remember that? It's the last thing I was thinking of.'

But she was right and the following morning I was down at school early. I was nervous for this was another first. I'd never taught an A level group before and you always doubted your competence, especially when you looked at past exam papers and saw questions that you knew your students would struggle to answer. And my students needed the grades so badly. Whatever happened, good or bad, it would be life-changing.

I saw Roger and the Deputy Head in the office poring over a table covered in papers. It was with Roger that I had shared the teaching of the Literature group so I comforted myself with the fleeting thought that I was only fifty percent responsible for their results.

Roger looked up. I tried to read his face. Then he nodded and raised his eyebrows, 'We did well. Great results.'

I scanned the list of names. There was a range of marks and in some ways it wasn't Stacey's and Kiera's A grades and Mark's B that I was most pleased with, but rather it was Michael Davidson's D grade. He had struggled for the two years of the course and I had never been confident that he would pass. He had talked of dropping out but I had coaxed and cajoled and worked to boost his confidence. He needed three pass grades to follow the college course he had chosen so his D was fine.

When the students arrived at the school an hour later, there were tears of joy for some and tears of angst for others. Michael was delighted. He caught my eye, nodded and waved his results paper. 'Didn't think I'd get it, sir.'

'But you did. Well done. So where are you off to?'

'Manchester. Accountancy.'

'Brilliant,' I said.

'See you, sir. And thanks.'

As for me, I breathed a huge sigh of relief. I felt I had finally come of age. I had taught A level English to A grade standard and I had a newly born son.

So play your song again Mr Taylor. Let's hear it for Sweet Baby James.

*

At a staff meeting in the spring of 1980 the Deputy Head made an announcement. 'We have a new problem. A number of fourth year boys are regularly truanting in the afternoon. It seems they're being lured by a new craze called 'Space Invaders'. Apparently it's what they call a video game. In Japan they say it's like a drug craze and psychologists are heralding the end of civilisation as we know it.'

There was a bubble of laughter at this comment. But in a way the psychologists were right. Space Invaders was just the beginning. Computer technology was about to start changing our lives in every way.

My focus that spring was not computers but helping my A level students to prepare for their Communication Studies orals. I didn't know of another A level subject where the student had to stand up in front of an audience and be judged on an oral presentation of her work. You could be an ace academic student in one of the traditional subject but if you couldn't hold your own in a face to face exchange you weren't going to get very far in the real world. Good oral communication was the key and my new A level made it part of the examination.

It was the first time we'd done this and it was nerve-wracking, to say the least. We assembled an audience of around a dozen sixth-formers in the library. They were primed to ask questions and Jean and I had to grade the candidates on the quality of their communication with the audience. We had talked about the importance of eye contact, the use of visual aids, clarity of diction and overall rapport. However the outcomes were surprising.

Some of the more intelligent students were so self–conscious that they gave very nervous stilted presentations. One boy froze in mid-sentence, his face drained of colour and I had to catch him before he fell in a heap on the carpet. Others talked away quite confidently.

The final student was Alison. We waited for her to appear and then one of her friends poked her head round the door. 'I think you'd better come,' she said.

Alison was sitting in the cloakroom outside the sixth form library clutching her prompt cards and shaking with nerves. 'I can't do it.' she said. She was normally so controlled, so organised, so meticulous with her written work and she had done a superb project publicising a local charity. There were cleverly designed leaflets, posters and badges and she had composed a script for a radio commercial and recorded it and here she was, on the morning of her oral, a dithering wreck. If she didn't do the oral we couldn't give her any marks and she would certainly fail to get a pass grade. Her place at Liverpool University to study English Literature would be lost. Much depended on the next half hour.

'I'll take her for a walk outside,' said Jean.

It was fifteen minutes before they reappeared by which time I too was something of a dithering wreck. Jean nodded. 'She'll be okay.'

Alison came into the library, carefully set out her project on a table at the front of the room. She picked up her prompt cards, looked through them and then looked squarely at her audience, breathed deeply and began.

It was brilliantly delivered. I couldn't believe it.

'What did you do to her?' I said to Jean afterwards. 'That was amazing!'

' I told her to become a tree.'

'A tree?'

'It's a sort of yoga technique. You think of your feet as rooted in the ground and then you channel the energy from your head down your body into your 'roots'. It's like earthing electricity.'

'Amazing. And it worked.'

'She was very responsive.'

'Takes a good teacher though.'

Three months later, on results day in August when Alison was smiling and her place at Liverpool was confirmed I remembered that morning when Jean turned her into a tree and rescued her future.

*

ITCHY FEET

What set me thinking was meeting Norman Hamilton at a teachers' meeting the following year. He taught English at the neighbouring Trinity School and he had done a year's teacher exchange in Canada. I'd never heard of the teacher exchange programme.

'You swap everything, apart from your spouse – job, house, car. The exchange teacher does your job over here and you do theirs over there. It's brilliant.'

'And salaries?'

'No, unfortunately you don't swap those and US and Canadian teachers get paid a lot more than we do. But, hey, it's the experience that counts. We had a great time.'

I lodged this idea away at the back of my mind for a while. I hadn't been at St. Aidan's long enough to justify such a change. But maybe in a couple of years time.

*

One break time, Jean put a piece of pink paper in front of me. It was the monthly bulletin of job vacancies.

'There's a job for you. I think you ought to apply.'

I put down my coffee and looked at the sheet. The job she'd circled was: *Head of English. Trinity School.*

I shook my head. 'I don't think I'm ready for something like that. It's a huge job. Anyway I like it here. And what about the A level we started? I can't just abandon it. The Head would go nuts.'

'I'm not going anywhere. I'll carry on with that. It's well established and getting great results and there are other people who could teach it. Don't let that stop you.'

I talked it over with Sue. In some ways it was a logical step and if we weren't going to move house, there was only ever going to be a limited number of opportunities for promotion in the area. But me, a Head of English? That was a difficult one for me to swallow.

If I was honest, though, I had been starting to get itchy feet for some sort of change. The talk in the staff-room was sometimes negative and depressing but then I had to admit, the new decade was tilting in curious ways. Argentina had invaded the Falklands and our illustrious Prime Minister, Margaret Thatcher, had dispatched her Armada to the south Atlantic to quash the invaders. At home there had been race riots in Brixton and Liverpool and I was reminded of the comments of the Priory student, Huey Morrison, when he talked of 'trouble coming to the streets of London'. The unions seemed to spoiling for yet another a fight with the government and all in all things were feeling pretty unsettled. Maybe it was time for a change.

Sue and I mulled over the teacher exchange idea but this new job opportunity at Trinity knocked that idea on the head. We had little spare cash and with inflation running at around nine percent things were not likely to improve quickly. Thinking of the two little faces who now sat at the breakfast table with us I supposed that I ought to think of my responsibilities to them and go for this promotion.

Somewhat half-heartedly I filled in the application form. I went to see the Head to ask for a reference. I imagined he would be far from happy. But I was surprised. He sat in his chair and nodded. 'They need some creativity in that place. You could do a good job there. Of course I'll give you reference.'

I was stunned. He was such a difficult man to fathom. I had fully expected a dose of vitriol yet here he was giving me a veiled compliment.

Two weeks later I received a letter inviting me for an interview.

'I got an interview,' I said to Jean, showing the letter.

'Of course you did, dummy. They're not choosy at that place.'

'Thanks,' I said. 'Still not sure I want it. I went to see Norman Hamilton over there last week. He's applied for it as well. He showed me round. It felt a bit dismal and depressing.'

'You see you've been spoilt by this place,' said Jean.

'I think I have.'

It was true. When I went for the interview and toured the school it so reminded me of the old grammar school I had attended in Birmingham as an eleven year old and which I had loathed. Situated in Aston near the Ansells brewery and the HP Sauce factory it reeked of both. It was a dark, oppressive place stifled with the ghosts of Victorian forbears. And when I toured Trinity, saw the wood-panelled staff-room in the upper school I remembered those old school masters in caps and gowns who wielded canes and a brutal chauvinism. Maybe I was being irrational but this place didn't feel comfortable.

The other four candidates were not particularly remarkable in any way but I knew that a traditional school like Trinity would probably be looking for a Curriculum Vitae which was more conventional than mine. At the main interview I felt distinctly uncomfortable.

'So you started in industry, Mr Day. Why did you leave?' The question came from an older man in a brown tweed suit.

'I found that the work became predicatable, uncreative, unrewarding. And I couldn't get excited about making exhaust pipes for the car industry.'

'Someone has to make them.'

'Of course they do, but it didn't have to be me.'

The whole interview verged on an out of body experience. I was watching myself go through the motions but I wasn't really fully committed. And when the five of us were waiting for the result and the door opened and the older candidate named Nigel was called back to be offered the job, I wasn't surprised.

'So what now?' asked Norman, whom I felt should have got the job as he was such a nice guy. 'Back to the old job or will you keep looking?'

'No, I think I've decided. Your exchange idea sounded tempting. I think I'll look into that.'

'Good luck,' he said.

'Thanks' I said. 'And good luck with your new Head of Department.'

*

LOOKING WESTWARD

'Florida! They've given us Florida.' I stared at the letter. Re-read it.

'What did you say?' said Sue.

'I wrote on the form 'East coast north of the Carolinas or west coast.' And they've given me a school in Miami, Florida. What was the point of asking for preferences?'

'What kind of school?'

'A junior high school called Ponce de Leon Junior High.'

I had applied for the exchange soon after the failed interview at Trinity. My request had been given the go-ahead by the Head and governors and the preliminary application to the Teacher Exchange Bureau had been successful. Now we had been waiting to hear from the exchange bureau about the details.

'Who's the person you'd be exchanging with?'

'Someone called Genevieve Gillen. It says here that if I accept the offer I should write directly to her to introduce myself.'

'So what are we going to do?' said Sue.

'What d'you reckon?'

'Florida would be nice for the children – sunshine, outdoor living. Could be exciting.'

I nodded, but I wasn't sure. Like going to Jamaica, it was a leap in the dark, but then that was just the two of us. With a three and a five year old in tow, it was a different matter.

'What about their schooling?'

Sue shrugged, 'I could always teach them if we're not happy with the local schools It's only a year and it'll be an adventure for them and for us.'

'So you're okay with this?'

'If you are. You're going to be teaching there.'

I nodded. 'Right, Genevieve Gillen. Here we come.'

It was two weeks later that I received a fat yellow envelope stamped on the back with *Genevieve Gillen, 325, Alesio Avenue, Coral Gables, Miami. Fla.*.

'Sounds exotic, doesn't it,' I said. I fingered the US Airmail sticker and the stamp showing some palm trees and a lighthouse.

'Go on, open it. Let's find out more about this lady and where we're going to live,' said Sue.

There was a neatly hand-written letter, some print-outs of book lists and teaching programs, a brochure on Ponce de Leon Junior High School and a booklet on Miami.

That evening when the children were in bed we reviewed more calmly the contents of the envelope.

'I can't believe she covers all this literature in one year. With her ninth grade she covered *Silas Marner, The Good Earth, Great Expectations, Macbeth, Cross Creek* and half a dozen others. How do you do that in a year? Takes me a term to get through one novel.'

'She's been teaching for quite a long time and has grown up children. I reckon she must be in her late forties or early fifties,' said Sue, reading from the information pack. 'No mention of a husband. Looks like she's on her own,' continued Sue. 'She's obviously very excited about the exchange, says it'll be the fulfilment of a life-long ambition to come and work in Europe.'

The following day I showed Jean the letter. 'She sounds like an intriguing person. Could be good for the school to have a bit of cross-cultural input. I'm looking forward to meeting Ms Gillen,' commented Jean. 'When will you meet her?'

'We fly into Washington and there's a meeting at the university. Then the American teachers fly over here and the British teachers go their separate ways.'

211

'What an adventure,' smiled Jean. 'It's going to be interesting for all of us.'

A few weeks before we left I contacted the weekly newspaper, the Cumberland News, told them of our trip and asked if they would be interested in some articles on our experiences in America. John, one of the young sub-editors, was keen on the idea.

'In the grand tradition we could call it *Letter From America*,' he said.

'You better wait to see the quality first,' I said.

'Just send some articles over and we'll see what we can do.'

I told Sue when I got home. 'I have my first commission as a journalist. How about that.'

'Do they pay you?'

'Didn't ask.'

'Fame but no fortune, eh.'

'We'll see.'

CHAPTER THE FIFTH 1983-84 Miami, Florida.

'I WANT TO BE IN AMERICA….la la..'

Two families from opposite sides of the Atlantic have swopped roles for a year

Pictures: LOFTUS BROWN and MIKE SCOTT.

● The Day family (left to right) ... Katie, Sue, Barrie and James.

● The Gillen family (left to right) ... Layton, Glen and Genny.

This is America!

Carlisle teacher Barrie Day and his family are living and working in Florida. In this, his first letter from the States, Barrie describes part of the exciting journey from Cumbria to Coral Gables, near Miami.

Feature writer Jane Loughran meets American Genny Gillen who lives with her two sons at the Day family's Kirkbride home and teaches at St Aidan's School, Carlisle.

TOURISTS, cocooned from reality by the all-embracing

Beyond the campus railings of Washington University, 'America' beckoned. I write the word in inverted commas because in my mind 'America' was not just the name of a country but it was an idea, a myth, a chimera. From the age of four it had tantalised me. My childhood friend, John Rose, had a Welsh grandpa who was a Methodist minister and every year he would go to this place called 'America' to do some preaching. And every year grandpa Lewis would bring back some new treats for John: a new Colt 45 cap gun, a leather holster, a cowboy hat with a wooden toggle, a leather cowboy waistcoat. I always hoped that one year his grandpa might bring me back some cowboy gear but he never did and to my four year old mind 'America' remained a tantalising enigma.

Then came the Sixties: *77 Sunset Strip*, Kennedy, Motown music, Vietnam and so much more via our television screens. And when we had left Jamaica we set foot on American soil and sampled something of its tastes and textures. But it was a fleeting visit. Now we were to live here and maybe we might unmask something of its reality. I gazed at the lights of the city from the window of our room, watched the tail-lights of the cars on the freeway. I couldn't wait to be amongst it all.

But wait I had to. We were to be three days at the university and it would be an important three days. I would meet Genny Gillen, my exchange partner and find out more about her school and her home in Coral Gables. There would be presentations on the American school system and tips on how to survive the year.

Genny was a short woman with thick wavy brown hair; she wore glasses and a rather earnest expression. She explained that grades were all important in the American school system. A student's average score or 'grade-point-average' was the passport to the future; nothing else mattered.

'Barrie, I only have to hold up my grade book and there is instant attention and order in my classes. I don't have to speak. The grade book says it all.'

'These book lists are impressive,' I said. 'You seem to cover so many major works of literature in a single year.'

'That's right, Barrie, we focus on the classics, British and American. American parents are very keen for their children to be immersed in good literature My Principal, Ms Martin, has been very supportive of this exchange and she was telling me that a lot of parents have expressed an interest in having their children taught by a real British English teacher. You'll be faced by some bright students, children of bankers, lawyers, doctors.'

'It's a slightly different demographic in Carlisle,' I said, thinking in particular of the Danny Flemings of this world.

'But teaching is teaching, Barrie, whatever the class, colour, creed, we're there to serve them.'

I was impressed. Here was dedication and an almost missionary zeal.

'And writing, what about children's writing? For us that's a starting point for their work in English,' I said.

'We get to that eventually, but for us a rigorous groundwork in English grammar is the building block for good writing. Then a well crafted paragraph is what I'm after.'

' I see,' I said.

We discussed setting up a pen pal project between our classes and then moved on to discuss domestic issues. She was having the use of our car and we would be using hers. I was looking forward to swanning down Interstate 95 to Florida in some flash limousine.

At the end of the three days we were itching to leave. Sue had attended some of the sessions but for the most part had been entertaining the children at the university crèche.

'Can't wait to get going,' she said. 'Three days stuck here is quite long enough.'

She had met another family, the Jaques, from Shropshire who were also travelling to Florida. Paul would be teaching art at a college in Orlando. He had sent money over to his exchange partner who had bought them a Chevy van. Nikky, his wife, was herding their three small children, Hugh and twins Stella and Eve who were a similar age to ours. We agreed to travel down to Florida together.

On the day of our departure we had a brief final meeting with Genny who handed over her car keys and told me where the car was parked. 'Forgot to tell you, it's a stick shift, not an automatic.'

'Same as mine,' I said.

'The roads are hell in Miami,' she said. 'Crazy Cuban drivers are the worst.'

'Ah well, Cumbrian roads are very quiet. You'll find it quite different.'

'Can't wait,' she said.

We shook hands and as we parted I felt confident that St.Aidan's was going to benefit from the arrival of the formidable Ms Gillen.

*

'This isn't it surely!' exclaimed Sue.

I looked again at the registration plate. 'The Sunshine State' it proclaimed on the number-plate.

' Fraid so,' I said.

'But how are we going to get everything in?'

We were looking at a little brown Vauxhall Chevette. First illusion blown. Not all Americans drive flash limos. We crammed our suitcases into the small boot and then piled bags and other packages in the space between Katie and James. They thought this was all good fun.

'I've got a little den,' said Katie.

'Can I have a den like Katie's?' called out James.

'Don't make it too cosy. It's going to get really hot later,' said Sue.

The previous day the temperature was in the eighties and the humidity was draining. The sooner we got out of the city the better.

We faced a journey of fifteen hundred miles. I hoped this little battered Chevette was up to the challenge. Interstate 95 ran all the way from Washington to Miami. For the first half of the trip, through Virginia and the Carolinas, the interstate was well inland from the coast but from Georgia onwards it hugged the coast. We could divert to the sea if the heat became overwhelming.

First we had to buy a tent. We knew we couldn't afford motels. My salary was pretty meagre and with the exchange rate falling against the dollar, Genny would be sitting pretty on her salary but we would find things tight. We headed off to a shopping mall on the edge of the city and had our first K-MART experience.

It was an emporium the size of a football field crammed with cut-price stuff – everything from lino to ladders and hammers to haemorrhoid relief balm. We bought a small nylon tent, a camping stove, some cooking pots and sleeping bags. This was exciting. It was the adventure we had dreamed about.

From the leafy suburbs of Washington we followed the Jaques family in their green Chevy van south for a hundred miles and camped the first night among the ghosts of Civil War battalions at Bull Run State Park. Bull Run was where the Confederate General Thomas J. Jackson stood his ground against the Unionists in July 1861 and received the nickname 'Stonewall Jackson'. The campground was a camper's delight with rustic benches, barbecue pit, good showers and a play area of rope and timber structures. We erected our new K-Mart tent while Katie and James and the Jaques children went running among the trees searching the campground for signs of Yogi Bear and Booboo.

After we had eaten, we piled more wood into the barbecue-pit, gathered the children round and read to them from Laura Ingalls Wilder's *Little House in The Big Woods*. It was the perfect book for nourishing our pioneering spirit and the sense that our adventure had really begun.

The following day it was into Virginia, via Richmond, the old Confederate capital where the children fed pigeons at the feet of the statue of Edgar Allan Poe. That night we were haunted by the first pioneers on the banks of the James River where in 1607 English settlers established their first permanent settlement on the north-American continent. They called it Jamestown but it barely survived as a settlement. One survivor wrote: *Our men were destroyed with cruell diseases, as Swellins, Flixes, Burning Fevers – but for the most part they died of mere famine.*

By comparison we were a load of pampered softies, complaining of ants in the corn-flakes and the showers not working properly.

Across the wide James River on a paddle-boat car ferry and down into North Carolina, we passed fields of parched corn ruined by drought and barns festooned with bunches of drying tobacco. The heat was building, the car's air conditioner whirred ineffectively against the thickening humidity and when I glanced in the rear-view mirror it was to see two little red faces beaded with sweat.

'Daddy, why did we come here. I want to go home,' moaned Katie.

So we turned off the interstate and headed towards the coast. By late afternoon we were splashing in the Atlantic rollers which crashed on to the sandy shore of South Carolina. There were families fishing from the sun-bleached piers and out at sea the shrimp boats moved slowly down the coast trawling their nets.

We continued on the coast road the following day making for Charleston, home of the famous dance craze and the place where the first shots of the Civil War were fired. Before Charleston however, there was the splendour of Myrtle Beach. Someone described Las Vegas as 'endless orgasm' – Myrtle Beach comes close but never quite makes it. It is a visual cacophony of billboards and buildings: plastic baroque jostling mock rococo; pseudo Georgian elbowing mock Hawaiian; smoked glass and steel nudging Doric column. The neon lights battle with the fluorescent – colour clashes colour – strawberry pink and lime green, turquoise and beige, orange and purple – one's eyes are blitzed with the delicious horror of it all.

To then encounter the benign tranquillity and elegance of old Charleston is to experience what is the essence of Americana; it is the country of sublime and ridiculous extremes. The eastern approach to the city of Charleston is spectacular. US 18 is carried by the amazing Grace Memorial Bridge, an iron cantilever bridge which soars on a gradient of 6% to a height of 150 feet above the Cooper River. At night the tail lights of the cars seem to be climbing into the night sky and hanging on the clouds.

Charleston is embedded in the map of American history. By the spring of 1861 the southern states had broken away from the Union and formed the Confederacy but Fort Sumpter, located on an island at the mouth of Charleston harbour, was held defiantly by a Union garrison. On April 12th Confederate forces under General Pierre Beauregard attacked the fort and thus began the American Civil War, a war which, over the next four years, was to claim the lives of over 600,000 Americans.

The streets of old Charleston are wide and shaded with avenues of oaks. There are faded clapboard houses with rickety wooden staircases, porches with climbing plants, rocking chairs and swing seats. Secluded squares and churchyards are brilliant with oleander, hibiscus and crepe myrtle but for us there is only one destination - an ice-cream parlour. It is James' fourth birthday and he has been promised ice cream. He has had ice cream before, the kind of bald, single vanilla scoop you get in English sea-side resorts. He has never experienced an all-American ice-cream.

As one carries a candlelit birthday cake, so James carried his mountainous 'one-scoop' cone out of the shop, eyes transfixed on this chocolate-chip wonder. Happy Birthday sweet baby James.

Whenever I listen to Randy Crawford singing *A Rainy Night in Georgia* I remember our next night. The drive down I-95 into Georgia had been intensely hot. The radio was reporting the first hurricane of the season moving up through the Gulf of Mexico towards Texas. We camped in a pine-wooded site just south of Savannah. It was well-appointed with swimming pool, playground and spacious pitches. Everything was set for a good evening: the tent was pitched, barbecue lit, food set out, wine glasses catching the glow of the setting sun. Then a warm breeze gusted through the trees and there was a noise like flapping wings in the high branches.

It was not like English rain. This was a prolonged deluge of sheeting, stinging bullets which kept us huddled in the car for half an hour watching helplessly as pizzas were peppered into a milky swill, grapes floated away in the rivulets of water which cascaded off the picnic table and the barbecue coals hissed, steamed and died.

By the time the rain ceased there was little to salvage. It was getting dark, the air was steamy and humid, the mosquitoes were cavorting for a night of riotous blood-letting and so with dampened spirits we zipped ourselves inside our nylon sweat chamber and prepared to endure a long, hot, restless night in Georgia.

In the morning, despite an uncomfortable night of broken sleep, our spirits were high. Today we would cross the border into Florida. Our destination was Daytona Beach just 290 miles from Miami. At each state line there is a Welcome Center offering restrooms and information leaflets. But at the Florida state line there was a difference. Here they gave away free Florida fruit juice, just what we needed with the temperature at 95 degrees and Katie and James squirming among the clutter of bags on the back seat.

We arrived at Daytona Beach early the following morning. It is a 23 mile beach of hard, flat sand where Sir Malcolm Campbell and others set successive automobile speed records on the 'measured mile'. Today, as on most days, the cars are lined along the beach a few yards from the water's edge. There is something dubiously decadent about driving on to a beach, parking within a yard of where the waves are lapping and then tumbling from your car into the surf. But this is what you do on Daytona Beach. And beyond the cars there were bronzed surf kids on fat tyred beach motor bikes, senior citizens pedalling tandems, planes overhead trailing advertising streamers, mothers and children flying kites and along the edge of sea the auto-sun-worshippers spread-eagled beside their low slung, twin-carb, turbo-assisted, tinted-windowed, wide-wheeled, fast-back furlined motors. Another slice of Americana.

We said goodbye to the Jaques family in Orlando and continued south towards Miami joining the Florida Turnpike with ninety miles to go. When we had told friends in England we would be living in Miami they were horrified. News about Miami was only ever about riots, shootings and drug-trafficking. I had told myself this had to be a case of media distortion but when I pulled in for petrol just south of Orlando and mentioned where we were heading, the girl behind the counter joked, 'Look out for the bullets flying.'

We passed signs to Palm Beach, Delray Beach, Boca Raton on what is called the Sunshine Parkway. The road is attractively lined with windbreaks of tall feathery casuarinas pines and low hedges of yellow hibiscus. Canals run by the roadside; the water is clear and patched with water hyacinths. People are fishing wherever there is a stretch of water – from bridges, from boat docks, from the backs of pick-ups – fishing seems to be one of the American obsessions.

Soon we see the skyline etched with high-rise blocks; hotels and offices, white against the blue sky and catching the afternoon sun. A green sign overhead says 'Miami - One Mile'. The freeway is eight lanes in each direction elevated on concrete pillars high above the Miami suburbs. The engine of Genevieve's trusty Chevette is huffing a little, and we are overtaken by the hiss of tyres from cars with darkened windows and faceless occupants. Will it be arid, sun-drenched streets and gunfights at noon? I'm not sure. But there's no going back now.

*

OF DONUTS AND DANGLING PARTICIPLES

On either side of the main entrance to Coral Gables Senior High School stood two senior students in green and white cheer–leading uniforms: girls who exuded that American sparkle of confidence – bright eyes, bright smiles and holding out a big rosy apple in one hand and a donut in the other.

'Hi,' they beamed, handing me an apple and a donut. 'There you go. Have a nice day.'

'Thanks,' I said.

How nice. How unexpected. This friendly gesture went some way to allay my feelings of nervousness. I was attending a pre-term training day for Dade County teachers and it would be my first encounter with the American teaching profession. I followed the throng of other teachers into the main auditorium. There were hundreds there bubbling with excited chatter and clutching files and bundles of papers. I scanned the sheet I had been given which outlined the programme for the day. There would be an opening presentation by the Superintendent of Dade County Schools followed by a choice of training sessions. I scanned the sessions on offer for 'Language Arts', the name they gave to English, and circled a session entitled 'Advanced Writing Skills' to be presented by a Professor Laurie Smithberger and another on Advanced Placement Literature by Jenny Krugman, the Head of English at Coral Gables Senior High. My school, Ponce De Leon Junior High, fed into this school so I thought I ought to get a feel of what the students would face when they were seniors.

The auditorium quietened as the Superintendent of Schools mounted the rostrum. Everybody stood up and I saw people placing their right hands over their chests. Then came a voice over the PA system leading the Pledge of Allegiance. I wasn't sure what to do.

'*I pledge allegiance to the flag of the United States of America and to the Republic for which it stands, one nation under God, indivisible with liberty and justice for all.*'

I seemed to be the only one not speaking and with his hands by his sides. It was the first time I had witnessed this pledge of patriotism and it was quite impressive. We sat down and then listened to the Superintendent exhorting us to 'raise our game, meet the challenges of the new year, raise the profile of Florida in the eyes of the nation, and to remember our young men and women doing service overseas'. After the presentations were over, we filed out to locate our different training sessions.

There were more donuts and coffee on tap, and helpful people with name badges and stickers indicating *I'm Here To Help. Just Ask Me.*

I found the 'Advanced Writing Skills' session and took a seat at the back. Professor Laurie Smithberger was a lady in her forties, smart tailored dark blue jacket and skirt, immaculate hair and make up, manicured nails.

'What I want to do this morning colleagues is to furnish you with some strategies for writing enhancement which will progress your students to a more advanced writing style. Now, you will all be familiar with the way good writing is predicated on the key role of the topic

220

sentence, a sentence being a grammatically self-contained speech unit consisting of a word or a syntactically related group of words that express an assertion, a question, a wish, a command or an explanation. You will, no doubt, have covered with your students the deconstruction of subject and predicate, you will have confronted the issues of dangling modifiers and the crucial role of the sentence demarcator without which the sentence can itself become dangling. What I intend to do this morning is to move us on to the issue of how we might combine sentences. It is through sentence combination that we move towards the construction of the paragraph.'

Was I in the right session? I wondered. Was Language Arts really the same as English?

A set of papers entitled 'Combining Sentences' was handed round on which there were questions and tick boxes.

The professor continued. 'Now these are the kinds of quiz sheets you might wish to use with your students to assist their understanding of the concept of sentence combination. The sheets are progressive, arranged from simple to complex. Take your time to work through them.'

The first sheet involved choosing whether to use 'and' or 'but' in a sentence such as 'In winter, it is cold ___ wet.' I flicked through to the last sheet. This sheet dealt with the words 'while' and 'during' - *We met___ the holidays*'.

I looked back at the lady professor and then at the three rows of teachers, heads bent over their quiz sheets. What was I was missing here? Was this classed as Advanced Writing Skills? It was all being taken very seriously and yet somehow I was missing the point.

After about fifteen minutes the professor tapped the table top for our attention.

'You will notice colleagues, that in the first example the choice is between the co-ordinating conjunction 'and' and the subordinating conjunction 'but'. Both are types of connectives. An understanding of the way connectives can embellish the topic sentence and introduce the student to the advanced concept of the compound sentence is a crucial aspect of progressing the student towards advanced writing skills.'

Had I misunderstood the fundamentals of what English teaching was about or was this a load of pretentious gobbledygook? I had to think about this. If this was what teaching English to American students was all about I was going to have problems. Back in England I had seen the way children could write brilliantly and it certainly wasn't dependent on knowing about subordinating conjunctions and dangling modifiers.

If the morning session with Prof. Smithberger was somewhat disconcerting, the afternoon session with Ms Jenny Krugman was like a balm of reassurance. There was none of the abrasive pretentiousness of the lady professor. No, Jenny Krugman was at ease with us, with herself and with her subject. A short, slim woman, probably in her early forties, she spoke with a voice which positively purred. And she talked the language I understood; of the transforming power of literature, the way it helped students to hold up a mirror to their own lives and a mirror to society. She glided confidently between references to Shakespeare, Swift, George Eliot, Arthur Miller and Jack Kerouac, and by the end of the session I felt less anxious about the prospect of slotting into the American school system.

'How did it go?' asked Sue.

I found her at the back of the house in the bathroom. She had run a cold bath for the children to try to cool them down. The level of heat and humidity was proving quite a trial.

'Interesting,' I said. 'A little unsettling. One session was with a scary professor lady who was ladling out some indigestible stuff on grammar and then the afternoon session on literature was wonderful. But the highlight of the day was getting a free apple and donut when I arrived.'

'You're easily pleased. We've been on the verge of expiring in this place. I took the children for a walk down the road and got stopped by the police. They asked if everything was okay. Seems people don't walk around here. Everyone drives. They were very courteous but James was a bit thrown by the sight of the officer's gun. And we've met the neighbours on the one side. They have two little girls, Carrie and Kristen, about the same age as ours so that'll be nice. What's next for you?'

'I have to go into the school tomorrow to meet the principal. And there's something called 'Back To School Night' on Thursday.'

'What's that?'

'Not sure. I'll find out tomorrow.'

*

I had to pinch myself as I set off the following morning through the quiet residential streets of Coral Gables. The early morning sun was a delight as were the over-arching clear blue sky and the palm-lined roads; this was a world away from cloud-shrouded England.

Coral Gables had been created in the 1920s by a designer named George Merrick. It was to be a Garden City, one of the nation's first fully-planned communities incorporating both commercial and residential districts and with architecture inspired by the Mediterranean. Hence the low-rise houses, generally single storey, with Spanish and Italianate touches such as terracotta tiled roofs, archways

and fountains, rough stuccoed walls, and landscaped gardens. The wonderful Venetian Pool, an open air swimming venue, was one of the gems of Coral Gables. Landscaped from a former quarry, it later became our place of respite after a tiring day in the heat and humidity.

Genny's house was a modest sized, single storey place with a living room at the front, a small kitchen and bathroom and two bedrooms at the rear of the house. There was a smudge of lawn at the rear and a small grassed area at the front with a poinciana tree shading the porch.

I navigated my way through this very pleasant neighbourhood before emerging on to a busy six-lane freeway. This was US 1, also known as Dixie Highway. The school was located just on the other side of the freeway. I had an appointment to meet the principal, Ms Martin, at 9.30.

I crossed Dixie Highway and stood on the corner of the street by a Burger King outlet across the road from the school; there were playing fields fronting the school on one side near the highway. I found the main entrance on a side street. It was a campus of low-rise buildings spread around a central area of tree-lined walkways and sitting areas.

'Can I help you? You look a little lost.' The voice came from across the car park. A young man in smartly pressed brown slacks and a cream polo shirt had just emerged from his car. He was tall and slim with a thick moustache and short brown hair. He smiled and then pointed a finger at me, 'Hey, you wouldn't be the British guy who's joining us would you? You look kinda, you know, English.'

'That's me,' I nodded. 'Barrie Day.'

He held out his hand, 'Kalinsky. I'm the Assistant Principal in charge of curriculum. Welcome to Ponce.'

'Thanks,' I said.

I had to get used to the name 'Ponce' without smiling. At home it had the English connotations of effeminacy, over here just the opposite. Ponce de Leon was one of the intrepid Spanish conquistadores who explored the Americas in the early 16th century.

'You'll be in to see Ms Martin, right? And then I'll give you a tour of the place. C'mon, I'll take you in.'

I followed him up the steps of the main entrance. It was quite an old building, painted cream, the frontage a line of square pillars supporting the canopy of the roof. Facing the main entrance was a pathway lined with small palm trees leading to another teaching block; on each side of the path were grassy sitting areas shaded by the broad spreading branches of oak and casuarina trees.

Like all those films set in American high schools, this was just the same. There was the reception counter and behind that, through a glass panel, the offices of the administrators. Kalinsky knocked on the principal's door and I was shown into a wood panelled office. There were framed certificates on the walls. The principal, Ms Martin, sat very upright behind her desk. Even though term had not started she was dressed smartly in a pale green dress and jacket. She was a woman in her early forties, dark hair carefully styled, small gold earrings, gold necklace. She stood up as we entered and extended her hand. She had a quick smile and piercing brown eyes which locked on to mine. Her hand shake was firm.

'Welcome to Ponce, Mr Day. Thank you, Mr Kalinsky, I'll give you a call when we're through.'

The Ponce Galleon

I noted the formality. No first names. Interesting.

'Take a seat, Mr Day. I have to say your arrival has been eagerly anticipated.'

'Really?'

'Oh yes. The students are excited. The parents are anxious to meet you. It's a big deal, you know, swapping teachers. Something of a gamble in a way. Genny Gillen is one of our most experienced teachers and she was keen to do this exchange. So we supported it and, I have to say that the idea of us having in return a British teacher of English is something of a coup for the school.'

'But still a gamble,' I said.

She smiled and nodded, 'But still a gamble. It's quite a challenge for you, but I sense that you're up to meeting the challenge.'

'I hope so.'

This was one formidable lady.

She continued, 'It may surprise you but despite our two hundred years of independence, we still revere the English in all sorts of ways. I have been inundated by requests from parents for their children to be taught by you. And we're talking here of some high-powered people – doctors, lawyers, businessmen. They're keen for their children to have the experience of a British teacher of English.'

'Wow,' I said, 'that is quite a responsibility.'

'It certainly is. And so you have a teaching schedule which most American teachers would die for. You have all honors classes.'

'Honors classes?'

'The best and the brightest, Mr Day. Most teachers would perhaps get a couple of honors classes alongside classes of weaker students. But you have been given all honors classes; bright, challenging young people. You'll find them interesting.'

She picked up a pair of glasses and scanned some sheets of paper on her desk, then placed the glasses back on the desk and looked up again.

'Oh yes, there's something else I have to put to you. We're in need of a soccer coach. Our previous coach left unexpectedly over the summer and I am wondering whether someone from the country who gave birth to the game would step into the position of soccer coach for the year.'

This was totally unexpected. Me coaching football? I had played all through my schooling and at university but that was twelve years ago. And playing was not the same as coaching a team. I vaguely knew the basic rules but the finer points of refereeing were distinctly hazy.

The voice continued while my thoughts gambolled around.

'You would be paid on an American teacher's rates and it would involve coaching both the boys' and the girls' teams. Ponce has a great reputation at soccer. We've been in the finals of the local schools championships for the past three years.'

Did she say girls' team? I'd never seen girls play football. In 1983 it was unheard of in England. I smiled to myself at the rather ridiculous image of girls running round kicking a football. But the idea of extra money to supplement our limited budget was certainly attractive.

'So do you need time to think about this Mr Day or can you give me a decision now?'

I hesitated for a moment and then said, 'I have to be honest, Ms Martin, I've never coached football before. I've played since I was a child but I've never coached a team. But if I can help out, I'll give it a go.'

'No it's not football coaching, we have a football coach; it's the soccer team I'm speaking of.'

'I'm sorry, we use the word 'football' for what you call 'soccer'. Don't worry, we are talking about the same sport.'

She nodded, 'I see. So that's a yes then. Wonderful. I hope you're going to be happy at the school. I'll call Mr Kalinsky and get him to show you around. Do you have anything you wish to ask me at this stage?'

I shook my head, 'I don't think so.'

And that concluded my first meeting with my new principal. Quite a woman.

Kalinsky collected me and took me round the school. In nearly every classroom there was a buzz of activity: teachers pinning up displays and clearing cupboards, student helpers carrying piles of books.

'It's busy,' I said.

'It's always like this the week before a new academic year. Everyone likes to be organised,' replied Kalinsky.

He showed me my 'home' room where I'd teach all my lessons. It was at the end of a long corridor and was a large airy room with windows filling one wall. The first thing I noticed was the American flag hanging from a small flagpole at the side of the black board. It was the same in every room I had passed. Patriotism was certainly high profile here.

'Can I see the types of books I'll be using?'

'Ah, your buddy, Ms Matheson, she's the Head of Language Arts, she'll be in later this morning to show you the books. That's not my brief. Not sure what they use in English.'

We'd been told of the American 'buddy' system at the briefing in Washington. It was like having a mentor.

Later that morning I met my new 'buddy' over a donut and coffee in the staff room. She was a tall, slim lady, late thirties maybe, coiffured and manicured like the principal but rather tight-lipped and distant. Not much eye contact with this one and not much conversation either. I followed her to the book room. There were piles of brand new books stacked on the floor and on tables.

'These are your books for ninth grade and those are for your eighth grade classes.' She looked up briefly and then back at a sheet of paper she'd taken from her brief-case. 'I notice you've been given all honors classes. That's most unusual, Mr Day. You're very privileged.'

I wasn't sure what that meant but I sensed the lady was not entirely happy. She didn't ask me any questions or volunteer much information. Seemingly my 'buddy' was not overly enthusiastic about my arrival.

I trundled my allocation of books down to my room on a trolley and started unpacking them. There was a basic course book for each year group supplemented by the types of literature anthologies I had used in Jamaica. The anthologies looked superb, the course books decidedly underwhelming – no eye-catching material, just a sequence of chapters on aspects of grammar.

I had brought maps and photographs of Britain and Cumbria for a wall display and I spent the rest of the morning starting to get my room organised. As in Jamaica, there were no separate desks and chairs, just the two combined into a chair with a small table top attached. There was a chalk board behind the teacher's desk but no audio-visual equipment that I could see. Next to the American flag at the side of the chalk board was a framed copy of the Pledge of Allegiance in gold italicized print.

Kalinsky had given me a folder of information. I found my timetable. There was an even mix of eighth and ninth grade classes. It was a six period day, four periods before lunch, two afterwards with half an hour for lunch. But then I noticed something. Every day was the same. Surely they'd got it wrong. I checked with Kalinsky later in the day

He nodded. 'That's correct,' he said. 'Each day's the same. No confusion.'

'So I see the same classes at the same time of day, every day?'

'You got it. Don't they do it like that in England?'

'No. Each day is different. It has to be to get all the subjects timetabled.'

He frowned. 'Don't your students find it confusing?'

'No, why should they?'

He shrugged, 'Never heard of anything like that before. We've always done it like this.'

'So students only take six subjects?'

'That's right. But they're planning to add an extra hour next year so that students can take another subject. Why, how many do they take in England?'

'Maybe ten or more.'

'Ten subjects?'

'That's normal.'

The prospect of teaching the same classes at the end of the day, every day, appalled me. It was so patently unfair on the students and on the teacher. No teacher is as fresh and energetic at the end of the day as at the beginning. The system was crazy.

My next hurdle that week before the term started was 'Back To School Night' - another unknown. Parents came into school to meet their children's teachers and find out what each teacher was planning to teach. And of course the teacher got a first taste of what the parents were like.

As the principal had said, the school drew students from many professional families and on the Thursday night in question I found myself standing in front of some very smartly dressed parents. I noticed a mix of races – a predominance of white, but also Chinese, Cuban and a few black couples. They took their places sitting at the desks, some had notepads and one man in a  smart beige suit had a dictaphone which he placed on the desk-top.

I smiled, greeted them and then outlined my teaching background, and then my ideas on education. I stressed the value of literature and of writing; the value of discussion and debate. They were very attentive and nodded at my comments.

One father, smartly dressed in a white open-necked shirt, black hair neatly combed back and with a darkly tanned face raised his hand. 'Jonathan Gonzalez, father of Joseph, Mr Day. I have to say we are delighted to have a British teacher teaching English to our children. It's a rare privilege for them. But would you say the British and the American ways of teaching English are similar.'

I thanked him for his compliment and avoided mentioning my reservations about the apparent preoccupation with grammar teaching. He seemed reassured when I said I'd taught American students in Jamaica. There was a general nodding from other parents.

'Obviously Mr Gonzalez, I haven't met the students yet but I shall be assessing their abilities in the first few weeks. If I have any concerns about their progress, I won't hesitate to contact their parents.'

He nodded, 'Thank you, Mr Day.'

Another hand was raised; a woman with short blonde hair and a pale peach-coloured top. 'Margaret Hess, mother of Katherine, Mr Day, my daughter has hopes of being a journalist but I have to say she was pretty bored last year with all the grammar exercises they had to do. She didn't do a lot of writing. What is your view of the place of grammar?'

Interesting. Someone on my wavelength.

'It's one of the tools of good writing, Mrs Hess, but it's only a tool. The desire to write is in children from a young age and it's this desire which must be nurtured and not stifled by a preoccupation with clause analysis and parsing sentences. That can be a real turn off for budding writers.'

A slight raising of the eyebrows and a nod.

Another hand from a very straight-backed coiffured lady in a plum coloured dress. 'But you're not saying grammar is unimportant then? Oh, I'm sorry Mr Day, I'm Beatrice Johnson, mother of J.J.. I mean correctness and accuracy are key components of good communication.'

I nodded. 'Of course, Mrs Johnson but appropriateness of style and tone are equally important. You have to think of your audience in any communication.'

She nodded, a slight frown playing around her forehead.

I ducked and dived, ladled out what I hoped was some old fashioned British courtesy and by the end there were some smiles and nodding alongside some more impassive faces.

They filed out, and the last to leave was a small woman whose face was framed by a mass of shiny black hair. She was clearly a little nervous. 'I just wanted to say, Mr Day, that my daughter, Shannon Martell, and her friends are so excited about you coming to Ponce. You've no idea.'

'Well that's great, Mrs Martell. I'll try to do a good job. Thank you.'

'So how did you get on?' asked Sue when I arrived home.

'Hard to tell. They were very attentive, asked some questions. Seemed pretty sharp, very polite but hard to tell what they were really thinking. I'll have to be on my toes.'

From the back of the house came a plaintive little voice, 'Daddy, here, daddy.'

I went to the back bedroom where the children were supposed to be fast asleep. They were wide awake. Two glowing faces with bright eyes looked up from the pillows.

'It's too hot. We can't sleep and James keeps fidgeting and wriggling,' said Katie.

'Can we go out in the canoe?' asked James.

229

'We don't have a canoe.'

'Yes, we do,' said Katie. 'We found one down the side of the garage.'

'What kind of canoe?'

'A red one and there are paddles.'

Then I remembered. Genny had said something about a canoe.

'We'll take a look in the morning.' I said. 'Now you two need to get to sleep.'

'Read us a bit more of the story,' said Katie.

They were utterly absorbed by *Little House in the Big Woods* which we had started reading on the drive south from Washington. It was the first in the wonderful series of books by Laura Ingalls Wilder about her growing up in a pioneer family in America of the 1870s.

'Okay, but just one chapter.'

Cue for immediate snuggling down and finger or thumb sucking as I started reading about life in the little log cabin on the edge of the Big Woods of Wisconsin: *It is springtime, the time of tilling the soil and planting. The days are lengthening and at night after another day of adventure in the Big Woods the three little girls Mary, Carrie and Laura drift into sleep to the sound of Pa's fiddle playing.*

Before I had finished the chapter, two pairs of eyes were closed and their little faces were flushed and puckered. I left the room and returned to where Sue was reading.

'I think I found a school for Katie,' she said. 'I met Mary our next door neighbour. She has two little girls, Carrie and Kristen about the same age as our two. She's going to show me their school tomorrow.'

'That's great, and what about James?'

'He's too young for first grade so we'll have to find a pre-school group.'

'He tells me we're going canoeing.'

'Oh really? You're not getting me in a canoe if we're liable to encounter alligators.'

'Who said anything about alligators?'

She thrust the evening copy of the *Miami Herald* in front of me. 'Just read that.' She pointed to a column headlined 'Alligator in the Alley'. 'Some man encountered an alligator in his garage, not a million miles from here. So think again. You can paddle your own canoe.'

*

Energy, excitement and enthusiasm – I remember the start of that first term so clearly. It was all bounce and vigour. The corridors or 'halls' as they called them, buzzed with excited youngsters pinning up posters and banners for the student council elections. Hustings were held at lunch time where candidates for the student council pitched their campaigns to the gaggles of onlookers who munched on burgers and slurped from cans of Pepsi. So many of these fourteen and fifteen year olds brimmed with a confidence and verve that I'd rarely seen in school back home. They were not afraid to pick up a microphone and hold forth on what they believed in. No-one sneered. There was no cynicism. Everyone took this seriously.

Apart from me. I hovered on the margins like some visiting extra-terrestrial. It was all so blindingly different. For the first two weeks I was faced with classes of forty eight! Forty eight bright-eyed, quick-witted, often precocious teenagers. This was because the staffing ratio in Dade County wasn't finally established until three weeks into the term. Only then would they know how many students were intending to join the school. Only then would they know how many teachers they needed. Teachers were employed by the county not directly by the school. If more teachers were needed, the county pool would supply them. That was the system.

I flew by the seat of my pants. I arranged the four rows of desks in a semi-circle and for many lessons I sat on a high stool in front of them and orchestrated the lessons like someone doing a cabaret act. This was not conventional teaching. I was constantly tripped up by the old adage – 'two countries separated by a common language'. Simple instructions backfired on me. Attempts to exert authority erupted in my face. In one encounter a student lobbed a ball of paper at his neighbour.

'Pick that up and put it in the waste-paper basket!' I said sternly.

He looked at me, looked at his neighbour, frowned, shrugged and along with half the class, erupted into sniggering.

What to do? Get angry at this insubordination or sort out what was going on?

I quickly learnt that things like 'rubbish' and 'waste-paper baskets' don't exist in America. Here it was 'trash' and 'trash cans' but getting my tongue round these unfamiliar words felt somewhat contrived and something of a betrayal of my avowed role as ambassador for the Queen's English. Clearly the English accent was held in high esteem and that gave me a head start in the kudos stakes but if the students didn't understand what I was talking about we had a problem. It was no good telling students to 'form a queue' - the word 'queue' doesn't exist in American lingo. Rather it's 'get in line'. A sentence doesn't end with a full-stop but a 'period'. They don't have 'canteens' but 'cafeterias' and when you're ordering food if you ask for 'chips' you'll get crisps – chips are 'fries'; biscuits are 'cookies'. If you ask for jelly you'll be given jam – if you want jelly, ask for 'jello'. And so on.

But nothing compared with my first fumblings as the newly appointed soccer coach. I designed some posters advertising 'Soccer Tryouts' scheduled for the second week of term. When I went to the office for drawing pins I was again greeted with frowns and blank looks. 'Oh you mean thumb tacks,' exclaimed one of the office staff when I described what I was after.

I nodded, 'For pinning up the football..., I mean soccer posters.' I had to remember that over here football was soccer and to them football meant American football. I was not a 'football' coach but a 'soccer' coach.

I had heard that, to an extent, sport defined itself on racial lines. Typically, soccer was popular with white and Cuban students but few blacks played. Basketball, American football and volleyball were more popular with black students. Swimming was dominated mainly by white students. So I wasn't surprised when, for the soccer tryouts. there were few black faces coming out of the changing rooms. What I was surprised by were the numbers. I'd expected a dozen or so as you'd get in England. But on the afternoon of the boys' tryout around forty boys appeared.

I blew my whistle. 'Right lads, line up at the end of the pitch and we'll start with some running.'

No-one moved.

I tried again. Maybe they weren't 'lads.'

'Okay guys, I want you to line up at the end of the pitch and then jog two lengths to get warmed up.'

David, a fair-haired lad whom I recognised from my one of my ninth grade English classes, came across. He'd encountered the language problems before in our lessons.

'They don't understand what you mean, Coach. You said 'pitch.' That's what we do in baseball. Do you want us at the end of the field?'I nodded. 'Yes, that's exactly what I want. Thanks David.'

Attempting to look confident, I tried again. 'C'mon guys, line up at the end of the field and jog two lengths.' I blew the whistle. Instant response. The line of soccer hopefuls set off down the length of the 'field' (note to self: must remember a 'pitch' is what you do with the ball in baseball).

I started with some warm-ups and some dribbling in and out of a line of cones. Then followed some shots at goal and finally some short games of eight-a-side.

Some of the boys had arrived wearing trainers. 'You need boots, boys, trainers are no good.' They looked at me with blank stares, looked at each other and I read the familiar frowns. 'Boots, on your feet boys, you can't play in trainers.'

David came to my rescue again. 'What d'you mean by 'boots', Coach?'

'Those things on your feet, football boots... I mean soccer boots.'

'Cleats, Coach, they're called cleats.'

The boys looked at each other; I saw raised eyebrows.

'Sorry, guys, there's a slight language problem here. In England, we use different terms. Over there we call these things soccer boots. But I get it, over here they're cleats. So let me start again; you can't play unless you're wearing cleats.'

This was turning into a real trial for me. But then, when the games started, things settled down a little. Several of the boys had played in the team the previous season and it wasn't difficult to start to make a rough selection for the roster. They were keen and talented; the defensive players were dominated by Carlos, a broad-shouldered, six-foot Cuban and there were some impressive attacking players - George from Texas and Patricio, another Cuban, who was something of a tearaway on the wing.

David helped me identify names of players and I started making some preliminary groupings of 'probables' and 'possibles'. It was not easy, they were all keen to show their skills and not backward in coming forward.

'I played defence last season, Coach.'

'Jimmy was one of our stars last year, Coach.'

'Coach, I played alongside Jimmy last year. He and me are one great combination.'

'See me there, Coach, impressive huh?'

And so it went on. Finally the quiet, towering figure of Carlos stood in front of me. 'When you posting the roster, Coach?'

'In a couple of days, Carlos. There's a lot of talent here.'

'We got to the county finals last year. We could win it this year, Coach,' he added.

These were serious players and the competition to make the squad was intense. Once again it felt like a 'seat of the pants' job. I'd seen American coaches in films and on television. They were hard-nosed, loud and ruthless. I was none of those things. But, heigh-ho, they were paying me to do this so I'd better somehow cultivate a Coach's swagger and bravado.

At the end of the session I sat on the grass for a while after the boys had left and looked over my lists. Across the playing field came the muted roar of rush hour traffic on Dixie Highway. The sun was hot in a cloudless sky and the humidity was still thickening the heat even this late in the afternoon. It was now four-thirty. I'd started teaching at eight o-clock that morning. There was only a break of half an hour for lunch and then back in the classroom until early afternoon when school finished. Then followed the two hour session in my new coaching role. If this was to be the pattern of the day, it was going to be a tough term.

'Just call me Coach,' I said to Sue when I arrived home. I swaggered in emulating a John Wayne walk and leaned on the kitchen worktop.

'And who d'you think you are then?' she said, unimpressed.

'I'm Coach Day, the new hotshot soccer coach at Ponce.'

She smiled and shook her head, 'Well don't start poncing around here, Mr Coach. Go and see to the children. They're in the bath. How did the football session go?'

'It's soccer, not football and they're cleats not boots and it's a field not a pitch and it's trash not rubbish. Boy, did I have a testing time today. You've no idea. And it's the girls tomorrow. Who knows what that'll be like.'

'Hi, daddy,' said Katie; she was squeezing out a sponge of water over James' head in the bath.

'Hi, you two, how was your day?'

James was wiping water out of his eyes, 'We went to the bank and there was....there was.... was...a police man and he showed me his gun, and it was a real....real gun.'

'James was really scared and hid behind mummy,' chimed Katie.

'I was not scared and anyway it was a real gun, so there.'

'How was school today?'

'It was fine,' said Katie, 'but we had to do this thing.'

'What thing?'

'Well you all stand up and you have to put your hand across your chest like this and then you spread your legions.'

'You do what?' I said frowning.

'It's about the flag. There's an American flag hanging at the side of Miss Gonzalez' desk and we all stand up and say this thing, 'I spread my legions to the flag of America' or something like that.' She giggled. 'I just said what the others were saying.'

I suppressed a smile for I realised what she was referring to. I faced the same ritual each morning. At eight-fifteen there would be a chime over the p.a. system and the voice of one of the student monitors would say, 'Please rise for the Pledge of Allegiance.' We would all stand, the students would turn towards the American flag which hung at the side of the blackboard behind my desk, and with hand on heart recite the Pledge of Allegiance. 'I pledge my allegiance to the flag of the United States of America.......'

The first morning I caused some consternation in my home room class when I didn't face the flag and didn't join in.

'You didn't do the Pledge, Mr Day,' commented Jocelyn.

'No, that's right, Jocelyn. I don't have any loyalty to your flag.'

The students were clearly shocked with my reply. They had never met anyone who didn't show allegiance to the American flag.

'Would you do the Pledge if it was a British flag?'

I shook my head. 'No, we don't have a Pledge of Allegiance. We're not as patriotic as you are.'

'Why not?'

'Good question. Our history is different. America is a young country. You fought for your independence. We never did. Maybe that's the difference.'

And now here was Katie trying to 'spread her legions.'

'Not sure you got it quite right, Kate. When you're out of the bath I'll explain about it.'

'Can you read more story?' asked James.

'Where did we get to?'

Katie cut in quickly before James had a chance: 'Pa was teaching Laura how to milk a cow and Ma said you do it from the right side and then they all had a drink of the delicious, warm milk.'

'Is that what it said?'

Katie grinned, 'I remember it said about the delicious warm milk.'

'Right then, a bit more story and then bed.'

'I had homework today,' said Katie.

'Really, what was it?'

'Oh nothing much, just a sheet I had to fill in. It was easy. And we played with the girls next door, Kristen and Carrie.'

'So you had a good day.'

'And we had a milk-shake at Burger King,' added James.

'Sound like a pretty good day to me,' I said. 'Right, let's get on with the story.

When I returned to Sue after settling the children, she held up a sheet of paper. 'What d'you reckon to this? Katie's homework.'

It was a worksheet with questions and blanks to be filled in:

We live in.................

This is the flag of ....

Washington is the capital of......................

...................is the greatest country in the world.

'Apart from it being far too easy for her, do we really want our daughter subjected to this type of propaganda?'

'Patriotism, my dear, it's big over here. I got ticked off for not saluting the flag the other morning. I'm supposed to 'spread my legions' to the flag each morning like Katie.'

'Did she tell you?' said Sue laughing.

I nodded. 'I've just explained to her about some of the problems I've had with the language. I just wonder how Genny's coping. She did seem rather earnest about things.'

*

OF SMELLY RUBBERS AND HEADLESS CHICKENS

The following morning I received a large envelope from Ms Gillen containing a bundle of pen letters from one of the classes she was teaching at St. Aidan's. There was a short explanatory letter from her, asking if I would get my students to reply to the letters and then bundle them all together and send them back to her. She said little about how the teaching was going but towards the end of the letter informed me that she'd had a collision in my car with a tractor. *Not too serious. And not too much damage. Your next door neighbour is fixing it.*

There was a ludicrous irony to this news. Here were we, driving her battered Chevette on the eight-lane freeways of Miami and there was she driving the quiet lanes of Cumbria and she collides with a tractor!

When I distributed the letters to my eighth grade English class there was great excitement. I just hoped they were neatly written and gave a good impression of the Carlisle students. Quiet descended for a while as the class eagerly read through the contents of the letters.

'Please, Mr Day, there's something here I don't quite understand.' It was Shannon, the daughter of the lady who had spoken to me on Back To School Night.

'What is it, Shannon?'

'This girl Tracey says one of her hobbies is collecting smelly rubbers.'

'Urgh! That's gross,' blurted Kathy. 'That's disgusting!'

This was not a good start. To an American the word 'rubber' refers to a condom.

Shannon showed me the letter. *'One of my hobbies is collecting smelly rubbers. They come in all sorts of flavours, strawberry, banana.....'* It did sound rather dubious. Then it clicked. Just before we left England there was a new fad among the kids for buying fruit scented rubbers or 'erasers' as they called them over here.

I laughed and handed the letter back to Shannon. I clapped my hands and quietened the class. 'Listen up. Another little cultural gem for you all. In England what you call an eraser, we call a rubber. So when Shannon's pen friend talks of collecting smelly rubbers she's referring to this craze in England for collecting different types of erasers which come in a variety of fruit flavours. It's certainly not what you might call a 'rubber'.'

'What about my guy,' said Aaron, waving his letter. 'He says his dad is a lorry-driver and he's just got back from a holiday in a caravan. What the heck's that mean?' 'A lorry is what you call a truck and a caravan is what you call a trailer.'

'How weird is that. I thought we all spoke English,' said Aaron.

'Not quite the same English, Aaron.'

*

That afternoon I watched girls playing soccer for the first time. In England in the nineteen-eighties there was little visible sign of girls in the sport but when soccer began to take off in America in the Seventies they never assumed it was a male-only sport. For me to see girls play soccer was a revelation.

What was also a revelation was the arrival of fifty girls on the field for the try-outs. Fifty! What to do with them and how to organise them – that was the question.

First I sent them off jogging while I set up lines of cones for dribbling practice. And it was quickly obvious that while some of them were quite skilful at ball control, others hadn't got a clue. They were brimming with enthusiasm but, unlike the average British boy, they certainly hadn't been kicking a ball around since they were knee high. Kicking a ball. Now there's a thing. I had always assumed it was a fairly obvious thing to be able to do. Not so, I realised. Some of the girls ran at the ball and then just ran into it. I had to start  rapidly trying to analyse the mechanics of a kick so that I could explain that it involved taking off on one foot, landing on the other and bringing the kicking foot through to connect with the ball.

When I started them on playing a game it was chaotic and the competition to get on the team murderous. Most of them ran in a huge gaggle after the ball – no sense of positioning or passing. They were desperate to be seen by the Coach and some of them seemed to treat the whole thing as an outdoor party, running past smiling as if that was going to get them on the team.

There were some pouts and glum faces when I started to separate the 'probables' and 'possibles' but in the last half hour I was encouraged to see signs of real skill and talent. It was a different game from the game the boys played - less physical, more reliant on skilful footwork and speed rather than physical strength. But some of them could kick and head the ball with power not so different from the boys. What a sin that girls in Britain had been barred from the sport for so long.

My final roster for the girls team had a racial profile similar to that of the boys – all white or Hispanic apart from Marie, the only black player in the squad. I knew Marie from my year eight English class. She was opinionated and feisty and on the field she was a strong defensive player - a force to be reckoned with by any attacking player.

'Did I make the cut, Coach?' she said, her face beaded with sweat.

'You'll have to wait until I post the list, Marie.'

'Did I do okay though?'

I nodded but remained non-commital. 'From what I could see you're more a defensive player than a forward.'

'You still didn't tell me if I did okay.'

'Wait and see, Marie. There were a lot of girls out there.'

'And a lot of dummies racing round like headless chickens.'

I smiled.

She watched me, looking for any hint at my decision. 'Okay Coach, so when you posting the list?'

'Maybe tomorrow.'

She stood, hands on hips, nodding slowly, weighing up whether to press me further. Then she turned, 'Cool. Catch you later, Coach,' and she was off jogging slowly to catch up with the other girls.

I spent all that evening going through my lists and making a final selection for the boys' and the girls' soccer rosters. And as I drew up the final lists I had Bob Dylan's quote from Abraham Lincoln running through my head: *You can please some of the people some of the time but you can't please all of the people all of the time.* I knew there would be grouses and grumbles but, hey, wasn't I The Coach, and didn't The Coach have the last say? I had to start growing into my Coach's breeches and assert myself.

As expected, there was a feeding frenzy round the notice board when I posted the rosters. There were squeals of delight, fists pounding the air and girls hugging each other. Others just walked quietly away. I spotted Marie hanging back behind the others waiting for the throng to clear. When she read her name she nodded to herself and then turned and caught my eye, 'Thanks, Coach,' she said. 'That means a lot.'

'Don't thank me, Marie, you were the player on the field and you did well.'

She nodded again, 'Doesn't always follow that you get picked though.'

*

MAKING THE GRADE

We had never heard of 'yard sales' and 'car-boot sales'; they didn't exist in the England of the early nineteen-eighties. But in America they were already a well established trading institution. Quite simply if you had stuff to sell you posted notices in the local paper or on lampposts and street corners near your house, set out your stalls and waited for the punters to arrive.

On a Friday we would check the *Miami Herald* for postings of local sales and then early on the Saturday morning set out on our treasure hunt. You had to be early to get the pickings and you never knew what you'd encounter. Sometimes the tables in a garage and front yard would display a modest selection of old household gadgets, a few cast off clothes and children's toys. But at other times, if there had been a death, the whole pavement could display a person's life story. There might be well worn woodworking tools, quality shoes and boots, jackets, shirts, bed linen, boxes of records, a rack of pipes and cigarette lighters, a typewriter and piles of books. You could almost piece together a sense of the person and the life. It was all rather sad to see it end like this.

But setting sentiment aside, for us it was a treasure trove. We acquired all sorts of goodies – a small pink bike for Katie, a bike for Sue with a seat on the back for James, a bike for me, toys, bits of camping and fishing gear.

Now, I was able to cycle to school and leave the car for Sue. I took the quiet back roads through the tree-lined streets of Coral Gables; along the curving Riviera Drive on to Vilabella where the houses backed on to one of the canals, along Blue Road and on to Granada which took me down to Dixie Highway. The early morning air was cooler, it took a while for the humidity to build up and I would arrive at school exhilarated and ready for the fray.

There was never a dull moment; frenetic, relentless but never dull. I was beginning to get to know the personalities in my classes. The eighth graders were full of exuberance and now that they had pen-pals in Carlisle, were full of questions about England. The ninth graders were more guarded. There was a self-conscious sophistication about these sons and daughters of lawyers and doctors.

With no uniform at Ponce it allowed lavish displays of designer clothes with attendant disparagement for those less wealthy students who wore what was sneeringly referred to as 'generic' clothing. Following the box-office success of *Flashdance* earlier in the year, a number of my ninth grade girls were adopting the sultry look that Jennifer Beals affects in the film – the loose-necked sweat shirt casually and teasingly draped off one shoulder.

These ninth graders were mature, sharp, and sometimes precocious. During a reading of Robert Frost's poem *The Road Not Taken* I initiated a discussion on choices in life.

'Are we getting graded on this?' came the immediate question from Rhett Baldwin, son of the Chair of the Parents' Committee.

'On what?'

'On this discussion?'

'No, Rhett.'

'Then why are we doing it?'

The question threw me for a moment.

'Do you not normally do discussions in English lessons?'

'Maybe for a test.' He shrugged. 'But what's the point?'

I remembered the impressive list of works of literature that Genny Gillen had sent me, books she would cover in a year. I looked away from Rhett to the rest of the class. 'Tell me, when you were given a literary text like *Jane Eyre* which you studied last year, how long did you spend on the book?'

It was Stacey who offered a response, 'Maybe two or three weeks. We had to read it then there was a test.'

'What kind of test?'

'Well, Ms Gillen would call each of us in turn out to her desk and ask us questions.'

'What type of questions?'

She shrugged, 'Maybe the names of the family who Jane grew up with or the name of the girl who died at the school.'

I nodded. 'So, mainly factual questions and then you were given a grade.'

'That's right,' replied Stacey.

'Then you'd move on to another book?'

She nodded.

Ah, so that was how they got through the list of so many texts in a year. No real discussion of themes or author technique. No written work as such. All that mattered was the grade. I remembered Genny saying, 'I only have to raise the grade book and they come to order'.

I was starting to realise the crucial importance of the grading system. Grades determined everything. They determined whether you made the Junior Honors list, which in turn would later influence your chances of being considered for a high status college; whether you were held back to repeat the year in summer school or if you failed that whether you were held back to repeat the whole year again. The average of your grades or Grade Point Average determined your educational destiny. That's why Genny only had to hold up the grade book and that's why to most students the only thing that mattered was the grade. All else was a waste of their time.

So I talked about the importance of discussion, of sharing ideas with each other, of taking risks to volunteer opinions without fearing the scorn of your peers. They were familiar with the formalities of a structured debate but not the more fluid cut and thrust of open discussion. This explained why in American schools the students sat in separate rows in those chairs which incorporated a small desk top for working on. In England desks would be in pairs and students encouraged to sit together and share ideas. Not so here, it seemed. Dialogue was one way only – between teacher and student not between students.

'So, to return to Rhett's question,' I continued, 'no, there's no grade for discussion but it's important that you share ideas, listen to each other and develop your thinking. And when we're exploring a literary text I'm not going to be testing you so much on the facts of what happened but more how the writer is working on you as a reader through the language used, the ideas woven into the text and the themes underpinning the story.'

Early on, I had abandoned the language text book prescribed by Dade County which focused on a heavyweight diet of grammar knowledge. These students were bright and responsive; it was an insult to condemn them to mindless grammar exercises. Stacey had shown me her eighth grade exercise book. There was pristine neatness and page after page of exercises on identifying types of clauses, adjectival phrases compared with adverbial phrases, and what was called 'sentence mapping' which was a way of drawing a diagram to show the parts of a sentence. It was grindingly boring, sterile stuff and I refused to encourage it.

But the other shock was that despite their quick thinking and their seeming sophistication, when it came to expressing themselves on paper they were painfully inhibited. It was as if the years of assimilating and regurgitating the rules of grammar had stifled their capacity to write freely. Initially I had set them a simple task of writing about their childhood, partly to get a fix on their ability but also because I was genuinely interested to learn about their backgrounds, America being such a melting pot of racial and ethnic diversity.

It was painful watching them trying to get started, pens poised over the sheet of blank paper, faces pinched with anxiety. I wandered up and down the aisles and stopped at Rhett's desk. He was shaking his head.

'What's the problem, Rhett?'

'Sir, I'm not sure whether I should be starting with a topic sentence and whether you're supposed to have subject and then verb or whether it's okay to maybe not start with the subject. And Ms Gillen warned us about some kinda dingling participles.'

'Probably 'dangling', Rhett. But forget all that. Try writing it as you would speak it; keep it sounding natural.'

It took a few weeks of encouragement and reassurance but after a while things started loosening up; more of the class were volunteering opinions and writing became less of a threat and more of a pleasure.

However, I'm not sure the Principal was so impressed. At first I was disconcerted to hear the door open and find Ms Martin standing in the doorway. She would say nothing, just observe for a few moments and then leave closing the door quietly. In England it was rare for a Head Teacher to look in on classes and give a teacher some feedback but here it was a regular occurrence. Later in the day I would find a yellow 'Post-It' note in my mail box.

'Engaging lesson, students interested, but a couple seemingly distracted. Keep a closer check. Ms Martin'.

This was something new and rather scary. But I was impressed by her. After three weeks she called me into her office.

'Just thought I should check on how you're settling in Mr Day or should I say Coach Day. I hear we have a good girls' team this year. The girls seem to like you. When's your first game?'

'Thursday.'

'Good luck.'

'Thanks.'

'I'm getting some good feedback from parents. The students are enjoying your lessons.'

'That's nice to hear.'

' I have to say I've noticed quite a lot of talking going on in your classes.'

I nodded, 'I encourage the students to discuss their work with each other.'

'Really? We don't normally do that.'

'Discussion allows them to clarify their ideas and test their opinions.'

'As long as it does not distract them from the task.'

'Exactly,' I replied.

She sat behind her desk, dark eyes locked on to mine, nodding slowly. 'Have you heard from Ms Gillen?'

'She sent some letters from her English students and we've set up a system of pen pals.'

'Wonderful,' said Ms Martin. 'D'you have any issues you wish to raise?'

'I don't think so. I'm beginning to understand the system over here. Quite a few differences but the students are very responsive.'

'Good. Expect to see me at your door every so often. I try to get round to see everyone regularly. But I won't intrude unless there's something particular I wish to impart. Thank you, Mr Day.'

She nodded, gestured with her hands as a cue that the interview was over and I got up and left.

*

It was two o'clock on a Tuesday morning when the phone splintered my sleep and woke us all up.

'Hallo?' I murmured.

'Barrie, what are you trying to do to me!' the voice screamed into my ear.

'Genny, is that you?'

'I distinctly told you to send the pen pal letters back to me directly and now the students are complaining they haven't had a reply. Are you trying to undermine me!'

'Genny, it's two o'clock in the morning.'

'I don't care. You've ruined this project for me.'

'But wait a minute, the project's not for you, Genny it's for the students and they seem to be enjoying it. My students have had some great letters from your students so I don't see what the problem is.'

'The problem is you've undermined my authority and...'

'I'm sorry, Genny, I'm not prepared to talk about this in the middle of the night. Phone me at a more reasonable time and we'll discuss it but I have school in a few hours and I need some sleep. Good night.' I put down the phone.

'What's she phoning for?' murmured Sue. 'Not to apologise about the car, I bet.'

'Sounds like she's under stress. Something about the pen pal letters.'

'Was she upset?'

'Just a little.'

The next lesson with my eighth graders I checked how the pen pal letters were going.

'I love it,' grinned Tracey. 'Sarah has invited me over to stay and my dad said we may go over in the summer.'

'That's great,' I said.

'And mine's telling me all about the clothes they wear,' added Kristen. 'They only just got *Flashdance* over there but she went with her 'mates' as she calls them and they thought it was incredible.'

They had all received a letter and all but one had replied.

'My dad says our great great grandfather came from Scotland. Is that far from Carlisle?' asked Alycia.

'Carlisle is called the Border City – it's only a few miles from the Scottish border,' I replied.

'They came from somewhere called Perthshire. My dad says we need to go and check it out one day.'

So what was Genny getting in a tizzy about? It all seemed to be going well. Maybe she'd just had a bad day and forgotten about the time difference but somehow I didn't think it was as simple as that. This was not encouraging. I hoped our exchange wasn't destined for a swift termination before Christmas.

*

THEN CAME THE ROLLERS

When we first visited the USA in the Seventies, after Jamaica, we were overwhelmed by the kindness and hospitality we received. Americans are known for this and we assumed we would find the same in Miami. Not so.

In the first few weeks when we met new people they would say, 'How wonderful to meet you. We must have you round.' But nothing ever came of it. We went several times to the local church hoping to forge some links but it seemed Miami was different. You never saw anyone on our street to say hallo to. Where they were, we had no idea.

But then the Rollers arrived and everything changed. They appeared one day on their bikes, knocked on the door and introduced themselves: George, Linda and their three small children. Linda was honey blonde with a mass of long wavy hair and George was dark and broad shouldered and bursting with energy. George taught English at Coral Gables Senior High in the morning, worked at his law practice in the afternoon and, on several evenings, drove up to Fort Lauderdale to do church work. They lived and breathed their Christianity in a totally

245

unapologetic way. It mattered not that we were non-believers, we were lost lambs who needed a little friendly shepherding.

'We have known Genevieve for years, heard about the exchange program and knew we must come and call on you,' smiled George. 'When can you come round for a barbecue?'

And so our lives were taken over. For us they were the essence of the American personality – positive, energetic, idealistic. They took us to their church in Fort Lauderdale, the First Presbyterian, an amazing modern structure of soaring glass, steel and pinewood. It had its own radio station, newspaper and network of international links spreading its evangelical message from downtown Fort Lauderdale to the wildernesses of eastern Europe and Russia. George would regularly do what he called 'witnessing' on the streets of Fort Lauderdale, talking to drug addicts, helping the homeless, searching out lost souls. But it was never patronising. It was about self-belief and dignity, looking forward not backward, finding the power of positive thinking.

At meal times we were introduced to the ritual of joining hands round the table, heads bowed and George saying the blessing and although it did nothing to enhance my belief in the Almighty, still I respected the way they lived and breathed their religion in a way that I had never before witnessed. This was no dressing up for Sunday church and token respectability while the rest of the week took its chances with the heathen hordes; on the contrary this was unself-conscious, seven days a week of living the faith with laughter and joy.

I confided in George about Genny's early morning phone call and the embittered tone of some of her recent letters. I mentioned the basic problems I'd had communicating with students because of the language differences and how undermining it sometimes was and the need for humour rather than indignation when a student laughed at something you said.

George nodded. 'I imagine Genny's having the same problems. I hope she's not taking it personally. My best advice is to kill her with kindness. I know it's hard when someone's sounding off like this. But don't respond in like manner. You'll feel better for it. Anger only eats you up.'

And he proved to be right. Over the coming months when Genny vented her frustrations on us, we simply wrote back with some practical suggestions and continued telling her what a great opportunity this was for all of us.

Standing back from the situation it was interesting to assess the differences in our two systems. I was faced with a highly structured system whereas for Genny it was much more fluid and laissez-faire. Over here teachers had little latitude to depart from the prescribed curriculum and the county adopted text books. There was the tight grading system and I noticed the teachers defined themselves as 'instructors' rather than educators. They delivered what the school system dictated. They were not employed by the school but by the county and so might be moved between schools quite regularly at the behest of the county administrators. I felt a close allegiance to the school community at St. Aidan's and worked under a free and easy system of curriculum content where I could decide what books and materials to use with my classes, whereas over here it was more of a straight-jacket.

I could begin to see why Genny might be finding it difficult. I was certainly kicking against the heavy diet of grammar the students were supposed to cover and I found the testing regime highly dubious. Unlike in England, there were no tests which involved extended writing. Here all the tests were done through multiple-choice questioning – lists of questions with a set of answers to choose from by shading a small circle or 'bubble'. This allowed the 'bubble test' then to be marked by an electronic marking machine. Dead easy for the teacher to administer but as a way of testing English it was laughable. I thought back to the projects and essays that my students in Carlisle produced and although it produced mountains of marking, it gave them a chance to show how to use language in a way that these machine-marked tests never could.

Genny and I were both roped to a steep learning curve. Frequently you lost your footing and clung on with your finger-tips but for me it didn't make the climb any less exhilarating. I hoped Genny felt the same.

*

HALLOWE'EN CAPERS

Second only to Thanksgiving and Christmas, Hallowe'en is the biggest extravaganza in the American calendar. By mid October, pumpkins and corn stooks were starting to appear on people's front porches; supermarkets were crammed with ghoulish masks, Dracula capes, pumpkin lanterns and witches' broomsticks. What I didn't realise was that the whole thing would spill over into the classroom.

On October 31st I cycled into school as usual. I was early and there was no-one around. I went into an empty staff–room and spent time collecting things for the morning lessons. Outside I could hear people arriving; there was chatter and laughter but then came squeals and cheering. The staff-room door opens and in walks a bizarre masquerade of costumed folk   There is the principal Ms Martin, usually so meticulously coiffured and manicured, dressed as a St. Trinian's girl with short skirt, school blouse and tie, a boater and a rather racy garter just above the knee. Anne, the garrulous Humanities teacher, appears in an off-the-shoulder toga, an ivy leaf coronet on her head. Helen, the Science teacher, is dressed up as a cow-girl, and Mike, the Technology teacher, as a pirate complete with eye-patch and parrot on his shoulder.

They look at me. 'Why aren't you dressed up?' says Mike.

'Nobody told me,' I answer feebly.

The bell for first lesson rings and I head for my classroom. There is the usual crush and bustle in the corridors but today it's different – I've stepped in through the looking-glass. I rub shoulders with bunny girls, witches and Sinbad the Sailor. There's a clown with a mop of bright orange hair, a red polka-dot suit and a big red nose chatting up baby dolls with nappies who are sucking on feeding bottles. Some of the boys wear grotesque zombie and Dracula masks dripping fake gore and entrails; there are harlequins and white mice and huge grinning teddy bears. I follow Tweedle-Dum and Tweedle-Dee and Humpty-Dumpty into the classroom.

And as the day progresses the sense of the bizarre continues. I stand at the front of the classroom trying to teach the finer point of English grammar and literary technique to a class scattered with a Spanish dancer in one desk, a caterpillar at another, a tramp talking to a witch at the back of the class, a baby doll making eyes at Superman in the corner.

When I arrive home Sue tells me the bank tellers were dressed up as bunny girls and James was sent from teller to teller collecting sweets which they were giving away.

In the evening it is 'Trick or Treat' time. Katie and James have been talking about this all week. They're not sure what it is but the children at school have been babbling on about it and the excitement is contagious. They hope that by knocking on doors and chanting 'Trick-or-treat' they'll be showered with sweets and other goodies.

Darkness falls on our street on a warm Hallowe'en evening. Pumpkin Jack-o-Lanterns glow on door-steps and luminous cardboard witches and skeletons hang from door knockers. James is dressed as a pirate with a black eye patch and carrying a plastic sword covered in tin foil. Katie is a pink fairy with a silver wand, silver wings and a pink tutu. They are joined by six other little children – Strawberry Shortcake in a mop cap, a French maid, Little Red Riding Hood, a highwayman, Wonderwoman and Orphan Annie. 'Trick or Treat!' they shout and off they go to the first house, James leading the way waving his sword and carrying a red plastic bucket for his booty. They're lucky and our neighbour across the road deals out sweets to each of them. They charge off to the next house and so on down the street.

By the end of the evening the children's bags and James' bucket are bulging with sweets, chocolate bars, apples and more bubble gum than James has seen in his life. But they're getting tired; Katie's silver wings are bent, her wand has lost its star, the silver foil has fallen off James' sword, Strawberry Shortcake is dragging her mop cap on the ground and the highwayman has fallen asleep on his father's shoulders. The chant has degenerated into 'Trick or treat, trick or treat, give us something good to eat. If you don't we don't care , we'll pull down your underwear.'

'Time for bed,' murmurs Sue and we herd our little trick or treaters back to the house.

'Do they have Hallowe'en in England, daddy?' asks Katie.

'It's not quite the same over there.'

'It's fun over here, isn't it,' she adds.

I nod and smile, and muse on the lunatic day I've just lived through.

'Certainly is pretty crazy at times.'

*

'IS IT BECAUSE I'M BLACK?'

As the term moved into December, the humidity eased, the temperature dropped and the students revelled in wearing their 'winter' gear. Shorts gave way to designer jeans; jackets and sweaters took over from tee shirts. My early morning bike ride to school was fresher, more exhilarating but by midday the sun was still pretty hot.

My two soccer teams were performing well. The boys had won five of their six games and drawn the last. The towering Cuban, Carlos held the defence together and allowed the forwards, with the fiery Mexican, Patricio on the left wing, to get the better of opposing defences. It was clear the boys knew each other's games and I just went through

the motions of orchestrating the team. In fact they could have operated quite effectively without me. Not that I let on. No, a sports Coach commands unquestioning authority and I was only challenged over the fact that I didn't yell enough.

It was half time in the girls' game against our rivals McMillan School. The team were gathered round me for a pep talk.

'You are allowed to yell at us, Coach,' said Nina, 'Most coaches give their teams hell.' Nina was our tenacious centre forward. She'd scored one and was itching for more.

'I don't work like that, Nina, it's not always the best way to motivate.'

She nodded and shrugged.

'You're doing a great job without my shouting,' I added.

'Thanks, Coach.'

Constantly I felt like a fraud, that I would be found out. I was starting to get the hang of coaching but compared to American coaches with their drills, their discipline, their detailed knowledge of their sport, I was an amateur.

McMillan were a strong team and today our defence was not hanging together. Several times Marie, at half back, had mis-kicked and let the opposition through and I was starting to have doubts about her. The Ponce girls' team had an impressive record. They had been Zone and District champions for eight years running but a number of them still lacked some of the basic skills. I had held sessions on dribbling and passing and trapping the ball. I tried to get them to look up when they were running with the ball, rather than simply focussing on their feet

'You must think about what you're going to do with the ball, looking and thinking about who you're going to pass it to. You've got to work together more. Now let's tighten up the defence or we're going to lose this game.'

In fact it ended in a 2-2 draw with Nina working a great move with Natalie on the wing to score in the last minute but it was not our best performance. I looked at the roster and my list of reserves and decided to try Catherine in Marie's place for the next game.

As well as playing in the soccer team, Marie was also in the eighth grade English class that I met last period each day. I had posted the team for the next game early the following week at lunch time.

At the end of the English lesson Marie hung back after the rest of the class had left.

'Could I speak to you, Coach?' she said. She clutched her books to her chest and stared at the ground.

'Of course, what is it?'

She hesitated and then said, 'I saw the team. You dropped me from the squad.' She continued staring at the ground.

'Marie, there are a number of other girls who haven't had a chance yet. And in the last game you made a number of mistakes. We almost lost.'

There was a pause and then she said, 'Is it because I'm black?'

It came like a bolt out of nowhere.

I had been told by Kalinsky, the Deputy, about the racial tensions in the school and in south Florida generally. It was a three-way split. Exiled Cuban immigrants vying for jobs with blacks. Whites feeling the pressure from energetic Hispanic entrepreneurs, feeling the pressure to move north away from Miami, Cubans moving in, blacks being ousted. Yes there were tensions.

'Never attempt to break up a student fight,' Kalinsky had said. 'Never step in. Get the other students to break it up.'

I used to watch the two Deputies, Kalinsky and Brennan, patrolling the grounds in the morning, keeping in touch via their portable intercoms like something from a scene from the new *Miami Vice* TV series. The use of walkie-talkies looked somewhat pretentious for I'd never seen a fight or altercation around the school but then what did I know about the realities simmering beneath the surface?

Marie stood there awaiting a response. My mind was somersaulting in giddy spirals trying to frame an answer.

'Marie, if you want to believe that I've dropped you from the team because you're black, there is probably nothing I can do to convince you otherwise. I'll tell you again that the reason I've replaced you is that you played a poor game, you let the opposition through a number of times and I decided I ought to give Catherine a chance. She's keen and she's good.'

'And she's white.'

I hesitated before I spoke again.

'Marie, when things go against you in life, you will always be able to play the race card and convince yourself that it's because you're black and the other person's wrong, not you. You've always got that get-out to fall back on. But you need to weigh up whether you're being honest with yourself. As I said, if you want to convince yourself that you've been dropped because you're black then nothing I can say may change your mind. I just repeat that it's purely about your performance. That's all.'

She barely looked up, just a flicker of eye contact, then she turned and walked out of the room.

I stood for a long while chewing over the encounter. I didn't know Marie well enough to judge how she would react to what I'd said. Maybe I'd gone too far.

*

As Christmas approached so the mood in the corridors or 'halls' as they called them, became more frenetic. There were rehearsals for the Christmas show, for parades and other events; the cheerleaders were practising for the special end of term football game, rooms were decorated, Christmas trees appeared. There was an energy about these students which never failed to amaze me. Maybe it was the effect of the weather, the sun and blue skies, I told myself. But really it was a fact of the school culture. Here they were energised, keen to take part. Most of them were involved in numerous school clubs and activities. Julie, one of my ninth graders was typical: she played on the wing in the soccer team, was secretary of the student council; she was in the National Junior Honor Society, played clarinet in the school band, sang in the Advanced Ensemble Chorus, was active in the Debate Club and the French Club and worked on the school newspaper. And she was not unusual. As well as being involved in clubs or teams, students could act as volunteers to help in the library, assist the office staff as 'Office Aids', get involved in community work, work on the school yearbook. It was an aspect of the 'Can do, Will do,' principle which seemed to underpin so much of American culture. And it was impressive.

There were exceptions of course. During one of my eighth grade English lessons Danny Fitzgerald fell asleep. Maybe he'd been overdoing it in other areas of school, but knowing Danny, I doubted it. Sleeping in a lesson was a cardinal sin and an affront to any teacher. Were my lessons that boring? Admittedly we were reading a section of George Eliot's *Silas Marner* which was a standard text in the prescribed literature anthology. Surprisingly it seemed to have caught the imagination of most of the class; they were very attentive or perhaps my reading had cast them into a soporific haze. Anyway, what to do with Danny, happily dozing through the latter part of my lesson?

As more students noticed, there were nudges and sniggers and I gestured to them to be silent, not to disturb the sleeper. When the bell sounded, he slept on and I motioned to the students to leave quietly and to warn the next class to enter quietly.

The next class arrived. I checked the register, the class opened their books, settled themselves around dozing Danny.

Ten minutes into the lesson Danny stirred. He opened his eyes and glanced around. Nothing registered at first. Then he frowned and looked around again.

'Your class left ten minutes ago, Danny,' I said quietly. 'Never fall asleep in my class again.'

He nodded, said nothing and left hurriedly to a crescendo of giggles and laughter.

On reflection was I unkind, a little sadistic? Maybe. But at least Danny wouldn't sleep in a lesson again and it was the end of a long, hard term.

If Hallowe'en had been spellbinding for Katie and James, Christmas was even more so. The shopping malls were decked and glittering, Christmas music fluted among the tinsel and baubles in every store and we saw something we hadn't seen in England: little candy walking sticks, in twisted stripes of red and white, 'candy canes' they were called. Small ones hung on the branches of Christmas trees, larger ones in shop windows and attached to street lamps. There were Santas on sleighs, reindeers, snow flakes, smiling snowmen but somehow, under a piercingly blue sky and in temperatures in the seventies, it all felt rather surreal. In downtown Miami the city council had hired a snow-machine to spray artificial snow in one of the squares. But against a backdrop of sailboats on a turquoise Biscayne Bay and people strolling in shorts and Hawaiian shirts, it didn't quite work.

At night, however, it was more magical; in places it was positively garish. On some streets there was competition to see who could display the greatest wattage of Christmas lights and gimmicks. Certain households were known for trying to emulate Walt Disney in their Christmas illuminations. And these displays were not static, it was all cleverly animated with nodding reindeers, swaying snowmen, Ho-Ho-ing Santas, sleigh bells jingling, elves tinkering with hammers in Santa's workshop. Specialist contractors were hired to set up and orchestrate these displays and clearly there was rivalry afoot to see which property would blaze the brightest. People drove for miles with their families to these streets to gaze at this electrical extravaganza. In England you might see the lights of a modest Christmas tree in someone's front window but nothing to compare with what we were seeing here.

When I left school on the last day of term it was with relief at the prospect of a two week break but also a feeling that I had coped reasonably well with the challenges. There were kind words on Christmas cards from appreciative parents, affectionate comments from students. But the most important to me was a card from Marie with a note which read:

' I thought a lot about your words, Coach, and I value that you gave me your time. I have to raise my game. You were right.

Thanks. Happy Christmas. Marie. '

*

UP THE CREEK AT CHRISTMAS

'And so if an alligator leaves the river bank and starts swimming towards you just bang your paddle on the side of the canoe. He'll soon go away.' The ranger nodded his head and smiled. James' little hand tightened in mine.

'Will we really see an alligator, daddy?' His troubled face looked up at me, eyes big.

'Sounds like it. But the ranger says it's fine, they normally just snooze in the sunshine on the river bank.'

The canoe had been loaded on to the car as soon as I'd arrived from school on the Friday afternoon when term ended. We had packed the camping gear and newly acquired fishing rods and then driven west out of Miami on route 41. We were heading for the Koreshan State Park on the Estero River just north of Naples on the Gulf coast. It had been recommended by Anne, one of the science teachers; apparently Koreshan was a great camping and canoeing spot and December in Florida is perfect camping weather – low humidity, high midday temperatures for sunning ourselves on a white sand beach – just what we needed.

A two hour drive from the Atlantic coast to the Gulf coast on highway 41 took us through the fascinating landscape of the Everglades. The highest point in the entire state of Florida is only 345 feet above sea level and that's up in the northern 'panhandle'. Central and southern Florida are flat, and I mean flat. Apart from the coastal strips, the Everglades occupy most of southern Florida from Lake Okeechobee for a hundred miles south to the tip of the state at Florida Bay. The bedrock is limestone and during the summer it runs with several inches of freshwater, for the Everglades is not a swamp but rather a freshwater river, 50 miles wide flowing slowly south. A haven for wildlife and rare plants, it is home to herons, deer, bobcats and raccoons and in the deeper ponds or 'sloughs' are the 'gator holes', home of the alligators.

Everywhere people are fishing. It's a type of religion in Florida. Wherever there is place to pull a truck off the highway next to a stretch of water there'll be someone with a long fishing pole. There are numerous canals and creeks of clear water but the eye is taken by the wide spreading 'river of grass', tall grasses and reeds which paint the landscape with swathes of green and gold. Breaking the sea of grasses are 'hummocks' – small mounds of tight packed trees, mangroves and tropical undergrowth.

The sun sets quickly in Florida, there is no lingering twilight like in Europe. Here the sun goes down fast and as the light fades so the chorus of cicadas rises in a zithering crescendo to vibrate the darkness. We work quickly to get the tent up and the barbecue coals lit. We'd been warned about mosquitoes and lather ourselves in an insect repellent called 'Off!'.

'We're like Indians, with the canoe and the tent and catching fish,' said Katie.

'I suppose we are,' replied Sue.

I had bought new paddles and life jackets from a 'wilderness' store in south Miami. It was 'Boys' Own Adventure' territory. There were regiments of fishing rods, racks of guns, crossbows, gleaming knives with bone handles, camouflaged hunting jackets. I was in the country where the 'right to bear arms' was indelibly embedded in the DNA and where the yearning to take to the woods to hunt still bubbled in the blood of many Americans.

We launched the canoe early the following morning under a pristine blue sky. I was beginning to realise that on most mornings there was a pristine blue sky – this was why northerners flocked south in the winter. It was typical Florida weather - day after day was wall-to-wall sunshine.

Sue took up her position at the front of the canoe, Katie and James sat in the middle and I was tail-end Charlie along with the picnic, fishing rods and our bait bucket. We had bought shrimp for our bait although the man in the bait shop did advise us that, 'You won't ketch no mullet with shrimp. They's vegetarian – only go for bread. You'll see em jumping and may ketch one but the meat ain't so good.'

We'd seen fish jumping the previous evening when the river was still and the fading light was hazy with spirals of flying insects. We assumed it was what fish did in the evening. But it was the same this morning. There would be a sudden slap as a large fish hit the water. You would look up and within a few moments there would be another shimmer of silver as a mullet took to the air and then the 'slap' as the fish re-entered the water.

'Alligator, daddy,' hissed Katie, 'over there!'

We were paddling in the middle of the river. The surface of the water was unruffled - no breeze - clumps of grey-green 'Old Man's Beard' hung from the branches of the cypress trees and the banks were dense with mangrove and saw-palmetto. Along the river bank were small sandy beaches and it was here the alligators lay with their ugly snouts close to the water.

'Just keep still and remember what the ranger said,' murmured Sue.

'He's moving,' hissed James. 'Will we bang the paddle on the boat?'

'Only if he starts swimming towards us.'

We all held our breath as the canoe slid silently past the black cobbled back of the alligator.

'Phew, that was scary,' grinned Katie, 'just like Laura seeing the black bear behind the cabin in the story.'

Further on, the river widened. A heron took off from a cypress stump and flapped languidly across the  river. Dead ahead a fish jumped; it was a quite a long way off, maybe forty yards or so. We drifted on and then it happened again, dead in line with the canoe, the fish jumping and entering the water about twenty yards ahead. 'It can't happen again,' I said to myself.

We glided on and I waited.

Then came the moment. Fish in mid-air, over Sue's head and 'plump' into the bottom of the canoe at the children's feet. Squeals and giggles, fish flapping, canoe rocking, me suddenly with the hunter's blood bubbling loud in my veins whacking the fish with the end of my paddle, Sue clinging on to the boat for dear life!

Never to be forgotten – that moment became etched into the archive of family memories to be re-lived a thousand times. In the re-telling, the fish never grew any bigger and I became somewhat shameful of my manic fish battering but that's the way it happened.

That evening we barbecued our prize and James poked and prodded the sizzling body of the fish with a stick.

But the fish had the last laugh, in a manner of speaking. The meat of the mullet was grey and dense with tiny bones. One attempted mouthful was enough.

'Sorry, guys, we can't eat this,' I said spitting out the bones.

'I bet the Indians would have eaten it,' said Katie.

'Well, maybe,' I conceded. 'But how about this for a backup plan? Didn't I spot a little old McDonalds not five miles down the road?' No more needed to be said. With whoops and unbridled glee the children raced to the car. Forget living like the Indians. Far better was a finger-lickin' feast at 'Mickey D's'.

*

'But how will Santa find us?' said James the morning of Christmas Eve.

He stood with hands on hips, a frown on his face.

'We're going to put up streamers in the trees and balloons on the top of the tent,' replied Sue.

'It'll be all right, James,' added Katie, 'Santa's reindeers are very clever. They'll find us.'

There was great excitement as we hung stockings from the guy ropes of the tent and put out a plate with mince pies for the reindeers, wove coloured streamers into the branches of the trees round the barbecue area and then settled Katie and James into their sleeping bags.

I read them the chapter from *Little House on the Prairie* about the Ingalls' Christmas when the creek was flooded and Santa sent the girls' presents with their neighbour, Mr Edwards.

'See, James, Santa always finds a way,' said Katie.

'I'm worried,' said James.

With the children settled, Sue threw another couple of logs on the barbecue fire and we sipped champagne and agreed that life was treating us pretty well.

'So we need to start thinking about this summer trip,' said Sue. 'D'you reckon it's feasible – coast to coast and back again in six weeks?'

I shrugged. 'It's about seven thousand miles plus a few hundred for detours. I'd like to try it. But we need to find a vehicle – some sort of van we can sleep in.'

Term would finish in mid June and the plan was to drive the three thousand miles to San Francisco and meet up with the Jaques – the Shropshire family with whom we'd travelled down from Washington. They would be setting off two weeks earlier as Paul's term finished in early June. We would then drive back east to Philadelphia ending up at the home of our friends from Jamaica, the Moyers, where we hoped to sell the van and all our accumulated gear at a yard sale.

'D'you think Katie and James will cope with such a trip?' asked Sue.

'Across the prairies in our own wagon? Of course they'll cope. It'll be the adventure of a lifetime.'

What was less easy to cope with was what happened during the night of Christmas Eve. The temperature dropped an extraordinary thirty degrees! When I awoke and smelt the air I knew something was different. It was freezing cold. There was frost on the ground, the water had frozen in our cooking pots.

'But they never have frosts in Florida,' said Sue.

'Well they just did. Santa's been working his magic.'

It was truly historic. December 1983 is remembered as the winter which caused the price of Florida orange juice to rocket as much of the orange crop had frozen on the trees and was ruined.

While the children shivered and giggled in their sleeping bags, tingling fingers struggling to open Christmas presents, we warmed milk in a billy can to pour on their breakfast cereal. It was far too cold to be camping and so we quickly packed away the tent, coaxed a reluctant car engine into life and drove up the coast to find a motel. There were palm trees and palmettos hung with icicles, orchards of orange trees dusted with frost. In residential areas gardens were ruined with tender sub-tropical plants brown and dying.

'This is unreal,' remarked Sue, 'these gardens are devastated.' There were swathes of manicured garden plots all displaying the same brown wash of dead plants – broad-leafed heliconia hanging like sticks of limp wash leathers; hibiscus and oleander bushes, ginger plants and, saddest of all, the 'Christmas rose' or poinsettia – all of them hanging as rags on their stems.

We pulled into a Howard Johnson motel and ordered breakfast: eggs, waffles, bacon and coffee. It was an unusual kind of Christmas morning.

After we'd eaten, Katie set her plate aside and took up her new colouring book while James was on the floor lost in his world of He-Man battling Skeletor. He loved the cartoon series and Santa had brought him some new plastic figures and a model of Castle Grayskull.

'Not quite as planned,' I murmured.

'Not to worry, let's open these.' Sue produced a wad of Christmas cards and letters which had arrived from England.

There were cards from family and friends in England and a letter from Jean. It was clear that Genny was not finding things easy at St. Aidan's, but Jean and Roger were trying to give her support and it was hoped that now we had reached Christmas, we would not be called back early.

'That's a relief then,' I murmured.

'Just hope we don't get any more phone calls in the early hours,' said Sue.

There was news of more IRA bombings. Ninety had been injured and a few killed in a bomb placed at Harrods just before Christmas. Jean grumbled about the continuing popularity of Prime Minister Margaret Thatcher and her cosying up to Ronald Reagan.

'I don't want to hear about it, thanks,' said Sue. 'Let's enjoy things over here while we can. We might be called back next week.'

After breakfast we drove up the coast. The sun was shafting through the morning mists and melting the frost. The temperature was finally rising. The waters of the Gulf of Mexico were a brilliant turquoise; far out near the horizon the shrimp boats were already at work even on Christmas morning.

'It says here that you can find sharks' teeth in the sand at Captiva Island,' said Sue. She was reading from a leaflet picked up at the motel.

We drove on for a while and then turned off towards the silver sand beaches north of Sanibel where we spent the rest of the day paddling along the shoreline, building elaborate sand castles and searching for sharks' teeth.

'Found some,' shrieked Katie, holding up tiny triangles of polished bone. Some were long and curved, others short and stubby with a clear line where the V-shaped root joined the sharp tooth.

'Why are they here?' asked Katie.

'Maybe it's where the shark tooth fairy buries all her loot,' I replied.

'Like pirates' treasure?' said James.

'Daddy's just being silly,' said Katie.

'Could be true,' I said.

'And pigs might fly,' said Sue.

'And Florida might get snow in December,' I added.

*

STEPPING UP TO THE PLATE

The Spring term was crammed with activity. My English classes would take their statutory Minimum Skills Tests in April. They were pretty basic multiple choice tests on aspects of grammar. No writing as such was involved but I had resisted doing much grammar work so far. With my ninth grade classes I hadn't opened the grammar text book I was supposed to work from. It was full of boring, mindless exercises and my students deserved more stimulus than that. So I had taught them through the themes we were encountering in literature. We looked at issues of ambition and loyalty in *Macbeth;* our readings from Mark Twain's *Life on the Mississippi* generated some brilliant personal writing on growing up. Robert Frost's poetry led us into a consideration of where people's choices in life lead them.

My students' writing was blossoming. There was no need for them to know about clause analysis or the danger of the dangling participle. These youngsters were smart, articulate and enthusiastic. They just needed opportunities to show what they could do. And so I launched The Great Ancestor Project.

During the previous months, my own perception of this country called 'America' had shifted radically. The term 'American' was so misleading in suggesting a commonality of character and personality. Apart from the Native Americans, this was a country of immigrants – refugees, adventurers; an ethnic and racial diversity which belied any single label. When I looked down the names of my students – Gonzalez, Schneider, O'Brien, Jaouhari, Jones - what was so clear was the rich cultural mix that made up this intriguing country. What was equally teasing was the question of how my students' ancestors had made their journeys to get here.

So, I set my ninth graders a research project to investigate their ancestry. They had to interview parents and grandparents, search out old photographs and documents, map their family trees. This would be an archive for them to create and cherish and I hoped that it would reveal the threads which connected the various branches of their families. Already I had gleaned that in my classes there were connections with Russia and eastern Europe, with Africa, south and central America, and the Middle East. But I was also aware that with some families this project might touch on sensitive areas so I sent a letter home to parents explaining the purpose and background to the project. There were no objections; that is apart from my tangle with the formidable Mrs Penn-Smithson.

Her son Todd was typical of many of my ninth graders. He was confident, intelligent and precocious. He liked to challenge me, to score points for the entertainment of the rest of the class.

'So, Mr Day, on the fourth of July will you be celebrating along with the rest of us?'

'Of course, Todd.'

'Celebrating, the British getting their butts kicked?'

'Probably celebrating the delights of American hospitality.'

'But the British got whooped.'

'And are you assuming some personal responsibility for the whooping, Todd?'

'Well, not exactly but my ancestors were some of the first pioneers. We'd have been there shooting at the British redcoats.'

'Well, my ancestors were selling fruit and veg in a Warwickshire market and weren't much interested in colonial adventures across the Atlantic.'

'They would if the price of tea had rocketed.'

'True but I don't think the Boston Tea Party was aimed at raising the price of tea in England.'

'Don't you have any pride in being British?'

'To an extent but not everything the British have done is commendable. You have to pick your way through your own history and decide for yourself what you're proud of.'

He frowned. Todd, like most young Americans, was raised on an unswerving patriotism to country and flag. There was the Pledge of Allegiance each morning, the American flag which hung at the side of every chalkboard in every classroom, the flags which hung out from the walls of many houses, the reverence for the stories of the Pilgrim Fathers, the heroes of the Revolutionary War, the architects of the Declaration of Independence. They all sustained the sense of unblinking pride. To hear my revisionist sentiments was something of a shock.

But that wasn't what stirred Mrs Penn-Smithson into booking an after school meeting with me. It was the fact that I'd been giving Todd lower that his usual straight As.

'But Todd doesn't get Bs; he's a straight A student. He's in the National Junior Honor Society.' Pursed lips and a piercing look from this coiffured and expensively tailored lady.

'Todd's coasting, Mrs Penn-Smithson. He's bright, extremely bright but he's lazy. He does enough to get by. He has the makings of a really good writer, a journalist or a barrister. But he lacks commitment. I'm trying to motivate him. I'm not going to give him As when he's not giving his best.'

And here was the crux of the difference in our two grading systems. It seemed that in the American system where most of the tests were multiple choice tests, you could achieve an A grade if you completed a set of correct answers. In the assessing of English in Britain we didn't set up a grading system based on right or wrong answers; the subjective judgement of the teacher was involved and, maybe at times, we were mean in saving the A grades for when a budding Shakespeare appeared on the scene.

'Did you see the letter about the Ancestor Project which I've set the students?'

She nodded.

'Here's a chance for Todd to achieve an A grade. I understand you're related to the early pioneer families.'

'That's right. We're connected to William Penn.'

'Of Pennsylvania fame?'

'That's correct,' she nodded again.

'I'll be fascinated to read Todd's work when he's completed the research and the writing.'

With that she nodded, got up and left, still unconvinced that her son should ever be blighted with anything less than an A grade.

*

Afternoons were still taken up with soccer training. There were only a few weeks to go before the soccer playoffs for the District Championship. The boys had already won the Zone Championship defeating Rockway and McMillan and now we were up against Arvida School the following week. The girls' team had also done well winning the Zone Championship. All we faced now was the District Championship against Glades in two weeks time. The girls were playing a wonderfully fluid game, weaving passes with the forwards showing great footwork. There was none of the aggressive physicality of the boys' game. It was often a pleasure to watch and in the past  six months I had been given a real shake-up in my chauvinistic assumptions about girls' ability to play good soccer. Marie had impressed me with some new found tenacity and as a defensive player she was now much more dependable. She was back on the team. But it was at the end of a practice session with the boys' team that I had one of my memorable moments.

Near the boundary of the playing field, close to the fence which bordered Dixie Highway, was the baseball triangle. This was where most afternoons the baseball team would be practising. Their coach was a young police officer who did some voluntary community work at the school. After the practice with the boys' team I wandered over to watch the baseball.

Kalinsky, the Deputy, was standing just behind Officer Karr who was pitching. He waved. 'Hey Coach, this is a bit different from that weird game you play in England.'

'You talking about cricket?' I shouted back.

'Never did understand what that was all about. Ever tried baseball?'

I shrugged and shook my head. In fact that wasn't quite true. In Jamaica I'd played some softball and baseball didn't look much different – same type of bat just a smaller ball.

'C'mon, let's see Coach Day face some mean American pitching.'

The boys laughed as I wandered across to the batter's box. I'd forgotten how narrow the bats were with only a small target area for connecting with the ball. But in Jamaica I'd never had a problem hitting a softball; it couldn't be so much different.

'I'll go easy on you, Coach,' smiled Karr as he lobbed me a fairly slow ball.

I hit it back to him without much effort.

'Hey, not bad,' crowed Kalinsky. 'I think we need to wind it up a bit, Mr Karr.'

The first few pitches had been gentle underarm throws. Now the young policeman started to pitch overarm and I started to hit with a little more effort. The baseball guys cheered every time I connected.

'This guy's played before,' said Kalinsky.

'Never played baseball,' I said, which was technically true; I said nothing about the softball.

By this time several of the boys from the soccer team had drifted over to watch. They'd heard the cheers.

Karr gestured to me, 'Okay Coach, I'm going to up the pace a little.' He started pitching with that slick flat arm trajectory that baseball pitchers use. Still I was connecting with nearly every ball, getting the feel of holding the bat high over my right shoulder and swinging through in a level sweep. It was totally unlike swinging a cricket bat but watching the ball on to the bat was the key.

Kalinsky was shaking his head and smiling. He'd expected a display of gauche slapstick but instead this English Coach was doing okay.

'Okay Coach, here's the deal. If you can hit one into the tennis courts in ten pitches, it's burgers all round for the soccer team,' he said.

There was whooping and cheering from the baseball players and more of the soccer team had arrived to watch. I glanced across to the tennis courts. They were beyond the soccer field which bordered the baseball triangle, so the distance was the width of the soccer field plus some.

'And Mr Karr, no holding back,' said Kalinsky.

The balls flew at me and the first three I missed completely. On the fourth I connected and the ball travelled a reasonable distance landing halfway across the soccer field.

'C'mon, Coach,' shouted Patricio, 'I'm tasting that burger.'

'Yeah, Coach, give it some!' shouted another of the soccer team.

The fifth ball I missed but then I watched the next ball right on to the bat, found the sweet spot, felt the kiss of the ball on the bat and watched it soaring high across the soccer field. It landed close to the touchline about twenty yards from the tennis courts.

'Go Coach!' cheered the soccer boys.

Four to go. I missed the seventh and also the eighth. The boys groaned. I was snatching at the ball. I was too tense. I eased my shoulders a little and waited before looking up at the pitcher. Then I was ready.

That moment lives on even now. The pitcher's arm, the swing, the light feel of the ball on the bat and then the ball soaring high in the air, over the soccer field, over the high fence of the tennis courts and bouncing on the tarmac.

The boys erupted with glee and ran over to congratulate me. Kalinsky came across shaking his head and smiling. He shook my hand. 'Pretty good, Coach. Never seen an Englishman swing a baseball bat before.' He turned. 'Okay guys, Burger King has it!'

And off we all trouped to the Burger King which fronted Dixie Highway.

'And you never played baseball before?' said Kalinsky as he set down a tray of Whoppers and fries.

'A little softball, in Jamaica but I never faced a baseball.'

'Impressive,' he nodded. 'I need to check out this game called cricket. Maybe it's not so different swinging a cricket bat.'

'Yeah, it's different,' I said. 'Quite different. I'll show you one day.'

OF CRABS AND CUBAN REELS

James and Katie were hooked. They were lying face down peering over the edge of the boardwalk and waiting. They watched for movement in the shallow water and kept very still holding the string. Out of the shadows, moving in that weird sideways scuttle, came their first catch of the day. They watched it move across the sand towards the wire mesh of the trap where the chicken leg was fixed.

'Now,' whispered Katie.

'Wait,' hissed James.

'Go on!'

James jerked on the string and up came the wire basket with the little blue crab locked on to the bait.

'Yeah! Got him,' squealed James.

This new obsession of catching blue crabs was ignited one Sunday on a visit to Bill Baggs State Park on Key Biscayne. We were first taken to the State Park by George and Linda in December and since then it had become our escape destination at the week-end.

Leaving the commercial district of downtown Miami, you crossed the Rickenbacker Causeway which connected the mainland to the island of Key Biscayne. The State Park was a world away from the mauling rush of city traffic. Here there were boardwalks, fishing keys, casuarina pines shading the picnic tables and a white sand beach curving round to the Cape Florida lighthouse which stood on a rocky outcrop at the southern tip of the island. The only drawback was the brazen arrogance of the racoons which could devastate a picnic basket and fling its contents in all directions within minutes of you turning your back. Vigilance was key.

Apart from ambushing crabs from the boardwalks, our other fascination was watching the Cuban fisherman fishing from the key on the calmer western side of the island. They were old men, short and squat wearing faded shorts, their rounded bronzed backs hunched over their work.

First they caught their bait using a circular cast net. They threw the weighted net in a high arc so that it landed flat on the water. It then sank slowly for a few minutes before being yanked closed with the central draw string. If it was a good cast, the net, now closed into a bag, would emerge from the water glistening with wriggling sardines. The sardines were then fixed as bait on a fishing line attached to a circular Cuban reel. The reel was held in one hand while the other hand swung the baited line like a lasso and flung it far out into the deeper water.

These fishermen knew what they were doing. Within minutes of throwing out the line they would be tugging it in with a fair sized fish flapping on the end.

James was fascinated. He peered into the buckets which stood on the boardwalk and viewed the morning's catch. One of the fishermen came across, put his arm on James' shoulder and pointed out the different fish, 'Blue Runner that one an' over here we got Snapper. You wan' try ketch one?'

He picked up a spare Cuban reel and then went to the bucket which held the sardines. James watched open-mouthed as the little sardine was threaded on to the hook. Then he stood on the edge of boardwalk and with the fisherman's help flung the baited hook out into the deep water.

'Hold him tight now,' said the old man.

James held on as the line moved in the deep water. Then his hands gripped harder, 'Daddy, I think I got one.'

I helped him wind in the line, coiling it back on to the reel.

'I see him,' shouted Katie pointing and hopping from foot to foot.

'Blue Runner,' said the fisherman.

The fish was vivid shades of silvery blue with sharp fins and a small mouth. James held him in his hands for a moment.

'You wan' tek him?'

James shook his head. 'I'll put him in the bucket.'

It was a crowning moment, imprinted for ever – the tug of the line, the first sight of the fish and then the silky feel of its skin on the palms of his small hands.

Stone crabs were a different matter though. On another crabbing foray, down on the Florida Keys, Katie pulled up something quite different from the small, finely shaped blue crabs. This was a mini monster. It had a bigger body, pale pink shell and vicious looking black claws, one much larger than the other. Katie dropped the crab trap on the boardwalk and jumped back as the creature started to scuttle towards the side of the dock.

Another fisherman snatched up the crab before it could escape. 'Oh no, you ain't gettin away little buddy.' He held the crab by the edge of its shell, its claws scraping at the air.

He turned to the children. 'This here's what we call a stone crab. Now they's different from the blue crab. You see this big claw here?' He pointed at the much bigger right claw. 'This is what we gonna keep. This is good eatin'' And with that he snapped the claw from the body and threw the crab back in the water.

Katie winced, her hand across her mouth.

The man stooped down in front of her, 'It's okay little miss. It don't hurt him none. And he'll grow back a new claw in just a few weeks. That's the beauty of the stone crab.' He held up the snapped off claw. 'Now what you need to do is boil up this claw for a few minutes, then get a little hammer to break the shell and then try the meat. I think you'll find it's a little touch of sweetness.'

He held out the claw but Katie was not sure. It was James who stepped forward to take it. 'Can we cook it, daddy?' He held the claw and touched the serrated edge with his finger.

'I think we need to catch a few more,' I replied.

That afternoon we caught six blue crabs but the stone crabs were not biting.

In the evening we boiled a big pot of water, dropped in our catch and watched the blue crabs turn a brilliant pink. Our single crab claw emerged on to the plate like a piece of exquisite porcelain tipped with polished ebony. It seemed a shame to smash it with a mallet. But our rule was: You have to eat what you catch. And so James did the deed. The white flesh was indeed sweet and tasted of the sea.

'So what do we think?' I asked.

Katie shook her head, 'I think it's cruel. If I catch a stone crab I'm going to throw him back.'

'Crabs don't feel things,' said James, 'and he'll just grow another claw.'

'I don't care,' replied Katie. 'It doesn't seem right, that's all.'

*

TRACING THE THREADS

'Listen to this for a conundrum. Fred Houstoun's distant ancestor was governor of Georgia in 1778 and then here's Fred's grandfather, who at age sixteen, is a top ranking pool player. He buys a cottage in the backwoods of Georgia with his winnings and then disappears in 1980. None of his family has seen him since.'

I was utterly engrossed reading the Great Ancestor Projects from my ninth graders. Marking papers and books was often tedious but these projects were intriguing.

I turned to Sue. 'These are the students who are supposed to be swallowing an undiluted diet of clause analysis and grammatical gobbledygook. And here they are producing the most incredible writing.'

Sue was clearing the dishes from our evening meal when she said, 'Katie and James were playing with Carrie and Kristen from next door today. Little Carrie comes up to me with a frown on her face and says, 'What I don't understand is elemeno.' I asked her what was 'elemeno'. And she says, 'It's in the rhyme: A,B,C,D,E,F,G…..H,I,J,K elemeno P.' Seems no-one's explained the alphabet to her.'

'There are certainly some loopy things about the education system over here. Some of it's great but the way they teach English is archaic.'

I returned the projects to my classes the following week and thereafter I never looked at my students in the same way again. I now had a glimpse of their history, the tapestry of adventures that their ancestors had woven.

Catherine, dark eyed, with lustrous black hair, who played defence on the soccer team – her great, great grandfather was the doctor in a small town in Honduras. He was hounded out of the country by political bully boys and set up his own radio station in Costa Rica. His sons became doctors after moving to America in the 1960s.

Vicky, who always sat near the front; pale complexion, long honey-coloured hair, neat, fine handwriting – her Swedish mother, a dentist, had married a young American naval officer in Spain and moved to America in 1968.

Robyn's ancestry was Russian. Her great, great grandfather, Louis, was born into a family of peasant farmers. He left Moscow aged 16 in 1905 to avoid getting caught up in the Russian war with Japan and lived with his aunt in Washington before becoming a peddler. For five years he travelled up and down the east coast selling his wares before finally settling in Georgia where he set up a store. But his young son Carl died in an accident caused, it was claimed, by his sister Rosa's negligence. Pauline, the mother, died two weeks later of a broken heart. Rosa, in her teens, married a gambler and was exiled from the family but her daughter, Sandra, Robyn's mother, progressed to teaching at the University of Miami.

Then there was Stacey's complex family history which started with Carlos, her great, great grandfather leaving Italy and travelling by ship to Argentina. He was a journalist, critical of the dictator Juan Peron whose secret police closed down his paper, *La Prensa,* and threw him out of a job. Stacey's aunt Margaret, a talented musician with the Boston Symphony Orchestra, met a tragic end when she died falling into the orchestra pit and breaking her neck during a rehearsal in Los Angeles.

But perhaps the most intriguing of the projects was that of Rebecca. There was Irish blood on her father's side. Her great, great grandfather, James, born in 1820, was an engineer and initially worked on Mississippi steam boats. In 1842 he constructed a diving bell to recover cargo from sunken boats and was then asked to advise President Abraham Lincoln on the use of ironclad ships in the civil war. He was famed for designing and constructing the cantilever bridge across the Mississippi at St Louis. On Rebecca's mother's side there was Spanish blood. Her grandfather led a revolution in Paraguay. He became Paraguay's ambassador to France in 1953, was appointed Secretary of State in 1959 and Senator in 1961.

And finally, what of Todd Penn-Smithson? As Todd's mother had said, there was some illustrious ancestry. On his mother's side the original James Smithson was a religious dissenter who was imprisoned in London and then in Belgium for his anti-Catholic views. He crossed to America sometime in the early 1700s and was among those to be granted land by William Penn when he married one of Penn's nieces. His son Richard got embroiled in anti-colonial riots in the mid 18th century in Virginia and further down the line we find a Penn-Smithson trading tobacco in West Virginia. Latterly a Jonathan Penn-Smithson was involved in giving legal advice to Henry Flagler when the railroad tycoon was bringing his railroad and hotel business south into Florida in the 1890s.

'So, quite a story, Todd,' I said when I handed it back to him. 'A brilliant piece of work. Well done.'

I could see he was surprised. After our various altercations over the past few months and the interview with his mother, the last thing he expected from me was glowing praise and a triple A grade. For once he was lost for words.

'Did you discover things about the family which were new to you?' I asked

He shrugged. 'I knew nothing of all this, sir. I've never much listened when my mother's been going on about the family history. But, yes, it's really got to me. I enjoyed working on it.'

'You write well, Todd. That project's a great achievement. Save it for your children to enjoy.'

He nodded and turned away, turning the pages of the project, 'Yes, sir, thanks, sir. My mother will be pleased.'

'I'm sure she will,' I added.

*

NOT WITH A BANG BUT A WHIMPER

It was a Thursday evening in February when the phone call from Jim Halloran came through. Jim was the husband of one of the science teachers at school. 'I got you passes for the shuttle launch on Saturday morning. They're like gold dust but they're yours.'

The launch of the shuttle 'Challenger' was scheduled for 8a.m. We set off straight from school on the Friday evening to drive the 200 miles north up the Florida Turnpike to Cape Canaveral on the east coast.

After a fitful few hours sleep at a friend's house we were up again at 5.30a.m. The children were fractious and bleary eyed so I was buzzing with my 'trip-of-a-lifetime' sales pitch to snap them into some enthusiasm.

The Kennedy Space Centre is built on the looped spit of land called Cape Canaveral which encloses the broad lagoon of the Banana River. It was across this stretch of water that we would view the launch of the shuttle. As we set off for the two hour drive my mind was filled with those classic images of rocket launches: the count-down, the explosive moment of ignition, the billowing clouds of smoke and steam, the column of fire thrusting the massive space rocket upwards. What an experience this was going to be.

By 7a.m. dawn had broken on a clear Florida morning and we were nose to tail with some of the other 200,000 shuttle seekers who had set out to view the 8o'clock launch. But we were in good time. The gate was now only half a mile ahead; there would be time to set up our camp chairs, eat some breakfast, get the cameras ready and drink in the atmosphere of this unique occasion before the actual launch.

By 7.15a.m. we were a few yards from the gate to the Kennedy Space Complex. The gate man was cheerily waving cars through and I followed, showing our gate pass. 'Hold it, buddy,' he said stepping forward with his hand up. 'Wrong gate. Back 3 miles, hang a left, across two bridges then another left.'

I couldn't believe it. After gasping in disbelief, I turned the car and headed back the way we had come, cursing our luck, cursing the state of Florida for its lack of clear signposts, cursing NASA for arranging its launch at such an ungodly hour, cursing all those other motorists who were smugly passing through the gate to set up their camp chairs, eat some breakfast and drink in the atmosphere.

Finally, when we had retraced the three miles and crossed the two bridges and taken the left turn, we cursed the never-ending stream of traffic which now snaked away into the hazy distance ahead of us. The minutes were ticking away. We scanned the horizon across the Banana River for something resembling the silhouette of a rocket. The shores of the lagoon were massed with people armed with binoculars, telescopes and telephoto lenses all directed towards the far side of the lagoon. But still we could see nothing.

On the radio the cheery voice of the commentator announced that all was set for lift-off in ten minutes and all was looking good. If only he knew!

Finally we passed beyond the lake shore and in through the gate of the Space Centre. No problem this time except the continuing jam of slow-moving traffic two miles ahead of us. And now our view was completely obscured by a neatly planted row of trees and bushes along the roadside. 'And everything's looking good for an 8 o'clock lift off...' bleated the radio, 'three minutes and counting...' I cursed again. So much for the leisurely breakfast and drinking in the atmosphere. Instead we were choking on exhaust fumes, Katie and James were fighting on the back seat and we were still stuck in this dumb traffic jam with no sign of anything resembling a space rocket anywhere in view.

'Two minutes and counting....'

We hurriedly pulled off the road, dragged the children out of the car, sat them on the roof and fumbled to find cameras and binoculars.

'Ten, nine, eight, seven...' and suddenly there it was, curling up from behind the trees and telephone wires – a tiny dark pencil-like object with a tail of fire climbing rapidly on a column of smoke. There was no sound at first, just the smoke snaking higher and higher with the small dark object at its head. I was watching partly through the movie camera lens while trying to aim the still camera in the right direction with my other hand. It was like watching bad television.

Then came the earth shaking rumble, the delayed sound of the lift-off, while high above us the booster rockets separated and then all one could see was the sun catching a tiny metallic object far way in the blue sky.

It was all over in seconds. I stood there staring. It was like that feeling you get on Guy Fawke's Night when you've paid a fortune for a Brocks Intergalactic Rocket Cascade which fizzes, then keels over and zooms into the vegetable patch.

I looked at Sue and shrugged hopelessly. Had we really driven 200 miles, spent a sleepless night, endured two hours of snarling traffic for this damp squib experience?

But then I got to thinking. Weren't we acting like typical 20th century media brats? One stopped short of saying 'It's not as good as on the telly.' But the feeling was there. We were spoilt by those close focus shots of other launches – the synchronisation between sound and vision, the camera following the ascent, the joy of the action replays, the countdown again, ignition from a new angle, those slow-motion vertical camera shots from the rocket gantry with the body of the rocket streaming past close enough to touch, the glorious technicolor, the choirs of angels, the stirring music.....

As it was there was only the pale imitation that reality could offer – this drifting column of white vapour being slowly folded by the breeze, the empty wastes of blue sky where the rocket had been only minutes before, the stream of cars heading back across the causeway.

Faith is somewhat restored later in the morning by the visit to the Space Centre itself. The Visitor Centre is superbly organised. There are many rockets and space vehicles on display, free viewing of films of the Apollo and Space Shuttle missions and the two hour bus tour takes you round the whole complex including a visit to the actual launch pad which was used only two hours earlier.

And perhaps what is most pleasing about visiting the Space Centre is that it is authentically and totally American. So much of what one sees in the country just isn't.

The Americans are masters of replica and so often one is confused and disorientated. Is this a genuine Venetian palace of the 15th century which has been transported from Europe or is it a clever 20th century copy. Often one never knows. There is for instance Washington Cathedral, a skilfully constructed Gothic place of worship built in the 1920s. There is Duke University in North Carolina, an ivy-covered

'Gothic Oxford College' built in the 1950s. In New York there is a medieval monastery full of atmosphere and the apparent charm of antiquity. In fact it was transported brick by brick from southern Spain and skilfully reconstructed. And somehow one feels deceived, taken in by a series of subtle 'cons'.

To the newcomer the only enduring reality seems to be the American highway with its hamburger chains, its pizza emporia, its chromium-plated car lots and the neon-lit all-night diners. Where is the real America in all this?

At the Kennedy Space Centre, there is an answer. This is authentic. This, America can call her very own. This is to be celebrated.

As we crossed the Banana River once more and turned the car south, the vapour trail had all but disappeared, merging with wisps of cirrus cloud. Challenger was on her way. Another successful launch.

Two years later, however, it would be a different story. On January 28th 1986 the same shuttle would break apart 73 seconds into its flight, killing the entire crew of seven. It would be NASA's darkest hour.

*

TO BE THUS HONOURED.....

The spring term was rolling along at speed and our thoughts were turning to our summer road trip. Coast to coast and back again in six weeks. Seven thousand miles, crossing through twenty one states. Miami to San Francisco, then back on a more northern route to Philadelphia to fly home.

The priority now was to find a suitable vehicle to survive such a trip. Our budget was very limited. My salary was half what Genny was getting in England, added to which the exchange rate was dropping miserably and we were getting fewer dollars for our pounds each month.

It was Rick Rodriguez, the workshop teacher, who caught me one day during lunch break. 'I hear you're lookin' for a van.'

'That's right,' I said.

'Neighbour of mine, Cuban guy name of Raul Guanci is sellin' a Ford window van. Might be worth lookin' at. He's an okay guy.'

'Thanks, Rick, that's kind of you.'

'No problem. Think you're crazy though, doing a trip like that in the summer. Me, I'm off down the Keys, fishing.'

I shrugged, 'Once in a lifetime trip, Rick. Gotta do these things when you get the chance.'

'S'ppose so. Good luck.'

Katie and James christened it the 'Smurfmobile.' It was a pale blue 2.5 litre 1973 Ford van; long wheel base, tinted windows, a long passenger seat behind the front seats and then an open space behind. It had a lot of miles on the clock, but Raul Guanci seemed an honest type of guy when he said, 'Yeah, this truck has quite a lots of miles but she go round the clock a lot more times yet, I promise you.'

'She won't die on us halfway across Death Valley?'

'You go to Death Valley in the summer? That is kinda crazy. They say the tarmac melts. I would miss Death Valley, go north or further south. Not Death Valley.'

'I'm joking, Raul, but I think our route across southern California would take us close to Death Valley. I'm just concerned that this van is up to the trip.'

'She's a good vehicle.' He shrugged, 'Never let me down for five years.'

I haggled a little on price but finally we shook hands and the deal was done.

'Will we sleep in the van?' asked Katie.

'That's the idea. I'm going to build a bed in the back and we'll look for a mattress at a yard sale.'

'And I'll take my fishing line and the crab traps,' added James.

'It's going to be quite an adventure,' I said.

'Like Laura in the story,' said Katie.

I nodded, 'Yes, our own four-wheeled little house on the prairie.'

*

With the temperature and humidity starting to rise again, I was relieved that the soccer season was over. My first fumblings as Coach hadn't exactly been a disaster. The girls' team won the Zone championships but in the County Championship were beaten 2-1 by

Miami Lakes School. And the same with the boys – Zone champions but beaten in the county playoffs by Arvida.

'Congratulations, Coach. You did a good job.' Ms Martin, the Principal, was pleased. She had called me into her office after school one afternoon. 'And Mr Kalinsky tells me you hit a pretty mean baseball.'

'Pure luck,' I said.

'I don't think so somehow,' she said. She handed me a large envelope. 'And now you're invited to be honoured by Dade County.'

'Honoured?' I said.

'Don't worry, it's not just for you. It's for all the exchange teachers in the county. It's down at County Hall next week.'

I doubted that there would be a similar civic presentation for Genny in Cumbria. In England people didn't like to 'make too much fuss'.

And this threw up another difference in our two cultures. Here, there was a distinct liking for formality and social etiquette. People were confident about standing up in front of an audience and making speeches. Students would readily pick up a microphone in an assembly or at a sports meet and address the audience. At George and Linda's church in Fort Lauderdale the pastor gave weekly broadcasts on the church radio. People would stand up and address the congregation with no hint of nervousness or inhibition. Americans seemed to value formality and ceremony.

When we had been invited for meals with new American friends, we always felt awkward at the start when everyone was expected to join hands round the table and a blessing was given. On one occasion Joe, our host, a church friend of George and Linda's, stunned me by saying, 'Barrie, we would be honoured if you would give the blessing.'

It was assumed I was a believer and that giving a blessing would be second nature to me. I stammered something about being thankful for their warmth and hospitality and in a curious way I began to warm to this formality of joining hands and acknowledging the importance of friendship. It didn't alter my doubts about the veracity of the divine but on a human level it was something I could appreciate. England, by comparison, seemed somewhat buttoned-up and overly self-conscious about such matters.

At another gathering with George and Linda's Christian friends I was thrown yet again. We were casually mingling, making polite conversation, sipping fruit punch and munching canapés, when Frank, the host, clapped his hands and said, 'Friends, I think it would be good to pray'. A circle formed in the middle of the living room and we shuffled to take our place. We stood with hands linked, eyes closed, heads bowed while Frank intoned,

'Lord, we thank you for this gathering and for all your bounty that you so freely give. And we especially thank you for bringing Barrie and Sue and their children to visit with us. We hope that your blessing on this home will go with them as they travel across this great country of ours. We ask this in the name of your son, Lord Jesus Christ. Amen.'

I had squinted and sweated through this little ceremony, hoping desperately that Frank didn't ask me to do a prayer or give a blessing. But it ended with nods and smiles and friendly banter and that was that.

The following week I travelled downtown to the Dade County office with the Principal to the honouring ceremony for the exchange teachers. It took place in the main assembly room. A group of local dignitaries sat on a raised dais while the audience of Fulbright exchange teachers and their principals sat in the main body of the hall. There were television cameras from the local TV station and reporters from the local radio stations. The Superintendent of Dade County Schools gave a brief address and then we paraded in front of the dais to be given our Proclamation Certificates. There were eight exchange teachers in Dade County and each of us gave a short vote of thanks to the assembly. It was all very formal, such was the American way.

'Will they do a similar ceremony for Genny in England?' asked Ms Martin.

'Possibly,' I replied. But I very much doubted that Carlisle's civic dignitaries would assemble to make a fuss of an exchange teacher.

When I got home I showed Sue my certificate.

'A bit over the top isn't it,' she said looking at me sideways.

'You see, that's a typical British response. This is the way they do things over here. They celebrate achievement,' I replied.

'Sounds like you're a convert.'

'Maybe I am.'

The Proclamation was designed to be framed and hung on the wall. It measured 14x20 inches and was embossed with gold lettering and in the bottom right hand corner there was a gold pennant with a blue ribbon bearing the Dade County Seal. The Proclamation read as follows:

WHEREAS, Barrie N. Day has come from Carlisle, England, to teach in a Dade County public school during the 1983-84 school year as a Fulbright exchange teacher; and

WHEREAS, at Ponce de Leon Junior High School, his American school, Barrie N. Day is providing the students, teachers and community

with a valuable opportunity to develop a better understanding of his country, while he gains greater understanding of the United States; and

WHEREAS, the opportunities for educational and cultural exchange serve to enrich young people on both sides of the sea with a broader, more expansive view of the world beyond their countries' boundaries.

NOW, THEREFORE, BE IT RESOLVED THAT:

The School Board of Dade Country, Florida, extends its warmest greeting to Barrie N. Day, a visitor to our country, and its sincere appreciation for his efforts as an exchange teacher.

A copy of this resolution is placed in the permanent records of this board.

Presented this 22ⁿᵈ day of February, A.D. 1984

'So my dear, a little more respect if you please for someone who has thus been so highly honoured,' I said.

Sue gave me a hearty shove and added, 'So you'll hang it on your office wall when you get home, will you?'

I shrugged, 'You see, again, there's the difference. Go into any of the offices of the teachers at school here and you'll see their certificates and accreditations proudly pinned to the walls. But for some perverse reason we frown on that and wouldn't be seen dead doing it in England. Why is that?'

'False modesty?' replied Sue. 'English reserve? I don't know but I can see what you're saying.'

'Maybe we're just too cynical. It's what we do to our celebrities and people who achieve things. One minute they're applauded, the next minute the tabloid press is tearing them limb from limb. Over here they celebrate success, they don't knock it like we do. I'm beginning to think our cynicism is not clever but rather sad.'

'Maybe it is, but I'll bet you fifty pounds you won't put that certificate on your office wall when you get home.'

'Right, you're on. We'll see whether or not the worm has turned.'

*

THEN CAME SPIRIT WEEK

There are no half term holidays in the American school calendar. Once school starts in September, apart from the odd day, there's no let up until the break for Christmas in December. In the spring, however, there is a week of what they call Spring Break but that's it until the school year finishes in mid June. Then there's the long three month holiday.

So to inject some respite into the weekly grind they build in events when students and staff can let off a little steam. In the autumn term we'd had the craziness of Hallowe'en. Now, in the summer term, we had 'Spirit Week.' And what a week of zaniness this turned out to be. With Hallowe'en I'd had classes of freaky ghouls, witches and goblins; in Spirit Week there was a different theme for each day but we were still expected to teach something resembling normal lessons.

Day One – this was billed as 'Punk Day.' Students turned up for  school in their version of punk gear. It was all rather bizarre. I remembered the true punks of the early Seventies: eyebrows and cheeks pierced with safety pins, ripped clothing, skin tight jeans and Doc Marten boots, wild hair colours spiked into Mohicans. The American versions were somewhat more tame but it was all good fun.

There was some good natured anarchy at times on the first day but I was able to regale my classes with stories of my encounters with real punks in England.

'You mean they really stuck safety pins through their eyebrows?'

' My god that's mega sick!'

'Can you imagine sticking a pin through your cheek.'

'That's mega gross!'

I recalled the Christmas when my fourteen year old nephew, James, arrived at the front door with his family to stay for a few days. He sported a luminous pink Mohican, perfectly groomed with spikes nine inches long, and a safety pin dangling from his ear. He wore a ripped tee shirt and ripped jeans. He had to duck his head to get through the doorway. Sue's father, Harry, who was somewhat Victorian in his outlook, took one look and his scowl lasted for the three days that young James was in the house. Katie was fascinated. She wanted to know how he didn't mess up his perfect hairdo at night.

'He sleeps sitting upright in bed,' replied his mother, 'propped up with pillows.'

Katie was open-mouthed.

'He's a bit of a soft punk, if you ask me,' added Sue. 'And he still says please and thank you. I don't think he's going to start a revolution.'

But Sue's father was never convinced.

Day two of Spirit Week was 'Tacky Tourist Day'. On this day, the halls were awash with students in Hawaiian shirts, straw hats, sun glasses, and various styles of beach wear and baseball caps. At lunchtime there was an outdoor concert in the quadrangle in front of the main school entrance. It

featured a range of performances. Theo Garner, one of the more quiet students from my 9th grade English class, was a revelation. Here he was alone on the stage playing keyboard and guitar and singing two of his own compositions to rapturous applause. Mild mannered and modest he just nodded and half smiled as he left the stage.

He was followed by a Michael Jackson tribute act performed by five girls dressed in black leotards, white boots, each wearing a sequined glove on one hand. They punched out *Beat It* and *Billy Jean*, spun, and gyrated a hip hop routine which had the audience whooping and clapping.

Day three was Blue/Grey day. Blue and grey were the school colours but on this day, the 8th graders had to wear clothing in some shade of grey while the 9th graders wore shades of blue. The final lesson of the day was cancelled and we all trouped into the auditorium for a concert.

First, the school band assembled with their splendid array of wind and brass instruments dominated by two huge tubas on the back row which looked like periscopes from some yellow submarine. Phyllis Compton, the band teacher, stood up on a small podium, settled them with a couple of taps of her baton and with an upward sweep of her arm set them exploding into the theme from *Rocky*. It was an impressive sound, utterly professional and confident. Next, followed the theme from *Star Wars* with all the players swinging their instruments in time with the music, the two tubas nodding back and forth to each other on the back row, the line of trombones swinging one way while the trumpets swung in the opposite direction. It was pure showbiz, utterly and wonderfully American. Playing in the band was not an extra-curricular activity as it would be in England. Here, they took 'Band' as a subject on the curriculum and these musicians were very accomplished. After *Star Wars* they played a medley of numbers while the cheerleaders, the Devilettes, (the school's sports emblem was a Blue Devil) performed a series of routines and cheers.

Until I'd witnessed Amy's cheerleaders in Jamaica, I'd always written off cheerleading as a silly girlie thing designed merely to enhance the macho mania of American football games. Now, watching it more closely, I had to admire the gymnastic skill and precision discipline involved in their routines. This was no silly girlie frippery but skilfully choreographed movement.

Finally, it was the turn of the school Chorus. Like Band, Chorus was also a subject on the curriculum – 30 to 40 singers came on stage and performed a series of songs from *Footloose* but by the time they got to *Let's Hear It For The Boy* it was clear the audience was getting restless.

Kalinsky, the deputy, took over the microphone in an attempt to restore some sobriety to the occasion. There followed the voting for Mr and Mrs Blue Devil: 9 boys and 9 girls lined up on stage and each took over the microphone for one minute to plead their case as to why they should get the vote. The decision would be based on audience response to their pleas.

'Hi, I'm Taylor, and I should get the vote for all the things I do round school to support the school community.'

Loud booing.

'Hi, I'm Gretchen, and I do a lot to help the administration by being an office monitor. I think I deserve your vote.'

Whistles and laughter.

'Hey guys, I'm just the best looking guy on the block.'

Loud cheering and whooping.

And so it went on. All rather cringe-making to my English eyes.

Finally Mr and Mrs Blue Devil were crowned to great cheering from the audience. The band ended the concert with a stirring rendition of *The Star-Spangled Banner* while the audience stood and mouthed the words in a rather half-hearted fashion. So ended Day Three of Spirit Week.

Day Four was a much more serious day. This was Student Leadership Day when students took over the running of the school. Prior to the day students applied for a range of school positions from Principal down to classroom teachers. They had to present their credentials before being selected. The students selected as Principal and Deputies for the day had to be appropriately mature and confident enough to be able to address the student body over the PA system, tour the classrooms observing lessons and command a modicum of respect rather than ridicule.

For each of my classes, students had applied to me to be considered for teaching the lesson. They had to submit a lesson plan and convince me that they could cope with the challenge without it degenerating into farce. So for example, my first lesson of the day with an 8th grade class was taught by Julie and Roberto. They had prepared a lesson on letter writing and they took turns to deliver the lesson alternating every ten minutes. The rest of the class showed due respect for what was quite a challenge and I was impressed by the maturity of these fourteen year olds. I doubted that my students back in England could handle the task with equal panache.

During one of my ninth grade lessons which was being taken by Susannah and Declan, who were leading a lesson on the poetry of e.e.cummings, the door opened and the Principal for the day, William Cooper, stood in the doorway with Ms Martin standing behind him. He looked impressive in a smartly tailored grey suit, white shirt and blue tie – a contrast to his usual jeans and tee shirt.

'Sorry to interrupt but can you just brief me on the lesson you're teaching, Susannah,' he said.

This was no pantomime. They were taking it all very seriously. I was impressed.

Susannah was nervous. 'Er, we are looking at a poem by e.e.cummings.'

'Oh, the guy who didn't like capital letters,' replied William.

'That's him. But his poetry is, er.., very captivating,' said Susannah.

281

William wandered round the class glancing at the students' work, nodded and said, 'Looks good, Susannah. Well done, class.'

At the door Ms Martin raised her eyebrows and nodded, gave me a half smile and followed the acting Principal out of the room.

'So what did you reckon to Spirit Week?' she said at a meeting the following week. 'Do you do that type of thing in England?'

'It was intriguing,' I replied. 'A mix of fun and good humour but also there was the contrast of Student Leadership Day. They took it very seriously. That surprised me.'

'Why?'

'There's a great energy and enthusiasm about the students here. They enjoy the fun and entertainment side of things but then the Student Leadership Day showed another side. William, your acting Principal, was very impressive and so were the students who taught my lessons. I don't know that my students back home would handle things so well.'

'Why is that?'

I shrugged, 'Maybe it's our cynicism.'

I wasn't sure why I felt like that. But there was this distinct difference again between our two cultures. There is an instinct in the British to see Americans as somewhat naive, almost childlike in their enthusiasms, their untrammelled idealism, their brashness. They were the new upstarts in the historical story, we had been there, done that, gained the wisdom, learned the lessons. We had real medieval monasteries. They only had copies of medieval monasteries. We had a thousand years of history behind us – they had a mere two hundred. I was as guilty as anyone about harbouring this instinct to make judgements from behind a mask of patronising cynicism. But I was beginning to question this instinct. Okay, so they only had two hundred years of history but what they had achieved in that time was mind-bending. South Florida had been a mosquito infested swampland until Henry Flagler opened it up in the 1890s with his railroad. And now look at it – cities, luxurious residential developments, Disneyworld, the Kennedy Space Centre and an extraordinary highway system which extended down to Key West via a series of remarkable bridges, the longest being seven miles long. There was an energy to get things done here which challenged the world weary cynicism and entrenched views of the old country. If this year in the USA was doing anything, it was blowing apart many of my prejudices.

*

THE END OF SOMETHING

'Will there be bears in the campsites, like in the story?' asked Katie. She had remembered the chapter in *Little House in the Big Woods* when Laura discovers a bear in the barn.

'Maybe, especially when we get into the Rocky Mountains.'

'Will we be safe in the van?'

'Hope so. I'm going to make grills for the windows and they say as long as you don't have food near where you're sleeping, you're okay.'

She nodded, raised eyebrows, not entirely convinced. But then neither was I. People passed round lurid tales of hungry bears ripping doors off vehicles and breaking through caravan skylights; of rampant grizzlies mauling people in their tents.

We couldn't sleep in the van with all the windows and doors closed so I set to work to fashion some steel grills for the windows. I bought some steel mesh from a hardware store and enclosed it in a wooden frame to fit in the window slot. I lined it with mosquito netting and also made a netting screen for the back of the van so that we could have the doors open but be safe from a mosquito invasion. A raised wooden platform was constructed in the rear of the van so we could store our gear underneath but have an area for laying out a folding mattress on top for Sue and the children. I would be sleeping on the bench seat behind the front seats. If we were not in bear country there was always the option of using our tent.

Katie watched my handiwork and helped with fetching tools, nails and screws. She loved the idea of our little home on wheels. James, for the most part, was lost in his world of cartoon adventures - He-Man, Skeletor and the mysteries of Castle Greyskull. He played endless games with his collection of toy figures and with the Battlecat figure I had made him out of ply wood on which He-Man rode into battle. These and their box of Lego would occupy both Katie and James for hours on our long trip from Miami to San Francisco.

There were end of term tests in early June. As usual these were expected to be 'bubble tests' – those mindless multiple choice tests that could be zapped through an optical mark reader and marked in seconds. *'Mark the sentence which uses a conjunction/ Circle the pronoun in this sentence/ Place speech marks in the appropriate place in this sentence.'* These types of test were an insult to the intelligence of my students, the students who had produced such brilliant writing during the year. I refused to use them and devised the type of writing test which I would

283

have used in England. In fact my end of year tests were the only ones in the school where students had to do any extended writing. All the other subjects used multiple choice tests.

Admittedly it took hours to mark them but I felt strongly that to be true to what I believed English to be about and, to be true to my students, I needed to leave with a clear conscience that I'd done the right thing. Throughout the year I had been forced to re-examine my assumptions about this subject called English. The American books told me it was about grammar, clause analysis, the mechanical dissection of parts of speech. My British background told me it was about developing thinking, imagination and the powers of using language expressively. The two approaches weren't mutually exclusive but I felt the American approach was stultifying and ultimately counter-productive in inhibiting students from expressing themselves effectively. To me the proof was in the enthusiasm of the students and the work they produced. We had played language games, devised role play scenarios, dramatised scenes from plays and novels; they had created poetry files, produced their remarkable ancestor research projects and written great stories. They had written and debated intelligently on the literature we had read and my mind went back to that early lesson when Rhett Baldwin challenged me about why we did discussions if they weren't graded. We had travelled a long way since then.

It is the rare privilege of the teacher of English to be allowed to get close to the hearts and minds of his students, more so, I think, than in any other subject. Literature by its very nature explores the whole spectrum of human emotion and endeavour – love, regret, envy, ambition, birth, death, pain – we discussed these, explored the way they were portrayed in plays, stories and poems and in their writing the students often revealed their innermost ideas and sensitivities.

Sean, a student in my first period eighth grade class, was a case in point. He rarely spoke or socialised with the others but revealed to me that he was moved to tears by S.E.Hinton's novel *The Outsiders* because he so closely identified with the motherless central character of Ponyboy. When we were moving towards the end of Daniel Keyes' brilliant short novel *Flowers for Algernon* with its heart-rending pathos, several students wrote that they found it hard to bear the tragic irony of the ending. I had used Cat Stevens' song *Father and Son* as a stimulus for imaginative writing and it generated some stunning pieces of work on family relationships. We laughed together at the caustic brilliance of Dorothy Parker's poetry and delighted in the sensuality of Hemingway's

The Big Two-Hearted River which triggered thoughts of summer and the great outdoors.

I had built up a relationship with these classes which was very special. They had poked fun at my accent, we had miscommunicated many times when I used English idioms they didn't understand and there had been a few altercations along the way but we had developed a bond which was rare for them and rare for me. To steal a title from Hemingway it was 'The End of Something' and I received touching messages from appreciative parents and cards from students.

'You've been quite a hit, Coach Day,' nodded Ms Martin at our final interview. 'I've had a lot of parents saying how great it's been for their children.'

'That's nice to hear.'

'How's it been for you?'

'It's been a challenge. I don't think I've ever worked so hard in my life.'

'But it's been worth it?'

'Oh, yes,' I replied. 'A year like no other.'

My American teaching experience
as drawn by one of my students

During the final term I had been approached by the school newspaper class to write about my experience of teaching at Ponce Junior High. I penned a fairly light-hearted piece and didn't mention my more serious reservations about the school system. During the year I had managed to send off eight articles for the *Cumberland News* with

285

photographs. They had published most of them with pleasing full page spreads – Jean had sent them over each time they were printed. I'd kept to humorous anecdotes about cultural encounters, family experiences and travels to various Florida hotspots.

But I did feel I needed to set down my observations in a more serious way before I left. During the final weeks I phoned the *Miami Herald* and spoke to one of the editors outlining what I had in mind. She was interested so I set to work.

I had profound reservations about the way English was meant to be taught as evidenced in the state adopted course books. Their approach was clinical, focussing on the mechanics of grammar and sentence construction. There was little or no invitation to stimulate thinking and to write at length. Brad, one of our Miami friends who taught in the Medical School at the university, complained of straight A honors students arriving for their degree courses and being unable to string a couple of paragraphs together. They were having to take remedial classes in writing. But should anybody be surprised when so little extended writing took place in any subject and where tests were based solely on multiple choice questioning?

My other main criticism was the crazy structure of the school day where every day was exactly the same – same teacher, same class at the same time. It was fundamentally unjust. The first half of the day was always more productive for teacher and students than the second half of the day – for obvious reasons. So to condemn period six students to the tired end of the day, every day, and similarly for a teacher to have to face that period six class at the end of every day – it was patently unfair and inefficient. It also restricted students to a maximum of six subjects, far fewer than their peers in other countries would be taking. Was it any wonder then that American students compared badly in their subject scores with their peers abroad? When I raised this with Kalinsky, the Deputy, he claimed the students would get confused if they had a different timetable on each day as in England. But clearly it was designed to make administration easier rather than to maximise the educational potential of the students.

I composed a lengthy article and sent it off to the *Miami Herald* not expecting much joy. But at least I'd given it a shot and pulled together some of the observations I'd drawn from my year teaching in the American system.

A few days later I got a call from one of the sub editors at the *Herald.* The article would be published the following week. I was delighted.

It appeared on the front page of the *Viewpoint* section of the Sunday edition. Apart from my *Cumberland News* articles, it was only my third time in print. I'd had a short story and a travel feature published in Jamaica but nothing on a serious subject. It was placed just below a feature on the debt crisis by none other than Henry Kissinger, the former Secretary of State. Not bad, I thought, to be placed alongside such illustrious company, not bad all.

*

On the last day, when the students had gone, I took down my wall displays – my pictures of Cumbria, my map of Britain with its various landmarks. I cleared my desk and binned all the 'trash' in the 'trash can'. I wheeled my bicycle along the hall and out into the afternoon sunshine and peddled across Dixie Highway for the last time.

'Go West, young man' – that nudging call gambolled round my head as I pedalled home. I needed no persuading. The van was almost packed; the route was vaguely planned and it was only three thousand miles to San Francisco.

Time to get the wagon rolling.

CHAPTER THE SIXTH Road Trip USA:summer 1984

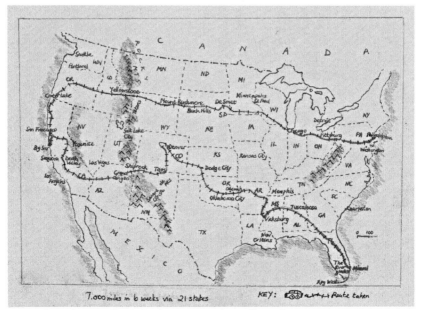

7,000 miles in 6 weeks via 21 states   KEY: 🚐 ✦×✦×✦ Route taken

(see Appendix 1 for larger version of map)

THE JOURNAL : A 7,000 MILE MEANDER ACROSS 21 STATES IN 6 WEEKS

June 15th Late afternoon. Finally pull out of the driveway and head north for the Florida Turnpike. Van jam-packed – fishing poles, bikes, spare wheels strapped to the outside. Interior equally over-stuffed. Sue is sorting maps and last minute paper work. Katie and James are setting up a den and play area on the folding mattress behind the long passenger seat. They have a lego board and plastic tubs of various toys and no idea of what we have embarked on.

Sky overcast; heavy rain falling. Turnpike snaking with slow-moving traffic. Gas tank is full but it's the temperature gauge I have to keep an eye on. I haven't really questioned the wisdom of this trip until now. The distance we've planned is maybe over-ambitious and the engine on this ageing 2.5 litre Ford always seems to run slightly hot - not good when we're heading for summer temperatures in Arizona and California.

Making for Tuscaloosa, where the grandfather of one of my teaching colleagues lives. He's offered to accommodate us for a couple of days and show us something of Alabama. Flick through my collection of cassette tapes. Head awash with a clutter of thoughts - last-minute people – students, teachers, friends – warm words and touching goodbyes. Now the prospect of this epic trip with my little family in this ageing van which could overheat - it's all mesmerising. Scan the box of audio cassettes and select Christopher Cross' *Sailing* hoping it will massage my mood.

Traffic eases north of West Palm Beach where turnpike heads inland towards Orlando. Sun sets quickly - within an hour we are enveloped in soft tropical darkness. I shall miss this back in England, this blanket of warmth which laps around you in the evenings.

What to make of this place – Florida – 'the man-made state'? They drain swamps to create land for buildings - make soil out of crushed limestone. Like the geology, nothing seems to go deep. People are transient. White Americans moving north to Orlando, Cubans moving in to take over south Florida. Retirement communities and new shopping malls spring up overnight instantly landscaped with fully grown palm trees and shrubs, a veneer of smooth tarmac masking the rubble. A hurricane can clear the lot in seconds.

Early evening stop at Fort Drum Rest Area south of Orlando. Sue cooks steak on our little camping stove while I go exploring with the children. Scent of orange blossom heavy on the night air. Pick sprig of the white flowers from orchard which borders car park - the start of our collection. Next, a rose from Georgia.

Towards midnight pull into rest area near Gainsville. We'll stay here for the night. Sue and children already asleep. I have been lulled by Mahler's *4th Symphony*, staring at the tail lights of the vehicles ahead in that semi-hypnotic state that night driving induces. Sleep comes easily.

June 16th 6a.m. Smell of cool pines. Orchards swathed in mist. Two racoons snuffle round garbage bins, pay no attention to me as I head for the washrooms. A trucker shaving at one of the washbasins. Tattoos down his arms. Shaves carefully round his bushy grey moustache. 'Atlanta Falcons' shirt hangs from a peg on the wall – reminds me we're close to the state line with Georgia.

8.30a.m. In a McDonald's getting breakfast. Not good. Coffee thin and tasteless, eggs the texture of rubber. Need to find local diners in future. Even so, Katie and James love the finger-licking mess of fast-food eating. Sue passes on the food and settles for fresh-squeezed Florida orange juice.

Back on the road and soon crossing the Swanee River made famous in the 1851 song *Old Folks At Home* written by Stephen Foster. This gleaned from a leaflet picked up at the Rest Area. Apparently the song is 'The Real State Song of Florida'. Explain all this to Sue and the children and lustily sing the opening line *'Way Down Upon The Swanee River...'* only to be greeted by hoots of derision and Katie shouting, 'Stop it daddeeeeeeeeee!'

Minutes later cross state line into Georgia. Road surface noticeably poorer. Land green and flat – peanut country. Along the road bleached clapboard shacks with rust red roofs.

Pass through Valdosta and Albany and stop to look at Confederate monument in Cuthbert. Buy a Cherokee rose, the Georgia state flower, at a small flower shop to add to our collection. It's late morning; sun is high and humidity stifling. Across the road is a beaten up Pontiac with bags of peanuts piled on the roof and bonnet. There's a sign 'HANK'S NUTS' and Hank sits in a camp chair, bleached  overalls, stained grey shirt, lined black face, grey hair under his cap.

'How much?' I ask.

'2 dollar a bag.'

'Are they roasted?'

'Sure. 30 minutes at 300 degrees. They's roasted.' He nods sagely, sucks at his pipe, spits tobacco juice. The brown gobbet rolls in the dust on the road. Katie and James stand and stare, not sure about all this.

'I'll take a bag.' Hand over two dollar bills. The bag is warm not just from the sun but from the peanuts still warm inside. James giggles as he puts his hand inside the bag and feels the warm kernels. They are crisp when you snap them, the nuts are a warm salty flavour.

I turn and nod at Hank. 'Taste good,' I say.

'Hank's nuts is the best,' he growls from under the peak of his cap. 'Best in Georgia.'

2.37p.m. Cross Alabama state line at Lake George. Bridge takes us across lake and into the town of Eufaula. This place is prosperous. Well tended parks and gardens, tree-lined roads; stunning white columned ante-bellum style homes squatting at the end of avenues of oaks and cedars. In contrast, on the edge of the town, clusters of teetering shacks, black families on the verandahs. Nearby are railroad sidings. Creepers and vines entomb three miles of rotting, rusting rail trucks, paint flaking from a sign on the sides of the trucks which reads 'Southern Gives The Green Light to Innovation.' A historic marker records the location of the riot of November 1874 at Springhill, nine years after the end of the Civil War. It reads: *On election day there was a shoot out after the polls closed which marked the end of Republican domination in Barbour County.*

Drive on through intermittent downpours. Road steams. When we cross from Macon County into Montgomery County road surface improves. Every mile or so there is a church – Baptist mainly – white clapboard with small towers and slender spires - all with roadside billboards peddling a different take on God's message:

IF YOU LOVE JESUS – HONK.

Be Ye fishers of men – You catch 'em – He'll clean em

FORBIDDEN FRUIT CREATES MANY JAMS

This must be what they call the 'Bible Belt'.

Pass south of Montgomery, state capital of Alabama, a key city in the history of the Civil Rights movement. It's where Martin Luther King started his ministry and where, on December 1st 1955, Rosa Parkes was arrested when she refused to give up her seat on a bus for a white man. At that time blacks could only sit in  the rear seats of the bus and had to give up their seats if all the white seats were taken. Rosa Parkes refused. This triggered the Montgomery bus boycott with blacks refusing to ride the city's buses. It lasted 381 days after which the Supreme Court ruled that segregation on buses was unconstitutional. This victory for civil rights inspired further challenges to the harsh segregation laws of the south. In 1965 Martin Luther King led the famous march from Selma to Montgomery in the face of violent opposition by whites and the police. It ended with King making a speech on the steps of the state capitol which ends with the words: 'How long? Not long, because the arc of the moral universe is long, but it bends toward justice.'

But we don't stop in Montgomery as our destination is still some distance away in Tuscaloosa.

Grandad Stuart Carver greets us with a firm handshake and a touch like a blessing on the heads of the children. He is a robust, stocky 81 year old, grandfather of Anne, a science teacher at Ponce. When she heard of our trip, she didn't hesitate to contact her grandad. He walks us round his garden, keen for us to catch the scent of his gardenias on the warm evening air and to watch the house martins swooping in and out of the eaves. I watch the thick forearms and the stubby fingers move to cradle the gardenia blooms as he bends to smell them. 'That there's the scent of an Alabama summer night,' he murmurs in that easy southern lilt which is almost like singing in the rise and fall of the cadences. No formality with this old man, just a quiet but comfortable gravitas.

He has prepared beds for us and a cold supper of chicken and potato salad. The children quickly warm to him as he takes them into the garden to see his chickens.

'This here rooster's been with me a good few years. I call him Red Neck. He's a proud fella and he keeps his ladies in order.' He checks the hen house for eggs and hands a speckled brown to James. 'Just cup your hands together and carry it carefully now.'

James stares at his treasure and waits for grandad Carver to lead the way back to the house.

After the children are in bed we sit on the porch and Stuart serves us iced lemonade. Darkness vibrates with zithering sounds of tree frogs and crickets. He tells us of his time in the lumber trade – he was young, head strong and he invested in the rights to three million feet of timber in an area of swampland. It was good wood – cedar and oak. But three months of rain ruined him. The level of the swamp rose to a height which drowned his tractors. He was unable to harvest the timber and was left penniless. That's when he moved to Tuscaloosa and got a job in the insurance business. But he still thanks god for his good fortune and his long life.

'I'd be favoured if y'all come with me to my church tomorrow. I'd like you to see it.'

June 17th Up early, before humidity has built up and while there is still freshness in the air. Scent of mimosa drifting from the tree close to the corner of the house. Fruit and cereal on the table and a coffee pot steaming on the hob. A television preacher declaims that *'abortion is murder'* and *'Brethren, there's a decision that has to be made. The Lord doesn't favour the waverer.'* I like his clever use of rhyme but not his sentiments.

Grandad Carver drives us to his church and on the way reveals that he's a tobacco chewer – even in church he secretly keeps a plug of Chattanooga Chew in his cheek, 'I never spit, well not on a Sunday, and nobody don't know but me. My little secret.' He winks at James and Katie.

The Tuscaloosa Primitive Baptist Church is a recently built brick building. Interior plain, no altar, no images, no candles, just pews and a pulpit for the preacher. They are a breakaway church of a dozen or so families who parted company with other local Baptists – some disagreement about religious practice. They raised money and built the church themselves. Stuart explains that Primitive Baptists are a branch of Baptists who firmly adhere to original (primitive) tenets of faith and practice as supported by the New Testament. They don't follow the teachings of Calvin but see themselves as strictly adhering to the original ministry of Jesus. So, no adornment in church, no musical instruments only acappella singing. Foot washing at certain times in the church calendar and in the communion service real unleavened bread is used.

Other families are already inside. We are introduced and they beam with pride that we have come to visit them. Before the service there is singing practice. Stuart stands at the front and launches into a rousing hymn, 'Lord the Time is Coming and We Must be Ready.' His rich baritone leads the small congregation and the unaccompanied singing gathers strength. Services consist only of singing and preaching; no ceremony or ritual.

The previous evening Stuart told the story of a famous preacher who came some years ago to one of the annual camp meetings. Services are held in tents and hundreds assemble to sing and listen to the preaching. This particular preacher climbs into the pulpit, stands and looks out over the congregation, hundreds of the faithful who have travelled great distances to hear him, faces turned to hear his words. There is silence and then he shakes his head. 'I'm sorry brethren, but the spirit isn't moving in me today.' And that's it. He stands down from the pulpit and makes his way past his disappointed flock.

'And let me tell you now,' said Stuart, 'if any preacher took out some notes to preach from he would be asked to stand down. The preacher is only a vessel, a conduit for the Lord's words.'

Next, our initiation into Bible Belt 'fire and brimstone', the first preacher being Preacher Livinstone. He is impressive; knows his biblical references, weaves them together with subtlety, uses his voice like a practiced performer, slowing the pace for emphasis, speeding up to raise the tension, that wonderful sing-song southern accent soaring and dipping as he sucks on the consonants and chews on the vowels working his audience like a skilful actor. *'An' I tell you, brethren, the Lord ain't waiting, the Lord ain't amusin' himself while you makin' up yo mind whether or not to commit. Yuh have to to make that commitment right now, right here, in this here church on this Sunday.....'*

His message about Sin, Redemption and Obedience by-passes me completely but as a performance I score him high in the Oscar stakes.

Second preacher, Preacher Ewing, is less experienced. None of the subtle tonal nuances of the first. Spills out the quotes and bible references in a nervous frenzy of quivering vibrato. He leans and sways over the edge of the pulpit nodding or shaking his head for emphasis, raising a hand here or pointing a finger there. It is poor theatre from an inexperienced actor.

It calls to mind the scene in *Footloose* where John Lithgow plays a preacher in a small southern town. Daughter, Ariel, sits in the empty church, watches her father rehearsing his sermon – learning the references, weaving them into his message, trying out his voice in difference ways to create the right dramatic effect. This may be preaching without notes but if you're under rehearsed it shows.

After the service – lunch: ham, okra, beans, ribs, fried chicken, corn bread and we 'visit' with members of congregation. They are smiling and polite and rather restrained. An all white congregation and both preachers are white. Wonder whether it's typical in many of the southern churches that races don't mix.

During drive back home Stuart describes his trauma at age four seeing his father baptising his mother in a river. Clothed in white 'like an angel' she was thrust under the water and he thought she was lost to him forever. His grandmother was half Indian and his grandfather was preacher on Sunday, bridge builder during the working week. As a boy, Stuart helped him to build bridges across creeks and rivers. He would swim with a line to the other side of the river, tether the line to a tree and use it to pull logs across for building the bridge.

'When my granddaddy was preaching he held the hearts of his flock in the palm of his hands. But I have to say that today my heart was not held by Preacher Ewing. He still has to find the voice of the Lord in his soul.'

We have grown close to this grand old man in the short time we've spent with him; have warmed to his easy manner, his quiet dignity, the warmth of his gravelly voice and when we wave him good bye there is a feeling that we have been blessed by this encounter.

June 18th 10.30a.m. Cross stateline into Mississippi, heading for Vicksburg just west of Jackson. Vicksburg lies on a meander of 'ol' man river' and I can't wait to see 'The Father of Waters' as Abraham Lincoln called it. We're in pick-up country – every other vehicle a Ford or Dodge pick-up, often trailing aluminium bass-boats with bulbous outboards clamped to the stern. In Kosciusko we fill up with gas. 80cents a gallon, that's 58p in English money - in England it's £1.75 a gallon.

3p.m. Vicksburg National Battlefield Park. Standing on a high bluff looking down on the mighty Mississippi, a wide brown highway of water snaking into the distance. James and Katie are climbing on the cannons which point towards the river. Vicksburg was crucial to Confederate control of the Mississippi during the Civil War - it became a key

battleground. Under cover of darkness on the night of April 16th 1863, Union ironclads sailed south past the line of defensive cannons and set up a bridgehead south of the city. 35,000 Union troops under Ulysses S. Grant faced 15,000 Confederate troops under Lt.  Gen. John Pemberton. Grant surrounded the city which was gradually levelled by Union artillery; the people were living in caves and holes in the ground and eating rats. After putting up sustained resistance Pemberton finally surrendered on July 4th.

Tour the park reading historic markers trying to make sense of the place for the children – trying to explain why the 'Blues' were fighting the 'Greys' over something called 'slavery'. At park exit we stand before a painting of a Union soldier meeting a Confederate soldier in heaven, both sheltered by an angel's wings. Something must have got through for

Katie says, 'I hope I die only when I'm old.' Collect sprig of magnolia from Vicksburg cemetery to put with our Florida orange blossom and Georgia rose. Tomorrow cross into Arkansas.

June 19th Today, rendezvous with Chris and her two little girls who were in same pre-school nursery as James. Her husband Brad is a plastic surgeon on placement at Miami Medical School. Chris is driving back to the family farm in Oklahoma for the summer and then on to their home in Denver. She's invited us to join them. We have planned to meet up at a campground in Arkansas near Blanchard Springs.

Take Route 61 north from Vicksburg. It runs teasingly close to the Mississippi all the way to Memphis but high levees mean we rarely get a view of the river. Fields mainly of soya and rice. Black workers hoeing in the fields, pink magnolias shading some of the white clapboard homes. Pass cypress swamps, the trees with curving trunks like grey skirts sunk into the water, Spanish moss hanging from the branches.

At Rosedale State Park we finally get down to the river and I fulfil a childhood whim of paddling in the great river and feeling Mississippi mud between my toes. At park shop they sell *Bottled River Water* with the instruction: *'No tap water added. To make muddy just shake. Bottled 1982'.* Or there is *'Mississippi River Sand – Guaranteed full of grit $1.50 a bottle.'* We are not tempted to buy.

12.30p.m. Cross river into Arkansas at Helena. Riverboat pushing 20 coal barges passes beneath the bridge. 'Is this the river Laura crossed in the book?' asks Katie. Each evening we read another chapter from *Little House on the Prairie*. At the start of the book the Wilder family cross the wide Missouri heading for the prairies of Kansas. We are travelling further south but we'll be in similar territory when we get to Oklahoma. For Katie and James our house on wheels has become a horse-drawn wagon heading for Indian territory.

Now we are in a new state, the road is immediately better. Pecan orchards, prosperous looking farms. Overtake two Goldwing motor bikes – his and hers. Husband and wife on a road trip chatting to each other via their radio mikes – small aerials project from their helmets. How cool is that.

North into green undulating countryside. Small farms, dairy cattle, woodland – reminiscent of England. Heading for campsite at Heber Springs. The Ozark escarpment emerges out of rain mist beyond the forests, a bleached grey outcrop of rock stretching across the horizon.

John Denver's *Rocky Mountain High* is becoming something of a signature tune to accompany this journey and we all sing along each time it's played. Katie has been sitting next to me in the front seat, feet up on the dash board, headphones on, listening to a story tape. Today it's *Swiss Family Robinson*. James plays with lego on the mattress behind the long passenger seat.   They are excited about   meeting up with Emmy (5) and Lauren (3), at the campsite. When we finally turn into   the   Heber   Springs campground their faces are close to the windows trying to be first to spot Chris' brown VW campervan.

Set up camp alongside them. Children race off into woods to collect sticks for campfire, their little voices ringing among the branches sending the chipmunks scurrying. Barbecue burgers and hot dogs and then in the glow of the firelight Chris reads another chapter from the story. She is the gentle earth mother, voice like buttermilk, easy on the ear with its light sing-song mid-western lilt. She and Brad lived for a while in Germany while Brad was continuing his medical training. She didn't care for life in Florida and is longing to get back to the farm in Oklahoma and their home in Colorado.

When children are tucked up in sleeping bags, we sip wine and Chris talks of Okemah, the little town in Oklahoma where she grew up. Her grandmother knew Woodie Guthries' family who also lived in the town. Describes them as strange and distant and recounts the time when Woodie's sister Clara poured petrol over herself in front of the house and set herself on fire. 'It seems the family suffered from Huntington's disease, a genetic neurodegenerative disorder which affects behaviour and probably explains why they were seen as strange,' explains Chris. Woodie Guthrie, the hobo folk legend, composer of the alternative national anthem *This Land is Your Land* and around 3000 other folk songs, was disowned by the townsfolk. 'I'll take you to see where his house stood when we get to the farm. There's nothing left of it now though,' adds Chris.

June 20th Drive a little way north to the town of Mountain View, centre for folk music, local crafts and antiques. Music comes from town square and on the porch of one of the houses a four piece bluegrass band playing *Green Back Dollar* – two guitars, a violin and a dulcimer. Katie and James are fascinated by the dulcimer; they've never seen one before.

They watch the fingers of the player sliding along the strings squeezing out exquisite sounds from this strange looking instrument.

Later, visit Ozark Folk Centre. Watch a furniture maker turning a length of hickory on a pole lathe worked with a foot treadle. Another craftsman hones thin pieces of maple and spruce for violins and guitars. In the old schoolhouse Miss Mary Gillihan, dressed in a long flowered cotton dress, sits children at old desks and explains about old time schooling. She writes their names using a quill pen and ink she has made from pokeberries – same berries used in ink for writing the American Constitution in the 18th century. In Folk Centre shop, while children nose among candy sticks, I find what I'm looking for: a thin yellow book *How to Talk Pure Ozark.* It's a gift at $2.00

Here's a sample:

Farred - *He farred his gun*
Ford   – *Don't be backard in comin' ford*
Gay-us –*Yoons use raggle or Ethyl in yore gay-us taink?*
Damlar - *Yuh kaint trus Billy Joe. He's a damlar.*
Paints – *Those girl bolly baw players have on tight paints.*
Wole   - *Many of the new cyars have white wole tars*

June 21st 9.30a.m. Heading west along I-20 following course of Arkansas River north of Little Rock. Cross stateline into Oklahoma at Fort Smith, originally established as a military outpost in 1817. It's the place where 'More men were put to death by the U.S. Government... than in any other place in American history.' This at the hands of one Judge Isaac Parker. He served as U.S. District Judge 1875–1896. Nicknamed the 'Hanging Judge' he imposed rough and ready frontier justice and sentenced 160 people to hang during the course of his career.

As we move further west into the state, I notice Oklahoma number plates have legend - *The Sooner State.* At rest area near Henryetta on the I-268 we sit round shaded picnic table and drink cans of cold Pepsi while Chris explains. 'It all started at noon on April 22nd 1889. They call it the Great Land Run. What had been Indian territory was opened up to settlers. Settlers with their wagons and horses lined up on the new state line and when the signal gun was fired they raced to claim their plot of land. But some people had hidden themselves over in the new territory and these 'sooners' then jumped up to claim their land sooner than they should have. That's why we call Oklahoma the 'Sooner State.' She goes on, 'They reckon 50,000 people lined up for the run and there were about two million acres available. By the end of the day both Oklahoma City and Guthrie had established cities of around 10,000 people and that had happened in a single day. Can y'all believe it? And within a day or two streets had been laid out, property lots marked and they had started to form a municipal government. They say that children started collecting buffalo dung to sell as cooking fuel. Within a couple of weeks schools had opened and do you know that within a month Oklahoma city had six newspapers and five banks.'

'What's dung?' asks Katie.

Chris smiles, 'Buffalo poo.'

Children grimace. 'Yuk!'

'But life was hard for those little children and they would do anything to help their families even a yucky job like collecting buffalo poo, drying it and selling it. There wasn't too much wood on the prairies and dried poo gives off a good heat, so you had to make do.'

'Like pa in the story,' adds Katie, 'he has to go to the creek to get wood to build the house.'

'That's right,' nods Chris. 'Now I grew up in Okemah, that was in Okfuskee County and it was my great granddaddy who named the county. He named it after a Creek Indian town in Alabama. You see a lot of Indians, or what we call Native Americans, had been forced out of their lands by white settlement and they journeyed two thousand miles along what is called 'The Trail of Tears' from the south eastern states into Oklahoma and the mid-west. I have to say it's not a part of our history that I feel comfortable with.'

June 22nd 6p.m. Sun setting over the farm lake. House Martins swooping for insects across surface of water. A flat bottomed aluminium boat is tethered to a stake on the bank. Rolling wheat land beyond. Warm wind blowing. Chris says the wind always blows in Oklahoma. Farmhouse is a solid stone building. Inside, a homely warmth – bookshelves, quilted throws on the furniture, old photographs and framed needlepoint on walls. Meet Chris' parents – Tom and Mary. Tom is thick–set, barrel-chested, wavy grey hair, a slow gravel-edged voice but softened by the Oklahoma lilt. Mary – petite with open kindly face, thick greying hair piled in a bun on her head. They greet us warmly. A meal has been prepared. Fried chicken, cornbread, cold ham and sliced tomatoes.

10.00p.m. Along lakeshore. Starlight pricking the surface, murmur of crickets, croak of a bullfrog; a beaver nosing a kite of ripples which catch shards of moonlight. Tomorrow we will lay out a trotline across part of the lake. James finds it hard to settle to sleep. The night is hot and he's excited about catching a catfish. Tom has said they can grow several feet long with mouths the size of a bucket. James will not sleep easy tonight.

June 23rd 11.30a.m. Sitting in one of Chris' old haunts – 'The Sooner Drug Store' soda fountain on Okemah Main Street where she came as a child. Little has changed. Formica tables, a soda bar with round swivel seats which the children clamber on with great excitement. Chris orders everyone her usual – cherry lime milk shakes. I try a root beer float – strange medicinal taste tempered by the sweetness of the vanilla ice-cream.

Chris has walked us through various parts of Okemah. First to site of Woody Guthrie's house. There's only an empty earth beaten foundation. The house had either collapased or burnt down. Guthrie was named after the President of the time, Woodrow Wilson. Last night I found on the bookshelf a copy of Guthrie's book *Bound for Glory*. In the early chapters he describes life in Okemah; the name comes from a Creek Indian word meaning 'town on a hill'. He talks of the friendly banter on the streets, small town talk and small town dramas. His politics were radical: 'Left wing, chicken wing – it's all the same to me,' and his songs protested the frustrations and yearnings of the common man.

Today Okemah main street is dusty and tired. Weeds poke through the pavers and flourish along the roadside. Gutters have broken glass, ancient bottle tops, squashed Coke cans – they have not been swept in months. There are faded street signs and empty buildings. It's a town struggling to survive. Stunted oak trees line each side of the street. Every other vehicle is a pick-up truck. Native Americans are distinctive with deep red-brown skin, black hair, dark eyes.

Buy two dozen minnows from bait shop - 99cents a dozen. James gingerly lifts the plastic bag half filled with water and tied with a knot. He looks up at me, eyes sparkling with excitement.

Back at the farm we unwind the trotline. It is about thirty metres long and has about forty hooks already attached.

'Be careful now, don't hook yourselves. Fish-hooks ain't easy to remove,' calls Tom from the bank.

James and I paddle boat to far end of lake near the dam where the water is deep. Attach one end of trotline to tree stump and paddle out trailing the line until we reach other side. Tie other end of line to stout branch of willow which overhangs the water. Next we pull up the line to find the hooks. The minnows are in a bucket and taking one at a time we thread a hook into the soft mouth of the tiny fish. It takes about half an hour to bait fifteen hooks. Save a few minnows to use with the fishing rods. When we have baited the last hook and dropped the line we paddle back across lake towards boat dock. Dragon flies with white wing tips hover over the water lilies and house-martins are back diving to skim the surface for insects.

June 24th 6.00a.m.   James and I up early before crickets and grasshoppers have started chirping. Sun is still below the horizon, grass glistens with dew, all is quiet. Untie boat and paddle across lake. 'What if it's a big catfish?' whispers James. I shake my head, 'We'll be lucky to catch a tiddler, don't you worry.'

Reach trotline which curves from the willow branch down into the water. I start to pull in the line. Nothing, just empty hooks. Then a little resistance; maybe the line snagged on something. But then feel movement through the tension of the line. 'Did we catch something, daddy?' I'm not sure. Keep pulling in line, hand over hand, the weight dragging now. 'I think we did.' The line vibrating and something strong tugging. 'Feel the line.' He stretches out his hand and touches the line, feels the tension. Looks up at me wide-eyed. 'Grab the net and hold it ready,' I say.

Then we see it. Flat, glistening, grey-black head, whiskers round the gulping mouth, the three sharp spines on its back which we mustn't touch. I pull it to the side of the boat and loop the net underneath it. It's heavy to lift and it flaps and struggles in bottom of boat. James claps his hands. 'We did it. We got a catfish!'

It is about 15inches long and unlike a regular fish. Has a wide bulbous head, whiskers and smooth tapering body. I hold the fish down with thick leathers gloves, remove the hook, careful to avoid the spines and drop the trotline back in the water. The remaining hooks are empty.

Paddle back and James is eager to cast his line and use up one more of the minnows. 'You'll be lucky,' I say.

He casts, the bait hits the water and he settles at front of boat. Then he is shrieking, winding in his line with a small wide-mouthed bass wriggling on the end. James' eyes shine with delight. 'Isn't this our lucky day,' I smile.

10.00a.m. Oklahoma City. Have driven from farm into Oklahoma City. And I am in awe of the energy and industry of Americans. It has taken less than 80 years for this modern city of classic Palladian buildings, flowing freeways, glass and steel skyscrapers and tree-lined boulevards to rise from what was barren prairie. Dominating the city centre is the magnificent capitol building, seat of the state government – a wide columned frontage like a Greek temple. Built on the riches of the oil fields which lie beneath the prairies, an oil derrick stands in front as a symbol of the city's wealth. Around the city the evidence is everywhere. From the city centre out to the wheat fields beyond, there are the 'nodding donkeys' – cleverly designed oil pumps made of steel beams, pulleys and weights which bring the oil to the surface; 'donkeys' because at one end of the horizontal beam is a weight shaped liked a donkey's head which rises and falls against the counterweight at the other end of the beam. Ingenious.

11.00a.m. Arrive at the 'Cowboys Hall of Fame'. 33ft bronze statue of Buffalo Bill Cody dominates main courtyard. Exhibition rooms house bronzes of scenes of western life, artefacts and representations of 'The Wild West': a replica chuck wagon, wigwams, collections of guns and Native American headdresses. There are oil paintings by Frederick Remington, the famous Harper's Weekly artist whose illustrations did much to create the mythology of the 'Wild West.' An auditorium shows clips from John Wayne films. Sit and watch scene from *The Man Who Shot Liberty Valance*. The children are fascinated. This is all new to them. While my childhood was dominated by cowboy heroes – Roy Rogers, the Cisco Kid, the Range Rider and clashes between cowboys and 'Indians' – James and Katie are the children of the *Star Wars* generation. They know little of cowboy legends. Stop by one particular glass case. I lift James up so that he can see. There is an arrow head on display. Alongside is the explanation: *W. Lewis, M.D. certifies: "On Tuesday July 17th 1882 in St. James Hotel, Kansas, I successfully removed this steel arrowhead from the back of George T. Reynolds of Fort Griffin Texas. It had remained in his body for 15 years when he was shot on the 3rd April 1867 after a battle with Indians."* Below the arrowhead is the bridle of the Indian who fired the arrow.

The Hall of Fame does much to reinstate the dignity of the Indian. My childhood presented the simplistic notion of Cowboy = goodie, Indian = baddie. It was only in the Seventies, with films like Ralph Nelson's *Soldier Blue*, Arthur Penn's *Little Big Man* and Dee Brown's classic book *Bury My Heart At Wounded Knee,* that the Hollywood image of the

302

heroic cowboy and the savage Indian was revised. Move into the Native American section. Glass cases show Indians from the eastern tribes – Creek, Choctaw, Cherokee, Chikasaw and Seminole from Florida who faced the inhumanity of 'The Trail of Tears'. Some photos show them wearing European clothing. One Robert Jones (1808-1873) was the wealthiest man in the Choctaw nation prior to the Civil War. He owned 5 plantations, 2 steamboats and 500 slaves and served as a delegate to the Confederate Congress - a far cry from the classic image of the half naked, painted Plains Indians which Remington tended to favour in his paintings.

7.30p.m. Tom has skinned the cat-fish. It's a female and the children are fascinated by the egg sacs. Katie says it's a shame we caught a female with eggs. James is indignant and says, 'We didn't know.' The meat is rolled in breadcrumbs and cornflour and fried in an iron skillet. It has a faintly earthy taste.

Chris presents us with a sprig of mistletoe, the state flower, to speed us on our way in the morning. We'll meet up with her again at her home in Denver.

June 25th 10a.m. Heading north west towards Kansas on Route 81. Open prairie country – big sky, red earth, nodding 'donkey' oil pumps dotting the wheat lands. We are on a section of the historic Chisholm Trail. Named after trader Jesse Chisholm, developed after the Civil War – an 800 mile drovers' trail to bring Texas beef from the Rio Grande to newly built railhead at Abilene in Kansas. It was used only from1867-1884 when quarantine law closed it. During those 17 years, 5 million cattle were driven from Texas to feed the appetites of those in the north and it launched the folk hero of the 'cowboy' – a figure who would ride across our television and cinema screens for a hundred years.

Pass contract harvesters – whole families in convoy of trailer, pick-up and combine harvester, en route to the next ranch. Cross and recross the Cimarron River. The flat plains are scrubby, treeless, tinged with blue from sagebrush. Road winds between flat-topped mesas, huge shoulders of rock which have thrust upwards from the underworld.

4.30p.m Arrive at Dodge City. Katie and James are excited. We've been spinning them tales about Dodge City – wild west frontier town of gunslingers, buffalo hunters and lawmen like Wyatt Earp and Bat Masterson. Turns out to be a disappointment. Town is dominated by rail terminus and grain silos. Main street lined with fast food outlets and motels. Museum is tacky, selling Chinese-made souvenirs. No flavour of the original town of 1872. Then it was a railhead and terminus for the Texas cattle drives, peopled by cowboys flush with pay at the end of long cattle drives, buffalo hunters cashing in on the government strategy to control the Plains Indians by killing off the great buffalo herds. In 4 years the vast herds had been wiped out and the Indians corralled in reservations. Visit site of the famous Boot Hill – cemetery for wayward gunslingers and drifters who were unceremoniously buried with their boots on – hence the name.

June 26th 6.30a.m. Sunrise over the wheat lands. On the road early. A few miles out of Dodge City stop near a spot where there are reputedly wagon tracks of the original Santa Fe trail. Children bleary eyed as we try to explain the significance of the ruts in the ground.

'Were they wagons like Laura was in?' asks James.

'Just like that,' nods Sue. 'Lots of families passed this way heading for a new life out west. Sadly they often didn't make it.'

'Why? Did the Indians come and kill them?'

'More often it was starvation or disease, rather than Indians,' replies Sue.

Pass several cattle stations. Bleak barren barns where thousands of cattle are housed prior to transport by train or road. Downwind from the cattle stations the stench is grim.

9.15a.m. Cross state line into Colorado. We have gained an hour having just passed into Central Mountain Time. No mountains yet just endless flatness. Katie has created a whittlers shop behind the passenger seat, whittling pine sticks with a pair of scissors and offering them to James to buy. But he's lost in his *Star Wars* book and tape; head phones on, eyes wide.

10.30a.m. 50 miles east of Pueblo, first sign of the Rockies emerging out of the heat haze. Such a relief after the endless flatness of Kansas.*12.30p.m.* Snow on the mountain peaks. Fast-flowing rivers down the mountain sides. Rain deluge as we approach Colorado Springs. Spirals of rain and forked lightning, low elbowing cloud. Then, south of Denver, rain clears to blue sky. Vivid green grassland clothing the lower mountain slopes. Follow a car with the sticker: ' *3 that set us free – Guns, God and Guts* ' .

3.15p.m. Route 87 crests a rise north of Castle Rock and there is the city of Denver spread before us. It is space age, futuristic with high rise glass and steel buildings backed by the grandeur of snow-capped Rockies.

Tape player sings out *Rocky Mountain High*, the signature tune of the trip and it's doubly appropriate. Henry John Deutschendorf Jnr. named himself John Denver after the city. Colorado was the state he chose to settle in and where he wrote most of his songs. Many are evocative of the Colorado landscape – the mountains, the shimmer of sunlight through the aspens, the snow-capped peaks, the star-studded dome of the night sky, the 'sunshine on my shoulder'.

Spend a splendid evening with Chris, Brad, Emmy and Lauren in their Denver home before preparing for our next excursion.

June 29th 9.30a.m. Heading for a night in the mountains. I'm excited to visit the city of Boulder in the foothills of the mountains at an elevation of over 5,000feet. When I was at Lancaster University in 1976 I learnt that it was twinned with Boulder University and that post-grads could continue their studies at Boulder. I've harboured the dream ever since. When I see the campus, the dream sparkles even brighter: Spanish roofed, ivy-covered buildings built of warm red sandstone. The mountain air clear and free of humidity up here, aspen leaves shimmer silver in the sunlight, students lie out on neatly tended lawns, bookshops have soft couches and aroma of freshly brewed coffee. One day, some day, maybe.
3.00p.m. Drive west from Boulder, higher into the mountains. Camp in the Roosevelt National Forest. Snow-capped peaks beyond the pines. A lake and a river where we fish alongside another camper whose name is Martha. She's a seasoned outdoors woman – colourful bandanna holding back her grey hair. James is intrigued by the array of fishing flies pinned to her fishing jacket. Today she's using salmon eggs for bait and catches three small trout in quick succession. We're not so lucky and return to the campfire empty-handed.
6.00p.m. Here we are at 11,000ft. Still snow lying in shaded parts of the woods. Temperature drops dramatically as sun sets. We have bought a sack of logs for $3.50. from campground shop. We need them. Blaze the fire and I tune the battered guitar I bought for $1 from a flea market in Boulder. Only four strings but still it makes an acceptable sound. Not sure that John Denver would appreciate our rendition of his songs.

June 30th 6a.m. Sun just touching the tops of the trees. It is bitingly cold in the shade. Cycle down to Brainard Lake. We are carrying two bikes on a rack on the front of the van, useful at times like this when the others are sleeping and I want to take off. Sound of an axe on wood echoes in the trees. One or two early campfires flickering. Lake surface a mirror. Fish nose the surface setting off circles of ripples. Alpine flowers carpet the grass which fringes the lakeshore. Cobalt blue sky.
9.30a.m. A minor hitch - van engine won't start. We phone AAA and after half an hour a truck arrives. It seems I should have had the carburettor adjusted for the altitude. Petrol doesn't vapourise so easily at 11,000ft. But the AAA guy is cheery and waves us on our way.

11a.m. Travelling down Clear Creek Canyon towards Route 70. Pass through Central City one of the old centres of the Gold Rush of 1859. Along the valley side are ancient spoil heaps and rusting mining gear. You can still pan for gold in the river and people are down there now trying their luck.

July 1st. 9a.m. Leave Denver in torrential rain, visibility appalling. A truck towing a long trailer starts to overtake us but then drifts into our lane. He hasn't reckoned on the length of his trailer and as he pulls in front of us I brake but it's no good. A sickening judder as the trailer strikes the side of the van. Skid to a halt and the truck almost jack-knifes across the carriageway. We are lucky. No injuries, no broken glass, just a cracked window and a big dent in the side. But the van is still driveable. Ted Richards, the truck driver, is shaken and very apologetic. Follow him to his head office. They tape up the window cracks with duct tape and we fill out paperwork for the insurance claim. They want to hold the van to get it fixed but we want to drive on. Still a long way to go and we're on a tight schedule.

July 3rd 8.30a.m. Delayed in Denver waiting to sort out insurance details on the van. Finally we're on our way again heading south on Interstate 25.
Today is special. Today is a day of pilgrimage and I'm very excited. We're heading for Taos, New Mexico and the final resting place of the writer who has been my lifelong inspiration – D.H.Lawrence. I have written before about how Lawrence seared into my imagination at school when I first read *Sons and Lovers*. Ever since, his voice in his letters, poems, essays and novels has resonated and inspired and set my mind reeling in so many ways. This will be a day of days.
11.15a.m. North of Trinidad and the New Mexico stateline. Landscape is parched, barren, almost desert. Tracks lead from the road to decaying shacks with blind, empty windows. We are dwarfed by this landscape of monstrous 'buttes' which sheer up from the flat desert to a height of several thousand feet. They are flat topped, steep-sided rock buttresses which squat on the landscape and round which the ribbon of the Interstate snakes its way south.

1.15p.m. Slow climb up the narrowing Raton Pass which peaks at 7,834ft. where we cross stateline into New Mexico. Emerge from town of Raton into a landscape of empty scorched plains with huge mesas like recumbent Sphinxes watching our insect-like progress westwards. Put on Mahler's *5ᵗʰ Symphony* while Sue and the children doze. It seems fitting for this bleak, brooding moonscape.

3p.m. 120 miles from Taos. And I wonder what led Lawrence to find peace in this forbidding, elemental land.

He had grown up in the small mining village of Eastwood, grown up in a miner's cottage. And maybe that's it, that here was space and freedom where in England there had only been imprisonment and persecution. *The Rainbow* had been banned in 1915 on grounds of obscenity. He and Frieda then escaped to Cornwall where he wrote a sequel – *Women in Love* in a small rented cottage in Zennor, west of St Ives. But even there they were hounded by the police who believed Frieda to be a German spy sending coded messages via her washing line to German U-boats.

They were forced out of Cornwall in 1917. It was in 1919 that Lawrence and Frieda finally left England forever to live in voluntary exile. They travelled to America via Ceylon and Australia arriving in New Mexico in 1922 to live at the Kiowa Ranch, 14 miles outside Taos. I'm itching to see the place. But it will have to wait until tomorrow.

5p.m. Stop to camp in Cimmarron – it stands on the Cimmarron River which roars its passage through the Cimmarron Canyon. This was a stopping place for pioneers on the Santa Fe Trail. I think of the landscape we have just driven through. Can't imagine how families with horses and wagons could have made it. Cimmarron, like Dodge City, was the haunt of outlaws and drifters – Billy the Kid was the most notorious.

9.30p.m Firecrackers and sky rockets split the desert air and wake the children. Of course - it's July 4ᵗʰ tomorrow – Independence Day.

July 4ᵗʰ 7.30a.m. Set off early. Over the lip of the canyon and we're into a different landscape – forests, cabins, mountain ski runs, clouds folding over the peaks like sea surf in slow motion. Eagle Nest Lake shimmers in sunlight and there are lupins and Indian Paint Brush plants amongst the clover spreading away from the roadside. Into the valley of the lush Carson National Forest. New log cabins being built and a runway for ski tourists. Over the head of the valley and before us spreads the plain around Taos. To our left the rocky surge of the Sangre de Cristo Mountains. To our right, scattered homesteads all built in the cuboid style of the adobe – some ancient where the clay is cracked and parched; others newly built in cream and ochre, with satellite dishes mounted on flat roofs.

9.30a.m. Taos town square. Tree lined, cool, shaded pavements in front of adobe shop fronts. There are galleries of Native American art, shop fronts blazing with the brilliant colours of woven blankets. I am

searching for the Hotel La Fonda which is located somewhere on the square. While I explore, Katie and James eat their breakfast of raisin bran and fruit juice sitting on a bench in the shade. Then I spot it, dominating the south side of the plaza, 'La Fonda de Taos' and on the wall a sign which reads:

This is the only showing of the D.H.Lawrence controversial paintings since his Exhibition was permanently banned by Scotland Yard when his show opened at the Warren Galleries London in 1929.

At reception desk pay $1 for big brass key which opens door of small lobby room. Here are the paintings which caused such a furore in 1929. They are signed 'Lorenzo' and seem rather childish in style. Fleshy breasts and buttocks abound as young men and women run through knee high grass. Dark beards, triangles of black pubic hair among the lavish swirls of peachy flesh – these are what obviously upset the refined sensibilities of the judiciary in 1929. As well as the paintings

there are letters and photographs: a photo of Lawrence and Frieda in the square at Taos. He wears a crumpled white linen suit and holds a straw hat. Frieda is buxom in an Indian skirt and shawl, face shaded by a wide sombrero. Another of Lawrence on a horse at Kiowa Ranch, a low cabin in the background. I am itching to see the place and tread the hallowed ground.

10.45a.m. Stop briefly at the Taos Pueblo, an authentic Pueblo Indian settlement. Local boy sits on steps of white adobe church, head nodding to the sound of his Sony sound system. Sleek modern cars parked alongside the square adobe homes; yards and window boxes blaze with colour – oleander, heliconias, hibiscus and bougainvillea. Young boys gather in groups around their motor-bikes.

The ranch is 14 miles west of Taos. Cross a treeless plain, mountains etched against a wide cloudless sky. The light is clear, vivid. We are on Route 3, the Kit Carson Trail. Stop at a roadside stall selling deep-fried corn bread smothered in syrup for $1.50 .

Turn off road at sign 'Lawrence Ranch' and follow gravel track which winds up from the plain for 4 miles towards the pines. Finally stop in front of two storey ranch house. Frieda returned here after Lawrence's death in southern France in 1930. She paid for the ranch by trading the manuscript of *Sons and Lovers* and lived here with her third husband, Angelo Ravagli, until her own death in 1956. The ranch is now owned by the University of New Mexico.

A short distance behind the ranch house is the small cabin where the Lawrences lived in 1922 and again in the summer 1925 when Lawrence was struggling to recuperate from a serious bout of typhoid and pneumonia. The Kiowa Ranch features as the location for the final chapters of his novella *St Mawr*. The cabin is low, single storey. And there, in front, is the towering pine tree which features in the book. It really exists! The girth of the tree must be around five feet. Bark is gnarled, peeling, deeply split. In *St Mawr* he writes: *That pine tree was the guardian of the place...a bristling, almost demonish guardian from the far-off crude ages of the world.* Beyond the great pine tree is the alfalfa field where Lawrence wrote of seeing the shadows of coyotes in the moonlight.

Follow a path behind cabin to find burial place. Although he died in southern France in 1930 and was buried there, Frieda had his remains exhumed and cremated in 1935 and brought the ashes back here to Kiowa Ranch. Katie and James are ahead of me following the zig-zag path which winds up a short hill between a plantation of young pines. At the top a small white building – the Lawrence shrine. The blood is ringing in my ears. My legs feel like jelly. Over the years I have traced locations associated with Lawrence's life – Eastwood, Cossethay, The Haggs' Farm, Zennor in Cornwall but nowhere compares to this place.

Of the view from the ranch down across the desert Lawrence wrote: *There are all kinds of beauty in the world...But for a greatness of beauty I have never experienced anything like New Mexico.*

In front of the small white building a slab of white marble - Frieda's headstone. A photograph of her inset into the side of the stone. Inside the shrine is a rectangular concrete block which houses the ashes. The letters **D.H.L.** are painted on the face of the block and decorated with sunflowers. On the wall behind is a sculpture of a phoenix rising from the ashes – the symbol which Lawrence adopted as his own. Above the sculpture a small round window filtering yellow light through the sunflower painted on the glass. It was painted by Dorothy Brett, the only one of the Lawrences' arty friends who came with them from England to set up their new community of 'Rananim.'

I am reluctant to leave this place. The wind in the pines whispers with the murmur of ghosts. Maybe they are just inside my head but I like to think they are part of the spirit of the place. In a lifetime of wandering, searching and questioning it was here that his restless soul found some solace. He wrote: *one can be quite alone and feel the living cosmos softly rocking, soothing, restoring and healing.*

3.15p.m. Route 84 west, crossing the San Juan mountains. Lush meadows, pine forests, dazzling pure light, stark mountains etched against the cobalt sky. It has certainly been my day of days. I have followed the arc of the Lawrence rainbow and touched gold.

July 5th 7.30a.m. Leave campsite at Navaho Lake after early morning swim. Mist rising off the lake surface. Stock up on provisions in Farmington. Most important is to buy bags of ice to fill the big cooler in which we keep water and other drinks. Today we'll be into desert as we cross into Arizona. Road passes through the town of Shiprock – the only place in the US where four states intersect – Utah-Colorado-New Mexico-Arizona. We are crossing a flat, arid land. In the distance the striking jagged outline of Shiprock itself – a volcanic plug which projects 1700 feet above the plain – so-called because as the sun rises and illuminates only the upper part of the mountain it looks like a ship riding across a shadowed sea and features prominently in Navaho mythology as a place of refuge. This is Navaho territory. Pass a Navaho mission school, Navaho Cultural Centre.

2.30p.m. Route 160. The brown, treeless desert landscape continues, tyres hiss on tarmac softened by the midday heat. Scattered Navaho hogans, dried up river courses in an inhospitable moonscape. I check the temperature gauge constantly, listen to the rhythm of the engine. This is not a place to break down. Bare red rock. Why would people choose to live in such a place where nothing grows?

4.00p.m. Keyenta – big Navaho settlement at southern end of Monument Valley. Drive a short way along the valley. So iconic with its great squatting mesas and rock pillars –echoes of John Ford's film *Stagecoach* and so many other westerns. Pull off the highway. I put Katie and James on the roof of the van and walk back to take photos of them against this classic backdrop of red rock wonderment. How dwarfed we feel.

8p.m. Navaho Monument State Park. Camped on a buttress of red rock which overlooks the plain. There is a flat area where we have the picnic table laid out. Scent of juniper from the pinyon trees which edge our pitch. Throw juniper twigs into the fire in the barbecue pit, air pungent with scented wood smoke. Sun sets across a rocky desert plain softened by low pines. As the orange glow deepens, so the blue-black dome of the sky becomes jewelled with stars. Katie spots the 'plough' or, as they call it over here, the 'roller-coaster'. Talk in whispers. So this is why people rave about the desert. Life stripped bare to the essences of earth and air. The light is pure, horizon draws the eyes across an uncluttered landscape. Mind takes wing.

James mixing sand and berries in a little cup and stirring them with a twig. This is his Indian drink, he tells us. Visited the Visitor Centre earlier, saw various pictures and displays of Native American life and now he and Katie are 'living like Indians' he says.

July 6ᵗʰ Last night slept on roof of van under the stars. Rolled out a sleeping bag but lay on top because of the heat. It was warm and still. Feared I might roll off but the risk was worth it. No bugs, the odd rustling in the undergrowth but the magic of the universe arrayed above my head with the desert spread below me was an image which will go with me to my grave.

9a.m. Hike down into the canyon to visit the Betatakin cliff dwellings. Like Mesa Verde, the buildings are sheltered under a huge sandstone overhang. Built by the Anasazi people around 1250AD. Katie is excited by the ranger's talk about plants, especially when she mentions that the soft juniper bark was used by the Indians to make diapers. Invites us to chew gum from the pinyon trees and smell juniper berries. James runs to the ranger's table and brings us samples of nuts, gum and berries. Later the ranger leads us along a winding trail which descends deep into the canyon. Temperature drops in shadow of vertical canyon walls. The air is less dry. Pines and aspens alongside the juniper. When we reach the cliff dwellings we are able to clamber up ladders and shuffle along narrow ledges to explore what remains of the homes of the Anasazi.

James loves the way the canyon has a double echo. His high voice rings round the canyon and he stares open-mouthed that it works every time.

2.00p.m. Heading for Grand Canyon on route 160. Air filled with red dust swirling off the desert. Road snakes through curious landscape of the Painted Desert – rocky hillocks almost like mining spoil heaps, composed of narrow bands of orange, pink and brown sandstone.

3.00p.m. Great excitement as we approach the south rim of Grand Canyon. Navaho market selling pieces of craftwork – weaving, sand paintings, carved wooden animals, jewellery. Katie pores over a table displaying turquoise bracelets. Nearby an old Navaho sits in a chair – head band, dark glasses, beads round his neck. Extends his hand toward Katie and murmurs to her. She is wary, looks at me and then back at the old man and dares not touch his gnarled hand.

Park close to Desert View Watchtower and walk to edge of canyon. Foolishly I had expected the great sculpted monoliths and mesas of the canyon to loom up before me like mountains. But of course they are down there, below the level of the desert plain – spread like a painted frieze in front of and below me. With the sun still quite high there are few shadows, no sense of depth or scale; distances are deceptively fore-shortened.

And I'm not the first one to be confused. The first Europeans who viewed the canyon in 1540 were a group of 13 Spanish explorers – part of the Coronado expedition searching for the fabled Seven Cities of Gold under the command of Garcia Lopez Cardenas. Like me they totally misjudged the scale of the canyon thinking the Colorado River in the base of the canyon was only about 6 feet wide. In reality it's about 300 feet wide.

You stand and gaze in muted wonder at this vast expanse of sculpted grandeur. You would have to trek down the Bright Angel Trail deep into the canyon or take a helicopter ride for $120 to get a clear sense of size and scale. We won't do either and so must stay bemused - eyes and mind unable to fathom exactly what we're looking at.

July 7th Gain an hour today having crossed into the Pacific Time Zone.

10a.m. Stop at a 'Rock Shop' south of Grand Canyon village. It is stuffed with amazing samples of crystalline rocks and fossils. Find what I never found during my two years as an A level geology student – a trilobite. In the first lesson of the A level course the teacher, Peter Frogley, threw out a challenge to the class: 'Over the next two years you will no doubt find a variety of fossils. But I'll eat my hat if one of you ever finds a trilobite.'

He kept his hat intact. But now Mr Frogley, sir, the tables are turned. I'm holding a trilobite fossil in my hand and I'm about to pay a wizened Navaho lady $6.00 for my little geological treasure. So eat your hat, old man, I'm going to frame this little beauty.

11.00a.m. Pass road sign – Los Angeles 436 miles. Ahead, 3 Harley Davidson veterans – bandannas, wind in their grey pony tails and beards. We'll be in California tomorrow. This is earthquake and volcano territory. Where the road cuts through a mountain side you see dramatic cross-sections of contorted and folded rock strata, dramatic fault lines. The mountains are steep, profiles irregular – sometimes studded with small volcanic cones.

8p.m. Dusk. End of a day of overheated desert air vibrating off a bleached treeless landscape. When we crossed the stateline, the border guard confiscated our collection of wheat from Oklahoma and Colorado. Katie was most upset. Didn't tell her I'd hidden some under the seat.

10p.m. Poolside – *Lazy 8 Motel*, Needles, the motel at the end of the universe. Just over the California stateline it stands as a bleak outpost on Interstate 40. Temperature still hot and even the pool is not refreshing. Trucks thunder past into the night heading east and west. Tomorrow 150 miles of desert - the Mohave Desert -before we get to Sequoia.

July 8ᵗʰ 8a.m. 100miles before the next gas station at Barstow. Temperature gauge running hot - not good news. Long haul up to Barstow. Rest Area sign warns: *Beware Rattlesnakes.* A crippled fellow with bent legs stumbles out of a beat up Chevy pickup. He is unkempt, grubby shirt and jeans, matted hair and beard.

Hear him asking for a container so he can bathe his feet. He is ignored. No-one meets his eyes. I go across – offer him a plastic jug. He shuffles towards the rest room entrance. Group of children run past him laughing and pointing. Sometime later he emerges, comes across to return the jug. Asks where in England we're from. Bloodshot eyes glazed and staring. Says he was in Scotland in '64. Wishes he was back there now instead of in this godforsaken place. 'Got banged up in Saigon,' he says. Could we give him a ride to the coast? 'I'm not armed, I'm not a druggie, I just take medication,' he says.

I'm glad I have the excuse that we're going to Sequoia as I feel sorry for this Vietnam war casualty but still I'm wary of him. 'Thanks for your help,' he says and shuffles back across the parking lot.

11.00a.m. Mohave Desert. Black lava flows on either side of the road. Lunar landscape.We are close to the San Andreas Fault. Edwards Air Force Base sign-posted to the south – one of the main landing areas for the Space Shuttle program.

2p.m. Beyond the town of Mojave landscape starts to soften as we descend on to flatter cultivated plain of San Joaquin Valley – orange trees, grape vines, orchards of almond trees and pistachio nuts. Engine temp. has dropped. I can relax a little. Katie and James are singing some song they've made up. Sue makes notes and calculates our finances using her little calculator. Feel we have 'come through' in a sense – having left the arid desert and the El Paso mountains behind – fascinating but not my kind of landscape. I crave trees and greenery - must be the rural England in my soul. Road side stalls selling fruit. We stop to buy grapes and peaches.

9p.m. Sequoia National Park. Having been dwarfed by brooding mountains in the desert we are now dwarfed by the soaring giant redwoods. Thought we had found the ultimate respite in the tranquillity of the forest. But not so. Chaos reigned earlier this evening. We were camped in a valley in the forest along with dozens of other campers. Campfires and barbecues smoking, tents pitched as people settled in for the evening. Then came the rangers with their loud hailer. 'Clear the Campground...Everyone has to leave!' We had noticed, pinned to the trees, signs warning: 'DANGER OF PLAGUE! DO NO FEED THE RODENTS'. The word 'plague' seemed somewhat anachronistic in such a place of sylvan delight. Didn't 'plagues' die out in biblical times?

Apparently not. A child who had camped in the campground the previous week had a confirmed case of bubonic plague. Campground had to be cleared prior to being fumigated. Much crashing of pots and pans and frantic stowing of camp gear as we made our getaway ahead of the pack. 3 miles to the next campground where we found one of the few remaining pitches. Others are not so lucky. All through the night hopefuls arrived and left disappointed. Site was full, thankfully plague-free. But the night was far from restful.

July 9ᵗʰ 6.a.m. Wake to the skitter of chipmunks among the fallen pine cones. Like being in an outdoor cathedral – stillness, quietude – just the majestic pillars of the trees. The bark is soft, a deep russet colour, peels easily into strips like soft leather. Pine cones are huge – some around six inches long.

10a.m. We are exploring the wonder of this amazing place. Ranger tells us these trees are some of the tallest living things on the surface of the planet at a height of 280feet and 36 feet in diameter. The General Sherman tree is the tallest and oldest with an estimated age of around 2,500 years old.

12.30p.m. Descend 6,000 feet in 20 miles into the lush San Joachim Valley. Wine is 4 dollars for 3 litres. Buy champagne in anticipation of rendezvous with the Jaques family who had been based in Orlando for the year. Drove down the east coast from Washington with them back in August and now we will hopefully meet with them, as arranged, in Yosemite National Park later today.

5p.m. Yosemite. So different from Sequoia – landscape of bare, grey sculpted granite peaks softened by pine woods and waterfalls. Find a camp pitch in the valley and it's not long before the woods echo with the excited screams of children – Katie and James have found their buddies – Hugh, Stella, Eve – the Jaques children. After a drive of around 4000 miles our paths have finally crossed again. Great excitement and so much to talk about around the camp fire this evening.

July 10ᵗʰ Here for 3 nights – glad not to be driving for a while. Explore the woods and waterfalls which drop from hanging valleys into the main Yosemite Valley. Some drop a thousand feet hardly touching the rock face but drifting in a vapour of white mist. Bridalveil Falls are the most distinctive with a wide swathe of cascading vapour dropping down a 600 foot precipice. The Ahwahneechee Native Americans called this waterfall Pohono, which means Spirit of the Puffing Wind; they believed the falls had magical powers.

*8p.m.*Whether there is magic in this valley or whether the Californian wine and champagne are working their own magic – who knows? But the evening is mellow after a barbecue of pork ribs and burgers. Firelight flickers on the faces of the five little children who huddle together listening to the chapter from *Little House on the Prairie* entitled 'Indian Camp' - the chapter where Pa shows Laura the moccasin tracks of the Indians. We tell the children that tomorrow they can search for animal tracks in the woods. 'Will there be bears in the woods?' asks James.

'Of course there are bears. Everyone knows that,' says Hugh.

James cuddles in closer and sucks on his thumb a little more vigorously.

July 11th Today cycled valley floor, explored the woods, got drenched in drifting spray from the cascade of Vernal Falls which drop over 300feet from the lip of the falls. Bathed in the crystal waters of Merced River and children searched for animal tracks but encountered only chipmunks and squirrels – no bears. Late afternoon drove up winding road which climbs

to Glacier Point. Here the bare granite landscape is spread before you. The mountains are stunning: El Capitan soars to 7,500 feet but it is Half Dome which takes your breath; as if a cone has been split cleanly down the middle and one half discarded leaving the severed other half sheering 4,700 feet down to the valley floor. The peaks and valleys are softened by the pine trees and by the white ribbons of the many water falls which drop from the hanging valleys into the main Yosemite Valley. It is a majestic landscape.

July 12th 7.a.m. Should reach the Pacific today. Once again cross lush San Joaquin valley. Roadside fruit stalls abound. We crave to see the sea but before that there is the forbidding barrier of the Diablo Mountains.

11.a.m Road is now two-laned, thunders with trucks, headlights blaze even in the middle of the day. Driving is anything but relaxed. Heat is intense. Signpost indicates 'Salinas' - remember the name from Steinbeck's *Of Mice and Men*.

1p.m. Now into another valley – bright swathes of geraniums, peach orchards, pecans, cherries, apricots, lemons. Farms well kept, prosperous. Pass through town of San Juan Bautista, once seat of the Mexican Government, site of one of the oldest Spanish missions.

2.p.m. San Francisco signposted to the right, *Salinas* and *Monterey* to the left. Branch left, air is cooler, excitement rises as we crane our heads to see the sea. Mist over the Sierra de Salinas, air almost cold.

And finally the sea, the sea, the smell of the sea. Sailboats on a blue-grey ocean, cliffs above golden beaches. Pacific rollers crashing on the shore.

We head south along the high coast road towards Big Sur - name derives from the Spanish 'el sur grande' or 'the big south'. It has been the haunt of artists for decades. In my twenties, I read the correspondence between Lawrence Durrell and Henry Miller, when Miller was living at Big Sur and had gained notoriety through his novels *Tropic of Cancer* and *Tropic of Capricorn*. Jack Kerouac spent a few days in Big Sur in early 1960 living in a cabin in the woods owned by the poet Lawrence Ferlinghetti. Later he wrote a novel titled *Big Sur* based on his experience.

So we roll along the amazing Highway 1, high above white Pacific rollers which crash on to gold sand beaches below.

We have made it from Atlantic to Pacific. I can't quite believe it.

July 13th 9a.m. Camped in the Andrew Molera State Park on bank of shallow river. Katie and James paddle and clamber among the boulders scattered in the river bed. Yesterday evening explored the beaches near the Point Sur lighthouse. Rock pools for dibbling – James trying to capture hermit crabs which scurry away from his little fingers. Katie jumping off rocks on to the sand. Beach wide and empty. Crests of the breaking surf fired with sun glow.

This morning we have driven a few miles north to explore Carmel and Monterey peninsula. Wind off the sea brings scents of sea wrack from the shoreline, aniseed from the bushes of fennel which grow on the coastal slopes, sage brush which grows at the roadside. Seals bask on the rocky islets off Devil's Cauldron where surf boils around rock arches. Pay $4 to drive the famous 17 Mile Drive round the Monterey Peninsula. Bay lined with grey bark cypresses. Wedding guests sip champagne on Pescadero Point. Back from the road luxurious homes nestle amidst exotic gardens. At Monterey Harbour buy fish and chips on Fisherman's Wharf. It is close to the old sardine packing factories of Cannery Row, made famous in Steinbeck's novel of the same name. Now there are chic eateries, coffee shops and souvenir stores.

317

July 15th. Yesterday a welcome day of relaxation round the camp site. Now we're off again, north to San Francisco. Low bank of fog hangs across the sea typical of this area where a cold offshore current hits the heat of the land. It is Sunday – cars are streaming south away from the city. But heading north twelve big Honda Goldwing motorbikes pass us – the last belongs to *"George & Thelma"* – names embossed in gold on the rear paniers.

The city like an amphitheatre around the Bay – small coloured toy town box houses stepped up the hillsides. The tops of the two main steel stanchions of the Golden Gate Bridge seem to float above the wall of fog which obscures the rest of the bridge and seeps into the bay. Find a city RV park fenced in by a high wire stockade – not very welcoming but it will do for one night. Into the city, we head for Fishermen's Wharf. It is half a mile of street theatre performers: break dancers, a duo in tuxedos on the back of a pick-up truck, one playing an upright piano, the other a trumpet; mime artists, 'living' statues painted head to toe in metallic gold or silver who stand rigid and then suddenly move to the shock and delight of the audience;

jugglers, a sword swallower, a pair of clowns. The back-drop to all this entertainment are the stalls where steaming pink crabs are drawn from vats of boiling water – beyond are the fishing boats and the blue waters of San Francisco Bay. The prison island of Alcatraz hazy in the mist. We devour monstrous cones of ice cream in Snoopy's Ice Cream Parlour where *'Life is like an ice-cream cone – you have to learn to lick it!'* Boat ride across Bay to Sausalito but still the famous bridge is shrouded in thick fog. Katie finds a ten-cent piece down the back of one of the seats. This is much more exciting than spotting famous landmarks.

After boat ride, drive the famous roller coaster roads up from city centre, then down again, through the gay district where men stroll arm in arm or sit at tables holding hands and on past the park where families fly multi-coloured kites of all shapes – from bloated whales and alligators, to razor light speedsters which cut and zip among the slender chords which their owners tug and nudge to tether the wind.

July 17ᵗʰ 8.30a.m. North on Highway 1 accompanied by Elgar's *Nimrod Variations* on the van's sound system. Some nostalgic yearning led me to choose this piece this morning. Maybe it's because soon we'll be turning east and home is in that direction. Cross the Golden Gate Bridge and it is fog free and magnificent in its rust red slung steel glory.

Last night we brushed against the darker side of the American dream on our city camp site.   Just settling the children down to sleep, curtains drawn, darkness falling – we hear the crunch of car tyres moving slowly past the front of the van; then movement brushing the side of the van. Peered through gap in curtains to see policeman stooped low to the ground, gun drawn and another following behind a slowly moving police car. He saw me and gestured to keep down. Scrabble of feet on gravel, a car engine, running footsteps, muted voices, another engine and then the whine of a siren coiling away down the street.

We listened, breath held.... all quiet save the even breaths of Katie and James lost in the oblivion of innocence. 'No more city campsites for us,' murmured Sue.

But this morning all is fine again, breathing the joys of Elgar and this highway which hugs the rugged coast. Pacific rollers crash along this coastline of rocky headlands, small coves shouldered by cliffs, long swathes of sand where fishermen stand in the surf and hope to reel in Ocean Perch. Redwoods teeter on the edge of the cliffs. Fallen ones lie on the sand like great dinosaur limbs washed smooth by the salt wind and the surf.

Stop north of Eureka at Trinidad Beach near the old whaling station to give the children a chance to play on the beach and for me to set up the crab traps under the boardwalk. Having met up again with the Jaques family we'll now travel together the 3000 miles back to Philadelphia. While the children build sand castles and dam the small stream which crosses the sand, I collect sea-washed fragments of red wood. Have it in mind to make some kind of mobile when we get back to England. Paul searches for a more solid piece of redwood to take back. He's a sculptor and fine craftsman. His vision is of something much more artistic.

July 18th 9a.m. Oregon is said to be the 'greenest' of all the states. No billboards permitted on the highways, recycling and care for the environment are central to state policy. Outside the city of Gold Hill is a sign which reads: *This is a quiet city. All unnecessary noise and disturbance prohibited!* The landscape is spectacular. From the giant redwoods on the coast to the jewel of Crater Lake. Arrive there late morning and climb to the viewing point. Snow still lying on some of the slopes of what was the ancient volcano of Mount Mazama. According to Native American belief, a battle between Skell the sky god and Llao the god of the underworld resulted in the destruction of the mountain. What is left is the jagged rim of the mountain and the circular lake which fills the crater. It is a classic example of what geologists call a caldera and the huge explosion occured some time around 5700BC. Like a giant's looking glass, the sky and clouds are perfectly reflected in the mirrored surface. A small volcanic cone called Wizard Island pierces the smooth surface of the lake close to the western rim. To the Native Americans it is a place of great spiritual power. It's not difficult to see why.

We drink in the wonder of the place but then the snowy hollows beckon. The children skate around in the snow and then we launch them down the slopes on pieces of polythene which make brilliant toboggans. The mix of a hot summer sun with sledging is an unexpected delight for us all. Cut blocks of snow to put in the cooler to keep the drinks cold.

4p.m. Late afternoon – stop appropriately at Dayville on the John Day river. The children search for branches to build yet another bivouac – this is their latest obsession – 'living like Indians.'

July 22nd 9a.m. We have lost three days. Struck down by some virulent bug. James started with something like the scene from *The Exorcist* – projectile vomit which amazed him and the rest of us. One by one, all nine of us succumbed to 48 hours of misery – squirming in and out of mithering consciousness and gastric upheaval. Feel squalid and grubby and crave for clean sheets and a proper bed.

But our hardships pale when we read a historic marker at Vale, close to the stateline with Idaho which records: *Here passed the ill-fated Whitman party in 1843. Marcus Whitman a physician and missionary with his wife Narcissa led the first party of wagon trains along the Oregon Trail to the West, a trail followed by hundreds of thousands of emigrants in the following decade. The Whitmans established a mission some distance north in southern Washington State ministering to the Cayuse Indians. However, the Cayuse blamed the Whitmans for the deaths of all their children and half their adults during a measles epidemic in 1847. Then followed the 'Whitman Massacre' in which the Whitmans and twelve other settlers were killed.*

Our hardships seem pathetic by comparison.

11.a.m. Cross the wide Snake River into Idaho and move from the Pacific into the Mountain Time Zone. Pass the Craters of the Moon National Monument – curious lunar landscape of old lava flows, volcanic spatter cones, craters, twisted black trunks of ancient trees – bare, brown rock unusually smooth and rope-like snaking along the roadside. But then the wider view is of a rift valley with volcanic cones. This is where the Apollo astronauts practised for lunar landing.

Excursion to the Visitors' Centre triggers the following exchange:

James: Is a volcano stronger than He-Man?

Katie: Of course.

James: Is it more powerful than God?

Katie: Maybe.

James: No it's not cos God could lift the earth and a volcano couldn't do that. Is it more powerful than Jesus?

Katie: No, cos Jesus is 3800 times more powerful.

Not sure where her statistics have come from but it silences James.

3.30p.m. Pass through Arco - in the distance framed by a backdrop of volcanic cones is Atomic City, the place of the world's first nuclear power plant, an oasis of concrete towers set in a bleak rocky desert.

Camp at KOA campground at Idaho Falls. After our bout of group sickness and flagging stamina we lift our spirits at Arctic Hamburgers. The children are indulged with hot dogs, burgers and fries. 370 miles covered today and we can enjoy hot showers and sort out our grubby laundry.

July 23rd Idaho is famous for potatoes. Huge barns, earthed up at the sides protect the harvest from frost; wide plantations of potato fields stretching across the broad Snake River Valley.

Long, slow climb up a narrowing canyon to the Teton Pass at 8500feet. Engine struggling, temp. gauge nudging red.

Cross state line into Wyoming and finally at Jackson see the grandeur of the snow-capped Tetons - jagged Alpine type mountains. At the roadside, meadows of wild flowers. Stop briefly. Flowers are waist high in places and the children's heads appear and disappear as they roll and tumble in the grasses. But we cannot stop - our sights are set on Yellowstone.

4.30p.m. West Thumb on Yellowstone Lake. The world's first National Park, established with such vision by the US Congress in 1872.

Steam rises through the trees, smell of sulphur. Boardwalks bordered by bubbling hot water springs and gloopy cauldrons of sputtering mud. The children are mesmerised by this land of magic - water sprites and goblins; strange hissing of steam issuing between the rocks, grass smoking with hot vapours. Ground rumbles and whirlpools of steaming water thrash and tumble in rock basins like water dragons.

Then the rumbling quietens and the waters settle for a while. Alongside the path are tiny aqua-marine basins which blurt small bubbles of steam. These are child-size and James pokes with a stick to provoke the water sprites. Katie, more wary, holds his other arm, just in case.

9.30p.m. Drive to Old Faithful Geyser. We sit waiting. Every 91 minutes they say it will erupt. We wait. Feel the rumble growing in the rock beneath us - the hissing - then suddenly a jet of hissing water and steam gushes over 100 feet into the air. After Disney World it's hard to believe this is a natural phenomenon. One imagines some clever mechanical wizardry below the ground. In the early days of the park less respect was paid to the geyser. It was often used as a laundry by placing garments in the crater of the geyser when the geyser was quiet. In 1882 General Sheridan's men found that linen and cotton fabrics after being soaked and then shot into the air were nicely laundered by the action of the water, but woollen clothes were torn to shreds.

But we are spellbound and check our watches and sure enough, 90 minutes and 10 seconds later the ground rumbles and the children dance and squeal as Old Faithful erupts on cue. James and Hugh thrust their sticks in the air and shout, 'By the power of Grayskull!' Katie, Stella and Eve just grin and shake their heads while the other bystanders clap this little piece of theatre.

July 24ᵗʰ 7a.m. Slept in a rest area near Mammoth Springs. All night the strange hissing of steam among the trees. This is a restless landscape, peopled with unearthly murmurings and ghostly conversations where shattered tree stumps squat like sentinels on an ancient battlefield.

9.30a.m. View the Yellowstone canyon and the Falls; the canyon walls formed of ancient lava flows are indeed a distinctive shade of yellow.

10.30a.m. We are passing the wide blue expanse of Yellowstone Lake when Katie lets out a sudden squeal. 'Buffalo, daddy, over there, see them!' Sure enough on the hillside beyond the lake there are the dark humped shapes of buffalo. 'It's like in the story, when they cross the creek and they're on the prairie, they see buffalo.'

We continue the second book of the Wilder saga, *Little House on the Prairie* and all the children are entranced. As we move east further into the prairie landscape of Wyoming, so much of the book resonates with what we're seeing around us.

'Will there be wolves?' asks James. 'Remember the wolves in the story that follow Pa's horse but they didn't hurt him, did they?'

'There are no packs of wolves any more,' I reply. His face is unsure but he nods and grips his He-Man figure a little tighter.

12.30p.m. Arrive at Cody. At the Buffalo Bill Historical Centre we learn that Cody on the Shoshone River is named after 'Buffalo Bill' Cody, one of the legendary figures of the Old West who helped found the town. Contracted to provide buffalo meat to the workers of the Kansas Pacific Railroad, William Cody earned his nickname after killing 4280 buffalo in 18 months. Later he became a showman and toured his Wild West Show across North America, Great Britain and Europe. The show included displays of sharp-shooting and rodeo skills, mock fights with Indians and featured folk heroes such as Chief Sitting Bull and Annie Oakley.

The historical centre features profiles of early pioneers and trappers. We are drawn to the statue of Jeremiah 'Liver-Eating' Johnston. A six foot giant of Scottish descent, he came west in 1840s as a trapper in Wyoming and Montana. Married an Indian of the Flat-Head tribe and they lived in a cabin on the Snake River. But his wife and unborn child were murdered by Crow Indians and Johnston set out to avenge their deaths by seeking out and killing Crow Indians for the next 12 years. After each killing he is reputed to have cut out and eaten from the livers of his victims.

Behind the Historical Centre is the historical Old Trail Town, a collection of genuine old buildings - saloons, ranch houses, blacksmiths, jails, a school house all of which have been lovingly transported from who knows where and reassembled here. There is the Hole-in-the-Wall Gang's adobe hideout and the log cabin of 'Curley' - General Custer's Crow Indian scout and the only person who survived from Custer's army after his defeat at the Battle of Little Big Horn. Inside some of the buildings are collections of rusting guns, dusty army uniforms, kitchen utensils, farm implements. These are not in polished show cases - they retain the aura of the moments when they were worn or handled. And the buildings, although relocated, have the scuffs and blemishes of the people who nudged their walls, pushed open their doors, spilt their beer, tethered their horses. But the town itself does feel like a film set and the children rush down the main street whooping and shooting imaginary guns as they search in and out of the old buildings - until they encounter the formidable Miss Belinda Edgar who stands hands on hips in the entrance of the old schoolhouse. 'You young hoodlums need corralling and if someone don't do it then I'll be locking you in the jailhouse! Now hush your noise you'll set the dogs barking.'

Hugh stops, looks at Katie who looks at Eve and Stella. James emerges from behind Miss Belinda. He's crawled past the 'No Entry' sign.

'You been scoutin' for cookies, young man?'

James looks at the ground, lost for words.

'Well you just better skidaddle before the Sheriff comes and locks you up.'

Our little crestfallen gang of hoodlums dawdle their way back to the car-park.

'She was bossy,' says Katie.

'Well James shouldn't have gone behind that No Entry sign,' puts in Hugh.

'Well you shouldn't have been shouting so much,' adds Stella.

'And anyway I wasn't looking for cookies,' says James.

'Well it's not a real town so they couldn't put us in jail,' states Hugh.

'Wouldn't like to be in her class,' says Katie. 'Just too bossy!'

4.30p.m. Heading east across wide, empty prairie. Sagebrush country. Then slow climb through the Big Horn Mountains up to Granite Pass at 9000 feet. Just beyond this point a Historic Marker records:

At this point Colonel J A Sawyers wagon-train and road-building expedition of 82 wagons fought the Arapaho Indians for 13 days in August 1865.

East of Buffalo across open prairie. Roadside markers record incidents from Red Cloud's campaign to stop the white man intruding further into the Sioux hunting grounds. The culmination was General George Custer's defeat at the Battle of Little Big Horn in June 1876.

7.30p.m. Sun setting behind us. Black Hills of Dakota ahead. Next stop is Rapid City and Mount Rushmore.

July 25th Breakfast in the car park of the The Mount Rushmore National Memorial. The children squat on edge of pavement and eat their bowls of cereal. Behind us the remarkable sculptures of the heads of four American presidents - Washington, Jefferson, Roosevelt and Lincoln. The 60 foot sculptures carved into the face of this granite outcrop were the work of Danish-American Gutzon Borglum, his son Lincoln and 400 assistants. The project was started in 1927 and completed between 1934 and 1939. It was  more an amazing feat of engineering rather than sculpture. The workers drilling the profiles were lowered by ropes over the rock face and blasted away at the rock with explosives before finishing with jack hammers. The detail which intrigues me is the eyes. They appear convex and seem to reflect the light as from a polished surface. In fact they are concave and the light is reflected off the face of a projecting carved beam of rock which extends from the back of the concave eye socket. Ingenious.

10.30a.m. Repair stop at a gas station – 20 minutes and $6 to remove a nail from a tyre and insert an inner tube by a mechanic in a cowboy hat, cowboy boots and spotless blue jeans. Impressive.

2.00p.m. Apart from the canyons and rock pinnacles of the Badlands, the landscape of South Dakota doesn't thrill the eye. Increasingly it is levelling out into gently undulating grassland and with it our spirits flatten. Our thoughts are 500 miles ahead of us, somewhere on the east coast ready to fly home. And the journey now must just be endured, the drama of landscape has gone. John Denver continues to punctuate the journey with his songs of the Rockies, of the forests, of woodsmoke and sylvan musings but the reality of all that is behind us.

7.30p.m. Rest area at Mitchell - centre of corn country. The Corn Palace is the centre piece - the whole structure covered in corn cobs. In the evening we watch the youngsters cruise the main street, sound systems loud, V-8 engines hunting the neon-lit darkness. It's a scene straight out of *American Graffiti*, George Lucas' 1973 film.

July 26th Today the children are excited. We're detouring to the little town of De Smet, the place where Laura Ingalls Wilder lived after her prairie adventures in Kansas. We find the house, now a museum and assemble in the parlour to listen to the museum guide. This is the actual house which features in her fourth book *By The Shores of Silver Lake*. Laura was 12 when she lived here. The Wilder family arrived in De Smet in the summer of 1879 when Laura's father came to get work as the paymaster and timekeeper for the railroad company. The girls were getting over scarlet fever and older sister Mary had become blind from the illness. In the opening chapter of the book Laura writes of Mary: *Her beautiful golden hair was gone. Pa had shaved it close because of the fever and her poor shorn head looked like a boy's. Her blue eyes were still beautiful but she did not know what was before them and Mary herself could never look through them again to tell Laura what she was thinking without saying a word.*

The guide leads us through the house. She points out the shelves and cupboards and a rocking chair which Pa had made. Replicas of Laura's dolls and her story books line the shelves in the upstairs bedroom. The children are especially fascinated by the trundle bed which Laura's little sister Grace slept in; it's like the bottom drawer of a chest of drawers. Pa had made it out of a packing case. In the kitchen are small stooks of twisted prairie hay which was the only thing available to burn in the dreadful winter of 1879 when they couldn't get coal or wood because the snow was so deep. The trains finally got through bringing mail and provisions in May and it was then that they were able to celebrate Christmas.

As we walk back to the road Katie says, 'Don't think I would like to live in a house with wolves sniffing round the back door like the lady said.'

'You could shoot them with a rifle,' says James.

'What if you ran out of bullets,' asserts Hugh, 'and the trains didn't come to bring in more supplies. Then what would you do?'

James shrugs, 'He-Man would know what to do. He'd get Battlecat to chase them away.'

Katie shakes her head. 'You're daft James. Just daft.'

3p.m. Cross the stateline into Minnesota. The landscape is more forgiving, less windswept, more trees. Around the well tended farms are tall concrete corn storage elevators. Roadside billboard shouts: *'Legalise Bingo - keep grandma off the streets!'*

8p.m. The children have Leggoed their way across Minnesota and now they're sleeping. Nothing to remark on about this stage of the journey. We are simply trying to gobble up the miles. Behind us the sun is going down, ahead are the tail lights of the Jaques' van and the flat, dead straight line of Interstate 90. Inside the glow of the interior light on Sue's book and the haunting strains of Gerry Rafferty's *Bring It All Home* drawing down the blinds on the day. The driving is mesmeric in this sort of landscape and at this time of day I suck on candy sticks to ward off tiredness, rotating them between my lips to create a point like a pencil, the challenge being how thin can I make the point before it breaks.

And it is the quiet time of day. I shall miss this womb-like experience of being enclosed with my little family in our home on wheels. Sharing the ups and downs, the closeness, the sense of adventure in an unpredictable landscape of people and places. In our bedtime reading a few nights ago we read of Laura and Mary's boredom in the back of the wagon as they trundled slowly across the prairie seeing only the hunched shoulders of Pa holding the reins and Ma with her hands folded in her lap. Katie remarked that it was a bit like her and James in the back of the van.

And this could be the last night we spend in the van. Tomorrow we'll be with friends of my parents in Chicago, then with Amy in Pittsburgh and the night after at Judy's in West Chester, PA.

And so, mile by mile, the trip is reeled in.

July 27th 8a.m Through Minnesota and into Wisconsin across the Mississippi at La Crosse. We stop at a rest area near an overlook of the great river. The children build dens from sticks and driftwood. This is their last chance to play together for this is where we part company. The Jaques are going south while we're heading for Chicago. We'll meet up again in Philly.

How much will Katie and James remember? Theirs has been the world in front of their eyes or in their imaginations not the grand vistas of landscape and maps which inform our image of the trip. Katie's memory of San Francisco is the place where she found a ten cent piece down the back of a seat on the ferry across the Bay. James remembers finding a piece of driftwood on the beach in Oregon which made a perfect sword.

10a.m. Cross into Illinois at Beloit. Not far now from Lake Michigan and our stop in Chicago.

2p.m. Chicago water front. Like looking out on an expanse of blue, blue ocean. There are impressive high rise blocks, stunning futuristic architecture, the Sears tower dominates. Behind the lake front promenade are gardens and fountains; in front a marina and sailboats far out on Lake Michigan.

9p.m. An evening of anecdotes with Margery, an old friend of my father. We are staying with her son, John and his wife. She tells stories of my father as a young man who had his own dance band, wore spats and thought himself something of a dandy. I've never seen my father in this light before. In the garden Katie and Rachel, John's daughter, are out collecting fireflies in jam jars.

July 28th 9a.m. Down at the waterfront again. The south shore beach throngs with bathers. Cyclists and roller skaters along the park paths. The lake waters are a deep, deep turquoise, white sails against the azure sky. Perry Como is appearing at the theatre at McCormick Place. He was a favourite of my father.

11a.m. Back on the road east through Gary into Indiana on the Indiana Turnpike.

3p.m. Cross into Ohio. Roadworks and thundering trucks on the James Shocknessy Highway round the southern shore of Lake Erie.

5p.m. Finally cross into Pennsylvania.

7p.m. Arrive at Amy's in Pittsburgh. We have travelled over 450 miles today.

*July 29th 8a.m.*We haven't seen Amy for 8 years. She's little different from when we taught her in Jamaica in the 70s except she now has two young children, Katie and Jimmy. Still the smiling, generous soul who first invited us to stay with her family when we left Jamaica. Nothing is too much trouble. She bakes blueberry muffins for breakfast and plies Katie and James with sweets from her 'candy cupboard'. Her husband Jim works at the car dealership he took over from his father. He works long hours, is out early and home late; we see little of him.

10a.m. Heading east across Pennsylvania, the state named after William Penn. Landscape is heavily wooded, mountainous. Pass through tunnels of the Appalachians. 150 miles to go. Pennsylvania Turnpike takes us through the town of Carlisle, just west of Harrisburg. Echoes of home and the school I must return to. Very mixed feelings.

12.30p.m. Sue is driving as we cross the wide Susquehanna River at Harrisburg. It is a chance for reflection. Glancing round the van I remember the Cuban who sold it to us and who assured me this van was up to the trip. He was right. 7,000 miles later our trusty 'Smurfmobile' is still purring along, the temperature still hovers close to red, the taped side window, cracked when we were hit by the truck leaving Denver, is still intact. It has worked well. Sad that soon we'll have to dismantle what has been our home on wheels.

I am stretched out on the passenger seat, my back against the cooler. Katie is up front while James is asleep on the little folding mattress which rests on the raised wooden plinth I constructed. Underneath, our suitcases are stored along with crab traps and other gear. The mattress folds into a little sofa during the day and opens into a bed at night. Against the rear doors are folding chairs and two milk crates which house the stove, gas light and cooking utensils. Behind the passenger seat are stored the children's games and my guitar. In front between the driver's seat and the co-driver's seat is a ply wood drinks table I made with holes cut out for cans  and cups to sit in. There is our box for music and story tapes and alongside is mounted the little fresh air fan which has been a godsend.

From underneath the drinks table hang the headphones which have been in big demand for listening to music and story tapes when others are sleeping. The clever seat pockets which Sue made and which hang from the backs of the seats have been invaluable. The pockets hold the children's books and games, the maps and reference books which have been in daily use.

Soon it will all have to be dismantled and the van sold when we get to Philadelphia. But we do have our little bag of souvenirs: the polished pieces of driftwood from the beach in Oregon, the fossils from Arizona, a fir cone from the giant Sequoia in California, a piece of rock from near D.H. Lawrence's grave in New Mexico, lava from the Mohave desert.

And of course there is our collection of flowers from each state pressed in a scrap book. They are dried up and fragile but still serve as a reminder of places we passed through: orange blossom from Florida, the rose from Poppa Carver's house in Alabama, wheat from the prairie near Dodge City, Black-Eyed Susan from Oklahoma, sunflower from Kansas, sagebrush from Arizona, the samphire from the cliff at Monterrey, cornflowers from Oregon, the cluster of small blue flowers from the geyser basin at Yellowstone.

7p.m. West Chester, PA. Judy, Zoe and Harold are on the doorstep to welcome us. Zoe was 14 and Harold 12 when last we saw them here in 1976. Zoe is now a striking young woman of 22 - a college graduate who works as an environmental health officer. I remember her so clearly as an impressive runner in my house relay team in Jamaica. Harold was then a scrawny precocious kid; now he's tall, amusing, articulate and soon to graduate from college. I wonder what the other Priory students are doing and how life is in Jamaica after the violence and civil strife of the late 70s. I know the Megevands left to go to Martinique where Katie experienced a bad car crash and now they're in the French Pyrenees running a small tea shop for what Katie calls 'the rich bitch set'. Maybe we'll travel to France to see them. So much is possible when we return.

Aug 1ˢᵗ. We are thrown into crisis. A phone call from England. Sue must return home immediately as her mother is very ill. I will stay with the children to get our scheduled flight. I have to sell the van and all our surplus belongings. But already our thoughts have crossed an ocean and now we are marking time.

Aug 14ᵗʰ. This curious hovering on the cusp. We are at the end of something here on the eastern seaboard of North America. This year has been momentous. Now it is shredding so quickly. The van is sold along with all our gear. We hold a yard sale on the front drive of Judy's house and get rid of most of the stuff. I hawk the van round several dealers and get a half decent price. And for Katie and James it seems like a betrayal to trade our travelling home for a bundle of dollar bills.

Aug 15th. John Denver's *Leaving on a Jet Plane* probably isn't the best choice to lift our spirits as we drive with Judy to the airport. But he's been with us from the Atlantic to the Pacific and back again, so we pay him due homage.

Now England beckons, the children are excited about 'going home'. I'm apprehensive about what awaits us. And as soon as the wheels of our aircraft leave the ground and we settle into our seats so our year in America starts to slip away into the shifting prisms of memory.

And what of Sue's mother's illness? And how has the house fared in our absence and the garden? And how will it be to see old friends and family and to slot back into my old job having experienced so much this past year?

Let all that wait. The children are bright-eyed and buzzing. Let's just focus on the here and now; the messy delights of our finger lickin' in-flight meal and, for old time's sake, a bag of pretzels and some cans of Coca Cola.

PART TWO

NOT IN FRONT OF THE INSPECTORS

1984-2006

CHAPTER THE SEVENTH   Cumbria 1984-2006

SETTLING BACK.... NOT!

September 1984.

'So, skiver, you're back. Swanning around all year while we got on with the real work. We read all about it in the newspapers. Suppose you reckon you're something of a journalist now.'

My first greeting as I walked into the St. Aidan's staff-room. Mike, the geography teacher. Still the same 'in-yer-face' attitude. Nothing new there then. But then I shouldn't be expecting a welcoming party. Roger and Jean were certainly glad I was back. Genny had not found the year easy and on a number of occasions they had had to salvage the situation.

But to walk back into my old classroom was disconcerting. Little seemed to have changed and it felt as though I was putting on a suit of old clothes that I'd cast off a year ago. There was the same chalk-dust, many of the same posters on the walls. The place looked dour and dowdy under a grey Cumbrian sky. My year away had given me so much; it had been so vivid, so energising. Now it was a world away and I was faced with a more sober reality.

England seemed a tired old country. People moaned and there was the usual cynicism about the state of the world. I missed the fresh-faced idealism of America. Yes, it seemed naive at times but it was positive, it was optimistic, it was infectious.

Margaret Thatcher had been cosying up to Ronald Reagan who'd won a second term as President and she was attempting to inject something of the American spirit of free enterprise into the sluggish economic culture of the UK. But it was done in a crude and brutal way. The miners' strike, which started in March, still dragged on with nightly news coverage of clashes between police and pickets. Mining communities in the north of England were being decimated by pit closures. Inflation was running at around 10% and the price of petrol was three times what it had been in America.

On the domestic front the house needed a lick of paint and our car was something of a wreck. It bore the scars of Genny's early accident, there were only three gears functioning rather than four and it was truly a sad old rust-bucket. The garden was completely overgrown. It was like something out of Miss Havisham's garden in *Great Expectations* - green creeper festooning and clinging to everything - trees, bushes, lawn, veg. plot. It all needed re-awakening.

In addition, we were still reeling from the sudden death of Sue's mother who had died two days after our return. Sue had nursed her for almost three weeks and it was as if she'd held on to see me and the children and then given up the fight. A wonderfully generous and spirited woman had gone and left a huge space in our lives.

At least Katie and James were excited to be home, to rediscover the toys and books they'd forgotten, to reorganise their bedrooms, although James was not quite so thrilled about starting school full-time.

After a few weeks back in the job, I sensed that there were some changes in the air. When I left for Florida in the summer of 1983 there was talk of getting computers into school. A year later there was now a dedicated 'Computer Room' full of BBC computers. It was financed by something called TVEI - Technical and Vocational Education Initiative, a government project aimed to raise the skills of those students not destined for the academic route. Money was showered on this project and those involved in the teaching seemed to inhabit a different realm from the rest of us. There were frequent training courses at swish hotels where good food and wine were lavished on the delegates. Methods of teaching were unconventional. The TVEI students enjoyed a special timetable and were given time to spend on technical experiments one of which involved a big new satellite dish linked to computer software to track weather patterns and satellites. They were given initiative tests - building rafts to ford rivers, constructing bridges out of bundles of straws. It was typical of the Headmaster at St. Aidan's to be at the forefront of new developments. He was certainly a man of rare vision and not afraid to allow people to take risks and try new things.

My only contact with computers was with a cast-off ZX Spectrum which James had been given by a friend. It had curious rubber keys and came with a tape player and booklet which showed how to do some simple programming. It was not wildly exciting as the tapes kept on being chewed up by the tape machine and what appeared on screen didn't seem to add up to much. But when I saw the word processing possibilities of these new BBC computers, I realised I was close to being able to ditch my trusty type-writer and dispense forever with using messy Tippex correction fluid.

In the English department, however, there was no investment in computers and we were barely touched by these developments in the new technology. I tried to hold on to that buzz of energy that I'd felt in America. I remembered George who so personified the American spirit - his passion for life, his boundless energy - teacher in the morning, lawyer in the afternoon, evangelical missionary in the evening. And also there was his business venture which he had revealed to me one evening.

'Barrie I want to show you a business opportunity you might be interested in developing when you get back to England.'

I thought to myself - I think you got the wrong guy here, George. Ever since I left industry I'd been trying to put some distance between me and the business world.

'Sounds interesting,' I had said, trying to be polite.

'Linda and I would like you to come to a motivational meeting where you'll meet some very successful business people but also some people like yourselves who might consider getting into the business.'

I had great respect for George and didn't think he would be luring us into some cult of the black arts or drug trafficking. So we went along to the meeting.

It was held in a posh Miami hotel and the conference room was filled with be-suited men and manicured women. Many of the men seemed to affect a slight nervous tic which involved taking out a small aerosol of Gold Spot Breath Freshener and spraying it into their mouths. This would happen every three minutes or so. Everyone had those perfect, gleaming white teeth, the women shiny lipstick and polished nails. On the stage there was a banner which spelt the name AMWAY. Amway was the name of the company all these people were connected with. They marketed a range of 'superior' cleaning products. I was reassured they weren't grooming me to become a Kleeneze man - one of those rather sad door-to-door salesmen I remembered from my childhood who hawked their wares around in a big suitcase knocking on doors and trying to flog their wares. My mother never bought anything but she always took the free gift they were offering.

No, Amway was different. You built up a network of your own salespeople starting with friends and family and you made money if they made money. They recruited their own people, which added to your network and gradually you built up this thriving pyramid of colleagues - the bigger the pyramid the more money you made.

On stage walked Tom and Annie, a so-called 'diamond' couple whose pyramid was one of the eighth wonders of the Amway business world. They talked movingly about their 'journey' out of penury to their present status of business royalty. The audience was very attentive. At the end there was applause, a standing ovation, the conference room buzzing with this energised and electrified audience of would-be diamond-geezers and their wives.

At first I was cynical - typical of the English who don't take to a public show of positivity. But George plied us with tapes of motivational speakers, of diamond couples like Tom and Annie and the more I listened the less cynical I became. Maybe it was 'all in the mind' whether you succeeded or failed. From personal experience I knew how easily you could talk yourself in or out of making a commitment to something. What if you only listened to the positive voice in your head and snuffed out the negativity which so often pulled you back from trying something new? That's what the Toms and Annies of this world seemed to have done. Why not me?

Admittedly America was a fertile landscape for trying out some positive thinking. So many people seemed to live by a 'can do' philosophy. It's what the country was founded on. England, by contrast seemed to sustain itself on a diet of grim acceptance that we were all wallowing in a mire of mediocrity and that's the way it had to be. 'Let's all sink together, it's cosier that way' seemed to be the prevailing mood. Anyone who popped their head above the parapet had to be prepared to get attacked by a barrage of cynicism and mockery.

But in the autumn of 1984, faced with the predictability of my old job, a salary which barely grew from year to year, a growing family and the feeling that the energy of the New World was still vaguely flowing in my veins, I decided to make the commitment to strike off down the road of Amway.

In my heart my real satisfaction came from nourishing the souls of students with the treasures of poetry, literature and drama. Selling cleaning products to build a business empire was like entering a parallel universe. Dressing up in a smart suit to attend a motivational meeting in Glasgow felt weird. But in good faith Sue and I travelled up the motorway to meet Trevor, an Amway contact George had located.

The Reverend Trevor Collinson and his wife Denise had 'gone diamond' the previous month. He was a Presbyterian minister and I wondered whether his congregation were all loyally using Amway cleaning products in their homes. His own home was glitzy with cut glass and silver in abundance, all polished to perfection. And that morning this little dynamo of a preacher held court in a local hotel to a lively audience of Scottish Amway devotees.

'As soon as you get some people together, Barrie, I'll come down to your home and we'll get your group up and running.'

The challenge was there.

At school if felt like I was nursing a secret. I didn't approach any colleagues to join the Amway club. I felt I should keep separate these two very different worlds. But at the Scottish meeting I'd been given the name of someone in Carlisle who might be an Amway candidate. This was a start and it was with a mixture of apprehension and excitement I knocked on the door of a small terraced house in Denton Holme. A thin woman in her forties with thick-lensed glasses opened the door. Yes, she was Molly Jameson. I explained how I'd been given her name.

'I wondered whether you might be interested to hear about a business opportunity,' I said.

'Well that sounds very nice.'

'It would involve coming to a meeting at my house.'

'Can I bring a friend?'

Another possible recruit. Brilliant.

'Of course and if your friend knows of anyone then we can include them as well.'

Molly didn't seem the most dynamic of personalities but for selling cleaning products maybe being dynamic wasn't a prerequisite for success. I drove away exhilarated. My business team was taking shape already.

The plan was that I would do the presentation and Trevor would be there to offer support. The presentation followed a set pattern. Flip chart showing the way you built your pyramid, calculation of potential earnings and finally a demonstration of key products - this would seal the deal. The killer demonstration was using a pot of Amway's metal cleaner. All you did was to take a copper coin from your pocket, dip half into the cleaning paste then withdraw it to show one side of the coin now gleaming as if new. It was like a magic show and never failed to draw gasps of surprise.

The stage was set for an evening in late November.

I picked up Molly and she directed me to her friend's house.

'I didn't mention Betty's in a wheel chair but her husband Terry will be there to help,' said Molly as we set off.

'Right,' I said. 'A wheel chair. Right.'

Betty was only partially immobile and she was able to manoeuvre into the car by sliding herself off her chair. She was a rather stern faced woman with severely cropped grey hair. Her husband was a short man with round shoulders and a bald, egg-shaped head.

'C'mon Terry, the man's waiting. Get that chair in the boot and get inside. We're going to be late,' she barked.

I helped Terry to fold the chair. 'Hi, Terry, I'm Barrie,' I said chirpily.

He grunted something and nodded, barely looking up.

'Hello, Betty, are you all right back there?' I smiled.

'It's a bit squashed but we'll manage. Is it far?' she said.

'We're just picking up Marjorie,' said Molly.

'Marjorie? What's she coming for?' said Betty.

337

'I thought it would be a nice change for her. She doesn't get out very often.'

We collected Marjorie from an old people's home. She was a bright little lady probably in her late seventies. She walked with a stick but took my arm as we negotiated the path back to the car. 'Hello, Mr Day. This is so nice of you. Molly's told me all about it. She says you're setting up a little business.'

'That's the idea,' I replied.

Trevor had already arrived at the house. He looked groomed and polished. His gold cuff-links and wrist chain and Rolex watch shone with stunning brilliance. His teeth gleamed and his breath was freshened every few minutes with a subtle puff from his Gold Spot Breath Freshener. 'Good evening ladies,' he beamed. 'So this is Barrie's little business team is it?'

They took their seats and I saw Betty jab Terry in the ribs with her elbow. He shifted along the settee and she scowled at him. Molly was gazing rather vacantly round the room through her thick lenses which had misted up; little Marjorie sat in the middle settling the hem of her skirt over her knees.

I adjusted my flip chart, checked that my sample of products was in the right place for my demonstration, felt the heat rising in my face and my collar chafing my neck. Then I started.

I had remembered the patter, drew the diagrams to show the business model, showed the figures for potential earnings and did the demonstrations. Marjorie was delighted with the coin-in-the-metal-polish routine. 'Well I never,' she exclaimed, 'it's like magic.' Betty never cracked her face, just stared, lips pressed tight. Terry sat hunched, his head slightly nodding. I wasn't sure whether he was agreeing with it all or on the verge of falling asleep. Trevor was there nodding sagely and beaming at my 'team'.

The atmosphere lightened somewhat when Sue came in with the refreshments. Her flapjack was a real hit as were the scones and jaffa cakes. And after their second cups of tea I felt it was time put the question. Were they on-board? Could I groom this motley crew into a dynamic sales machine?

'Well what do you think?' I said.

Trevor cut in before they could answer, 'As you can see, the business model is certainly a winner and the products are second to none. They sell themselves. Everyone needs cleaning products so it's just a case of talking to friends and family, work colleagues, showing what the products will do and you're away on the road to prosperity. And with Barrie at the helm you could really be going places.'

There was some nodding. No-one spoke for a moment, then Marjorie raised her hand.

'Yes, Marjorie,' I said.

'I did tell them I wouldn't be back late. It's been very nice, Barrie. And I'm sure you'll be very successful but I need to be getting back. Thank you for a lovely evening.'

'Right, Marjorie,' I replied. 'Yes, I'll run you back.'

Betty nudged Terry with her elbow again. 'C'mon, Mr Day's taking us home. Get yerself shifted.'

I looked across at Trevor who simply smiled, raised his eyebrows a little and said, 'Well Barrie, I think we've made a start here. I need to be getting back to Glasgow as well. Give me a call and we'll talk things over.'

After I'd dropped off Betty and Marjorie I finally drew up outside Molly's door.

'There's just one thing,' said Molly. 'I wonder if you would take one of my leaflets and be prepared to go on a mailing list.'

'No problem,' I replied, 'and you'll let me know how many products you want to order,' I added.

'Oh yes,' she replied. 'Thank you. It was a nice evening.' She wrote down my address in a little note book and gave me a leaflet.

I watched her front door close and then looked at the leaflet:

Dianetics, Your Road to Clear.

Thank you for joining the Church of Scientology.

*

ONWARDS AND UPWARDS

'And to cap it all she sees me as a recruit to the Church of Scientology, whatever that is.'

Sue just rolled around on the settee stifling laughter. 'I don't think Betty Brimstone is going to attract many customers. What a dragon she was. And dear Marjorie was just enjoying an evening out.'

'About the only success of the evening was your flapjack. The whole thing was a farce, an absolute farce. I don't know what Trevor thought.'

Sue put an arm around me, 'Just see it as practice for next time.'

But I wasn't sure there would be a next time. Positive thinking was all very well but it had to be applied to something I believed in. I wasn't sure I could ever feel honest about persuading people to part with their money for a range of cleaning products.

Hope came in early February when Jean showed me a copy of the Times Educational Supplement. 'There's a job for you. About time you moved on from here.'

'Gee thanks. Nice to be wanted.'

'You know what I mean. You're ready for something new. Have a look.'

The post of Head of English at the nearby Newman School was advertised for Easter. It was a small Catholic school of around 600 pupils, half the size of St. Aidan's. Whenever I had been there for meetings I'd always liked the atmosphere of calmness which seemed to pervade the place, very different from the cut and thrust of St. Aidan's. But I wondered whether it would matter that I wasn't a Catholic.

I applied and waited for a response.

Our Amway adventure stumbled along. We sold a few products to friends but as for building my pyramid of dynamic sales people I had to admit it was more like a molehill.

I channelled my energies into more building work. The barn at the rear of the house was being converted for Sue's father to live in and while a team of builders worked on that, I started digging foundations for a kitchen conservatory. The house was terribly draughty. The west wind funnelled under the front door, floated the carpet a little on its way through the living room and found its way out of the back door. During the winter Katie had been mesmerised one evening by seeing the carpet lifting next to where she was sitting. She patted the carpet down and asked, 'Is it a ghost?' It was then I decided a conservatory might be the answer to keep the ghosts at bay.

In the first week of March a letter arrived. I'd got an interview. I tried to adopt the mantra of positive thinking but I was nagged by doubts. What would they think of my wayward career so far? Doing the wrong degree. Off to Jamaica after only one year of teaching; a year in Florida and now wanting to move jobs almost as soon as I'd returned. It read like the career of someone who was unreliable. But then on the positive side, I'd established a new A level course, worked as an examiner, successfully taught A level and O level, managed difficult classes and retained my sanity. But then, I wasn't a Catholic and maybe that mattered.

It was an all day interview and the more I walked around the school and met the staff, the more I wanted this job. The buildings were modern and well kept, the main hall had a sunken parquet floor which was polished to a high sheen and smelt of bees wax. It was light and airy and the buildings spread out in four blocks so that at no time were hundreds of children all shoving past each other when the lessons

340

changed. The Head was a man in his forties. He was short and slight and had long wavy grey hair. He spoke with a quiet voice and often there was a smile playing around his mouth. The Deputy Head was just the opposite: tall, broad and robust, he had a gruff voice but a hearty laugh. They made a good duo. Yes, I could work in this place.

A number of people taught English including the Head. It seemed he always elected to teach a bottom set of fifth years. This was indeed a far cry from Piggy Hardcastle at Lichfield. There was humanity here, good humour and I warmed to it all.

When the interviews were over I waited with the other four candidates in the staffroom. I sighed at what might have been. Surely they would choose one of the others.

The door opened and the Deputy Head came in. He looked around and his eyes fell on me. He nodded, 'Mr Day, could you follow me please.' I could have hugged this bear of a man and danced a sailor's hornpipe. No more trying to flog floor cleaner and build pyramids. I was going to be a Head of English.

I valued the six years I'd spent at St. Aidan's; the place had been inspiring and the English Department was a wealth of talent and good humour. I'd tried myself out in a range of projects - not always successful, remembering my Hallowe'en embarrassment but I had banished the doubts that I'd had about being a good English teacher. I would miss them but with Newman only a short distance away I wouldn't be losing touch. I was intending to set up the A level Communication Studies course at Newman and, doing the same English GCE course, I was bound to see Jean and Roger at training meetings. We were also planning a joint trip to Stratford for the A level English students.

'This is just what you were ready for,' said Jean. 'You're going to be just fine.'

But teaching is a funny old profession. You get promoted into a management position but nobody tells you how to manage or even what management is.

'It'll take you three years to get established,' said Duncan, the outgoing Head of English, whose job I was taking. He was going off to join Her Majesty's Inspectorate. 'Three years?' I thought. 'What does he know.'

But he knew all right. Teaching young people is one thing. Managing adults is something quite different.

*

I started the job after the Easter holidays. It was an odd time to start, like stepping on to a stage when the play's almost over. I was covering the last stages of revision with Duncan's exam classes and trying to pick up the threads of the work he had planned with other classes. But that didn't matter too much. What mattered was the sign on my office door: 'Head of English'. Admittedly the office was small but it was my domain, all mine. I felt I was now standing on a plateau looking out over the vista of where I'd come from. It had been a journey of hiccups, false starts and deviations but now the road ahead was much clearer. I had a department of six to organise and manage. There was a stock of reading books and exam texts to check out, staffing to organise for September, stationery to order, two designated English rooms to keep an eye on. It was the term which rolled down to the summer holidays and when life became less frantic.

My soul is intact, dear Mr Freer and we're ready to rock and roll.

*

And, yes, size does make a difference. With 1200 students at St. Aidan's we never had whole school assemblies. Apart from the sports hall there wasn't a room big enough to accommodate everyone. Newman was a different matter. With only 600 students whole school assemblies were held each week. The Head and Deputy had devised a fascinating opening ritual. There were seats for everyone and Bill, the Deputy, would stand on the stage as the students were marshalled in by their form tutors. A certain low buzz of noise was tolerated until everyone was assembled. Then at a given signal the school was told to 'Please stand for the Headmaster'. Everyone rose, there would be an expectant silence, a hiatus and then the Head would stride down the hall and up on to the stage. He would rub his hands together, peer out at the congregation and then say, 'Please sit down.' He was always polite, always courteous.

There were no hymns, the assemblies were devised by each of the four House Heads who worked on a rota. An assembly might involve a piece of drama or role play; there might be some music, a poem, a reading but whatever it was, the Head always took the opportunity to end the assembly by addressing the school. And his recurring theme was 'Newman is a good school'. He would repeat the phrase, 'a good school'. It was about being positive, upbeat and he was a great speaker, a natural raconteur. But he chose his anecdotes skilfully, there was often a touch of humour but always a moral pointer to leave in the minds of the

342

students. I liked this man. He seemed to have got the balance right. I was going to enjoy working here.

*

REUNION EN FRANCE

In May a letter arrived from the Megevands which prompted us to think about driving to Europe that summer. They were living in Geneva having moved yet again: Haiti, Jamaica, Martinique, Perpignan - now Geneva. It was time we saw them again. With my new salary we could afford to buy a decent car. The rust bucket could go. We had 'arrived' and could now join the exodus of fellow teachers who headed for France in the summer.

At home, the conversion of the barn for Sue's father was almost complete and we now had a conservatory off the kitchen warmed by the morning sun. The thought of France and warm sun, grapes and wine prompted me to invest in a grape vine from the local garden centre. Apparently to grow grapes in a conservatory you planted the roots outside and brought the vine stem inside. I chiselled a hole in the wall to bring in the vine. This could work. In ten years we could be treading grapes with our feet, squeezing grape juice between our toes and bottling our own wine.

'You are joking,' said Sue.

'Grapes?' said Katie. 'Don't be silly, daddy.'

'Just you wait. You'll eat your words and our grapes in a few years time.'

'What about some chickens?' added Katie. 'I think we should have chickens.'

'Right,' I nodded. 'Let me think about that.'

So that summer we drove to France. We camped on the south side of Lake Geneva. Warm French bread, croissants and pain au chocolat each morning, village markets loaded with fresh produce - moist lettuces, succulent tomatoes and peaches plucked from some nearby allotment. Bitter French coffee and pain au raisin, soft oozing Camembert and pink blushed grapes washed down with local Burgundy wine - how I loved all things French that holiday.

The Megevands drove from the city to see us. The reunion was tinged with sadness at the catalogue of circumstances which had brought them back to Philippe's home country of Switzerland. They had money and property still locked up in Jamaica which they couldn't access,

Katie's car accident in Martinique had left her with neck and back problems and Philippe's health was not great. The verve and energy they had displayed in Jamaica when they were running one of the top restaurants in Kingston had been sapped. There was a bitterness in Katie's voice when Jamaica was mentioned. Philippe still retained something of his wit and good humour. He mesmerised little Katie and James with his magic tricks and his jokes but at times he was edgy and tense. Regine, who had been a rather gauche and earnest eleven year old in Jamaica, was now a sharp, engaging young woman of twenty who was studying law at the university in Geneva. Her sister Katarina, who had been in my GCE group in Jamaica, was now married and living in Paris. It was their generation who were preparing to take over the reins in the working world while the parents withdrew into the shadows.

After a few days we said goodbye and drove south into the Alps, along the valley of the Arve, through the tourist trap which is Chamonix and further up the valley to Argentiere. There we took the cable car up to the high meadows where the air was crisp, the grey mountain peaks still capped with snow and the hiking trails edged with gentians and wild azaleas. Standing on the edge of the Argentiere glacier it was easy to see how myths of monsters and magic had grown to haunt the firesides of ancient peoples. We listened to the strange subterranean growling and grinding of the glacier beneath our feet. Katie and James were intrigued. It was hard for them to understand that this huge swathe of shattered crevasses and boulders was a moving river of ice. Only the dull earth tremors and the distant grinding sounds hinted at the scale of this massive ice dredger.

Turning north after a few days, we headed to the bucolic delights of the Meuse valley. The children paddled our little inflatable dinghy on the tranquil creeks and backwaters while Sue and I relaxed by the tent reading and sampling some of the local white wines of Alsace.

I had brought away a copy of George Bernard Shaw's *St. Joan*. It was one of the set texts for the O level Literature exam and as well as reading the play for the first time, I planned to do a little local research while we were away. Joan had grown up in the small village of Domremy. It was in the fields near the village when she was 12 that she first saw her visions and heard her 'voices' which told her to lead the French army and drive the English from French soil. At 16 she travelled to the local town of Vaucouleurs to get permission from the garrison commander, Robert de Beaudricourt, to go to the French court at Chinon and see the Dauphin. I wanted Katie and James to hear the amazing story of this young girl and see the places associated with her life - Domremy, her birthplace, Vaucouleurs where she was finally given a horse to ride to Chinon; Reims Cathedral where it was said her suit of armour was on display and finally the square in Rouen where she was burnt at the stake.

The village of Domremy-la-Pucelle is in the valley of the Vair River which, further north, joins the grandeur of the River Meuse. Jeanne D'Arc's house lies near the centre of the village. It is untouched by tourism. There were no other visitors on the morning of our visit. The cream stone house with its strangely asymmetric shape and sloping roof was open for us to explore. It was empty of furniture. No attempt to recreate the past for visitors - just cool, lime-washed walls, stone floors and low oak-beamed ceilings.

A mile away and close to the wooded coppice where Joan heard her 'voices' is a church. It houses the huge paintings which depict Joan's progress from naive country girl to national icon, feared by the English army and burnt at the stake.

From here we drove to Vaucouleurs where Joan pestered de Baudricourt for a horse to ride to Chinon. The cobbled streets of Vaucouleurs and the castle which looked down on the valley of the Meuse still evoked something of the flavour of France in the 15th century.

But most poignant was to stand in Reims Cathedral and gaze at the tiny suit of armour which Joan wore in battle.

Katie was transfixed. 'Is it the real suit of armour that she wore?'

'The actual one,' I replied.

'Can I touch it?'

'Not supposed to but go on, no-one's looking.'

Tentatively Katie stretched out a finger to touch the skirt of the upper body armour. 'It's very cold,' she said.

'She was a very small person,' said James. 'How could she lift a sword?'

Finally we stood in the square in Rouen and looked at the brass plaque which marks the site of the pyre where Joan was burnt.

'I think it's nasty what the English did to her,' said Katie.

'Was she really a witch?' asked James.

'I don't think she was,' replied Katie. 'I just think it's a shame, what happened. Burning someone on purpose is just horrible.'

James gave a small sigh and then, looking across the square towards the shops said, 'Can we have frites for tea? I'm hungry.'

Sorry, Joan, but the attention span of small boys was ever thus.

*

FLY-FISHING IN THE CLASSROOM

When I saw the images on the evening news in the autumn of 1985, Huey Morrison's words from 1976 came back to me - 'trouble comin' to the streets of London'. I recalled that he had just obtained a copy of Linton Kwesi Johnson's *Dread Beat and Blood* and had read me a couple of the poems. And now here on my television screen was the reality. Streets of London and Birmingham in flames, young blacks rioting and the front page of the Daily Express showing a black youth brandishing a petrol bomb with the headline 'ENGLAND 1985'. The riots started when the mother of a black suspect was shot during a house search.

At school people tutted and some trotted out the usual racial platitudes about immigrants and 'sending them home'. Carlisle was predominantly white English, there were few ethnic groups and there seemed to be a strong current of xenophobia embedded in the culture of the city. One of the older teachers frequently used the phrase 'nigger in the woodpile' when he was declaiming about some problem or other, quite oblivious of the racist undertones in the phrase.

'You can't use that phrase,' I said to him on one occasion. 'It's blatantly racist.'

'Just a saying, that's all. Doesn't mean anything,' he retorted, somewhat miffed at being challenged.

But having been out of the country, things like this screamed at me. Britain had to wake up in the way that America had woken up to the civil rights abuses in the southern states in the 1960s. There were rumours that the extreme right wing National Front were recruiting at school gates and I'd seen their leaflets littering the pavements on several occasions. Some of our fourth year lads were flirting with the appeal of the Front's racist agenda. Opinions expressed in class were often simplistic : 'I think they should kick em all out,' said Jamie Stevens one afternoon. Jamie was in my lowest 4th year set.

'Who's 'them' Jamie?' I replied.

'You know, all them nignogs and pakis who are kicking off in Brixton and Liverpool.'

Where to start in unpicking all his undigested prejudices? Should I start with 'nignogs' and challenge the use of the word itself? Should I ignore that and go to the issue of the riots - the high unemployment rates among urban blacks; their hatred of the way the police used the 'stop and search' or 'sus' powers; the fact that the idea of 'kicking them out' was absurd as these were second and third generation black British. Where to start with someone like Jamie Stevens on a rainy afternoon with only half an hour to go before the bell.

I made a stab, 'Where would you kick them out to, Jamie?'

'Back where they came from - nignog land.'

Others in the class were smiling and shaking their heads. Jamie was enjoying the attention of my questioning. 'C'mon let's be serious about this, Jamie. Most of the rioters were born in Britain, like their parents. Maybe their grandparents came from the Caribbean in the fifties when the British government encouraged workers to come from Commonwealth countries to work in what they called the 'mother country'. So the idea of 'kicking them out', as you put it, is daft. They're black British; Britain is their home. They just want a better deal.'

'So you agree with the rioters?' said Peter Johnson, one of the more thoughtful lads in the class.

'No, I don't agree with rioting, Peter, but I think I understand something of why they're rioting.'

'Didn't you once live in Jamaica, sir?' asked one of the girls. 'You talked about it once.'

'Yes, Debbie, for three years, I was teaching there.'

'What was it like?'

'It was a place of extremes - the rich were very rich , the poor very poor. There were places of great beauty and places of ugliness. There were shootings - a high murder rate in some areas of the country while in others it was a tropical paradise like you see on the Bounty adverts. And it was a bit scary at first being in a minority surrounded by people of a different colour. Took a while to get used to. So I understand something of what it's like for people in this country when they're a racial minority surrounded by white people.'

'Muhammad Ali's okay,' said Jamie, 'and he's black.'

'He's clever as well,' added Peter. 'Did you see him when Parkinson interviewed him and he did that kind of rap thing?'

'And there's that John Barnes,' piped up Terry Fields, 'he was in the cup final last year - played on the wing for Watford. He's black and he's okay.'

'You don't support Watford. What a crap team,' laughed Jamie.

'No I support Everton,' replied Terry. 'I'm just saying Barnes was good on the wing that's all and that he's black. So some blacks are okay.'

The discussion jumped around like a firecracker as usual. No particular logic, little real progress in developing their understanding. When the bell went all I could do was think that at least they had voiced some opinions, they had listened to each other, we had parted amicably and that Jamie Stevens didn't have the last word.

I made more progress with my A level Communication Studies group. The newspaper coverage of the riots was perfect for analysing the way news was packaged. Whenever a major event took place I'd buy all the newspapers of the day, share them out and get groups to compare the treatments of the same news story across the tabloids and broadsheets. Contrasts in headlines, space given to the story, space given to pictures compared with text said much about the news values of particular papers. Then there was the way the reports were written. There were always differences in statistics quoted, uses of emotive language, opinions stated. It made clear that no news reporting is free of bias. The class of twelve was working in four groups poring over their selection of newspapers.

'So where's the truth in all this?' asked Mel. 'How do we know what's really going on if there's all this distortion?'

'Truth doesn't come into what newspapers do, does it, sir?'

Raymond Vickers had replied for me. I left Mel's question hanging in the air to allow the others to join the discussion.

'It says here in the Mirror that there were around 200 rioters,' said Rebecca.

'I've got around 700 in the Daily Mail,' added Simon.

'Guardian gives it at 150,' quoted Annie.

'My dad says you can't believe what you read in the papers,' said Raymond. 'This proves it.'

This was a new course for the school. I had launched it back in the summer term when I'd visited all the 5th year classes who were about to take their final exams. To get 12 students on an A level course was pretty good for a school the size of Newman. I was pleased with the way it was going. Several of the students like Mel and Raymond combined the course with A level English Literature so I saw them several times during the week. They were a joy to teach: lively, good humoured and sharp. What was always a challenge was getting a new sixth form group to gel and feel comfortable to voice their opinions in front of each other. It was often the brightest who were the most inhibited especially the girls. I remember a conversation after class one day with Diane, an extremely intelligent English Literature student. Her essays were brilliant, her insights mature beyond her years and yet she would never speak up in class.

'It's not er... cool, sir, to say too much,' she said, eyes averted.

'Cool - what d'you mean?' I asked.

'Not good for a girl to be seen as too intelligent.'

'You're kidding me. I thought Women's Lib. had trampled on all those social barriers,' I said.

She half-smiled and shook her head. 'C'mon sir, this is Carlisle, not west coast America. Still in the Dark Ages here.'

Teaching an A level group was very different from a class of thirty unpredictable teenagers. Having said which, the more I taught, the more I realised good teaching was not about telling students things, giving them packages of knowledge, it was about asking appropriate questions, questions which helped students to connect with the ideas and understanding towards which you were trying to lead them. With younger students the questions might be more accessible but whatever the age you were trying to stretch their thinking. I likened it to fly-fishing, not that I've ever tried it. But the image of casting the bait just ahead of the fish and getting it to swim towards the bait was the image that I had in mind.

It was also about a kind of classroom theatre where you floated a question and then let it hang in the air; where you allowed for moments of silence and didn't rush to fill them. That's when students were forced to think, were forced to swim harder. It didn't always work if you had some pubescent numskull who wanted to fill the theatre with his or her crass performance. But generally if you treated students with respect for their intelligence or flattered them with language more complex than they were used to, then remarkable things might happen. Unlikely students would surprise themselves and their mates by the maturity they could assume. They would voice ideas and views which they wouldn't normally dare to do for fear of ridicule by their peers. It was all about creating a safe atmosphere in which they felt they could drop their masks and be themselves for a few minutes.

Then when they left the room you'd hear the banter:

'What happened to you then, swallow a dictionary?'

'Get lost moron.'

349

But I knew that that person who had ventured to go for the bait, had grown a little in his own eyes and in the eyes of others in the class and that's what I was aiming for.

*

THROUGH THE LOOKING GLASS

Spring of 1986 and I was getting more and more irritated by having to put up with smoke in the staffroom. It was a small staffroom and although there was only a handful of smokers they were enough to cause real annoyance. Some people didn't seem to bother about it but I was becoming increasingly intolerant.

Some years ago I'd banned my father from smoking in our home. One Christmas when Katie was still a baby I'd come into the living room where she was sleeping in her carry-cot to find my father reading the paper and smoking one of his small Mannekin cigars. Smoke hung in layers across the room. My new little daughter was still sleeping and my father was oblivious that anything was amiss. He was of the war-time generation when the government gave free cigarettes to the troops. Smoking was a way of life. At the end of a meal he was used to saying, 'Anyone mind if I smoke?' and proceed to take out his tin of small cigars. When we replied, 'Yes, we do mind,' he was taken aback. 'Well you did ask,' added my mother. 'You'd better take yourself outside.' My father was not happy about it, but attitudes had to be changed and home was where we could make a start.

I can remember when I was at school going to the staff-room at break-time to take a message. You'd knock on the staff-room door. After a while it would open but you could barely see anyone - the place was just a fug of dense smoke.

By 1986 things were different though. Increasingly there were murmurings in government about banning tobacco advertising on the television and in magazines. I'd started getting posters and stickers from the ASH anti-smoking organisation and putting them up in various parts of the school. At a recent staff meeting I'd waited until the end and under 'Any Other Business' had raised my hand and said quite simply, 'I'd like the right to breath clean air in the staff-room.'

'Oh, right,' replied the Head. 'Now let's think about that one, er..' He was somewhat thrown. 'Maybe you should come and see me, Barrie.'

So I went to see him, put the case and the outcome was that an extractor fan was put at one end of the staff-room and the other end designated as a smoking area. The smokers grumbled and glowered at me about this 'infringement of their rights' . The overall effect was that the extractor fan pulled the smoke from one end of the room to the non-smoking other end before it exited. Not satisfactory but at least it was a start.

March 27th was 'National No Smoking Day' and I'd been busy distributing badges and leaflets round the school in an attempt to galvanise more support for the cause. I came in early that morning to finalise a display that I was erecting in the foyer. When I opened the door of the staff-room there sat Gareth Jones, one of the science teachers, puffing smugly on a fat cigar and waiting for my response.

'Nice one Gareth, and what d'you do for an encore?' I said as I swept past him. There was no point having a slanging match. Time was on my side.

But in fact it would be another 20 years before smoking was finally made illegal in the workplace.

*

If progress was slow on the anti-smoking front in1986, there were exciting developments in the new technology. It was the year when the English department acquired its first computer. There was already a room in school full of BBC computers allocated to teaching the new subject of Information Technology. For other departments to get computers was a piece of history. Initially, English, Science and Maths got priority.

The machine was a BBC Master model with 128KB of memory. Not that I understood anything of the technicalities of computers. All I knew was that the first BBCs had been 32KB, then came the 64KB model and now the 'Master' had arrived with its 128KB memory which all sounded pretty impressive to me.   The question was how to use a single computer in the classroom. I bought a computer trolley to be able to wheel our prize from group to group. New software was generally being marketed on 5.25 inch floppy plastic discs although you could get a word processing chip to put inside the computer. Word processing was the new revolution for me. No more messy ink blotches or fading type from a worn out typewriter ribbon; no more messy correction fluid. Now deleting was a joy. You could cut paragraphs, move them around, reinstate them. This was true liberation for a writer.

Then there was something called DTP or 'Desk Top Publishing'. The DTP software was another kind of magic. It allowed you to produce newspaper formats with different fonts, layouts for flyers, adverts, greeting cards. The potential for using this with English classes was just amazing.

Some of the educational software used a gaming format - solving puzzles to improve spelling or grammar. But for me, the most interesting find was some software called *Developing Tray*. It had been devised by a London teacher called Bob Moy and the name was taken from the photographic process of an image gradually emerging in a developing tray. You typed in a poem or piece of text which would then appear on screen as just a series of dashes, all of the letters having been removed. By predicting letters or buying them the words slowly started to emerge on the page. It was brilliant for students to have to mentally scan for words, check spellings and I used it with students from first year to 6th formers. It held students' attention like nothing I'd ever seen before.

For my A level students' first attempt I tried them with D.H.Lawrence's short two verse poem *Discord in Childhood*.

Outside the house an ash-tree hung its terrible whips.
And at night when the wind rose, the lash of the tree
Shrieked and slashed the wind, as a ship's
Weird rigging in a storm shrieks hideously.
Within the house two voices arose, a slender lash
Whistling she-delirious rage, and the dreadful sound
Of a male thong booming and bruising, until it had
Drowned
The other voice in a silence of blood, 'neath the noise
of the ash.

The poem appeared on the screen as a series of dashes and then they started the process of prediction. It was interesting watching the group dynamics. At first Raymond assumed the role of leader but as more text was revealed on the screen and the context of the poem became clearer so it was some of the quieter members of the group who started to shine. They picked up Lawrence's powerful use of alliteration and metaphor and the word 'thong' drew a giggle from Raymond until I explained that it did not refer to a skimpy under garment.

'It's describing the man's voice, you idiot, like a sort of club beating down the woman,' said Diane.

Raymond frowned and then nodded, looking somewhat chastened.

'And that contrasts with the woman's voice compared to a 'lash',' added Mel.

I nodded but said nothing.

'Isn't there that thing we did in Shakespeare where nature seems to copy people's actions?' said Diane.

'Pathetic something,' added Anne, 'oh, what is it?'

'Pathetic fallacy,' said Richard triumphantly.

I nodded again. 'Well done.'

They continued putting in their predictions until they had fully revealed the text. I had barely said two words but what I had witnessed in the last forty-five minutes was extraordinary. These students had wrestled with language, meaning, inference, imagery and in a strange way had lived the creative process that Lawrence must have experienced in composing the poem. The level of engagement was intense, fuelled by some healthy competition within the group but most important was the way the quieter members had found their voices.

This was truly a revolutionary way of working and I was intrigued by the potential that these first computers were offering to change our style of teaching.

I had also decided it was sensible to buy a BBC computer for home as well so that I could preview software, word process worksheets and get Katie and James involved. It didn't take long. When they discovered games like *Chuckie Egg* and *Killer Gorilla* and James found he could drop bombs on ships in *Bomb Alley* they were both hooked.

That year a new Head of Music arrived at Newman. Avril was an unusual musician. Not only was she a great instrumentalist but she was acutely tuned to the potential of the new technology. She ordered new electronic keyboards, digital drum machines, brought in her own Atari computer and introduced the students to the mysteries of multi-tracking.

After school one day I needed to discuss arrangements for a forthcoming drama/music evening. I tracked her down to the science lab where she was in close discussion with the Head of Science over some new electronic gadgetry. They were staring at a screen on an impressive piece of equipment. The dialogue went something like this:

Head of Science: I can't understand where we've got this wave pattern from.

Head of Music: We've got lots of sub-oscillation going on, so we'll use the VCF to get rid of the frequencies we don't want. You see, this machine uses subtractive synthesis so we can filter out the sound we don't require. Look at the oscilloscope and we'll be able to see the different wave forms: saw tooth, square wave and so on of the various sounds we're generating.'

H.of Sc. : Well how is this one different from the Casio ?

H of M: This one is an analogue synth whereas the Casio digital model uses phase distortion.

H of Sc. : What about the Yamaha?

H of M. : That's pure FM synthesis where the sounds are created solely by binary digits or bits.

A musician talking to a physicist? This was something new. Times they were definitely a-changing.

And more changes were afoot that year. The government announced they were phasing out GCE O levels and CSE exams to be replaced by something called the General Certificate of Secondary Education or GCSE. It was due to be examined for the first time in 1988 so we had to start the new curriculum with 4th year groups in September. It was intended to be more egalitarian and encompass the whole ability range. No more the stigma of being labelled a 'CSE kid'. Students would be slotted into the higher or lower tiers of the new exam.

There was a good response to this change from the members of my department. The Head, who always taught a bottom set English group, agreed to continue under the new exam system. He enjoyed pitting himself against the recalcitrant ne-er-do-wells of the school and they seemed to like his drole wit, his fund of colourful anecdotes and his quiet authority.

'Basically, I just tell them stories,' he said at one departmental meeting. 'They love it. Probably most of them were never read to when they were little and they're like putty in your hand when they hear a good story.'

And he was a great story teller. Some of his assemblies were legendary but the performance which still resides in the annals of Newman relates to a disastrous sports day.

As usual the whole school had been marched down to the Sheepmount sports stadium near the city centre. But, before more than two races had been run, the heavens opened. The track was flooded and all 600 students were crammed into the small covered stand. The roof of the stand was leaking under the deluge and the decision was taken to march the students back to school. There was still an hour and a half to go before the bell so they couldn't be released to go home. Corralled and driven into an untidy procession by a grumbling staff, this bedraggled crocodile of soggy individuals stumbled its way back to school.

Then what to do with them? A huddle of senior staff argued heatedly about what was best. Meanwhile the hall was filling with a steaming mass of miserable and restive students.

'Get them sat down,' said the Head.

The senior staff remonstrated, 'Then what?'

'Faith and hope,' said the Head. 'I'll deal with it.'

And he did. He settled them down, told them to listen and, in a broad Yorkshire accent, launched into a recital of the 13 verses of *The Lion and Albert*, the monologue made famous by the late Stanley Holloway.

There's a famous seaside place called Blackpool
That's noted for fresh-air and fun,
And Mr and Mrs Ramsbottom
Went there with young Albert, their son........

The students stared, not sure what to make of this. The teachers stopped pacing and stared, not sure what to make of this either. But the Head was warming to the task leaning forward from the stage, gesturing like a true cabaret pro......

A grand little lad was their Albert
All dressed in his best; quite a swell
'E'd a stick with an 'orse's 'ead 'andle
The finest that Woolworths could sell.

And you could feel the tension in the hall ease as the story ran its comic course with Albert getting eaten by the lion and his mother being mildy annoyed at the inconvenience of it all.....

The Magistrate gave his opinion
That no-one was really to blame
He said that he hoped the Ramsbottoms
Would have further sons to their name

At that Mother got proper blazing
"And thank you, sir, kindly,"said she
"What waste all our lives raising children
To feed ruddy lions? Not me!"

The Head finished his performance with a flourish, and spontaneous applause erupted in the hall. He bowed, smiled, calmed the excitement, looked at his watch and said, 'I think we may be able let you out a little early today for good behaviour. Well done, school

IT'S AN ILL WIND.......

That year we were touched by the ripples of two global disasters. Back in January we had been shocked by the explosion of the space shuttle Challenger seconds after lift off. We had watched this same shuttle rise into the Florida sky back in 1984 and then toured the launch pad at the Kennedy Space Centre just a few hours after the launch. James had bought a badge from the souvenir shop which commemorated the flight and showed the names of the crew. It was stitched to his old tracksuit top.

After we'd watched the news coverage and stared open-mouthed at the coiling vapour trails and clouds of white smoke where the shuttle had once been, James went and found his old track suit top. He'd remembered and he fingered the surface of the badge with a frown on his six year old face. 'Did all the people die?' he asked.

I nodded. 'Yes and sadly there was a lady teacher on board, the first teacher to take part in a space launch.'

Then in April came the Chernobyl nuclear explosion at a power plant in the Ukraine, 1600 miles away. But it wasn't until the autumn that we saw a news report on the television which clearly worried Katie.

'What about the chickens,' she asked, 'will they be okay?' She was worried about her new chicken project.

We had bought six Warren chickens from Roger, my old Head of English at St. Aidan's. His smallholding near Ivegill was still flourishing. How he ran the English department, maintained his herds of sheep and Belted Galloway cattle and had time to write his weekly column on Cumberland wrestling for the Cumberland News still amazed me. He was the true Renaissance man.

'D'you want a cockerel?' he asked.

'I don't know, do we need a cockerel?'

'Depends whether you want chicks. I've got a little bantam fella here you could have.'

'Yes, we want chicks,' said Katie, 'don't we James?'

'Yes. Does a cockerel give us chicks?' asked James frowning.

'Certainly does,' replied Roger, 'but ask your dad how that comes about.'

'Thanks,' I said. 'I'll keep that conversation for some other time. Let's get these chickens back to their new home.'

The idea was that Katie and James would look after the chickens like a little business. Katie would keep a tally in a notebook, sell us the eggs, buy the feed and she and James would clean out the coop and keep an eye on things. That was the plan.

The previous weekend we had spent the day building a chicken coop against the wall of one of the outhouses which bordered the field. In the evening there was a news report about the fallout from the Chernobyl explosion. There was evidence that areas of Wales, Cumbria and Scotland were being contaminated with radiation blown by easterly winds and brought down by several days of torrential rain. It was unbelievable. Now the government was preventing movement of livestock on around one thousand upland farms.

'Don't worry,' I said, ' It's only the farms in the high fells that are affected. I'm sure our chickens will be okay.'

'I hope so,' said Katie. She took out her little notebook and wrote something down. 'I'm going to have to keep an eye on them.'

'And me,' said James. 'I'll help.'

'They should be laying in a couple of weeks time,' I said.

And they did. Our little bantam cockerel strutted his stuff around his harem of six Warren ladies who started producing fine brown eggs each morning. James cradled them in his hands and carried them to the kitchen like new found treasure.

But as for Chernobyl, we had no idea that it would be another 26 years before the government lifted its ban on the movement of sheep in the upland farms of Wales, Cumbria and Scotland.

*

THE GREAT DESCENT OF THE DURANCE - Summer 87

We sat on the river bank mesmerised. The great Durance river surged past us in a wide swathe of grey snowmelt water. There were wave peaks crested with surf, side currents which boiled in whirlpools: it looked monstrous and dangerous.

'What d'you reckon?' I said.

Doug nodded, 'As you know, my eyesight's rubbish but I reckon we could give it a try. Catherine will go crazy of course.'

We were back in France after my second full year as Head of English at Newman, on holiday with Doug, my lawyer friend, and his family. After much searching we had finally found a site at a place called Baratier in the southern Alps, south-east of Grenoble where the Durance river enters the massive Serre Pencon lake. Doug and his wife Catherine and their three young children had never camped before and I was feeling responsible for the success of the holiday. During the dark days of winter I had enthused about the delights of camping in France and they had agreed to join us and give it a try.

A few days earlier we had driven south through the Alps looking for a likely place to camp. By late afternoon we had found nothing. The N94 south of Briancon follows the Durance through a bleak rocky Alpine landscape which is anything but welcoming. Finally we arrived in the medieval town of Embrun and looked for a small hotel for the night. We'd search for a campsite in the morning.

But in the morning events took a bizarre turn. I got up early to fetch something from my car which I'd parked alongside Doug's in the main car-park. The car-park had been full but now it was empty and a gendarme was about to lock the gate. It was market day and cars were not allowed to enter as the stallholders were setting up their stalls. Some were already established and when I motioned that I wanted to drive my car out the gendarme grunted something in French and waved me through. My car and Doug's were the only ones there and I quickly reversed out of my space, manoeuvred past some of the market stalls and out of the gate.

Poor Doug wouldn't be so lucky. His car had been turned into a market stall. A canopy was attached to his roof-rack, a blanket laid out on his bonnet on which were arranged neat rows of plastic jars filled with different coloured bath salts. That car was going nowhere.

'You are bloody joking,' he said when I reported back.

'Go and see, but don't make a fuss, they might fine you. Cars are not supposed to be there on market day. There's a sign.'

'In French?'

'Of course, we're in France.'

'But I don't speak French!'

'They don't know that.'

'Well they should bloody well think of the visitors.'

After a quick breakfast we all trouped down to the market. The children thought it was hilarious when they saw the car.

'Listen you lot, don't let on that it's our car. They could fine us,' said Doug.

'How d'you know that?' asked seven year old Amy.

'There's a sign over there on the gate.'

'But dad, you don't speak French.'

'I'm a fast learner. Now just keep away.'

Amy giggled. 'I want to see what's happened to our car,' and she was off.

We wandered round the market, all the time watchful for the local gendarme.

'You don't want to be here when the market closes,' advised one helpful market trader. 'That's when he'll be back and believe me he will fine you.'

'Your English is very good,' I commented.

'Thanks. Probably cos I'm English.'

'Oh sorry,' I said, 'thought you were a native.'

'I'll take that as a compliment. Moved over from Dagenham fifteen years ago. Just love it over here.'

The children dared each other to go up to the stallholder who was using Doug's car and ask 'Combien?' about the jars of bath salts.

'You'll do no such thing,' said Doug.

'I'll go,' chirped Amy and she was off before Doug had time to grab her.

She waltzed back a few minutes later with a jar in her hand. 'Douze, he said, but then I told him it was our car and he laughed and gave me a jar free.'

'And now we're going to get a fine. They know who we are,' remonstrated Doug.

'Stop making a fuss,' said Catherine, 'and these bath salts smell divine.'

Two days later and Doug and I are sitting on the banks of the Durance weighing up whether it's worth risking our lives. We had watched the big rubber inflatables carrying eight people and an instructor breasting the surging water. They wore life-jackets and helmets and probably paid handsomely for this 'thrill-of-a-lifetime' experience. It looked exciting but not as exciting as it would be in our little plastic two-man inflatable.

'I've noticed, it's quite calm near the bank. We could always bottle out of the main current if it gets too hairy,' I said.

'You reckon?' said Doug. 'Should we tell the girls or should we just do it?'

'We'll need someone to take photos of whatever happens, so yes we'll need to tell them,' I replied.

When we got back to the campsite we inflated the dinghy we'd bought for the children and were now intending to use for our grand adventure.

'You're planning to do what!' cried Catherine.

'It'll be fine dear, we know what we're doing,' said Doug.

359

'And what happens when I'm left a widow to bring up three children. What happens then?'

'Don't be so dramatic, dear. Barrie knows what he's doing.'

'Don't blame me, you old bugger,' I murmured.

We drove up river to where the river bank was shallow and we could launch the dinghy. Sue, Catherine and the children were at various points further down river ready to watch the drama and pick up the pieces.

'The river looks higher than I remember,' I said. 'Seems to be more water than before.'

'No good asking me,' said Doug, 'I'm as short-sighted as a mongoose and my glasses will steam up before we've gone 10 yards. I'll just sit in the back and dabble my paddle to keep us straight. You go at the front and look out for rocks.'

We waited until there was no sign of any of the big professional inflatables and then pushed off the bank into the slack water. Ahead the grey surge swept past in rolling swathes of surf. 'Are you ready?' I said.

Doug was leaning back in the rear of the dinghy sitting low down with his knees sticking up holding his little plastic paddle, his glasses already steaming up. 'Ready, captain.'

I paddled us out further into the main current, careful to stop the dinghy turning sideways which could be disastrous. But once into the main current we were picked up by the great river and swept along at speed.

'Can't see much but it feels great,' shouted Doug.

The river bank glided past at increasing speed, the grey snow melt water surged around the sides of our little vessel but we were rolling along in fine fettle. That's when I heard the shout. I turned to see one of the big yellow inflatables bearing down on us.

'Hey, you stupide! C'est tres dangereux. Allez, allez!' It was an instructor waving his paddle at us from his high position in the rear of the

boat. I nodded and pointed at the river bank and we steered out of the main current back into the slack water. We waited a few minutes until the bigger boat had disappeared.

'Sod that, we were doing so well. Let's get back in there,' said Doug.

I steered us back out into the main current and we were off

again, flying down the centre of the river. Down stream on the river bank I could see the little gaggle of our children jumping and waving. As we sailed past, Sue waved, Catherine shook her head and I heard James shouting, 'Me, daddy, I want to do it.'

I nodded back and checked the river bank for a good place to pull in. We steered into the slack water and the children charged to meet us.

That afternoon there were several more descents of the great river. James said it was the best thing he'd ever done in his life, Katie wasn't so sure when the bottom of the dinghy started to part company from the sides. Sue reckoned she'd got some great photos but Catherine was still unconvinced by the whole escapade.

'I could have been left a widow on my own with three children,' she mumbled.

'But darling you haven't been,' cooed Doug. 'I'm still here and it was great so why not go and have a nice hot bath and use some of the bath salts which Amy got for you.'

'Don't you humour me,' huffed Catherine. 'You men are like little boys sometimes.'

Doug nudged me, 'Yeah, it's great isn't it. Who wants to grow up.' He turned to the children. 'Hey, you lot, who wants to go fishing and catch our supper?'

'Me, me, me!' came a chorus of squeals.

We'd spotted a trout farm close to where we were camping. It would be a great way to end a memorable day. We paid the fee for rods and bait for the children and then the lady in the fishing shop handed them each a small length of rubber hose.

'What's this for?' asked Amy.

The madame gestured with her hand holding the piece of rubber hose and lightly tapped it on the back of James' neck.

Amy shook her head and frowned. 'I don't understand.'

'It's for killing the fish after you've caught it. You smack it on the back of its head,' said Doug.

'Urrgh, that's cruel,' said Katie.

'Well getting a poor innocent fish to swallow a worm with a hook attached and pulling it out of the water, that's not exactly the height of kindness,' said Doug.

The enthusiasm on the five little faces dimmed for a moment. Then James said, 'Well I'm going to fish and I don't mind hitting it.'

There wasn't a lot of skill in fishing the little trout pond. No sooner had the children lobbed their baited lines into the water than a small trout was tugging on the line. The landing caused great excitement but dispatching the catch somewhat quelled the glee.

'Just give it a whack,' said Amy.

'I can't look,' said Katie.

'Well you'll miss hitting the right spot if you don't look,' replied Doug.

'Give it here,' said Amy. She took the piece of rubber and walloped the fish on its head. 'There, didn't feel a thing.' And she turned to bait another hook.

'Remember,' said Doug, 'you have to eat what you catch. That's the rule.'

'But I don't like fish,' said James.

'Then you can't catch any,' replied Doug.

'Maybe I'll try just a bit,' answered James as he cast his line back into the pond. In less than two minutes he was reeling in a fair sized trout. He held it down on the ground to stop it flapping and Amy delivered it a smart whack on its head. 'There,' she said. 'There's your tea, James.'

That evening Doug and I cleaned and gutted the fish ready for cooking. We pulled up a couple of chairs and settled down with some cold beers. The barbecue was lit, we were glowing after our day in the sun, the children were doing some quiet colouring in the tent and there was time for some musing as we tinkered with the charcoal and put the fish on the griddle.

'Did I tell you about this amazing new machine we got at work? You might be interested,' said Doug. 'It's called a fax machine and it will send a document down the phone line which you can print out at the other end.'

I shook my head, 'I don't quite follow.'

'Well you dial the telephone number of where you're sending the document, feed the document into the machine which scans it; then you press a button and the document is printed out at the other end.'

'So no need for stamps and envelopes,' I said.

'Exactly. For us it means we can send a contract to some guy in Australia and it's there and back signed and sealed the same day. And it can't get lost by the post office.'

'Wow, they talk about the paperless office. This is what it means.'

We sipped our beers and nudged the fish that we were barbecuing.

'I need to come and see one in action,' I said. 'Maybe there's some way I could use it at school.'

And that's how Doug sowed the seed of a new venture in my career in education. It would turn into the great Cumbria Fax Project; a global first.

*

JUST A TOUCH OF MALARKEY

Back in school that autumn I contacted the technical support department at the education office to investigate more about these new fax machines. The local adviser was Eddie Morgans and I floated my idea with him. Fax machines were new in the business world but were unheard of in education. He hadn't seen them in use.

'So what's your idea?' he asked.

'If we could get fax machines into a group of local schools, we could maybe put together some sort of publication where each school contributes a section which is faxed to each of the other schools,' I explained. 'A kind of co-operative magazine or newspaper using desk top publishing software and this fax technology which hasn't been used like this before. Could be a global first for Cumbrian schools.'

He nodded. 'Sounds interesting. Leave it with me. But don't hold your breath. Not much money left in the budget for hardware this year.'

There was plenty more on my agenda that year. A group of troublesome tearaway lads were causing mayhem in a number of classes. In lower school they had been dispersed in our mixed ability groups but now in 4th year they were in ability sets and I had elected to take set 4 - always one of the most tricky groups to take. Set 5, which the Head took, was always a small group of less able, often quietly disaffected students

363

who followed a much less demanding syllabus in English. Set 4, by contrast, was a much bigger group and they were expected to follow the new GCSE syllabus and complete a folder of assignments like everyone else. I hadn't encountered them in lower school but now they were 4th years, flexing their hormones, baiting teachers, scoring points off each other, vying for attention, contemptuous of the others in the class who wanted to learn. They brought with them all the hassles they encountered daily in the neighbourhoods where they lived and the rancour which issued from dysfunctional family lives. When they entered the room you never knew what mood they'd be in, or how volatile the lesson might become.

The four ringleaders in my English set were Gerald Maloney, an uncouth lump of a lad, who bullied the others; Stevie Layton, who was knocked around at home by a drunken dad and who craved attention by being constantly disruptive, shouting out and acting the fool and with an attention span of a gnat. Then there was Michael Mallard. At times he was biddable and capable of some half decent work but he was Maloney's stooge, lived in the bigger boy's shadow and stoked the class disruption in subtle, devious ways.

Finally there was Alan Richards, a loner who had already been in juvenile court for petty crime and was like an unexploded bomb in the classroom. Often he was quiet and could get engrossed in word puzzles or illustrating the cover of a project. But there was something strange about Alan. One day, when we were standing outside the classroom waiting for the previous class to leave, he dropped his pen and I accidentally trod on it. It was only a cheap plastic thing but the vehemence of Alan's reaction was shocking.

'You did that on purpose. My dad'll have you! He'll put you through that window and hang you by your ankles. You see if he doesn't!' All this spat at me through gritted teeth and narrowed eyes.

I had nightmares about this group. Often, in those hours before dawn, I would sit bolt upright in bed sweating, caught up in the warped reality of some dream about Maloney or Richards or the whole group wreaking some havoc.

'It's okay,' Sue would say, 'shh.. it's okay.' She would slowly lower me back on to the pillow and wait for my breathing to slow down.

I had no control over these dreams and they coloured my feelings about teaching this group. Even so, I would attempt to disarm them at the beginning of each lesson by being overly polite and good humoured as they came into the room, not bearing any grudges over some fracas in a previous lesson. 'Hey, Stevie, how's it going today?'

'It's bollocks, sir. Just had that Miss Jefferson for maths and she's stuck me in detention for nowt.'

'Didn't do yer homework,' said Maloney.

'Couldn't do it. Anyway she hates me.'

As Head of Department I couldn't be seen to be failing to control my classes and by a mix of humour and quick-wittedness I usually managed to defuse explosive situations although it didn't stop me dreaming about them. Other teachers were not so lucky. There was a female maths teacher who frequently ran out of classes in tears and the miscreants were sent to the Deputy Head for punishment. In time past corporal punishment might have been used on the likes of Maloney or Richards but that all came to an end the previous year. New legislation came into force in 1986 banning the use of corporal punishment in state schools. The story of that legislation is worth telling.

It was the Conservative Education Secretary, Kenneth Baker, who steered the legislation through parliament, but only just. There was a lot of backbench opposition. Several pro-caning Tory MPs missed a key vote in July 1986, which was won by 231 votes to 230, because they were stuck in a traffic jam caused by preparations for the wedding of Prince Andrew and Sarah Ferguson. Prime Minister Margaret Thatcher, didn't vote either as she was having dinner with Nancy Reagan, wife of the US president.

So now schools had to come up with alternatives. There was after school detention in which some mindless activity was imposed such as copying out lines. There was an attempt to get the parents involved but the problems of students like Maloney and Richards were often the result of parents not caring so there was little mileage in bringing them into school.

Avril, the music teacher, told the story of her lively encounter with Michael Mallard's mother back in the summer term. The music room at Newman is in a far corner of the school next to the sixth form block. In the mid 1980s security was taken less seriously than it is now and the side entrance into the block was always open for 6th form students to come and go.

Just after lunch Avril spotted Mrs Mallard passing her window followed by a tall girl and a slightly shorter boy. She noticed the girl was carrying a rolling pin and the boy a baseball bat. The outer door was flung open and in strode the diminutive, roly poly figure of Mrs Mallard. Despite her height she had a screeching voice to compensate.

'Is this it then?' she shouted. 'Where is she?'

Avril emerged from the music room and smiled, 'Can I help you?'

'Did you call my boy a lazy pouf. Did you? I'm goin' to ave you!'

By now, Avril was beginning to get jelly legs but still maintained an outward show of calm. 'Now Mrs Mallard...'

'Don't give me that bleedin' Mrs Mallard malarkey.'

Just then Michael appeared in the doorway looking rather pale. 'Mam, mam. That's not her. You got the wrong teacher.'

His mother turned round, 'What's that you say?'

'It's the wrong teacher, mam. Can you leave it?'

'You said it was music, you little shit. Where's the eadmaster? I'm not avin teachers calling you a pouf, even though you act like one sometimes.'

She and her storm troopers headed out of the door and back round the side of the building. Avril took a short cut and sprinted off to warn the Head.

By the time the Mallard posse arrived at the main entrance there was a welcoming party of the Head, the Deputy and one of the senior male teachers.

The Head stepped forward, 'Hello Mrs Mallard. Would you like to come into my office and tell me what the problem is?'

Just then a police car drove down the main drive.

'Mam, it's the police,' said the tall girl, nervously scratching her leg with the end of her rolling pin.

'Don't worry, Mrs Mallard, just their afternoon routine. They always drop in to see how we're doing,' said the Head, smiling. 'Will you come this way.'

'It's one of your teachers been rude to my boy and I won't ave it.'

'I'm sure I'd feel the same, Mrs Mallard. Now can I get you a cup of tea.' He turned to the two minders, 'And I think we'll leave the cooking and sports equipment outside, shall we. Just give them to Mr Smith.'

The rolling pin and baseball bat were handed over and the Deputy followed the Mallards inside the Head's office. The door closed.

What happened inside the office Avril never found out. But in the next lesson with Michael, Avril greeted him with a friendly, 'Hi Michael, how's things. How's your mam doing?'

He shook his head, 'She's just embarrassing, miss. Off her trolley at times.'

Avril nodded, 'Pretty scary lady when she's angry.'

'You're telling me, miss. Didn't know she'd come up to the school like that.' He shrugged in a kind of hopeless way.

And you quickly realised the sad reality behind the boy's often appalling behaviour. You couldn't ignore it but you had to try to understand where it was coming from.

*

WINDS OF CHANGE

I wasn't alone in coping with stormy weather. Mine was in the classroom but elsewhere it was more real. In October 1987 there was The Great British Storm when 120 mile an hour winds killed 23 people and brought down 15 million trees in south-east England. In Jamaica, Pat Bourke, the gentle philosopher-king and Deputy Head of Priory School, a man who inspired my belief in the transformative power of education, was tied up and murdered in his home in Kingston; a tragic waste of a great mind and a charismatic personality.

At the same time storms started brewing across the teaching profession in England when the Education Reform Act of 1988 was published. They were talking about introducing something called the National Curriculum but more importantly 5 extra days were to be added to the 190 already being taught. Kenneth Baker, the architect of the Reform Act, lent his name to these 5 extra days. They would be known as 'Baker Days' and used for in-service training. A waste of time and an imposition was the verdict of many teachers in the weeks running up to the first Baker Day. Resentment was running high and I was in the eye of this brewing storm.

As well as my main role of Head of English, I was also the SDO or Staff Development Officer, responsible for in-service teacher training. With the arrival of Baker Days it would be down to me to organise the programme for the day. Each school was assigned to a consortium of four or five other schools, the idea being that teachers could work together to develop their skills.

The local Headteachers in their wisdom had decided that to launch the first Baker Day all the consortium schools would get together under one roof. Then all the subject teachers could be grouped together in subject groups to explore the novelty of their first Baker Day.

In the weeks leading up to this momentous event I attended a number of meetings with other anxious SDOs to try to come up with a programme for the day which might be useful and which might cool the cauldron of teacher anger which was still brewing over the dictat of 5 extra days.

367

Then I remembered Miami. I remembered the surprise and delight I had felt when I attended that first teacher training session and was given a free donut and a polished red apple.

'That's it,' I said to my SDO colleagues. 'After the first session when they break for coffee we give them all a freebie - something like a Danish pastry, to have with their coffee. However angry they are I guarantee it won't last when they're having to navigate their way round a ring of flaky pastry. And anyway nobody ever gives teachers treats so let's surprise them.'

It worked, after a fashion. On the day, it was the woodwork and technology teachers who were particularly frosty and fuming when they came out of their first session. One bearded veteran was sounding off about 'Thatcher and Baker and the bloody Tory mafia' when a plate of Danish pastries was held in front of him. He stopped his tirade and a few minutes later when he was fumbling with flaky pastry in his beard and down his shirt front, even he melted into some reluctant amusement.

Thus were born 'Baker Days' and at Newman, what I called the Danish Pastry Syndrome. Initially the training days were grudgingly endured but as time passed they became a part of every teacher's conditions of service.

*

Winds of change were blowing through education, but I was feeling the breeze in other ways. For years I'd tried and failed to master the sport of windsurfing. During our year in Florida I'd hired a windsurfer at a beach at Bahia Honda, on the Florida Keys. But although I was competent at dinghy sailing, at windsurfing I was pathetic. Just couldn't get the hang of it. Even if I managed to haul the sail out of the water, I generally nose-dived off the board before getting any sense of balance or forward movement. Either I had to forget the idea completely or invest in some half decent equipment of my own and get some guidance. One Friday I spotted an advert in the Cumberland News for a used windsurfer. I phoned the number. The owner said he would meet me on the Saturday morning at Talkin Tarn, a local lake just east of Carlisle.

When I arrived I saw that he had bought himself a spanking new board and sail. His old one looked in good condition but it wasn't this which fired me up to master this elusive sport. It was the size and shape of this man. If he could do it then so could I. He was a man in his fifties, around 5'6" in height and weighing in at about 15stone. His wet suit ballooned round his belly and his squat little legs made him look like a Michelin man.

But forget all that. When he stepped on to his board, adjusted his position, leaned back on the boom of the sail and smoothly glided away across the surface of the lake, I was lost for words. I was hooked. Clearly you didn't have to be a honed and toned Adonis to master this sport. You could windsurf into your retirement. This was the sport for me.

And it didn't take long. Like learning to ride a bike, once you get the feel of balance it becomes second nature. Now windsurfing is definitely more tricky than riding a bike. You have to read the wind, watch the surface of the water ahead of you to check for approaching gusts; you have to negotiate tricky changes of direction by tacking or gybing which involves swapping sides with the boom of the sail, transferring your position on the board. But let me tell you that the surge of speed, the hiss of the water beneath the hull, the pull of the sail through the boom, the balancing of your body against the strength of the wind – it is like orchestrating the gods of air and water. There is something pure, something elemental this harnessing of the wind with a simple board and sail to take you skimming across the surface of a lake. And it didn't matter if the sun didn't shine. In fact the best winds were often on a stormy day; cacooned in a good wet suit the outdoor temperature mattered little.

This was me, then, in the spring of 1988 – each day watching the movement of the trees, checking the strength of the wind, itching to get back on the water and feel the thrust of the wind in the sail. With the promise of another summer in France I was keen for the rest of the family to get involved. I didn't want Sue to become a windsurfing widow like some wives become golf widows. So I bought a junior rig for the board which was a smaller sail and mast. This would help Sue, Katie and James to get started and maybe, like me, get bitten by the windsurfing bug.

Before we could take off for France that summer the closing rituals of the school year had to run their course. And none was more memorable than the prize-giving ceremony of that year.

Now one thing that was set in stone at Newman was how the student body should conduct itself at assemblies. Frank, our venerable Headmaster, saviour of wet sports days and appeaser of the Mrs Mallards of this world, was far from amused at this years prize-giving assembly. He was very precise about how such an assembly should be conducted. 'Applause is fine but no whistling, absolutely no whistling,' he said at the outset.

Names were read out, students filed up to the front of the hall to receive their awards and all was going well until the final award. This was the award for the house which had won the overall sports trophy for the year. The house captains of Durham House went forward to receive the trophy, held it aloft to excited clapping. Then from nowhere came a couple of whistles. The Head's face froze. He stood up, came to the front of the stage, leaned forward and hissed, 'Who whistled! C'mon, whoooo whistled!'

This insubordination had clearly struck a chord. He marched off the stage and came down the central aisle between the seated assembly of 600 students. He leaned to this side and that side hissing, 'C'mon, I want to know whoooo whistled!'

No-one moved. The teachers who were standing down the side of the hall scanned the heads of the students to try to spot the culprit. Then the Head uttered the words that no-one wanted to hear. 'No-one leaves this hall until the person who whistled owns up!'

I glanced at a couple of my colleagues. They were inwardly groaning like me. We shook our heads at each other. No, Headmaster, that's not what you should have done. No fool is going to own up in front of the whole school. But the Head persisted, digging us all deeper into the mire.

'I mean it. No-one leaves. Now I'll say it again: whooo whistled!'

We waited. No-one moved. The Head scanned the assembly, eyes narrowed, jaw thrust forward. It was so unlike his normal kindly demeanour.

Then a miracle occurred. From the back of the hall where the 5th year boys were sitting, a hand was raised. Tony Warburton, one of the wayward comedians of the year group stood up. 'It was me, sir.' Like some slow-motion scene out of *Oliver Twist* the Head swivelled on his heels, raised his arm and shouted, 'Out! To my office.'

But it was not over. Another hand was raised just along the row from Warburton. Simon? He was only the son of Pat, my close colleague in the English department. How embarrassing was that. I daren't look at

Pat who was hoping a hole in the floor would open up so she could disappear.

The two boys slunk off to the Head's office and he returned to the stage. He looked out over the assembly and said quite calmly, 'Now where were we before we were so rudely interrupted?'

A week later I was holding my usual end of term social gathering at home for members of the English Department plus one or two other colleagues like Avril whom I'd worked closely with on music/drama events. Frank, the Head, always enjoyed coming to these gatherings. He could relax and enjoy the banter and a glass of wine. But Avril and I had decided to mark the Head's triumphant 'no whistling' assembly with a little entertainment. We had written a musical ditty in the style of Chas and Dave, a Cockney duo who specialised in pub sing-along type songs. They wore flat caps and working class clothes so Avril and I did likewise. We weren't quite sure how Frank would react to us sending up his bravura performance in the assembly but we decided to take the gamble.

Avril sat down at the piano and played the intro in a honky-tonk style. Then we launched our homage to Frank.

> *I was walking past this school the other day*
> *Feeling quite transported and at ease*
> *When all of a bloomin' sudden some geezer gave a shout*
> *That scared the livin' daylights out of me.*

> *He said:*
> *Oooooo whistled, that's what I want to know*
> *Ooooo whistled don't be so bloomin' slow,*
> *Own up now or I'll smack your little bum*
> *And I'll kick your little backside from here to kingdom come*
> *Tarara, tarara..........*

There were several other verses and all through I was glancing at Frank's expression. A smile was playing around his mouth and there was a twinkle in his eyes so I hoped we were safe.

When the applause had subsided he simply said, 'I wonder if you'd perform that at the end of term staff luncheon. It might go down quite well.' Good old Frank.

Following the final school assembly the students were dismissed and the staff made their way to the staffroom for the usual buffet and glass of plonk. There were one or two presentations to staff who were leaving and when the formalities were over Avril set up the keyboard, we donned our flat caps and I announced our little entertainment. No-one, apart from the English staff, knew anything about it and the rest of the staff certainly didn't realise Frank was in on the act. So when we launched into the song several pairs of eyes swivelled to observe the Headmaster's reaction. Some of the older, more restrained staff were frowning and clearly not amused at this mockery of the Head's authority. But at the end he stood up. Even now some staff were unsure about his reaction.

He nodded, 'Bravo to our cabaret duo and I admit to commissioning this little entertainment.'

The tension broke in the room and there was a burst of applause. He held up his hand and continued, 'Oh the power of theatre. I have to say that when I uttered those words in the assembly I realised I'd dug myself into a hole. So I have to commend Pat for inculcating honesty in her son Simon. I was so relieved when he and young Warburton raised their hands. I was torn between giving them both a hug or booting their backsides. So colleagues, don't take yourselves too seriously during the summer break, laughter is nearly always the best medicine.'

It was certainly a great summer. Correction, not true if you happened to be one of the doves being released at the opening ceremony of the Olympics in South Korea. When these 'doves of peace' were released and the cauldron ignited, quite a few doves went up in smoke. Not a good omen for the Games.

However, we were not plagued by such ill luck. We travelled to the south of France towing a small trailer which carried our camping gear and with two canoes and a windsurfer strapped to the roof bars. By then Katie and James and Sue had all mastered the basics of windsurfing. The previous Whitsuntide break we had driven up to Arisaig on the west coast of Scotland and it was there, despite frequent tumbles into a chilly sea, they all got the hang of this new sport. In France, windsurfing on calm inland lakes under a hot sun was pure delight.

First stop was the Cevennes region, on the Gard river at Anduze where there are plunge pools deep for swimming and rapids which bubble fast over the shallows and will carry two people in an inflatable dinghy at some speed. At the hottest part of the day the shallower pools are crammed with lazy, sluggish fish. With a tent peg tied to a bamboo cane you can attempt to spear fish for the evening barbecue. We sailed, fished, swam, ate warm baguettes and croissants in the morning, barbecued and supped local wine in the evenings. We took a trip to the Pont du Gard – the amazing Roman aqueduct built in the 1st century AD to carry water to the city of Nimes. Swimming in the Gardon River under the three tiers of its towering arches we could only marvel at the magnificence of this ancient structure and at our own good fortune.

Then it was west to the Haut Languedoc region, for more indulgence in the pleasures that France always provides. Finally, reluctantly, we decamped and headed north to the ferry but not before a brief stop in Paris. I wanted Katie and James to stand on one of the bridges across the Seine and see the Eiffel Tower in the distance, watch the Bateaux Mouches, those long passenger boats, glide the river, and then drive them up the Avenue des Champs Elysees and round the Arc de Triomphe through the crazy circus of traffic at the Place de la Concorde.

We waved goodbye to 'la belle France' as the cross-channel ferry eased its way out of the dock at Calais. It was now back to Cumbria and the reality of a new school year.

*

'SUN, FUN AND PLENTY OF WILLY'

The end of the decade was fast approaching and the pace of changes in our lives seemed to be accelerating. I hit the age of forty in December 1988 and didn't cope particularly well with the thought of it. To be in your thirties is still to be bathed in the afterlight of your twenties. To be forty is to anticipate the shadowed greying of your fifties. But it was only a temporary blip and once back on my windsurfer, skimming across the windswept surface of Derwentwater or Moricambe Bay the momentary shadows were dispelled and I convinced myself I still had a vestige of youth in my blood. There was stuff to get done and the world was not waiting for me to catch up.

Apart from turning forty, I remember December 1988 for another reason. We were going out carol singing on the night of the 22nd. It was just after 7pm and Katie was standing at the open front door waiting for us to get our coats on. It was a clear starlit night but for just a moment the sky was curiously illuminated by a bright orange glow in the distance. It was there for just a few seconds and then it was gone. I assumed it must be the flood lights across the Solway at the Chapelcross nuclear power plant. But then a short while later we heard the report of a plane crash at Lockerbie. What I had in fact seen was the moment when Pan Am Flight 103 flying from Frankfurt to Detroit was blown up by a terrorist bomb. All 243 passengers and 16 crew were killed and 11 local people were killed on the ground.

Years later, I still remember that moment, when the sky lit up with a strange orange glow. No sound, no rumble of an after-shock, just the glow and the horror of what it represented.

*

When Katie started at Newman in September of 1989 she laid out the rules of engagement.

'If we meet in the corridor, dad, there's no eye contact. You don't know me, okay?'

'Right.'

I must have betrayed a slight smile for she came back with, 'I'm serious, dad. I don't want any favours. It's bad enough going to a school where your dad's a teacher, let alone people thinking I'm getting treated better than they are. So, no eye contact. Understood?'

'Understood.'

For both of us it was something of a trial. Katie was just desperate to fit in. So I had to keep my distance, whatever was happening. And when it turned out that she'd been placed in a form group of particularly rough-and-ready characters my colleagues urged me to move her to a different class where the pupils were better behaved.

I shook my head. 'She wouldn't hear of it,' I said. 'And anyway, it's good for her to rub shoulders with all types.'

I received some wry looks but they didn't know Katie. She was a survivor.

The two years which ended the nineteen eighties I remember as vintage years in my teaching career. Maloney and his cronies were still giving me sleepless nights as they barged and blundered their way through their last year in school. But then the Head devised a cunning plan. Maloney was bragging to anyone who would listen that he was going to join the SAS. He had already joined the Territorial Army and this only added to the swagger he cultivated around school. He had outgrown the world of desks, exercise books, chalk and talk. He wanted to go commando and face the world with an AK47 in his hands. So, in the spring and summer terms, the Head devised for him a training regime which took him out of school under the watchful eyes of an ex-army physical training instructor.

With Maloney gone my 5th year class was transformed. Stevie Layton became a shadow of his former mouthy self. He had been kicked out of his home by an abusive father and was found one night by the police to be camping in a small tent on a piece of waste ground in

Botcherby. He drifted away from school and rarely put in an appearance for the rest of the year. With the leading ghouls of the group gone, the remaining students were happier and so was I. My nights were no longer haunted and my days with the class tolerable.

However, the real joys of those two years were my 6th form classes. A number of students were taking both A level Literature and A level Communication Studies which meant I saw them on several occasions during the week. The girls outnumbered the boys: they were sharp, witty, intelligent and the boys struggled to hold their own against this bevvy of sparky, female talent. One English Lit. lesson on *Tess of the D'Urbervilles* went something like this:

Leanne: I could slap that Angel Clare.

Helen: What a wuss.

Anthony: He's just a sensitive kind of chap.

Leanne: Sensitive? My pencil case is more sensitive than Angel Clare.

Kate: And poor Tess, I could cry for her. That poor baby.

Leanne: And that arch swine Alex D'Urberville. I'd swing for him after what he did.

Debra: Typical though isn't it. Has anything really changed?

Me: What d'you mean?

Debra: Well look at him, he pretends to be a reformed character but then he's only after one thing, like so many men.

Anthony: What's that then.

Helen: To get inside your knickers.

The group laughed.

I held up my hands and spoke with mock gravitas. 'Helen, thank you. Let's not lower the tone of this intellectual exchange. So are we saying that Hardy's plot and characterisation are pretty authentic? Does the novel read as a reflection of real life? Are there 20th cent. girls like Tess being exploited by manipulative men like Alex D'Urberville?'

'Of course,' said Helen. 'Just read the Sunday papers. It's full of stories about sex slaves, young girls being forced into prostitution.'

'Are you saying Tess becomes a kind of prostitute for Alex?' I asked.

'Not exactly.'

'But he does set her up like a high class mistress,' I added.

'She's only getting her own back,' said Leanne.

And so the cut and thrust would continue. These girls were feisty and challenging but always good humoured. Anthony, the lone male voice in the group, gamely held his own and managed not to be cowed by the scattershot of female voices.

Over the two years that I taught them we wrestled with Shakespeare's *Hamlet,* the poetry of Ted Hughes and Willy Russell's brilliant two-hander *Educating Rita.* The superb film of Russell's play had come out a few years earlier. Directed by Lewis Gilbert and starring Michael Caine and Julie Walters, it tells the story of Susan, an uneducated hairdresser, who adopts the name Rita when she enrols on an Open University course in English Literature. Her tutor, Frank, is played by Michael Caine. Willy Russell's brilliance as a dramatist lies in his ability to move the mood from the comic to the tragic within a single line or a gesture.

The class loved the play. They took it in turns to read the parts with Anthony generally taking on the part of Frank. We dramatised certain scenes in the classroom and at times we were almost rolling on the floor with laughter, especially when Leanne was reading Rita's part. But there were also the poignant moments as when Rita's marriage ends, her husband throws her out and yet she still persists in her struggle to cope with the demands of the course which is her lifeline to a better life.

Similarly with the Shakespeare, we wrestled with and shared the anguish of Hamlet struggling to cope with the death of his father and the betrayal of his mother who has married the murderer, Claudius.

It was this sharing and exploring the many strands of the human condition which was the joy of teaching English Literature. In their teens, when young minds are primed to be triggered into new ways of looking at the world, their emotions are often raw and volatile. Literature helps to crystallise and give shape to their thinking. Reading their essays I saw their minds beginning to weave thoughts and make connections. And through my comments on their work I would try to boost their confidence and nudge their thoughts towards greater clarity of thinking.

That summer I had organised the annual trip to Stratford for an intensive four day diet of all things Shakespearean. It was a joint trip with students from my old school St. Aidan's and a chance to spend some time with my old colleagues Roger and Jean who were organising their part of the trip. The six girls from my literature group jumped at the chance for what they called an 'out of school jolly'.

'What's the club scene like in Stratford, sir?' asked Leanne.

'No idea, Leanne.'

'It has to be better than what's on offer in Carlisle.'

'Have you ever been to the Pagoda, sir?' said Helen.

I shook my head.

'Don't bother, it's the pits!'

'Well I have to disappoint you, girls, we're not going to Stratford for the clubs. It's Shakespeare for breakfast, dinner and tea. No clubbing.'

That summer they all fell in love with the young Mark Rylance who was playing Romeo in a stunning production of *Romeo and Juliet* at the newly opened New Swan Theatre. Designed like the Globe Theatre and only opened in 1986, the Swan had a projecting stage and seats mounting in tiers on a curving timber structure. It was close and intimate and it wasn't surprising that the girls were quickly swooning at the young Romeo. To Rylance's Romeo there was the brilliant young David O'Hara playing Mercutio. But the girls took an instant dislike to Georgia Slowe, who played Juliet.

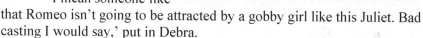

'Her mouth's just too big,' said Leanne.

'And she's not pretty enough for Juliet,' added Helen.

'She certainly wouldn't 'teach the torches to burn bright',' added Kate.

'Hey get you,' said Helen. 'Who's been learning quotes from the play then?'

'I mean someone like that Romeo isn't going to be attracted by a gobby girl like this Juliet. Bad casting I would say,' put in Debra.

They bought photos of Mark Rylance from the theatre shop and posters to stick on their bedroom walls. And that memorable week, they devoured three Shakespeare plays and a Restoration comedy by Ben Jonson. We toured the Shakepeare properties, had afternoon tea at Mary Arden's farmhouse, hired rowing boats on the river Avon and took a trip out to Kenilworth Castle where I sat them down at the foot of the castle walls and read them a spooky Roald Dahl story.

Each night when we got back to our small guest house we would chew over the events of the day, before my colleague, Helen, ushered the girls up to their rooms. Only then would I relax. Being in charge of six lively, sparkling seventeen year old girls was quite a responsibility and I was never really relaxed during the four day trip. Helen and I didn't attempt to chaperone the girls every hour of every day. They were trusted to behave sensibly and they seemed to respect our trust.

It was only on the last night that we had a slight hiccup. All was quiet in the small lounge of the hotel. It was around 11.30pm and everyone had gone up to their rooms. I finished the last of my cup of coffee and was just about to turn in, when I heard a creak on the stairs; a creak and then a suppressed 'shushing'. I sat back in my chair in the corner of the lounge and waited. The six girls appeared led by Leanne, shoes in their hands, tip-toeing towards the door. They were dolled up and ready for some evening action.

'Evening girls,' I murmured. 'Going somewhere?'

They gasped, turned, looked at eachother and then Leanne said, 'Oh, go on, sir, it is the last night. We'll be good. You can come too. We'll take you clubbing.'

'You are joking.'

'Don't be a party pooper, sir,' put in Kate.

I shook my head.

'Go on, sir, we won't tell, ' added Debra.

'Back to bed, girls. It ain't gonna happen. More than my job's worth. Now skiddadle. I need to get to bed.'

They sighed and fussed and moaned and finally went reluctantly back up the stairs. I sat for another half hour listening but I think the 'Stratford Sextet' as they had dubbed themselves had got the message.

The following year, when they were planning their Communications Studies projects, Helen decided to use the Stratford experience as the basis for a promotional campaign to persuade other students to go on the trip. She prepared flyers, posters and set up a stall in the sixth form common room. The banner headline across the top of her stall captured something of the flavour of the Stratford trip: 'SUN, FUN AND PLENTY OF WILLY!'

*

'LOVE IS A WORD'

Duncan, my predecessor, had been right when he said it would take three years to get on top of things. I was now four years into the job and felt I was doing okay. My exam classes had performed well each year, I was getting the measure of handling the Maloneys of this world (even though my subconscious told me otherwise) and I felt I was managing my department reasonably effectively. The one area I still hadn't mastered, however, was putting on a drama production. I was still haunted by the embarrassing debacle of the St. Aidan's Hallowe'en drama night. Somehow I had to knock that ghost on the head.

378

With such a spirited sixth form group and knowing of other talented performers lower down the school I started to work on an evening of music, drama and dance on the theme of the 'battle of the sexes' to be held at the end of the Christmas term. I spent hours scouring books for poetry and prose extracts. I had a notion that a scene from *The Taming of the Shrew* might work with, maybe, Leanne as the fiery Katherine opposite Paul, the Head of History and a talented amateur actor, playing the part of Petruchio.

I put my idea to the Head and with his approval I set things in motion. This had to work. I had to lay those ghosts.

I had never pulled together a show of any sort before and this one with its twenty assorted performances was anything but sraightforward. There were dance routines, drama sketches, poetry and prose readings, and finally a tape/slide sequence with music and a voice-over of poetry. The slide sequence was somewhat experimental. I'd seen the technique used in an art show some years earlier. Using acrylic oils you dripped the oils between the two surfaces of a photographic transparency. Clipped together, the two surfaces kept the oils in place. Then when the heat from the slide projector heated up the oils they began to move in all sorts of exotic ways. The technique was probably a legacy of the psychedelic light shows of the nineteen sixties but my idea was that it would create a memorable end to the show. While the slides worked their visual magic so there would be disembodied voices distorted via an electronic echo chamber reciting fragments of the poetry used earlier in the show. It could be a mesmerising finale. The show was entitled 'Love is a Word'. The first half would focus on 'Young Love', the second half on 'Marriage' and finally 'Memories'.

For the opening of the show, set in a disco, I penned a kind of rap which the sixth formers chanted to a pulsing bass beat.

> *Love is word, it's quite absurd*
> *The power of L-O-V-E,*
> *It'll set you up and it'll knock you down*
> *That word is like a devil.*
> *Playing the game that drives you insane*
> *The minute you start to meddle,*
> *It'll make you quiver, make you quake*
> *You'll start to shiver, start to shake,*
> *It'll spin you around, feet off the ground,*
> *Hooked by the crook of Love.........*

It continued for a couple more verses and then there were some sketches and poems based around the disco setting. One of these was an hilarious exchange set in the disco toilets, between Helen, wearing an enormous Dolly Parton-style blonde wig and Leanne wearing a long black wig. As they touched up their make-up in imaginary mirrors so they bickered and bitched about boys, other girls and eachother. The audience loved it. This was followed by some dance routines, songs, and a short play set at a railway station involving a female busker and a young man waiting for a train. The first half ended with a brass ensemble playing a jazz piece they had composed.

I was relieved. It seemed to be going well. However, the second half was a lttle more challenging.

There was the scene from Shakespeare's *The Taming of the Shrew* with Leanne and my colleague Paul in the parts of Katherine and Petruchio. At one point Leanne slaps her rival across the face. The audience loved it. A student doesn't often get the chance to slap the face of a teacher.

At the end of this drama scene I swapped places with the music teacher and sat myself at the piano at the side of the stage. This was the part of the show which I had been dreading. Would my nerves get the better of my fingers as they had on that fateful Hallowe'en drama night? I was to play a twelve bar blues sequence to a song called 'Housewife's Blues' that I had composed. Debbie, one of my lower sixth students, was to play the part of a harrassed housewife who is bemoaning her boring life of grinding housework. Towards the end of the song she was meant to symbolically rip off her housecoat and headscarf, jettison her bucket and broom and emerge as a newly liberated woman. It didn't quite work that way. Although my fingers were successfully working the piano keys, Debbie's fingers were fumbling with buttons and bows which wouldn't undo, a broom which she trod on and which shot up and whacked her on the head and a bucket which she stumbled over. My prize scene ended as something of a lame duck. But I sat back relieved that at least I hadn't messed up on the keyboard and my blues composition sounded half way decent.

What followed was a year 8 dance/drama piece which included daughter Katie stepping on to the Newman stage for the first time. Throughout her life she had never sought the limelight or chosen to be centre stage. She was nervous and I was nervous that she was nervous. But parents are suckers for watching their offspring performing from the time that they first walk, and I sat there quietly nodding with delight as she went through the routine without a hitch.

Now came the final challenge of the evening - my multi media extravaganza. While the brass ensemble was performing, I made my way to the balcony at the back of the hall to where the slide projector was set up. The music teacher had recorded a sequence of rather weird electronic noises over which some of the poems from the show had been dubbed using a voice distortion technique. She assured me the audio would be suitably atmospheric. I waited. The house lights dimmed, then a dull reverberating noise filled the hall. I switched on the projector. My first slide of oily colours filled the screen at the back of the stage. The coloured blobs began to move, sluggishly at first and then more fluidly as the oils heated up from the heat from the projector lamp. Every ten seconds or so I changed the slide to give a different colour mood. The disembodied voices reciting the poetry snippets came and went while my oily coloured shapes moved slowly around the screen. It was certainly different and somewhat mesmerising. What I hadn't expected were the shapes the moving blobs of oil would create. A recurring shape was an elongated sausage shape which showed, at one stage, an uncanny resemblance to a rising penis. I quickly changed slides but the forces of heat and gravity seemed to be conspiring against me. These oils had a definite predilection for penis and boob shapes!

The impression was not lost on the Head who, the following day, called me into his office. 'Well done, Barrie,' he said. 'You put on a good show. But I wasn't quite comfortable with that rather erotic light show towards the end. Some of those shapes were highly dubious, don't you think?'

I looked innocently at him. 'Not sure what you mean. It was all quite colourful and a little hypnotic. Not sure about the 'erotic' though. But then they do say that with art, the meaning is all in the eye of the beholder. You must have seen things I wasn't aware of.'

He gave me one of his wry looks. 'Anyway, well done. A good end to the term.'

The ghosts of drama production had been laid. Well, somewhat, anyway.

*

FACING THE FAX

The decade had turned. We were into the nineties. It would be a decade of monumental change in education driven by the revolution in computer technology and by major political decisions about how children should learn and how teachers should teach. On the home front it would be a decade when Katie and James grew into adults and left home to forge their way in the world.

Margaret Thatcher's controversial 11-year reign as Prime Minister ended in November 1990 after a back-stabbing campaign by some of her ministers. Her tumble from power was hastened by the Poll Tax riots in London in March over this new tax that Thatcher had championed and which hit the poor hardest. There were riots in Trafalgar Square between mounted police and a crowd of 150,000 angry protesters slinging missiles. Missiles of a different sort were being fired in the deserts of Iraq following the invasion of Kuwait by Saddam Hussein's army in the summer of 1990. The allied campaign called Desert Storm was about to start. The new decade had certainly started with a bang.

However my sights were set on June 27th, probably the world's first Faxday. Ten schools were on board and each had been supplied with a fax machine. We were experimenting with the new Desk Top Publishing software which was revolutionising the way text and images could be combined on paper. The students were excited by the range of different fonts which were available and with the ways pages could be set up. We now had our hands on the techniques which had previously only been available to professional printers and publishers. It was heady and exciting stuff and the prospect that the finished work would be viewed by students and teachers in other schools spiced up the need to get it right.

In the run-up to the Faxday various year groups worked on the

****

THE
FIRST
CUMBRIAN
FAX
NEWSPAPER
PRODUCED ON JUNE 27TH
1990

****

design and lay-out of their pages. Each school was allowed three pages with the hopeful outcome being a thirty page newspaper. I had recruited a team of helpers from Katie's year group and the week prior to the

Faxday we held after school meetings to crop and re-jig layout and content of our pages. Tension was palpable with students poring over the computer screen and arguing over the finer points of layout and design. The new National Curriculum for English, which was just being phased in by the government, stressed that 'audience' was the key determinant of the style and content of any communication. And here we were, at the eye of a project, where our audiences in nine other schools would be looking critically at our work.

For the Faxday itself each school had been given a time slot of 25 minutes in which to fax its three news sheets to the other nine schools. Timing was tight and the first school was due to start faxing at 9 a.m. We waited, watching the second hand on the clock. A light on the fax machine winked, there was a whirring and a clicking and then a sheet of paper started to emerge from the machine. It was from Beaconside Primary in Penrith. There was a cheer. We were up and away!

One of the intriguing news reports of the day was by Claire Armstrong from Caldew School, in Dalston. She reported on a school drama trip to London to see *Blood Brothers* at the Albery Theatre. The students and their teachers unwittingly found themselves caught up in the poll tax riots. She wrote: ....*cars and shops were totally demolished. Looting was going on, cars were on their roofs and ablaze. Police sirens could be heard for miles around and lots of screaming people. Mounted police were chasing people up and down the street. I stood and watched as a man stood in front of a smashed shop window and leaned through the window and pinched lots of things..*

Apart from news reports there were quizzes, snippets of local information and photographs. Looking at it now The First Cumbrian Fax Newspaper looks a little crude – the quality of the reproduction and printing is not what we would accept today. Back then, it was cutting-edge stuff and our trophy newspaper was proudly displayed in the window of the Cumberland News Office alongside a news report and photograph by a reporter from the paper. Even the prestigious Times Educational Supplement published a full page spread of an article I had sent in and for a brief period we all felt we were media stars.

DOWN A LANE OF MEMORIES

If, on a winter evening, you walked past the barn conversion at the back of our house you might be forgiven for thinking nobody lived there. No lights on, no sign of life. But if you looked more closely you might see a misty grey glow from the corner of the living room and a ghostly face illuminated by the dim light from an old black and white television set. Sometimes there might be child's face staring at the TV set. Ghosts? No, just James and his grandfather watching the snooker.

When Sue's father, Harry, came to live with us in 1985, James was six years old. Over the next few years a routine developed whereby James, at tea-time would go across the yard to 'Poppa's house' and bring him over for his evening meal. Often Harry was glued to his little black and white TV set watching the cricket in the summer or snooker in the winter. We pleaded with him to give up his black and white set for a colour one but he was not one for change. 'But you'll be able to see the colours of the balls, Poppa,' James would say. Harry would tousle James' hair, tap out his pipe on the hearth and reply, 'Ah, but if you know the colour sequence in a snooker game you can work out the colours. That's the test, you see.' He would refill his pipe with some more Erinmore Flake, light a paper spill from his coal fire, set his pipe going again and give James a wink.

He demanded little of life. His pipe, his coal fire and his black and white TV set were his staples. Beyond that he was as content as he would ever be now that he'd lost his lifelong partner.

When Sue's mother died in 1984 the light went out of Harry's life. She had been his inspiration, his energy, his source of fun and laughter. She was 62 when she passed her driving test. Prior to that they had never had a car but she was determined to be able to drive up to Cumbria to see us and to establish some independence for them both in their latter years. They bought a trusty dark blue Morris Minor and it lasted them for years. Sue's mother, Florence May, never went by her real name. Everyone knew her as 'Bunty' a name coined by some dubious friend who likened her shape to that of Billy Bunter, the fat boy in the comic book stories by Frank Richards. Bunty was certainly not fat, she had a cuddly roundness, abundant good humour and a generosity of spirit which was infectious. I felt it instantly the first time I met her.

Sue and I were still at school and had started dating in the sixth form. I had just bought my first car, a black Ford Anglia with a curious side-valve engine which had cost me £70. I drove round to show off my new 'wheels' and was invited into the house. Harry was sitting by the fire cleaning nicotine goo out of his pipe. He stood up and offered his hand. He was tall and upright with a head of neat white hair, and a trimmed moustache. He could have passed for an army officer but was, in fact, an accountant. Bunty was short and bubbled with energy. She laughed and scolded Harry to put away his 'dirty old pipe'. 'It's not dirty,' he said, 'I just gave it a spring clean.' Their warmth, coupled with Bunty's deep crust apple pie and fresh cream, worked their magic on me. At Christmas a large ham hock would be delivered and I would be plied with thick wedges of ham sliced fresh from the ham bone, a dollop of Colman's mustard and a wedge of crusty bread. Little wonder that I always looked forward to my visits to the family home.

They had visited us once in Jamaica in 1974 accompanied by Sue's auntie Edie. They were excited about their visit and raised the question as to whether we had come across someone called Robert Lightbourne on the island. They had known Robert or 'Bob' years ago when they were all much younger. His black face would have a been a rarity on the streets of Birmingham in the 1930s when he was starting out in the world of heavy industry. Harry, Bunty and Edie had met him through their shared love of dance music. Bob was a talented pianist, Edie was a singer and Harry played a mean clarinet. They were keen to try to locate Bob again.

What they didn't realise was that the Robert Lightbourne of 1974 was now in the top rank of society. In the sixties he was tipped to be leader of the Jamaica Labour Party and prime minister to fill the vacancy created by the death of Donald Sangster. He was now an MP in the government and had been involved at government level for many years furthering Jamaica's international trade and industry. He was a person of eminence and importance and many also knew him as the person who had composed the music for Jamaica's national anthem, *Jamaica, Land We Love.* I doubted that he would have the time or inclination to meet up with Sue's parents and her aunt. Their lives had followed very different tracks and anyway it was forty years ago. Nevertheless, just prior to their arrival we had written to The Right Honourable Robert Lightbourne, MP outlining the situation and raising the question of a possible meeting. We were surprised, some weeks later, when we received a positive response. Yes, we could arrange a visit.

Edie mentioned it again soon after they arrived. 'Have you managed to find if Bob is still around? He was such a smart young man. Doubt that he would even remember us now though.' When we told her that we were taking them to his house for tea she couldn't believe it.

And so one afternoon the five of us, crammed into our little orange VW beetle, arrived at the gates of the home of the eminent Robert Lightbourne. I was not sure about this meeting. People change over forty years. It could end up in awkwardness and disappointment.

We went up the drive and the front door was opened by the housekeeper. Behind her came a tall, lean figure. His face, the colour of polished ebony, broke into a wide smile. He extended his two hands in greeting. Edie was nervous and hung back. It was Harry who went forward and shook his hand rather stiffly. Bunty, ever the effusive one, said: 'Hello Bob, can we call you Bob?'

He was grace personified. He nodded, 'Of course, wasn't I always 'Bob' in those days. It's only over here that I'm The Right Honourable Robert.' He broke the ice gently for them but for a while there was still a distance and a nervousness. Tea was brought in and we fussed with cups and cakes. The years had opened up a gulf between them and I doubted that we could bridge that gulf. Maybe this wasn't such a good idea after all.

Then Harry started reminiscing about music. 'Do you still play?' he asked. He gestured towards the grand piano which stood by the window.

Bob nodded, 'Not like I used to but, yes, a little.'

'Would you..' said Edie, 'play for us?'

And that was the key which unlocked the years. Bob sat at the

piano and started to play. It was a forties dance number. Harry's head started to nod and his fingers to click and Edie closed her eyes and began to hum and murmur the words. Bob warmed to the music and his hands worked their magic on the keys. Harry got up and came and put his arm on Bob's shoulder, leaning in over the keyboard, head swaying to the rhythm. Bunty was tapping her feet, moving her shoulders and tapping her hands on her lap. Edie was still murmuring the words of the song, eyes closed, mind drifting down her lane of memories.

The spell lasted until Bob played the last song. We applauded, he nodded and smiled and stood up shaking his head, 'A long time ago,' he said. 'Thank you for reminding me.'

That afternoon Sue and I glimpsed something of a past of which we knew nothing – Birmingham, England of the 1930s when the lives of these four ageing people had come together by chance and been held together by their love of music.

Harry and Bunty were Sue's adoptive parents. She was 'extra special' they said as they'd chosen her from the nursing home when she was 6 weeks old. They were wonderful parents. So when Bunty died prematurely of heart failure soon after we returned from our year in America in 1984, Sue was devastated and Harry became a lost soul. He lived with us for five years until the autumn of 1990. James was eleven and had just started at Newman and one October evening went across to bring Harry over for his evening meal. James came back shouting, 'Poppa's on the floor.' Harry had suffered a stroke and was hospitalised for the next six weeks. Finally he started pulling out the feeding tubes and without words made it clear he'd had enough.

When parents die you lose more than your loved ones. You lose that comfort blanket which has shielded you from confronting your own mortality. You shiver and feel just a little bit older.

*

Now both Katie and James were at Newman. James had laid down no 'rules of engagement' in the way that Katie had. If we met in a corridor he would smile and wave. He wasn't going to be phased by the fact of his dad teaching in the same school. 'He's not like Katie,' said several of my colleagues to Sue at James' first Year 7 Parents' Evening. Annoyed at the implied criticism, Sue would bite back, 'No he's not, he's a boy, he's almost two years younger and he's got different talents. What point are you making?'

Even though there was just a school year between them, James was almost two years younger. But they were great companions. Every Friday evening we would drop them at the Brook Street Music Centre for band practice with the Carlisle Concert Band. Katie was learning the flute and James the saxophone. While they were safely occupied there Sue and I would escape for an hour to Gianni's Italian Restuarant in Cecil Street. It was a chance to step out of the hectic routine of coping with work, homelife, evening marking and lesson preparation and review the week.

'How about an Easter trip back to Devon,' I said one evening. 'I'd like to show the kids some of our old haunts; try out the new caravan.'

Devon was a place of warm magic in my memory. I was eight years old when my father roused me and my elder brother from our beds at 5 a.m. on a spring morning. It was the Easter holidays and we were staying in a caravan in Brixham, a small fishing port on the southern tip of Torbay. The morning was chilly with the woods cloaked in mist and the sea like cold green glass shifting out of the fog. We dutifully padded along the cliff path, through what they called the Battery Gardens, not knowing where our father was taking us. 'Just wait,' he said, 'you'll see in a short while.' Down the steps from the cliff path and we were into the town which huddled on steep slopes around the harbour.

The fish quay was already busy with men in blue aprons smeared with blood and fish guts. They were shifting wicker baskets and stacks of wooden trays. The first trawlers were already unloading and baskets of wriggling fish were being tipped from the trawlers on to the floor of the fish quay. The fishermen in their short yellow rubber boots stepped into the mess of glistening bodies and started sorting them, flinging mackerel into boxes in one direction, haddock in another, sprats into the wicker baskets. I have never forgotten that morning: the trawlers with their small rust red stern sails emerging out of the sea mist and chugging into the harbour, the glistening rainbow patterns of the mackerels' skin, the sheen of fish blood on the fishermen's aprons, the smell of fish and salt water – the memory is indelible.

Now I wanted my own children to share something of the Devon magic. I wanted to take them to the shingle beach at Fishcombe where my brother and I used to set off in our black and white canvas canoe to paddle round the rocky shoreline to the harbour. I wanted to see what had happened to Laurie George, the old painter who was a fixture on the quayside when I was a boy. He was always there at his easel in his paint-smeared fisherman's smock, a coloured handkerchief tied round his neck, a beret on his head and a curving Meerschaum pipe clamped between his teeth. He was a rare and exotic figure in my childhood memory and I would stand and stare at the way he painted, not with a brush but with a small trowel which he dipped into the coloured oil paints on his palette and smeared on to the canvas. He was quite old even then and I doubted that thirty five years on he would still be alive.

But there was also a younger painter, Terry Burke, who arrived on the scene much later. He painted in a style more accessible to my boyhood eyes. Laurie George's paintings had seemed abstract and blotchy, Burke's were more realistic. I liked them. I wondered if he might still be there.

We trailed our caravan that long drive from Cumbria to Devon down the M6 and the M5 motorways. Finally, south of Exeter, the old names started to appear on road signs – Newton Abbott, Torbay, Paignton, Goodrington, Brixham – the names took me spiralling down a tunnel of childhood memories. I wondered how much would have changed. Going back to cherished places can be a mistake.

After that initial visit in 1956 when I watched the trawlers coming in, my parents bought their own caravan and had it permanently sited at Brixham. We would visit three or four times a year travelling the 207 miles from our home north of Birmingham. In the late fifties and early sixties there were no motorways, just a tedious seven hour journey down the A38. The first motorway, the M1, was opened in 1958 but it would be another ten years before a motorway route to the southwest was operating. There was little to amuse us in the car. My older brother, Ian, and I would play endless games of I-spy. We would wave at people in other cars and try to make words from the letters on car registration plates. No seat belts in those days and squashed on the back seat next to my baby brother's carry cot it wasn't long before we would start to squabble and my father would threaten to stop the car and 'box our ears'. After six hours came the slow crawl up Telegraph Hill, near Exeter where we would get our first glimpse of the sea. Then the last hour just slipped away in the excitement of arriving.

Katie and James in typical teenage fashion had yawned and feigned utter boredom when I tried to conjure in them some enthusiasm for this trip down memory lane. 'Yes dad, you've told us before,' said Katie. 'But that was then and this is now. It may all be different. You might be disappointed.'

We set off from the campsite at Churston Ferrers and hiked along the coastal path and into the woodland which led to the small bay at Churston. This was the bay where I used to spend hours with snorkel and mask searching the rocky shoreline for caves and sea creatures, imagining I was Lloyd Bridges in the TV series 'Sea Hunt'.

At Easter we would pick primroses and at Whitsuntide it would be armsful of bluebells which Ian and I would carry back to the caravan and present to my mother to be put in jam jars.

And here they were – the primroses; small clumps of the pale yellow flowers nudging the sides of the path, scattered amongst the trees and dotting the grassy slopes which led down to the shingle beach. This was my first time back to this little bay for almost thirty years and yet it was just the same – a horseshoe shaped bay with two beaches separated by a rocky outcrop. I jogged over the rocks with Katie and James following. I remembered the handholds and the steps in the rock face where you had to place your feet to climb from the beach at Churston to the other beach at Fishcombe. By some curious trick of memory I was my eight-year old self - leather sandals, khaki shorts with turn-ups and a blue and white striped tee shirt, scampering over the same rocky outcrop.

But it was when we arrived at the harbour that my joy was complete. Near the statue of William of Orange and marking the spot where the Mayflower set sail for America in September 1620 stands the Strand Gallery, the home of a group of local painters. We went inside and there he was - Terry Burke, sitting at an easel working on a canvas. He was obviously older but I recognised the style of his paintings immediately. I told him my story and asked about the old painter, Laurie George. 'Died quite recently,' said Terry. 'Grand old trooper.'

Much to Katie's embarrassment I got Terry to sketch her portrait in charcoal while Sue and I chose one of his paintings to take back to Cumbria. It was like completing a circle, forging this connection between my childhood and that of my own children. And the journey didn't end there. Next there was Sue's childhood to connect with.

For years she and her family spent holidays just along the coast at Salcombe, a picturesque town located at the rocky mouth of the Kingsbridge Estuary. It is a place of yachts, sailing dinghies, fishing boats, houses clinging to the steep slopes of the shoreline and, on a blue sky day, a sea of pearly aquamarine. Each summer they had taken the train from New Street station in Birmingham and travelled down to Devon to the village of Malborough where they stayed at a small guest house. It was close to the coastal path which led to Salcombe and the fine sandy beaches of East Portlemouth and Gara Rock.

We retraced those footsteps of years ago along the path to Bolt Head, the rocky headland on the south side of the estuary, then through the woods at Overbecks and into the town itself. We ate fish and chips on the quayside and watched the sail boats, and the ferry taking passengers across the estuary.

Katie nodded and murmured, 'Devon's nice; not sure about the magic but, yes, it's nice.' She wasn't speaking to anyone in particular, just nodding and gazing out across the water.

OF CARPETS AND CATS

There was the whiff of grapeshot in the air, the first hint that all was not happy in the world of English education. I had attended an inservice training programme on the new National Curriculum in January 1991 and the general mood among teachers was quite positive about this attempt to introduce some standard entitlement for students in England and Wales. What people were less happy about was the proposed testing regime at ages 7, 11 and 14. There was talk of using the results of these tests to rank schools in 'League Tables'; to use the results to affect funding of schools and on the right wing of the Tory party there was talk of linking test results to teachers' pay.

Until now I had been enjoying a fairly laissez-faire educational culture in which teachers had a degree of freedom to experiment with new ideas. This was bound within the constraints of the school's internal testing regime and the GCSE examination system which were the means of assessing whether our teaching was effective or not. But beyond that teachers could be imaginative and experimental. There was guidance on national initiatives from the Local Educational Authority advisory teams who were generally helpful and supportive of new ideas coming from teachers. My Faxday initiative had been welcomed both locally and nationally and there were many new opportunities arising from the exciting developments in computer technology. But there was certainly a whiff of something new in the air and it didn't sound at all exciting.

However on the technology front things were much more interesting. My colleague Eileen, who taught Business Studies, kept referring to something called 'e-mail'. I had never heard of it until recently so one afternoon I went down to her room to see how it worked. The room was equipped with a number of BBC Master machines and after typing in various codes and then a short message, Eileen assured me that this message would be transmitted electronically within seconds. Unlike the fax machine no paper was involved. 'They talk about the paperless office,' said Eileen, 'but it sounds like science fiction to me.'

This 'e-mail' looked a bit complicated with its esoteric codings and special phone line. Fax, on the other hand could use existing telephone numbers for sending documents and seemed to me much more straighforward. I still only had two computers on trolleys in the English department so for now e-mail would have to wait.

However what I did need were carpets. The rooms in which we taught our English lessons were far from ideal. Often we were timetabled in the dining rooms which were poorly equipped for teaching. They had

391

old blackboards which needed painting. The chalk skidded across the shiny surface when you tried to write and when the sun shone it was impossible to read what was written. After lunch the dining-rooms would be grubby, the floors scuffed, the students typically restless and teaching could be a trial. In the other three English rooms things were slightly better. One was carpeted which deadened the noise and made for a sane teaching environment. The other rooms had lino which echoed and magnified every chair scrape, every cough, every bit of chatter. We needed carpets on the floors.

'Not possible, too difficult to clean,' was the reply of the Deputy Head i/c Buildings.

'What's more important, the quality of the teaching or the cleaners having to use a hoover instead of a mop?' I replied.

'Sorry, it's not going to happen, not on my watch.'

'You don't have to teach in there day in day out,' I retorted.

He shook his head, 'Sorry, not possible.'

He didn't hear the string of expletives uttered as I closed the door of his office. Teaching was stressful at the best of times and noisy classrooms were not what we needed for good education. But it looked as if my carpet idea was going nowhere. That is until a few months later.

It was a sunny afternoon and I was teaching a second year class in Room 23 which was on the ground floor and next to the main drive. The class was quietly working on some questions on Nina Bawden's novel *The Twelfth Day of July*. A green van came down the drive and stopped. It's rear doors were open revealing rolls of carpet tied to the back doors with string. I didn't hesitate. I was out of the door in a flash. 'Are you selling these?' I asked.

'End of rolls, good quality, good price. What d'you need?' said the driver.

'Give me a minute,' I said.

I hopped back into the class and paced the dimensions of the room.

'What are you doing, sir?' said one child.

'Tell you in a minute. Just carry on with your work.'

I gave the man the dimensions.

'Perfect,' he said. 'I've got beige and dark blue.'

'How much?'

'Fifty quid.'

'Give me a minute,' I said.

I skipped along to the Head's office. 'Frank, there's a man selling carpets from the back of his van. Is it okay if I buy one for room 23? Fifty quid.'

Frank nodded. 'Sounds a good idea. I know you've mentioned it before. Yes, go ahead.'

Within minutes the deal was done and the man off-loaded a roll of carpet. He helped me carry it through the door towards my teaching room. From behind some coat pegs the Deputy Head i/c Buildings appeared. 'What's going on?' he demanded.

'Just bought some top quality carpet for my English room from this kind gentleman.'

'What did I say about carpets?' he said.

'Go and see the Head, he gave me the go ahead,' I said and, turning away, proceeded into the English room with my prize.

The Deputy was furious but I didn't care. By the end of the following week a local carpet fitter had glued the carpet to the floor and the acoustics in the room were transformed. The teachers in my department were delighted but the Deputy never forgave me.

*

My confidence for producing drama events was increasing and I had an idea for a dance drama based on T.S Eliot's collection of cat poems – *Old Possum's Book of Practical Cats*. This would be part of the Christmas show. Not to be confused with Andrew Lloyd Webber's *Cats*, I called our production *Skats*. What helped to crystalise things was the arrival of a new music teacher fresh from college. Jim was one of the new breed of music teachers who was  using computer technology in very creative ways. One lunch time I explained to him my ideas for the themes of the dance routines and he set up a meeting in the music room later that week.

I was intrigued to see the process of multi-tracking for the first time. Using a synthesizer linked to his computer, he started by laying down a bass beat; then he added chords and musical phrases, layering the sounds in a kind of sound 'sandwich'. The results were astonishing.

By the end of the session I had some preliminary dance soundtracks which I could hand over to Christine, the dance teacher, to work out the choreography. There would be four routines: a starting chorus, then two more individualised pieces based on *Gus the Theatre Cat* and *Skimbleshanks The Railway Cat*. Finally the climax would be based on Eliot's *The Battle of the Peaks and the Pollicles*. For this piece I wanted a gang fight scenario which echoed the routines of the Jets and the Sharks in the 1961 film of *West Side Story*, and Michael Jackson's routine for the 1982 video of *Beat It*. In addition I wanted to incorporate a lighting technique I had seen used by the Black Light Theatre Company at St. Aidan's in the 1980s. Using UV lights and fluorescent colours on a black background you could create all sorts of stunning illusions and dramatic effects. Objects could appear to float in the air, skeletons could appear to be dancing if the costume was black with a fluorescent skeleton shape painted on it.

For several weeks I experimented with various ideas. The result was cat costumes, masks and makeup which used vivid fluorescent colours. Coupled with Jim's superb sound track and the choreography which I had worked on with Christine and the dancers, the end result was impressive. For the actual performance I was sitting directly in front of the stage working the UV strip lights. The final 'Peaks and Pollicles' scene commenced with a pulsing bass beat followed by a driving rhythm over which the poem was narrated. The dancers appeared first in silhouette and then the UV lights picked up their fluorescent masks, black leotards streaked with white paint and fluorescent strips. Then came the stylised fight routine between the two gangs and finally the climax featuring the great figure of the Rumpus Cat, resplendent in a striking fluorescent mask and cloak.

I was well pleased. It was my best drama production to date. The bonus, of course, was seeing Katie performing as one of the cat dancers and James featuring on saxophone in the school rock band in the second half of the show.

When we watched the recording of the show sometime later Katie commented, 'Don't think I'll ever make a great dancer, dad. I look too gangly. Think I'll stick to the flute.'

James, on the other hand, was really chuffed with his first appearance in a rock band. 'Whadya reckon, dad. Pretty cool, huh?'

*

394

CHICKEN TALES

The little chicken enterprise which Katie and James were managing had been running well for several years now and when Zoe and Scott arrived from America at Easter, their little daughter Corey was delighted to chase newly hatched chicks round the garden. It was hard to believe that this young American mother was the same Zoe we had taught in Jamaica when she was 13 years old. It was their first trip to England and we wanted to treat them to the best of English. Zoe's husband Scott, a professional photographer, was in seventh heaven. There was so much to photograph, so much that was different. We were in London for a couple of nights and of course there was the river, Big Ben, the Palace, the Mall – photo opportunities were endless. Then by train to Cumbria and the wonder of the Lakes. We hiked from Borrowdale via Watendlath where it snowed, then on down the gorge of Lodore Falls to Derwentwater.

From Cumbria via Hadrian's Wall we took them to the Northumberland coast – Holy Island and Lindisfarne and a stay in Bamburgh where we sunbathed on the dunes under the gaze of the majestic Bamburgh Castle.

'Your country is just amazing,' remarked Zoe. 'Back home you can drive two hundred miles and the landscape doesn't change. Here you drive 20 miles and you're in totally different country. I love it.'

It's always good to see the familiar through the eyes of a newcomer. You're reminded of the wonders of this 'green and pleasant land' of ours which we so often take for granted.

Katie's worries about the fall out from the Chernobyl disaster affecting the chickens had been calmed although the high lakeland farms were still affected and there were serious restrictions on the movement of stock. At lower levels it wasn't a problem although we did have problems of a different kind.

Recently we had been given a young cockerel from a neighbour and he scurried on the heels of our long serving bantam cock who lorded it over six brown Warren females. Each day when the eggs were collected, Katie would record in her notebook the numbers, James would check the level of chicken feed in the feed bin and we would pay them for the eggs.

Then one day things took a turn.

'One of the chickens isn't right,' said Katie. 'I think it's Mildred. She just stands there and doesn't eat and hardly moves.'

I went out to have a look. The chicken's comb on the top of its head is a sure sign of the state of health. In a healthy chicken it is a bright red and stands up fairly erect. The comb of this particular chicken was decidedly limp and a pale purple colour.'

'Might be egg bound,' said Jill, a colleague at school who kept chickens and knew a thing or two about them.

'So what do I do?' I asked.

'You have to massage the egg duct.'

'How do I do that?'

She smiled. 'Warm olive oil, finger, egg duct. But make sure you find the egg duct and not the anus. They're right next door. I'll lend you a book.'

'Right,' I said. 'Sounds like a challenge.'

The next evening I re-read the chapter in the *Backyard Poultry* book Jill had given me. 'James, I'll need your help,' I called. 'Just stand behind me and tell me how Mildred is reacting when I start the treatment, okay?'

He nodded. 'What are you going to do?'

'Well, I have to get some of this warm olive oil on my finger and massage the egg passage.'

He grimaced, ' You mean up its bum?'

'Well, yes, where the eggs come out.'

'Yuk. That's gross!'

'It may be 'gross' as you put it, but keeping animals isn't always pretty.'

I picked up the chicken, holding it under my arm like a rugby ball, its head facing behind me so that I could locate the egg passage. I moistened my finger with olive oil and then proceeded to lubricate the passage. This curious intimacy with a chicken's nether regions felt a little unsavoury but if this was the recommended treatment it had to be done. The chicken didn't move and I continued the 'massage' for a few minutes.

'What she doing?' I asked James over my shoulder.

'Nothing much, just smiling,' replied James.

Over the next week or so we watched Mildred's progress but she still looked rather forlorn. I tried various strategies to spark her into action. I placed her on the top of the fence thinking she would at least have to fly to the ground. But she just clung on until a gust of wind came and she fell off in a heap.

'Poor Mildred,' said Katie. 'What are we going to do?'

I took her into the middle of the field at the back of the house where the other chickens were foraging, then called them and banged the tin lid of the feeder. This always brought them scampering back to the coop. Sure enough they all hurried through the grass to the fence, all except Mildred. She just stood where I'd set her down. The wind blew, it started to rain and still this sad chicken just stood there.

Finally, I retrieved her and brought her back to the coop. I looked at Katie. 'I think Mildred is going to have to go to the big chicken coop in the sky. She can't go on like this.'

'What about the vet?' asked James.

'Mildred's no spring chicken, so we're not going to pay vet's bills for an old chicken who is half dead already. Sorry. You go inside and I'll see to Mildred.'

'I think you're mean,' said Katie.

'We can always get another chicken,' added James.

They went inside and I filled a bucket of water from the outside tap. I'd never killed a chicken before. I'd killed turkeys but then there was nothing endearing about a turkey. But chickens who had loyally provided us with eggs for so long – that was different. I couldn't face wringing Mildred's neck. The feel of her warm skin under my fingers was too much to cope with. Drowning was the best option. I held her gently, looked at her one last time and then thrust her under the water and looked away.

How long does it take to drown a chicken? I had no idea. So I gave it a good five minutes. There was no movement so I assumed the job was done. I turned my head and looked down into the bucket. There was Mildred, eyes open, mouth still opening and closing. It was like that scene in the 1987 film 'Fatal Attraction' when Glenn Close, the supposedly dead lover, drowned in the bath, suddenly rises up out of the water and attacks Michael Douglas. Surely Mildred wasn't about to do the same!

'Just the twitch of the nerves,' said Jill, when I reported back to her at school. 'Remember, chickens will run around a yard with their heads chopped off. They have a network of nerves in the spinal cord programmed to control muscles. So they don't need signals from the brain to move their legs.'

I was partly reassured. Even so, the image of Mildred's eyes open and mouth moving under the water, after five minutes of total immersion, still haunts me to this day. Katie would have said, 'Serves you right,' but I spared her the details of Mildred's final moments.

Some weeks later I was confronted by another chicken situation. When I arrived back from school my neighbour came out of her house. 'Something going on with your chickens today. Terrible squawking and clucking for a good ten minutes then it all went quiet. Never heard anything like it.'

It was a case of 'The king is dead, long live the king.' We hadn't noticed that our young cockerel had grown. He was no longer scrawny and clearly his hormones had been triggered. There had been a vicious fight for control of the Warren harem. There were feathers everywhere and the young usurper was now strutting his stuff round the clutch of females.

'Where's the other cockerel gone?' asked James. 'I can't see him.'

We searched around for the little bantam cock who had lorded over his ladies for so long. He had always been a proud little fellow and you could see where the phrase 'cock-sure' came from when you watched him strutting among the females. But now he had been literally 'knocked off his perch.'

Eventually we found him, a quivering mound of feathers, head and body tightly squeezed into a corner of the coop for protection. He was still alive but now an outcast. For the next few days we watched him, a shadow of his former strutting self. He was cowed and shamed, frequently being nipped by the new young 'cock-of-the-walk' if he ventured too close to the flock.

'Nature's cruel, isn't it,' said Katie.

'Nature's nature,' I said. 'Nothing lasts forever. The old have to give way to the young just like this old cockerel has had his day.'

Eventually the old guy went the way of Mildred. Pecked and taunted daily by the others, it was a case of putting the sad old bird out of his misery.

*

TIMES THEY ARE A-CHANGIN'

Freddy Mercury, the iconic lead singer of the rock group 'Queen', had died. The pernicious disease of Aids had cut down King Freddy. He had strutted in crown and ermine at the Wembley concert of 1986 and mesmerised the stadium crowd. And then we had watched his final video to the song *These Are The Days Of Our Lives*. It was hard to watch. The lyrics themselves were poignant but the video shot in black and white showed a thin, gaunt Freddy trying hard still to be a showman. But he was a shadow of the man he had been. The verve and vitality had gone. He died a few months after the video was shot. It was the end of an era of great music which had punctuated our lives during the seventies and eighties.

Now, closer to home, more change – Frank, the long-time Head of Newman was due to retire in the summer but in the spring of '93 he was faced with a rebellion. Girls were agitating to be allowed to wear trousers to school. There had been murmurings for years about this but schools in general were resistant to change. Now revolution was in the air. Championed by a new parent governor, Jim Joyce, who had three girls at Newman, a petition was circulating among parents and a pressure group was gearing up for a showdown.

Sue had championed a similar battle back in 1976 when we were living in Lancaster and she got a temporary job at a local secondary school. She was told she couldn't wear trousers to school and she objected that she didn't have the funds to buy a new wardrobe – it was either trousers or she would resign. The regular staff begged her not to back down and after a minor standoff, the Head and governors gave in and Sue was the toast of the staff-room.

Nearly twenty years on and school girls still had a fight on their hands. At first the Newman governors were standing firm but parents and their daughters were beating at the door of change and finally they won. I think Frank saw that this wasn't the only change on the horizon. New style exams, a new inspection regime, a more clinical approach to teaching - a new educational culture was flooding the landscape. It was time to call it a day and that summer we said goodbye to the man who had been Newman's youngest Headmaster.

The old was giving way to the new but this included the arrival of John Patten, a new hard-boiled Tory education minister in the government of PM John Major.

John Haggitt Charles Patten, Cambridge educated, former Oxford don and a devout Roman Catholic navigated by the philosophy that individuals choose to be good or evil and the only way to engender goodness was to dangle the threat of Eternal Damnation over the miscreant. 'I believe in God. I worry about him. I think that he probably worries about me', he was quoted as saying in a *Spectator* article. This new minister was shunting in a new educational culture. He started issuing dictats about Christian assemblies. He believed a lack of belief and lack of fear of damnation encouraged criminality, indiscipline and bad behaviour in schools. He felt that English teaching should go back to grammar basics, that Victorian novels exemplified true morality and that frequent testing and grading were 'liberating' for ordinary people. He studiously avoided tarnishing his mission by not giving interviews, not speaking to unions or large groups of teachers but is said to have commented that he 'looked forward to shutting down a lot of duff schools'.

Since going back to full time work, Sue had been feeling the weight of the new National Curriculum for primary schools. It was unwieldly, over prescriptive and impossible to administer. Now it was hitting secondary schools with the first English tests for 14 year olds being rushed in for summer 1993. From universities, to independent schools and state schools, the educational establishment was in uproar about the new education minister and the narrow English curriculum with its emphasis on standard English usage, the rules of correct grammar and a prescribed diet of dead, white, male authors – Twain, Defoe, Keats, Browning, Tennyson – writers who would really inspire our disaffected 14 year old boys!

This was the climate which fomented a boycott of the national English tests for 14 year olds in 1993. We were erecting barricades to fend off this onslaught on the way we taught English. The tests were becoming the narrow focus of our teaching. Everything became geared to these tests which asked mindless questions on the compulsory Shakespeare texts and gave our students little scope for demonstrating their skills.

I fired off a letter to the *Times Educational Supplement* congratulating John Patten on being the first education minister to really unify the teaching profession (against him). We organized meetings with parents to explain the problems with the new testing regime in the hope that, like Scottish parents the year before, they might keep their children away from school on the day of the English tests. It was the start of a new culture in education. Times, they were certainly 'a-changin' and not for the better.

Into this heady maelstrom of frustration and rebellion strode the new Head of Newman. Tall, wiry and reputedly an expert golfer, he was certainly no kindly patriarch like Frank had been. He wouldn't be dressing up as mother goose for the school pantomime or holding the entire school rapt with a recitation of *Albert and the Lion*. No, he represented the new breed. Something 'corporate' about him. In his first assembly he spoke of 'my school'. The word 'my' sent shivers of resentment through me. We were a 'family' weren't we? That possessive pronoun was seriously offensive and I sensed the loss of the cosy days of Frank's regime and the arrival of something much more cold and bureaucratic.

Within a short time my job description was changed. As well being Head of English I had also been the Staff Development Officer. I had a small budget which went on organising inservice training sessions and providing opportunities for individual staff to develop their careers. I enjoyed the interaction with colleagues across all departments but now this was to end. My new role would be to set up and organise a new PSE (Personal and Social Education) programme for the whole school. One lesson a week was timetabled for PSE which was supposed to cover everything from healthy eating and drug abuse to environmental issues and sex education. The last was the trickiest. We were a Catholic school and I was a non-believer. I knew little about the current Catholic thinking on contraception, abortion and homosexuality. A large percentage of the students were non-Catholic and I was supposed to design a PSE programme which steered through a minefield of moral issues. I had seen sex education videos showing students unrolling condoms over plastic penises. Highly commendable I thought, but I couldn't see the Newman parents and governors accepting this type of thing. I would have to tread carefully.

I had been treading carefully on a another front that year. James had been in my Year 9 English group and I was acutely aware of not showing him any favouritism. Unlike Katie, he appeared quite relaxed about having his dad teaching in the same school and didn't seem to mind having me as a teacher. English wasn't his strongest subject so there was no question of him being near the top of the class. But not being seen to treat him differently was always uppermost in my mind. It was probably weird for him and it was certainly weird for me this detached relationship we had to display during school time. I didn't want to give his peers any ammunition for nagging or baiting him.

One evening on the drive home he opened up about a problem he was having. He fancied a particular girl in another class and they had once met in town to go to the cinema. But that morning the girl's monster of a cousin had cornered James and threatened that he 'better not mess her around or you'll have me to deal with.' The cousin was a big, hefty lad and James was small for his age. And James was a country boy, used to open skies and green fields not the hard edged street lore of the kids who grew up in the city. He'd never encountered physical threats like this before and wasn't sure how to react. Neither was I.

Then I had an idea. A scene from an old black and white American film came to mind, one where the dad gets out his old boxing gloves and teaches his son to box so that he can stand up to the neighbourhood bullies. I hadn't got any old boxing gloves but I did remember the basic karate course I had done in Jamaica. Maybe that was the answer.

So I enrolled myself and James on a course in Karate-Do Chojinkai at the Sands Centre in Carlisle. In so-doing we entered the esoteric world of of the 'dojo' and the 'sensei', a world of mystery and curious ritual. It wasn't a club it was a 'dojo'. The man in charge, Doug James, wasn't a teacher he was a 'sensei'. He taught us moves which were precise and stylised, no free movement or liberal punching as in boxing; this was a kind of choreography of stepping, kicking, punching and blocking. We had to learn strange utterances to accompany our punches and lunges. We wore a special white jacket and knee length pants tied with a belt. There was a particular way of tying the belt, symbolic of the journey we had embarked on. You started with a white belt and graduated to ever darker colours as you progressed up the ladder to the ultimate black belt status. It was all about mental and physical discipline. We were to be equipped with knowledge which was potentially lethal. Our fists and feet would become our secret weapons, never to be unleashed unless it was a matter of life and death. According to the sensei, the most important weapon we would acquire was the confidence to walk away from a fight. To this end we had to sign a vow:

"I promise to uphold the true spirit of Karate-Do and never to use the skills that I am taught against any persons, except for the defence of myself, family or friends in the instance of extreme danger or unprovoked attack, or in support of law and order."

I liked the sound of all this and felt a parental glow that I was doing the right thing for young James. Thus we started the journey from white belt to yellow belt. This involved learning a routine of steps, kicks, blocks and punches which would be closely assessed in a few months time. There were a lot of youngsters like James in the dojo and a number of honed and toned young men sporting darker belts. Their strength, quickness and skill were a little intimidating to an ageing greenhorn like me and, compared to the balletic grace and fluency of the lithe youngsters, I felt something of a clumping old carthorse.

As the weeks passed my enthusiasm for this venture began to wane. I was never going to be much good and the thought that I might fail my yellow belt assessment in front of James and the assembled dojo filled me with dread. On top of this came James' announcement that the girl friend had been dropped and that he was now 'good mates' with her monster of a cousin. This rather undermined the whole purpose of the project and I began to think that maybe James would be better cultivating his natural sense of fun and good humour to disarm the bullies rather than becoming a super-fit fighting machine.

The day of the assessment arrived. We assembled in the gym as usual checking we had tied our belts correctly and bowed to the sensei. Then we waited our turn. The routines were done in pairs in the middle of the gym, watched by the 30 or so other members of the dojo. I had been secretly practising the routine in front of the mirror in the bedroom trying to remember the sequence of moves. I was not confident that I could pull this off.

Finally our names were called and James and I went out on to the floor. James knew the routine backwards and I was glad he was slightly in front of me so that if I was consumed by nerves and forgot what to do I could always copy his moves.

It wasn't a disaster but I was seriously out of my comfort zone. Forty-five year old joints don't flex like those of a fourteen year old and I probably looked rather foolish out there on the floor kicking and punching the air and grunting 'Keyaye!' at every lunge.

As we drove home and James was fingering our new yellow belts he said, 'Thanks dad, we did okay, didn't we. But you know you don't have to carry on with this just for me. I'm okay, you know.'

Another lesson in parenting, when your son offers you an escape route from further embarrassment. 'Well, if you don't mind then. Maybe we'll concentrate on tennis now the weather's getting better,' I replied casually.

I don't know if he gave me a wry smile. But he probably did.

*

'...SONOFAGUN WE'LL HAVE BIG FUN ON THE BAYOU'   (OR NOT!)

94% humidity. No air conditioning, just a sluggish paddle fan. Night time temperature of 74F. Mosquitoes like B52 bombers drilling holes in the night air. Cicadas jangling our nerves with their incessant rhythms. Clouds of insects round the outside lights. We were entombed in the cabins of 'SS Athena', an old Mississippi tug boat which had been reassembled on the banks of Bayou Sorrel in the Atchafalaya River Basin of Louisiana. This was our accommodation for three days kindly arrange by Chris and Brad, our old friends from Miami. We had stayed at their  farm in Oklahoma during our drive across America in the summer of 1984 and now, almost ten years later, we were enjoying a grand reunion, although 'grand' wasn't quite how we felt on this particular night.

It was the third week of our summer holiday. The term had ended on a high note. The boycott of the first English SATS had worked and the education minister's reputation was starting to melt. And now there was a five week holiday revisiting our friends in America.

We had spent the first week on the New Jersey shore with the Moyers family: Judy, her three children and now four grandchildren. Life had moved on for us all since our time in Jamaica but the connections of friendship were as strong as ever.

We had driven from New Jersey the 1000 miles to Tulsa, Oklahoma, for our reunion with Chris and Brad. And they surprised us with an unexpected addition to our trip – a flight down to Houston, Texas and then a road trip to Brad's childhood home in Morgan City, Louisiana. But before that we would divert into the Louisiana bayou country with accommodation in the saloon and wheelhouse of a Mississippi tug boat, the aforementioned 'SS Athena'.

On that first night on the bayou, I woke out of a fitful sweat-soaked sleep to hear someone crying. I nudged Sue. 'I think Chris is crying,' I murmured.

'Who's that?' whispered Katie who was also struggling to sleep.

'Ssh!' I hissed. We listened. There it was again.

'She's not crying,' said Sue. 'Chris is giggling!'

I got up and switched on the light. It was like a teenage sleepover. We had all dragged mattresses out of the small stifling cabins and on to the floor of the tug boat's more airy saloon. Chris was shaking her head, hands over her face. 'I'm so sorry, guys. You drive 1000 miles to see us and we end up in this heap of vintage crap. It sounded so exotic in the brochure – 'SS Athena, a genuine 'ol man river' tug boat' - but I reckon they should have sunk the old gal instead of resurrecting her and dumping her on the side of this croc infested swamp creek. Oh my lord, what must you be thinking?'

We reassured Chris that it was just part of life's rich tapestry and in the morning it all looked very different. The sun filtered through the cypresses and their branches hung with 'ol man's beard'; there were exotic butterflies and birds, fish jumping, the locals fishing and small boats busy on the silky brown waters of the bayou.

This was 'swamp country' a rather off-beat world where life focused entirely on the creeks, bayous and backwaters and whatever swam or crawled there. The local eateries boasted such exotics as 'Crawfish Etouffee, Blackened Catfish, Bayou PonPon Chicken, Lump Crabmeat  Cocktail'. There were 'Swamp-Boat Tours' with invitations to view ferocious Snapper Turtles, Alligators and Anacondas. The swamp lands sucked you into a labyrinth of snaking creeks and channels where hermits lived in floating shacks and hung snake skins out to dry; where hunters tracked alligators and fishermen wrestled with huge spike-backed catfish. It was a land that time forgot, different from any place I had ever visited.

From the bayou we drove to Morgan City, the place where Brad grew up and where his parents still lived. A bit like Huck Finn, Brad's great grandfather, as a young man, had drifted down the Mississippi from Ohio to Morgan City to seek his fortune. He and his family had fled the Gettysburg battlefield in 1863 when their farm was over-run by the Confederates. And now we were sharing a table with that young man's descendants, a table groaning with an array of southern cooking, courtesy of Brad's dear mother. There was fried chicken, cornbread, crawfish bisque, jumbo shrimp and baked okra, followed by Mississippi mud pie and ice cream. This was Louisiana summertime and the livin' was certainly easy.

A few days later after our return to Tulsa we were back in the hire car driving the 1000 miles east to the Washington. It was our first time back to the capital since 1983 when we were en route to our year in Miami. But this time the tourist sites beckoned – the Lincoln Memorial, the Washington Monument, the Capitol building, The Smithsonian Institute. We were staying, appropriately, at a Days Inn, on Connecticut Avenue and what was memorable about that visit was not so much the impressive marble buildings with their grand columns and towering majesty but something else.

In the hotel lobby, in the elevators and in the lounges were groups of men - loud, back-slapping buddies all wearing red tee shirts, shirts which bulged with biceps and pecs and barrel chests. On the backs of the shirts were printed the words: 'Mike's Company'. It was obviously some sort of reunion and there was laughter and banter and the typical swagger of men meeting up for some sort of 'jolly'.

It was only later that morning that I realised my naiivety. We had walked the short distance from the Lincoln Memorial to see the Memorial Wall for those killed in Vietnam. Nearby on the grass there was a service of remembrance taking place fronted by an army chaplain. He was reading out names, the names of 'Mike's Company' who had not returned. The veterans, in their red tee shirts, stood with their families, heads bowed, holding small American flags. Some were openly weeping and being comforted by their wives. The children held their fathers' hands and looked confused. And when the service was over, they progressed down the line of the Memorial Wall searching for names, sometimes kneeling, sometimes just leaning their heads against the wall.

The architect of the Memorial Wall, Maya Lin, was just 21 and an undergraduate when she designed it in 1981. Constructed of black gabbro rock mined in Bangalore, India, the surface of the polished wall displays the names of the 58,267 dead soldiers, listed in the order in which they died. It was a controversial design which met with a lot of criticism at the time. One veteran, Tom Carhart, described it as 'a black gash of shame and sorrow.' To appease the criticism another memorial was added, a statue of three young soldiers designed by Frederick Hart. The statue of the three men is intricately detailed in bronze and was unveiled on Veterans' Day in 1984. Of the two memorials Hart said, 'I see the wall as a kind of ocean, a sea of sacrifice that is overwhelming and nearly incomprehensible in the sweep of names. I place these figures upon the shore of that sea, gazing upon it, standing vigil before it, reflecting the human face of it, the human heart.'

*

THE INSPECTORS COMETH

I was looking at Windows for the first time. The colours were stunning, the graphics out of this world. Bill Gates' company, Microsoft, had pulled off a coup like no other. They had launched a computer system, Windows 3.1, which completely changed things. Up until now I had used our ageing BBC Master computers for word processing, desk top publishing and for educational games. Beyond that I wasn't able to fathom the type of programming to go any further. But now, wow! Windows 3.1 was a system which was simple. There were pull down menus at the touch of a button, you could switch from one 'window' to another effortlessly. And the new computers were 'multi-media' – they didn't use the old bendy 'floppy' discs but smaller rigid 3.5 inch wide discs and they would play what were called CD Rom discs. Up to now there had been the audio CD discs which had been rapidly replacing cassette tapes for listening to music. CD Rom discs, however, were able to store graphics, data and audio files. You could get CD Rom encyclopedias which presented information with sound, film clips, coloured diagrams. It was truly revolutionary - a window on a brave new educational world.

The school was being equipped with what were called PC (Personal Computer) machines and the old BBCs were being unceremoniously dumped. I had to jump on this new band wagon and get myself one of these multimedia PCs. I scanned the computer brochures and finally decided on a machine made by CLASSICL. For purposes of comparison with modern machines here's the spec. for my *'powerful 486 Multimedia PC'* in 1993: Processor 25MHz , RAM 4Mb, Hard Drive 120 Mb, Sound: 16 bit card and speakers. Pre-installed with Windows 3.1 Cost? £1299+ VAT.

In addition there was a bonanza of glitzy software you could buy but for me it was Microsoft Word and Microsoft Publisher which were my new babies. They opened up a world of print and graphic options which made our FAX newspaper of 1990 look decidedly amateurish.

Add to these developments the arrival of the new ink-jet printers and better photocopying machines and the possibilities stretched away into an exciting educational future.

What was not so exciting was the prospect of a visit from the new government inspection regime of Ofsted (Office For Standards in Education) established by an Act of Parliament in 1992. Prior to this there had been a fairly relaxed system of inspection by HMI (Her Majesty's Inspectorate) or by local inspectors. But Ofsted was different. Ofsted was rigorous, aggressive and under the leadership of its first chief executive, Chris Woodhead, ruthless. He reckoned there were 15,000 incompetent teachers and it was his mission to weed out the weak. There would be no hiding place for poor teachers, incompetent Heads or senior managers – the Woodhead mantra was: 'I am paid to challenge mediocrity, failure and complacency'. For him the gloves were off and there was a major shake-up coming.

Woodhead was in, but thankfully John Patten was out. This hapless education minister resigned in 1994 having alienated so many in the educational world, the ultimate ignominy coming when he described the brilliant Birmingham education chief, Tim Brighouse, as 'a madman...wandering the streets, frightening the children'. Brighouse sued and won substantial damages and not long afterwards Patten resigned.

So we waited for the letter from Ofsted announcing when they would pounce. We would get two months notice, two months in which the worms of neurosis and paranoia could squirm as the countdown clock ticked. But it gave us a chance to set our house in order, to prepare glossy departmental files and brochures, tidy up stock cupboards, spruce up display boards.

In the days before our first Ofsted inspection the tension in the school stretched to snapping point. Nerves were shredded, and blood pressure soared.

I tried to reassure my department that we had nothing to fear. Our exam results were exemplary; we were innovative, enthusiastic. But that wasn't enough to allay the fear of having your lesson scrutinised by a faceless bureaucrat sitting at the back of your class. Nobody was immune to that. And the fear was fuelled by the stories which circulated about Ofsted inspections in other schools. How the inspectors waited at the school gates and interrogated the pupils as they went into school. How one Headteacher suffered a heart attack and died during a debriefing. How Ofsted inspectors hid in cupboards and spied through keyholes. Some schools resorted to bussing their bad lads out for a school trip on the day of the inspection to avoid lesson disruption. Others tried to mask and massage the obvious deficiencies in the school. The nightmare stories swirled like fallen leaves in a graveyard. And there was no halting the day of reckoning.

They arrived early, eight of them, with files and brief cases and wearing sharp suits – six men, two women, one of whom wore black stilettoes. Ronnie, the site manager, was the first to voice his displeasure. 'If she marks my waxed floors with those bloody pointy shoes she'll have me to answer to!' Ronnie was well known throughout the caretaker fraternity for the shine on the wooden floors at Newman School. The first whiff of grapeshot was in the air.

As it happened, these 'faceless bureaucrats' turned out to be not unreasonable people. The school did feel strange during those four days of the inspection. A foreign presence had infiltrated the very air we were breathing and you never knew when an inspector would pop out of from behind some coat pegs or emerge from one of your rooms. You tried to read their expressions after a lesson observation but they gave nothing away, no hint, no feedback. Had the lesson gone well? badly? What was their assessment on the scale of 'Unsatisfactory to Outstanding'? We were told nothing. We would have to wait for their final report on the last day.

With my own lessons I debated whether to take risks or play safe. The inspectors were looking for pupil participation, interaction, not some safe lesson with heads down doing some writing task in total silence. So I gambled. The inspector for English had hinted that he would probably drop in on my Year 10 GCSE group so I decided to bite the bullet. We would use a brilliant new book that I had just bought: *Shakespeare's Insults: Educating Your Wit* by Wayne Hill and Cynthia J. Ottchen. It was a compilation of quotations from Shakespeare's plays but all the quotes were a delicious use of strong insulting language. The students would work in pairs and put together an exchange of insults which they would then perform in front of the class while circling each other as if preparing for a fight. It would be used as part of their GCSE oral assessment and hit the syllabus criterion of 'Knowledge About Language' as well as being a piece of drama.

The students filed into the class followed by the inspector who took his place at the back of the class. This was a top set year 10 group who were great to teach. They were bright, sharp youngsters and I'd established a good rapport with them over the past few months. I outlined the task and they were given twenty minutes to put together their script. There was a buzz of banter but heads were down and pens were busy.

Finally, I stopped them and asked for volunteers to perform their 'Dialogue of Declamations'. There was a pregnant silence as they waited for someone to go first but then two of the girls, Steph and her friend Jo, raised their hands. They were both in the school drama club and had the confidence to take the floor. I had said they must circle each other and try to lock eyes while still reading from their scripts. Their exchange went something like this:

S: What ho, pernicious blood sucker of sleeping men, malicious censurer!
J: Dunghill groom, you fat and greasy citizen!
S: You quintessence of dust, carcass fit for hounds!
J: Oh well, King of codpieces, you vile worm, hodge-pudding!
S. Huh, a pox of wrinkles, you are a needy hollow-eyed wretch. Go hang!
J. You idle weed, iron-witted fool, poisonous bunch-backed toad! Away with you...'

While they continued I glanced at the inspector. He was watching and then making notes, his face betraying nothing. I might have made a gross miscalculation here. If he was humourless, this lesson might be judged 'Unsatisfactory' and for a Head of Department that was going to be very embarrassing.

Steph and Jo finished to rapturous applause but the inspector was still po-faced. I felt like slinging one or two Shakespearian expletives in his direction. The class was responding brilliantly and deserved to be commended. They were gaining confidence and realising that Shakespeare could be fun. That alone was a breakthrough for many of them who found the mention of Shakespeare intimidating.

At the end of the lesson the students filed out and the inspector got up. He came towards me, face still impassive but as he caught my eye he nodded, 'I enjoyed that. Well done.'

I could have hugged him, kissed him, shined his shoes. They weren't supposed to give anything away but his words were like gold-dust and I breathed a sigh of relief. Maybe there was hope for us after all.

The week didn't go well for everyone. There were smiles and tears but the overall judgement for the school was Satisfactory with Good Features. That would do for now; it would keep the Ofsted wolves from the door for another couple of years. There were targets set which the school had to meet but we could breathe again. At least we knew what an inspection felt like and a new verb had been coined – we had been 'Ofsteded'.

We celebrated with one of Ronnie's legendary barbecues. Our big-hearted site-manager had, for a while, been doing a monthly barbecue for the Newman staff and their families. Come rain or shine, winter or summer, Ronnie would set up his barbecue on the small covered patio just outside the staff-room and cook mountains of sausages and burgers. It was a generous gesture which helped to engender the 'family' feel of the school and staffroom.

'So how was Ofsted for you, Ronnie?' I asked.

He prodded a couple of sausages with extra vehemence. 'Don't talk to me about Ofsted. That woman inspector lady with the nails and the stiletto shoes, she tells me the hall floor might be a health and safety risk. Too shiny she says. Well I told her. It's taken me years to get that shine on that floor and everyone who comes comments on that hall. It's known throughout the city. Go to Newman School, people say, and just take a look at Ronnie's floors. That's the way to polish a floor, I told her.'

'What did she say?' I asked.

'I didn't give her much chance. I was very polite and I said, 'Maybe your shoes are something of a health and safety risk. Wouldn't do to turn your ankle during an inspection'. And then she just walked off, muttering to herself.' He shook his head and offered me a bun. 'Ketchup on your burger?'

*

Summer of 1994 – a time for reflection. Katie had completed her GCSE course and results day in August was a day of smiles. She had done well. Now it was James who would start his final GCSE year. The summer had been spent once again in France and the Jamaica connections lived on. Our Pennsylvania friend Judy was travelling by train round Europe with husband Boyd. We trailed the caravan through France to a campsite on the south side of Lake Geneva and then drove to Geneva station to pick them up. From there we drove for lunch to a restaurant on the shore of the lake. James insisted we ordered frogs' legs. We didn't know the French for 'frog' and when we pointed to the menu the waitress nodded, 'Ah, kermit.'

'Kermit?' I replied, frowning. 'Sounds like a German word.'

'As in the Muppets, dad,' said Katie, groaning. 'You know, Kermit the frog?'

'Ah, Kermit,' I nodded and smiled at the waitress. 'Oui, une assiete de kermits, s'il vous plait.'

'A plate of Muppets?' said Katie. ' That's what we are, a load of Muppets not bothering to learn the language properly.'

We spent a week camped by the lake, swimming, wind surfing and celebrating our reunion with Judy and Boyd. But it didn't end there. We drove into Geneva and collected another of our close friends from Jamaica days, Katie Megevand, who was now living alone in Geneva, her husband, Philippe, having recently died. There was a sadness about her. Gone was the 'joie de vivre' that Katie M. had shown in Jamaica when she and Philippe ran one of the finest restaurants in Kingston. They had had to leave during the violent civil strife of the late 1970s, leave their home, their business, most of their savings and start over. And now Katie had lost her soul mate and there was a vacancy and sadness about her. She hadn't met Judy before and there was much for them to share about their time in Jamaica. I had taught Katie's elder daughter Katarina who was in the same class as Judy's daughter, Amy.

'Why you mus' teach them that *Henry the fifth* play?' asked Katie M. 'Katarina hated that one. Why not *Romeo and Juliet* or *Antony and Cleopatra*? Now those are plays she would have liked.'

'Yes, Amy found the Shakepeare hard going,' added Judy.

I shrugged, 'No choice, I'm afraid. That was the play for the exam they had to take. I didn't find it easy I can tell you, trying to teach a play which was written to stir the hearts of an English audience in the 1600s.'

'That Priory School was a great school though. My kids loved it,' said Judy. 'They still talk about it.'

'And mine,' said Katie M. 'Those were special times for us all.'

It was a rare meeting, this warm reunion on the shore of Lake Geneva and I felt pleased that Katie and James were able to hear something of those special years in Jamaica.

Katie Megevand had lost Philippe and I was now losing my father. Little by little the early stages of dementia were stealing him away. He had been a big personality throughout my life, always centre stage at social gatherings, a brilliant pianist who could turn his hand to a Chopin Polonaise, a Rachmaninov Prelude or a repertoire of dance tunes. But now his repertoire was shrinking. My mother reported that he tended to play the same tunes over and over. He had stopped initiating conversation. He would still respond but he was becoming increasingly passive and my mother, who had for all her married life lived in his shadow was now taking over the reins of their lives. It was a curious reversal. He was retreating into the shadows and she was emerging.

At their golden wedding celebration at a hotel in Beverley in the spring of 1995, it was she who made the speech and it was she who steered my father's hand to cut the cake. There was a grand piano in the lounge and, inevitably, my father was drawn to the keyboard. He played from memories locked deep in his brain and it was touching that he could still play at all, so much had been lost.

In an attempt to try to assess how much had been lost I tried a little test during a visit to Cumbria. He had sat at the keyboard of my piano and started his familiar dance tunes when I placed in front of him a copy of Sibelius' *Finlandia* which he used to rattle off with ease. He frowned and stared at the music and then tried to find the chords. His fingers stumbled and hit wrong notes. He became agitated.

'Don't worry, dad, carry on with what you were playing,' I said. I felt dreadful and removed the sheet music.

'Just out of practice,' he said and went back to playing his dance tunes.

I could have wept that I'd pushed him too far. I had to accept what was, not what had been.

*

Easter 1995, and we were on a mission, a literary mission. James was due to take his GCSEs in the summer and in an attempt to aid his English Literature revision we would travel to Thomas Hardy country. He was studying *Far From The Madding Crowd*, the same novel I had taught to my O level class in Jamaica. I had shown them John Schlesinger's wonderful film of the novel which captured the sweep of the Dorset downland in a way which lodged in my memory and in my heart. I had devoured several of Hardy's novels when I was sixteen and I was anxious for James to experience the same enchantment.

After the long drive south towing the caravan, we set up camp on a cliff-top site just south of Dorchester. Here we were well placed to be able to visit key locations in Hardy's 'Wessex'. There was a museum in Dorchester with a reconstruction of Hardy's study; there was the beach at Durdle Door where Sergeant Troy fakes his own drowning. There was the iron age fortress of Maiden Castle where Troy shows off his dexterity with his razor sharp sabre to the amazement and trepidation of a quivering Bathsheba Everdene. And finally there was the birthplace itself, the cob and thatched cottage at Higher Bockhampton where Hardy had actually written the novel. From our caravan pitch high on the cliff top I could look out over the rolling chalk downland and imagine Bathsheba carrying the milk pails from the milking shed and see Gabriel Oak herding his sheep down to the sheep pen in the valley. This was enchantment indeed. How long before James would fall under the Hardy spell?

We started off in Dorchester, touring the museum and the clever reconstruction of Hardy's study. There was his writing desk and chair; his pen, his blotter, his ink well, his book cabinet. James didn't say much but I imagined he was quietly imbibing the ambience and the spiritual presence of the great author.

Then we were off to Maiden Castle, the magnificent Iron Age hill fort, one of the largest in Western Europe, where Hardy sets the scene with Sergeant Troy and Bathsheba. The fort is a series of steep grassy banks and ditches, rising in several tiers to the crown of the fort. In the film Terence Stamp simulates a cavalry charge, cantering down the bank towards Julie Christie on his imaginary steed and sweeping his sabre close to her face in a series of passes which leave her quivering with excitement.

It was clear to me that in order to bring Hardy's dramatic scene to life, Sue and I should re-enact the scene for the benefit of James and Katie. They seemed a little distracted and complained that it was past lunchtime but I felt sure that the drama of our performance would refocus their attention and certainly help James with his exam preparation. I hadn't access to a real 19th cent. sabre so I had to make do with a stout bracken stem from which I stripped the leaves. I got Sue to stand on one of the lower tiers and adopt a suitably demure, maidenly pose while I cantered up the slope to prepare for my Sergeant Troy routine.

From a distance of about thirty yards I signalled that I was ready and Sue signalled back. This was it then. Holding my bracken stem aloft I set off at speed galloping down the slope uttering a high-pitched roar appropriate to that of an attacking cavalry officer and pointing my sabre in the direction of Sue's quivering Bathsheba. I made two passes before stopping to demonstrate my sabre skills in front of her. It was only when my sharply erect bracken stem bent into a flaccid wand and Sue collapsed giggling on to the grass that I felt that maybe the spell of the drama had been broken. As for Katie and James they seemed unamused and just shrugged and shook their heads at me.

The climax of our Hardy odyssey was a visit to the hallowed ground of the birthplace. I had been recording our visit on my new video camera knowing that when we returned home this audio-visual record would be useful in the run-up to James' exam. We approached the cottage at Higher Bockhampton along a rising woodland path and I could see the outline of the thatched roof through the trees. Katie and James were some way ahead so I called for them to stop while I got the camera ready. I wanted to record their approach to the house and hopefully James opening the door and stepping over the threshhold.

They stood at the top of the rise with their backs to me waiting for my signal. I checked the camera and peered through the viewfinder, finger at the ready to start recording. I signalled with my hand and called out, 'Action.'

They both bent over, lowered their jeans and presented me with a pair of pale moons.

'What did you expect?' said Sue, shaking her head and laughing.

Katie came down the hill, grinning. 'Is that in the can, dad, or should we do a re-take?'

I kept a straight face and replied, 'Maybe we should adjourn to the Gabriel Oak tea rooms and review this morning's footage over a Bathsheba bap and chips.'

'Now you're talking dad. Let's do it,' said James. It was the first time he'd shown much enthusiasm all morning. 'Oh yeah, I meant to ask,' he continued. 'In the museum there was something about his mistress. Did she say, 'Kiss me, Hardy' ?'

'Wrong Hardy, James,' said Katie. 'That was Nelson at the battle of Trafalgar. Better not put that in your literature exam. Don't think they'd be impressed.'

*

DOWN THE TUBE.

September 1995 and I was sitting in a small Information Technology room we had just set up. I was staring at a monitor, waiting. If Fax had been a revolutionary development for the school in 1990, we were now on the cusp of something even more exciting – video conferencing. To be able to actually see the person you were talking to was truly amazing. And what about the possibilities for the students? We could share ideas and experiences with students from John O'Groats to Lewisham. There could be international links with Spanish and French schools. Sixth formers could have tutorials with eminent professors on far flung university campuses. The possibilities were endless.

Meanwhile I waited for our call from a school on the other side of the city. It was part of a pilot project which had connected three schools around Carlisle to foster links for teachers and students. I adjusted the camera which was clamped to the top of the monitor, checked that I looked presentable and then heard the ring tone. The monitor flickered and then the face of Tony Roper, a senior teacher from

415

William Howard School, appeared on the screen. He waved, I waved back. We exchanged pleasantries and then wondered what to do next. It was obvious there had to be a visual focus for the connection, otherwise you might just as well pick up a telephone. It certainly was novel seeing the person's face as well as hearing his voice but the money invested for this pilot project had to be justified on educational grounds. It wasn't enough just to smile and wave and congratulate ourselves on how clever we were.

We decided to organise a project with a small group of year 10 students. They could develop their Speaking and Listening skills which was a key area in the new English National Curriculum. That would impress any passing Ofsted inspector.

The first obstacle that cropped up was that our year 10 students didn't have English lessons at the same time as the William Howard students, so special arrangements were made and the following week a group of six Newman students clustered round the monitor and waited for the call. They were to take it in turns asking questions of the other students, questions they had prepared themselves. This would be a first for our schools, students sharing their knowledge on a video-conference link-up. It was certainly worthy of a write up in the local press.

The clock ticked towards the appointed time for the call. The students were nervous and so was I. Then the call tone rang out. I clicked the mouse button and, hey presto, there was Geoff Meadows, the William Howard English teacher surrounded by a cluster of students.

'Who wants to go first?' I asked my group.

'I'll do it,' replied Richard, eager to sit in front of the monitor. I moved out of the way and he took over the 'hot seat'. The others clamoured round behind him.

'Okay,' I said to the faces in the monitor. 'This is Richard and he's going to ask some questions. Who's he talking to first?'

There was a clamour of 'Me, me..' coming from the monitor and then a girl took her place in the chair. 'Hi, I'm Michele.'

Suddenly, boy meets girl, eye to eye down a video conferencing link. Immediate embarrassment and giggling. Richard consumed with shyness fumbling with his piece of paper. The girl takes the initiative.

'What are your favourite subjects at school?'

Richard is squirming. The others are nudging him.

'Er, English, and, er, history.' Richard is looking down at his paper. He can't take the girl's eyes and smile. It's all too close for him.

'Can't stand history,' giggles the girl. 'I like French. Can you speak any French? Parlez vous francais?' she smiles.

'I can,' says David, 'here let me have a go.' Then I hear him whisper to his mate John. 'She's okay, her. I fancy that.'

David muscles into the hot seat and Richard moves out of the line of fire, relieved. 'What bands d'you like then?' asks David, all smiles, drinking in the eyes of this vivacious girl in the monitor. 'Foo Fighters, me.'

'They're garbage,' says Michele. 'D'you watch *Friends*? It's the best.'

'S'okay. Jennifer Aniston's cool. What footy team d'you support?'

'ManU,' shouts a voice from behind Michele. A cheer goes up.

'I hate them. Everyone supports them. What about Carlisle?' asks David.

'Carlisle are rubbish,' shouts another voice.

It's all getting rather messy. There was meant to be an orderly process of question and answer not this hormone fuelled free-for-all with faces of students thrusting themselves into the frame of the monitor and more riotous giggling.

'What's *her* name?' says a new face in the monitor, pointing a finger. Michele appears to have been unceremoniously elbowed aside. 'The one with the long blond hair.'

Shy Annie Duckworth is thrust into the line of the camera by David who yanks her forward into the hot seat. 'This is Annie,' says David.

'Hi Annie,' says the new face, 'I'm Kev. What sort of music d'you like? D'you go clubbing?'

Annie has lost the power of speech. She shakes her head and shrugs.

'Sorry, Annie, this is a bit in-yer-face isn't it,' says Kev. 'Maybe we could meet up.'

At this point, Geoff intervenes. It's not quite going to plan. His face appears in the monitor. 'Well, Newman, this was a first, probably a global first for video-conferencing in schools. Thank you for taking part but it's lunch time for us so we'll have to rearrange for another time.'

There is a collective groaning from both sets of students. Clearly they are just warming up.

I thrust my face into the eye of the camera. 'Thanks to you all. This was just a trial run. I'll be meeting up with Mr Meadows to see how we can develop this further. Bye for now.'

My students were not happy. 'That was just getting interesting, sir,' said David, 'why did you cut it short?'

'Wasn't too happy with the sound quality, David. It was a bit iffy. And I need to speak to the technician about improving the visuals. There's a lot of money invested in this project.'

Video-link pupils focus on the wider picture

It was all lies but also an unsettling lesson in how quickly youngsters could hijack the new technology and make it their own.

Later that day I ran into the Head. 'How did it go?' he asked.

'Great,' I said. 'It all worked splendidly. The students were very enthusiastic.'

'How did you organise it? What exactly did they talk about?'

'Oh, they had prepared questions on various subjects and they, er, took it in turns to question each other.'

'Like a debate?'

'Something like that. Very impressive I can tell you.'

'Good. Well done.'

If our initial try-out with video-conferencing was somewhat anarchic, we followed up with a more civilised link between two groups of sixth formers. At the Newman end there was Katie and her friends Ella and Dawn exchanging pleasantries with some boys from William Howard School. BBC cameras were there at both ends of the link to capture this 'global first' for the Look North programme and there was coverage in the Cumberland News of the event. We were well pleased with out latest efforts to harness the new technology which was exploding in so many new directions.

In fact in the autumn of 1995 a new word entered the vocabulary of computerspeak. It was the word 'Internet', a word which had just been given official approval by the FNC (Federal Networking Council), an American forum which monitored new developments in technology. Apparently this 'internet' was a way of linking computers world wide. It was all a mystery to us and when I mentioned it to the Head of Science at Newman he was pretty cynical, 'It's just a fad, it'll never catch on.'

Later in the term I caught up with the Head again. 'I'd like you to look at some PSE material that's just been sent through; on sex education. I need your opinion.'

He raised his eyebrows and nodded. 'Will you see my secretary and make an appointment.'

I had been scratching around for new material for the PSE course and some sample booklets had arrived which I thought were brilliant. They were cartoon strips of various aspects of sex education but they included sketches of male genitals, female genitals, masturbation, menstruation – it was all there, clearly explained and presented with a sensitive lightness of tone and humour but without underplaying any of the issues. Would the Catholic fraternity tolerate such 'subversive' material? I wondered. I certainly wasn't going to authorise the purchase and distribution of these little books without agreement from a higher authority.

I was pleasantly surprised and reassured by the Head's response. He flicked through the booklets, shrugged a little, sighed and then nodded, 'I suppose we have to go down this route if we're going to be delivering something which is honest and realistic.'

'I think so,' I agreed. 'Thank you.'

When the books were handed out to the Year 9 classes some weeks later in their PSE lesson it was like giving out gold dust. After a few initial 'oohs' and 'aahs' and a few sniggers, you could have heard a pin drop for the full duration of the lesson. I'm not sure the tutors were so comfortable with fielding questions on such a tricky subject area but I was less bothered about their discomfort than I was in improving the understanding of the students.

How to help them make their way through the jungle that is puberty? That was my challenge and this material was certainly an improvement on what I had encountered at the same age. I remember at age 14 my friend Terry Hardwick producing a brand new hardback copy of *Lady Chatterley's Lover* from under his coat. His father had given it to him with the blessing, 'Read that son, and you'll be all right.' Those were the bad old days of utter ignorance about sexual matters apart from illicit pickings gleaned from biology books or lurid tales passed down by older boys.

Knowledge was power, knowledge was control and it was my aim to try to help these youngsters with what they needed to navigate the tricky world of relationships. Not easy but at least I'd made a start.

*

COMING OF AGE

The police car arrived at around 11.30. No-one heard it. There were no flashing lights, no siren. The car just purred down the lane and stopped. Two young officers appeared at the gate.

It was Katie's 18th birthday. The garden was full of people, there were lights in the trees, faces glowing in the firelight from the fire-pit, bubbles of laughter, the clink of glasses. My older brother had just done a toast to Katie and then the music had been cranked up and Katie and half a dozen other girls cavorted under the pine trees singing a wild version of Queen's *Bohemian Rhapsody*. That was probably the clincher which triggered the complaint to the police from someone in the village.

'Sorry, but we have to follow up these calls,' said one officer.

'Stop and have a drink,' said Katie, 'we won't tell anyone.'

The office smiled, 'Thanks, but we'll leave you to it.'

'We'll be quiet as church mice,' added Sarah, Katie's cousin.

'I somehow doubt it,' replied the officer. 'Just keep it down a bit.' He closed the gate and got back in the car.

'He looked a bit tasty,' said one of the girls. 'Something cool about men in uniforms.'

18 years old. It was hard to believe. So much had happened at this old house of ours. Katie had been born four weeks after we moved in and now she was on the verge of taking wing. Literally. After A levels next summer she was planning to do a 'gap' year somewhere. She'd spoken of Mexico where she could use her Spanish. We'd always encouraged her to be adventurous and independent. Now the chickens were coming home to roost. When she was first born I made a vow to myself that she must be brought up to be as fearless and confident as any boy, confident about swimming, sailing, climbing mountains. It didn't always go according to plan of course. A few weeks ago she had asked me to move the car out of the drive.

'You can do it,' I said casually and threw her the keys. She'd just started driving lessons and this was a chance for her to try herself out. She hesitated. 'Go on,' I said, nudging her just that little bit further.

Ten minutes later she was back in the kitchen in tears. She flung the keys on the table. 'Sorry dad, I hit the wall.'

As a parent you win some, you lose some. There wasn't a lot of damage to the car, more to Katie's pride but it was a lesson for me. It's good to push them but not too fast and not too far. Although Mexico did sound a long way away.

We'd pushed the two of them out of the nest the previous summer. Off to America on their own as soon as the GCSE exams were over. This was to be a major initiative test for them and when we waved them away down the corridor to Passport Control at Manchester airport it was James who was striding confidently leading the way and Katie who was looking back giving a last wave. She was to stay in Delaware with Zoe who had just had her second child. James was to live with Judy and Boyd, in West Chester PA and work as a bag-boy at their golf club. He would turn sixteen in August, the month of his GCSE results.

We had joined them a few weeks later when term finished. It was good to see each of them away from home, on their own turf, establishing themselves without our help. I marvelled at the way that decision back in 1973 to apply for the jobs in Jamaica had now brought us to this point and to this place.

That first week we sipped the delights of Cape Cod. Our rented cottage was on the southern shore, not far from the Kennedy's summer retreat at Hyannis Port. It was roofed and clad in grey cedar shingles. It looked south towards the sea and, to the rear, a balcony faced one of the 'ponds', those shallow inland lagoons edged with marsh grass where the egrets perch on the salt-bleached docks and dive for fish. From the docks we dangled chicken bones on lengths of string into the water and caught blue crabs. Plunged into a pan of boiling water the crabs turned pink and then, with a small wooden hammer you cracked the shell and eased out the soft white flesh from the body and sucked it from the claws. It was an initiation into one of the many simple pleasure that Cape Cod offers – sifting through sea-shells on the shoreline, listening to the breeze in the marsh grasses of the salt pond, fishing on the dock of the bay, watching the drift of sailboats out on the blue haze of sea and sky – this was therapy indeed after a long school year.

But it was the boat trip out to Martha's Vineyard which was particularly significant for me. For years I had harboured this yearning to be a published writer. I had some early success with a short story published in the Jamaican Daily News and then, from the year in Miami, a series of travel articles, and more recently some education features. Two novels failed to secure publishers but I lived in hope. And now here was Martha's Vineyard, playground of the rich and famous and surely territory ripe for exploitation by an aspiring writer. I took notes, recorded impressions and the result was the article which follows, published in the *Times Educational Supplement* of March 1st 1996. It was written to lift the spirits of dispirited English teachers.

STUFF AS DREAMS ARE MADE ON

You see I have this fantasy about being a writer. That one summer I'll go away on holiday and never come back. That I won't have to give that soul-shuddering groan in the last week of August and resign myself to just being an English teacher who pretends that one day he might be a writer but in the mean time gets this masochistic buzz from teaching the successes of other writers. No! One day the prostitution will be over and I'll be a bona fide writer myself. That's the sneaking fantasy I carry around with me. That's my secret route out. No escape committees for me. I'll go it alone.

And last year I almost convinced myself that I'd arrived. I went with American friends to Cape Cod where real writers have lived – Eugene O'Neill had his first play performed in Provincetown; Hemingway, Emily Dickinson, Robert Lowell, Thoreau – all the literary boys and girls have stayed there at some time or other. I was on promising territory this time.

Now on this particular day we went by ferry across to Martha's Vineyard. If you're a child of the Sixties you must have heard of the place. It's an island about the size of the Isle of Wight just off the south coast of Cape Cod. It's the playground of the beautiful and famous – James Taylor, Carly Simon, Jackie Onassis and Bill Clinton .

We cross Nantucket Sound by ferry to Vineyard Haven and there are yachts and power-boats and lighthouses called East Egg and West Egg and I can see Daisy and Robert Redford waving to Scott Fitzgerald across the water and it's all so exciting – a great place for a writer. There has to be a best-selling article or short story in all this, I tell myself.

So, here I am taking notes like writers do; recording impressions on my little Sony tape recorder, snapping photos; doing the kind of 'research' that writers do. The ferry docks and we all clamber off eager for adventure. Well, we get on this bus to go round the island but I suddenly realise my 16 years old son is having trouble with his co-ordination. He is dribbling and panting and behaving in a very strange manner. We think it's sun stroke, but then it transpires he's just spotted the actress Michelle Pfeiffer in a car across the street and doesn't know what to do about it. 'Michelle Pfeiffer? Are you sure?' I ask. He nods, points and pants some more.

I spend some time hunting round the shops doing a little more research, looking at blondes, taking notes, that sort of thing but Miss Pfeiffer seems to have escaped me.

Anyway, we get on this bus heading for a place called Gay Head. Sounds kind of interesting. The bus is driven by a young fellow called Dave who proceeds to give us a commentary on the history of the island from glaciation to Bill Clinton's golf problems. There are anecdotes such as how this year Carly Simon's annual concert sold out in 18 minutes. He points out the field where the great event is to take place. How Diana Ross likes to be incognito but rides around in a white chauffeur-driven Rolls Royce. I'm scribbling madly in my notebook as I imagine real writers do. And I'm fizzing inside. This is it! On my way down the escape tunnel. Sorry kids – couldn't finish the syllabus. Decided to become a writer instead.

It's all going swimmingly when suddenly Dave comes up with a real howler. Get this. He says that Martha's Vineyard was the inspiration for Shakespeare's play 'The Tempest'. Well, as you can imagine my English teacher's hackles rose. It was like the first shot of the War of Independence being fired all over again. The cheek of it! So Dave goes on with his smug little tale..... and I have to confess it begins to sound vaguely plausible.

You see, the first Englishman to claim territory on Martha's Vineyard in 1602 was Bartholomew Gosnold who came from Falmouth. It was he who named the island after one of his daughters. The 'vineyard' refers to wild grapes which grow on the island. Well, apparently a number of recent Harvard PhDs have claimed that when Gosnold returned to England he met up with Shakespeare in London. Shakespeare read his notes on the trip and was inspired to write 'The Tempest' which was published in 1611.

It was a teasing theory all right. The sort of novel idea which a real writer could use. I was on to something here, what private detectives call a 'lead'. While the rest of the party was gorging on clam chowder and choc-chip ice-cream I was playing Philip Marlowe or maybe Raymond Chandler. I was sniffing around for more information.

I went to the bookshop in Vineyard Haven and browsed the history section. I was after Bartholomew Gosnold's original diaries. They would hold some clues to the veracity of this theory. The book clerk checked the computer. Not in print since 1605. He suggested I went to the Vineyard Museum in Edgartown – 15 miles away. I checked my watch and then noticed the family going towards the ferry back to the mainland. 'C'mon dad, your ice-cream's melting,' yelled my son. He was still looking around for Michelle Pfeiffer. Surely real writers didn't have to worry about ferry times and melting ice-creams. Didn't they just drift around cafes and the salons of wealthy widows?

On the ferry I decided I'd phone the museum in the morning. In the meantime the hunt continued. That evening I got hold of a copy of 'The Tempest' and started looking for clues: you know, references to 'vineyards', that type of thing. My pulse quickened when I found Prospero talking about 'the green sea and the azur'd vault'. That certainly matched the colours of sea and sky around the island. And then I found Caliban referring to 'all the qualities o' the isle/The fresh springs, brine-pits, barren place and fertile.' Hadn't we passed such places on the bus-ride earlier in the day! And what was this – Stephano referring to 'Indians' when he says to Caliban in Act Two, "Do you put tricks upon us with savages and men of Ind?" Now I'd read that the early Plymouth settlers had many encounters with local Indians and reported them to be rather weird looking. It mirrored Stephano's meeting with Caliban exactly.

This was dynamite. I had here the nugget of a notion which could set the academic world alight. Shakespeare inspired by the Americans! It was as sacrilegious as Eurodisney doing an animatronics version of Rodin's 'The Thinker'. All I needed now was some solid data from the Vineyard Museum and my writing career was launched.

Early the following morning I phoned the Vineyard Museum in Edgartown. First I enquired about Gosnold's diaries. 'Gosnold's diaries?' said the voice of the curator. 'Sorry not available.' Then I played my trump card. 'I'm doing a little academic research into a new theory that there's some connection between Shakespeare's 'Tempest' and Martha's Vineyard.' There was a pause. He was clearly impressed. Then I heard him clear his throat, or was it a chortle? 'Pure fantasy,' he quipped. 'But....' I mumbled. 'Some American academic wish-fulfilment,' he added, rubbing salt into my ears. 'A little myth-making. Nothing in it.'

I put the phone down. I was mortified. He had exploded my material, the most original lead I'd ever had. My escape route. The start of my career as a real writer. All gone. My fantasy vaporised in an instant. Like a summer romance fading and in its place the dark caverns of the September classroom beckoning, gremlins at the helm once more.

So I give in, Prospero buddy – we are the stuff that dreams are made on. But then let's face it, writers don't live happy lives either. There are the critics, they're never satisfied. You write a best-seller and they're waiting to guillotine you on your next effort. Then there's the paparazzi at your gate – I couldn't do with that, all those telescopic camera lenses ruining my dahlias.

And then the gloom began to lift as I remember 3B on a Friday afternoon, the most appreciative audience for stories you could get. I picture the scene. 'Stop writing. Did I ever tell about the time when I was *on this bus with Michelle Pfeiffer. We were going to visit Carly Simon and talk about Shakespeare.' Their mouths are open, eyes agog. And for the moment I'm king of the story-tellers.*

Who needs to be a writer?
T.E.S. 1.3.96

*

The holiday didn't end at Cape Cod. We drove north through New York State to Alexandria Bay on the Canadian border. It was where the St. Lawrence River fed into Lake Ontario and where the river was dotted with a thousand islands. This was the original birthplace of Thousand Islands  Dressing, reputedly created by the chef of George Boldt, proprietor of New York's Waldorf-Astoria Hotel and frequent summer visitor to the area. This was the place where Judy's family had vacationed for years. It was always a big family affair – Amy and husband Jim and their four children, Harold and wife Deirdre and Zoe and Scott and their two. We stayed in simple wooden cabins at a place called Pine Bay, a circular inlet off the main St. Lawrence River. It was a sheltered bay edged with granite outcrops and ringed with pine trees, the waters of the bay fresh and clear. There were power boats, sail boats and canoes and a small sandy beach where the toddlers could build sand-castles. It was an idyllic spot to spend a vacation.

We'd first come here with Judy's family in the summer of 1984 after our trip across America, when Katie and James were small. It was a place that didn't change. Always the lap of the water on the rocky shoreline and against the boat dock, the leisure craft in and out of the islands and docking at Alexandria Bay for supplies and sometimes, in the distance, a tanker making its way down the main Ship Canal heading for Lake Ontario. Little changed except that we were all getting a bit older and the children were growing up fast.

*

That Christmas I stepped outside my comfort zone again with my production of *The Dracula Spectacula*, a 'spooky musical'. It was the first full length production I'd produced on my own. Previously I'd dabbled with bits of this and that – the *Skats* dance production and the *Love is a Word* mix of music, drama and poetry were parts of bigger events, whereas this *Dracula* was a full blown production for which I carried the can.

There was a big cast drawn from all sections of the school. Katie's sixth form friend Dan played the leading part of Count Dracula with all the other year groups being involved down to first years in the the Brides of Dracula dance troupe. Rehearsals stretched through the term and a legion of helpers worked on set construction, dance choreography, costumes and lighting. I was anxious that the production should be visually impressive. I experimented with back-lighting, smoke machines, an ultra violet bubble machine and sound effects. I'd acquired a couple of huge silk parachutes from a parent at the Border Regiment and these I slung from the ceiling of the hall to create a cavern-like setting for the scenes in Transylvania. Dracula would have a laboratory with luminous liquids bubbling and steaming in bell jars. Smoke would billow up from an underground lair. Cackling laughter would be scattered from the four corners of the auditorium by quadrophonic speakers. Of course, the danger with all this technical wizardry is that something goes wrong and you end up with a damp squib of a production.

However, it didn't fail. The show ran for three nights and was a resounding success. Finally, I'd laid the ghost of past failures and learned much about stage direction and the potential for using sound and lighting effects. But above all there was the challenge of working with the students and drawing out their talents, their energy and, as with Katie and James and, as with me, building confidence to step into unknown territory and try things which hadn't been tried before.

*

IN MEMORIAM – Spring 1996

The floors of the school had lost some of their shine and there was a chill about the place. Ronnie had died. It was sudden and unexpected and we felt the loss. He had been a key figure in the Newman 'family'. This short, barrel of a man, who feigned truculence but had a heart of gold, had been Frank's right hand man when the school first opened. Under the new Headmaster he had a new title – 'site manager' - but Ronnie was still the same – a little abrasive on first meeting but then the twinkle in his eye which meant 'Let me think about it.' His family barbecues for the Newman staff were legendary and colleague Paul said he'd carry on with this tradition of Ronnie's. But I felt something else was needed, something to mark Ronnie's great contribution to the school.

That spring of '96 the pall of sudden death not only hung over the school but shrouded the airwaves and the pages of newspapers. Sixteen children had been gunned down by a local man in the town of Dunblane in Scotland. This massacre was mind-numbing in its brutality and, like the death of Ronnie, reminded one of the fragility of life and the waywardness of fate.

Then it came to me one day during an exam invigilation in the hall. I was wandering up and down the rows of students who were bent over their exam papers. It was always a tedious way to pass an hour and my attention was soon drawn to the small quadrangle which was enclosed by the hall windows on one side, a science lab and offices on the other three sides. There was a silver birch tree in the middle of this area which was slabbed with grey concrete paving stones; a few scrubby bushes and shrubs filled what passed for flower beds. It was a sad, neglected area which was never used but into which the sun streamed at midday. One of the windows overlooking the area had been Ronnie's office. I had a vision of a secluded garden, a quiet place for colleagues to escape to - a wooden bench, bubbling water, granite boulders and raked gravel - Japanese style, and flowers. Ronnie would have approved, I'm sure. He would have frowned at first, stroked his chin and then given me the skeptical nod of approval.

I wasn't sure the Headmaster would be so enthusiastic, however. There was no easy way in or out of this area. I had just completed installing a stream and a pond in the garden at home and I knew the implications of this type of landscaping project. There would be a tree and around forty paving slabs to be removed along with other debris. Then there would be landscaping materials – soil, maybe some rocks,

427

cobbles and gravel to be brought in with wheelbarrows along narrow corridors and through the print room, which had the only door that opened on to the quadrangle - past the new photocopiers and computers – there was the distinct possibility of some expensive catastrophe; the logistics were horrendous. This was not going to be an easy project to sell to anyone.

I arranged a meeting with the Head. I don't think he knew much about gardening and I underplayed the details about how the project would be carried out. I just presented the idea of a memorial garden which could be a communal facility for staff to enjoy and maintain. He nodded and said that as long as the work took place after school he had no objections.

I left his room somewhat stunned. This romantic vision on which I had been musing during a boring exam invigilation might become a reality. Spring was in the air and it was the right time to embark on such a project. The thought of doing a couple of hours of hard manual work after a day's teaching seemed, on the face of it, a little crazy. However, the reality was quite different. It became a kind of end-of-the-day therapy, donning my overalls and trundling a wheelbarrow. And I was not alone. I had floated the garden idea with the staff and there was a growing team of enthusiastic helpers.

Over the next month we wheeled out the forty concrete slabs, chain-sawed and removed the ageing silver-birch tree, wheel-barrowed in soil, gravel, cobbles and twelve craggy Lake District boulders donated by the Head of Science who lived near Ullswater. Miraculously, there were no collisions between wheelbarrows and Xerox print machines and finally the staff were invited to bring and plant bulbs and plants and shrubs. A group of Design Technology students built wooden planters and I worked on the construction of a rustic bench. In late spring there

was a planting session which was touching in its innocence. Some staff had never had their fingers in soil, had never planted anything in the ground and for them this was a revelation. Finally there was a simple service of dedication which rekindled some fond memories of Ronnie and renewed something of the 'family' feel the school had always fostered but which I felt was being increasingly shredded by a colder culture seeping into education.

Of course, invigilation during the summer exam season now became more difficult. Rather that keeping an eagle eye on the students, my attention was constantly being spirited away to the garden – to the glint of sunlight on the bubbling water, on the brush of a green pine branch against a granite boulder, on the brilliance of the yellow and blue pansies. And at lunch time my rustic bench was in big demand by several colleagues who gathered there for some respite, to close their minds to the classroom and their eyes to some sun warmth for a few stolen moments.

There may have been tranquility in my little memorial garden but in the wider world it was anything but tranquil.

A hundred miles further south a nightmare erupted in the centre of Manchester when, on June 15th, the IRA exploded a 3,300 pound bomb which devastated a section of the central shopping area in Corporation Street. The area had been evacuated after a telephoned warning but over two hundred were injured.

Against this backdrop Katie was taking her A levels and looking to leaving school. Maybe it was also a good time to be leaving the country. She had applied to the 'Gap' organisation to work in Mexico and was awaiting the results of her application. James was ending his first year of A levels and he was in one of my groups for Communication Studies. We had used the news coverage of the Manchester bombing for an analysis of the way the news was being reported. These kinds of national events were useful for comparing news values of different newspapers and then comparing the television and radio coverage. The broadsheet papers were typically more detached, less emotive in their use of photographs and their style of reporting. The tabloids, by contrast, wallowed in the drama with close up shots of blood-soaked victims and personal stories of survivors. Teaching James was never a problem. He was easy-going and a popular figure in the sixth form, not at all self-conscious about having his 'dad' teaching the class which certainly made life easier for me.

But the making of him that year was working at Gianni's, an Italian restaurant in Carlisle. By now he was nudging six feet in height, his face was becoming more chiselled and he had to deal with the overtures of parties of women out for a good night and who, after a few glasses of Chianti, weren't beyond pinching the backside of a young waiter. He took it all in good humour and on several occasions we ate at Gianni's when James was working. To see our son on his own turf, coping so well with the real world of work and other people was great.

As a parent you start to relax a little, knowing that your children are going to be okay without you.

However, on one particular night when we were there, a hen party had ordered glasses of sambuca and requested that they be flamed in the traditional way. James had struck the match, lit the surface of each glass but had not reckoned on one of the girls knocking her drink so that flaming sambuca started running all over the table top. On impulse, James blew on the flames which only spread them further. It was Sue who grabbed a towel and threw it over the table top to smother the flames. There was applause all round, James was a little red-faced but he was still the darling of the ladies who thought this was the best floor show ever.

When he arrived home just before midnight he put his head round our bedroom door and whispered: 'Thanks, mom, you saved my job tonight and I got my biggest tip so far!'

'That's all right,' murmured Sue, half asleep. 'Nice to know we still have our uses.'

*

'I'LL TELL YOU WHAT I WANT,
WHAT I REALLY REALLY WANT…'

I spied my old colleague, Andrew Austin, from Appleby School, high up in the Dress Circle. He'd been Head of English at Appleby when I was first interviewed there back in 1977 and he was still at the

school. Today he was dressed to kill – fish-net tights, a crimson and silver basque, stiletto heals and a fabulously coiffured black wig. He waved and some of his students wearing equally outrageous costumes waved and blew kisses to our students. This was like a performance in itself and the real show hadn't even started.

We were at the Blackpool Grand Theatre for a performance of *The Rocky Horror Show,* the zany 1973 musical by Richard O'Brien which crosses the Frankenstein story of mad scientists creating monsters with B movie Sci-fi and Horror films of the 1950s. The main character, Dr. Frank N. Furter is the bisexual cross-dressing mad scientist who preys on an innocent young couple, Janet and Brad, when they arrive at his castle during a rainstorm. For my students this had distinct echoes of our recent *Dracula Spectacula* production but without the sexual eccentricities of *The Rocky Horror Show*. It was customary for the audience to dress up in costumes from the show. Andrew had bravely gone for the transvestite look; I was more cowardly and wore a tailcoat and top hat.

The Newman students sported a range of styles: elaborate eye and face make-up with black lipstick, fluorescent hair gel, knee length boots, fish-net tights - and that was just the boys! I had checked out the suitability of the show by watching the 1975 film version which starred Tim Curry. Being from a Catholic school you couldn't be too careful and

with the Headmaster's three teenage children attending I had to tread warily. I didn't want to end up on the streets without a job. The film version was pretty outrageous in places but didn't cross any serious moral lines, apart from the start of the second Act, where a disguised Frank seduces first the innocent Janet and then her boyfriend Brad. In the film there is a scene of oral sex but I was sure that for a 'family' show they would leave out such a scene.

The first half of the show went well and the audience were having a ball although an over-strident heckler was singled out by Frank N Furter at one point and told in no uncertain terms to 'shut the f*** up or get out!'. At the interval the students were buzzing with the craziness of it all. There were lots of schools there and the bizarre range of costumes was entertainment in itself.

My mind turned to the opening of the second half. The Headmaster's son was sitting two seats away from me and was, I sensed, a little out of his comfort zone with all this zaniness. The lights dimmed and the curtain came up on a circular cone of light. The silhouette of Frank N Furter appeared face to face with the silhouette of Janet. There was some obvious gyrating and humping of bodies which I hoped was not too shocking. I glanced to my left to check the reaction of the Head's son. He was as attentive as everyone else. So far so good, I thought. But then came the scene with Brad, and the silhouette performance was so obviously one of oral sex with little left to the imagination. With a quiet intake of breath I glanced to my left to hear the comment, 'I don't find this very amusing.' The Head's two daughters were sitting two rows behind me and I wondered how they were reacting and what they would report when they returned home that evening.

Already I had pictured the headlines in the local newspapers, imagined myself hung out to dry – 'Teacher in student corruption scandal......' I could see it now.

I don't remember much about the rest of the show apart from the finale and a riotous rendition of the show's signature song *Time Warp* which had the whole audience on their feet and doing the actions.

Back at school the following week I waited for the call to the Head's office. It never came. He just stopped me in the corridor one morning and said, 'Oh the girls enjoyed the show.' I nodded, slightly dumb-struck and mumbled, 'Yes, the students certainly rose to the occasion.' Some imp in my brain added gleefully, 'And so did Brad in that silhouette scene,' but I stifled the thought and managed to continue with, 'they were very well behaved.' The Head nodded. 'Good,' he said and walked on. I grinned back at that imp. The show goes on, I thought. I still have a job. And I went off to my next class with a skip back in my step.

That summer the air waves buzzed with 'Girl Power.' This was linked to a new band which had exploded into the media spotlight. Five feisty girls known as the Spice Girls released their debut single *Wannabe* and all the young girls in school were singing it. At the Newman summer talent show there were Spice Girl lookalikes for Sporty, Baby, Posh, Scary and Ginger. The first music interview with this new female pop phenomenon appeared in *Music Week* magazine in July of '96 where journalist Paul Gorman wrote that this, *all-girl, in-yer-face pop group have arrived with enough sass to burst the rockist bubble.* Their debut single topped the charts in 31 countries.

Now the girls in school walked with more swagger and confidence chanting the lyrics, 'I tell you what I want, what I really really want.....' and the boys would step back a little non-plussed at this brashness. Some of my students started relating 'girl power' to characters from the literature we were studying – Beatrice in *Much Ado About Nothing*, Katherine in *The Taming of the Shrew*. If it helped the students articulate their thoughts about literature I didn't mind the latest buzz words from the pop music world infiltrating our discussions of literature.

'Only I wouldn't talk about 'girl power' in your GCSE exam answers,' I suggested to my year 11 group. 'The examiner might not know what you're talking about.'

That summer the planet of one of the Spice Girls, Victoria, aka 'Posh Spice' was definitely in the ascendancy, destined to collide with that of a young soccer player who had just scored the most audacious goal ever seen. At age 21, David Beckham, playing for Manchester United against Wimbledon in the opening game of the new season, received a ball at the half way line, noticed the Wimbledon goal-keeper was well off his line and launched a shot half the length of the field which went over the head of the keeper into the goal. Beckham had announced himself to the world of football as Posh Spice had announced herself to the world of pop music. Their planets would collide more permanently a few years later. 1996 was just the start.

Of course there was some 'girl power' going on under my own roof. Katie was leaving for her 'Gap' year in Mexico in early September. Her placement was in a home for mentally handicapped children in the city of Puebla, south east of Mexico City. She had been paired with a girl called Jo, from Yorkshire. They had met only once at the time of the original interview and now, at the airport in Manchester, it was crunch time. This was it. No going back. They were both excited and nervous and eighteen years old. It was going to be some adventure.

Also for us. Seeing our daughter hoisting her enormous rucksack on to her back and with a final wave heading off to 'Departures' was something of a heart-stopping moment. I glanced at Sue, she gave me a shrug and a moist, wistful look and said, 'I never really considered what our parents must have felt when we took off for Jamaica.'

'We were a bit older than 18, though,' I said.

'Still not easy.'

I nodded. 'She'll be fine,' I said. 'We'll call her as soon as we get a contact number. I'm sure they'll cope.'

*

INTO THE UNKNOWN

I had been teaching about the media for almost twenty years now. Starting with the Communication Studies 'A' level back in the late Seventies, media education had gradually moved to centre stage in the curriculum. There was now to be a 'media' component to GCSE English as well as GCSE Media Studies and a new A level Media Studies syllabus which I was attracted by. It had taken a long time and the subject still faced a lot of prejudice from the traditionalists who so often labelled Media Studies a 'Mickey Mouse' subject. 'Watching films and TV all day. What a doddle that is,' my colleagues would say. I would

433

shake my head and smile and cling on to the belief that it was crucial for freedom of thought and democracy (yes, I thought it was that important) that youngsters should be able to disentangle the power of the media; to understand the techniques used by advertisers, by newspapers, and by television programme makers to influence their audiences; to appreciate the subtle devices used by a film-maker to create mood and move an audience to laughter or to tears; to understand something of the magic of radio or a film soundtrack. The world was moving beyond the 'Gutenberg Galaxy' when print was king to a world dominated by image and sound and with the revolution being swept in by computer technology, education had to reflect those changes.

The inclusion of media study as a component of the English curriculum was a huge leap forward, so it was with great excitement that I attended an in-service training course in Harrogate with my old colleague Jean, from St. Aidan's. We both felt the curriculum was finally 'coming of age'.

'They're finally catching up with where we've been for the past fifteen years,' said Jean during the coffee break. 'I just wish there were some better books on the subject that we could put in front of the kids,' she added as she thumbed through the books on display.

It was during the drive home that the thought slipped into my mind. It was a tentative thought, a somewhat pretentious thought. 'Why don't we write one?' I ventured.

Jean looked at me, 'One what?'

'A media course book.'

She frowned and then nodded, 'Yeah, why don't we. There's some crap stuff out there at the moment.'

'Are you serious?' I said.

'I don't know, are you?'

'Let's jot down some ideas, some possible chapter headings. See what we've got.'

We met a couple of times to collect some thoughts and run our minds over this audacious idea. Neither of us had any experience of writing a book. I had attempted to penetrate the ivory portals of the publishing world on several occasions with fiction manuscripts, only to be met by standard rejection letters or what seemed like some grudging encouragement to consult *The Writers' and Artists' Yearbook* for help. It felt like a closed shop, available only to those who had 'contacts'.

By coincidence, a week later, the book rep. from Oxford University Press was in the staffroom setting up a book display. I swallowed my doubts and went across to him. 'If I had an idea for a coursebook who would I contact?' I asked. I watched for the hint of a smile or a snigger but there was none. He rummaged in his brief case and pulled out a business card. 'There's a phone number on there,' he said. 'No harm in trying.'

'Thanks,' I said.

I carried the card around for several days. 'Oxford University Press', one of the most prestigious publishing houses in the world. What was I even thinking? At the bottom of the card was the name 'Helen Giltrow, Senior English Editor.' I imagined some blue-stocking intellectual, refined, Oxbridge educated. There was a telephone number alongside her name. I felt like some country hick, standing at the door of the squire's country house. Had I the cheek to knock on the door? Then I remembered George in America – positive thinking George and those motivational tapes he gave me which had nudged my English cynicism with their message that negative thinking defeats you before you've taken a step whereas positive thinking can open doors you never dreamed of. And here I was close to my 50th year, dithering about making a phone call. If I couldn't pick up the phone and dial that number at my age, then I never would.

I waited until I had a free period in the afternoon and went into my office. Looked again at the phone number and picked up the phone. I took a deep breath and punched in the number. Waited. Heard it ringing. Then a woman's voice, 'Hello, Helen Giltrow here.'

It was the lady herself. I explained how I'd got her number and that I had an idea for a media course book. I waited for the call to be politely terminated but she said, 'I'm in a meeting at present, but it sounds interesting. Can you call me back in an hour?'

Almost lost for words, I replied, 'Of course, yes, in an hour then.'

In the next phone call my image of a frosty, blue-stocking intellectual changed. She sounded friendly, interested, encouraging. 'Send me some sample ideas,' she said. 'It doesn't have to be detailed just an outline of topic areas.'

I reported back to Jean. 'Wow,' she said surprised, 'we better start taking this a bit more seriously then.'

We held another couple of meetings to put together some ideas and I dug out some of the material I used with students on film analysis and deconstructing adverts. The problem was that so many books on media looked dated within a few years of publication because the illustrations they were using were out of date so quickly. I wanted to come up with a different approach, to devise a method for reading and analysing the media which would be relevant now and in ten or twenty years time – an approach which was fundamental and which could be applied to any medium, whether it was a news report, an advert, a feature film or a television programme.

I wrestled with various ideas and various approaches but finally decided it was semiology which held the key. Semiology is associated with the 19th century Swiss linguist Ferdinand de Saussure and I had first encountered his theories during my MA course in Lancaster. Semiology is about the reading of signs, a sign being anything which carries a meaning. So you could have verbal and non-verbal signs, language signs, graphic signs, moving image signs like camera angles, props, costume. There was the whole range of sound signs such as the pace and rhythm of a film soundtrack, the use of sound effects – all of these conveyed meaning. But how to translate these theoretical concepts into a form which a 14 year old student might be able to grasp – that was the challenge.

For weeks my waking hours were taken up with trying to tease out an approach which might work. Even when teaching a regular day, some back-room in my brain was ticking away, chewing through various ideas of how to translate media theory into something palatable for students and their teachers. I was waking at 3a.m. with my head swirling with some new idea or some notion of a possible way forward. I had a note book at the side of the bed and until I had written the idea out of my head I couldn't get back to sleep.

Finally a framework for the book started to crystallize and I prepared some sample pages with text, questions and illustrations. There would be four basic sections focussing on what I would call the four 'codes' used in media messages: the codes of written language, sound, moving images and graphic images.

I showed Jean the sample just before sending it off. She studied it closely and after a while she looked at me and nodded, 'Pretty good, professor. I think this might just work. It's not an approach I've ever seen in a media studies book before. Quite revolutionary. Just hope friend Helen sees its value. But let's also be honest about this whole thing. This is not a joint book, this is your book, your ideas. I'll just be a sounding board from now on.'

A week later I received an email from Helen at OUP to say the sample had arrived. She was fairly non-commital, saying only that it looked 'interesting' but that it now had to be sent out to various key schools for 'review'. The responses would determine whether the book would progress to the next stage.

There was clearly nothing straighforward about bringing a book to publication. The whole process was a huge unknown; I was only at one of the early hurdles at which it could quite easily fail.

News from Mexico was not good. In mid-September we phoned Katie and sang 'Happy Birthday' down the phone. The voice from the other end was a voice of desperation, 'Dad you've got to get us out of here. The conditions are appalling. It's cruel and it's not what we signed up to do.' She was in a home for children with physical and mental disabilities. It was run by a private trust and the trustees, to save money, had just dismissed most of the paid staff and left Katie and Jo virtually in sole charge. They were expected to sleep in the same dormitories as the children, prepare their food, wash their clothes, clean up the urine and faeces as well as working with them all through the day. Effectively they were on a 24 hour shift. One of the toddlers was almost permanently strapped to a small chair from which he struggled to escape but where he must stay, said the housemother - it was a way of controlling and disciplining him.

'Katie, you've got to refuse to do all this,' I said.

'Dad, it's hard trying to use my A level Spanish to argue a case against these people who don't seem interested in the welfare of the children. They just get money from the families who want these disturbed kids out of the way. When we have tried to object we're just told it's our Christian duty to get on with it.'

'What about your Gap supervisor? Can't he do something?'

'We've no way of contacting him.'

We felt utterly helpless and, when we put down the phone, looked at each other for a hint of a way out.

'What about Jean's son Joel?' said Sue. 'He works in a school in Mexico City. Maybe he could contact the Gap man in Puebla.'

Later that day we got a call from Jean. She had spoken to Joel who worked alongside the Gap co-ordinator for Mexico City. She had phoned the Puebla agent and things were starting to move.

Within the week Katie and Jo had been relocated to the Salvation Army Children's Home in Puebla where they worked for the rest of their six month placement. It was still tough work but not so intolerable as their first stint had been. Katie was consumed with guilt for abandoning a group of children who were desperately needy. We tried to reassure her and say that challenge is all very well but with no experience of dealing with such extreme needs and no staff to look to for support, it was not a situation that two 18 year olds could be expected to deal with. I'm sure she was not convinced for I know her sense of guilt troubled her for a long time afterwards.

NEW LABOUR, NEW HOPE?

In the Spring of 1997 the Labour Government of Tony Blair replaced the tired regime of the Tories which had been in power for 18 years. At age 43 here was the youngest British prime minister of the century promising us hope and sweeping changes. The country was riding on a euphoric high. The newspapers dubbed it 'Cool Britannia' and Tony Blair tried to tap into the mood by throwing a reception at Number 10 Downing Street for various celebrities, including Noel Gallagher from the Manchester band, Oasis, currently riding high in the world of popular music.

In education we fully expected that the draconian inspection regime of Ofsted under the rigid fist of its Chief Inspector, Chris Woodhead, would be swept aside for something more sensible and humane. At present schools were inspected every six years; they were given two months notice and then an inspection team of around eight inspectors would descend on a school for a week. They would observe and grade teachers' lessons, make judgements about the ethos of the school, its pastoral system, its relationship with parents as well as give close scrutiny to exam and tests results. The school would then be graded on a scale from 'Unsatisfactory' to 'Outstanding'. The whole process drove blood pressure levels to bursting point, disrupted the normal running of the school and led to judgements on schools which were anything but consistent.

However, the general election brought no welcome change. Woodhead remained, patronising and as iron-fisted as ever and the so-called New Labour government seemed to be embracing many of the Tory education policies. This was not the humane, empathetic socialism of the past, this was something more clinical and unbending. A new corporate ethos was now running the show driven by target-setting, data analysis and rigid application of strategies more associated with running a business. Headteachers were now 'managers', the old philosopher-king Headteacher of Frank's ilk had been consigned to the scrap-heap..

Under the Ofsted inspection regime, schools would be 'named and shamed' and senior managers of schools would be fired if they didn't turn a failing school around within two years. Standard Achievement Tests or SATS taken at age 7, 11 and 14 would be used to rank schools in league tables so that parents could make judgements about a school's performance.

Gone were those days when we had freedom to devise our lessons and improvise teaching strategies. Now there would be 3-part lessons comprising 'Starter', 'Main' and 'Plenary' sessions. This was the education straight-jacket into which we all had to squeeze ourselves. Maybe there was a case for bringing in some standardized approach to ensure the students everywhere would get their 'entitlement' to a reasonable education. But for me the straight-jacket chafed and cramped my style of teaching and I kicked against it at every opportunity. In addition, the New English Curriculum Framework was being introduced which dismembered English into bite sized chunks of grammar teaching and so-called 'skills-based' learning that would then be tested under the new testing regime. I was definitely out of step with these changes. Creativity, the life-blood of inspired teaching and effective learning was being throttled. Only that which could be measured and tested was seen as valid. Those lessons where I would hold a class spellbound by reading them a story for thirty minutes would be classed as a 'failed lesson'. Students had to be seen to be 'engaged', 'interacting', 'on task'. How did you gauge how much a student's imagination was 'engaged' by their listening to a story? If it couldn't be measured, if there was no 'evidence of learning' then in 'Ofsted-speak' it was not valid education.

Thankfully, I was partly distracted from this philistine transformation of the education system by focussing on developing my media course book. After a wait of three months I received some feedback from Helen Giltrow. She sent me a selection of the reviews from the schools which had examined my sample material. They ranged from the ecstatically positive to the claim that it was 'too hard'. There were a couple of lack lustre responses but Helen reassured me that the project hadn't been jettisoned. However we needed to get clear about the age group this book was targetting. So much could be done by phone and email but maybe, she said, it was time that we met face to face, sometime in the autumn.

*

That autumn of 1997 was memorable for a number of reasons. There was the aftermath of the car crash in the Pont de l'Alma road tunnel in Paris which killed Diana, Princess of Wales and her boyfriend Dodi Fayed. On the home front, Katie was off to Stirling University to study psychology while James was going to York St John University.

Katie's return from Mexico in the spring had not been easy for her. She and Jo were the last passengers to emerge from the 'Arrivals' at Manchester airport. We were anxious to see them but they held back not wanting to break the spell of their trip by having to reunite with the more mundane world of parents and home. Since surviving the six month placement in the children's home in Puebla they had travelled to Puerto Escondido on the Pacific coast for some relaxation, then up through the jungles of the Yucatan to the beaches of Cancun. Was it any wonder they were reluctant to return to the grey skies and predictability of England?

Katie was restless on the journey home. She wanted to listen to a tape of Mexican music and was slow to open up to us about her experiences. When we stopped at a motorway services and she walked through the café area she remarked that it was a relief not to be whistled at, propositioned or 'touched up' by Mexican men. It was the first time in six months that she could relax and not have to look over her shoulder all the time.

It took a long while for her to adjust to life back home. She was critical of the grumbling British public who didn't realise how well off they were compared to those on the streets in Mexico. She had come back with few belongings having given most of them away to the kids on the streets. We would never know what she had experienced during those months in Mexico and how it had affected her. It was two years before she could bear to read her diary and we sensed there were things deeply locked away about her Mexican experience which we could barely fathom.

Now James, too, was taking off. I had enjoyed teaching him and watching him grow in stature and confidence. He was playing county standard tennis and first team soccer. York was his destination for the next 3 years to study sports science and psychology. He and Katie were very close and had shared a lively group of friends at school. Now they would go their separate ways. James was already talking about applying to the Major League Soccer organisation to coach soccer in America the following summer. Sue and I would now be coming come home to a quiet house and a meal for just two. It was quite an adjustment.

The death of Princess Diana in Paris in August and the news frenzy which followed was intriguing from a media perspective. On September 3rd both The Mirror and The Guardian ran stories about Henri Paul, the driver of Diana's car. The Mirror's feature was headlined: *SPEED FREAK – Bike nut could down nine whiskies a night* while The Guardian's article, entitled *Mystery of a quiet man*, spoke of a *self-effacing man who only drank occasionally, had never been seen drunk and lived for his passions of flying and sailing.* This was dynamite for my book – perfect examples of news bias. I just had to obtain permission to use the articles.

And this was now the main issue I was facing. It was one thing to find media material to illustrate some concept or principle I wanted to

440

explore, it was another to get permission to use it. In one newspaper there was an excellent example of the digital manipulation of news photos. It was a group picture of the royal family but seemingly it was difficult to get a picture which flattered everyone in the group. The newspaper had run a feature showing the way the head of Prince William had been digitally removed from one group photo which had been rejected and inserted into the final official group portrait. Again, perfect for my purposes but when OUP tried to get permission to use it, the royal decree was a very definite 'No – on pain of death' etc..

*

'Crewe station.10.30a.m. Under the information screen. Wearing blue coat.' Those were Helen Giltrow's instructions. This was it then. I was to meet the person I'd been emailing and phoning for the past year.

It was a cold, sharp autumn morning and I was there early. So much hung on this meeting. We had made some progress on the book but there were still questions, reservations. The publishers wanted a specific target audience so that they could market the book effectively. Was it aimed at Key Stage 3 or for 15 and 16 year olds to equip them to handle the new media component of GCSE English? Or was it for GCSE Media Studies?

I didn't want to be so specifically tied down. The book I had in mind was a general handbook for anyone starting to analyse the media. I saw this book as being useful even at A level as a starter. But this wasn't what publishers were interested in and Helen made that very clear that morning.

I finally spotted a figure in a blue coat standing with a brief case not far from the information screen. She was slightly built, short, light brown hair. I went tentatively across to her. 'Helen, is it?'

She smiled, 'This is a good test of reading signs. It's good to finally meet you, Barrie.' We shook hands.

We spent the morning in the lounge of a nearby hotel and Helen had a clear set of queries she wanted to sort out. She didn't waste any time putting her cards on the table.

'At last week's English Subject meeting,' she said, 'it was agreed that this needs to be targetted at Key Stage 3, lower ability students. At present what you've produced is certainly very promising but it's too difficult. If we're going to run with this book you'll have to adjust the way the material's presented to suit that readership.'

I thought of the framework of the book, the key concepts which I wasn't prepared to jettison. My colleagues had tried out the sample material with their lower ability Year 9 classes and it had worked well.

Helen sat back and gave a slight shrug. 'I'm only going on the feedback I've been getting from the trials in other schools. They seemed to find it too hard. And remember you're familiar with media work; for some teachers this is all completely new.'

We spent around two hours in discussion and by the end I was swallowing the pill that some major revision would have to be done if this book was going to be acceptable to the ultimate arbiters at Oxford University Press – the Delegates.

On the train home I tried to decide whether I should be encouraged or depressed. Helen knew the business, knew the market but I felt I knew how kids' minds worked but also what ingredients had to be included in the book to equip them to unpick a range of media texts.

It wasn't exactly an impasse but clearly there was still a lot of work to be done.

*

TESTING TIMES

'What about this, sir?'

Tom had found a red cloak and a Hallowe'en mask and Richard had thrust a woolly tam on to his head.

'Not bad, Tom, not sure about the red cloak. A bit bright,' I said.

'Could be a symbol, sir. Y'know like the blood on her hands which she can't wash off,' suggested Rachel.

'Brilliant, Rachel. Great idea,' I nodded. 'Okay, the red cloak can stay.'

Two of the other boys, David and Robert, were enthusiastically pulling bits of costume from the costume cupboard. 'How about this?' said David holding up a pirate's hat and plastic machine-gun.

'Not really in the spirit of the play,' I said.

This was my year 9 group, attempting to deal with the new Key Stage 3 curriculum. The study of a Shakespeare play was now compulsory, to be tested in the summer SATS tests. These were the tests we had resisted and boycotted back in 1993. But now they were firmly part of the culture of testing and assessment which Tony Blair's new government was championing. The challenge for my department was how to make Shakespeare enjoyable and palatable for some less than enthusiastic 14 year olds.

So here we were in the main school hall, about to embark on what the class had dubbed 'the hubble bubble scene' when the witches meet with Macbeth.

We had a choice from three plays. For me 'Macbeth' had the ingredients which might hold the interest of 14 year olds and with some inspired improvisation things weren't going too badly.

'I think it's Lady Macbeth who causes all the bother,' offered Tony. 'Macbeth was okay at the start until his wife started getting at him.'

'Wait a minute,' replied Julie. 'He was the one who had the idea to kill the king in the first place.'

'No, it was the witches,' said David, 'they put a spell on him and that was it. They did for him, good and proper.'

'I don't think so,' retorted Julie. 'They just looked into the future, told him his fortune.'

'Yeah but that's what put the idea in his head. No, it was the witches, I'd put money on it,' said David.

They used a litter bin for a cauldron and huddled round it throwing in bits of this and that as they read their lines; ' *Eye of newt and toe of frog.. Wool of bat, tongue of dog....* ' The rest of the class sat on the floor and watched with commendable interest.

This was to be the pattern of our Year 9 teaching from now on. Choose your Shakespeare play in September and start preparing for the SATS which would take place the following summer. And the results had better be good as they would determine the school ranking in the new League Tables. The government, with Ofsted riding shot-gun, now had its manacles on the teaching profession. Our wings were being firmly clipped and we were being shackled to a treadmill of testing and assessment which offered little room for manoeuvre.

The government had also abolished the wonderful 100% coursework GCSE syllabus which had inspired so many English teachers and their students for the past decade. Now the emphasis was on more traditional exams. I decided to pull out of my work as a GCSE examiner. The coursework-based syllabus had been an inspiration and great opportunity for me to rise through the ranks to the position of Assistant Chief Moderator, chairing meetings of thirty or forty teachers, running training programmes and feeding off the enthusiasm generated by a huge network of energetic and passionate teachers of English. Now we were to be cowed and brought into line. Standardised testing, a standardised curriculum and standardised models of teaching were now the pills we were expected to swallow.

I started looking for more creative outlets. Things had gone quiet from OUP. I had heard nothing for several months and although I had been doggedly working on the final two units of the media book, I was increasingly pessimistic that anything would come from this venture. Supposedly, some selected schools were trying out my material but there was little news coming from Helen Giltrow into my e-mail file.

To cap this downhill trend I came back to school to find the cherished carpet, bought off the back of a van several years ago and installed in one of the English rooms, had been removed during the holidays.

'Lino is so much more hygenic, easier for the cleaners,' said the Deputy i/c Buildings. 'And anyway that carpet was of such poor quality.' He stood with a somewhat smug, self-satisfied expression, a slight raising of the eyebrows challenging me to respond.

'You could have replaced it with some better quality carpet then. You've no idea what a difference carpetting makes when you're teaching. And who are these classrooms for anyway, the cleaners or the students?'

'It is cushioned lino,' he said unmoved. 'In fact I think they call it 'cushion-flooring'. It'll last a good while.'

'It'll be like teaching in a cave again. Thanks a lot!'

He gave a slight shrug, and turned away. He'd finally got his own back. He said he would when I originally pulled a fast one and went behind his back to have the carpet fitted. Not a good start to the term.

*

While teaching lower school English and GCSE was more constrained, my A level teaching of literature and media studies still inspired me. In A level literature there was a coursework element which allowed students to choose the texts they could compare, while media studies was opening up in several new directions. Students had to produce a practical project as part of the course and the new computer software for manipulating images and editing video opened up a wealth of creative possibilities. I was also beginning to explore the genre of science-fiction.

Apart from the brilliant short stories of Ray Bradbury, I'd never been drawn to the sci-fi genre. However, I was starting to realise that it could be used to explore some intriguing philosophical ideas. One of the driving principles in my teaching career had always been to broaden the thinking of my students. Literature was a great vehicle for exploring personal and social issues but science-fiction, by way of its detached perspective, could also ask some far-reaching questions about man's place in the world and the interface between the world of nature and the world of the machine.

My love of D.H.Lawrence's work was partly rooted in his exploration of the tensions between man and machine and the impact of industrial development on human sensibility. Two of his short poems come to mind:

THINGS MADE BY IRON
Things made by iron and handled by steel
Are born dead, they are shrouds, they soak life out of us.
Till after a long time, when they are old and have steeped in our life
They begin to be soothed and soothing: then we throw them away.

THINGS MEN HAVE MADE
Things men have made with wakened hands, and put soft life into
Are awake through years with transferred touch and go on glowing
For long years.
And for this reason, some old things are lovely
Warm still with the life of forgotten men who made them.

I now realised that films like James Cameron's *The Terminator*, Ridley Scott's *Alien* and *Blade Runner* threw up searching questions about human values in a world dominated by science and technology. *Terminator*, despite its overt action/adventure billing, carried interesting quasi-religious overtones with the character of Sarah Connor fighting to protect her future son, John, the unborn child/saviour of mankind. *Alien* grips the audience with its claustrophobic mood of lurking terror but also challenges sexual stereotypes in Sigourney Weaver's powerful character of Ripley. *Blade Runner* is a complex conundrum which throws up some intriguing moral and philosophical questions about the dominance of sophisticated technology.

Here, indeed, was an exciting new area I could get my teeth into to offset the loss of creative freedom in other areas of my teaching.

*

We were all nervous that first year of SATS, wondering whether we had interpreted the specification for the test correctly and prepared our year 9 students adequately. There were three test papers – Reading, Writing and Shakespeare. We had spent months on practice questions, on revising key scenes from *Macbeth* and the learning of key quotations.

We didn't favour this 'teaching to the test' style of teaching but so much hung on the results that the reputation of the department and ultimately the school would be judged on the outcome.

When the day of the test came, I opened the question paper envelopes with great trepidation. What I saw made me furious. We had spent all year preparing for this new test but I hadn't anticipated how limiting the test questions would be. They gave little scope for students to demonstrate their talents and worst of all was the Shakespeare paper. We had explored in depth the themes of *Macbeth*, the characters, their relationships, what motivated Macbeth and Lady Macbeth to embark on their blood-soaked progress through the events of the play. And what did the test ask?

'Why are villains entertaining? Write about a villain and say why this person was interesting.'

There was also a rather lame question about Lady Macbeth and that was it. Our months of preparation and revising were distilled into this superficial pap! We were furious. If this was the government's so-called new 'rigorous testing regime' it was a joke, a cruel joke on the nation's teachers and their students. And that wasn't the end of the story.

When the marked papers were returned three weeks before the summer holiday it was clear there had been a gross travesty in the marking. Some of our best students had scored much lower than our weaker students. The marking was inconsistent from student to student. It was clear that the marker was some unqualified numbskull.

With the Head's approval I parcelled up the test papers and sent them back for a remark. When they were returned several weeks later our doubts were fully justified and a large swathe of marks were adjusted upwards. Over the next few months it became clear that nationwide the English SATS had been a disaster and rumours filtered out of markers being recruited who were incompetent or inexperienced.

This would be the pattern for the next ten years until the tests were finally scrapped in 2008. Out of the those ten years we sent tests papers back for remarking on six occasions. It was always a blot on the end of the summer term waiting for results and then having to check they had been marked accurately.

Not a great way to end each school year but our hands were now firmly tied. If the results were poor, the gnomes of Ofsted might come knocking on the door and threaten the school with closure. There were no hiding places anymore for incompetent school managers and classroom teachers. And that was no bad thing. It was the tone of it all which disturbed me. The patronising, castigating pronouncements of Chris Woodhead, the Chief Inspector, seeped into the management style of a lot of new Heads and senior managers. A bullying, mechanistic culture was being promulgated and it was poisoning the humanity and good humour which had been the hallmark of good schools.

*

BEYOND THE SHADOWLAND

7a.m. The phone rings. The line is crackly but it's obviously James' voice. 'Dad, I'm at a bus station in San Francisco. It's midnight and the place is full of weirdos - hookers, druggies.'

'I imagine that's pretty typical of American bus stations at midnight,' I replied unsympathetically. Sue frowned with concern. Her boy was not happy.

'But it's really dodgy,' he went on.

'Why are you there?' I asked.

'They've changed my placement. I've got to get a bus to Portland, Oregon.'

'Well at least we know where you are.'

Sue took the phone from me. 'Are you going to be all right?'

'Well it's not the best.'

I shrugged at Sue and mouthed, 'Nothing we can do. He'll be fine.'

'Well, just keep yourself safe. Make sure you've got your passport and your money well hidden.'

'Okay, mom. Oh, bus has just pulled in. Betta go. Love you.'

'Love you too.'

Sue put the phone down.

'It's Mexico all over again,' I said. 'I don't know what they expect us to do.'

'They just need to touch base now and again. But he didn't sound happy.'

James had just completed his first year at university in York and he had been taken on by MLS (Major League Soccer) to coach in America for six weeks. This was going to be character-building stuff, travelling on his own and surviving. His first placement was on the west coast then he had to fly back east. Katie, Sue and I were flying out to meet him at the end of his second placement in Connecticut. We would then drive north to the Thousand Islands for a weeks holiday with our American friends.

447

At 5p.m. that evening the phone rang again. 'Hi dad, just had a great trip north. I'm in Portland and it's brilliant. Met this girl on the bus and we had a really good chat.'

'Well, that's a relief,' I said. 'Just reassure your mother that everything's okay.' I handed the phone to Sue. 'It's our long lost son and he's having a ball. Told you, didn't I.'

School was forgotten as we all sank into the comfort blanket of an American summer. There was water-ski-ing and sailing at the Thousand Islands, barbecues on the beach at Pine Bay and, just like the Nat King Cole song, endless lazy, hazy, crazy days with sodas and pretzels and beer.

Then it was south through New York State with Judy's family for two nights in New York. They showed us the sights – Staten Island ferry, Statue of Liberty, the Twin Towers, Radio City and food at the Carnegie Deli in midtown Manhattan, a place famous for its bulging pastrami sandwiches and luscious cheesecake.

But perhaps one of the great delights of that summer was seeing the affection for James from the boys and girls he'd been coaching and their parents at a farewell party for him in Connecticut. They had clearly enjoyed having him around and it seemed that he'd done a good job. MLS wanted him back the following summer.

And the good news didn't end there. When we got home to England there was a letter waiting for me from OUP. It was a 'Letter of Agreement'. It looked as if they were going ahead with my media book and this was the first stage in sealing the deal. A contract would follow. I couldn't believe it. What was taking the time was getting permissions from the various companies whose material I wanted to use. Aardmann, the makers of the Wallace and Gromit animations, had just published a book of some of their storyboards. It was perfect material to illustrate the unit on film. I didn't hesitate in phoning them. They made some encouraging noises and a month later permission from them came through. Finally things were beginning to gel, or so I thought.

The contract came through in November. It committed me to producing *'a draft manuscript for a Key Stage 3 Media coursebook'* but its publication was *'subject to the approval of the Delegates of Oxford University Press'*.

Another hurdle was passed but I wasn't home and dry yet.

Sue was busy planning a celebration for my 50th birthday at the end of December when news came through of a deterioration in my father's condition. All year my stoical mother had been coping with him at home with the daily help of care workers who would hoist him out of bed and in and out of his chair. He inhabited a shadowland, partly in our world but mainly somewhere else. The dementia had stolen what had been a big-hearted, gregarious personality and left a shell; it had stolen his memory apart from some confused recollections from a misty past. Sometimes he would sit at the piano and his fingers remembered snippets of what had been a fine repertoire of classical and popular music. But most of it had gone.

Then a week before Christmas my mother slipped and fell, breaking her arm. She was taken to Hull Royal Infirmary and my father was taken to Castle Hill Hospital a few miles away. The doctors warned us that he was slipping away. My mother pined at the loss of him but was in no state to move from the hospital to see him. I drove over to join my younger brother at his bedside only to arrive fifteen minutes too late.

Christmas didn't really happen that year and the celebrations for my fiftieth were postponed while we dealt with the funeral. I asked myself why I wasn't consumed with grief. But then I realized I had been quietly grieving for the past few years as, month by month, the dementia stole another piece of the man who had been my father, leaving us with someone who was like a stranger in a waiting room.

*

PUBLISH AND BE DAMNED

I'd signed a book contract and received a small advance for my work. It felt like I had arrived at some sort of destination. How wrong could I be. This was just the start. What followed was a year of intense e-mail cut and thrust with Helen, the commissioning editor at OUP.

Firstly, I would need to change the format of the manuscript for editing purposes. I had submitted the original using Microsoft Publisher and included illustrations, sample layouts for pages with graphics and artwork. Now I was told it all had to be submitted in Microsoft Word. Cut all the design stuff, they just needed the text. That alone was a massive re-typing task.

Furthermore, the units were still deemed 'too hard' for Key Stage 3 and needed simplifying. There were problems with obtaining permissions to use certain leaflets, adverts and news photos. Could I find

449

alternatives and write new questions around them? We needed to obtain some radio scripts for the Sound Unit and an illustrator for drawing storyboards for the Film Unit. There were questions and tasks for the students on virtually every page and the wording of these had be precise, engaging, grammatically correct but friendly. We were down to the minutiae of each page, each question, each word.

It was like doing a degree course with a very exacting tutor. But as Helen said, OUP were investing a lot of money in this project and they didn't want the book to sink without trace. We had to get it right. The ding-dong of emails continued all year like a protracted electronic conversation as the manuscript was honed again and again.

In the meantime there was the day job. Ofsted came in April. Unlike the latest regime where they give you just 48 hours warning, back then we still had notice and so there were weeks of nervous preparation with the blood-pressure rising as the inspection day approached.

Then the inspection team would descend like a flock of dark suited ravens. For three days they would peck in our cupboards, sit beady-eyed in our classrooms, flock together in their designated room to compare findings while we waited, sniffed the air and tried to sense their mood as they skittered around the school. Finally the judgement came that overall we were 'Satisfactory' with certain targets for improvement. They would return the following year to check on our progress but at least we could all begin to breathe again.

The little memorial garden became a great place to retreat to at lunch times. The flowers and shrubs were developing nicely and for some snatched moments I could sit back on my rustic bench, close my eyes to the sun and dream of a saner life. It was there that I had the idea for a drama production at Christmas. I chatted to my History colleague, Paul, himself a keen amateur actor who had produced several school productions. He was keen to assist me as was Alain, our very talented Head of Music. Why I would want to saddle myself with another major project seems rather perverse, but that's what I did. It would be a big production, glitzy and bold. We would do that high-school favourite – *Grease.*

The production of the media book staggered on and I was now working with a freelance editor for the final stage. I never met Becca in the twelve months that we worked together. It was all done by email. She had no backround in media and so asked the most fundamental questions about each unit of the book, each exercise, each task. It was probably deliberate on OUP's part so that I would be forced to clarify every assumption, eradicate any confused thinking. Becca was sharp, surgical in the way she worked but that was good for me – hard but somehow exhilarating. We were into the final stages, permissions were coming through at last and the re-jigging of the book seemed to have passed the approval of the OUP Delegates.

In September Helen informed me they had contracted a top notch designer to work on the colour and print layouts. The title of the book had been an issue for months. We had tossed various ideas back and forth. I wanted something with a double-edged impact like 'Media Exposure'. Helen reckoned this might have the wrong connotations for year 9 boys, given the popularity of page 3 girls in the Sun newspaper. Finally we agreed on *Mixed Media.*

Thinking we were into the final stages I had happily embarked on my production of *Grease.* Surely I could now keep another plate spinning in the air.

There had been auditions in the summer term generating great excitement among the senior students who were vying for the key roles of Pink Ladies or T-Birds. Feelings were running high, especially among the girls until the final selection was made.

I published a rehearsal schedule for the autumn term, recruited the assistance of the technology department to build some semblance of a car which we could get on and off the stage and started working out the staging. But the biggest challenge would be the dance routines. There's a great dance sequence at the end of the film 'Footloose' and I loved the music. Somehow I wanted to work that into the opening of our production of 'Grease'.

I found dance fascinating but I was no choreographer. I was relying on some of the sixth form girls and my colleague, Christine, from the PE department. The dance routines would make or break this production and in the early weeks I was having my doubts. Choreography was harder than I'd thought, especially with boys who were reluctant to make fools of themselves. So although the gang of T-birds were fine doing 'cool' stuff like strutting around in leather jackets, when it came to rehearsing complex dance moves a couple of them started murmuring about leaving the show. Most of the key actors were upper sixth formers, preparing for A level mock exams in January so I could sympathise. I'd also had comments from some of their teachers that such a production was a really bad idea for them to be involved in.

Then into the mix came Matt. He was a student at the college, a friend of Zoe who was playing the part of Sandy and he was a dancer and choreographer. Here was a very talented, charismatic young man who was willing to help. Suddenly the rehearsals started to buzz with new life. The doubters were back on board and the production started to come together.

By half term things were progressing well. But then came a bombshell from OUP. The designer had set the parameters for the book. It would be 128 pages, a typeface size of 14pt, larger than usual but easy for less able students to read. She had also restricted the amount of text on each page so that the layout was open and attractive. What did this mean for me? Massive cuts in content. And I was given two weeks to make the cuts and send back the revised manuscript.

Sue was feeling the pressure as Senior Teacher at her school and we had booked a holiday in Majorca for half term to give us a break. I now had to pack the bulky manuscript into my suitcase and anticipate having to spend the week with a red pen slashing swathes out of the manuscript to get it to fit the requirements laid down by the designer at OUP. I was far from happy!

After a frenetic two weeks of 'slash and burn' whilst desperately striving to retain the integrity of the book, I dispatched the cut down version and awaited developments at OUP.

Meanwhile there was a show to put on. Sue was busy sewing jackets for the Pink Ladies.

The dance routines were beginning to take shape and the actors were finally getting round to learning their lines. A team of colleagues was helping with set construction, lighting and sound issues and Alain was busy rehearsing his rock band. All the music for the show would be performed live. Matt's work with the dance routines had been like sprinkling gold dust on the production. The dances were slick, complex and starting to look like something from a professional production. The buzz of excitement among the cast was infectious.

The three nights of that production rate as one of the high points of my teaching career. As I watched from the back of the auditorium, I remembered those first hesitant fumblings with drama productions years ago. Now I had progressed to this - this brilliant extravaganza of colour, music, acting, and stunning dancing from a group of students who had found talents within themselves they'd never dreamed of. The quieter ones had grown in confidence. The whole cast had shared an experience which they  would probably never forget. Its impact was incalculable. There was no way of measuring its value against any of the criteria which Ofsted deemed worthy of consideration. To them, if it couldn't be measured it was of minor importance. But I knew different. I saw it in the eyes of the students, on the faces of their parents and in the eyes of my colleagues who had worked on the show. For a while we had all escaped from the world of targets, assessments and data measurements into that unique world of artistry and imagination. That's the world I valued; that's the world I wanted to hold on to.

'As good as a West End production - well done,' commented one of my colleagues after the final night's performance.

'Thanks,' I replied, nodding. 'I have to say, it was pretty good.'

*

NEW MILLENNIUM – NEW DICTATS

'Could I see you after the lesson about my essay?'

It was an innocent enough question from Diane, one of my sharp, sparky A level students. I'd just returned her essay on *Waiting For Godot* and she clearly wasn't happy with the grade I'd given. I'd taught her for two years to GCSE and now for a year in sixth form. I knew her well. English is a subject that lets you into the minds of your students in a way that most other subjects don't. Students write about their ideas, their thoughts and feelings in their work and you get close to the way a young person ticks. I had a good rapport with Diane, had done for three years now. Seeing her after the lesson for ten minutes was never a big deal. Until now.

At the last staff meeting the Head had issued a new dictat. 'Never allow yourself to be alone in a room with a student, especially a male teacher with a female student.'

The bell for the end of the lesson and start of morning break rang and the class started filing out of the room. Diane's friend Gill was near the door.

'Could Gill just er.. stay behind while I see you.'

Gill looked at me, looked at Diane, 'You want to see me as well?' she asked.

'Well, not exactly,' I said. 'There's a new rule that we mustn't be seeing students on their own.'

The elephant was suddenly in the room. Gill frowned. Diane tilted her head and looked at Gill. 'Why is that?' she said looking back at me.

I had introduced a wedge into the situation which had never been there before. Diane was suddenly wary, so was Gill. They were looking at me differently. 'Is this to protect me from you or you from me?' she said.

I shrugged a little. 'It's a new rule and you got it in one,' I said. 'Child protection, they call it. Situations do arise.'

'C'mon, Mr Day, I've known you for years.'

'It's the rule,' I said.

Diane looked at Gill. 'Sorry, you've gotta stay by the sound of it.'

'Seems daft to me,' said Gill, 'but go on, just pretend I'm not here.'

Relationships with students were complex. 'In loco parentis' they termed it – 'in the place of the parent'. Teachers trod a tricky path every day. From the time they arrived in Year 7 you watched students growing and changing. You helped to nurture them in various ways. You shared their emotional turmoil, their highs and lows. But there was always that invisible line you respected and didn't cross. *Don't Stand So Close to Me* Sting had sung in the 1980 song by The Police. He knew. He'd been a teacher himself, just briefly.

Now it had been formalised with the new dictat. Maybe in the past we had all been too casual leaving ourselves vulnerable and the students vulnerable. I'm not sure. But in that moment, when I got that look of confusion from Diane and Gill, I felt something had intruded which didn't deserve to be there.

There are certain vintage years in teaching when, as a teacher, your students inspire you with their wit and their promise and you inspire them to discover their potential. This was such a year. A class of thirty young individuals can gel into a community who laugh together and sometimes share tears together when moved by a poem, a piece of literature, a scene in a play or a film. One of the plays I often used as a drama text was Willy Russell's *Educating Rita*. Reading the text and watching Lewis Gilbert's brilliant 1983 film of the play starring Michael Caine and Julie Walters was guaranteed to move you to laughter and to tears as you watched the vulnerable character of Rita struggling to find her voice and realise her ambition to get an education.

Romeo and Juliet could have an even more powerful impact with its theme of forbidden teenage love and untimely death. For years I had used Zeffirelli's 1968 film which endured because of the brilliance of the filming, the fight choreography and the innocence of the two lovers played by Leonard Whiting and Olivia Hussey. Classes loved the play but then came the Australian director Baz Lurhmann in 1996 with a new version starring the young Leonardo Di Caprio and Clare Danes. This was modern, this was visual jazz, the camera work and editing were startlingly original, the soundtrack unashamedly contemporary. And yet Lurhmann respected the original Elizabethan text. The film is so driven by the action that you barely notice the Shakespearean language which people often complain is impenetrable. Not so with this version. The students loved it and it made engaging with the written text so much easier.

To share the emotional temperature of plays, poetry, films and literature with students was what made the teaching of English so rewarding. Even with the constraints of the new curriculum revisions, it was still possible to navigate through a syllabus and find inspiring material to ignite the imagination. We could still laugh and cry together even with the Ofsted wolf knocking at the door. I would be sorry to say goodbye to some of this year's classes.

*

When Big Ben chimed the stroke of midnight and the new Millennium was welcomed, the dreaded Millenniun computer bug did not strike us down, networks did did not crash and life continued into what became awkwardly called the 'Noughties'. What did strike me down was the latest bombshell from Oxford. 'We will need a Teachers' Book to accompany the course book', chimed a New Year e-mail from Helen. It was the first I'd heard about it. She went on: 'Imagine a teacher new to media work. This book will explain how to handle each section of the student book, what possible answers might be given for the questions you've set on each page and suggestions for extension work. And we need it within two months if we're to meet the publishing schedule. The book is due out in January 2001'.

Why on earth had they not alerted me to this a year ago when I was formulating the questions and thinking through the tasks for each section? I could have written down the answers then! As it was I would have to think my way right back to the very first page and plough my way through again with the clock ticking loudly in my ears.

*

INTO THE WALLED GARDEN

Across the water, the Grand Gateway, the O-torii of the Miyajima Shrine seemed to float on the high tide. The changing light shifted the colour from red to pink to a luminous orange as the sun started to set. As the tide dropped and the mud flats emerged so the people came with their baskets and trowels to hunt for shell-fish. Then the great O-torii stood even higher with its feet of camphor wood firmly embedded in the silt of the bay. Ten days into our trip, this sacred island of Miyajima, just over the water from Hiroshima, was a place which had quickly cast its spell over me. But then the whole trip was a trip like no other.

It was a couple of months earlier that my older brother, Ian, had mentioned that he and Pat, were flying out to visit son, Andrew, and his wife who were in Japan for a year. They were taking part in the JET (Japan Exchange and Teaching) programme where English-speaking teachers worked alongside Japanese teachers to help students improve their spoken English.

Although we only had two weeks holiday at Easter we leapt at the opportunity. My old friend Will, a colleague from that first year teaching in Lichfield, had been teaching in Japan for years and married a young Japanese lady. He always spoke warmly of the Japanese culture and its intriguing contrast to that in the West. Now I knew something of what he was talking about. Everything was different. Like entering a parallel universe, all assumptions about how to live were challenged. Here are some starters:

- The Japanese betray little in their faces – all is politeness and courtesy. To show anger is seen as a weakness. To say 'No' to someone is a gross insult. They always hedge round a disagreement to avoid hurting feelings.
- Bowing – everyone bows. The air hostesses bow when you enter the plane. The ticket collector bows as he enters and leaves the carriage of the bullet train. The angle of the bow mirrors the level of respect shown to the other person. The lower the bow, the greater the respect.
- Japanese show reverence for age. The older you are the more respect you deserve. (Quite a contrast to attitudes in the West!).
- Never enter a building in your outdoor shoes. These must be removed and replaced by indoor slippers. In hotels there are different slippers for the bedroom and toilet areas.
- Using a hotel bath. Traditional baths are cube shaped, deep enough to cover your shoulders when sitting. They will be full of hot water when you enter the washing area and covered to keep in the heat. Never enter the bath without prior washing. Sit on the stool in front of one of the showers and wash yourself before bathing. Leave the water in the bath covered for the next person.
- Social drinking. You are not expected to drain your glass before leaving a bar. Whenever you take a drink it will be immediately topped up by your host. Never top up your own drink, this is impolite. This routine led to Andrew getting hopelessly sozzled when taken out drinking with a colleague during his first week. He kept finding his drink topped up and felt he had to drain his glass each time. He only made the mistake once. And don't say 'chin chin' as a drinking toast – this is Japanese for male genitals.
- Beware of showing off your skill with chopsticks – pointing with them, sticking them in your food is impolite.
- If sitting on the floor, never point your toes at another person. This is an insult. Cross you legs.
- If receiving a present, never open the gift in the presence of the giver in case you betray your feelings about the gift.
- Public use of handkerchiefs is frowned upon. It is more polite to sniff, this being an admirable sign of self-restraint. Masks are often used by people with colds or coughs so that they don't spread their germs to others.
- Don't be afraid to slurp your noodles. This is expected.

The list could go on. While your mind is assaulted by these confusions and differences of etiquette, so are your senses and your sense of history.

Journal entry: Wed. April 19th 2000. Bedroom balcony - 8th floor of the International Youth House at Aster Plaza. I am looking out across the city of Hiroshima, mind wedged with confusion. I see a modern city, built on the rubble of the city which was flattened at 8.15 a.m. on August 6th 1945 when a nuclear bomb was detonated 1900 feet above the ground. 70% of the city was destroyed on that day, 80,000 killed. And what of the radiation? Surely radiation survives for millennia? But here I am in my white cotton kimono (I have remembered to tie it left over right – the other way is only used for clothing corpses) and towelling slippers, sipping tea, looking out over this modern city trying to fathom a myriad of confusions ignited by just being here.

I feel a kinship with what I see of the Shinto and Buddhist practices, where religion is not rooted in a church and a hierarchy but seems to be insinuated into the very air and the landscape. We come upon statues and shrines in woodland glades or on the edge of reflecting pools; the elegant design of temples, gardens and pagodas speaks of a quiet contemplative spritual tone, not the strident declamations of Roman Catholicism or Anglicanism back home. Shinto speaks of the interconnectedness of living things, a reverence for nature and connections with the past. D.H.Lawrence would have been at home here, I'm sure. He wouldn't have been seen as the heretic that he was in promulgating his belief in the flame of nature as the ultimate truth. Here in Japan, that reverence for the flame seemed to be a given.

It is a conformist culture. No-one likes to stand out as different. The grey-suited 'salary-men' follow their bosses for after-work drinks for as long as it takes to demonstrate their loyalty. There is an on-going fear of 'dishonour' which leads to suicides among the salary men who lose their jobs and generates a pressure-cooker tension in schools. Failure in school can lead to dishonour for the family.

My nephew invites us to visit his school at the end of a working day. He describes his frustration with the job. He's a trained drama teacher but finds the students will not make eye-contact with him in the classroom. Strong eye-contact is not the Japanese way. Outside the classroom it is different. Then the students are smiling and friendly. Inside the classroom is a different regime. There is no obligation on the teacher to ensure learning is taking place. That obligation rests with the student who faces 'dishonour' if he or she fails. Look into any Japanese classroom during a lesson and you will see a teacher at the front of the class, pointing at or writing on the blackboard. Look at the class and you may see some students involved in the lesson but you may also see students sleeping (typically the soccer players who are held in high esteem), girls at the back of the class who have set up their mirrors to do their make-

up, parents who have come to sit in the lessons because their child is ill and must not miss the day's lesson.

At the end of the school day the students and teachers set to the

task of cleaning the school. Equipped with mops, brooms and buckets there is a collective duty to make sure the school is left tidy for the next day. There is no fuss about this. It is the Japanese way to conform and carry out your obligations with good humour. And there is lots of humour. The students smile and laugh readily. They wave to us as we tour the

school and the grounds, and are desperate to have their photos taken.

After school there is an hour or so of extra-curricular activities. Everyone takes part and it is all unsupervised. The students run the whole thing themselves. The soccer players are smartly kitted out and start their drills on the soccer square. Lined up along the outside wall of the gym, five meters apart, stand members of the school orchestra separately practising their instruments. We pass through a strange cacophony of noise from trumpets, trombones, flutes, clarinets and

violins and make our way to the baseball field. There are ten lines of boys pitching, hitting and throwing. As we approach the edge of the field, they spot my nephew and all activity stops as they bow to him. We bow in return and then the activity resumes.

Inside the gym there are more activities: volleyball teams squaring up for a game, groups jogging round the perimeter of the gym, gymnasts doing vaults and complicated flik-flaks, others doing tricky routines on parallel bars. In some of the side rooms there are karate, judo and tai-quando sessions. And again, I am amazed there is not a teacher in sight.

'It's just what they do,' says my nephew. 'Part of the group thing to take part, be involved, conform to what is expected.'

It seems enviable, this group ethos, this eagerness to take part. I think of the reluctance back home; how students sometimes have to be dragged to get involved in school teams, how it's seen as 'uncool' to get enthusiastic about school clubs and activities. As for cleaning the school – how unhip would that be! The Japanse system is controlled, regulated, orderly.

But there is always the flip side to these things. The conformist culture in Japanese schools is highly pressured. The fear of 'dishonour' probably accounts for the high suicide rates among students. The teaching hierarchy does not expect to be challenged and so the system is rigid. In recent years there have been cases of students in revolt against this inflexibility. Some are hammering at the doors to let in change.

One evening, at rush hour, we were walking back to our hotel in Hiroshima. We crossed a one-way street jammed with four lines of slow-moving traffic. Suddenly, there were car horns and a siren and flashing headlights. Driving down the centre of the road straight into the on-coming traffic at a slow, steady speed was a powerful motor-bike. The rider wore a red jump suit and black helmet. Behind him, standing on the seat was a young man in a bright yellow jump suit, arms folded, head held high. Cars swerved to the left and the right as the bike ploughed its furrow of defiance against the tide of the oncoming traffic. It was a dramatic gesture of rebellion which I'll never forget.

On the flight home I spent a long time standing at the rear of the plane gazing out of one of the windows at the snowy wastes of Siberia. No distractions in a white wasteland. Good for contemplation. Good for trying to digest something of what we had just experienced. To live in a culture of order, control and group conformity, if only for two weeks, is to enter a world of calm predictability. Initially it seems quite attractive compared to the chaotic individuality which often characterises British society. Ultimately, I suppose it is the choice between a tidy walled garden or a wilder landscape of pitfalls and promise.

*

VINTAGE TIMES

Each summer term there was a residential week for Cumbria's gifted year 9 students held at the Brewery Arts Centre in Kendal. For years it had been organised by Ron Creer, the Head of English at Coniston School. I had taken six students the previous year and been inspired by the programme of creative activities which Ron had arranged. There were writing workshops with professional writers, poetry sessions, drama activities and opportunities for the students from a dozen Cumbrian schools to mingle and work together.

Just after Christmas I had received a call from Ron asking if I would be prepared to organise this year's course as he had other commitments. Here was a major challenge and an opportunity. I hoped to complete the Teachers' Book for OUP before Easter so I'd have some space in my head to take this on. And for the students who were invited to attend, the course was a great antidote to the mindlessness of preparing for SATS tests. I readily agreed.

If I ever want a reference point for what great education can be I think back to that week in Kendal. Admittedly I was working with bright, self-selected students but to see the creative potential that can be unlocked by having the right environment and stimulus from talented professionals was inspiration indeed.

I had a team of three other teachers helping. We had students from ten Cumbrian schools and I'd recruited the novelist Janni Howker, *(The Nature of the Beast)*, Misha, a black performance poet from London, Martin Plenderleith, a BBC Radio presenter, each of whom devised some challenging sessions for the thirty students.

Early on, as an 'ice-breaker', I'd used my *Shakespeare's Insults* book (Hill & Ottchen) and mixed the students in pairs to create and perform a dramatic dialogue they had composed. There were some hilarious offerings and it was immediately apparent that we had some talented young people here for the week. It progressed like a series of fairground rides; lots of high octane moments of humour and drama then times of quiet contemplation when the students would lose themselves in the nooks and crannies of the old Brewery building or out in the gardens to work on individual or group tasks.

In the evenings, after our meal at the Youth Hostel, we would trek up to the park overlooking Kendal and play wild games of rounders. On one evening I booked us all in to the Brewery cinema to see Albert Finney and Julia Roberts in the brilliant new film, *Erin Brockovich*. To bring down the excitement of the day and hopefully settle them down for

461

some sleep we would gather the students in the youth hostel lounge and I would read them a short story: something like Roald Dahl's *The Hitchhiker* or Ray Bradbury's *The Other Foot*.

At the end of the week the students prepared a presentation for when their parents arrived. There was drama, music, readings, audio-visual projects and, when it was all over and I'd offered my thanks to one and all for the efforts and achievements of the week, there were the hugs and a few tears, an exchanging of addresses before they went their separate ways. The bubble of the week leaked away leaving us all a little sad but richer that we had shared something rare and special, something that all young people deserved to experience.

That summer term was also veiled in sadness at the sudden death of Frank, my first Headmaster at Newman, he of *Albert and the Lion* fame. Since his retirement in 1993 he had travelled widely in Africa and South America doing voluntary work with CAFOD (the Catholic Overseas Development Organisation). His death was sudden and unexpected. He had set the tone for the school during the 21 years of his leadership; for a Catholic school it was not overly doctrinaire but it practised a philosophy of humanity and compassion. For me it made coming to work a pleasure. The spirit of 'family' which Frank had engendered in the school still lived on in the good humour of the staff room and in the relationships between teachers and students.

I was also sad to see the departure of my sixth form groups. These multi-talented youngsters, several of whom had starred in my *Grease* production were destined for interesting futures. We had shared an intricate journey through some challenging literature texts – the poetry of Ted Hughes, the prose of Hardy and the gripping narrative of Charles Frazier's 1997 novel *Cold Mountain*. The students in the A level Media Studies group had produced impressive projects using sophisticated graphics and digital photography. We had wrestled with the writings of Ferdinand Saussure and Roland Barthes and their theories of semiology, explored the genres of film noir and science fiction, delved into the debate over the impact of media violence. For the two years I had taught these young people I had watched them grow; at first taking tentative intellectual steps, then finding their feet, gaining in confidence and self belief and finally starting to really flourish. I would await their exam results in August with great anticipation but not without the usual trepidation.

Katie was in Spain that summer working as a holiday rep learning to handle tourists who paid for budget holidays but expected 5-star treatment. It tested her skills of diplomacy and tolerance. She would off-load to us down the telephone about how appalling the job was but we later learned from a friend she was lodging with that she was the darling of the coach drivers, being the only rep who spoke in courteous Spanish, the other reps speaking to the drivers loudly and slowly in English as if they were addressing naughty children.

James was back in America coaching again for the summer but that autumn it was his graduation from the university in York. The ceremony was held in York Minster. The sun shone on the wonderful Gothic edifice of the cathedral as we proudly took photographs of our son in his cap and gown. Afterwards as we made our way to a restaurant to celebrate, my dear mother walked hand in hand with James down the street looking like 'the-cat-that got-the-cream'. Her expression of pride and delight has lived with me ever since.

The school A level results were especially good that year but what capped things was receiving a letter from the Examination Board saying that Jennie, one of my English Literature students, was in the top twenty students in the country. She had won a place at Oxford and was off to Magdalen College to study law.

Vintage times indeed.

*

INTO THE WOODS

My baby is born! After a protracted four year pregnancy the postman has delivered a first copy of *Mixed Media* and I am on cloud 999! It wasn't entirely unexpected. Just before Christmas I had received a copy of the flyer for the book which was going out to schools announcing the publication date - April 2001. And here we are, finally, after so much blood, sweat and gnashing of teeth. I have a renewed respect for every name on every book on every bookshelf. Getting a book published is hard, hard graft, let me tell you.

I ordered a couple of sets for school and, the first time they were placed in front of the students, I glowed with satisfaction and waited. It took a while and then a girl spotted the name on the front. My name. She frowned, looked up, looked back at the book.

'Did you write this book, sir?' she said.

Queasy mix of pride and embarrassment. 'Er, yes I did.'

'How d'you write a book?'

'It's a long story.'

And, apart from me, would anyone buy it? That was the question. The deal was that I would get a statement half yearly in July and January with any attendant royalties. Royalties were set at 10% of the price which initially was set at £8.00. So 80p for each copy sold. I certainly wasn't going to get rich quick and retire to that Caribbean island of my dreams. But the money mattered little. The satisfaction of seeing it in print was worth a treasure chest of gold bullion. And it looked good. The cover was colourful and contemporary, the interior airy, easy on the eye and full of vivid illustrations. The designer, for all that I had cursed her when she set me to slash and cut the content, had done a good job.

Time would tell whether other teachers agreed.

However, my euphoria coincided with a nightmare scenario which was unfolding across the Cumbrian countryside and beyond. Following an outbreak of 'foot and mouth' disease which threatened to destroy livestock farming across Britain, the government embarked on a slaughter of cattle in an attempt to control and eradicate the disease. The slaughter target was 21,000 cows a day.

A few miles south of Carlisle near the village of Great Orton a huge burial site for carcasses was being prepared on the old airfield. Driving home one night after a parents' evening I remember seeing the distant glow of a funeral pyre, black smoke billowing into the night sky. As I got closer to the fire I stopped the car and stared. It was like something from a Hieronymus Bosch painting: carcasses, legs and heads silhouetted against the brilliant orange of the flames. It seemed positively medieval in its crude brutality. The cull continued for the next few months and for Cumbrian farmers it was a living nightmare. The countryside was a 'no-go' area for walkers and at Sue's school the children from farming families were for a time marooned inside their farms, prohibited from leaving in case they unwittingly spread the disease on their shoes.

It was a suffocating time and I needed to breathe some different air. Following the completion of the book my head had been de-cluttered of all the spirals and tangles of words, thoughts, issues which accompanied the writing, editing and the production of the book. It was time for some therapy. I decided to renew my dabblings in rustic furniture-making.

Back in the spring of 1996 we had gone to the horticultural show at Holker Hall in south Cumbria. Apart from the plant exhibits, what had intrigued me were the stalls displaying rustic furniture. I'd never seen a bench made from limbs of green wood. I didn't realise that there was a craft tradition of making rough hewn chairs, tables and tools from unplaned wood. This appealed. This touched a chord. This was a style of woodwork which spoke to something in my DNA. *'Things men have made with wakened hands and put soft life into...'* came the echo from Lawrence's poem *Things Men Have Made*. I'd never been much good at real precision joinery but with this way of working you get away with literally a 'bodged' job. They were actually publicising a course in 'chair bodging'. I sat at the feet of one of the craftsman who talked about traditional methods of working. No power tools, just age-old methods of using hand-tools. He talked with a slow, gentle gravitas which spoke of a wisdom and a knowledge honed and gilded over a lifetime. This was an antidote to my weekday world of computers, spread-sheets, data

processing, and target-setting. This was just what I needed. I wanted to be on the receiving end of this old craftsman's wisdom. 'Whatever your course is, I want to do it,' I decided.

So I had signed up for Colin Simpson's course on 'Wooden Hay Rakes and Gunpowder Barrels' to be held along with fifteen other courses at Hay Bridge Nature Reserve, near Ulverston in south Cumbria.

It had been a blissful, bucolic long week-end. After school on a Friday afternoon I drove down to Hay Bridge and pitched my little tent in a meadow below a farmhouse barn along with other campers in horse-drawn caravans, Mongolian yurts, tents ancient and modern. Then for three days I worked with Colin learning how to use my hands, read the grain in a piece wood, feel the difference between the tough fibrous core of a rod of hazel compared to the fine, dry grain of ash which split

465

cleanly with one stroke of a cleaver. I learned to slow down as Colin reined in my exuberance which often led to a shoddy standard of 'bodging'. He would look at some part of my hay rake that I'd been rushing to finish, and say simply, 'I don't think we're happy with this are we?' I would nod, knowing he'd found me out and return to a slower, more measured approach.

During the coffee breaks I drifted through the woods where the pole-lathers were working. They bent to their work, rhythmically toeing their treadles to turn the wood, shaping it with the blade of a chisel. On the hill below the barn sat the willow weavers making baskets, fashioning exquisite patterns from different shades of willow. Down in the meadow a column of steam and smoke rose from the yurt makers who were steam-bending lengths of ash and by the river were the coracle makers weaving frames of ash which they would later cover with tarred canvas.

I had returned home after that weekend with two hay rakes and a small gun-powder barrel made from strips of oak. The barrel was bound together by thin strips of hazel which were ingeniously woven. No nails could be used for fear of sparks igniting the gunpowder. Clever, those craftsmen of old.

Now, five years on, it was time to renew my rustic connections. Enough of the world of publishing and cerebral stress. I needed to be under the greenwood tree.

My close friend Andy, Head of one of the primary schools in Carlisle, was a fine woodworker but was keen to sample the world of rustic bodging. After a little research we found a week-end course at the Beamish outdoor museum in County Durham. We could make our own 'shave-horse', a traditional rustic device you sit on to clamp and shape wood. The course tutor was a craftsman called Maurice Pyle. It sounded interesting.

And so, after school one Friday afternoon in May, Sue and I loaded up the caravan, collected Andy and his wife Lily and drove across the Pennines to the Bobby Shaftoe Caravan Park located within walking distance of Beamish.

The following morning while Sue and Lily went off to discover what Durham had to offer, Andy and I made our way along a small river path to a meadow where an ancient stone barn stood. It was below and out of sight of the main outdoor museum area and it felt like stepping back in time. Inside the doorway of the barn a blackened kettle steamed on a charcoal brazier and we were greeted by our teacher for the weekend, Maurice Pyle. There were seven others on the course and after a brief introduction to the component parts of a shave-horse we selected a metre length of ash which we had to split to form the main seat. This then had to be shaped and smoothed using small axes and chisels.

Through the weekend the work moved from some crude chopping and splitting of wood to fine chisel work on a pole lathe which stood in the centre of the old barn. The ancient stone walls were stacked with varying lengths of wood. The air was pungent with the scent of resin and woodsmoke, the light hazy with shafts of sunlight streaming through gaps in the barn roof. Time had shifted and I felt like some character from a Thomas Hardy novel, some estate worker relying only on the skill of my hands and the tools I was using.

By the Sunday afternoon Andy and I made our way back along the river path carrying our trophies on our shoulders.

'So what is it?' asked Lily.

'It's a shave horse, of course,' replied Andy proudly.

'What does it do?' asked Sue.

'D'you sit on it when you're having a shave?' said Lily, winking at Sue.

'This, my dear,' said Andy, 'is what the traditional woodsman would set up in the woods to craft his chairs and other fine wooden utensils.'

'Do we really need one though, when we've got IKEA just up the road?' said Lily.

We didn't rise to the baiting but, casting disdainful glances in the direction of our wives, loaded our prizes into the boot of the car. For two days we had been steeped in the esoteric world of 'bodging'. Only other 'bodgers' could understand the simple joys of that silvan world.

*

'I've decided on teaching. I'm applying to Liverpool for a PGCE.' This was James, out of the blue, on the phone from America.

Since graduating he had been over there coaching full-time.

'Thought you'd said you'd never be a teacher having seen how many hours we put in,' I replied.

'Well, I've been thinking. I like the buzz I get from the kids when I'm coaching.'

'The world needs good teachers, so go for it,' I said.

By coincidence, Katie was on the phone from Stirling later that same day. She was in her last year majoring in psychology. 'Thought I wanted to be an educational psychologist,' she said, 'but I think I need some experience with children first. So I'm applying for a teacher training course at Leicester.'

'Right,' I said. 'You've seen what it's done to us,' I added.

'C'mon dad, you know you love it really.'

'Seriously, it's hard work, long hours, piles of marking, frustrating government policy changes every other year, but yes, there's no other job which is as creative and rewarding and there's always shelf stacking in Tesco if it doesn't work out.'

'Thanks, dad.'

Katie's graduation from Stirling was another great milestone. The sun shone as we took photographs on the edge of the campus lake. We had listened to the actress Diana Rigg give her address as Chancellor of the university and now it was time to celebrate. This was the year of our 30th wedding anniversary and we were planning to meet up with James in America and the four of us would do some kind of road trip.

August 7th, the day of our anniversary, found us drenched in spray in a boat at the base of Niagara Falls. We had flown into Toronto, driven round Lake Ontario to Niagara to stay with some old friends who had recently emigrated from Cumbria. From there we drove across New York State to the coast of Maine to sample some of the famous clam chowder and lobster then down to Boston where James was desperate to

go and spend some of his earnings at the Abercrombie and Fitch store in Faneuil Market.

Finally we met up with our American friends, Judy and Boyd, in New York City. They insisted we took a ferry ride on the Staten Island ferry. It is one of the great New York institutions. There is no charge and the ferry runs round the clock between the southern tip of Manhattan Island, past Ellis Island and the Statue of Liberty, to the St George Terminal on Staten Island. On that August day as we returned across the waters of the Upper Bay, the setting sun was glinting on the faces of the iconic Twin Towers in Lower Manhattan.

Less than a month later I was coming out of the staffroom at school at around 2.15pm. My colleague, Paul, called to me from the doorway of the office. 'Come and look at this,' he said. There was a small TV monitor in the corner of the office which normally monitored the CCTV cameras. Now it was tuned to the BBC channel which was taking live footage from the American channel CNN. There were the familiar Twin Towers again, but now black smoke was billowing from the top of one of them. 'What's happened?' I asked. Paul shook his head, 'Must be a fire or a bomb or something.' We both stared at the screen. Then, from the right of the picture a small object, a plane appeared. It flew straight into the second tower slicing into it half way down. There was a massive explosion of flame and debris and then clouds of smoke.

In those seconds the axis of the world tilted, the planet shifted, the earth trembled and that evening as Sue and I watched again the agony of the events – the first plane crashing, then the second, then the collapse of the towers, the people running ahead of the billowing clouds of debris, then emerging like so many ghosts covered in grey dust, you knew that the world had changed forever.

*

BONKING DINOSAURS

If the wider world had changed forever, in a small way so did my working world change that autumn of 2001 by a chance discovery. My former colleague Avril, who had been Head of Music at Newman, was now part of the Cumbria advisory team. In November she organised the first of a series of impressive annual conferences on the theme of creativity. Held at the Lowood Hotel on Lake Windermere this was just what was needed to counter the increasingly philistine policy changes which were forever spilling out of the government's Education Department.

That first conference, entitled 'Inspiring Minds', started with some inspiring key-note speakers. Then followed two days of fascinating workshops: creativity in writing, computing, drama, fine art, dance, music, sculpture, as well as a chance to meet and discuss ideas with other teachers in a pleasant working environment. During the breaks between workshops and seminars you could browse the stalls of books, computer software and other teaching aids. It was then that one stall in particular caught my attention and changed the course of my career over the next few years.

469

The computer company Intel was demonstrating a small video camera for use in classrooms. It looked like a small toy gun and sat on the desk in its plastic base. I had been using a big Sony video camera in the classroom for a number of years for recording drama, news simulations and role play but these new cameras were obviously designed for students to use. I knew only too well that cameras in classrooms could be a disaster and huge waste of time. Youngsters tend to fool around when a camera is pointed at them so this wasn't what drew my attention. It was a reference in the product brochure to 'Stop-Frame Animation'. This was intriguing. Stop-Frame Animation was the painstaking technique used to make animated cartoons. In recent years Aardman Animation had achieved great success with their Wallace and Gromit animations. I had used some of their storyboards in my media book. I wondered if animation could work in the classroom.

I ordered one of the cameras and over the Christmas holidays played around with this new technique. The software which accompanied the cameras was stunning, allowing you to add sound, text, graphics and special effects to whatever you had filmed. The filming was a slow, concentrated process of setting up a scene with some toy figures, moving them slightly, capturing each minute adjustment and finally running together the sequence of shots to create the animated movement. But how could this work in a classroom of thirty students and would it meet the approval of an Ofsted inspector?

Over the past couple of years I had invested a portion of my departmental budget in buying some of the new generation of slim laptop computers. These could provide the flexibility I needed. Fixed computers were really too restrictive for what I wanted. I envisaged groups of students working round a small stage-set mounted on a table. With my six laptops I could accommodate groups of five students. It might just work. I took a gamble and ordered six of the cameras.

During the next few weeks I scoured charity shops and discount stores for cheap toy figures, cars, animals, anything which the students might find interesting for creating an animated story. Eventually I had four large plastic boxes full of these tiny props. It was launch time.

That year I had a particularly interesting Year 8 class with a group of bright, lively boys who were well into computer gaming. I was sure it would work with them but I was keen to see if it would catch the imagination of the girls. Typically, girls were not drawn to playing computer games and I hoped this might be an alternative way for them to access the IT (Information Technology) curriculum.

I had a lesson with this Year 8 class after lunch on a Wednesday afternoon, so during the lunch break I set up the computers in six areas of the classroom. Each group had a piece of art board they could set up as a screen or back drop for their filming. I would leave it to them to choose their props.

When the students came in they were understandably bemused.

'Find a seat and just sit down for a moment,' I said. I called the register and then continued. 'We're going to try something new today. You'll be working in groups of five or six. Each group has a computer and one of these new cameras. First I'm going to do a quick demonstration.'

I showed them a couple of simple animations I had made a few weeks earlier and then demonstrated the principle of stop-frame filming.

'Right, first you need to choose your toys. Keep it simple for now.'

They were intrigued. They were being invited to play with toys in an English lesson. They didn't have to write anything or read anything. This was weird, Mr Day.

I watched them. Listened to the buzz of discussion. No-one fooled around, even the usual malcontents who struggled with literacy were there, choosing their toy figures, discussing possible scenarios, settling down round the table, setting up their little stage for the filming.

At odd times a hand was raised to sort out a technical problem but apart from that I was not needed. They were utterly immersed, some concentrating on carefully adjusting their toy figures, while others operated the computer to catch each movement.

I did a quick mental check of what is supposed to be in evidence in a good lesson, according to Ofsted criteria. There was lively discussion, interaction and problem-solving; there was a high level of IT skill involved in using the computer software; they were constructing a narrative sequence and working towards a final presentation to an audience – all valid criteria in the New Literacy Framework for English which had just been published and to which we were expected to pay homage. I could be on to a winner here.

During that year I tried out animation work with all age groups from my 11 year olds in year 7 to my A level group. Amazingly it worked at all levels. Typically the 11 year olds put together simple scenarios of heroes and villains, damsels being kidnapped by pirates, knights in castles fighting off marauding dinosaurs. With the older students the storylines became more subtle, ironic, comic even.

Some of my A level media studies students decided to choose animation for their examination project work and things got really interesting. The most ambitious project was by two talented students, Damian and Carly. Damian was a keen musician and his friend Carly was an aspiring poet. Since year 9 she had been showing me her poems and by sixth form she was deep into the complexities of Sylvia Plath's work.

Their animation was a spoof on the 2001 Lara Croft film *Tomb Raider*. It was called 'The Quest For The Blind Eye' and involved a main character called Cara Loft. They wanted to experiment with special lighting effects and needed a dark room. The only possible place I could think of was a type of broom cupboard beneath the lecture theatre. And so, every week, for one of our lessons, they would troop off to this cupboard with their lights, camera, computer, music player and props to make their film.

This was all unknown territory for me and for them. Their A level results and possible university places hung on it being successful. Every so often I would go and check how things were going and find them squashed in this tiny space, stepping round equipment shooting some scene, adjusting lights, character positions and camera angles. I hoped the final result would do justice to their time and effort.

I wasn't disappointed. The final film was skilfully constructed. They had painted backdrops for a range of scenes, edited in real-time footage of jungles and tropical animals, used camera angles and lighting for dramatic effect. Damian had composed part of the soundtrack and edited it together with other music tracks and sound effects. They had written a script which was witty and full of comic touches. I hoped the exam board would be as impressed as I was, for this was a first for me and something of a gamble.

It paid off. The examination board had never had a submission like it and they were impressed. The technology to produce animated films in a school was utterly new. We were probably among the first in the country to be experimenting with it. The film was highly commended and earned them a top grade. It was even showcased in an event at Tyne Tees TV studios in Newcastle which was celebrating new achievements in using digital media.

If this was one of the high points in my new animation venture, there were other more dubious moments. That same year I had a particularly tricky year 9 group with some boys who disguised their limitations in literacy by shows of bravado and disruptive behaviour.

Should I gamble with letting them loose with an animation project or not? It could be mayhem.

They tumbled into the classroom as usual and stopped when they saw the changed set up.

'What's happening, sir?' shouted Chris. He was a tall lad, one of the stars of the school football team but not so good at English.

'Just sit down, Chris and I'll explain.' The lads went through their usual pantomime of pushing and barging each other to find a seat. When they were all settled I explained about this new project. I showed them Carly and Damian's animation and a couple of the best ones from my year 8 group.

'So that's what year 8 can do,' I said. 'I'm sure you can better that.'

'Just watch us,' said Brian, nudging his mate Ricky.

I invited them, group by group, to choose the toys they would work with.

'It's like being back in playgroup,' laughed Chris. I watched the lads sorting through the boxes of toy figures. They were the last to settle. The other groups had already got started, positioning their figures, adjusting the camera, checking how it looked on the computer screen.

For the next forty-five minutes there was just a low murmur of voices, eyes concentrating on their desk-top stage-sets. Even my group of wayward lads was working intensely on their scenario which involved some plastic dinosaurs and a piece of string which Chris had attached to one of them. I had no idea what their storyline was but they were working well and I wasn't going to interrupt their concentration. I'd never seen them so involved, so focussed, in any of my previous lessons.

'Sir, have you got any of that blu-tak stuff, you know, for sticking things,' asked Chris.

Along with my boxes of toy figures I had also assembled an assortment of paper clips, sticky tape, blu-tak, string, scissors – the sorts of things which might be useful.

'Yes, Chris, blu-tak's here.'

Then he gave a curious smile, glancing at Brian. 'Have you got it in white, sir?'

'You mean 'white-tak'? Yes I've got some of that too.'

He came out and took some and returned to the group. There was a burst of laughter from the lads and then they settled down again.

I'd given the class forty-five minutes to produce some sort of animated sequence so that we had time to view each group's work. The lads were the first to put up their hands. 'Finished, sir, come and look at this.'

They were clearly pleased with their efforts and they had worked extremely well. I sat down with them and Ricky clicked the computer mouse to run the sequence.

One dinosaur moved across the screen. Another appeared from the top of the screen dangling from a piece of string. This one then landed on top of the other dinosaur. From a technical point of view the next sequence must have been a painstaking one to film as the movements of the two dinosaurs were choreographed very smoothly. The climax came as the humping movement of the dinosaurs speeded up and then a string of white tack appeared from between their legs. End of sequence.

The boys looked at me and waited. I nodded. Looked at them with a frown. 'Boys...,' I hesitated for effect, 'this is technically brilliant.' They were not expecting this and glanced at each other and then back at me. I continued, 'Technically brilliant but I don't think bonking dinosaurs can really go on general release. I think we need to censor this.'

'Smart though, sir?' ventured Chris.

'Technically smart, Chris. As for the content, I think you can do better. But good work lads. You concentrated really well.'

They were not expecting praise and didn't quite know how to respond. I got up and left them and went to view the other groups' work. They tidied up their equipment and then waited for the bell. As the class left the room it was Brian who came across to me. 'Will we be doing that again, sir?'

'Yes, Brian, this was just a start. But maybe go easy on the white-tak next time, eh?'

He smiled and nodded. 'Smart lesson, sir.'

And, bonking dinosaurs apart, I'd proved something with this lesson. Even with muddle-headed adolescent boys and all their attendant hormonal mood swings, this animation work was a winner. They had concentrated, co-operated, negotiated and fathomed the intricacies of the computer software with great skill. They had revelled in handling toys again. In what other context could it be 'cool' for a testosterone-fuelled teenager to be seen playing with plastic dinosaurs and toy pirates? I needed to spread the word about this way of working. I would put pen to paper.

*

AND BABY CAME TOO

In July 2002, the OUP statement fell through the letter box showing the sales to date of *Mixed Media*. It was 16 months since publication:

Student's Book   Home - 7,448   Export -   640
Teacher's Book   Home – 478   Export – 49

The book really was selling but apart from the numbers what fascinated me was where they were selling. Outside the UK there were sales in South America, the Caribbean, Africa, Asia, the Middle East, India, Australasia. Who were these teachers in faraway lands who were teaching about the media? What sort of institutions did they teach in? It was all a wonderful mystery.

At school, however, we were struggling to make sense of the so-called New Literacy Framework for English which fragmented the Year 7 curriculum into 98 separate skills areas. I volunteered the department to pilot this new approach, redesigned our departmental scheme of work to accommodate the teaching of the 98 skills, devised short, medium and long term plans and agreed to embark on the model '3-part-lessons – Starter/Main/Plenary'. It was anathema to me - mechanical and formulaic but I thought I'd better give it a try so that I could evaluate it from experience rather than prejudice.

After a term my colleagues and I were exhausted, dispirited and sapped of the inspiration which had made us such a successful department prior to this new government initiative. I fired off articles of complaint to various educational publications but to no avail. However, in the autumn, the Times Educational Supplement in their magazine section published my article on using animation in the classroom. It was a pleasing full-page spread with a nice colour photo of Stephen, one of my sixth formers operating the equipment.

My teaching veered from the sublime (animation lessons) to the ridiculous (trying to teach to the new Literacy Framework). But school itself felt a little strange that year. We seemed to be adrift. A colleague likened it to being on a ship without a captain. The Head was often absent from school, apparently involved in the Cumbria Secondary Heads Association. Finally news came through that he was leaving at Easter. That probably accounted for his absences – interviews I assumed.

Who would we get to take his place? That was now the question.

*

'Hello, Mr Day.'

There were two girls at the main door of the school with prams.

'Barbara?'

'We thought we'd bring our babies in, show everyone.'

Barbara and Jennifer had left the previous summer after failing to turn up for their GCSEs. Now I knew why.

Barbara was a sharp but headstrong girl. I'd never taught her but remembered a dramatic encounter when she was in Year 9. One of my colleagues called me out of my lesson one morning. 'Barbara's kicked off again. She's refusing to budge. I can't do anything with her. Can you come?'

I went down the hallway to the next classroom. There was Barbara in the middle of the room, arms folded, lips pursed, eyes on fire. What had gone on I had no idea but the rest of the class had retreated to the sides of the room. It was like entering a gladiatorial arena. One wrong move, the wrong look, the wrong tone of voice or choosing the wrong words and the situation could explode. My strategy was not to provide any ammunition to spark the explosion. I had no idea what had gone on so, as I always tried to do, I was respectful and spoke quietly and courteously hoping I could prise her out of the room.

'Could I speak to you for a minute, please, Barbara?'

It was a frozen moment. The seconds ticked. Would she move? Would she hold out? She was certainly strong-willed enough. I stood in the doorway waiting. Nobody spoke and I hoped my colleague wouldn't say anything to fuel the fire.

With a kick of a chair for good measure, Barbara stood up, glared at my colleague and strode out of the room. 'Thank you, Barbara,' I said, as she passed in front of me.

It was always difficult dealing with these situations. You had to support your colleagues but over the years in different schools I had seen so many instances of injustice against students when a teacher would be unreasonable, sarcastic, patronising or insensitive. Was it any wonder that a teenager, with all the problems that comes with that tricky stage of life, holds her ground and challenges her teacher.

Students are rarely unreasonable but they have a sharp sense of injustice and unfairness and what they value most is their self-respect. Challenge that and things can kick off big-time.

It turned out Barbara was having a tough time at home, her parents were splitting up, her brother was on drugs and she'd just been spoken to by my colleague in a way that had really touched a nerve. She agreed to apologise and the situation was defused.

Now, two years on, aged 17, she was pushing a baby. I bent over the pram and made polite noises about how lovely the baby was but all the time thinking what a shame this was for these two 17 year old girls. There was a high incidence of teenage pregnancies locally and I had tried to address this in my role as PSE co-ordinator. I had provided all the form tutors with material on contraception, sexual relationships; there were videos on teenage pregnancy but how the issues were handled in tutorials and whether the message ever made any impact I had no way of knowing.

'So how are things with you, Barbara? It can't be easy. New babies never are.'

She looked away for a moment, shrugged, 'Pretty rubbish really. Didn't get to do any GCSEs. Got on a college course but I've had to give that up. And none of my friends want to know me now I've got a kid.' She looked back at me, shrugged again, 'So, yeah, it's rubbish.'

'How would you feel about bringing your baby in and talking to some classes about being a young mother?' I said.

'Yeah, if you like.'

'It could be really good for them to hear it from you.'

'From the horse's mouth.'

I smiled, 'I wasn't going to put it like that, but yes from someone who's been there.'

Three weeks later Barbara was standing in front of one of the Year 11 classes. It was a PSE lesson. She had brought in the baby.

'Who has ever held a new baby?' I asked.

Quite a few of the girls but none of the boys put up their hands. I had agreed with Barbara that we should try this out. She handed me the baby and I looked around the class. On the front row was a lad who was really popular with the girls – good-looking, sporty – his current girlfriend was sitting next to him. He would do. I offered him the baby.

'Here,' I said, 'have a go?'

He froze for a moment then looked at the baby. His girl friend nudged him. 'Go on,' she said, 'he won't bite, he hasn't got any teeth yet.' Tentatively the lad took the baby and cradled it awkwardly in very stiff arms. Then he started to relax a little and Barbara continued talking, continued to tell how it was being a single mother.

'You lose your friends, you know. They pretend they'll keep coming round but they don't. Who wants to be around someone with a baby when you can go out clubbing with your mates. I used to imagine all the things I was going to do, be a fashion designer, have my own shop. I used to be good at art but I can't do any of that stuff now. It's pretty shitty really.'

The class hung on her every word, the baby slept quietly in the boy's arms. The lad's face and his shoulders had relaxed. He looked around at some of his mates. 'Didn't think I ever be doin' this,' he said.

'Well you might if you keep your brains in your trousers,' said Barbara.

This broke the ice and people laughed. A few now felt comfortable to ask questions and for the next twenty minutes there was a lively exchange.

'Thank you so much for coming in,' I said as Barbara carried the baby out to the pram. 'You've no idea the effect you may have had on that class.'

'S'all right. I quite enjoyed it.'

'You handled it better than some professionals I've seen. Could I book you in for some more sessions?'

She shrugged, 'If you think it's worth it.'

'Thanks, I'll be in touch.'

'See you,' she said and strode off up the school drive pushing her pram.

*

SOME BEGINNINGS AND SOME ENDINGS

The Atlantic rollers roared across Gunna Sound. Tiree was a distant stretch of low land misted by the sea surf. We were looking out from Calgary Point at the most westerly tip of the Scottish island of Coll. Here was a necklace of white sand beaches backed by heathered moorland. It was a raw, wild landscape, perfect for sweeping away the trivia of the working world. This was the island which inspired Mairi Hedderwick to write her wonderful series of 'Katie Morag' stories for children. She had lived for many years in a cottage just along the coast from Crossapol Bay where we were staying. Her daughter still ran a handmade pottery store in the little port of Arinagour where many of the stories are set.

We had left the car in Oban and crossed on the ferry with our cycles and rucksacks to spend a week of the summer holiday cycling and island hopping with our friends, Andy and Lily.

This was a great place for some quiet reflection, to skim stones across the water, to lie back, feel the sun on your face and work your fingers into the warmth of the fine, white sand.

I had just completed the first draft of a novel which I had started in America two summers ago. I had always craved to get a novel published. The media book was one type of writing but there was something more pure, more basic about writing fiction. It came from the heart, from the labyrinth of the imagination. You played with the rhythms of language, the tone and colour of words, and inhabited the emotions of your characters – all very different from writing a school text book. The story had been inspired by my time in teaching. I wanted to take the reader into the world of the classroom but I also wanted to see if I could get inside the mind of a troubled adolescent and add that to the mix. I had wrestled with the story for almost three years and now it was finished. Time to throw it to the wolves in the publishing world and see what would happen.

After a few days on Coll, we took a ferry across to the Isle of Mull on a morning of a flat calm sea with cormorants diving for fish in the wake of our small boat. I was musing on endings and beginnings - the novel was completed, Katie and James were both teaching and had bought a house together in south Manchester and for me the year had meant a new Headmaster. I hadn't seen much of him at the time of the interview, so this new regime was something of a question mark.

He had spent the first term interviewing the whole staff, one by one. Probably late forties, John was a tall, strongly built man with a gentle voice which carried a Geordie lilt. I liked the tone of his early assemblies. He spoke of the inclusiveness of the school, the community ethos he wanted to encourage. He would be looking to a Student Council for guidance and he would be listening to the staff and students for ways of moving the school forward. After feeling that we had been adrift as a school, now we were being driven. This new Head was a visionary, not one of the corporate clones who seemed to be taking over so many schools. Here was a man of empathy and sensitivity and with a clear sense of how he wanted to shape the school.

During his first year he had shaken things up. The roles of the senior managers had been changed, there were plans underway for modernising the dining hall and, to my delight, for carpeting teaching rooms and corridors. Table tennis tables were bought for the students' use during lunch breaks, there was new equipment for the PE department and the creation of a drama studio from an old, rather shabby teaching room.

He showed a particular interest in my animation lessons and within a short while was showing me plans for a new English and media teaching room to be fitted out with a bank of the latest computers. He was keen for me to run film animation sessions for our feeder primaries and by the spring we had groups of primary pupils in for half day animation sessions mentored by our year 10 and 11 students.

They talk about 'winds of change'. Things were certainly being shifted and shaped by this Head's new brand of leadership.

Sadly on the home front the cruel hand of fate slapped us down. Over Christmas my mother had stayed with us. She had joined in our walks, worn silly hats in games of charades, eaten heartily and relished the hugs of her grown up grandchildren. She waved us goodbye on January the 4th and was struck down with a devastating stroke two days later. It left her weakened but, worst of all, stole her power of speech. She tried to communicate her feelings through her eyes, her face, the lifting of her eyebrows but there was no way of checking that she was understanding all that we said to her. She could not write as usual with her right hand and her left-handed scrawl was never clear enough to decipher. For a person who loved conversation it was the ultimate cruelty.

From hospital she moved to a residential home in Beverley. She struggled on until November with her bright eyed resignation and her philosophy of 'what will be will be'. The week of her death coincided with the week of our Ofsted inspection. I went in each day, closed the door on my personal emotions, determined to get through the week.

The inspectors were thorough, their scrutiny was surgical. They commended the new Head on the changes he had made but in their words, 'You needed another 6 months to sort things out. We came too early.' They had unmasked weaknesses in various departments and in former management practice which could not be overlooked and we were placed in the dreaded category of 'Special Measures'.

For John, the Head, this was a body blow and what it now meant for everyone was constant monitoring and scrutiny. Local Authority inspectors would be in and out every few weeks to check on the progress of the school's Action Plan. There would be scrutiny of attendance figures, financial accounts and policy documents. At a departmental level the focus was on schemes of work, lesson planning and quality of teaching, not just for those departments judged to be 'failing' but for everyone. Lessons would be regularly observed, judgments made, individuals targetted and competency proceedings initiated if necessary. And of course, the public and the parents would now view us as a 'failing school'.

'Special Measures' was a stigma which fostered fear and paranoia. The Head tried to rally the staff by stressing the positive judgements in the Ofsted report and refocussing us on what now had to be done to get us out of Special Measures but in the final few weeks before Christmas there was little of the usual ebullience in the staffroom and there was no Christmas production to lift our spirits.

On the last day of term after the students had gone and the school was quiet I wandered round just looking at this 'failing school'. The Head had certainly put his mark on the place in a very short time. The new dining rooms with their modern furnishings and new kitchen and servery were impressive. The carpeted corridors and classrooms had transformed the feel of the school and had calmed the behaviour of the students. There was the new computer suite, the new library extension brightly lit and colourfully furnished with art work and easy chairs. And there was my new multi-media suite of computers and surround-sound cinema. It wasn't really a cinema but with the new digital projector, I could project a film from a DVD on my laptop on to a screen at the front of the class and give the students a quality cinematic experience. The students had joked that popcorn should be provided and then their lives would be complete.

What a transformation this was from the days when we wheeled a 23inch TV monitor and VHS video player round on a trolley and expected students to be captivated by movie magic. Now, with the new digital equipment, it was possible and I had plans to install surround-sound film projection in all the English teaching rooms.

I returned to the staff room via the main hall. It was set out for the A level exams which were due the first week of January. Rows of desks set out in single lines, the low winter sun casting a bright sheen across the polished parquet floor. Ronnie would have been proud to see his floors still showing off their shine.

Yes, the inspectors had come too early but it was no use telling ourselves that. To Ofsted, we were in the mire and we had to pull ourselves out.

*

Family and friends had come together at the little church in Leven for my mother's funeral and her ashes were placed next to my father's in the small burial site in the corner of the churchyard. Strange how the mind serves to sponge away the pain and leave the more positive memories. I rarely picture my mother during the year of her struggle after the stroke when she was so weakened and unable to give voice to her thoughts and feelings. Rather, I remember the smiles, the jokes and the good humour of her latter years. But the loss of both parents brings with it the shiver of one's own mortality and that Christmas I probably hugged the children a little harder and more consciously cherished our time together.

Just prior to Christmas, Sue and I took ourselves off to Cologne for a few days to see the Christmas markets. It was a welcome escape. The lights and colour of the market stalls under the spires of the splendid cathedral, the scent and taste of gluhwein and strudel, the comfort of a Bavarian 'Wurst' hotpot and a 'dunkel' bier in a crowded bierhaus – all these were as balm for our bruised emotions.

What finally put us back in the Christmas spirit was getting tickets for a German production of Ben Elton's rock musical *We Will Rock You* which celebrates the music of the Freddie Mercury's band 'Queen'. It didn't matter that we couldn't understand the German dialogue, the production was brilliantly staged and the sound of those classic Queen hits lifted our hearts for days afterwards.

*

THE DAY THE RAINS CAME DOWN

Rain had been pouring off the fields all night, incessant rain for four days now. The fields were saturated and water was flooding the road in front of the house. It was the first week of the new year and we were due back in school after the weekend. Then on the Saturday came power cuts and we had to heat a kettle and boil soup on our camping stove by candlelight. Normally the power would resume after a couple of hours but the cuts persisted and the rain continued to fall.

Early on Sunday morning the phone rang. It was Katie. 'What's happening in Carlisle? Have you seen the news?'

'We have no electricity so we're out of touch,' I replied.

'The city's completely flooded. I saw it on the news just now. Hardwicke Circus is under water and so is Warwick Road. What about the school?'

'We've heard nothing,' I said. 'I'll make some phone calls.'

And that was how it started. The realisation that something catastrophic was happening in Carlisle, something which would change things forever.

On that Saturday night of the 8th of January 2005 the equivalent of 2 months rain fell in 24 hours. In some places the flood water rose about four feet in one hour. The three rivers which flow through Carlisle, the Eden, the Caldew and the Petteril, all burst their banks and this, coupled with a high tide in the Solway, meant disaster for the city. 10,000 people were made homeless and nearly 5,000 homes, schools and businesses were flooded.

I knew the school was vulnerable. It stands close to the River Eden and is supposedly protected by high flood banks. But on that fateful Sunday morning the flood defences were overwhelmed and the school

was deluged to a depth of 5 feet. All the ground floor rooms – classrooms, offices, main hall, gym, new dining hall, computer suite – all were wrecked by contaminated flood water.

By Monday the waters had receded enough that I was able to get to see for myself. School was a place of utter devastation. The site manager's new bungalow which stood to the right of the main drive was fronted by piles of debris – broken furniture, fridge, washing-machine, books, clothes, television, dish-washer – all piled in a heap on the front lawn. I could see where the flood had reached by the tide line on the walls of the school. It was around shoulder height. Inside the front entrance the real devastation was clear. In the main office some of the office equipment was still in place but covered by a film of mud. Elsewhere the force of the water had pushed over filing cabinets and bookshelves and spilled their contents into a sodden, stinking heap.

From the front office I went to look into the main hall, a place which was so much the heart of the school where students and staff came together for assemblies, celebrations, performances. Now the tables and

chairs which had been set out for the A level exams were strewn across the well of the hall, piled by the water into a heap in a corner. The small rectangular blocks of wood which formed the parquet floor were strewn as if fired from a scattershot gun. The staff-room, another place where the pulse of the school normally beat

loudly, was now a wreck of overturned chairs and tables, sodden papers, school books and coursework folders.

I moved through the school from room to room. Now and then I met colleagues. We barely spoke. Just shook our heads at the hopelessness and tragedy of it all. There were no words. The new dining hall was a tangle of upturned furniture, floor covered in mud, servery still intact but smeared with grime. In the music room the keyboards were mostly in place but covered in the brown stains of the floodwater. The art room was still puddled with water, paintings and sculptures heaped in corners by the pressure of water. Upstairs where my office was located all appeared strangely normal. I was lucky, unlike my colleague, Paul, whose office was down below and which housed his library of rare books, history videos and slides. All now lay in a tangled, sodden heap on the floor of his office.

I learned later that on the Sunday, when the waters dropped a little, he and Peter, one of the deputies, had forced their way into school to rescue the main computer server and the A level examination papers. It was just one of many heroic acts which had gone on throughout the city during that fateful weekend. Firefighters in rescue boats chugged along Warwick Road and Corporation Road rescuing stranded people from flooded houses. A fleet of small boats, from canoes and rowing boats to the RNLI lifeboat, helped in the rescue. Helicopters winched frightened people from roof tops.

The drama of the flood and the rescues and seeing it reported on the national news held us for the first few days but, like all news, the searchlight quickly switches to other events. Clearing out the sodden debris of the flood and the quiet human misery that follows doesn't make the headlines but that's when reality really starts to bite.

We had no school to house our 600 students some of whom were due to take their A levels. John, the Head, had been stranded over in the north-east at his family home and news filtered in that the apartment in Caldewgate where he lived during the week was completely wrecked.

Our first staff meeting was a sad, muted gathering in a local church. With the Head absent, Peter, one of the Deputies, led prayers and then spelt out some of the practicalities. The exam papers had been saved and the A level students would take their exams as intended but at Harraby School a few miles away. As for the start of term that was being postponed for a week.

While he was speaking, I was looking round at this gathering of my colleagues. We had, somehow, to hold things together, hold on to the notion that we were the essence of what made the school function.

Without the building, without all our usual resources it wasn't easy to see a way forward but for the sake of our students we had to come up with something. Many of them had been driven out of their homes by the flood waters and were staying with relatives or in local hotels and guest houses. They may be getting an extra week's holiday but for many it was a miserable time.

The Head arrived the following day. As he turned into the car park I noticed a row of suits, shirts and ties hanging in his car. He was literally 'living out of a suitcase' and sleeping at one of the local hotels. We had been told to meet at the local college where we would be informed of the latest developments. Rumours were already circulating that the school might have to close permanently.

The flood coincided with plans to demolish and rebuild the front section of the local technical college. At present it was empty and we were offered the use of six empty classrooms on the 3rd floor. Harraby School three miles away on the south side of the city had offered us the use of their sixth form block which consisted of four classrooms and a gymnasium. Newman itself was a no-go area as the whole of the ground floor was unsafe on health and safety grounds.

Within the first couple of weeks the contractors were in, filling a line of huge builders' skips with debris and ruined equipment. New computers, printers, keyboards, and photocopiers were dumped unceremoniously into these skips along with the rustic bench I'd made for Ronnie's garden, parquet blocks from the main hall and all the timber from the floor of the gym.

The initial plan was to bus years 11, 12 and 13 to the Harraby site each day and house the rest of the school in the old technical college block. The main challenge was to devise a timetable which would allow teachers to move between both sites and be able to continue teaching the classes they had taught in the autumn term.

Some of the early timetables failed to work properly. Colleagues would find themselves teaching at Harraby and were then expected to be in front of a class three miles away at the college five minutes later. The same set of text books might be needed on both sites. There were no blackboards or whiteboards in some of the college rooms and we had to make do with flip charts and improvised lessons. At Harraby the A level students were all taught in the gym. It was divided into sections with tables grouped in the corners and along the sides of the room. Four or five 6th form lessons might take place simultaneously, just a low murmur of voices or activity coming from each part of the room. It was impressive to see the way colleagues improvised to make things work. My colleague Alain had lost all of his music equipment and introduced

485

singing and rhythmic movement into his lessons. Anything to keep the students engaged and smiling.

With a shortage of proper resources, I decided that for the lower school students it might be productive to use the flood experience as the basis for an extended project. We were, after all, living through a unique historical event, something they might look back on in years to come and be able to say, 'I was there and here's my diary or my photomontage of the events.' We set the students to capture their experiences of the flood in a variety of ways. There was personal writing, photo diaries, interviews with flood victims, newspaper reporting and the drama of TV news presentation.

What I wasn't expecting was the intensity and vividness of some of the writing. A number of students who had first hand experience wrote movingly about their own fears, the shock of seeing parents in tears, the suffering of grandparents and neighbours, the grief of losing treasured mementos and the tragedy of losing your home and having to live with strangers in a hotel or temporary accommodation. On another level the project seemed to work as a kind of therapy. The students were able to put their feelings into words, to share their experiences with others in the class and this seemed, in a small way, to help them cope.

The Ash Wednesday mass was held in the gym at the college. This is where we met for assemblies for years 1-4 who were based at the college. That service was particularly poignant. Nearly all the students came forward for a blessing and to have the ash cross marked on their foreheads. The feeling of shared emotion and shared compassion was powerful and uplifting at a time when we all needed some spiritual reassurance that God was still on our side.

Under the new arrangements the Head redeployed various staff to take up extra responsibilities on the two teaching sites and in those early weeks there was what might be called a 'Dunkirk spirit' - backs-to-the-wall, fighting on all fronts, everyone desperate to try to make these new arrangements work for the students and for our own sanity. The daily stresses were immense but the cumulative effect was difficult to predict. When the Ofsted report became public knowledge, the local paper posted a headline 'Flooded and Failed'. Just the 'kick in the teeth' that we all needed!

Each morning I had to talk myself into getting through the day. I would drive to work playing Queen's *The Show Must Go On* at peak volume in the car. I told myself I had to keep strong and positive for whatever the day might throw at me. There were my own staff to support but you also never knew what might erupt at either of the sites. At Harraby the year eleven students were under pressure to get exam coursework completed and literature texts revised, while at the college with 400 students crammed into a small area on the third floor with no playground for them to let off steam, the likelihood of some child losing the plot was high.

For safety the stairwell of the college had been boarded to the ceiling so that as you went up the stairs to the third floor it was like climbing a vertical tunnel, oppressive and claustrophobic. When you reached that floor the classrooms were small and cramped, not designed for classes of thirty students. At break time the students couldn't go outside, they had to sit in the corridors and eat their snacks while the staff tried to get a breather.

As the weeks wore on and spring temperatures rose, the college became a tinderbox of increasing tensions. One afternoon as I was teaching, I looked out to see reams of coloured copier paper being flung out of a nearby window. The paper fanned out and cascaded through the air and down into the quadrangle below like so much oversized confetti. I raced into the room next door to see Chris, one of our more volatile year 9 students, shouting, 'Don't wanna be here, pissin' waste of time.'

Jim, who had been put in charge of the college site, was there ahead of me and already talking Chris down off his perch on top of a desk. 'None of us wants to be here, Chris, but we don't have a choice. We do have a choice about how we behave. C'mon, let's go,' and he escorted the boy out of the room.

Chris was the exception. Generally, the students were immensely tolerant of all the disruption. Many of them had lost their own homes and there was a great mood of co-operation as we all struggled to get through each day.

My solace each evening was to pick up my guitar and soothe away the stresses of the day. I had always promised myself I would learn classical guitar when I retired but then the previous year Sue had surprised me by buying me some starter lessons as an incentive. My guitar had helped me get through the year of my mother's decline and once again it was helping me retain my sanity. So it was Queen and Freddie Mercury at full volume to fire me up on my way to work each morning and in the evening my fingers worked at some Giuliani and Fernando Sor to prepare me for sleep.

487

Back at Newman, the clean up continued. A temporary office had been set up in a portacabin at the front of the school. Inside the main building the air hummed day and night to the noise from industrial driers and dehumidifiers. Plaster was being been chipped off all the walls to a height of 2 metres, debris removed and floors hosed down.

Who was pulling the strings behind the scenes I have no idea but major things were happening. The tennis courts were being pressure washed and cleared and foundations laid for a dozen temporary classrooms to be installed. They arrived one day on an armada of low-loader trucks, one half of a classroom on each truck. They were lifted into position by cranes and an army of contract workers. This was to be the 'Newman Village'. It sounded quaint and cosy. The reality was somewhat different.

I saw little of John, the Head, during these months. He was a man under strain. The school that he had started to shape had fragmented overnight and he was now trying to oversee three different sites as well as negotiate the future of the school itself. He was still living in a hotel somewhere, his wrecked apartment still being uninhabitable. Ofsted had given the school some respite before returning but the county inspectors were never far from the door.

By the summer term the Newman 'village' was up and running and we were able to leave the claustrophobic confines of the college. The main school building was still being replastered and refurbished but a few rooms on the ground floor had been made ready for use. However, as the summer temperatures climbed so a problem arose. The floor tiles of the rooms had been floated away by the flood leaving the bitumen adhesive as a floor surface. In cold weather there hadn't been a problem but now it was warmer, if you were teaching in those rooms, you couldn't stand still for long as you soon found yourself glued to the floor!

By now the aftermath of the flood was taking its toll. Signs of stress were showing among the staff. Some were looking to get jobs elsewhere and others were increasingly absent. When a colleague took me to one side and, gripping a table to stop from shaking, asked 'When d'you know you're having a nervous breakdown?' then I knew that although we had come through a lot, there was probably worse yet to come. Despite our best efforts to keep the spirit of the school alive, week by week that spirit was haemorrhaging.

*

JAMAICA MEETS UMBRIA

Whit week break. A chance to escape. Saturday 28th May. 7a.m. flight from Stansted to Forli in central Italy. We were taking our annual Jamaica reunion to Italy this year. Usually we rotated round the houses in England but not this year.

Since leaving Jamaica in 1976 we had reunited annually with a clutch of close friends. The bonds we formed with each other back in the early Seventies on that beautiful and volatile island had remained strong.

Thirty years on and we were off for a week in the hills of Umbria. Eight of us – Jim and Jenny from Wakefield, Alan and Marion from Whitehaven and Ruth and Tony from Dalston, south of Carlisle. It was pure coincidence that six of us settled in Cumbria after Jamaica, a touch of curious synchronicity.

We land at Forli at 9a.m. and collect three hire cars. Like a scene from *The Italian Job*, we snake along the winding road to Mercatale. Then it's up the long gravel track to Rudi's villa at Canalecchia. Rudi is a German friend of Jim's who has rented us his hillside villa for the week.

It is a dream place built on terraces of olive trees; stone built with an abundance of oak beams and exquisite features. Our bedroom on the ground floor opens on to a small terrace and lawn. We use the outside bathroom which was an old wine cellar and has a vaulted roof of curving stone blocks. Walls and floor are tiled in small coloured mosaic tiles which create a spacious wet room in which to shower.

Outside the grounds step down in a series of terraces. There are numerous shady places to sit, to read, to doze. I have brought my small travel guitar and my musical fumblings are sometimes enhanced by the dribble of birdsong from the woods or interrupted by the frogs that chorus gruffly from the pond on the upper terrace. There is a large spreading mulberry tree shading a long table and chairs where we have breakfast and another table under the pergola outside the main door for

489

our capacious lunches. Ancient vines lean against the uprights and bright green shoots and tendrils coil round the wires of the pergola.

In the afternoons Jim is engrossed in Anthony Beevor's *Stalingrad*. After Jamaica he left teaching and re-trained as a lawyer. He was my close ally at Priory School. We both taught Social Studies and enjoyed a friendly rivalry as House Heads. Jim was Head of Princeton House and I was Head of Oxford House. When our sports teams were competing there was some sharp needling and pointed banter but beyond that there was a close, unspoken bond. With our wives, Sue and Jenny, we had trekked together and got lost in the infamous Cockpit Country of central Jamaica. We had shared the gastric misery of 'Montezuma's Revenge' in Mexico and Jim and I had dived for lobster from the coral reef off Hellshire's Beach on Sue's 26th birthday.

During those three memorable years all eight of us had shared some stunning times together, times which were imprinted strongly in the bank of remembered joys.

Since then, children had come and grown and sometimes kept us apart but we had always ensured that at least once a year we would meet together and muse on old times. So here we are, sharing the delicious drift of each day. For me it is a welcome world away from things back home. Here, there are no sudden shocks of weather change. The days feel seemless. Each morning you wake to the warble of birdsong, you open the shutters and see the sunlight on the trees, the blue sky; you feel the stillness, sense the humming murmur of the bees, catch the distant cuckoo, the momentary woodpecker.

Some days we stay around the villa and walk the hills; other days we take the track down the hillside and forage among the delights of Umbria. There is ice cream on the foreshore of Lake Trasimeno, the place where on June 21st 217BC, Hannibal and his Carthaginians defeated the Romans under the consul Gaius Flaminus. There is local wine and pasta at Mimmi's Restaurant in Mercatale. Midweek, Sue and I head for Assisi while the others go to San Gimignano. We join groups of American students and other tourists wandering the town. The architecture of the three storey basilica with its detailed frescoes is intriguing and a complete contrast to the simplicity of Saint Francis' own plain white church. I know nothing about St. Francis and the Franciscans and so decide that my holiday reading will be a biography written by GianMaria Polidoro, which is among the stock of books at the Caffe Duomo.

In the evening Rudi takes us to Cortona, a medieval town stacked on a hill, high above the valley of Valdichiana. The streets are narrow and we are plunged into cool shade until the street ends, opening into a spacious piazza. After a fine meal we join the local youngsters of the town who sit in the square chatting and eating cones and tubs of gelato. Apparently gelato is not the same as ice cream but whatever the ingredients are, this, coupled with an Italian espresso, is the perfect dessert.

Back at the villa the following morning I find in my reading about St. Francis, echoes of the early life of Siddharta, the Buddha. Both young men were born into wealthy families and turned their backs on materialism to find enlightenment. I thought of the Buddhist temples in Kyoto, the tranquil gardens, the mirror lakes, the notion of a world beyond, which you could sense through quiet reflection in such places. I remember turning my back on the world of industry back in my twenties, looking for something which I could believe in and live for. It turned out to be teaching and trying to live the creative life. Initially D.H.Lawrence had inspired me with his belief in the 'flame of being' and his rejection of the dead hand of materialism and the industrial behemoth. Our voyage to Jamaica had opened my eyes to myself and the wider world. The year in America and our drive across the vast space of that continent in the summer of 1984 were important reference points for how I viewed the world and my life in it. There was a space beyond the immediate, a place for contemplation and meditation which the Buddha and St Francis had both been searching for. That space beyond helped to frame things in a wider perspective. It was probably what was helping me to cope with the distress of my place of work back home and to which I was about to return.

*

THOUGHTS OF MOVING ON

I had made the decision. I would leave full-time teaching in the summer of 2006, a year from now. It wasn't a sudden decision but one that I had been mulling over for a while. Maybe the experience of the flood crystallised my thoughts. I never failed to be inspired by the resilience and resourcefulness of my colleagues. There was grit and determination to get through this nightmare time and keep positive for the students. But it was taking its toll. Some were struggling to cope and in danger of going under. A few years ago I had seen two colleagues die within a short while of retiring. That was not going to happen to me, I told myself. No job was worth my health and my sanity.

I wanted to leave teaching on my terms, with my sanity intact and the energy to pursue some new interests. Rejection slips from publishers who had looked at my novel were sometimes accompanied by encouraging comments so all was not lost there. The previous year, for my work using film animation, I had gained an 'Excellence in ICT' award from the county and this year I'd been shortlisted for a national award from BECTA (The British Educational Communication and Technology Agency) for promoting computer technology in the classroom. Clearly there was more to do to spread the potential of this type of work in primary as well as secondary schools. My plan was to continue part-time at Newman teaching my A level group after summer 2006, while setting up workshops and training in film animation on a freelance basis.

Leaving in 2006 would allow me to take my Year 10 GCSE English group through to their final exams. They were a very talented group of lively individuals who had coped with untold disruption this year. I was determined to do justice to their talents and do the best I could for them.

New initiatives were coming thick and fast from the newly re-elected Labour Government. Tony Blair was in for a third term as Prime Minister and he was intending to extend the changes to education he had set in motion during his previous terms. Ofsted would now only have to give two days notice before an inspection, compared to the previous two months notice. There was a revision to the Literacy Strategy which many eminent writers criticised as 'sterile'. For us it was more prescriptive and tied our hands even further. Writing in the Guardian newspaper about the Key Stage 2 primary school tests, the writer Phillip Pullman wrote: *'They were confronted with four crudely drawn pictures of a boy standing in a queue to buy a toy, and they then had to write a story about them, taking exactly 45 minutes. It was a task of stupefying worthlessness and futility, something no one who was serious about the art of storytelling could regard with anything other than contempt.'*

We were faced with the same stupefying dictats at secondary level. The lessons I used to love where I read to a class for twenty minutes and transported them in the spell and wonder of story-telling would now be viewed by Ofsted as a 'failed' lesson. 'Not enough pupil interaction, not enough evidence of engagement' they would say. They needed 'evidence, evidence, evidence' that learning was taking place.

That which couldn't be quantified by 'evidence', such as being lost in the wonder of a story, was seen as worthless. I was maddened by such philistine thinking which struck at the heart of what English teaching should be about. I wanted to transport my students, to take them on flights of fancy, to stir their creativity, fire up their imaginations whereas Ofsted and government education policy seemed only concerned with 'skills', making sure students were well trained for the world of work.

It was time for me to consider stepping off the treadmill.

I arranged a meeting with the Head to tell him of my plans. I hadn't seen him for a while and we walked round the Newman building looking at the progress of the refurbishment. Walls were being re-plastered and the industrial driers were working well. There was no longer the dank, earthy smell of sodden floors and walls. The air was warmer and drier and progress was in evidence. The new floor joists for the main hall were in place and some of the rooms were being plastered.

He nodded when I told him of my plan to finish full-time teaching in 2006 and teach part-time for a year to take my A level groups through to completion.

'I'll put it to the governors. I'm sure they'll approve it,' he said.

'And how are you?' I asked him.

He hesitated, shrugged a little, 'Still living in a hotel but it's tolerable.'

He looked weary and shook his head, 'What a time we're living through, Barrie. Good material for a play or a novel. There's been real drama going on, I can tell you.'

But he pulled back from giving any details and, with a stiffening of his back and rubbing of his hands together, said, 'Just got to soldier on and see it through.'

This year of such trials and hardships had taught me some lessons. Nothing was permanent. Nothing should be taken for granted. But above all I marveled at the fortitude, the resilience, the acts of compassion and tolerance which I had witnessed during the year, not only from my colleagues but also from the students. Small acts of heroism by unlikely people who stepped in to solve a problem, take responsibility during a crisis, show initiative in ways which I couldn't have predicted. It taught me much about not prejudging what people could cope with.

But the other side, the sad and tragic side of the year was seeing colleagues damaged by being pushed beyond their limits. To talk about being in or outside one's 'comfort zone' has become a cliché. But there is a truth there; we do operate within a zone of comfort and confidence.

Change the parameters of that zone and individuals can rise to new heights or fall into a well of confusion, anxiety and doubt where the damage can be profound.

As the end of term approached, Sue and I decided we should throw a garden party for the Newman staff. They deserved something after this nightmare year. We brought in a caterer and people contributed to the cost. A large number turned out on a fine summer's evening and sat in the garden, ate heartily, drank and chatted until it was time to light lanterns and put a match to the wood in the fire-pit.

The old Head, Frank, used to talk about the Newman 'family'. Since his leaving, something of that family ethos had gone. But then I remembered that first staff meeting back in January, when we all huddled in a chilly church and tried to face up to the loss of our school. Now I looked round this group of people who had helped each other come through it all. There was a long way to go yet but clearly, the 'family' spirit was not quite dead.

*

THE YEAR OF 'LAST TIMES'

As I drove to school on the first day of the autumn term of 2005, I realized this was the last time I would do this; after almost 35 years this would be the last time I would start a new school year as a full-time teacher. But like every year I felt excited about going back, seeing the students and being part of the school again.

It would be different this year though, a year of 'last times'. The refurbishment of the school had been almost completed, we were all back on the Newman site and there was a new deputy and senior teacher under the Head's leadership. Inspection teams from the county and from Ofsted would be knocking on the door more frequently now that the school was seemingly back to normal. I say 'seemingly' because some of the staff were still fragile and vulnerable. The summer break may have given us all some respite but the emotional scars of the flood were still there.

For me *summer came like cinnamon so sweet* – that alliterative gem of a line comes from Corinne Bailey Rae's 2006 debut album – an album which became the soundtrack for my final year. I always associate cinnamon with the taste and feel of America. They have cinnamon toast, cinnamon buns, the smell of cinnamon in the coffee shops and bakeries. That blend of sweetness and spice is 'America' for me and that summer

494

we had returned to spend time with our American friends at the Thousand Islands in upper New York State. It was a healing place, Pine Bay, where the fresh river water of the St Lawrence laps the granite shoreline. The cabins are spaced among the pine woods and our cabin this year overlooked a rocky bluff from which, each morning, I could dive into ten feet of clear water and swim to the rocky island in the middle of the bay. I had taken my travel guitar and it seemed that the local chipmunks didn't much mind my plucking and strumming. They would scurry around the verandah of the cabin while I amused myself with my musical therapy.

That holiday set me up for my final school year. I was back in my 'multi-media' teaching room where I could have Corinne Bailey Rae crooning from my surround sound system to greet my classes in the morning. There was a digital projector which I could link to my laptop and project whatever I chose on to the spacious white board at the front of the room. There was artwork and samples of students' work on the walls, potted plants by the window, carpets on the floor. I'd had a vision of this kind of quality teaching environment for a long time. Now it was a reality.

My Year 11 group were back. We had shared the trials of the flood, the improvised teaching at the college and now, when we came to our study of *Romeo and Juliet*, we could watch Leonardo Di Caprio and Clare Danes on the big screen with Baz Luhrmann's brilliant soundtrack filling the room. I had taught this play so many times with classes over the years and it never failed to grasp and twist their emotions. I recalled showing the video of Zeffirelli's film to my class in Jamaica on a small TV monitor and was reminded how far the technology had moved over the past 35 years. Now we could do justice to the film-maker's art and spend time not only exploring the skill of the camera work but also the power of musical soundtrack on affecting mood and atmosphere.

Thankfully blackboards and chalk had gone some years ago and now I had the flexibility of a laptop and digital projector, I could use Microsoft's Powerpoint software to put together text and photos and moving film footage. The possibilities of stimulating the interest of a class were endless. The pitfall however, as I had found at recent in-service training sessions, was 'death by Powerpoint.' The technology was no substitute for the cut-and-thrust of a lively verbal exchange with a class. You still had to 'read' a class, note the ones who never contributed, draw them into a discussion, feed their confidence and self-belief by encouraging whatever small offering they dropped into the mix. Show them a Powerpoint presentation and they could continue to hide in a corner. Set up a lively discussion, however, and this could work wonders.

Educational astrologers might tell you that the future lay in programmed learning using computers but I still maintained that you needed inspiring teachers to catch and hold the attention of a class.

That final year my classroom buzzed with the creative energy of students and the magic of teaching. One afternoon, during a lesson with my Year 10 media studies group, Fionuala, one of the really sharp girls in the group, presented me with a CD disc – 'Finished my project, sir.'

For several weeks she had been working on an idea for a film trailer for her GCSE project. 'A bit like that *Blair Witch* film, that's what I'm after,' she had said.

I used the 1999 film *The Blair Witch Project* as a case study on the way the internet had been skilfully exploited to generate a global audience for a newly released film. This film was first released as 'found footage' of real events involving the ghostly disappearance of three student film-makers in the Black Hills of Maryland in 1994. Only their film equipment and 'recovered video footage' was supposedly ever found. In fact, this was a case of clever 'drip-feeding' information via the internet by the architects of the whole 'con', Daniel Myrick and Euardo Sanchez, prior to the film's release. And it worked. Sanchez reported the initial budget for the film as being around \$20,000. It finally earned a remarkable \$248m worldwide.

Fionuala wanted to create the same kind of mood for her film trailer. What she presented me with was a remarkable piece of work for a 15 year old student:

Fade in to red caption on black background
If you go down to the woods today....
(Woodland setting. 3 teenage girls. Close up on worried faces)
Distant high-pitched mournful soprano voice

It may not be your kind of picnic....
Girls running through undergrowth. Dark silhouettes of trees.
Music quickening with sonorous bass beat.

Beneath the trees where nobody sees.....
High level shot looking down on girls. Their faces smeared with mud
They cling together in fear

They'll hide and seek as long as they please....
Girls running, camera following. Intermittent screams

Music continues, getting louder

It's creepy down in the woods today.....
Low level shot of dark canopy of trees. Sound of screams.

But safer to stay at home...
Medium shot. Girls flailing their arms as they stumble into a shallow
lake.

At six o'clock their Mummies and Daddies...
Girls dragging each other out of muddy water, still screaming.
Music slowing to a tick tock beat

Won't take them home to bed.
3 motionless blood-stained bodies lying on shore of lake
Music fades, tick tock beat slows and stops

Don't miss this summer's chiller at a cinema near you...

Apart from the clever twist on the Teddy Bears' Picnic rhyme,
the construction and filming of this sequence were amazing. I died
several deaths seeing how risky it was with the shots of girls submerged
in muddy lake water but then it was shot at a weekend and not with my
knowledge. The dreaded 'Health and Safety Risk Assessment Procedure'
would have killed the whole idea before it ever came to stepping on a
blade of grass. As it was, it was done, 'in the can' as they say and
certainly A* quality. It was just one example of student brilliance that
year.

As part of GCSE English Literature the students had to be
primed on an anthology of *Poetry From Other Cultures*. I always
enjoyed teaching this part of the course. It took the students and myself
into foreign lands and unfamiliar cultural territory. For some of the
Caribbean poetry like Grace Nichols' *Island Man*, I retold anecdotes of
Jamaica, showed slides of the Blue Mountains, downtown Kingston and
palm-fringed beaches and indulged them with my attempts at Jamaican
patios and the poetry of Louise Bennett. And when it came to Edward
Kamau Brathwaite's poem, *Limbo*, I brought in a broom-stick and the
video of the superb 1977 TV series *Roots* based on the book by Alex
Haley.

'What's that for, sir? Spot of army discipline is it? Ofsted
coming in are they?' quipped Michael when he saw me brandishing the

broom. He was one of the livewires of the group, tall, gangly with a ready smile.

Limbo was a serious poem about the slave trade but we started on a lighter note as I explained about the limbo dance. Michael was keen to try himself out. Two of the other students volunteered to hold the broom stick while Michael, a big grin on his face, approached the 'bar'. What followed was an hilarious ten minutes while he and the others tried their skill at shuffling their way, legs and knees spread wide, under the broom stick, the rest of the class clapping encouragement.

From the frivolity of the opening ten minutes, the mood quickly changed as I explained the theme of the poem which deals with the nightmare of the 'Middle Passage', that part of the slave trade when slaves were transported by ship from Africa to north America and the Caribbean. The students knew little of the slave trade, when, where and why it happened and that's where *Roots* helped to fill in the gaps. This TV mini-series, first screened in 1977 to a record viewing audience of 130million, was adapted from the novel by Alex Haley, a novel reputedly based on Haley's own ancestry. I just showed the opening episodes where the central character, Kunta Kinte, is captured on the Gambian coast in 1767, transported by ship to the slave auctions in Maryland and then to his first plantation as a slave. It is said, that when first screened, the streets of America were empty whenever the series was being shown. Americans of all colours were glued to their TV sets as they learned, probably for the first time, something of the brutal reality of their own history.

It had a similar impact on my own students. They had seen few screen dramas which featured black characters as central to a story and this story was powerfully filmed and powerfully acted. When each episode ended the class was quiet and pensive. They were puzzled by what they were seeing; it was a revelation this history of white exploitation of the black race and it was not easy to digest. Some stared out of the window, some doodled on their work books, others talked quietly. Deliberately, I didn't intrude for a while and left them to reflect on what they had seen.

One of the paradoxes of teaching is that you never really know what is going on in the thirty separate minds in a class. You design a lesson with the intention that your students will experience something significant both emotionally and intellectually. You try to test their reaction by a discussion or a written task, but whether you ever get close to knowing the impact you're actually having on each student remains something of a mystery. Years later you may meet an ex-student who will remind you of some lesson where you said this or that. Often it was the throwaway line they remembered rather than the main thrust of the lesson.

*

Now that things were back to some kind of normality the Head was keen to bring in groups of primary school children for an experience of film animation. It was good education and good publicity for the school and for a school in 'Special Measures' good publicity is vital to combat the negative headlines like 'Flooded and Failed'. So every few weeks I would see another little column of smartly uniformed youngsters arriving at the school gates and making their way down the drive and up to my room.

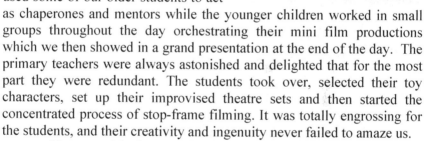

It worked like a charm. We used some of our older students to act as chaperones and mentors while the younger children worked in small groups throughout the day orchestrating their mini film productions which we then showed in a grand presentation at the end of the day. The primary teachers were always astonished and delighted that for the most part they were redundant. The students took over, selected their toy characters, set up their improvised theatre sets and then started the concentrated process of stop-frame filming. It was totally engrossing for the students, and their creativity and ingenuity never failed to amaze us.

That year I had a very interesting year 8 group who wanted to start a film animation club after school. Every week they would arrive at the door of my room soon after the bell went for the end of school. Without needing any supervision they would set up their stage, assemble their toy characters and props and then start filming. Their productions were clever, witty, skilfully designed and deserved a wider audience.

I wrote to the *Times Educational Supplement* about a planned training day involving eight local schools. One teacher plus two students came from each school and they were trained alongside each other. Again we used our older students as mentors for the day. A reporter and photographer from the TES arrived and spent a couple of hours observing. Their feature appeared in the TES some weeks later under the title *Animated Training*.

It was clear that film animation could be used to circumvent some of the sterility of the national Literacy Framework. It dealt with an understanding of narrative structure, and the nature of storytelling using sound, vision and speech. It required group planning and co-operation and a lot of verbal interaction. The students were using ICT skills at a very sophisticated level and, set against Ofsted criteria, I was confident this would rate as 'outstanding' learning.

*

And now another 'last time'. The last time I would read *Of Mice and Men* to a class. The last time I would see the stunned silence of a whole class as they realised in the final chapter what the character George was about to do – shoot Lennie his best friend, the friend who trusted him. This masterpiece of story-telling by the American novelist John Steinbeck worked every time and at every level of ability. I had used it for thirty-five years and I had read it numerous times to classes. It set up a moral dilemma on the scale of a Greek tragedy. Should George allow his simple-minded friend Lennie to be hunted down by the vengeful figure of Curly, or should he carry out a 'mercy-killing' and do the job himself?

My low ability year 10 group were upset and disturbed by it as I closed the book for the last time.

'But couldn't George try to save him, they could hide and then run away,' said Karen.

'Don't be daft, Curly would have gone after them. He was really mean,' said David.

'But it's so unfair. Poor Lennie. He had the mind of a child,' added Leonie.

'And George did it, kindly like. He told him the story of the rabbit,' said Jimmy.

'And then blew his brains out,' added Colin.

'Yes but Lennie would've been thinking of the rabbit. Just think if Curly had got to him first and shot him.'

'He's still dead,' said Colin.

'Yes but he died peaceful, like,' replied Jimmy.

The classes would wrestle in their own way with these moral dilemmas and therein lay the power of literature. And therein lay my joy of being a teacher of English. I could take students on a journey into the minds and into the worlds of strangers. They could explore foreign places, times past and times present and together we could reach into the hearts and minds of the characters. We could share their struggles, their loves, their losses, their hopes and dreams and maybe it would touch chords in the hearts of my students. Maybe. For you never knew. You could only hope.

*

THE CLOSING OF THE CHAPTER

They have seated me on a chair in the middle of the lawn. In front of me, standing and sitting in the garden is an audience of family, friends, close colleagues and some of my former students. Sue has

arranged this surprise retirement party for me and I am dumb-struck. Andy, my old friend and woodworking buddy stands and presents my life story in education. There are letters from old colleagues and friends, recorded messages from those in far away places. I feel honoured, humbled, delighted to be reminded of all that had gone before and how I have arrived at this point in the calendar of my life.

It is autumn and I am finally closing a lengthy chapter. There have been some emotional moments. The summer leavers' assembly had been held in the gym. These were the students who had endured the flood and its aftermath during their GCSE years. There was a strong bond between them, strengthened by all that they had shared. As they came into the gym they were each given a candle to hold. The first was lit and the flame passed from one to the next until eventually all the candles were alight. It was a simple but supremely symbolic gesture. The Head addressed the group, reminded them of all they had witnessed, endured and triumphed over. When the formalities were over there was the leave-taking – signing each others shirts in marker pen, photographs, hugs, tears. They were off to start their exams and the next phase of their lives.

That summer was the last time I would wait with trepidation for the results day. It had happened every year of my career, this nervousness, this hope, this responsibility that you had helped your students to reach their potential and do their best. And, with the group of

talented youngsters that I had been blessed with for two years, my hopes were high.

I was not disappointed. Lots of A grades and lots of smiling faces. At their Leavers' Ball at a local hotel, they were decked out in their finery: tuxedos, ball gowns. These survivors of the flood were stepping out in style and it was a joy to see and to share.

Ofsted came again and finally approved the progress the school was making. We were out of 'Special Measures' and the burden of 'failure' finally lifted.

But there was the cost. Colleagues had been broken by the flood and its aftermath and the exacting changes that Ofsted demanded. Some had left the profession with ill health, others lost the confidence to stand in front of a class; some found jobs outside of education.

So here am I, a survivor, sitting on the lawn in my garden being feted by my family and friends. I count my blessings and good fortune several times over. I look down the tunnel of time and think of my inspirational English teacher, Allen Freer, who worried about my soul; I think of my many adventures with Sue during our Jamaican years and of Amy and her family who first invited us to America and initiated a friendship which still continues. I think of our epic drive across America with Katie and James as small children and the joy of sharing their growing over the years. I think of the many classrooms in which I have looked out over a sea of expectant faces and wonder if I have met their expectations. I will never know.

But as I read through the cards which people have sent me, one in particular catches my eye. It contains a quotation by George Steiner and, as I read it, I nod to myself:

"the calling of the teacher. There is no craft more privileged. To awaken in another human being powers, dreams beyond one's own; to induce in others a love for that which one loves; to make of one's inward present their future; that is a threefold adventure like no other."

Yes, that sums it up exactly.

POSTSCRIPT

In 2008 I learned of the whereabouts of my inspirational English teacher, Allen Freer. He was living in Cheadle, south of Manchester with his wife Beryl. For years I had wanted to contact him to express my gratitude at the way he'd inspired me. I wrote a letter and the day afterwards received a telephone call from him:

'You've no idea the joy your letter gave me,' he said.

'I think I do,' I replied. 'I too know what it's like to receive messages of gratitude from students. I know that same joy.'

Some weeks later there was a poignant reunion. Sue and I went to the Freer's home for afternoon tea. Now in their eighties, Allen and Beryl were still inspiring company.

We had no idea of the extent of his influence in the world of art and pedagogy. He pioneered the use of fine art and poetry in the teaching of English and, in his role as English Inspector for Manchester schools, encouraged young writers and artists to work with pupils and teachers. Allen was, himself, an artist, writer and craftsman.

When we said goodbye, he gave me a gift of one of his paintings and a special edition of a D.H.Lawrence short story bound and illustrated with fine ink lithographs.

It was the closing of a wonderful circle, begun all those years ago when I first sat in his English lessons, aged 14, mesmerised by his teaching which stirred such murmurings in my young mind.

For further information go to : archiveshub.ac.uk/allenfreer
Or visit the John Rylands University Library, Deansgate, Manchester to see the 'Papers of Allen Freer'.

*

APPENDIX 1 Road Trip map

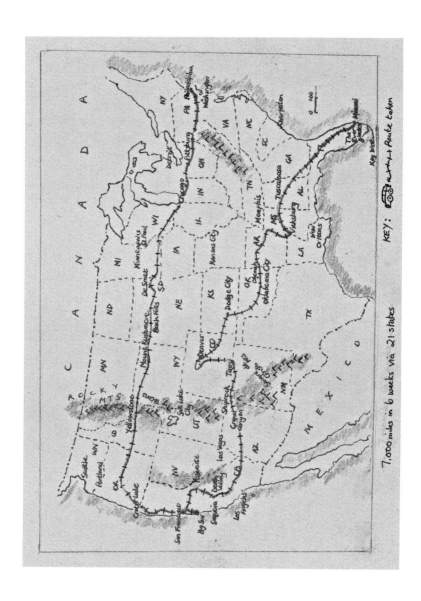

Printed by CreateSpace.com

Available from Amazon.com and other online stores

Available on Kindle and through other retail outlets.

Made in the USA
Charleston, SC
11 February 2016